THE
JOURNALS
OF
FRANCIS PARKMAN

VOLUME I

Francis Parkman at Twenty
From C. H. Farnham's Francis Parkman
(Little, Brown, and Company)

THE
JOURNALS
OF
FRANCIS PARKMAN

Edited by MASON WADE

Author of

FRANCIS PARKMAN: HEROIC HISTORIAN

ILLUSTRATED

VOLUME I

NEW YORK AND LONDON

HARPER & BROTHERS PUBLISHERS

MCMXLVII

KRAUS REPRINT CO.
New York
1969

Reprinted with the permission of the original publisher
KRAUS REPRINT CO.
A U.S. Division of Kraus-Thomson Organization Limited

Printed in U.S.A.

TABLE OF CONTENTS

VOLUME I

VOLUME II

LIST OF ILLUSTRATIONS

VOLUME I

VOLUME II

Preface

FRANCIS PARKMAN is the greatest writer among American historians; the "climax and the crown," as Van Wyck Brooks has pointed out, of that notable nineteenth century Boston school of historians which included Jared Sparks, John Gorham Palfrey, George Bancroft, William Hickling Prescott, and John Lothrop Motley. He is alone among this goodly company in that his books still live today, while those of his greatest rivals, Prescott and Motley, seem stiffly rhetorical and unduly romantic. As history his work has also stood the test of time, for much later research and investigation have disproved only a detail or two in the vast field in which he was a pioneer. History has become more factual and scientific since Parkman's day, but the new historians have not been able to make sound scholarship dramatic and exciting, as this romantic rationalist did. Parkman's newly rediscovered journals have a twofold importance: they constitute both a partial autobiography of one of America's greatest writers and the raw material of his work. From them emerges a remarkable picture of North America in the mid-nineteenth century, as seen by a great writer who was familiar through long and loving study with the history of the regions he describes. They are of enormous literary and historical interest, since they reveal the development of the vivid style for which Parkman is famed, and his methods of research and investigation. The journals constitute one of the finest descriptions and interpretations of the American scene of the period; and they throw a great flood of light upon Parkman's books, which are so notable a part of the American cultural heritage.

Francis Parkman was a Boston Brahmin, and his New England reticence allowed little of himself to appear in his formal works, the seven-part history of *France and England in North America* and its epilogue, *The Conspiracy of Pontiac*. But like so many of the great figures of that nineteenth century Boston which has set a lasting mark upon American thought, Parkman revealed himself more fully in his private journals than it was ever possible for him to do when writing for the public. And like Emerson, Thoreau, and Hawthorne, once the wall of Puritan reticence had been broken down in private, he was too much of a literary man to let his words go unread; and so he made use of passages from his journals in works destined for an audience. Thus his first book, *The Oregon Trail*, a youthful effort which has been more widely read than the formal histories, is wholly based upon the diary that Parkman kept during his great adventure in the West; and his only novel, the forgotten *Vassall Morton* in which is buried his personal philosophy, takes over much material and many incidents recorded in unfictionalized form in the journals. Most of the few personal references which Parkman permitted himself in his historical works are drawn from the journals, which enable us to follow his intellectual development and to discover the reticent man who hid behind the objective historian.

The main function of the journals was to record Parkman's researches in the field. The historian early settled upon his lifework, and his youthful journals were a part of the exhaustive preparation which he imposed upon himself for the task that lay ahead. One of the teachers of his boyhood, Thomas Cushing, recalls somewhat ponderously that his pupil shone "in the rhetorical department," and that "he might have excelled in narrative and descriptive poetry (the poetry of action) had he not early imbibed the historical idea." Poetry was indeed Parkman's first love, but considering the faultiness of his ear, witnessed in the journals by extremely rough phonetic equivalents for unfamiliar foreign words and names, it is doubtless fortunate that he decided, in his own words, "to confine his homage to the Muse of History, as being less apt than her wayward sisters to requite his devotion with a mortifying rebuff." But his early fondness for Byron, Scott, and Cooper never left him, and their romantic influence is evident in his lifelong love of the dramatic and the vivid. Once history had been settled upon as his chosen field, there remained the choice of a subject. This was strongly influenced by

Parkman's early passion for the wilds and by the active interest of
his Harvard history teacher, Jared Sparks, in the American past,
which had previously been neglected and largely forgotten in a
colonial culture's preoccupation with the European tradition.
Sparks, a Unitarian minister turned editor and writer, was the first
American academic figure to concern himself seriously with the history of his country. Parkman fell under his influence as an under-
graduate; did further historical work under his guidance while
nominally studying law; and acknowledged his assistance in *The
Conspiracy of Pontiac* by dedicating that first-written of the histories
to the new president of Harvard "as a testimonial of high personal
regard and a tribute of respect for his distinguished services to
American history." But however great the influence of Sparks may
have been, the choice of subject was primarily Parkman's:

Before the end of my sophomore year my various schemes had crystalized
into a plan of writing a story of what was then known as the "Old French
War"—that is, the War that ended in the conquest of Canada—for here,
as it seemed to me, the forest drama was more stirring and the forest stage
more thronged with appropriate actors than in any other passage of our
history. It was not until some years later that I enlarged the plan to include
the whole course of the American conflict between France and England,
or, in other words, the history of the American forest; for this was the
light in which I regarded it.

—Letter to Martin Brimmer, 1886

Thus from an early fascination with the wilderness and with the
obscure border battles of the Seven Years' War developed Parkman's
great historical epic, which covers a much broader canvas.

John Fiske, who habitually ranked Parkman's work with that of
Herodotus, Thucydides, and Gibbon, stressed its scope: "The book
which depicts at once the social life of the Stone Age and the victory
of the English political ideal over the ideal which France inherited
from imperial Rome, is a book for all mankind and for all time."
Fiske's judgment of Parkman's work is somewhat excessive, for
France and England in North America lacks the unity of the great histories
of Herodotus and Thucydides and the sweep of Gibbon's master-
piece. Parkman was plagued by ill-health, both mental and physical,
during his entire writing life; and though he early planned out his

lifework as a whole, he was forced to do it piecemeal, struggling against almost overwhelming odds that he would never live to complete it. He did finish the last link in the chain of volumes, and revised many of the earlier ones, but he had neither time nor energy left for the final revision in which he planned, on Henry Adams' advice, to weld the parts together into a single work. The theme was essentially episodic, for the conflict between France and England was fitfully waged over half a continent for a century; and most of its major episodes could be grouped about single central figures, a method which Parkman, with his romantic devotion to the great-man theory of history, found the most satisfactory principle of organization. What Parkman thus lost in majestic perspective over the chain of events, he gained in the vividness of the episodes. Fiske justly referred to the seven-part series as a book, for *France and England in North America* has a dramatic unity which offsets its division into studies of individual figures or topics. Parkman thought of it at first as the epic of the struggle between "feudal, militant, and Catholic" France and "democratic, industrial, and Protestant" England for domination of the New World. But later he saw that the American Hundred Years' War was a "contest for colonial and maritime supremacy," and that the struggle in America was intricately linked with the struggle for power in Europe. One of Parkman's great historical contributions was the demonstration that obscure events in America had a vital effect upon the course of history in Europe, as those in Europe did in America. Parkman was one of the first historians to take a continental view of North America, but that view did not prevent him from recognizing the influence of nationalism and internationalism.

The great history extends from the dawn of French colonization in America to the eclipse of New France with the English conquest of 1760. The first part, *The Pioneers of France in the New World*, deals with the tentative settlement of Florida and Carolina by the French Huguenots and their bitter struggle with the Spaniards in the latter half of the sixteenth century; and with the enduring colonization of Champlain and his associates in Acadia and Canada at the outset of the seventeenth century. The second, *The Jesuits in North America*, carries the story on to 1675, with a moving account of the missionaries' heroic but short-lived effort to convert the Hurons and the Iroquois, and to make Canada a New Paraguay rather than a New France. The third, *La Salle and the Discovery of the Great West*, is the story of the French exploration and token colonization of the Great Lakes and the Mississippi Valley, the heart of the continent. It is also an account of the conflict of the religious and commercial ideals in New France, the incompatible ideals of the Jesuit and of the fur trader. The fourth, *The Old Regime in Canada*—a pioneer American essay in social history—falls into three divisions: the first dealing with the semifeudalism of Canada, the second with New France as a mission, and the third with the royal exploitation of the colony for the benefit of the mother country. The fifth, *Count Frontenac and New France under Louis XIV*, is an account of the colony in its heyday, with the conflict between State and Church already straining its top-heavy structure as England and France formally began their great American struggle in King William's War (1689-97). The sixth, *A Half-Century of Conflict*, covers the years between 1700 and 1748, which were filled with border strife as well as Queen Anne's War (War of the Spanish Succession, 1702-13) and King George's War (War of the Austrian Succession, 1744-48). At the outset of this work, Parkman indicated that he had adopted a broader view of the great struggle which he was chronicling. He considered Queen Anne's War to be "the second of a series of four conflicts which ended in giving to Great Britain a maritime and colonial preponderance over France and Spain. So far as concerns the colonies and the seas, these several wars may be regarded as a single protracted one, broken by intervals of truce. The three earlier of them, it is true, were European contests, begun and waged on European disputes. Their American part was incidental and apparently subordinate, yet it involved questions of prime importance in the history of the world." The seventh and final work, *Montcalm and Wolfe*—considered the finest of the series—is an account of the climactic struggle of the Seven Years' War (1756-63), that "Old French War" on which he had first planned to write, ending in the downfall of New France on the Plains of Abraham. This conflict, unlike the earlier ones, started in America with Washington's attack on Jumonville on the Monongahela in 1754; an "obscure skirmish began the war that set the world on fire" two years later. *The Conspiracy of Pontiac*, which is not formally a part of *France and*

England in North America, fills out the story of the English conquest with an account of the subsequent Indian uprising against the new rulers of North America. It was Parkman's first historical book, written when he thought himself doomed to death before he could write the greater work on which his heart was set; and so its introductory chapters briefly sum up the great three-cornered struggle for the continent among the Indians, the French, and the English. If only one of Parkman's books can be read, this is perhaps the best choice, for it is at once a summary and the crown of the great epic of *France and England in North America,* and an excellent introduction to the pre-Revolutionary history of America. As that acute critic Theodore Parker pointed out to his young friend, however, it was unjust to the Indians and the Quakers; it lacked the dramatic unity which so notably characterized most of Parkman's later books; and its style was too florid, inexact, and hasty—characteristics not evident in the later books, in which his early tendency to overwrite and to be romantically picturesque was restrained.

So vast a project demanded the broadest sort of preparation, and Parkman was blessed with the social position, means, and opportunities which could provide it. He was the son of a leading Unitarian minister in Boston, the grandson of one of Boston's merchant princes, and an heir of the Brahmin tradition, with its pride of learning and its pride of power. His ancestry gave him a personal interest in the early history of America, in which his forebears had taken notable parts. His share of his grandfather's wealth relieved him of the necessity for making a living and enabled him to devote his life to a self-imposed task for which he received only a slight return—and that in reputation rather than in money. As a boy he roamed the Middlesex Fells near his grandfather's Medford farm and developed his lifelong fondness for the wilds. At Harvard he slighted all studies that did not further the purpose he had formed, and eagerly pursued those which promoted it. At eighteen Parkman set about preparing himself to treat the great theme which obsessed him. He did a vast amount of historical reading outside his college and law school courses, being blessed, as Sparks had been, with access to the collections of Harvard, the Athenaeum, and the Massachusetts Historical Society, which afforded facilities which then could not be enjoyed elsewhere in America. He also undertook a rigorous program of physical training designed to harden him for research in the field, for it was evident to him that "other study than that of the closet" was necessary for success in his attempt to write the history of the American forest. Rowing, riding, and boxing were supplemented by long walks and hunting expeditions through the countryside about Cambridge during term time; and all his college vacations were devoted to more ambitious and strenuous expeditions, for Parkman was determined to know the wilderness as well as the heroes of his history. Such was the origin of the series of forest journeys recorded in the early journals. In them research and recreation were combined, for most of the scenes of the struggle that dominated Parkman's thoughts lay in frontier regions, still almost untouched in the mid-nineteenth century by the advance of industrial civilization, and were in any case the places to which his innate love of the wilds would have led him. Indians and pioneers, two great categories in his cast of characters, could still be found on the New England frontier in the 1840's; and it was to these regions that Parkman first turned.

After his freshman year at Harvard, he spent the summer of 1841 in the wilds of northern New Hampshire and Maine; in the following year he visited Lake George and Lake Champlain, the scene of so many battles in the French and Indian War, and then followed the Canadian border eastward to the sources of the Connecticut River, returning home by his 1841 route. In the following summer he inspected the old forts on the lakes once more, and then passed northward by the Richelieu to Montreal and Quebec, returning by way of the White Mountains and later visiting an Indian reservation in Maine. In his desire to emulate the life of the hardy heroes who preoccupied his mind, he drove himself too sternly and nearly ruined his health; and so was packed off to Europe by his family for a rest and change. There, while touring Sicily, Italy, Switzerland, France, and Great Britain, he took advantage of his opportunity to familiarize himself with Catholicism, a potent force in his chosen field of history, and thus rid himself of some of the provincialism inherent in his make-up. In the summer of 1844, following his return from Europe and the completion of his college studies, he wandered through the Berkshire Hills, rounding out his acquaintance with the old New

England frontier. During the following summer he visited the Alleghany frontier and the old forts and trading posts of the Great Lakes, returning by way of the Mohawk Valley, the home of the Iroquois who played a role second only to that of the French and English in his history. And then in 1846 he made the greatest of his expeditions, a seven months' trip in the West over the Oregon and Santa Fe trails, in order to perfect his knowledge of the Indians. This journey brought about the collapse of a constitution already strained by ill-advised attempts to strengthen it, and so ended the series of wilderness journeys which gave Parkman a firsthand knowledge of the chief scenes of his history. No historian has ever covered the ground he was to write about as thoroughly as Parkman did, and none has left so rich a record of his preparation for his lifework.

With the long illness that followed, whose mental and physical manifestations tried his fighter's heart, Parkman lost much of the energy and vitality which make the early journals such absorbing reading. When interludes of improved health permitted travel for historical research, he was content to jot down rough notes and references in his notebooks, rather than to write full narratives, as before. All his slender store of impaired sight and diminished energy had to be concentrated on the production of the histories; there was none to squander on journalizing. These later notebooks, which record his frequent visits to Canada, his occasional forays to the French and British archives in Paris and London, and an expedition late in life to Carolina and Florida (to correct the descriptions of the one book he wrote without first going over the ground himself), are of less interest to the general reader than the early journals, though they are occasionally lit up by flashes of the prose poetry which has given an enduring vitality to Parkman's books. But they will delight the historian, who can form from them a remarkably detailed picture of Parkman's methods, sources, contacts with fellow workers, and the shoptalk of a master of the craft. And then, since Parkman was a pioneer in a virtually untouched field of history, his notes have a certain documentary value.

After 1862, when the illness which Parkman called "The Enemy" had been mastered and he began to write the books for which he had been so long preparing, he turned to the early journals for firsthand

impressions and observations to supplement the facts he had labori-
ously mined out of the mass of manuscripts, books, and pamphlets
bearing on his subject which he had accumulated. This practice does
much to explain the extraordinary vividness of his descriptions:
through the use of the journals he was able to recapture the freshness
of vision with which he first saw the chief scenes of the great historical drama. He had lived the same adventurous life as the *coureurs
de bois*, partisans, and missionaries whom he wrote about, and thus
he was able to invest his accounts of them with an immediacy and
vigor which make novels pall. The journals also served him well in
another more personal fashion: through rereading them when house-
bound by illness he could relive the strenuous days of his youth amid
the wilderness of which he was a lifelong lover. First ill-health and
then age barred him from the life of action that would have been his
choice, but he never ceased to regret being obliged to hold "the pen
with the hand that should have grasped the sword." He found compensation for his confinement in imaginative journeys, and this
mental habit stood him in good stead when he described the epic
wanderings of the French explorers and missionaries. Sometimes he
regaled his family or a close friend with a reading from one of the
early journals; sometimes, as in *Vassall Morton* or his *Harper's* articles,
he reworked these early writings for publication. The journals were
always at hand when the little world of Boston pressed too closely
upon him; he kept them in a drawer of his desk in the Beacon Hill
attic study which was decorated with trophies from the expeditions
they chronicled: an Indian shield and lance, bows and arrows, a
calumet, and pictures of some of the far places he had known in his
youth, before being confined in what he called the "Dungeon of the
Spirit." After necessity made him an armchair traveler, he developed
a great fondness for travel books. He also carried on a large correspondence with explorers such as E. G. Squier, Adolph Bandelier, and
Captain John Bourke, whom he aided in the field researches which
he himself would have liked to pursue. In his closing years some
improvement in his health permitted him another taste or two of
wilderness life: in October 1883 he made a six-day horseback trip
from Portsmouth, New Hampshire, to Crawford Notch and back, and
reported proudly that "although I am a sixty-year-old grand-

father, I was not upset by the adventure." Again, three years later, he spent the month of June camping on the Batiscan in Quebec, canoeing amid the furious eddies of that wild river, fishing, and trying his hand once more as a marksman, though his lameness confined his shooting to target practice—tame sport for one who had hunted buffalo on horseback! He spent the latter part of that same summer on the Rangeley Lakes in Maine, not far from the scenes of his youthful adventures on the Magalloway; and here he hoped to return each summer, but his health never again permitted it. His dying words concerned a dream he had had of killing a bear; his last thought was of the American forest which he has immortalized for those who can know it only by the printed page. There is no better picture of the wilderness among all Parkman's writings than that found in these journals, which are also the unassuming record of a lifetime's devotion to a single purpose that was fulfilled with a completeness rare in the annals of American letters.

II

Some account of the history of these journals is demanded by the fact that, with all their obvious value and importance, they have gone so long unpublished. Parkman's will provided that his historical papers should be turned over to the Massachusetts Historical Society upon his death, while his historical library and maps went to Harvard. The historical importance of the journals was not fully recognized by his family and early biographers. They were duly put at the disposal of Charles Haight Farnham, a former secretary who was appointed official biographer shortly after Parkman's death in 1893. Confronted with this treasure trove and a vast mass of correspondence, Farnham astigmatically characterized the materials for a life of Parkman as "extraordinarily scanty." The second biographer, Henry Dwight Sedgwick, saw the importance of the journals far more clearly, and used as many excerpts from them as the brief scope of his sketch in the American Men of Letters series permitted. It is not clear, however, whether he or Farnham ever saw all the notebooks, for they neither mention nor quote from some of them. After 1904 the journals dropped out of sight and out of memory.

In 1940, when the present writer set about the preparation of a new life of Parkman, he was unable to find any trace of these documents so essential to his purpose. They were not with the rest of the Parkman Papers at the Massachusetts Historical Society, nor among his books and maps at Harvard. The Parkman family knew nothing of their whereabouts, and was firmly convinced that all his papers had been turned over to the Historical Society. Further research in the United States and Canada offered no clue, except the evident fact that a considerable and important part of Parkman's correspondence was not with the rest of his papers at the Historical Society. Finally a visit to Parkman's old Boston home on Chestnut Street, by the kind permission of Parkman's niece, Miss Elizabeth Cordner, resulted in an inspection of his attic study, closed for the summer in 1893 and, because of his death that fall at his country home at Jamaica Plain, never since disturbed except for use as a storeroom. Parkman's Indian trophies still hung on the walls; the bookcases still held the well-worn editions of Byron, Cooper, and Scott which were his lifelong favorites; and in the center of the room, covered with a dust sheet, stood the desk on which the great histories had been written. This desk was two-sided; the drawers on one side had obviously been inspected and emptied of most of their contents, though in one was found the wire grid he used to guide his pencil when he could not see to write. The drawers on the other side had been overlooked; they contained the missing journals and a great mass of correspondence, including some of the most important letters Parkman wrote and received. Evidently, when Sedgwick returned the materials loaned him for the writing of his biographical sketch, the manuscripts had been returned to their accustomed place in the desk; and with the death of Parkman's sister, who had acted as his secretary, their hiding place had been forgotten. Miss Cordner graciously put the rediscovered material at my temporary disposal for the writing of my biography of Parkman; and then the manuscripts passed into the possession of the Massachusetts Historical Society, where it was agreed that they belonged under the spirit of Parkman's will.

III

The editing of the journals has presented certain problems. Some may consider the verbatim publication of such material, largely written in youth and for the author's eye alone, as a disservice to the memory of a great writer. But the polished and revised version of many a passage from the journals may be found in the standard sets of Parkman's works; and much of the special quality of these informal notes taken on the spot would be lost if the text were edited in accordance with modern usages. In addition, the historian would not be served, since he prefers the original text. Therefore, since the general reader (for whom Parkman wrote, scandalous as that may seem today) will not be particularly inconvenienced by slight variations from modern usage, and may be consoled by the discovery that even the greatest writers fall prey to slips of the pen, it has seemed best to present the text of the journals as Parkman wrote and hastily revised it. Punctuation has been modernized and such emendations made as were demanded for clarity. All such editorial emendations are in brackets, while parentheses have been used to indicate the omissions practiced in modern or correct spelling of the text. Parkman's footnotes are signed with his initials; those of the editor are indicated. Alternative readings rejected by Parkman have not been preserved, except in the 1870 Notebook, as a sample of his method of writing. Proper names have been given in their correct form in brackets upon their first appearance in each journal, and identified on the same basis in the footnotes when necessary or possible. Page references to the original MMS. are supplied in the running-heads.

Since the book is intended both for the general reader and the historical student, the editorial notes have not been allowed to encumber the text, but have been grouped at the back of the book, except for those necessary to follow the text, or cross references. In the course of six years' work on Parkman, the editor has accumulated considerable detailed information which, while wearisome to the general reader, may prove of service to the student not familiar with the mass of Parkman manuscript material or with the bypaths of Canadian history. This accounts for the fact that the notes sometimes bulk larger than the text of the terse later notebooks, which are largely concerned with historical matters. This material has been relegated where it will not obstruct the path of the general reader, while it remains accessible to the specialist or the curious. An introduction to each journal places it in relation to Parkman's life and works, and supplies general background material. Since the journals so closely approximate an autobiography, a chronological table is the chief biographical material here supplied. Further facts and theories on Parkman's life are available in the editor's *Francis Parkman: Heroic Historian* (New York, 1942). All references to Parkman's books are to the Frontenac edition, the last revision by the author.

The journals are published with the permission of the owners, the Massachusetts Historical Society, and with the consent of the Parkman family. For permission to reprint excerpts which have already appeared in print, the editor makes grateful acknowledgment to the Viking Press, the Limited Editions Club, Little, Brown & Company, and the Houghton Mifflin Company. The illustrations, aside from those by Parkman and the portrait of him, have been drawn from the William H. Coverdale Collection of Canadiana at the Manoir Richelieu, Murray Bay, P.Q., by courtesy of Canada Steamship Lines, Montreal. The editor is greatly indebted to the Western historical scholarship of Bernard DeVoto for aid with the Introduction and Notes of the Oregon Trail Journal, and to the cartographic knowledge of Norman Fee of the Public Archives of Canada for map references. The maps of Parkman's travels have been drawn by Van H. English of the Department of Geography, Dartmouth College. The editor welcomes this opportunity to express his thanks to a host of individuals who have aided his work and made this book possible; he is under particular obligation to Daniel Sargent, Bernard DeVoto, the late Eugene Saxton, Allyn B. Forbes, J. Bartlet Brebner, Antoine Roy, Père René Baudry, Joseph Belleau, and Alexander Laing. He is indebted for assistance and many courtesies to the staffs of the Massachusetts Historical Society, the Harvard College Library, the Dartmouth College Library, the Public Archives of Canada, the Archives of the Province of Quebec, the McGill University Library, and the Quebec Literary and Historical Society. He particularly thanks Mlles. B. Binet and B. Labrecque for assistance in preparing the manuscript, and Miss Caroline Neef for reference work.

MASON WADE

Quebec 1943–
Cornish 1946

Chronological Table

1823.   Born September 16 on Beacon Hill, Boston, eldest son of the Rev. Francis Parkman and Caroline Hall Parkman, descendants of Elias Parkman and John Cotton.

1831-35.   Parkman lived during these years on his grandfather Hall's farm at Medford and developed an interest in nature while roaming the Middlesex Fells.

1838.   Family moved to grandfather Samuel Parkman's mansion in Bowdoin Square, Boston.

1840-41.   Entered Harvard. Spent summer vacation of his freshman year in the White Mountains and Maine with Daniel Denison Slade.

1842.   Spent his summer vacation with Henry Orne White visiting Lake George and Lake Champlain, northern Vermont, the Eastern Townships of Quebec, the Connecticut Lakes, and then retraced the course of the previous summer's journey.

1843.   First trip to Canada: Lake George, Lake Champlain, St. John's, Chambly, Montreal, Quebec, White Mountains. After return to Boston, visited Penobscot Indians at Bangor, Maine.

1843-44.   European Tour, November-June: Gibraltar, Malta, Sicily, Italy, Switzerland, France, and Great Britain.

1844.   Visited Berkshire Hills. Graduated from Harvard College and entered Dane Law School.

1845.   Visited Pennsylvania, western New York, Detroit, Mackinac, Sault Ste. Marie, and returned home by way of the Mohawk Valley. Wrote sketches of frontier life for the *Knickerbocker Review*.

1846-47.   Wrote first version of *The Oregon Trail*, which appeared serially in the *Knickerbocker* during 1847-49.

1849.   *The Oregon Trail* published in book form.

1850.   Married Catherine Scollay Bigelow, daughter of Dr. Jacob Bigelow of Boston.

1851.   Published *The Conspiracy of Pontiac*, first historical work. Wrote on Indians for the *Christian Examiner*.

1852.   First contribution to the *North American Review:* critical article on Fenimore Cooper.

1856.   Published only novel, *Vassall Morton*. Visited Montreal, Quebec, and Ottawa Valley.

1857.   Only son, Francis, Jr., died.

1858.   His wife, Catherine Scollay Bigelow died. Parkman spent winter of 1858-59 in Paris under treatment of French neurologists.

1858-63. Worst period of health. Chief concern horticulture.

1863-64. Contributed a revision of his 1841 journal and advance chapters of *The Pioneers of France* to *Harper's* and the *Atlantic*.

1865.   Published *The Pioneers of France*, Part I of *France and England in North America*.

1866.   Published *The Book of Roses*. Visited Montreal and Quebec. Began to review historical books in the *Atlantic*.

1867.   Published *The Jesuits in North America*. Visited Middle West and Great Lakes region for La Salle material.

1868.   Elected overseer of Harvard. Wrote preface for William Smith's *Historical Account of Bouquet's Expedition against the Ohio Indians*. Spent winter in Paris and London.

1869.   Published *The Discovery of the Great West* (later called *La Salle*). Began contributing to Godkin's *Nation*.

1870.   Visited Mt. Desert and Grand Manan.

1871.   Professor of horticulture, Bussey Institution, Harvard. Visited Acadia.

1872.   Visited Europe, working in Paris archives.

1873.   Visited Quebec, lower St. Lawrence, Acadia.

1874.   Published *The Old Regime in Canada*.

1875.   Chosen Fellow of Harvard Corporation, President of Massachusetts Historical Society.

1876.   Developed *lilium Parkmanii*.

1877.   Published *Frontenac and New France under Louis XIV*.

1878.   Visited Lake George, Lake Champlain, and Quebec.

1879.   Visited Quebec, Louisburg, and Acadia.

1880.   Summer trip to Europe.

1881.   Summer trip to Europe.

1884.   Published *Montcalm and Wolfe*.

1885.   Visited Beaufort, South Carolina, and Florida east coast to revise *Pioneers*.

1886.   Camped on Batiscan River in Canada. Visited Rangeley Lakes in Maine.

1887.   Last journey to Europe.

1888.   Began to spend summers at Portsmouth, New Hampshire.

1890.   Published revision of his Roman journal in *Harper's*.

1892.   Published *A Half-Century of Conflict*, thus completing *France and England in North America*.

1893.   November 8, died at his country home at Jamaica Plain, near Boston.

1841 Journal

White Mountains and Maine

Introduction

IN THE summer vacation of his freshman year at Harvard, Parkman made the first of that remarkable series of journeys which were a major part of his self-imposed preparation for his life-work. For he never could have written so vividly of the forest if he had not known wilderness life at first hand; and this excursion of July and August 1841 to the White Mountains and Maine was no mere pleasure trip, though it fulfilled Parkman's strongest desires. In an autobiographic letter, written in 1864—with characteristic reticence, in the third person—to his friend Dr. George Ellis, Parkman thus describes his youthful preoccupation with the wilderness: "His thoughts were always in the forest, whose features possessed his waking and sleeping dreams, filling him with vague cravings impossible to satisfy." But in concluding this spirited journal of his holiday, he stresses his basic purpose: "My chief object in coming so far was merely to have a taste of the half-savage kind of life necessary to be led, and to see the wilderness where it was as yet uninvaded by the hand of man." He was already thinking of that "history of the American forest" which he later planned out in detail.

So, with his classmate Daniel Denison Slade, who was equally fond of the wilderness—at least in theory—Parkman spent a month traveling by stage, foot, and skiff through the then unfrequented wilds of northern New Hampshire and Maine, indulging his liking for fishing and hunting, and living the life of the forest dweller. Journeying by train from Charlestown to Dover, New Hampshire, the two young men took first to a stage and then to shank's mare, reaching Lake Winnipesaukee in the midst of an overpowering hot spell. Thence, by way of Conway and Bartlett, they continued to Crawford Notch, long to be Parkman's favorite center for excursions in the White Mountains. Here he scrambled about the cliffs

3

in the Notch, almost killing himself in one climb which he describes so vividly that it is clear that at seventeen the future historian knew singularly well how to paint action in words. Then he rode up to the summit of Mt. Washington on the newly opened Crawford bridle path. (Incidentally, he was so charmed by the "strength and spirit and good humor" of one of his companions here, a Miss Prentiss of Keene, that he became her devoted admirer for some five or six years.) Then he and Slade walked over to Franconia Notch, where they saw the sights and tried their hand with rod and gun.

Having been told of the existence of Dixville Notch while at Crawford's, and learning that moose and other big game were to be found there, Parkman dragged the increasingly reluctant Slade northward by way of Lancaster and Colebrook. At Lancaster he fell in with the State Geological Survey party under Dr. Charles T. Jackson, and got a full account of the country to the north and of the requisites for those who would travel there. Slade found this alarming, "as if we were bound for an exploring expedition to Hudson's Bay," and displayed a strong desire to go home rather than into the wilderness. But by means of alternate taunts and appeals he was induced to continue. After the pair left Colebrook, they were really in the wilds, for there was then only a handful of settlers in this region. Passing through Dixville Notch, where a road of sorts was first opened in this same year to Bragg's Settlement (Errol), Parkman and Slade followed the Androscoggin upstream to its source, at the juncture of the Magalloway River with the outlet of Lake Umbagog, near the Maine border. Somewhere below the present Wilsons Mills, Maine, they and their guide took to a skiff and followed the Magalloway northward to its forks, not far from the Canadian boundary. It is impossible to trace the route on a modern map, since the damming of the Magalloway above Wilsons Mills has covered Parkman's path with the waters of Aziscoos Lake. Without proper equipment and supplies, Parkman and Slade journeyed much as the Jesuit missionary and the *coureur de bois* had done, depending upon fish and game to swell their meager larder. Only the absence of blankets and bread, and the complete discouragement of Slade, deterred Parkman from continuing on to Canada by way of the St. Francis or Chaudière rivers.

Turning back, they retraced their route as far as Lancaster; and thence Parkman proceeded to Boston by stage down the Connecticut Valley, through Littleton, Haverhill, Hanover, and Windsor, and then to Nashua, where he took the train. Despite the rigors of this journey—no small feat for a gently nurtured seventeen-year-old, accustomed to the soft life of a student—Parkman viewed this journey "as the beginning of greater things" and "as merely prefatory to longer wanderings." Far from being worn out or weary of the wilderness, he expressed a wish soon to pass another month as pleasantly, as he initialed the last page of the journal with two triumphant flourishes. This hope had to be deferred until the following summer, when he returned to Boston by the Magalloway route after a far more ambitious journey along the Canadian border.

Aside from its interest as an early account of the best-known places in the White Mountains by one of their most ardent and eloquent admirers, this journal is notable for its picture of Parkman as a man and as a writer at the age of seventeen. Here are revealed the qualities of solitary courage and perseverance which enabled him to accomplish his lifework despite the almost insuperable difficulties which beset his path. And here, in this joyous and vivid narrative set down with only a few slips of the pen, is the measure of Parkman's precocious ability to use words effectively, and to make the unfamiliar world of the wilderness come alive for the armchair wanderer. The historian still had much to learn, but the writer was ready for the task that lay ahead.

The journal is written in ink in a $6\frac{3}{8}$ by $7\frac{7}{8}$ inches copybook, with marbled paper covers. In September, soon after his return to Boston, Parkman rewrote the account of the Magalloway portion of the journey in ink on gray paper. This revised version is inferior to the original, losing the simplicity and vigor of the first in an effort to be literary; and since it incorporates no new material, it is not reproduced here. Twenty-three years later Parkman published in *Harper's Magazine* for November 1864 (XXIX, 735-41) an anonymous sketch, "Exploring the Magalloway," which is based upon these youthful notes, and those of the 1842 journal. His companion Slade wrote an account of the trip ("In the White Mountains with Francis Parkman in 1841," *New England Magazine*, New Series, Vol. XI, 1 [September 1894], 94-9), supposedly based on his own diary but really on Parkman's. Slade's essay has little value, since it romanticizes in retrospect: "The entire journey was a delight to us"!

1841

July 19ᵗʰ, Monday. I was disappointed of one of my companions, Tower,[1] who fell sick this morning, having imprudently gorged himself with pie yesterday. Dan Slade's[2] horror at so inauspicious an occurrence damped his own ardor and somewhat retarded his preparations, insomuch that I watched from the window, quarter of an hour after the specified time, without beholding the approach of either of my fellow travelers. At length Dan appeared alone, striding along like the colossus; and truly there was need, for we had just five minutes to reach the depot of the railroad, three-quarters of a mile off. By a special providence, a hack was passing; we jumped in, exhorted the driver to use his best speed, and reached the railroad boat at the instant she was leaving the wharf. This was at seven o'clock—at ten we were at Portsmouth—at half-past eleven we were at Dover,[3] and at twelve, *cibo et poto graves,*[a] were on the way to Alton. Our conveyance was none of the most agreeable. A little carryall, whose legitimate freight was four persons, was doomed to transport seven, with baggage more than proportional. Four ladies, or women, were deposited behind, politeness, of course, forbidding Dan and myself to lay claim to back seats. The front seat was all that remained and the driver was a portly man—imagine, then, our condition—uncomfortable, at any rate, but almost insufferable when it be considered that beside being jammed by our disagreeable propinquity, we were obliged to sit bolt upright, for two of the "ladies" occupied the seat just behind, so that we sat back to back with these fair ones, with no guard between; consequently an attempt on our part to lean would have pitched the nymp(t)hs, head first, into the laps of their neighbors opposite. This state of thing endured for twenty miles, but the driver being pleasant, civil, and accommodating, the matter

[a] "Full of food and drink."—Ed.

7

was not so bad as it might have been. This "extra accommodation"—for such it was—carried us within twelve miles of Alton.⁴ Here we got out, glad of any change, strapped on knapsacks, and entered upon our pedestrian experiences. The way was long and the burden heavy; I particularly had, beside my knapsack, a heavy gun, a ponderous double shot-pouch, well filled, an[d] a powder flask. We travelled on at a tolerably easy rate, until Dan, seating himself on a stone, complained that his darned knapsack hurt his shoulders. He accordingly carried it in his hand a space, but finding this method still more annoying, he again restored it to its rightful position.

"How far to Alton Bay?" we inquired of a rustic who was raking hay in a field. "Two mile strong." "Two miles what?" said we in astonishment. "Two mile strong—rather more nor two mile"; and, accordingly, we found ourselves entering a valley between two ranges of high hills which had appeared to us first, a few hours before, like blue clouds in the distance. The road, flanked by thick woods, wound downwards through the valley; at length we turned an angle of it and saw the waters of the lake glistening through the trees. "There!" cried Dan in exstacy, "there's the lake at last—hope we shall get some good supper—Frank, is my face clean?" Having satisfied Dan on the important subject of his question, I proceeded down with him to a most unpromising-looking tavern on the lake shore. Nevertheless, our lodgings are good and our supper was excellent. We have travelled upwards of a hundred miles today, twelve of them on foot.

July 20ᵗʰ. The Winnipissiogeeᵇ steamboat foundered last year, the only sail-boat at Alton was out of repair, and our only alternative was a walk to Senter [Center] Harbor. There runs a road along the western banks of the lake, but little travelled, for the first eight or ten miles at least, and commanding fine views of the water and mountains. We left Alton by this path in the morning, doubting nothing to reach Senter Harbor by night, albeit it was a distance of nearly thirty miles. At first we were cool enough, for the road was flanked by deep and dark forests and shaded by wild hills, winding

---

ᵇ *Winnipisseogee* was the most common variant spelling of *Winnipesaukee* in nineteenth-century usage.—Ed.

at one time along the edge of the lake and then passing through
shaded vallies. But this happy condition of things was not destined
to last. The sun grew hotter and hotter and the road more and more
open. For the first hour or two, we passed no dwellings but a few
log-cabins, with a little clearing in the forest around them. But, alas,
the little pathway was widened by the junction of others, and farm
houses began to appear, first singly, then in clusters, with clearings
extending for miles. The road, too, began to turn from the edge of
the lake and to run inland, so that the scenery was no ways so interesting as before. It was almost noon and we toiled up the scorching
road, sweating and grumbling at the folly which had deprived us of
shelter and comfort by ridiculously burning the forests, in the zeal
for making clearings, though the burnt land lays utterly waste and
the sole effect of the operation is to ruin the scene and lay the road
open to the baking sun. The thermometer was at about 90° and the
road had become most disgustingly hilly and dreary. We reached
the lake again and bathed—no small relief, for our clothes clung to
us with sweat. Next we stopped at a farm house and got some bread
and milk, and next made a temporary encampment in a cool piece
of wood and rested some time. Then we journeyed on again, and
that part of us left undissolved by the heat arrived early in the afternoon at Meredith Bridge, where we lost no time in establishing ourselves at the tavern, wisely relinquishing our purpose of proceeding
further. "Last time you catch me walking this time of day," said Dan
from his easy chair in the tavern parlor. "Amen," said I, "we will
set out before sunrise tomorrow." Meredith Bridge, by the way, is a
disgusting little manufacturing village, with no single point of attraction, either as concerns scenery or anything else, if we set aside the
six-pound trout somctimes taken there. Indeed, we heard an apocry-
phal story of a trout of ten pounds caught a day or two ago.

July 21ˢᵗ, Wednesday. Agreeably to our resolutions of last night we
were up early; nevertheless, the sun from its very rising was insufferably hot, and every well we passed was called upon for our relief.
The inhabitants were a kind and hospitable race, to talk like the
geography. When we stopped at the cistern, a white-headed brat
would generally be despatched out to us with a mug, that we might

quench our thirst with the greater convenience, or the master of the house would come himself and hold a talk with us.

We toiled on to Meredith Village—nine miles—where we breakfasted, and finding that we were losing flesh with astounding rapidity and gaining nothing to counterbalance it, we hired a waggon and rode the remaining four miles to Senter Harbor. Here we got rooms, and finding it impossible to stir on account of the heat, we amused ourselves indoors as we best might, Dan with snoring on his bed and I with reading the *Alhambra*[5] on the balcony. There I sat watching the heated air rising from the road and fences, and the lake as it lay enduring the heat with Christian resignation, with its surface like glass and all its trees wilting over it. There has been no rain here for weeks; the crops are dried up and all the grass of a straw color. The evening brought some relief, for a party of us, having obtained a leaky boat with infinite difficulty, went out on the pond and landed on some of the islands. Returning, we bathed, to the indescribable horror and inexpressible consternation of a party of ladies who had been out in a leakier boat, and who were advancing in the darkness directly into the midst of us until we signified the peculiar delicacy of our situation by splashings in the water and unequivocal callings to one another. Then, indeed, arose a suppressed murmuring of "Oh's!" and "Ah's!" and "Did you ever's!" as the boat sheered off.

July 22nd, Thursday. We set out before sunrise this morning for Red Hill[6] in a waggon. The waggon and the early hour were both adopted from prudential motives, for we remembered our roasting of yesterday. We arrived at the foot of the hill a little after sunrise, fastened our horse, and began the ascent. The road is still shadowed by the forests, though it is extremely doubtful how long it will remain so. The unsightly "cleared land" is constantly extending its bounds up the side of the hill, and the smoke of the fires which are destroying the chief ornament of the country fills the air. So much for the Yankee spirit of improvement. The path at first is not steep. Half way up the mountain stands the house of the Cooke family, of whom we found only the deaf and dumb daughter at home. We made her comprehend that we wanted something to eat, and by imitating the

motion of milking and other pantomimic representations, that bread
and milk was what we particularly desired. She bestirred herself
with the greatest alacrity, and we pursued our journey upwards
marvellously refreshed. We reached the top but were disappointed.
The air was filled with vapour, and thin dull clouds were hanging
around the mountains. Even the near ridge of Ossipee looked like a
huge, indistinct, ragged wall, and the lake—visible in clear weather
through its whole extent—could now scarcely be seen at a distance
of ten miles. The whole landscape was dim and dull as if seen
through smoke. I had seen it once before in its perfection,[7] and knew
what we lost; as for Dan, he appeared to care little one way or other.

He sat him on a stone, and gave one glance at the view—"First-
rate prospect!—I tell you what, Frank, I guess my shoes won't stand
this much longer." "Dan," said I, as we went down, "I shall start for
the White Mountains this noon—you had better wait here a day or
two for Tower; you can join me again, if you want to, at Crawford's." "Darne it!" responded my fellow traveller, "you don't
suppose I am going to stay alone in this dirty hole, do you? If you
go, I'll go too."[c]

At two o'clock we took stage for Conway, having spent the interim
since the morning in sleeping and reading, for the heat is Tartarean,
and being out of doors at noon is out of the question. The country
was extremely wild and beautiful—more so than my recollection of
my former journey had prepared me for. Ossipee Pond is a magnificent sheet of water, girt by mountains, and not choked up, like
Winnipissiogee, by a too-great number of islands. We passed, too,
Chicoriuya, alias Chorcorua, Mountain, the highest peak of a noble
range, from whose summit the Indian chief who has given it his
name flung himself in dispair at the encroachments of the white
men.[8] But all these scenes are impaired by wide patches of burnt
wood and the half-cultivated lands which increase continually and
disfigure them more and more. We arrived at Conway at eight, and
I occupied myself with writing a letter home.

[c] Ten lines have been inked out here in the journal, and are largely illegible. They
open with a regret that Tower had not come along, so that Parkman could have left
his companions whenever he felt like it.—Ed.

July 23rd, Friday. Set out from Conway at six, breakfasted at Bartlett at eight, and proceeded onward for the mountains. The weather was cloudy and threatening, and passing a valley in the mountains, it began to rain. It soon ceased and we kept on through a country ten times wilder and more mountainous than we passed yesterday. The forests were untouched, and the hills, in place of the coat of green woods, were broken with precipices and crowned with shattered crags. The clouds were around most of them, and the view was indistinct with the mist, yet sometimes the more interesting on that very account. We reached (the) old man Crawford's,[9] eight miles from the Notch, and it began to rain in good earnest. I was on the outside; so was Slade; so were two ladies. At first we put up umbrellas; but the rain came down like a thunder shower, and I, who sat on the driver's seat, and whose umbrella, consequently, conducted a small torrent of dirty water directly into the laps of the ladies behind, judged it expedient to lower my miserable shelter and receive the bounty of heaven in full. This, indeed, subjected me to no additional drenching for, in the situation in which I was, the umbrella was like a dam of bulrushes against the Nile. We made sport of the matter, although the driver averred he had not gotten such a ducking for four years—the ladies especially exhibited much philosophy, though of the kind denominated "laughing philosophy," and, altogether, the ducking was an extremely agreeable affair. We entered the Notch; the clouds lay over the mountains from top to bottom, but occasionally, as some heavy mass was rolled aside, we caught a view of the craggy and savage hill, scored with avalanche tracks, and white with torrents. The little streams, parched up by the heat, were swoln on a sudden and went foaming about us, and rising every instant more and more. We reached the Notch House[10] in pretty plight. For myself, not a thread of my thin clothing was dry, and the heroic ladies were wet to the skin. A little brandy and water, with a change of clothing, revived us, though a reviving process was almost needless.

July 24. This morning I went fishing, following downwards the stream of the waterfall which comes down through the Floom [Flume]. I basketed about thirty trout. The weather was dull and cloudy; the clouds hid the peaks of the mountains and rolled in huge masses along their sides. Early in the morning the mist was rolling, in a constant stream, from the narrow opening of the Notch, like a furnace disgorging its smoke.

This afternoon I achieved the most serious adventure it was ever my lot to encounter. I walked down the Notch to the Willey House[11] and, out of curiosity, began to ascend in the pathway of the avalanche on the mountain directly behind. This pathway is a deep ravine, channelled in the side of the mountain which in this place is extremely steep. In the bottom of this gulf a little stream comes down from a spring above and renders the precipitous rock as slippery as clay. The sides of the ravine, which runs directly up and down the mountain, are of decaying granite, while the bottom is formed by a trap-dike. I ascended at first easily, but the way began to be steeper and the walls on each side more precipitous. Still I kept on until I came to a precipice about forty feet high and not far from perpendicular. I could see that this was followed by a similar one above. Professor Silliman,[12] a year or two ago, ascended in this place, until, as he says, "further progress was prevented by inaccessible precipices of the trap rock." The exploit of the professor occurred to me as I stood below and I determined that "inaccessible precipices" which had cooled his scientific ardor should prove no barrier to me. I began to climb; and with considerable difficulty and danger, and with the loss of my stick, which went rattling and bounding down the ravine many rods before it found a resting place, I surmounted both precipices. I climbed on; but finding that I was becoming drenched by the scanty stream, and seeing, moreover, a huge cloud, not far up, settling slowly towards me, I bethought me of retracing my steps. I knew that it would be impossible to descend by the way I had come, and, accordingly, I tried to get out of the ravine to the side of the mountain which was covered with wood, which I could grasp hold of to assist me. But I was enclosed between two walls, (of) fifty feet high and so steep and composed of such material that an attempt to climb would only bring down the rotting granite upon my head. So I began to descend the ravine, nothing doubting that I should find some means of getting out before reaching the critical point. But it was impossible, and I found myself at the top of the precipice with no alternative but to slide down, or clamber the perpendicular and decaying walls to the surface of the mountain. The former was certain destruction, as I proved by suffering a rotten log to slide down. It glanced by the first descent like an arrow, struck at the bottom, bounded six feet into the air, and leaped down the mountain, splintering into twenty pieces as it went. The other method was scarcely less dangerous, but it was my only chance, and I braced my nerves and began to climb. Down went stones and pebbles, clattering hundreds of feet below and giving me a grateful indication of my inevitable fate in case my head should swim or my courage fail. I had got half way up and was clinging to the face of the precipice, when the two stones which supported my feet loosened and leaped down the ravine. My finger-ends, among the rotten gravel, were all which sustained me, and they, of course, would have failed, had I not thought, on the instant, of lowering my body gradually, and so diminishing its weight, until my feet found new supporters. I sank the length of my arms and then hung, for the time, in tolerable safety, with one foot resting on a projecting stone. Loosening the hold of one hand, I took my large jack-knife from my pocket, opened it with the assistance of my teeth, and dug with it a hollow among the decayed stones large enough to receive and support one foot. Then, thrusting the knife as far as possible into the wall to assist my hold, I grasped it and the stones with the unoccupied hand and raised my foot to the hollow prepared for it. Thus, foot by foot, I made my way, and in ten minutes, as time seemed to me, I siezed a projecting root at the top and drew myself up. During the whole time of climbing, I felt perfectly cool, but when fairly up, I confess I shuddered as I looked down at the gulf I had escaped. A large stone, weighing, perhaps, a hundred pounds, lay on the edge. I thrust it off with my foot and down it went, struck the bottom of the ravine with a tremendous crash, and thundered down, leaping from side to side, until it lodged at last, far below, against a projecting rock. I descended the mountain by means of the trees and bushes; cut a fishing pole at the bottom; and, having amused myself with an hour's fishing, went to the tavern, and astonished the company with a recital of my adventure. Crawford expressed considerable astonishment at my escape, and the young lady in whose company I got my ducking on the stage transferred an account to her journal, but refused to let me see it, promising to send me a copy the moment her book was out of the press. Crawford's house, by the way, is full of pleasant company, and an ascent of Mount Washington is in agitation tomorrow.

July 25th. This morning proving tolerably fair, we set out for the mountain—an army of ten strong, horse[13] and foot, male and female. The first two miles (the entire distance is six miles) are through a dense forest—an ascent the whole distance. As we went on, the trees grew smaller and smaller, until we arrived in two hours at a height where the path ascended through a forest of the gigantic height of two feet—a complete miniature of the larger wood we had passed. Ten minutes more and we were on the summit of Mt. Clinton [Pierce][d] with a long succession of wild and rocky peaks stretching before. We descended Mount Clinton and mounted the higher summit of Mount Pleasant, and here a most glorious scene presented itself to us. On each side, thousands of feet below, stretched a wide valley, girt with an amphitheatre of mountains rising peak after peak like the black waves of the sea, the clouds now sinking over their summits, now rising and breaking, disclosing yet more distant ranges, and then settling thick and heavy so that nothing was visible but the savage rocks and avalanche slides of the neighboring mountains looming dimly through the mist. At length the clouds closed around and we could not even see one another and we descended Mount Pleasant in darkness. But as we mount[ed] up the steep ascent of Mount Monroe [Franklin] the sun broke out bright and clear; the mists gathered themselves and rolled down the mountain sides, quivered an instant, then boiled up through the ravines and gorges, scattered, and were borne along glistening in the sun, among the thousand mountains that lay beneath and around us. At the same moment, a peal of thunder sounded below and a rainbow arched, for an instant, the peak before us. I stopped my horse on the ridge where we stood and watched the rest, as they wound in a long line up the mountain. The side was steep and the path ran zig-zag up. No scene among the Andes could have been wilder or more picturesque. They moved, one by one, up the steep, bending and winding in twenty directions, the outlandish habits of the gentlemen and

[d] Mt. Pierce was known at this time as Mt. Clinton.—Ed.

the fluttering shawls of the ladies suiting well with the scene, until they stood against the sky on the summit. I followed, and the scene appeared yet sublimer and more extensive. The mountains were like a sea of lashing waves; the valley of the Connecticut was visible for fifty miles, with the river winding through it like a thread; while in the valley below, the forests seemed, from the tremendous height we stood upon, like fields of mown grass intersected by the channels of streams whose waters, at intervals, flashed in the sun. Two peaks were still before us, the highest and most distant topped with clouds, and this was Mt. Washington. We reached the first, Mt. Franklin [Monroe], and the path led along a ledge on a high precipice at its summit. The ledge overhung the valley beneath—deeper even than that on the other side, and in place of the extensive prospect there visible, a huge range of mountains, marked with avalanches and capped with clouds, heaved up like a wall.

We passed the Lake of the Clouds, near the summit of the Mountain—the source of the Amonioosack [Ammonoosuc] and another large stream. The lake is small but very deep and its waters extremely cold. Mount Washington now rose before us, still covered with clouds, and with patches of snow laying in its sheltered hollows. We mounted, and in a moment entered the clouds again. We could hear each other's voices but see nothing. The path wound among bare rocks scantily covered with moss, with here and there a stunted blade of coarse grass, and no other sign of vegetation. The wind was strong and cold and sleet was mixed with the mist that drove along the mountain. We reached the top at last—a pyramid of huge rocks through which the wind was whistling like the shrieking of a storm and faintly bore down to us the voices of some of the party who had reached the top before us and were singing "Old Hundred" to the winds. Crawford brought us provisions, with a stock of brandy, which he served out to us in a sheltered spot, as we sat round a flat rock which was his table. We remained there three-quarters of an hour in the vain hope of its clearing, but a storm of sleet and rain came on and we began our descent. We soon reached warmth and sunlight, and the scenes we had passed in ascending appeared to yet greater advantage now. Two of the party fell from their horses, three of the ladies were faint-hearted, and all of them tired with one exception—Miss Prentiss[14] of Keene, whose strength and spirit and good humor would have invigorated at least a dozen feeble damsels. We passed the mountains, entered the forest, and reached the tavern, having set out at ten in the morning and returned at seven in the evening. I walked, from choice, all but a mile in going, and all but about twice that distance in returning, the entire distance being twelve miles of ascent and descent.

July 26. A dull rain. It held up in the morning and I ascended the High Rock[15] in the Notch, whence I had a noble view. As in my former more critical adventure, ascending was passable, but coming down abominable. The way was through a tangled wood, rocky, bushy, and strewed in all directions with rotten trunks, many of which, when stepped upon, straightway burst to pieces, and, unless I was extremely careful, seated me among their rot. There was a path, but I did not avail myself of it. Coming down, I found dinner over and all the pleasant company gone to Franconia, whither I shall go tomorrow, weather permitting. And now, having made up for former neglect by writing 9 pages at a sitting, I begin to feel tired and more disposed to curse the weather than ever before, and the prospect of an evening almost solitary in no wise tends to improve my temper. Heaven send that I be not obliged to spend another day here at the Notch House—a place which, though one of the pleasantest in the world at other times, is the perfection of dulness in bad weather.

July 27th. We spent the last evening in the desirable company of Mr. and Mrs. Plummer—a couple of the most consummate fools I ever saw. They set out for the mountain this morning, though the lady uttered the most piercing shrieks her limited power of lungs could compass the instant she was seated in the saddle. A fit person she is, truly, to climb a mountain of seven thousand feet!ᵉ We left Crawford's early this morning, on foot, for Franconia. The morning was the finest we have had yet; so was the road. At Fabyan's, where we stopped a few minutes, we heard that our intended companion, Tower, had arrived before us, having recovered from his illness; and

ᵉ Mt. Washington's real height is 6,288 feet.—Ed.

was then gone, with a party, to Mt. Washington. He passed Crawford's without thinking to inquire there for us. We found, to our
surprise, that George Cary, Henry Parker, and Wheelright[16] were
at the tavern in the morning, but were now absent on the mountain.
We walked on. I shot a partridge and a wild pigeon, and we stopped
at noon in the woods on the bank of the Amonoosuck, kindled a fire,
cooked our game, and made a good dinner with the assistance of
some crackers. Eight miles further on, and we arrived at Franconia
Village—a distance of twenty-two miles from our morning starting
place.

July 28th. Left Franconia Village for the Notch this morning, having
first committed my imbecile shoes to the care of a competent cobbler
and substituted a new straw hat—the only one in the town—for my
damaged old one. We reached the Notch and dined on bread and
milk, then visited the curiosities of the place. The Old Man of the
Mountain scowled as fixedly as ever, and the mountains, with their
forest-covered sides and bare white peaks, presented the same aspect
as when I had seen them three years before. We found a boat on one
of the little lakes and circumnavigated it for some time, at the great
risk of capsizing, for the boat was a wretched affair. Spite of its fine
scenery, the place began to grow dull, and we walked on to Lincoln,
in order to see the Flume in the morning.

At Lincoln the sole tavern and the sole house presented rather
discouraging aspect; nevertheless, enter we must and make the best
of it we could. The interior arrangements in no wise belied external
appearances. In company with a most comical looking Yankee
pedlar, we were served with a supper whereof the chief item was
raw cucumbers, backed by an anonymous pie with a crust like
lignum-vitae. We survived it, not being fastidious, and having the
anticipation of a good breakfast, provided it be not spoiled in the
cooking, for I shot on the road a large partridge and several wild-
pigeons which I delivered to the hostess for preparation. In addition
to the other slight drawbacks to comfort, we found the host[f] drunk;
and it was with difficulty that we made him comprehend that clean
sheets, a couple of chairs, and a table were indispensable requisites.

[f] Referred to as Gurnsey in the 1842 Journal.—Ed.

As to a washstand, there was no such thing in the house; so we must e'en be content with the pump.

July 29th. We set out this morning, before breakfast, to see the Flume. Half-way through the woods, we missed the path, but, guided by the roaring of the water, we found the banks of the Pemigewasset and determined to follow them up until we reach the Flume. Now we were making a grievous mistake, for the Flume is not on the main stream, but on a branch of it in an opposite direction from the one we were pursuing. The forest was dense and dark, and the ground strewed with fallen trunks in various states of decay. The ground was rocky, moreover, and full of ravines and deep holes; and the thick matted undergrowth in nowise facilitated our progress. On we went, stumbling amongst piles of rotten logs, and switched in all directions by the recoiling twigs. The forest was almost impassable, so we essayed the bank of the river. But the river was full of huge rocks and stones, amongst which the water came racing and foaming down, so that even wading up its bed was impossible. Cliffs (of) sixty feet high, damp and green with moss, and with pine and birch trees growing from their fissures in many places, overhung the water; and along their edges and up and down their sides we must make our way. I was encumbered with gun and shot pouch, which was a still farther aggravation of my difficulties. Dan stopped short: "Hang your dirty Flume! I move we go back to the house and get the old man to show us the way as he said he would." "We could not find the house, Dan; our only way is to keep on till we come to the Flume. It can't be more than a few rods further."

There was a kind of natural pathway at the foot of the cliffs and we followed it, making our way with difficulty between the rocks on one side and the roaring water on the other. A projecting rock and a slight bend in the stream prevented our seeing further before us, but we heard a loud heavy plunging of water. By swinging from a projecting branch and making a long leap, we gained a flat rock in the middle of the river, and beheld a scene which paid us for our trouble. A broad circular basin[17] of water was before us, so deep that its waves were of a dark green, with huge perpendicular cliffs rising on each hand above it. From the top of the cliffs, trees started out obliquely against the sky and dripping festoons of moss were hanging from every cleft. In front, these same cliffs swept round until they almost met, leaving a narrow passage for the river, through which it plunged, over a wall of rocks, into the basin below. Above, it might be seen again, foaming over a bed of steep rocks, and closing the perspective with a smooth unbroken fall contrasted well with its lashing and white rapids. We looked at it for some time and then began to devise some method of proceeding. It was no easy matter, for the cliffs rose directly from the water and their sides were so steep and smooth that they offered no hold to one passing them. Our only alternative was to scale them where they were less steep, a little way below. We got to the top and began to force our way through the forest again. "Damn the Flume," said Dan, when we had proceeded about quarter of a mile. "We must have missed it," said I, "it can't be farther on than this. This river strikes the road about a mile from here—we had better keep on till we reach it." "Devil take the Flume —I wish we had never come, or else had brought a guide." Thus profanely spoke Dan, but we kept on for half an hour, with toil and suffering, and emerged at length on the road, two miles from the tavern, having forced our way through a mile and a half of forest in the whole, and having two miles more, on the road, to walk before we reached the tavern again. We got there at last, took breakfast, procured a guide, and set out for the Flume a second time. We found, to our great satisfaction, that visitors seldom attempted, unattended, to find the place we were searching for, and that when they did they usually returned discouraged and frightened, or else became lost and had to be searched for with shoutings and firings of guns. This Flume is a huge natural trough of rock through which runs, in a succession of falls and rapids, a branch of the river Pemigewasset. On each side of the stream high cliffs rise perpendicularly and run for many rods facing each other. Their black sides are smooth, and continually dropping moisture, for the forest above extends its branches from their edges so that the light of the sun can scarcely penetrate the ravine. Standing on the rocks at the bottom and looking up, you see huge decayed trunks and branches extending across the narrow strip of sky visible between the edges of the cliffs, and the edges themselves overgrown with masses of wet and green moss which hang dripping from them. Knotted and distorted pines, rooted in the crevices, fling their boughs across; and even these, though living, are covered with damp mosses. Midway between the top of the cliffs and the water, and closing the spectator's onward view, hangs a rock, hurled by some convulsion down the ravine and intercepted between its approaching sides. Just beneath this, the stream foams down over a bed of rocks into a deep basin at their foot, then leaps from the basin and rushes forward among the stones and accumulated trunks of trees which intercept its course.

We returned from the Flume and walked back to Franconia Notch, where the tavern is kept by a man named Fifield.[18] He went with us fishing in the afternoon to a little brook at some distance in the woods. I followed the stream upward, while Fifield and Slade went in an opposite direction. Just before sunset, I was half a mile up the brook, with a long string of trout and with the full belief that I knew the direction in which the road lay. I accordingly made all speed through the forest, lest I should be overtaken by the dark. I travelled about a mile, guiding my course by the sun, but the forest seemed deeper and wilder the further I went. At length I caught sight of a mountain peak which I knew, and shaping my course by that, in a few minutes reached the road.

July 30th, Lancaster. It was a week ago that I first heard of the existence of a pass in the mountains, in the town of Dixville, said by those who have visited it to be equal or superior in grandeur to the Notch of the White Mountains. Mr. Prentiss[19] from Keene, whom I met at Crawford's, first told me of it and advised me to visit it. The country about it is a wilderness where moose and other wild game are still common, though it is traversed by a new and almost impassable road. I determined from the first to go if possible, and came to Lancaster today to secure the services of an Indian named Anantz [Annance][20] as a guide. He was by far the best hunter in this part of the country, and lived, in part, by guiding parties through the wildernesses on the borders of New Hampshire and Canada. He was an educated man, moreover, having passed through Dartmouth College, and celebrated through the country for his skill, faithfulness, and courage. But arriving at Lancaster, I found that he was absent in Vermont and that there was no other man to supply his place. Luckily, Dr. Jackson[21] and his assistants in the state survey were in the town, and from them I got a full and accurate account of the country and of the requisites for my expedition. Mr. Williams,[22] one of his assistants, hunted there under the guidance of Anantz last season, and, between them, they shot two moose! He showed me a map of my course, of which I took a copy; told me the places where temporary guides might be engaged; and, more than all, acquainted me with the usual prices of their services—a most valuable piece of information, for otherwise I could not guard myself against imposition. As for Dr. Jackson, he most kindly gave us the full fruits of his experience—and a most ample one it has been—in the matters of provision, camps, canoes, guns, guides, and a thousand other things, as if we were bound on an exploring expedition to Hudson's Bay. Dan Slade was frightened by the formidable catalogue. He muttered several dark hints about his "not entering into the spirit of it," his "not engaging to come so far," "starting off without any preparation," &c., &c. I was obliged to accuse him of a tendency to "funk out" and open upon him a full battery of arguments before he would yield a reluctant consent. I took such pains for a double reason—first, I am unwilling to travel wholly alone through the wilderness, and I do not propose to secure a guide until I have visited the pass and penetrated yet deeper—secondly, the hire for transportation and guides will amount to just half the sum; that is, I shall pay one half, and he the other.

Our course lies first to Colebrook, a town thirty-five miles north of this place, on the Connecticut; thence we proceed on foot in an easterly direction by a road little travelled which brings us to the pass. Thence keeping on, we strike the Umbagog Lake and the Ma(r)galloway river. Here there is a small settlement, where a guide may be had, and from here our journey lies—the Lord knows where. We have just engaged a private waggon for Colebrook, for no public conveyance is to be had, and we leave Lancaster for that town at seven tomorrow.

By the way, we met Tower at Littleton today. He is sick and discouraged and on his way home.

Sir William Johnson, Baronet
Engraving
(Coverdale Collection No. 72)

July 31ˢᵗ, Colebrook. We reached this place at two o'clock. It is a town of a few hundred inhabitants—the largest north of Lancaster— and lies on the Connecticut opposite Monadnock Mountain on the Vermont shore. It is watered, moreover, by the Mohawk River, a mighty stream at present about four inches deep. Our journey hither lay along the east bank of the Connecticut, through a country fertile and by no means thinly inhabited. The high mountains in the town of Stark lay on our right, and the river, fallen extremely low and full of rapids, on our left. We found a neat little tavern where we are at present stopping.

Sunday, Aug. 1ˢᵗ. Sunday in the country is a day of most unmitigated and abominable dulness. By a strong and desperate effort, I nerved myself to endure, being greatly assisted in my resolve by the discovery of several numbers of a Baltimore magazine[23] in the house. I went to church in the morning, but the minister being unfortunately an Unitarian, the dulness of his discourse and the squall of his choir were not varied and relieved by any novel fanaticism or methodistical blunders. This being the case, I determined not to go again but to stay at home and amuse myself with writing a letter.

Aug. 2ⁿᵈ, Captain Brag[g]'s Settlement [Errol, N. H.].[24] We left Colebrook and civilization this morning, and now a new epoch of this interesting history commences. Our journey lieth not, henceforward, through pleasant villages and cultivated fields, but through the wild forest and among lakes and streams which have borne no bark but the canoe of the Indian or the hunter. This is probably the last night for some time which we shall spend under a roof. Our road ran eastward towards Maine. A few farm houses were at first scattered along its side, but they became more and more distant as we went on, and at last the way was flanked by a forest so thickset and tangled that we could scarcely see two rods in any direction, excepting before and behind. We were traveling what was called a road, but the term was grievously misapplied. By dint of great exertion, a strong waggon might possibly be forced over the stones and stumps and roots and through the overhanging boughs which formed a complete arch overhead, but the attempt would be destruction to a carriage or chaise. Ruts on each side showed that it was occcasionally travelled, but that this was very seldom was evident from the grass which almost covered it. As we were sitting on a log to rest, we heard a clatter of hoofs, and in a moment a man, mounted and bearing a gun, appeared through the trees, advancing towards us. He was from Brag's settlement, thirteen miles further on, and going to Colebrook for employment. The pass, he told us, was but a few miles before us, and accordingly, through an opening in the trees, we saw the mountains extended before us like a green wall and apparently blocking our passage. A little further, and we emerged upon a plain almost free of wood; and now a gap in the range appeared, with bare and pointed rocks starting upward from the forests that covered the mountains and looking down upon us as we entered the passage. These rocks were many hundred feet high and the pass between extremely narrow. Looking upward on either side, the mountains were almost perpendicular. Fire had stripped them of their verdure and left them covered with blackened trunks and rocks rolled from the sharp peaks above. In picturesque effect the scene was superior to the Notch of the White Mountains, but in grandeur it fell far below it. Instead of the vast rounded summits of the Notch, these mountains were surmounted by peaks and needles of rock, which from below looked like ruined towers standing out in relief against the sky.

We were in want of a dinner, and so, catching some trout and shooting some pigeons, we cooked them after a style wholly original, and stayed for a time the inroads of appetite. While Dan sat still to digest his dinner, I ascended one of the mountains and had a fine view of the pass and the neighboring country. We proceeded, passed some few houses, mostly log cabins, and reached at sunset the settlement of Capt. Brag on the Amorescoggin [Androscoggin]. Here we got tolerable accommodation, and slept to the roar of the rapids of the river which ran close to the house.

The Captain slew a bear day before yesterday, and his fresh skin was nailed on the barn to dry. I write this on the morning of the 4th—having got somewhat behind-hand—by the blaze of our campfire in the forest.

And now, the life I have led for the past week having prevented my recording my experiences from day to day, I take this first opportunity for making up for former neglect. Beginning where I left off:

Tuesday, Aug. 3rd. Brag's settlement is on the Amariscoggin River, not far from Lake Umbagog and a few miles west of the mouth of the Margalloway. The Amariscoggin at this place is a succession of rapids extending more than a mile. On the Margalloway, too, some miles above its junction with the Ameriscoggin, are rapids of two miles in length and passable only by means of a rugged and difficult portage. Our intention was to take a boat and a guide at Brag's, ascend the Margalloway as far as the rapids, have the boat drawn round them and launched above, and then keep on up the river, which is navigable for thirty miles above without serious obstruction. But we found it impossible to procure here a good guide and boat, though both, they told us, were to be had at settlements on the Margalloway. Could they convey us to these settlements? Brag had but few men with him and these occupied in necessary work; moreover, there was a path through the forest several miles less than the passage by water, and by this we might reach the settlements in half a day. We determined on this route, and Brag accompanied us a mile or two on our way to point out its difficulties and to prevent our plunging into quagmires or mistaking a rabbit track or a cattle path for the road.

"The first house," said he, "is five or six miles further on. When you get about a mile, you will have to cross a brook.[g] On the other side there are logging paths and one thing another branching out like, right and left. All you have got to do is to pick out the one that you see has been most travelled by the cattle, because all the others run a little ways and then come to nothing. Then go on a little further and you will come to a guzzle that they say is pretty bad this season, though I ha'nt seen it myself. However it a'nt more than two rods wide, so I guess you can get across. Just keep, all along, where the cattle have been most, and you can't miss the way."

With these direction we set out. The path was about four inches

[g] Probably Bennett Brook.—Ed.

wide, through the dense forest, choked up with undergrowth, and obstructed by logs that had fallen across it. As may well be imagined, five miles by such a road were equivalent to twenty by any other. We crossed the brook, and following the cow-tracks, fortunately took the right turning and found to our infinite satisfaction that the path became a little more distinct and passable than before. Passing over a swampy tract, we saw deer and bear tracks in abundance. Two miles further (which two miles it took us as many hours to accomplish) and we had our first view of the Margalloway—a broad, still river whose sloping banks are, and for centuries will be, clothed with deep forests. We had forgotten the threatened "guzzle," and our very ideas of its nature were somewhat vague and mystified, though the Captain had been at great pains to explain it. But now we came upon it and our doubts were set at rest. A kind of muddy creek, very deep and dirty, extended from the river directly across the path. It was, as the Captain said, about two rods wide, with muddy and slippery banks and no earthly means of crossing but two slender poles, laid one from each bank and resting on a floating log in the middle. On the opposite bank, however, lay a heap of logs with their ends in the water, and bearing to the careless eye an appearance of tolerable solidity. With a commendable spirit of prudence, I induced Dan to make the first attempt. He cut him a long pole to steady himself, and, adding two or three additional supports to the frail bridge, essayed to cross. He planted his pole firmly in the mud and leaned hard against it, but he was not a foot from shore before the bridge began to sink, inch by inch. Daniel's ponderous frame was too much for it and, wherever he stepped, down sunk logs, poles, and branches, and resting place for his foot he had none. Dan got flurried. He splashed here and there, lost his balance, gave a leap in desperation at the treacherous pier of logs on the other side, they tilted up, and in plunged Dan, floundering among the fragments of the demolished bridge and sputtering the dirty water from his mouth. He gained the bank and shook himself like a dog. "Ha! Ha! Ha!" laughed I from one side. "Haw! Haw! Haw!" responded he from the other. "Now let's see you cross," said Dan. I accordingly rearranged the bridge with his assistance and succeeded in getting over, though wet to the knees.

We at length came to a log house with a small clearing about it, where dwell a famous hunter in those parts, one Mr. Bennet[t][25]; a man strong and hardy and handsome, moreover, though I never saw an Indian darker than exposure had made his features. He should like nothing better than to go, he said, but he was in the midst of his haying and could not think of leaving home. "I know who will go with you, though. There's Joshua Lumber [Lombard][26]—he's got a boat and a team of oxen to drag it round the falls." "Where does Joshua Lumber live?" "Just at the foot of the falls, about five miles from here." Bennet's son paddled us over the river, for the path to Lumber's was on the other side; and passing a log cabin or two, we arrived in due time at that sturdy farmer's abode. His house was the last but one on the river, Captain Wilson[27] holding a "clearing" a mile further up—all above as far as the Canada settlements is one vast forest varied, as yet, with not the slightest trace of man's hand, unless it be the remains of the hunter's encampment. Lumber's habitation, like all in these parts, was of logs. He was blessed with a wife and a number of stout boys to whose charge he confided the farm during his absence. His place is situated just within the borders of Maine. A high and picturesque mountain rises on the west, with summits some rounded, some steep and broken. The river flows at its base through fertile plains which Lumber's industry has cleared of timber and covered with a growth of grain and grass. Asesquoss [Aziscoos] is the name of the mountain.[h]

As an initiation into the mode of life which we were about to enter upon, we determined to spend the night in the forest. Accordingly we repaired thither, built a fire, and arranged our camp. Soon we received a visit from Lumber and his sons, and with them came another man whom by his speech I discovered to be an Indian, for our fire cast but a dubious light on the assembly. This Indian [Jerome],[28] who was a nephew of Anantz and an excellent hunter, said that he was going on a hunting expedition up the river in the course of a few days. Thinking that his services might be useful, I appointed a place thirty miles up the river where he should meet us, and where we might engage him to guide us through the forest to

[h] If to the west, this must have been Halfmoon Mountain. Aziscoos is to the east.— Ed.

Canada, in case we should prefer that course to returning the way
we had come.

Aug. 4th, Wednesday. Early in the morning, a light skiff, built after
the fashion of a birch canoe and weighing scarce more, was placed
on a sledge and drawn up the portage by a team of oxen. The length
of the portage was three miles and so encumbered was it with logs
and fallen trees that the axe had to be employed more than once to
open a way. "Considerable of an enterprise, sir," said the farmer
when his oxen at length stood panting on the bank of the river above
the rapids. Here lay the canoe of Jerome, the Indian, ready for his
hunting expedition.

Our boat needed some repairs after its rough passage, but in the
course of half an hour we were embarked and on our way up the
river. Our stock of provisions was exceedingly limited. Six pounds
of bread, some salt, and some butter were all we had; but there was
a certainty of procuring fish and a chance of meeting larger game.
The Indian, moreover, had a large stock of dried moose-meat concealed near the place where we were to meet him. After half an
hour's paddling, we reached the mouth of a cold stream which
entered the river; and here we got a dinner of trout, the chief draw-
back to the pleasure of fishing being that the flies bit infinitely more
than the fish. After a paddle of an hour or two more, we stopped;
and cutting down wood, built a fire and made a tolerable dinner of
our fish. Then resuming our course, we kept on until dark, when we
stopped, hauled the boat on shore, cleared a space of a few yards in
the forest, built a roaring fire, got ready a scanty supper, and prepared to spend the night as comfortably as circumstances would
allow. Our bed was a heap of spruce boughs and our fire warmed the
cold night air. Several trees were cut down to maintain the blaze
and our camp being of [on] a bank elevated far above the river, there
was little apprehension from the cold. Soon the moon came up and
glistened on the still river and half lighted the black forest. An owl,
disturbed by the glare of our fire, sent forth a long wild cry from the
depths of the woods and was answered by the shrill bark of some
other habitant of the forest. Thus far, the river bank has been clothed
with huge trees and the summits of considerable mountains appeared

on the right and left; but tomorrow we pass "the meadows," a flat and marshy tract of ground covered with low bushes through which the stream runs in a winding course for many miles. We have paddled today eighteen miles. Along the banks, moose and bear tracks have appeared in abundance—not so, unfortunately, the animals themselves.

Thursday, Aug. 5th. We resumed our journey but our rate of proceeding was slow, for, by reason of the bends of the river, five miles by water were equivalent to one in a direct line. The stream began to grow shallow, too, and the current swift—so much so that the united force of paddles and poles was barely sufficient, in some places, to propel the boat. We often ran aground on shallows or among rocks, and were obliged to get out into the water to lighten our bark. Once we were stopped by a huge barricade of timber, over which we lifted the boat by main force. The bites of the flies were intolerable, so we made a fire of rotten wood in our frying pan, and, placing it in the bow of the boat, its smoke prevented any further annoyance from that source. We could get no trout today and were obliged to rest content with a dinner of chubs, of which we took some very fine ones. We passed the meadows at length, and again our way was through the forest, and a most wild and beautiful appearance did the river shores present. From the high banks huge old pines stooped forward over the water, the moss hanging from their aged branches, and behind rose a wall of foliage, green and thick, with no space or opening which the eye could penetrate. The river was not here, as some miles below, an expanse of still deep water, but came down over a rocky and gravelly bed in a swift current and some times broke in cascades—a change which, how much soever it might improve the effect of the scene, was of no advantage to the navigation. However, we reached our destination at last. This was the fork of the river, where, branching to the right and left, it preserves on the one side its original title and, on the other, takes that of the "Little Margalloway."[i] This was the place we had appointed to meet

---

[i] Probably the place where the western branch of the Magalloway leads to the New Hampshire line and the eastern to Parmachenee Lake and thence to the Boundary Mountains.—Ed.

the Indian and where he was to appear at sunrise the next day. We made our camp—this time with a little more care, for Lumber erected a shed of boughs as a protection against the dews. We procured a mess of most magnificent trout, none of them being less than a foot in length, though this is an unfavorable season for them; supped, and went to sleep. Our camp was on the tongue of land between the two streams, and the tumbling of the water was no ways unfavorable to repose. As usual, our chief annoyance was from flies

and mosquitoes, of which the latter swarmed in numbers unprecedented, but their attacks were as nothing in comparison with that of clouds of black flies—animals not much larger than the head of a pin, but inflicting a wound twice as large as themselves and assaulting with such eagerness that nothing but being in the midst of a thick smoke will keep them off. They seemed to take a special liking to me, and I was bitten to such a degree that I am now—nearly four days after—covered with their wounds as if I had the small-pox. There is another cursed race, yet smaller, denominated from their microscopic dimensions "no-see-ems." Their bite is like the prick of a needle, but not half so endurable, and they insinuate themselves through pantaloons, stockings, and everything else.

We slept in spite of them. Morning was on the point of breaking when a shout sounded from the river, Jerome's canoe touched the shore, and in a moment he was amongst us. He had seen a moose, he said, as he came up, had fired at and, he believed, wounded her, and he would go down in the morning to see if he could find her. He wrapped him[self] in his blanket, head and all, and in two minutes was fast asleep. Well he might be, for he had been paddling since nine o'clock of the morning before.

Friday, Aug. 6th. Our bread had almost failed and, still worse, we were unprovided with blankets; we therefore abandoned our half-formed intention of going on to Canada,[j] and determined to return by the way we had come. My chief object in coming so far was merely to have a taste of the half-savage kind of life necessary to be led, and to see the wilderness where it was as yet uninvaded by the hand of man. I had had some hope of shooting a moose; but that hope seemed doomed to be disappointed, although, had we kept on, there was a very considerable chance of finding them. Slade, however, became utterly discouraged and refused to proceed; and this alone would have prevented me, even if there had been no other obstacles. We breakfasted, cleared out the boat, and began our return voyage, the Indian having set out before us, whirling down the swift current like a bubble in his bark canoe. Our descent was nothing compared to our ascent. The mist was rising from the river, and the scenes we had passed the day before with toil and difficulty bore an appearance twice as inviting, now that we were borne by them with no effort.

The canoe was quickly out of sight. We had gone about five miles when a sudden splash into the water arrested our attention, and we saw a young moose, far in front, leap from the bank and wade the river. He ascended the opposite shore, shook the water from his flanks, and disappeared in the woods. I dropped my paddle, cocked my gun, and stood in the prow of the boat. We bore down swiftly and silently to the spot where he had disappeared, but there was no trace of him but the broad tracks which marked the place where he had left the water. A bend in the river prevented our seeing farther on. An instant after we heard another plunge. The snap of a gun missing fire followed, and, sweeping round the bend, we saw a large moose on the point of climbing the bank, while Jerome stood on the

---

[j] By way of the eastern branch, Lake Megantic, and the Chaudière; or by the western branch, Salmon River, and the St. Francis.—Ed.

opposite shore hastily and eagerly picking the lock of his gun. The bank was steep, and the moose stood half way up, nearly hidden in the bushes. I took a quick aim at the back, fired, and the moose tumbled into the river with her spine severed by my bullet. Jerome had fired at her the night before and wounded her in the lower part of the belly. He had just tracked her by means of his dog; she had leaped into the river and he had aimed at her as she was wading across; but, his gun missing fire, she had gained the shore and was attempting to ascend the bank when we approached. The poor beast lay an instant in the water and then, with a convulsive effort, staggered to her feet and stood in the river where it was about a foot deep. Jerome aimed at her head, fired, and missed altogether. I reloaded and, aiming at the eye, struck the head just below the root of the ear. Still the moose stood motionless. Jerome took a long aim and fired again. He hit her fair and full between the eyes. For an instant she did not move; then her body declined slowly to one side and she fell, gave a short plunge, and lay dead on the bottom. Being a female, she had no horns, but her body was larger than a horse's. Each siezed a leg and she was drawn to shore. Jerome shouldered the huge dead trunk of a tree, brought it from the forest, chopped it up, and kindled a fire to keep off the flies. He and Lumber then flayed and cut her up—a process which occupied an hour or more; and then we got under way again, taking with us as much of the meat as we had occasion for. Jerome stayed behind to load his canoe with the rest.

We stopped at our camp of the first night, and, finding our fire still smouldering, we rekindled it and cooked a dinner of moose meat. Getting again under way, we reached our starting place at the head of the rapids half an hour before sunset, having paddled almost unceasingly since early morning and travelled, by the river, a distance of more than thirty miles. We walked to Lumber's and, though he offered beds, preferred the fresh hay of his barn to the chance of what we might encounter in the shape of log-cabin sheets.

Saturday, Aug. 7th. We determined, if the thing was practicable, to reach Colebrook today, although the distance by road was forty miles. Leaving Lumber's an hour before sunrise, at half an hour after we were at Bennet's, where we hired a light skiff and paddled down the river for Brag's—a distance by water of ten miles. We reached the settlement at about half past ten; devoured a monstrous breakfast, for which we paid the enormous sum of nine-pence; and began our journey across the state to Colebrook. Now it so happened that that breakfast, our first civilized meal for some days, relished so extremely well that we both demolished several pounds of the pie, cake, and bread of which it consisted, and, in addition, imbibed

Sketched from the summit of one of the mountains of the Dixville Notch, representing the appearance of the cliffs opposite.

about a quart and a half of rich milk apiece. In consequence, we found ourselves more disposed to lie down and go to sleep than to continue our journey, and Slade became absolutely sick. A freezing-cold bath in a mountain stream effectually expelled my laziness, and relieved him to such a degree that he was enabled to continue his walk; and in the course of half an hour every evil symptom had vanished. It was long past noon when we entered the "Dixville Notch," and the scene appeared to much greater advantage on entering from the west than when seen from the opposite side. The road, which has been constructed within a few weeks, adds greatly to its effect. It is a causeway strongly built of stone against the side of the steep precipices which on the one hand rise abruptly from it, while on the other a shallow ravine, the bed of a winter torrent, is interposed between the road and the crags which overlook it.

These, steep as they are, afford in their crevices root-hold for large trees and a thick growth of saplings which, over-shadowing the road, make with the rocks above a beautiful perspective to one entering the pass. Further on, the rocks rise higher and fire has stripped them of their woods, so that in the heart of the defile nothing meets the eye but the tall pinnacles shooting upward

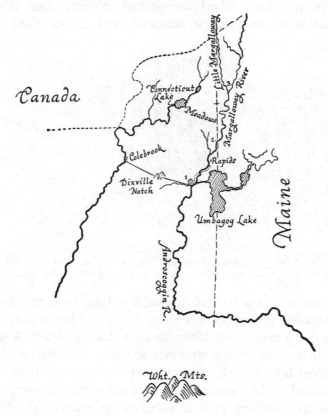

abruptly and with black and fire-scorched rocks scattered about their bases. Long after nightfall we reached Colebrook, having travelled thirty miles on foot and paddled ten miles!

Sunday, Aug. 8th. After our recent exertions, we were glad of a day of rest. My chief occupations have been sleeping and writing my journal for the preceding week.

This sketch is very inaccurate, but it may give some idea of our course. Leaving Colebrook, we reached in one day Brag's settlement, marked *1*, near the junction of the Margalloway and the Androscoggin. The distance is twenty-two [fifteen] miles, the road passing through the Dixville Notch. Thence to the foot of the rapids, though barely fifteen miles, occupied the greater part of another day. It was here that the memorable adventure of the "guzzle"[k] befel. The boat having been drawn round the rapids, we proceeded up the stream and reached at night the point marked *2*—the place of our encampment. Our camp of the next night was at *3*, and from this place we commenced our return the next morning. Just below *2* is the deserted camp of an old Indian, named Mettallic,[29] who lived here many years and subsisted by hunting, but, being striken blind by a disease, he was found on the bank in a starving state by a hunter.

Monday, Aug. 9ᵗʰ. The imperative necessity of my clothes undergoing a cleansing operation detained us, although most unwilling, at Colebrook. The day was dull and rainy; books were few—entertaining ones none at all; and the writing of a letter or two was my chief defence against an unwonted attack of blue-devils. Tomorrow we set out, on foot, for Lancaster.

Tuesday, Aug. 10ᵗʰ, Lancaster. Today we first turned our footsteps homeward. For myself, I am loth to abandon so soon the excitements and enjoyments of the few past weeks, though many of them have been purchased with "toil and sweat." My pilgrimage, however, must come to an end, and next Saturday will find me at home. I regard this journey but "as the beginning of greater things" and as merely prefatory to longer wanderings.

We left Colebrook early this morning and travelled fifteen miles down the valley of the Connecticut. Stopping to lunch at a little tavern, a couple of barouches drove up to the door; and, to my no small gratification, they were freighted with Dr. Jackson and his assistants. They were going on to Colebrook, but remained an hour and a half at the tavern, which space was occupied, most satisfac-

[k] Probably the "guzzle" was the outlet of Round and Long ponds.—Ed.

torily to me, in conversation upon backwoods matters. Among other kindness, Mr. Williams offered me the use of the note-book of his journies of last year, in which he has preserved a considerable number of Indian legends taken from the lips of Anantz, who is well versed in the traditions of his tribe. I shall certainly avail myself of his offer. Taking a waggon at this place, we proceeded to Lancaster, through the towns of Stratford, Northumberland, &c. Lancaster is thirty-five miles from Colebrook. We passed on our way a mountain of very peculiar appearance, situated, I believe, in the township of Stark. Avalanches had laid bare its sides and exposed a surface of white, glistening rock, which, with the black stains and fissures and, here and there, the stunted verdure which relieves it, affords a strange contrast to the forest-covered mountains around it. As through the greater part of the valley of the Connecticut, the level and beautiful meadows through which the river flows are shut in by parallel ranges of hills, some high and craggy—all wild and beautiful in their appearance. Distant mountains of considerable elevation overlook Lancaster on the east.

Wednesday, Aug. 11ᵗʰ, Littleton. Left Lancaster at two this afternoon— at 4 tomorrow morning leave Littleton for Windsor.

Windsor, Friday [Thursday], Aug. 12ᵗʰ. Leaving Littleton at 4, we reached Hallowell [Haverhill] at 10—a beautiful ride, especially the latter part. Thence we proceeded to Hanover, and thence to Windsor, where I now am, and where I deem it expedient to retire immediately to bed, since I must be off at two in the morning. Ascutney Mountain overhangs the village.

Boston, Saturday [Friday], Aug. 13ᵗʰ. Starting at two this morning from Windsor, I reached Nashua in time for the last afternoon train, and in two hours found myself in Boston[30] after an absence of a month. And a joyous month it has been, though one somewhat toilsome— may I soon pass another as pleasantly.

Windsor, Friday. Aug. 12th Leaving Littleton at 4, we reached Hallowell at 10 — a beautiful ride, especially the latter part. Thence we proceeded to Hanover, and thence to Windsor, where I now am, and where I deem it expedient to retire immediately to bed, since I must be off at two in the morning. Ascutney mountain overhangs the village.

Boston. Saturday. Aug 13th. Starting at two this morning from Windsor, I reached Nashua in time for the last afternoon train, and in two hours found myself in Boston after an absence of a month. And a joyous month it has been, though one somewhat toilsome — may I soon pass another as pleasantly.

F. P.

*Facsimile of Final Page
of the 1841 Journal*

1842 Journal

Lake George & Lake Champlain

Green Mountains, Eastern Townships

White Mountains & Maine

Introduction

WEARY of books after his sophomore year at Harvard, and acting on his lifelong conviction that "For the student there is, in its season, no better place than the saddle, and no better companion than the rifle or the oar," Parkman set off on another expedition as soon as his summer vacation of 1842 began. He had enlisted Henry Orne White, who was in the class above him at Harvard, as a companion for the strenuous journey he proposed to make. Starting from Albany, he planned to proceed northward by Fort Edward and the battlefields of the Seven Years' War about Lake George and Lake Champlain; then to follow the Canadian boundary eastward across northern Vermont and New Hampshire, returning by way of Mt. Katahdin in Maine. The itinerary was clearly designed to gratify both the student and the lover of the wilderness, for acquaintance with the classic invasion route of the French and Indian War was essential to Parkman's studies, while the final part of the trip would take him through frontier or untouched forest regions. It was a daring effort for an eighteen-year-old, and it is clear from Parkman's lively account that he rejoiced in the dangers and hardships which he encountered. It is worth noting that on this journey, as on that of the previous summer and others still to be made, Parkman wore out his companions, who lacked his almost fanatical zeal for hardening himself and for experiencing the same primitive living conditions as his historical heroes had known. In later years Parkman was to pay dearly in ill-health for trying the flesh so sorely in his youth.

The journal is primarily a spirited account of adventure, which displays Parkman's precocious ability as a writer, particularly in the brilliant descriptions of nature. But it also affords some interesting historical insights in its pictures of Albany, Schenectady, and Saratoga Springs a century ago; in its careful account of the ruins of Fort

41

William Henry and Ticonderoga, the old English and French out-posts on the lakes; and notably in its record of life along the Canadian border when war between the great neighbors of North America was not unthinkable. In fact, when Parkman passed back and forth across the boundary, a dispute over a considerable section of northern New Hampshire was just dying down, after the now forgotten incident of the Indian Stream Republic. On the American side of the border, Parkman, with the mark of Harvard on him, was suspected of being a British agent. On the Canadian side, he found small garrisons established in the frontier towns. But the essential thinness of the tension is evidenced by the charming incident of the singing of "America" with the refrain of "God Save the Queen" by a Yankee landlord presiding over the company in a Canadian inn. At this period the Eastern Townships of Quebec were of distinctly New England character in aspect and in population, and even today they remain a transition ground between New England and New France. Then there are also vivid glimpses of the religious and political ferments at work along the frontier, Millerism and Jack-sonian democracy, and of the rude life of the settlers who were gnawing away at the wilderness through which Major Robert Rogers' Rangers had fought their way home after the attack on the St. Francis Indians in 1759.

Forced by his companion's lack of funds and enthusiasm to abandon the plan of returning by way of Mt. Katahdin—first explored by white men only five years before—Parkman consoled himself with the little less ambitious project of cutting across the wilderness from the Connecticut Lakes to the headwaters of the Magalloway, and thence retracing his route of the previous summer. This enterprise—even today not one to be lightly undertaken—he succeeded in accomplishing with considerable toil and hardship and some real danger; and then concluded his summer's outing by passing quickly homeward through his beloved White Mountains.

The journal is clearly written, chiefly in ink but with some passages in pencil, in a $6\frac{3}{8}$ by $7\frac{3}{4}$ copybook with marbled paper covers. The latter part of the journal, describing the trip down the Magalloway, supplied much of the material for a *Harper's* article, "Exploring the Magalloway" (November 1864—XXIX, 735-41).

1842

July 15ᵗʰ, [18]42, Albany. Left Boston this morning at half past six, for this place, where I am now happily arrived, it being the longest day's journey I ever made. For all that, I would rather have come thirty miles by stage than the whole distance by railroad, for of all methods of progressing, that by steam is incomparably the most disgusting.[1] We were whisked by Worcester and all the other intermediate towns, and reached Springfield by noon, where White[2] ran off to see his sister, and I staid and took "refreshment" in a little room at the end of the car-house, where about thirty people were standing around a table in the shape of a horse-shoe, eating and drinking in lugubrious silence. The train got in motion again, and passed the Connecticut. Its shores made a perspective of high, woody hills, closed in the distance by the haughty outline of Mount Tom. The view from the railroad-bridge was noble, or rather would have been so, had not the Company taken care to erect a parapet on both sides, which served the double purpose of intercepting the view, and driving all the sparks into the eyes of the passengers. A few miles farther, and we came upon the little river Agawam [Westfield]; and an hour after, high mountains began to rise before us. We dashed by them; dodged under their cliffs; whirled round their bases; only seeing so much as to make us wish to see more,[a] and more than half-blinded meanwhile by showers of red hot sparks which poured in at the open windows like a hail storm. I have scarcely ever seen a wilder and more picturesque country. We caught tantalizing glimpses of glittering streams and waterfalls, rocks and mountains, woods and lakes, and before we could rub our scorched eyes to look again, the scene was left miles behind. A place called Chester Factory, where we stopped five minutes, is beautifully situated among encircling moun-

[a] This wish was gratified in 1844. Cf. the Boston & Berkshire Journal.—Ed.

tains which rise like an amphitheatre around it, to the height of many hundred feet, wooded to the summit. It almost resembled New Hampshire scenery. I learned the names of some of the mountains— Pontoosac—Bear—Becket—The Summit [Washington]—the last being the highest. The road here is ascending for a considerable distance through the townships of North Becket, Hinsdale, &c. The whole is a succession of beautiful scenes. The Irishmen who worked on the road made a most praiseworthy selection of places for their shanties, which many of them are wise enough to occupy still. Three or four of these outlandish cabins, ranged along the banks of a stream flowing through a woody glen extending back among the hills, made with their turf walls and slant roofs a most picturesque addition to the scene. We crossed the boundary line to Chatham, the first New York village. The country was as level as that about Boston. We passed through Kinderhook and Schodack—or however else it is spelled—and at half past six saw the Hudson, moping dismally between its banks under a cloudy sky, with a steamboat solemnly digging its way through the leaden waters. In five minutes the spires and dirt of Albany rose in sight on the opposite shore. We crossed in a steamboat and entered the old city, which, indeed, impressed us at once with its antiquity by the most ancient and fish-like smell which saluted our shrinking nostrils, the instant we set foot on the wharf. We have put up at the Eagle Hotel—a good house. Nevertheless, we are both eager to leave cities behind us.

July 16th, Caldwell [Lake George]. This morning we left Albany— which I devoutly hope I may never see again—in the cars, for Saratoga. My plan of going up the river to Ft. Edward[3] I had to abandon, for it was impracticable—no boat beyond Troy. Railroad the worst I was ever on; the country flat and dull; the weather dismal. The Catskills appeared in the distance. After passing the inclined plane and riding a couple of hours we reached the valley of the Mohawk and Schenectady. I was prepared for something filthy in the last mentioned venerable town, but for nothing quite so disgusting as the reality. Canal docks, full of stinking water, superannuated rotten canal boats, and dirty children and pigs paddling about, formed the foreground of the delicious picture, while in the rear was a mass of (of) tumbling houses and sheds, bursting open in all directions; green with antiquity, dampness, and lack of paint. Each house had its peculiar dunghill, with the group of reposing hogs. In short, London itself could exhibit nothing much nastier.[4] In crossing the main street, indeed, things wore an appearance which might be called decent. The car-house here is enormous. Five or six trains were on the point of starting for the north, south, east, and west; and the brood of railroads and taverns swarmed about the place like bees. We cleared the babel at last, passed Union College,[5] another tract of monotonous country, Ballston, and finally reached Saratoga, having travelled latterly at the astonishing rate of about seven miles an hour. "Caldwell stage ready!" We got our baggage on board, and I found time to enter one or two of the huge hotels.[6] After perambulating the entries filled with sleek waiters and sneaking fops, dashing through the columned porticoes and enclosures, drinking some of the water and spitting it out again in high disgust, I sprang onto the stage, cursing Saratoga and all New York. With an unmitigated temper, I journeyed to Glen's Falls, and here my wrath mounted higher yet, at the sight of that noble cataract almost concealed under a huge awkward bridge, thrown directly across it, with the addition of a dam above, and about twenty mills of various kinds. Add to all, that the current was choked by masses of drift logs above and below, and that a dirty village lined the banks of the river on both sides; and some idea may possibly be formed of the way in which the New Yorkers have bedevilled Glen's. Still the water comes down over the marble ledges in foam and fury, and the roar completely drowns the clatter of the machinery. I left the stage and ran down to the bed of the river to the rocks at the foot of the falls. Two little boys volunteered to show me the "caverns," which may be reached dry-shod when the stream is low. I followed them down amid the din and spray to a little hole in the rock which led to a place a good deal like the Swallows' Cave, and squeezed in after them. "This is Cooper's Cave, sir; where he went and hid the two ladies." They evidently took the story in *The Last of the Mohicans*[7] for Gospel. They led the way to the larger cave, and one of them ran down to the edge of the water which boiled most savagely past the opening. "This is Hawkeye's Cave: here's where he shot an Indian." "No, he didn't either," squalled the other, "it was higher up on the rocks." "I tell you it wasn't." "I tell you it was." I put an end to the controversy with two cents.

Dined at the tavern, and rode on. Country dreary as before; the driver one of the best of his genus I ever met. He regaled me as we rode on with stories of his adventures with deer, skunks, and passengers. A mountain heaved up against the sky some distance before us, with a number of smaller hills stretching away on each hand, all wood-crowned to the top. Away on the right rose the Green Mts., dimly seen through the haze, and scarcely distinguishable from the blue clouds that lay upon them. Between was a country of half cultivated fields, tottering houses, and forests of dwarf pines and scrub oaks. But as we drew near, the mountain in front assumed a wilder and a loftier aspect. Crags started from its woody sides and leaned over a deep valley below. "What mountain is that?" "That 'ere is French Mounting"—the scene of one of the most desperate and memorable battles[8] in the Old French War. As we passed down the valley, the mountain rose above the forest half a mile on out right, while a hill on the left, close to the road, formed the other side. The trees flanked the road on both sides. In a little opening in her woods, a cavity in the ground, with a pile of stones at each end, marked the spot where was buried that accomplished warrior and gentleman, Colonel Williams,[9] whose bones, however, have since been removed. Farther on is the rock on the right where he was shot, having mounted it on the look-out—an event which decided the day; the Indians and English broke and fled at once. Still farther on is the scene of the third tragedy of that day, when the victorious French, having been in their turn, by a piece of great good luck, beaten by the valorous Johnson[10] at his entrenchment by the lake, were met at this place on their retreat by McGinnis,[11] and almost cut to pieces. Bloody Pond,[12] a little, slimy, dark sheet of stagnant water, covered with weeds and pond-lilies and shadowed by the gloomy forest around it, is the place where hundreds of dead bodies were flung after the battle, and where the bones still lie. A few miles farther, and Lake George lay before us, the mountains and water confused and indistinct in the mist. We rode into Caldwell, took supper—a boat— and then a bed.

July 17th, Caldwell. The tavern is full of fashionable New Yorkers— all of a piece. Henry and myself both look like the Old Nick, and are

evidently looked upon in a manner corresponding. I went this
morning to see William Henry.[13] The old fort is much larger than I
had thought; the earthen mounds cover many acres. It stood on the
southwest extremity of the lake close by the water. The enterprising
genius of (of) the inhabitants has made a road directly through the
ruins, and turned bastion, moat, and glacis into a flourishing cornfield, so that the spot so celebrated in our colonial history is now
scarcely to be distinguished. Large trees are growing on the untouched parts, especially on the embankment along the lake shore.
In the rear, a hundred or two yards distant, is a gloomy wood of pines,
where the lines of Montcalm[14] can easily be traced. A little behind
these lines is the burying place of the French who fell during that
memorable siege. The marks of a thousand graves can be seen among
the trees, which, of course, have sprung up since. Most of them have
been opened, and bones and skulls dug up in great numbers. A range
of mountains towers above this fine forest—Cobble Mt.—the
Prospect, &c., the haunt of bears and rattle-snakes. The ruins of Ft.
George[15] are on a low hill of lime-stone a short distance southeast of
William Henry—of stone, and in much better preservation than the
other, for they are under the special protection of Mr. Caldwell,[16]
the owner of the village; but they have no historical associations
connected with them. I noticed some curious marks of recent digging
in William Henry and asked an explanation of an old fellow who was
hoeing corn in a field close by. He said that some fools had come up
the lake with a wizard and a divining rod to dig for money in the
ruins.[17] They went at midnight for many successive nights and dug
till day light. I undertook to climb the Prospect—three miles high,
without a path. I guided myself by the sun and summits of the mountains, and got to the top almost suffocated with heat and thirst. The
view embraced the whole lake as far as Ty [Ticonderoga]. All was
hazy and indistinct, only the general features of the scene could be
distinguished in the dull atmosphere. The lake seemed like a huge
river, winding among mountains. Came down, dined, and went to
church. The church is a minute edifice, with belfry and bell exactly
like a little school-house. It might hold easily about sixty. About
thirty were present—countrymen; cute, sly, sunburnt slaves of
Mammon; maidens of sixty and of sixteen; the former desperately

ugly, with black bonnets, frilled caps, peaked noses and chins, and an aspect diabolically prim and saturnine; the latter for the most part remarkably pretty and delicate. For a long time the numerous congregation sat in a pious silence, waiting for the minister. At last he came, dodged into a little door behind the pulpit, and presently reappeared and took his place, arrayed in a white surplice with black facing. He was very young, and *Yankee ploughboy* was stamped on every feature. Judge of my astonishment when he began to read the Episcopal service in voice so clear and manner so appropriate that I have never heard better even in Boston. He read the passage in Exodus—quite appropriate to the place—beginning "the Lord is a man of war." In his sermon, which was polished and even elegant, every figure was taken from warfare. One of Montcalm's lines ran northwest of the tavern toward the mountains.[18] Two or three years ago, in digging for some purpose, a great quantity of deer, bear, and moose bones were found here, with arrows and hatchets, which the tavern keeper thinks mark the place of some Indian feast. The spikes and timbers of sunken vessels may be seen in strong sunlight, when the water is still, at the bottom of the lake, along the southern beach. Abercrombie [Abercromby] sunk his boats here.[19] There are remains of batteries[20] on French Mt. and the mountain north of it, I suppose to command the road from Ft. Edward. This evening visited the French graves. I write this at camp, July 18th. Just turned over my ink-bottle and spilt all the ink.

July 18th, Camp at Diamond Island. Set out this morning in an excellent boat, hired at Caldwell. The sun rose over the mountains like a fiery ball of copper—portending direful heat. The lake was still as glass; the air to the last degree sultry and oppressive. Rowed to the western side and kept under the banks, which were rocky and covered with birch, spruce, cypress, and other trees. We landed occasionally, and fished as we went along. About ten o'clock stretched across Middle Bay and got bread, pork, and potatoes at a farm house, with which and our fish we regaled ourselves at a place half-way down the Bay. Here I wrote my journal for yesterday; we slept an hour or two on the ground, bathed, and read Goldsmith, which Henry brought in his knapsack. At three we proceeded to explore the bay to its bottom, returned, made for Diamond Island, which is now uninhabited, prepared our camp, and went to sleep.

July 19th. I woke this morning about as weak and spiritless as well could be. All enterprise and activity was fairly gone; how I cannot tell, but I cursed the weather as the most probable cause. Such has been the case with me, to a greater or less degree, for the last three or four weeks. Rowed today along the eastern shore. Explored several beautiful bays, in one of which was a curious cave in the rock. Heat suffocating. The water of the lake is equal to most spring water, and we drank it in great quantities. The scenery thus far, though extremely fine, had disappointed me, probably on account of the extravagant ideas I had formed of it; but now it grew continually more imposing. A strong south wind, too, sprang up and raised the glassy flat surface of the lake into waves, and, in part, dissipated the mists that hung over all the mountains. The boat began to pitch and plunge with an enlivening motion, and the motion in the air strengthened and invigorated us. We dashed through the water at a rapid rate. At last we saw a little white flag fluttering among the trees, by way of sign to a tavern. We landed, dined, and set out again. The wind almost blew a gale. The little boat was borne up and down with such violence that we judged best to keep near the shore, so as to be able to get our baggage in case of an overturn. White sat in the stern grunting a German song, about as intelligible to me as to him, while I rowed. We reached what in the War-time was Cankasky [Northwest] Bay, close to the Narrows. Here the storm grew so furious that we landed at the point of the bay—the extremity of Tongue Mt. The lake plunged and foamed like the ocean. At this point it is full of islands and flanked by noble mountains. This is the scene of the canoe-chase in *The Last of the Mohicans*.[21] While White had gone off shooting, I swam across the strait to one of the islands, from which the view down the lake was the finest water-scene I ever saw. It was a perspective of mountains towering above the narrow sheet filled with islands, against which the white breakers were now fiercely dashing. But everything was obscured with mist. When the wind became less violent we rowed to an island in the middle, where we are now encamped.

Wednesday, July 20th. Entered the Narrows this morning, and rowed among all the islands and along all the shores. White trailed a line behind the boat, by which means he caught a large bass. Scenery noble, but mists still on the mountains. Passed along the rocky and precipitous shore of Tongue Mt.; stopped and fished, and caught so many that we flung several dozen away. About 11 o'clock landed on a little island, built a fire and prepared a dinner, White officiating as cook with considerable skill. We rowed down the lake again, and soon cleared the Narrows. On our right rose the ridges of Black Mt., the loftiest summit on the lake. We stopped at a log cabin at its base, where an old man of eighty was splitting shingles under a shed, surrounded by a group of women and children who, with becoming modesty, fled at our approach. The old man lost no time in informing us that he did not belong there, but had only come to work for the family. We went up to the house—one of the most wretched cabins I every saw—inhabited by two families, French and American. Shepherd,[b] the American, was the most deformed abortion I ever set eyes on—his lip split up to the nose and his mouth twisted round the wrong way, so that he spoke from the side of his face, instead of the front, and that in such a sputtering mumbling style that he was perfectly unintelligible. We returned to the old man, who talked politics with great fury, and with more knowledge than I believe falls to the lot of many a state representative. He seasoned his discourse with stories—one about Ethan Allen[22] was exceedingly characteristic, but scarcely to be put in writing.

We left him and kept down the lake, with a fierce wind sweeping down after us, and driving the mists before it. The water was a dark glistening blue, with lines of foam on the crests of the waves; huge shadows of clouds coursed along the mountains. The little islands would be lighted at one instant by a stream of sunshine falling on them and almost making their black pines transparent, and the next moment they would be suddenly darkened and all around be glittering with a sudden burst of light from the opening clouds. We passed under Black Mt., whose precipices and shaggy woods wore a very savage and impressive aspect in that peculiar weather, and kept

[b]Known as the "King of Black Mountain," according to a note on the end paper of the journal.—Ed.

down the lake seven miles to Sabbath Day Pt. High and steep mountains flanked the lake the whole way. In front, at some distance, they
seemed to slope gradually away, and a low green point, with an
ancient dingy house upon it closed the perspective. This was Sabbath
Day Pt., the famous landing place of many a huge army.[23] We
noticed two abrupt mountains on our left, and steering under them,
found them the most savage and warlike precipices we had yet seen.
One impended over the lake, like the stooping wall of an old castle;
its top was fringed with trees, which seemed bushes, from the height,
and great fragments of broken rock were piled around its base. We
ran our boat on the beach of Sabbath Day Pt. and asked lodging at
the house. An old woman, after a multitude of guesses and calculations, guessed as how she could accommodate us with a supper and
a bed, though she couldn't say nohow how we should like it, seeing
as how she war'nt used to visitors. The house was an old, rickety,
dingy shingle palace, with a potatoe garden in front, hogs perambulating the outhouses, and a group of old men and women engaged in
earnest conversation in the tumble-down portico. The chief figure
was an old grey-haired man, tall and spare as a skeleton, who was
giving some advice to a chubby old lady about her corns.

"Well, now," said the old lady, "I declare they hurt me mighty
bad."

"I'll give you something to cure them right off."

"What is it? I hope it a'nt snails. I always hated snails since I was
a baby, but I've heered say they are better for corns nor nothing else
at all," etc., etc.

The old man was a revolutionary pensioner, Captain Patchin[24] by
name, and stout-hearted, hale, and clever by nature. He is the owner
of the place, but the house is occupied by another family—old man,
old woman, and a numerous progeny of youthful giants and ogresses;
but the whole "calculate on" removing to Illinois in the fall. There
were visitors of the family, also, the most conspicuous of whom was
a little Canadian Frenchman[25] with his family, who professed himself a mighty adept at angling, but whose pretensions we found on
trial greatly above his merits. The whose household presently
gathered under the old portico, where stories of Revolutionary
campaigns, rattlesnakes, deadly beasts, and deadly diseases flew

from mouth to mouth with awful rapidity. After a few rifle trials with the aforesaid youthful giants, we took supper, and went on the lake after bass, with the Frenchman in our boat, and the young men following in their own. We had good success—Henry and I caught a dozen apiece, some of very large size, while the vainglorious Frenchman had to be content with one wretched perch. The Captain tonight sent his dogs to the mountains, in the care of a neighbor of his, in hopes that a deer may be roused and driven to the lake in the morning. One of the children is playing with the tail of a rattlesnake, killed last night by one of the men in the middle of the road.

Thursday, 21ˢᵗ. Fished for bass off-shore with rifle and fowling piece ready, in case the deer should take to the lake. But we waited in vain. It turned out afterwards that the hound had proved unmanageable and refused to follow the scent. We caught fish enough, landed, and with Myrtle Bailey, one of the young Brobdignagians, a simple, goodnatured, strong-handed, grinning son of the plough, set out on a rattle-snake hunt on the mountain back of the Point. Here was the summer den of a swarm of these beasts, who thence infested the whole country. Myrtle told us that they went to their winter den in autumn; then repaired to their summer den in spring, where they educated their children; which parental office being discharged, the[y] scattered at large over the rocks. We climbed through tangled woods and steep sunscorched ledges till we came to the edge of a lofty precipice which towers above the lake. We looked down upon piles of confused rocks and forests of blasted and stunted trees along the foot of the cliff and washed by the lake on the other side. Some crows were wheeling and cawing over the tree tops, looking like black beetles from the height above. Steadying myself by putting one arm round a gnarled tree I leaned from the precipice and discharged "Satan"ᵉ into the gulf. The crows ceased their cawing and took themselves off with all speed. We soon reached a still higher point, which commanded the noblest view of the lake I had yet seen. It stretched north and south between its mountains, visible for two thirds of its length, its waters glistening in the sun, dotted with a

---

ᵉ Parkman's rifle, which was named, after the custom of the pioneers who personalized the weapon so vital to their lives.—Ed.

hundred green islands. As it wound down through the huge valley, it seemed like a still clear stream in the bottom of a deep glen, rather than a lake. The waters dwindled to nothing in comparison to the towering mountains that environed them. There would be no finer place of gentlemen's seats than this, but now, for the most part, it is occupied by a race of boors about as uncouth, mean, and stupid as the hogs they seem chiefly to delight in. The captain's household is an exception.

We found the den, but no snakes—they had already dispersed. We looked long and anxiously among the rocks, but in vain, and we had to descend. Near this Mt. is another—mentioned before—still more steep and rocky, called Buck Mt. from the exploit of a hunted deer, many years ago, who being hard pressed on the top by hunters, leaped from the precipice for the lake, but fell whirling upon the rocks at the bottom and sprinkled them with his blood for rods around. Afternoon: fished again—evening: fished again, and caught a very large bass—all in company of Myrtle, whose luck not satisfying him, he cursed the "darned cursed fish" in most fervent style.

Friday, 22nd. Left old Patchin's this morning, he having previously exhorted me to come and buy his place, which he says I may have for $5,000!! A strong south wind compelled us to run towards Ty. We rowed six miles down the lake—mountains less high than before—lake broad—in front lay a confused mass of precipitous mountains, apparently stretching across and barring the passage. On the left was a hamlet at the foot of a range of hills, for which we steered in order to put a letter into the post office, which we knew to be there. We broke an oar when within about half a mile, and paddled to shore with great difficulty through a considerable surf which was dashing against the beach like the waves of the ocean. We found the post office a neat little tavern kept by one Garfield,[26] entitled the Judge. He referred us to a carpenter who promised to make an oar forthwith, and worked six hours upon it, an interval which I spent chiefly in wandering through the country. I followed the course of a rocky brook which came down a valley, with a little road running along its side, with an occasional cabin, or mill, or narrow clearing breaking upon the forest. One old mill stood by the roadside where the stream tumbled in a broken line of foam over a mass of rock into a basin beneath, above which the building stood. Fantastic rocks, crowned with trees and shrubs, leaned above the basin and darkened the whirling waters below, while the dripping logs and walls of the mill on the other side, and the high rock and waterfall in front, gave a sort of picturesque aspect to the place that I never hoped to see the companion of any Yankee edifice. Going on farthur, I found other mills in abundance, and at last one which stood on the top of a steep descent of rock, flanked by the woods, down the surface of which the water came gliding in a thread so small that I wondered what had become of the stream I had seen so large before. Listening, I heard the heavy plunging of water, apparently from under ground. I looked all about, and could see no channel; but the noise grew louder as I approached the woods on the left. I forced my way among the trees and came to the edge of a ravine not ten feet wide but so deep that, leaning over, I could distinguish nothing but dark moss-grown rocks, while the noise of the water came up from the gulf with an appalling din. I went to the foot of the rocks and found the place where the water came glancing furiously out from the shelter of rocks and bushes; and following this guide by means of fallen logs and timbers, entered what seemed the mouth of a damp gloomy cavern. The rocky walls of the ravine rose on each side some sixty or seventy feet, dripping with continual moisture. When I had got a little farther on, I could see a mass of rocks piled up in front, with the water tumbling over it in a sheet of foam. The cliffs leaning towards each other over head and the bushes that projected from them rendered the place almost dark, though here and there the jagged rocks were illumined by a faint stream of sunshine. Just above the cataract could be seen the old green timbers and wheels of a mill, built across the ravine. The whole very much resembled the Flume at Franconia.

Returned to Garfield's and found there Mr. Gibbs with his wife, the "vocalist." Presently the man appeared with the oar finished. White undertook to pay him with a Naumkeag Bank[27] bill—the only bills he had. "Don't know nothing about that money: wait till Garfield comes and he'll tell whether it's genuine or not." "There's the paper," said I, "look and see." He looked—all was right. "Well,

A View of Ticonderoga
(Coverdale Collection No. 2250)

are you satisfied?" "How do I know but what that 'ere bill is counterfeit? It has a sort of counterfeit look about it to my eyes. Deacon, what do you say to it?" The deacon put on his spectacles, held the bill to the light, turned it this way and that, tasted of it, and finally pronounced that, according to his calculation, it was good. But the carpenter was not contented: "Bijah, you're a judge of bills; what do you think?" Bijah, after a long examination, gave as his opinion that it was counterfeit. All parties were beginning to wax wroth when the judge entered and decided that the bill was good.

We pushed from the beach and steered down the lake, passed some islands, and beheld in front of us two grim mountains standing guard over a narrow strait of dark water between. Both were of solid granite, rising sheer from the lake, with a (a) few stunted trees thinly clothing their nakedness. Behind each, stretched away a long train of inferior mountains, like satellites of some gloomy despot. One of these mountains was the noted Rogers' Slide;[28] the other, almost as famous, Anthony's Nose, Jr. Both had witnessed, in their day, the passage of twenty vast armies in the strait between; and there was not an echo on either but had answered to the crack of rifles and screams of dying men. We skirted the base of the Nose—for which sentimental designation I could find no manner of reason— till we arrived opposite the perpendicular front of his savage neighbor. About a mile of water was between. We ran the boat ashore on a shelving rock, and looked for a camping place among the precipices. We found to our surprise, at the side of a steep rock amid a growth of cedars and hemlocks, a little enclosure of logs, like a diminutive log cabin without a roof. We made beds in it of hemlock boughs— there was just space enough—brought up our baggage and guns, eat what supper we had, and essayed to go asleep. But we might as well have slept under a showerbath of melted iron. In that deep sheltered spot, bugs, mosquitoes, and "no-see-ems" swarmed innumerable. Our nets protected us from mosquitoes only. A million red-hot needles were gouged into hands, faces, everywhere. White cursed the woods and me for leading him into such a scrape. I laughed at the bugs and him as long as I could, but at last my philosophy gave way, and the utmost point of my self-command was to suffer in silence. It grew dark, and the wind came rushing along the side of the mountain and stirring the leaves of the trees over our head with a lulling sound, and we were well tired with the labor of the day; so we fell at last into a sort of inquiet and half-conscious doze, ever and anon interrupted by a muttered grumble or a motion to scratch some severely affected part. Late in the night, I was awaked from this blissful state by sounds rather startling in that solitude—the loud voices and shouts of men close by. I sat up and listened, but the moaning of the wind and the dash of the water against the shore prevented my distinguishing a syllable, until there came, louder than the rest: "Now then, G——d damn it, pull for your life—every stroke helps." In an instant it flashed across my bewildered brain that some scoundrels were making off with our boat; and I got clear of my blanket and ran down to the shore, first shaking White to wake him. All I could see through the darkness was that our boat was safe and that another was drawn up beside it, when a man sprang up suddenly from the grass with a startled curse, and demanded who I was. We made mutual explanations. He had tried to run up the lake from Ty, with a companion in another boat, but his strength had failed against a strong contrary wind and he had landed, leaving his friend, who had a less distance to go, to keep on.

The wind drove the bugs from the shore and made it a much more comfortable resting-place; so thither we adjourned, and spread our blankets near the ragamuffin boatman. We built a little fire, and our new friend and White enjoyed a social pipe together. As the light fell on his matted hair; his grisly unshorn countenance, haggard with drinking; and his tattered and patched clothes; and then again flared high up on the cliffs and savage trees, and streamed across the water, I thought that even that shore had seldom seen a more outlandish group—we in our blankets, he in his rags. He told us that the camp where we had been sleeping was made by a man last summer, who lived here for the purpose of fishing. "He was a sort of a villain-like character," said our acquaintance, "he went and stole fish off my grounds, damn him; and then again he killed his own son right down here in this place. The old man got drunk, and said he would have the boy over to this camp, and so he got him in his old boat with him, though the boy's mother cried about it, and said she'd keep him at home, and the boy himself felt afeared to go. Well, the old fellow was

so far gone that when he got to the landing-place—there, just where
your boat is drawed up on the rock—that he forget he had his son
with him, and ran his boat agin the rock and tumbled himself out
of it in such style, that she overset, and pitched the boy into the deep
water. The instant the old man heard his son holler, it sobered him
up in no time, but he nor the boy neither couldn't swim a mile, and
so he stood on the rock and see'd him drown, and then came over and
telled the folks of it in the morning. That 'ere cured him of his
tricks for one while, but within a week or two he has been up to
them agin, and I ketched him on my fish grounds last Sunday—may
I be d——d if I didn't dress him."

With this dismal legend did our new friend beguile the hours of
the night-watch. At length we all fell asleep, and did not wake till
day. The ragamuffin said he was hungry, on which we gave him a
piece of bread, got all things on board our boat, and set out again
for Patchin's, where we had left some linen to be washed. This
morning was the most toilsome we had passed. The wind was dead
against us; the waves ran with a violence I had never seen before
except on the ocean. It required the full force of both arms to hold
the boat on her course. If we slackened our efforts for a single
moment, she would spin round and drive backwards. We had about
twelve miles to row under these agreeable auspices. "Well," said
White, "you call this fun, do you? To be eaten by bugs all night and
work against head winds all day isn't according to my taste, whatever
you may think of it."

"Are you going to back out?" said I. "Back out, yes; when I get
into a bad scrape, I back out of it as quick as I can"—and so he went
on with marvellous volubility to recount his grievances. Lake George
he called a "scrubby looking place"—said there was no fishing in
it—he hated camping, and would have no more of it—he wouldn't
live so for another week to save his life, etc., etc.

Verily, what is one man's meat is another man's poison. What
troubles me more than his treachery to our plans is his want of cash,
which will make it absolutely necessary to abandon our plan of
descending through Maine. His scruples I trust to overcome in time.

We reached Patchin's at last, and were welcomed by the noble
old veteran as cordially as if we were his children. We dined, and sat

in his portico, listening to his stories. He is eighty-six. Three years ago he danced with great applause at a country party, and still his activity and muscular strength are fully equal to those of most men in the prime of life. He must once have been extremely handsome; even now his features are full and regular, and when he tells his stories he always sets his hat on one side of his head, and looks the very picture of an old warrior. He was several times prisoner. Once, when in Quebec, an English officer asked him, as he tells the story, "'What's your name?'" "'Patchin.'" "'What, Hell-Hound Patchin!' says he."

At another time an officer struck him without any provocation but that of his being a rebel. Patchin sprang on him and choked him till he fainted, in the streets of Quebec. He served in the Indian campaigns of Butler[29] and Brant[30] about Ft. Stanwix[31]—at the recovery of Ft. Ann[e][32] after it was taken by Burgoyne—was present when Sir John Johnson[33] fled from the Mohawk with his property, and tells how narrowly that tory made his escape from the pursuing party on Champlain. He wants us to come back and hear more of his stories.

We left him and his family and ran down the lake again, bathed at an island, and, White still continuing contumacious, I left him at Garfield's, and proceeded to camp by myself at an island two or three miles off. I hauled the boat on shore, and prepared to wash my pantaloons—an operation I could commit to no one else, since I should have to wander breechless in the interim. I put the breeks in the water to the windward of the island, and, having suitably pounded them down with stones, left them to the operation of the waves while I made ready my camp. Presently taking them out and wringing them, I strung them on a tree hard by to dry, wrapped myself in my blanket and laid down. I read a book of White's as long as I could see. Two boats passed by me as I lay, and the occupants turned a wondering gaze upon me, especially one old lady in green spectacles whom her son was rowing down the lake. I slept comfortably, and in the morning went back to Garfield's, where I found White, Gibbs, and his wife. The Judge was hospitable and kind, and we instantly planned a fishing party for the next day. Today being Sunday, I have staid at home for the most part, written letters, journal, etc. The family are essentially "genteel" in the true sense of the word: the Judge a gentleman, his wife a lady, both polite by nature. The lady has a pretty flower garden—with no sunflowers in it. There is an old Irish gardener, whose department is managed in a most exemplary manner, and who has spent half the afternoon in expounding the superiority of the shamrock over the rose and the thistle. In short the whole establishment is to the dwellings around it what Mr. Cushing's[34] place is to a common farm.

Monday, 25 July. Breakfasted at nine and went shooting with Gibbs —the ostensible object being a robin pie, the true one our own amusement. We made a great destruction among the small birds. The weapon I carried was used in the Revolution by Garfield's father. It was six feet long, slender, small bore, light breech of polished oak, flint lock. It had sent many a fatal charge of buckshot. In the afternoon went fishing with Gibbs and White and witnessed the arrival of the great Nabob, Mr. Caldwell,[35] the founder and owner of the village of that name, who comes here on a long promised visit in a little barge of his own, with flags at prow and stern, and a huge box of wines for his private refreshment. Ask anybody here what kind of a man Mr. Caldwell is, and he will answer with a shrug of the shoulders, or if he is unusually delicate or cautious, it will be, "Oh, he is a very good sort of a man," or else, in the emphatic tone of one defending an accused person, "He is a very clever man, sir, a very clever man." But the truth is that he is a consummate tyrant and fool. He refused to patronize the steamboat unless it was called after his name, and fired a salute on approaching the village, whenever he was present, which is accordingly done. It is impossible to get any favor from him without the humblest deference. He treats the townsmen, his vassals, with favor or the contrary according as they yield him due reverence. Tonight the report of a piece from his boat gave the signal of his approach. Patrick, the Irishman, stood on the beach with the Judge's best gun and answered with a salute, for so it must be, or the great man would be displeased. Somehow or other, the Judge himself, though I believe him as sensible a man as I ever met, seems to regard his humble roof as honored by the mighty presence. Caldwell is of course reported vastly rich, as perhaps he is, but he got all his property from his father, an Irish emigrant who built himself a fortune by trading at Albany.

We were to have gone towards Ticonderoga tonight, but an easterly storm with rain prevents us and compels us to remain here, and sleep under a roof.

Tuesday, July 26th. The great man and his retinue occupied every nook and corner of the little tavern. Two of his satellites were quartered in the same room with us, and entertained us all night with snorings so diversified and so powerful that I wished myself at camp in spite of the storm. Garfield has a very good rifle, which he wanted to "swap" for mine. As his has some important advantages over mine, especially in size of bore, and is only inferior to it in roughness of mounting and in being rather worn by use, I agreed to make a trial with him, which occupied half the morning and showed no marked superiority in either gun. I therefore declined the "swap." Left Garfield's at noon and rowed down to Ticonderoga. Passed close under Rogers' Slide, whose bare perpendicular sheets of granite, with their deep gullies and weather stains and the stunted shrubs in their crevices, present as dismal and savage an aspect as I ever saw, except at the White Mts. Found the steamboat at her wharf at the outlet of the lake and were welcomed on board by old Dick[36] whose acquaintance we made at Caldwell, who now composed her whole crew, the rest being seated under a tree on shore. Dick showed us his rattlesnakes again and told us how a fellow once stole them, shut up in their box, mistaking the rattling for the sound of some valuable piece of machinery; but when he examined his prize and found the truth of the case, he dropped the box in the woods and ran for his life. We consigned our boat to the captain, to be carried back to Caldwell, and got on a stage we found at the wharf which carried us to the village of Ty. It is a despicable manufacturing place, straggling and irregular—mills, houses, and heaps of lumber— situated in a broad valley with the outlet of Lake George running through the middle—a succession of fierce rapids, with each its saw- mill. I bespoke me here a pair of breeches of a paddy tailor, who asked me if I did not work on board the steamboat, a question which aggravated me not a little. I asked a fellow the way to the fort. "Well," said he, "I've heerd of such a place, seems to me, but I never seen it, and couldn't tell ye where it be." "You must be an idiot," thought I; but I found his case by no means singular. At last I got

the direction, and walked about two miles before I saw the remains
of a high earthen parapet with a ditch running through a piece of
woods for a great distance. This, I suppose, was the place where the
French beat off Abercrombie's army.[37] Further on, in a great plain
scantily covered with wood, were breastworks and ditches in abundance running in all directions, which I took for the work of
Amherst's besieging army.[38] Still further, were two or three square
redoubts. At length, mounting a little hill, a cluster of gray ruined
walls, like an old chateau, with mounds of earth and heaps of stone
about them, appeared crowning an eminence in front.[39] When I
reached them, I was astonished at the extent of the ruins. Thousands
of men might have encamped in the area. All around, were ditches
of such depth that it would be death to jump down, with walls of
massonry sixty feet high. Ty stands on a promontary, with Champlain on one side and the outlet of Lake George on the other; his
cannon commanded the passage completely. At the very extremity
is the oldest fort of the fortress—a huge mass of masonry with walls
sinking sheer down to the two lakes. All kinds of weeds and vines are
clambering over them. The senseless blockheads in the neighborhood
have stolen tons upon tons of the stone to build their walls and houses
of—may they meet their reward.

Wednesday, 27th. In Yankee land again, thank heaven. Left Ty this
noon—after going over the ruins again—in one of the great Champlain steamboats,[40] and reached Burlington at night. Visited the
college.[41] It was term time and the students were lounging about the
ugly buildings or making abortive attempts at revelry in their rooms.
The air was full of their diabolical attempts at song. We decided that
they were all green, and went back, drawing comparisons by the way
between the University of Vermont and old Harvard.

Thursday, 28th. Left Burlington this morning, knapsack on back, for
Canada. Saw the falls of Onion [Winooski] River—ruined by dams;
passed the villages of Essex and Jericho. Far on our left front rose the
peak of the Camel's Hump, the highest in Vt. A long line of wild
mountains bounded the horizon. In the midst of them, directly
before us, was Mansfield Mt., second only to the Camel's Hump in

height.[42] Passing the village of Underhill, we descended into a little woody glen, near the road, with a rocky stream running through it, where we consigned ourselves to repose, having walked about 16 miles. Late in the afternoon we started again, and journeyed on several miles, White making by the way several abortive attempts to shoot birds and squirrels. The country was rather hilly, tolerably cultivated near the road, but covered with woods elsewhere. On a hill before us stretched a line of forest, remarkably dense and lofty, and over the tree-tops and among the boughs dozens of crows were wheeling about, croaking in hoarse concert. Ascending this hill, we found ourselves going down into a deep valley on the other side, flanked by barren rocky hills, with flocks of sheep perambulating among the rocks and stunted trees. In front of us was a noble spectacle of mountains, with an intervening country of low hills, forests, and cultivated fields. We turned an angle, and descended into another valley. Mansfield Mt. appeared through an opening on the right, and on the left was a succession of high rolling hills, one behind the other, all covered with forests, with the sinking sun blazing among the trees on the summit of the most distant, and flinging streams of light and shadow over the whole. We followed the road through a deep wood, and when we emerged from it, the village of Cambridge lay before us, twenty-five miles from Burlington. We stopped here for the night. At the supper table was an old farmer who seemed determined to find out all about us and asked, among other little matters, who we were, where we came from, and where we were going. Wrath kept me silent, but White answered his questions, upon which the old fellow, looking fixedly at us, said he should think that whoever we were, we had some kind of prospects to look forward to. The desired explanation not coming from us, he turned to me and asked me if I was not an Indian! I assured him that I was not, on which he coolly shook his head and said that he made it a principle never to contradict any man. He did not consider it any disgrace, for his part, to be an Indian: he had knowed Indians well edicated, afore now. He was very far from meaning to offend. He proved, after all, a fine old fellow; his sins being all of ignorance. Far from being offended, I favored his belief, for the joke's sake, and he firmly believes us both to contain a large share of Indian blood. He invited us to his house, if we passed "his way." We have been taken, on this journey, for people of almost every nation on earth, but this is a consummation we hardly expected.

Friday, 28[9][th]. From Cambridge we walked on to Johnson. A fellow in a waggon pulled up as we passed and inquired if we did not belong to the British army—apparently in earnest. The Lamoil[l]e River crossed the road several times. Coming to some deep woods, we were astounded by a confusion of shrieks and cries from them; and approaching, half a dozen hawks, at least, flew off in different directions among the trees. We saw the remains of several of their victims scattered among the rocks and decayed trunks. Yesterday a hawk flew over us, chased and harassed by five or six kingbirds, who would pull his feathers, squall in his ears, and dodge whenever he turned on them. The hawk seemed in high dudgeon.

At Johnson we took the stage for Stanstead, in Canada. The "stage" was a broken-down carryall, into which six passengers with luggage were stowed, and the thing set in motion—under the auspicious influences of two sick horses—over a road of diabolical roughness. By mountain, lake, and stream, we lumbered and wriggled along, the way being made about twice as grievous by a passenger, sick, apparently, of consumption, who could not bear fast riding. He was going home under the protection of his sister—a pretty woman of twenty-five, who seemed all-accomplished, having been, as she said, a traveller all her days, and never down-hearted whatever turned up. She was lively and talkative, though she had been watching the night before, and her country phrases sounded very gracefully from her lips. We rode through a wild and mountainous country. Cliffs of hundreds of feet would sometimes hang over the road. Now and then, there would be a spot among the wooded hills which had just been cleared and burnt, and lay in all the dismal deformity of charred trunks and stumps. Stopped for the night at Troy, near Lake Memphramagog. At supper with us was a girl of sixteen or seventeen; a pretty, innocent little thing, too timid to speak above a whisper. She kept her great black eyes always turned downwards.

Saturday, July 30th, *Stanstead, Canada*. Resumed our journey this morning in the same "stage." A furious unintermitting rain. The air was full of mists, rolling along the hills, and entangled among the trees. Every mountain was hidden among clouds. We passed through tracts of half-burnt forests, steaming and smoking; some blasted trunks standing upright, others prostrate among charred trunks and tangled underwood, all looking supernaturally dismal through mist and rain. Here and there a dripping and miserable log house, dimly seen, would break the monotony of the forest. The road was made up of "corduroy," rocks, and water. One of the horses came down on a hill side, and we had all to get out in the rain. At last we saw Lake Memphramagog—a direful composition of great sheets of leaden water, scarce distinguishable from the fogs that enveloped it, and a border of melancholy trees which stood apparently lamenting and pouring forth copious tears above it. All nature was in a fit of the blue-devils. At length, ten miles farther on, we passed the line and entered the town of Stanstead, under the same agreeable auspices. The place is large, with several handsome churches. There was nothing in particular to distinguish it from a flourishing Yankee town till we pulled up at the tavern, where were two or three British soldiers, in their undress, standing in the porch. There were thirteen of them, with a cornet, quartered at the house, as there now are in all the border villages.[43] They were good-looking fellows, civil enough; natives of the province. They were gathered round a fire in the barroom, smoking and telling stories, or else indulging in a little blackguardism and knocking one another about the room. They invited us to drink with them, and the liquor being mead—the house is temperance—we consented. They have just clubbed to buy a barrel of cider.

Sunday, July 31ˢᵗ. Last night we were kept awake by the din of bugles and drums with which the soldiers were regaling themselves in the entry, singing and dancing meanwhile. This morning rainy and dismal. Soldiers and all gathered round the stove in the barroom. Their conversation was about as decent and their jokes as good as those of a convocation of Harvard students. They started a conspiracy, headed by the corporal, for making their cornet—who detests smoking—a slave of his pipe; an object to attain which various ingenious expedients were proposed. I went to their roll call, and then to church, dined and wrote letters, ate supper and walked out, the weather clearing up. Our driver of yesterday told us some stories of smuggling. Chase,[44] the landlord, asked us to hear some private psalm singing, in his kitchen. We went and found Mrs. C., her daughter, son, and another youth with a mouth like a gaping oyster seated along a table with their psalm books before them, humming, coughing, and *do–ra–me*–ing preparatory to the commencement. The cornet, who painfully professed himself fond of music, with a few of his soldiers, were in the room; the family stood up behind the singers, except Chase himself, who established himself in front to dictate and pronounce judgment. They sang well, especially the son. With every pause the old man—a downright puritan— would criticize the performance; and the unfortunate cornet declare that it was very good music indeed. They finished—having previously been reinforced by a long-faced individual, apparently a deacon,—with the tune of "America," singing, in order to satisfy all the auditors, the stanzas of the republican song, and adding to each one "God save the Queen." The cornet succeeded in retiring before the end, but his men seemed to like it and crowded into the room.

Monday, August 1ˢᵗ. Chase had promised to get us a waggon to advance us on our journey. He had it ready quarter before seven and we set out to seek Indian Stream and the Ma(r)galloway, that being now our destination, seeing that we are unable to go to Mt. Ktaadin [Katahdin]. Chase drove us as far as the town of Barnston, through Stanstead Plain, a very level and fertile country. He says that he should think Stanstead contained 6,000 inhabitants. Dismissing him and his waggon at Barnston—where four or five more soldiers are stationed—we set out on foot for Canaan, which promised land some told us was twenty miles distant, while others reckoned it thirty. The road for a few miles was good, but we were soon compelled to leave it and take a path through the woods. A beautiful river— smooth and rapid—ran across the road under a bridge of logs, between forest-covered banks. Not far from Stanstead, we had crossed a furious stream, answering to the sentimental designation of the Nigger River. We had walked but a few miles when the clouds settled on the hills and it began to rain. We went to a log cabin for shelter. The "old man" was frank and hospitable like all his genus I ever met, and the "old woman"—a damsel of twenty two, who sat combing her hair in the corner—extremely sprightly and talkative. She seemed somewhat moved at heart by the doctrines of Miller,[45] whose apostles are at work all along the Vermont frontier. We abused that holy man to our content and, the rain ceasing, left the cabin. High rolling hills bounded the horizon, all covered with an ocean of forest. The clouds hung heavy upon them, but would break every instant and admit a stream of sunshine, which would pass across the great carpet of woods, illuminate it in spots for an instant, and then give place to the black shadows of the clouds. Soon after leaving this place, we entered the afore-mentioned path through the woods. Now and then there would be a clearing with its charred stumps, its boundary of frowning woods, and its log cabin; but, for the most part, the forest was in its original state. The average depth of the mud in the path was one foot. Scarce a ray of sunlight ever reached there through the thick boughs overhead. The streams that ran through the wood had no bridges, and most of them seemed to have preferred the artificial channel afforded by our path to the one they had worked for themselves among the mossy stones and decayed trunks of the forest. So we had to wade in deep water about two-thirds of the way. Of course, we were soon covered with mud to the eyes. It was not long, however, before we emerged upon a broader path—one practicable to a stout waggon. This, too, led through a dense forest. We stopped at a log cabin at three o'clock and asked for dinner. A decent one was given us. During the process of eating, the "girls" were working at the spinning wheel and giggling among themselves, the boys sat stiff and upright in their chairs—homemade —and contemplated us with great attention. "How far to the next clearing?" we asked. "Eight mile!" and a long eight miles it was to us—a dismal slough of despond the whole way—mud to the knees. But the path was a singularly wild and impressive one—cut through a wilderness. Huge trees flanked and arched it—maple, pine, cedar, cypress, and a thousand others; bending over it, and intertwined with one another, two high walls of foliage and wooden columns. Below, a fringe of high bushes along the path hid the base of the trunks; but, looking through, the ground was hid with matted masses of green mossy logs, and heaps of rot, with a tangled undergrowth, all wet with the moisture that never leaves a forest like this. The day was showery, with occasional glimpses of the sun; so that we were alternately wet and dry. Late in the afternoon we reached a clearing, with a couple of cabins. Two men were mounting their horses to ride through the woods. We gave the accustomed shake of the hand, etc., walked through another two miles of forest, and came to another clearing, of an aspect so wild and picturesque that a painter might have won the credit of being an astounding genius by only copying things as they were. At the farthur end of this clearing was a stream, swift and cold, into which we walked in order to wash off the superfluous dirt. Thence, passing various dwellings, and holding various colloquies with the inmates, we reached Canaan, and a good tavern. The landlord has quartered [us] in his hall—large as a barn. Canaan is a microscopic village, the houses scattered through a valley among low mountains, all covered with forest. We saw here the Connecticut for the first time—rapid and full of rocks and foam. We follow its banks tomorrow.

Tuesday. Weather still cold and blustering. Thick clouds all over the sky. Set out after breakfast for the Connecticut Lake, twenty miles distant. The road ran along the river, about as good as a cart-track through the woods about Boston, and shadowed by the boughs of the trees. The Connecticut went roaring along on our right. When we had gone about two miles White found he had lost his powder-flask, and had to go back and look for it, an accident which detained us an hour and more. We passed several houses, cabins and others. At one where we stopped for a drink and a talk—for the men regularly turned out and shouted to us as we passed—I rested my rifle against a hogshead standing by a pump trough. A sudden jar knocked it down. It fell so that the muzzle struck with great force upon the trough. I picked it up and walked on, without imagining that it had been much hurt, till some way further, when I found the stock split, the breech-pin broke short off, and other damage done which made the gun almost useless. This was worse than anything that could have happened, short of the loss of our cash, but we determined to keep on to the Margalloway still, and make shift as we could. White seems to have lost his apathy and is now quite ready to proceed. Reports of the Margalloway trout have inflamed him. The road was still hilly, narrow, and, [a] great part of the way, flanked by woods. The valley of the river looked, as it always does, rich and fertile, but the hills and mountains around presented one broad unbroken expanse of forest, made the more sombre by the deep shadows of the clouds. In the afternoon, we reached a hill top and a vast panorama of mountains and forests lay before us. A glistening spot of water, some miles to the north, girt with mountains which sloped down to it from all sides with a smooth and gradual descent, was Lake Connecticut. As far as we could see, one mountain of peculiar form rose above the rest which we afterwards learned was the Camel's Hump [Rump Mt.]. Passing a river with rapids and a saw-mill, at the end of the day we reached the lake, where are two houses, Barn[e]s's[46] and Abbot's.[47] There are steep rapids at the outlet, with a mill, of course. We went to Abbot's house, and asked for lodging and a supper. Abbot, a stout, round shouldered, frank-looking man, was in his hay-field. I inquired of him for a guide to lead us across to the Margalloway, and he at once said that he would go himself, first confessing that he had never been before, and did not know the country in that direction. This was nothing to the purpose. A compass was guide enough. I hired him for a dollar a day.

We went in to supper, which was served in rough style, but had the virtue of cleanliness, as did the whole place—children excepted. There were some eight or ten imps of both sexes, the youngest called Henry Harrison, whence I divined that Abbot was a Whig.[48] There was a schoolmistress from Canaan in the house—plain, but of decent manners and sensible. Abbot was a rough-hewn piece of timber enough, but his wife was a perfect barbarian, as far as the entire absence of all manners can make one, but both were equally open and hospitable. Henry tried the polite, but I judged it best to do at Rome as the Romans do, and I believe got along best. We spent that evening about their enormous cavern of a fire place, whence a blazing fire gleamed on rows of suspended stockings, the spinning wheel, the churn, the bed, and walls covered with an array of piled up cheeses, plates, milkpails, and clothes; all clean and all in order; while the older children were dodging about the furniture of the crowded room and the younger ones venting precocious snorings from a box under the bed. Abbot soon began to rail against Tyler,[49] etc.; then diverged to stories, which we kept going among us, the little school-mistress taking her part, till a pretty late hour, when we were shown to a good bed in the opposite room. Abbot says that one of his relatives, Kenfield by name, fought at William Henry, and, at the massacre, seeing an Indian about to strip a fallen officer, caught him, raised him in his arms, and dashed him to the ground with such violence as to make him senseless.[50] Our host greatly exults in the bodily strength for which his family have been eminent—he himself no way dishonors his race in that respect. These settlements are of old date,[51] but have hardly increased at all for many years.

Wednesday. We devoted today to loafing about the place. White and I went out in an old "dug out" of Barns's on the lake, but caught no fish. The season is unfavorable, but we afterwards caught a few large trout at the foot of the rapids. There is in this lake and in Memphramagog a fish I have never seen, called the lunge.[52] There are moose, bear, and wolves on the mountains; and a beaver has long dwelt, spite of trap, in Indian Stream above the dam we passed two miles before we reached the lake. We lived in backwoods style today— sugarless tea for dinner—water drank from a mug common to all the company, etc. We liked it—I did, at least. Abbot sat cobbling his shoe against his projected expedition towards evening, but as I came up he turned round and remarked that he was not a disciple of St. Crispin[d] but only an occasional follower. As I was marvelling at this unexpected display of erudition, his wife thrust her head from the door, and exclaimed, "Here, supper's ready. Where's that other man gone to?" We accepted the elegant invitation and walked in, where Abbot astonished us still more by comparing the democrat levellers to Procrustes, who wished to reduce all men to the same dimensions by his iron bedstead. All this was while he was squatting on his homemade chair, one leg cocked into the air, shirt-sleeves rolled up to his elbows, bushy hair straggling over his eyes, and eating meanwhile as if his life depended on his efforts. I have since found that he has read a vast amount of history, ancient and modern, and various

[d] Patron saint of cobblers.—Ed.

other things—all fact, however; for fiction, he says, he cannot bear. When twenty-five—he is now thirty-six—he defended himself against a good lawyer in a court, and won his case, his opponent confessing himself outmatched by Abbot's general knowledge and quick memory.

Thursday. Started this morning to strike the Little Margalloway. We proceeded first toward the north, with a path for the first few miles. It soon failed us, and we had to force our way through tangled woods. At about ten o'clock we reached the west bank of the Second Lake. Connecticut is a string of three lakes, on the first of which Abbot's house and all the other settlements are. At this place we met an unexpected delay. The raft, on which we were to have crossed, had broke loose from the bank and gone over the rapids down to the first lake. There was nothing for it but to build another, an operation which took up two hours. We paddled over at last, the mountains which lay between us and the promised river heaving up, ridge over ridge, before us, covered with an unbroken and pathless forest, never trod except by hunters. We landed on this dreary shore— White tumbling over into the water in the attempt—shouldered our packs, and taking a southeast direction by the compass, plunged into the woods. Ten thousand decayed logs scattered here and there, piled one on other, a thick growth of strong and tangled under-wood, rocks, fallen trees, gullies, made the forest almost impassable. It was a constant straining of muscle and sinew. Boughs slapped us in the face, swarms of flies stung us; we trod on spots apparently solid and sank to the thighs in masses of rotten timber. White had hurt his foot the day before and constantly lagged behind, so that we had to wait for him every minute, the prey of torturing flies. At length the ascent of the first mountain made the way still more laborious. When at length we reached the top, we could see nothing on account of the thick growth of trees. We passed through a singular piece of boggy ground, of an oblong shape, enclosed in a fringe of cedars, rising one above the other, all hung with tassels of white moss. There was another place, partially open, near the summit. As we passed it, a large buck sprang from the ground, and leaped with long bounds down the mountain, before my rifle was at my shoulder. We

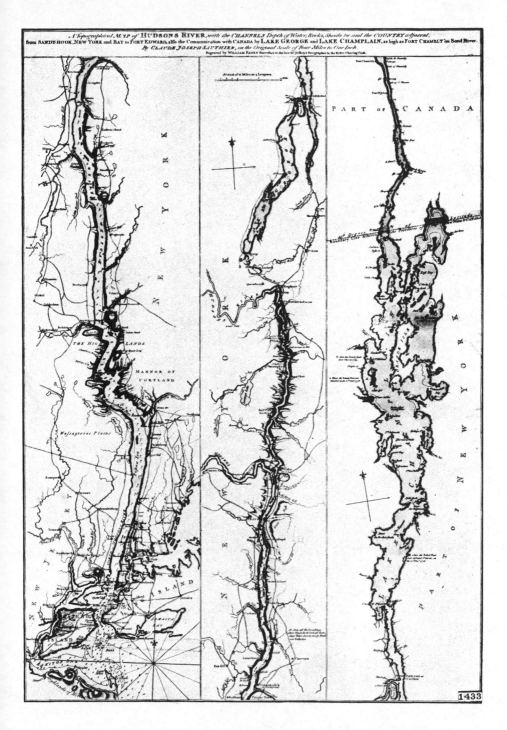

A Topographical Map of Hudson's River from Sandy Hook . . . as high as Fort Chambly, 1776
Engraved map by William Faden after Claude Joseph Sauthier
(Coverdale Collection No. 1433)

heard him crashing the boughs far below. In this spot were several springs of clear, cold water, in broad cup-shaped hollows in the ground, which had probably attracted the deer. We went down the mountain and found a little stream flowing through the valley at the bottom. Both Abbot and myself were for proceeding, but White said he could not go on on account of his foot; so we found a convenient spot and encamped. It was by the stream, flowing half-concealed beneath brushwood and fallen trees, in a thick growth of firs, spruces, and birches. We made a fire, and proceeded to cook our supper. We had brought with us seven pounds of bread, six and a half of rice, and a quantity of butter. We had beside about an ounce of tea, and salt, of course.[e]

We made our fire in the middle of the grove, cut spruce boughs for a bed, lay down on our blankets, and with our knives speedily made way with a mess of rice placed on a broad piece of birch bark amongst us. Then we heaped new wood on the fire, and lay down again, cooled by a gentle rain which just now began to fall. The fire blazed up a column of bright flame, and flung its light deep into the recesses of the woods. In the morning we breakfasted on rice, bread, and tea without sugar and cream, and then—Friday—prepared to resume our course. Abbot led the way, forcing himself with might and main through the bushes and trees, with us following behind. He carried White's blanket, for White professed himself unable, on account of his lame leg. The direction was southeast by compass, up the declivity of the second mountain. White was eternally grumbling and lagging behind. We had to wait for him every few minutes. The guide cursed him to his face, and said he never knew a fellow of so little pluck. At length, after some hours of tedious labor, we stood on the summit, and saw—nothing. The trees crowded round us so dense and thick that our view was confined to a circle of about a rod around, and a few little patches of cloudy sky above; but by climbing to the top of a tall maple, a noble prospect of mountain and wilderness lay before us. Far off rose the Margalloway Mountain, with a sea of smaller hills about it, all pale and indistinct in mist. Lake Connecticut glisten(en)ed among them like a surface of polished silver. Right beneath us was the valley of [Dead] Diamond Stream.

[e] "Written at Camp, without shelter, during a shower of rain."—F.P.

A line of steep and lofty bluffs marked its course, for the river itself was buried too deep among mountains to be visible. In front, close to us, heaved up a long ridge of mountains sloping away to the left down to the Margalloway.

We set the compass and found the river lay still to the southeast of us. We came down, and pursued that course again. We soon began to ascend [descend] the mountain on the side opposite that which we had ascended. The way was rough and precipitous. White lagged more and more, and provoked Abbot and myself beyond measure. After journeying many hours in this painful style, we heard the plunging of waters in a valley below us, and joyfully turned towards the sound. It grew louder and louder. In five minutes more we emerged from the gloomy forest and stood in the rocky bed of a wild stream that came down in a succession of rapids and falls over broad shelves of granite. Just then the sun came out from the clouds and lit up the long avenue of trees that followed the course of the stream, and made the water sparkle and glisten in welcome contrast to the sombre shades we had just left. We had struck a branch of the Little Margalloway. White's lameness seemed mysteriously to leave him; he siezed his fishing tackle and rushed up and down the rocks, pulling a trout from every deep hole and the foot of every waterfall. I soon followed his example. Abbot built a fire by the bank and cooked our fish. We made a plentiful dinner, and then began to follow downward the course of the stream. At first, it was a matter of no difficulty. We could walk well enough down the channel without wading much above the knees in any place, but soon the brooks that poured in from the mountains on all sides increased the depth of the water, so that we had to betake ourselves to the woods again. Four miles below where we struck it, the river was navigable for a canoe; a mile further, and we heard the loud plunging of a fall. We found a ledge of some four feet high stretched across the river, with the water tumbling over it into a deep basin of dark waters. On the right bank, close to the fall, were traces of an old encampment. Night was coming on, so we determined to establish ourselves here, though we had hoped to have reached the forks of the Margalloway, the place where its two branches meet, and where Slade[f] and I made our

---

[f] Daniel Denison Slade, Parkman's companion in 1841.—Ed.

last camp a year ago.[g] In the middle of the fall there was a rock, to which we waded and caught in ten minutes a dozen of trout averaging a foot in length. We built our fire, split open the fish, broiled them on forked sticks, boiled some rice, made some tea, and supped in very luxurious style. We lay down on our beds of spruce boughs and the monotonous plunge of the falls quickly lulled us to sleep.[h]

Saturday, Aug. 5[6][th]. The morning opened with a grand council. How were we to get down the river? Abbot could make a raft, thought he could make a spruce canoe, and was certain that he could make a log one. I told him to make a log one. We roused White from the spruce boughs where he persisted in snoring, in spite of our momentous discussion, and then prepared and ate our breakfast. White went to fishing. Abbot shouldered his axe, and he and I went off together for a suitable pine tree to make our canoe of. He found one to his satisfaction on the other side of the stream, some distance down. I built him a fire to "smudge" the flies, waded back across the stream, and as I ascended the farther bank heard the thundering crash of the falling pine behind me, bellowing over the wilderness, and rolling in echoes far up the mountains. I went back to camp, where White had again betaken himself to his diversion of snoring, took my broken rifle and set out on an exploring expedition to find the basin where the two branches of the Margalloway unite, which I knew could not be far distant. I waded a considerable distance down stream in the water, which varied in depth from the knees to the waist, but finding this method of progression somewhat unpleasing, I took to the woods, forced my way through them in a southerly direction for half a mile, and found at last the object of my search. The old place, though in the midst of a howling wilderness, looked to me quite like home. It was the spot which had listened to Slade's lugubrious lamentations, the extreme point of my last year's pilgrimage; the place where Jerome[i] had joined our party; and to crown all, it was scarce five miles distant from the scene of that

  [g] See 1841 Journal, p. 29.—Ed.

  [h] "*Friday, Aug. 5th.* Saw three moose-yards of last winter—known by the marks of teeth on the young trees and by the heaps of dung in every direction.—F.P."

  [i] Parkman's Indian guide in the preceding year.—Ed.

astounding exploit of knocking over the wounded moose. There lay the great black basin of dull waters, girt with its fringe of forests, but the appearance of things was altered since I had seen it before. The basin was fuller, the water blacker and deeper. Some hunter—Jerome, we found afterwards—had visited it since Slade and I had been there and made a good camping place of split boards. Two or three vessels of birch bark, a setting pole, and a fishing pole were scattered around. There was a fragrance of rotten fish in the atmosphere which told that the visit had not been many months back. I sat down, dipped a cup of water from the basin, took a biscuit from my pocket, and made a most comfortable luncheon. I took Jerome's pole, went to fishing, and in an hour caught large trout enough for several meals for our whole party. As I went back to camp, I found that Abbot was not at work on his canoe. While I was marvelling at this, I stumbled upon a half-finished sp[r]uce canoe, which Abbot had set about making, having found the pine tree, which he had cut down for his log boat, rotten. I was not much pleased at this change of plan: nevertheless, as the thing was begun I lent him [such] assistance as I could, so that by nightfall we had finished something which had the semblance of a canoe, but, owing chiefly to haste and want of tools, had such a precarious and doubtful aspect that White christened it the *Forlorn Hope*. We put it into the water. It leaked. We took it out and stuffed the seams with pounded spruce bark, chewed spruce gum, and bits of cloth. It still leaked, but we hoped it would do, with diligent baling; so, fastening it to the bank, we cooked our supper, rolled ourselves in our blankets, and went to sleep before the fire.

Sunday, Aug. 6[7]th. We were obliged perforce to adopt the sailor's maxim, "No Sunday off soundings," for our provisions were in a fair way of failing, and starvation in the wilderness is not a pleasant prospect to look forward to. So we prepared the last meal we were to take at the Rapids of the Little Margalloway. White, acting as chief cook, arranged the trout on forked sticks before the fire. Abbot filled his little copper kettle with water, and boiled some rice, which being poured into a tin dish and suitably buttered, made way for the tea which was afterwards boiled in the same kettle. The dish was set amongst us, the trout piled on a piece of birch bark close by, and the kettle of tea steamed on the other side. We soon demolished the repast, one item, at least, of which would have been considered an extreme luxury at the breakfast table of the richest man in Boston. I mean the Margalloway trout, which are the noblest in appearance and the most delicious in taste I ever knew. After breakfast we packed our luggage, and proceeded to make the dubious experiment of the canoe. All were embarked; White in the middle to bale, Abbot at the stern, I in the prow. "Push off." The canoe glided with a quiet and gentle motion down the swift stream, between the tall walls of forest on each side, but soon the ripple and tumbling of a rapid appeared in front and the hour of trial came. She quivered and shook as she entered the disturbed waters; at last there was a little grating sound. She had struck upon the stones at the bottom, but the peril was past; the water grew smooth and deep again, and again we floated quietly and prosperously down in the shadows of the woods. At last another rapid came. She entered it, grated heavily over the stones, and struck hard against a large one before her. The water spouted in like a stream from a pump. It would not do. The experiment was an utter failure. We left Abbot with the canoe to conduct that and the baggage as [best] he could down to the basin, and waded to shore ourselves, to walk there through the woods. We had not gone quarter of a mile when "Hallo, here" came from the river. "What's the matter now?" shouted we in return. "The canoe's burst all to pieces!" Sure enough, we found it so. Abbot stood in the middle of a rapid, up to the knees, holding our baggage aloft to keep it dry, while the miserable remnant of the demolished vessel was leisurely taking its way down the current. We pushed through the woods towards the basin, deliberating what to do next. Abbot was sure he could make a raft which would carry us down to the settlements, and yet draw so little water as to pass the "rips" in safety. The navigation would indeed be slow with such a machine, but it could be made in an hour or two, and this would more than counterbalance the want of speed. The river was high; the plan seemed eligible, and we proceeded to execute it. Meanwhile it began to rain furiously. We walked into the water to our waists and held the timbers in place while Abbot withed them together. Jerome's camp was demolished to furnish materials, his setting poles and birch-bark vessels appropriated to our use. After about two hours of aquatic exertion, during which we were wet equally by the rain above and the river beneath, the raft was finished. Owing to the badness of the timber, it drew twice as much water as we expected. We pushed from shore in a deluge of rain. Like its luckless predecessor, the raft passed the first rapid in safety, only venting a groan or two as its logs encountered the stones beneath. The rapids in the main river were, of course, much deeper than those of the Little Margalloway, above the basin, where the canoe had met its fate. When it came on the second rapid, the machine seemed to shiver in direful expectancy of its approaching destruction. Presently it grunted loud and dolefully. We set our poles and pushed it into the deepest part. For a while it bumped and blundered downward; at length there was a heavy shock, a crash, a boiling and rushing of many waters. The river spouted up between the logs. We were fixed irrecoverably aground. The water coursed savagely by us, and broke over the end of the raft, but it could not be moved. The result of this second experiment was more dismal than of the first. We were in the middle of the river; the trees on both shores loomed gloomily through rain and mist, and a volume of boiling and roaring waves rolled between. However, there being no remedy, we walked in and, by dint of considerable struggling, waded safe to the western bank, where I directed Abbot to try no more experiments but to work on a log canoe till he had finished it. He accordingly felled another tree, while we were, with great difficulty on account of the rain, building a fire. Abbot worked with great perseverance and skill. Before night, his canoe was nearly hewed out. We plied him with tea to keep his spirits up, relieved him of the cooking and all his other duties, so that his task was accomplished in what seemed an incredibly short time. That afternoon I went back to the basin to get fish for the public benefit. At night the rain, which had ceased for awhile, began to pour afresh. We put up White's blanket, which was wet, for a tent and, spreading mine on the ground beneath, made a great fire before it, ate our supper and lay down. As soon as we were quiet, the continual dropping and plashing of rain through the forest had a sound singularly melancholy and impressive. White dropped asleep, after his established custom on all occasions; but Abbot and myself, both of us wet to the skin, chose to lay and talk before the fire till past midnight. Our guide is a remarkably intelligent fellow; has astonishing information for one of his condition; is resolute and as independent as the wind. Unluckily, he is rather too conscious of his superiority in these respects, and likes too well to talk of his own achievements. He is coarse and matter-of-fact to a hopeless extremity, self-willed and self-confident as the devil; if any one would get respect or attention from him, he must meet him on his own ground in this matter. He is very talkative. I learned more from his conversation about the manners and customs of the semi-barbarians he lives among, than I could have done from a month's living among them. That night in the rain, leagues from the dwellings of men, was a very pleasant one. We slept a few hours towards day; and rose before it was fairly light, he to finish the canoe, we to prepare breakfast. We launched the boat soon after, embarked, and paddled down stream. Dull leaden clouds covered all the sky. The rain fell heavily and steadily. We determined to reach the settlements, if possible, that night; and accordingly we paddled continually all day, only stopping, about noon, to eat our last biscuit. White paddled lazily and unskilfully, and showed much of that kind of resignation which consists in abandoning one's self to fate, instead of fighting with it. Abbot gave him something more than hints of what he thought of him; and when I proceeded, in a truly Christian spirit, to bestow a little friendly advice and exhortation, that he should be up and doing, he flung down his paddle, wrapped himself in his blanket, and sat down listlessly in the bottom of the canoe. As night approached, we began to feel rather uncomfortable at the notion of spending it in the open air at such a time. At length we saw, on the left bank, a camp built of logs for the use of "loggers." We went ashore. The place was dry, the roof being slant and thatched waterproof, with a hole at one side to let out the smoke of the fire. A cart path led from the place towards the settlements, which we knew could not be far distant. In a desperate hope of reaching them that way, we left the certain to pursue the uncertain good. We walked and ran, with our heavy packs and guns, about a mile along the wretched path, which seemed only to lead us deeper into the wilderness. Wading through bogs, stumbling over logs, pitching into gullies, bruising our skins, running against trees, but still hurrying on, we came at last to where the path divided into three; and following the best, we came to other ramifications, till the path seem[ed] almost to disappear and we to be buried in a trackless wilderness. This was a pretty condition of things for a stormy night. It was too evident that the roads we had been following were the work of a party of enterprising loggers, none of them leading, as we had thought possible, to the settlements, but [rather to] the depths of dismal swamps, where the best timber grew. There was still, however, one little path which seemed of older date than the rest, and which, that no stone might be left unturned, we resolved to follow. It was getting dark fast. What was done must be done at once. We dashed on at almost a run. The trees overhead made the way about as dark as midnight; and the roaring of wind, the beating of rain, and the creaking of boughs shut our ears against all ordinary sounds. At all events, it was without much warning that we all plunged up to our necks into a gulf of muddy water that, swollen suddenly by the storm, was slowly eddying along through the forest in the channel which, the day before, held a little brook. As we scrambled up the bank, after this delightful immersion, we thought of warm taverns, hot suppers, soft beds, and brandy and water. But none of these desirable comforts awaited us. We took the best course the circumstances permitted and retraced our way to the logging camp. Fortunately I had secured my matches in a tin case, and this in my water-proof knapsack, so that we were able to build a fire with the aid of some dry birch bark we found in the hut. The floor was covered with clean straw which made us beds. We built a furious fire, which burned down one side of the hut and might have burned the rest, had not the logs been well soaked in rain. Hanging our superfluous clothing to dry, we laid down in the rest and slept comfortably all night.

*Tuesday, Aug. 8[9]*th. We did not rise till late this morning, so comfortable was our bed of straw. We found our clothes dry and our limbs active and pliant with the steam which filled the hut. We had eaten nothing of any consequence since the morning before. Now we got ready our last mess of rice, boiled all our tea, seasoned the breakfast with all the butter we had left, and made a very fair and satisfactory meal. When we got out of the hut, we found the forest about us glittering in the morning sun with the rain drops of last night; mists floated above the river and among the trees; the clouds that half covered the sky were light and thin and promised to scatter soon. We could hear, in the stillness of the morning, the rumbling of the distant rapids. We baled the water from our canoe and pushed it from the shore. After paddling about three miles down stream, the hoarse sound of the falls growing louder every instant, we saw before us the line of white foam, stretched across the river, which marked their commencement, and turning towards the bank, found the true pathway to the settlements. A walk of an hour brought us to them. The old logging camp, where we passed the night, was not more than six miles distant from them, so that [it] is not impossible that we might have reached them the night before, had we been lucky enough to have chosen the right turning in the labyrinth. The first man we met was the Indian Jerome, who was cleaning a moose-hide in a field. He shook hands with me very fervently, probably expecting a donation for old acquaintance' sake, but the rascal was disappointed. Jerome is an outcast from his tribe for various misdeeds, too many and too gross to particularize. White, after muttering a salutation which Jerome did not hear, and half extending a hand which Jerome did not see—or pretended not to—stood fixed in awe and abhorrence at the sinister look of the fellow's face, the dia-bolical size of his mouth, the snaky glittering of his deep-set eyes, the hollowness of his cheeks, and the black marks dissipation has made on his countenance. Jerome is an admirable hunter. He killed more than twenty moose this spring.

We next proceeded to the familiar cabin of my old guide Lombard, or as they all pronounce it about here, Lumber. His wife was in the house and gave us quite a cordial welcome. I asked her to get us some luncheon, and we demolished a miraculous quantity of her bread, milk, and cheese. I found the "old man" at work on the road—which needed it—at quarter of a mile's distance. He was as dirty, big, rough, ogre-like, and hearty as ever. He and a train of his sons went back with me to the house, where he took down from the rafters, amongst suspended stockings, yarn, bladders, etc., the ears of the moose I shot when with him last year. He said he had kept them a whole month in his chimney to dry, and meant to send them to Boston by the first opportunity he had, but such opportunities are not of very frequent occurrence on the Margalloway. I pocketed the valuable relics.

We next followed the "road"—so called by courtesy—down the river towards Capt. Brag[g]'s, where we meant to spend the night. Meanwhile the weather had changed. "Old Esquoss" [Aziscoos], and all the other mountains that flank the valley, stood out in dismal relief against black clouds. Thunder began to grumble and mutter. At length the storm burst over some of the more distant peaks, and the descending rain shut them from sight, like a grey curtain drawn before them. The clouds seemed satisfied with this ebbullition of wrath. They broke, the sun streamed through them, and we hoped to spend that day at least in a dry skin. At last we came to a place where it is necessary to cross the river. There is no regular means of so doing, so that passengers have to depend on the mercy of the farmer who occupies the log-house on the opposite side. We shouted for a boat at the extent of our lungs. No reply. We called the man by name. Presently a voice was heard—"A'nt got no boat—the boy's gone down the river with it arter a schoolmistress." No sooner was this sentence uttered, than White quietly seated himself on the bank in helpless resignation. We had flattered ourselves that now we had reached the settlements our difficulties were over, but here was no contemptible one in the outset. I ran back about a mile to the last cabin we had passed—no boat there. When I returned, I found the indefatigable Abbot looking among the trees for timber to make a raft, but everything seemed to oppose us—all the wood was so heavy as scarcely to float. We now roused White from his torpor and told him that if he had any spunk left in him, he would swim the river and apply for help at some houses we could see lower down the river. He made a flat refusal, but being suitably reviled, and accused of cowardice, want of spirit, etc., etc., etc., at length reluctantly consented. Abbot made him a little raft, of such wood as he could find, to put his clothes on and push before him. We saw him climb the opposite bank, and then set about preparing another resource in case this one should fail. We had already put all the baggage on another little raft, made by Abbot; and, maddened at White's long absence, were stripping ourselves to swim across with it; when Bennet[t], the owner of the house opposite, came down to the bank and called to us to search a little muddy creek near to us, where he said there might possibly be a boat hid. We did so, and found a broken log canoe, in which we embarked and contrived to keep afloat, by constant baling, till we got to the other side. After some time, White made his appearance, bringing with him a tall, long-faced fellow who had a boat, but was afraid to let it to us for fear we should not pay. We quieted his apprehensions on this score by liberal promises, so that at last he agreed to row us down the river to Capt. Brag's—ten miles—for a dollar. The late rains had made the path through the woods by land perfectly impracticable. We set out. The weight of the party sunk the gunnel of the little skiff to within an inch of the water. Mr. Hibbard, of whom we hired the boat, had declared that he hated to go, that he was a delicate man who always took cold when he was wet, and would not stir on any account if he thought another shower was coming. Abbot rolled his eyes learnedly over the firmament. "No, sir," said he, "it won't rain tonight. When you see a white streak in the clouds like that 'ere over the mountain, it's a sure sign of no rain for twenty-four hours." In spite of the white streak, there was a perfect certainty of a furious shower, if black lowering clouds and muttering thunder are any signs; but Abbot's sage remark closed Hibbard's mouth.

Beside the pair of oars, we all paddled, except White. The boat made rapid progress. We had gone about a mile, and there was a long reach of river stretching before us, when the forked flash sprang out from a huge black pile of clouds, and forth burst the thunder like a battery of ten thousand cannon. Then came a deep hoarse sound, apparently from the furthest depths of the forest. It grew louder and louder, nearer and nearer, till down came a deluge of rain on us that seemed as if it would beat our skiff and us to the bottom. Even the sound of the thunder peals seemed stifled in the dismal hissing and roaring of this portable cataract. It fell with such violence that the whole surface of the river was white. Our view was confined to a few rods round us. The wall of trees on each side could only be seen dimly and indistinctly, as if in the night. Feeling somewhat uncomfortable, we ran the boat ashore and waited in the woods till the first fury had past, and then drove down the river in double quick time towards our destination. There was a long line of dead pines, rising up high above the other trees, and flinging their knotted and twisted arms in such fantastic style through the mist and rain that they looked like so many tall imps of the devil, stationed there on purpose to plague and torment us. In about two hours, straining our eyes through the vapors, we saw a line of white objects in front of us, rising, sinking, approaching, falling back, and apparently performing a sort of ghostly dance across the river. These were the waves dashing against the rocks, at the head of the rapids of the Androscoggin, and spouting into the air as they struck. We moored our boat at the head of the portage, siezed our baggage, and ran, waded, plunged, and crawled, through mud, water, and slime, till we got to Brag's and dashed pell mell into his kitchen, inundating it plentifully. Mrs. Brag was full of commiseration. We were soon steaming before a huge fire; half an hour after, eating a hot supper; and half an hour after that, comfortably in bed, listening to the impotent malice of the rain as it beat on the windows. The delicate Hibbard preferred to sleep on a buffalo [robe] before the fire.

*Wednesday, Aug. 9[10]*ᵗʰ. Left Brag's this morning to walk to Colebrook. I had to carry about thirty pounds weight, including my blanket which, having covered White's shoulders through all the storms of yesterday, had become saturated with moisture; and as he had neglected to take any measures for drying it, it was about as heavy, when rolled up, as a log of hard wood. Abbot carried his for him. The day was overcast and showery. When we had got about six miles, we overtook an old fellow in a waggon, who was jolting along over stones, logs, gullies, and all other impediments towards Colebrook. White got in with him and rode the rest of the way, Abbot and I going on together, first committing the baggage to his care, except my knapsack, which I chose to keep with me. We soon entered the Notch. Its appearance is much finer when seen from this side than from the other. There you see nothing but bare cliffs, rising all around you and shutting out everything else, but here a host of green trees spring from every crevice, overhang the road, and half conceal the crags on each hand, and in a ravine on your left a little brook comes down in a succession of foaming waterfalls. We reached Colebrook early in the afternoon, having walked twenty-two miles. Abbot had previously taken a by-road which led to the north, and we saw no more of him.

Thursday, Aug. 10[11]^{th}. Stayed at Colebrook today, for want of means to get off. In the villanous little hole of a tavern there, there is never anything stirring to break the dismal monotony. Every day is a Sunday. There may be a whole week without any customer. Everything is scrupulously neat, the old lady starched and precise and, of course, grossly stupid. There is no fishing or sporting of any kind about the place. She had some old magazines in the house which she hunted up for us, and these were about our only amusement for the whole day.

Friday, Aug. 11[12]^{th}. The stage came by this morning from Canaan. It is called a stage, but is in reality a milk-cart. We got in. At noon we reached Lancaster, where White stopped, being reduced to his last quarter of a dollar, to see his uncle and borrow the needful of him. I kept on to Littleton; where I now am.

Saturday, Aug. 12[13]^{th}. Started for home by way of Plymouth. Riding down through the Franconia Notch, the mountains—rolled up, heads and all, in their blankets of mists—the lake, the martial countenance of the Old Man, and all the other familiar objects of that noble pass seemed to press me to stay in a manner that nothing but necessity enabled me to resist. All but the scenery, however, is changed since I was last here. Oakes[53] has left the tavern at the village, which Fifield has taken, having abandoned his last year's stand at the Notch House, which is now empty. The drunken scoundrel Gurnsey[54] has surrendered his house to one Knight(s),[55] and remains a sort of useless fixture on the premises. With an accommodating driver and a pleasant party of ladies and gentlemen—one of the former exceedingly handsome, romantic, and spirited—we rode on towards Plymouth and got there late at night. There was a general on board, a man of exalted character and vast political influence which he exercised on the righteous side of radical democracy, fiercely maintaining that ninepence was better than a million dollars, insomuch that the possessor of the first is invariably a good man and contented with his lot, while the owner of the last is always a grasping, avaricious child of the devil. When the general alighted at his own tavern, he saluted the first loafer who met him at the door as "major"; the next but one was "colonel," while our driver answered to the title of "captain."

Sunday, Aug. 13[14]th, Plymouth. Went this morning to church where a toothless old scarecrow, who had been a preacher twenty-five years ago, mumbled a sermon which nobody could hear. A sentence here and there reached my ears, and seemed to indicate something worthy a better delivery. A son of Deacon Punchard[56] is the settled Congregational minister here. Walked, after church in the afternoon, to see Livermore's Falls, where the Pemigewasset tumbles over a mass of combined mill dams and granite rocks in a furious "burst of yellow foam."

1843 Notebook

Lake George, Montreal, Quebec

White Mountains & Maine

Introduction

THIS was really the first of Parkman's long series of journeys for historical research. The excursions of the two previous summers were largely pleasure trips, though coupled with the love of adventure and of the wilderness which inspired these arduous expeditions was the historian's desire to experience for himself the life led by his heroes. In attempting to match the hardihood of those bold pioneers, and to strengthen a constitution none too robust by nature, Parkman had damaged his health to such a degree that this journey of 1843, except for a few active days in the White Mountains, was perforce that of a student rather than that of a man of action. His ill-health, mirrored in the incompleteness, terseness, and bad temper of this notebook as opposed to the joyous detail of the earlier journals, was such that his family sent him abroad soon after his return to Boston from this journey, rather than back to Harvard for his senior year.

The cryptic quality of this notebook is tantalizing, for here Parkman records his first impressions of the chief scenes of his history, the places which he was later to make celebrated by his spirited accounts of the events that brought the little-known settlements of colonial North America into the European eye. In the Hudson and Mohawk valleys he sought out oral tradition of Sir William Johnson, that wild Irish baronet who ruled the Iroquois for England; of the old Dutch settlers who founded Albany and Schenectady when New York was New Holland, and left their imprint lastingly on the land; of Joseph Brant, that most civilized of Mohawks, who was educated by Eleazar Wheelock, the founder of Dartmouth College, entertained by Boswell, painted by Romney, and commissioned a colonel in the British Army for his services to the king. At Lake George, Parkman wandered again over the much disputed battleground which he had first visited the previous summer, and was to enjoy revisiting until his death fifty years later. At Montreal he had his first contact with the French Catholicism which played so great a role in the history he planned to write. "Roman" institutions and "popish" customs were strange to the young Puritan son of a Boston Unitarian divine, and it is clear that he took more pleasure in his first sight of British regulars and of the forts which defended the much traveled invasion route of the Richelieu and Champlain valleys. At Quebec he was stirred by the old walls—not old enough, however, to have witnessed the actions he was to immortalize—and by the monuments to the great generals whose deeds he was to chronicle forty years later in *Montcalm and Wolfe*, perhaps the greatest single link in his chain of histories.

Always a Yankee, with the true home of his heart somewhere in the wilderness of the White Mountains, Parkman then left the strange new land of Quebec behind him and revisited the scenes of his travels during the two previous summers. This time, however, he was in search of historical information rather than adventure; and so he pumped the old tavern keepers, the antiquarian lawyers, and the garrulous stage drivers of the region, noting down the rich store of legends with which the White Hills abound. His notes proved useful for *A Half-Century of Conflict*, published in 1892. As always, Parkman liked the land rather better than the people; and his notes on the caverns in Crawford Notch and on his horseback excursion to the summit of Mt. Washington are free from the patronizing superiority which characterizes his accounts of fellow travelers. And constantly he jotted down the titles of standard works on colonial and frontier history which might serve his purpose—a necessary method in an age when the compilation of a bibliography demanded more reliance on hearsay than on reference work.

Returning briefly to Boston, he soon set off again with his sister Caroline for Maine, where she was to visit friends and he was to study the Penobscot Indians, the last remnants of the savage population of New England. At the reservation near Bangor he eagerly questioned the Indians about their ancient customs and traditions; but found the most talkative far more concerned with the urban delights of Boston than with the "out of date" ways of his forebears, who had once taken Mohawk scalps. Parkman's failure to gain here much firsthand acquaintance with savage life drove him two years later to visit the Great Lakes, and then in the following year to make the greatest of his journeys, the Oregon Trail trip.

The incomplete record of this summer's journey is found in a small maroon leather notebook, measuring $2\frac{1}{2}$ by 4 inches, written in pencil on both sides of the page with many abbreviations and omissions of punctuation because of the smallness of the page. The writing is fairly clear.

1843

Giles F. Yates,[1] Esq., Schenectady—"The best of Am[erican] Antiquarians"—that is, with an extensive knowledge of the colonial hist. of N.Y.

Rev. Mr. Williams[2]—Schenectady

Kerney—Clergyman—Clermont,[3] Columbia county, N.Y. A grand nephew of Sir W. Johnson.

The Germans of the Mohawk know much of Sir William and family. About Fonda, especially.[4]

The gent. who told me the preceding told me also what follows. He was a man of most extensive and minute information on similar topics.

His ancestor's house, together with one other, were all that escaped the Schenectady burning—for this reason: His ancestor, an old Dutchman, saved a Jesuit priest whom the Mohawks were about to burn at their "burning place" near Schenectady. The priest was secretly packed in a hogshead, boated down to Albany, and thence sent home to Canada. The old man accounted to the Mohawks for his escape by the priest's omnipotent art, magic. This priest accompanied the war party, and protected the house.[5]

The grandfather-in-law of this gent. was saved when at the stake by Brant.[6] He made the Masonic sign. Brant was a Mason, and so interfered.

As for the "burning place,"[7] he said he had dug there, and found a fragment of a skull and some bones.

Lake George. On a little hill, by a pine tree, near Ft. George,[8] I saw a flat rough stone with an inscription as follows "1776 Here lies Stephen Hodges" and more unreadable. Other apparent graves are near.

Close by, on a fresh ploughed [field], a boy with me found a buck-shot and a coin about the size of a 50 ct. piece. I myself picked up a musket ball and a copper coin.

Montreal—Friday. Visited the nunnery of the *Soeurs Grises*.[9] Hospital for invalids. School for children. Patients hideous to look upon— nuns worse. Buildings of the same rough grey stone generally used here. Large—with dismal courts and flanking walls—long passages, rough but neat—a chapel with altars and confessional, and hung with pictures and a piece of the true cross in an ornamental frame. The school rooms and hospital were hung likewise with pictures, etc., and over each door was the name of a saint. A host of pauper children, in a huge room—unpainted—sang a French hymn, looking like so many diminutive washerwomen. We visited the cathedral[10]—visited it again in the morning and saw the service—elevation of the host, etc., priests in abundance.

Two regiments are in town—71st Highlanders[11] and the 89.[12] A part of the 43rd [13] are on the island a short way off.

At St. John's is a small fort and barrack.[14] At I(s)le-aux-Noix a strong and admirable establishment.[15]

"Hope Gate,"[16] Quebec, is defended something in this manner:

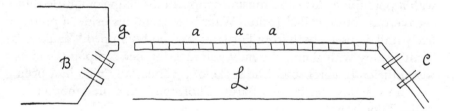

G—Gate. *B*—Blockhouse, stone below, with loops for musketry— wood above, and portholes for two cannons commanding the street. *L*—which is a precipice on one side. *a a a*—loop[hole]s all along the walls. *C*—two more guns on the wall, also commanding the street. The whole struck me as precisely resembling the *description* of the place where Montgomery[17] was killed.[a]

---

[a] "It does not resemble the reality."—F.P.

Wolfe and Montcalm. Inscription on their monument[18]: "Mortem virtus communem famam historia monumentum posteritas dedit."[b] "Here died Wolfe victorious."[19]

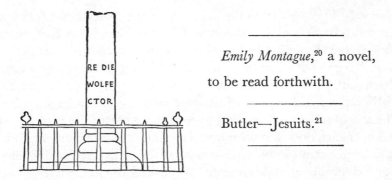

Emily Montague,[20] a novel, to be read forthwith.

Butler—Jesuits.[21]

Saturday night rode up from old Crawford's,[22] starting at sunset. The whole scenery, at that hour, especially about the entrance of the Notch, wild and exciting to the highest degree.

Old Abel tells me that *he* is the "first of the Crawfords." Settled in a log cabin about fifty-five years ago where Fabyan's now is, having got a grant from the state. Ethan Crawford[23] has returned from Guildhall and occupies Dennison's[24] near Fabyan's. Saw a dog at the old man's which had its face dismally swollen from a battle with a porcupine. Also an amusing couple in the shape of a little thin cadaverous youth, called Joshua Waterhouse, and his bride, a pretty, lively, tall damsel—both from Portland, and both stamped "Yankee." Went fishing with them, the lady volunteering her company, which was sufficiently agreeable. She spoke of a young lady who had been at Tom's a day before as "Sarah Thornton," and her mother as "Miss Thornton."

This delicate little flower, whatever it be, I place here in memory of the grimmest, dismalest den on earth, where it grew among moist precipices and rotting logs.[c]

I write at the bottom of a den more savage yet than the last. Turn

---

[b] "Valor gave them a common death; history a common fame; posterity a common monument."—Ed.

[c] A flower, resembling a violet, was here pressed in the notebook.—Ed.

to the left, as you approach Crawford's, enter a gateway of rock, and you will reach two dens that look like the very bottom of Hell. Nothing but great piles of damp mossy rocks, rotten timber, huge black cliffs fencing you in, with trees stretching across from their edges. A stream is plunging somewhere under ground, and breaking out into a black pool among the moss. Behind is a great heap of rocks where you descended. In front a steep descent, choked with fallen timber, and such a tangled mass of vegetation that a bear could scarce get through.

These ferns shall be a memento.[d]

Edifying specimens of humanity are staying here at Tom Crawford's.[25] Two botanists, each styled "Dr.," tall long-legged fellows, go about with tin cases and press boards all over the rocks. They actually reached the top of one of the Notch Mts. today, though one of them nearly killed himself in the attempt, and, as he elegantly remarked, "got sick as a horse, and puked." He stretched his ungainly person on the parlor sofa tonight, grunting with fatigue, and occasionally assisting a sentimental lady who was journalizing and arranging flowers, somewhat as follows: "Here—that ain't the way to press"—"That's the Coribla Em [?]" "I don't know what that is—let's look"—struggling with a groan into an erect position, etc.

Also mineralogists in abundance—tough broad-shouldered men, apparently schoolmasters.

Two pedestrians from Maine arrived last night, one of whom had gone three years ago as lieutenant in the Aroostook expedition.[26]

Rode up to the mountain on Monday morning alone, starting at six and getting back just too late for the stage—so that Crawford had to take me on in a waggon. Was about six hours gone. Laid down, thrust my head into the Lake of the Clouds, and drank a copious supplement to a gill of brandy wherewith I had previously regaled myself. My horse fell twice. Had a glorious time of it.

A man named Russel[l][27] carried me in a waggon from Bethlehem, discoursing deeply all the subjects of religion. Meeting a minister in another waggon, Russel pulled up and they began a conversation

---

[d] Pressed in notebook.—Ed.

about a debt due from one to another. My companion pronounced the minister a "loud one" and expressed great admiration of him.

***

Green Mt. Boys[28]

***

Have spent two very agreeable days at Franconia Notch at the house kept by Knapp.[29] He is a very good fellow. Have hunted, speared fish, etc. Coming to Plymouth, had a driver who expressed, in a very sensible manner, an enthusiastic admiration for the scenery of his route—a perfect phenomenon in his way. In other respects, too, he was an admirable fellow. He always, he said, "felt a kind of comfort as he rode through the Notch."

Stopped at Senter [Center] Harbor.[30] Saw, at the lawyer's, quite a collection of Indian relics—gouges, pestles, arrowheads, etc., found in the neighborhood. They told me of Indian graves about 4 miles off. The "mineral spring," on Ossipee hills, was evidently a place of resort.

***

M.S. *Wars of Canada*—C. F. Hoffman[31] knows.

***

Hoffman's *Wild Scenes in Forest and Prairie, Winter in the West,* etc.

***

Barstow's *New Hampshire,*[32] Dunlap's *N. York,*[33] Whiton.[34]

***

From Senter Harbor to Fryeburg; spent Sunday, and visited the Pond. Paugus's[35] gun, so-called, is shown at the Academy. Went back to C[onway]—thence to the Mountains again, stopping at Old Abel's. Found there a pedestrian named Wells. I heard downstairs a tremendous noise of tongues and found this gent. reading aloud from the *Northern Traveller*[36] and catechizing Old Crawford, usurping all the talk to himself, and making noise enough for a dozen. This done, he read us a piece in the newspaper. He had been something of a traveller, loved to talk of his experiences, and assumed the chief command: "Now, Mr. Crawford, we are all rather tired with our hard day's work and, if you please, we will retire to our rooms. What do you say, gentlemen, shall we protract our sitting?"

Mr. Stedman and Mr. King[37] are here.

Stayed a day or two, and rode on to Ethan's to spend the night. Mrs. C[rawford] soon produced her history of her husband's adventures, etc.—a manuscript which she means to publish.[38] Nash and Sawyer,[39] she says, discovered the Notch in their attempt to find a road from Upper Coos southward. They received the grant of land in consequence, on certain conditions. Her description of the Willey catastrophe is excellent. She tells, roughly and simply enough, but very well nevertheless, various characteristic stories of the early settlers. Her grandfather, Mr. Rosebrook,[40] settled before the war at the site of Colebrook—near 80 miles from settlements. Ethan's original seat was by the "Giant's Grave," where his house was burnt.

On the night of the slide, their situation was tremendous. In the morning, their fields were flooded, all the bridges for a score and more of miles swept away, great part of their roads torn up—and a bright unclouded sun showed the extent of the desolation. In the still morning they heard the waters pouring from the mountains. Ethan carried an impatient traveller across the swollen Amonoosuck, and left him to find his way to the Notch. He struggled on to the Willey House—found it empty. The children's beds had been slept in—the others had not. The house was started from its foundation and fallen in. The horses were dead—the oxen still alive, and he found an axe and released them. This done, he crept into one of the beds and slept till morning, hoping the family had escaped to old Crawford's. A dog of Willey's, which at first refused him admission, was his only companion.

Next day he found they were not at the old man's, and he passed on carrying the news to Bartlett and Conway. The neighbors and the relatives of the Willeys assembled—a dog pointed out the first body—the flies moving about the drift timber, the rest. The night after the traveller had left, when several people had assembled, Ethan C., who was there and anxious to get back to his own house, probably on account of his own loss, groped his way up the Notch in the darkness, though the road was ruined.[41]

Captivity of Mrs. Johnson,[42] Windsor, Vt., 1807. A book worth getting. Frontier Life in '54, etc.

Riding down to Conway, met Mr. Stephen Meserve[43] in the stage. He told the following particulars relative to the Willeys. On the alarm, he brought his dogs to the Notch at the desire of Willey's brother. They searched all the morning in vain, but on their suspending their efforts and assembling in front of the house, the dogs did not follow, but lay down by a heap of logs, rocks, etc. An old hunter was of the party and exclaimed "that means something." They went to where the dogs lay, and observed flies passing and repassing about the drift timber. Looking closer, a hand appeared clenched tight round a bough, and soon the naked body of a man was drawn out. The avalanche had torn away every shred of his clothes. The dogs no sooner saw it than they whined—then turned and ran the whole way back to Meserve's house in Bartlett. The other bodies were got out by means of the flies.

Riding from Conway to Dover, old Mr. Willey,[44] father to the sufferer, was in the stage with his daughter. He was more than eighty, had served in the Rev[olution]. He was suffering from a cancer in the lip, and was going to Nashua to get it cured.

He and his daughter gave the true version of the Nancy's Brook story. Old Colonel Whipple,[45] some 60 yrs. since, hired her and a young man to take charge of his house in Jefferson, hoping that they would be content to remain there as settlers on his grant—perhaps he thought of matrimonial results, to hold them closer. They "courted," in fact, but next year Whipple came up there with a party, and found his two settlers, though satisfied with each other, very loath to remain in the wilderness. He agreed to take both back with him. He however broke his word and left the girl, who was perfidiously deserted by her lover. The party went down through the Notch. The love-stricken girl was in despair. The few neighbors could not restrain her from setting out in pursuit, though it was winter. She did so; reach[ed] Whipple's deserted camp, at the site of Tom Crawford's, struggled through the Notch, and died near the Brook.

The Colonel was a close old fellow, so honest, however, that he kept a bag of half-cents to make change. He was disliked by the settlers on his grant. He once refused them corn when they were starving, and they took it by boring a hole in the floor of his granary, and letting it leak out into bags. They dressed as Indians and came round his house to frighten him; so that he took to the woods in terror.

He [was] captured in earnest, during the latter part of the Rev., at his Jefferson house by a party of English, Tories, and Indians. He managed to get permission to go to a back room for some clothes, squeezed through the window, and escaped.

The driver of the same stage told me of large eagles on Squam Lake which he saw sieze a lamb (see Jos[s]elyn).[46] Also he pointed out a brook in Ossipee(?) where he said Lovel [Lovewell][47] had ambushed some Indians, and mentioned the Pond in Wakefield which goes by his name, from a fight of his there.

Robert Southey had in his possession the whole of Wolfe's correspondence.[48]

Having started afresh, with C[aroline],[49] reached Gardiner, where I left her and proceeded to Bangor. Rode in a waggon behind the stage, which was full, in company with a stupid young downeaster who had been in the coasting and logging business, and was now going to recover a lost trunk. Broke the axle and had some trouble. Cursed my companion, and told him to run for help. Nothing moved his stolidity. He walked off at a snail's pace, in spite of my exhortations to "fly round." Got righted, left waggon, and went on in the stage to B., the downeaster forgetting his trunk. A miserable old wretch of a speculator and an ex-ship captain were my companions.

Went over to see the Indians.[50] One of them says he thinks there are about 400 in all, but many are gone away. Saw François and others—some squaws extremely good looking, with their clubbed hair and red leggins. Two fellows paddled me a mile or two up the river. The Indians use the genuine wampum. I saw a collar of it— said to be worth $6—round a squaw's neck.

There are a number of loggers in their red shirts seated in the bar; some of them have been to see "The Lord's Supper."[51] One expressed his disapprobation of the character of the exhibition as follows: "G——d d——n it, I should like to take that fellow by the nape of the neck, and pitch him into the road. He's no right to serve that 'ere up for a show in that way."

Bought some wampum of F.'s squaw, which he says he bought

from the Caughnawagas[52] near Montreal, 25 yrs. ago. It is however sometimes made by the whites in Canada.

I mentioned the Mohawks. "You no 'fraid Mohawks?" asked François' brother. "We 'fraid. They bad Indian—look too cross." Whereupon François began the following story, which he told with some excitement, mixing up the name of Castine[53] with it in a way I did not understand. Several hundred "Mohogs" (as he called it) came upon the Penob. and took prisoners and killed a large number. Many of the old prisoners were burnt—the young thrust upon sticks which were stuck in the ground. Soon after the Mohogs were famine stricken. Fifteen P. prisoners were left who volunteered to go out and hunt. The M.'s consented. The P.'s brought in plenty of game, feasted their enemies till they were overpowered with repletion, then fell upon them and killed all but one, whose ears and hand they cut off and sent him home.[54]

A fellow named Mitchell, whom I met in old Nicolas' house (his son), seemed to be a perfect adept in all the vices of cities. He showed me an advertisement of a firm in Boston, printed like a bank-bill. I asked him what he meant to do with it. "Me make some Indian take him—spose he don't know nothin'! Spose me have two, three in my wallet, then they think him bank bill—I get good credit."

He said he liked the city, and talked learnedly about the mysteries of Ann Street, appealing to me if his reasonings were not correct. He was much more practicable in conversation than most of them. It would have been hard to cheat him, with his quick observation and cunning.

He tells me that wampum is made of the sea clam, called *cohog*. The French Canadians, as well as the Indians, make it.

Speaking of the change in the manners of Indians, he says: "What use fight—take scalp—no do any good. Spose me kill snake—no get nothing at all. Spose um kill man, they no get anything."

François says he is glad Indians have left off fighting; "ought to be peaceable," he says. Even hunting, he added, is getting out of date, on account of the loggers, and the Indians are now farmers.

European Journal

1843–1844

Introduction

THE GRAND TOUR was an accepted part of every well-to-do young American's education in the mid-nineteenth century; and when Parkman's health showed signs of collapse under the rigorous regime of Harvard in his senior year, and under the Spartan extracurricular life that he had set for himself, nothing was more natural than that his family should send him to Europe. A sea voyage was the sovereign remedy of the day for the nervous exhaustion which was his chief symptom; and the change of scene and contact with the foreign world might both restore his health and round out his education, so far somewhat unduly provincial in character.

Parkman remained all his life a New Englander of the New Englanders, a Puritan among Puritans. But this early European journey, together with many later trips made both for recreation and for historical research, did much to relieve the provinciality of his environment and heredity, and to give him some understanding of Latin and Catholic civilization, to whose attempt to colonize the New World he devoted his life. Indeed he made a conscious effort, at the age of twenty, to prepare himself for his future work by seeing as much as he could of a world very foreign to that of Boston. It was not mere love of adventure that led him to spend a week in a Roman monastery, but a desire to achieve firsthand knowledge and understanding of the life led by the Catholic priests who played such a great role in the development of New France. In Sicily he visited all the monasteries along the way, "but a more intimate acquaintance with them and their inmates was needful for my purpose. I was led into a convent by the same motives that two years later led me to become domesticated in the lodges of the Sioux Indians at the Rocky Mountains, with the difference that I much preferred the company of the savages to that of the monks." So Parkman wrote nearly half a century later, when he published a revised version of his Roman journal in *Harper's*. But there is a later rationalization and alteration of his youthful motives in this account, for it is clear from the European journal that at this period Parkman was drawn to the Catholicism which was then anathema in Boston. He was in revolt against the arid Unitarianism of his father and the canting Puritanism of his forebears, both systems uncongenial to a temperament that fed on romantic and colorful ideas. In later life Parkman became an agnostic, without ever losing a certain militantly Protestant outlook, but many passages in *The Jesuits* and *The Old Regime* reflect the same attraction to the colorful Catholic tradition and the same conscious resistance to it which are found in the European journal. Parkman, the descendant of a long line of New England divines, was always an anticlerical, and far more anticlerical than he was anti-Catholic. Since one of the vexed questions of Parkman's place as a historian is how far a strongly Protestant writer could understand and appreciate the essential role of Catholicism in New France, this early Roman interlude is of major importance.

The European journal is also a valuable record of the impact of European civilization on a young American of the period. A lover of the past, who distrusted the new notion of democracy and despised the morality of commerce, Parkman found the Old World more to his taste than the New: "Here in this old world, I seem, thank heaven, to be carried half a century backwards in time." He was prepared to dislike the British military, and found to his surprise that he felt more at home with them than with many of his fellow countrymen. This is not inexplicable, for the New England Federalism in which Parkman was bred, and which he largely preserved through a life isolated from the new movements and ideas of his time, is closely akin to English Toryism. This son of the Puritans shared many of the ideas of the Cavaliers. But he was enough of an American to loathe tyranny, and his reaction to the rule of Ferdinand of Naples and of the Austrians in northern Italy anticipates the American sympathy with the revolutions of 1848. This sympathy was very closely akin to that with the Republicans in the Spanish Civil War and with other antifascists of our own time. Parkman's reaction against Austrian tyranny is revealed more fully in his novel *Vassall*

Morton than in this journal, but his lack of sympathy with absolutism is notable, considering the dominance of that system in New France. Then the fact that Parkman was already an able writer, if not a fully qualified historian, makes this youthful record of the Grand Tour more interesting than most; and the journal of a slightly homesick solitary traveler is more self-revealing than most of Parkman's writings, even among these diaries written for his own eye.

The journey was by no means the conventional Grand Tour, which doubtless had little appeal to so energetic a young man as Parkman. He sailed from Boston in November 1843 as the sole passenger on one of the small American merchant barks then so active in the Mediterranean trade. The tedious and rude voyage gave him ample opportunity to recuperate from his nervous exhaustion—reflected in his confusion about dates and his unreasonable impatience at the slow passage—and to jot down vivid descriptions of the sea in full fury, which pleased him so much a dozen years later that he incorporated them almost bodily in *Vassall Morton*. At Gibraltar and Malta he delighted in the pomp and circumstance of British military power, which was to be one major theme in his lifework; but he soon wearied of conventional sightseeing along the beaten path, and so, early in January 1844, he set off on muleback for an arduous tour of Sicily, alone except for an effervescent guide. Here the born historian reveals himself as he marvels over the successive waves of civilization which washed over that strategic island, and as he takes pleasure in tracing the remains of each. Parkman was a romantic, but he had been bred in the classical tradition, as this journal reveals. He was also learning to judge men of a different stamp than his own, to appreciate their foibles, and to sketch the salient elements of their characters with penetrating understanding, if not without the sense of superiority appropriate to a Boston Brahmin. There are evidences of Parkman's enduring Anglo-Saxonism, with its usual condescension to "lesser breeds without the Law."

Having covered Sicily thoroughly, he turned to the Italian mainland, to the home and center of that Catholicism which was so outlandish to a Boston Unitarian and yet so attractive to one whose ideal of life was "a little medieval." Italy rather than France was then the favorite refuge of American expatriates and the goal of tourists who sought European culture at its source; and Parkman encountered many fellow countrymen there. He saw little more of Naples than the average tourist, but after leaving the Kingdom of the Two Sicilies he had uncommon experiences in Rome, thanks largely to his cousin Coolidge Shaw, lately converted to Catholicism and then studying for the priesthood as a member of the Society of Jesus, that Jesuit order which played a major role in Parkman's chosen field of history. Because of the company at Rome of Theodore Parker, that exceedingly learned and most liberal of Unitarian clergymen, Parkman was not completely bowled over by his first real contact with the Catholic Church, but the journal reveals how strongly he was impressed by it; and even the mockeries suggest that he was consciously resisting an influence that he felt was almost too strong for him. Two years later he was still sufficiently concerned with Catholicism to keep up a correspondence about it with his cousin, who had not yet despaired of converting him.

During his Roman stay, this lover of the hills and the wilds wearied of the round of sightseeing among the ruin-dotted lowlands. He fled into the Apennines with his college friend, the painter William Morris Hunt, for a few days of a hardier and simpler life. Then, after the gorgeous pageantry of a Roman Holy Week, it was with eagerness that Parkman left the Papal State and turned northward to the Alps; such eagerness, in fact, that he hurried through the rich old cities of the duchies of Tuscany, Modena, Parma, and Austrian Lombardy with but little regret for the briefness of his stay. Though he was glad to quit Austrian territory and enter a free country, the Alps somewhat disappointed him; he found Lake Como inferior to Lake George and the Splügen Pass hardly more impressive than Crawford Notch. But perhaps these views are best explained by the homesickness that Parkman felt after long months of solitary travel, so evident in the Swiss passages of his journal. He hurried on to Paris, where a knowing uncle showed him the gay capital of Louis Philippe with such thoroughness that no time was left for journalizing—most unfortunately, since a record of this first impact of French civilization on the historian of France's greatest colonial effort would be of absorbing interest. Nothing that he would have been apt to see in the

Paris of that period would have tended to increase his regard for the tradition of absolute monarchy, whose sway in New France he later judged to be one of the main causes of the French disaster. Then Parkman, stricken with colic, short of sleep, and full of worldly wisdom beyond his years as a result of his stay in Paris, crossed the Channel to a Britain already familiar to him from much reading of Dickens and Walter Scott. London both fascinated and repelled him: his were the typical reactions of a young American of the period, who was at once drawn to the civilization which had given birth to his own and irritated by the superior attitude of the English toward transatlantic cousins and all their ways and works. Like many another American, he liked Scotland better than England. The measure of Sir Walter Scott's influence on Parkman is best indicated by the frequent references to the Waverley novels in this journal, and the evident thrill that Parkman experienced in seeing the places whose names had long been familiar to him from his reading. He wandered the border country, visited Edinburgh and Glasgow, regretted that there was no time for the Highlands, and hurried on to Liverpool to catch his ship. Finally there is a vivid account of the voyage home, with its sharp picture of the friction between Americans and Britishers at this period, when relations between the two countries had been strained since 1837 by differences over the New England boundary and the Oregon question. In his delight at being home once more, Parkman did not conclude his journal with any summary of his impressions of Europe, but references in the later journals indicate how keen an observer he had been, and how much this journey had done to free him from provinciality and to make him a citizen of a larger world than that of Boston.

Much material from the European journal went into *Vassall Morton*, the novel with which Parkman distracted his sick mind during 1854-55. For extended discussions of this book, see W. L. Schramm, "Parkman's Novel," *American Literature* (IX, 218-27); and M. Wade, *Francis Parkman*, 328-41. The portion of the journal devoted to Parkman's stay in the Passionist monastery served as the basis of an anonymous article, "A Convent at Rome," in *Harper's* for August 1890 (LXXXI, 448-54).

The European journal is written in ink in two large notebooks:

one, with leather spine and marbled boards, $9\frac{1}{4}$ by $7\frac{1}{2}$ inches, and a second, $8\frac{1}{4}$ by $6\frac{1}{2}$ inches, with purple paper boards, which was purchased in Strasbourg. There is also a small leather pocket memorandum book, of the type that Parkman favored for his travels, which contains penciled notes on the passage from Gibraltar to Malta, and on the Sicilian excursions, as well as fragmentary accounts of its expenses. Its contents are given in the Appendix to this journal.

1843-1844

December [*November*] *16ᵗʰ*, [*18*]*43*. Barque *Nautilus* (Devil of a sea—cabin dark as Hades). Got under weigh from Central Wharf about 10 A.M. of Sunday, Dec. [November] 12ᵗʰ—fine weather, and a noble west wind. Soon after the Pilot left us, we saw the frigate *Cumberland*, coming round a headland, bound for the same destination with us, but she chose to follow a more southerly course, and we soon lost sight of her.

Before long, we were pitched up and down on an execrable swell—the fruit of yesterday's east wind. The barque tossed about like a cork, snorted, spouted the spray all over her deck, and went rushing along like mad in a great chaldron of foam she raised about her. At the same time, it grew cloudy, and the wind became stronger. The sea rose and fell in great masses, green as grass—the wind driving the spray in clouds from their white tops. As I came from the cabin, I beheld, to my great admiration, a huge wall of water piled up in front, into which the vessel was apparently driving her bows; a moment more, and the case was reversed—her bowsprit and half her length rose straight from the waters, and stood relieved against the sky. In consequence of which state of things, I, like a true greenhorn, grew sea-sick by the time we were fairly out of sight of land. Accordingly I got into my birth as soon as it was dark, and staid there twelve hours.

When I came on deck in the morning, the weather had changed, nowise for the better. The same short seas were running—the vessel flung herself about in the same villanous style—a great black cavern on one side, and a huge mountain on the other, and a great pile of water rolling after her stern—but the wind had become contrary, and the whole sky was black with clouds. Two or three land birds fluttered about the ship, driven by the wind from shore, which the

107

unfortunates were destined never to see again. I wrapped myself in my cloak, and sprawling on the poop-deck read *The Bible in Spain.*[1] A schooner, with only top-sails set, went scouring past us, before the wind, homeward bound—also, in the afternoon a brig, tossing so that her keel was almost visible. A troop of porpoises went tumbling about us, and I ransacked the vessel in vain for a musket to get a shot at them.

The next morning opened under direful auspices. I came on deck, disconsolate with sea-sickness, when I was straightway saluted by about two hogsheads of water which came dashing over the gunnel, accommodating me with a most unwelcome morning shower-bath. It was showering a compound of snow, sleet, and rain—all was cold, dark, and wretched—the crew enveloped in oil-cloth, looking like drowned rats—the wind dead ahead, and blowing savagely. Foam and spray were spouting over the bows, far up among the sails, and every moment, with a thump, a torrent of water would come against the side, fly up, and innundate the decks. I got an old india-rubber cloak belonging to a former captain, in the stiffened folds of which I enveloped myself to the chin; and, braced in a corner, stood contemplating the crew, listening to the wind, and admiring the savage aspect of the ocean. At length, with a fluttering report, the jib flew to ribbons, and was hauled in. I spent most of the morning in my birth, reasonably miserable with sea-sickness—cogitating, meanwhile, on things human and divine, past, present, and to come. When dinner time came, I heard the captain's invitation to dinner, and staggered to the cabin door, determined to accept it, in spite of fate, when lo! the ship gave a lurch, the plates and the rack which should have secured them slid together from the table, in a general ruin, to the floor. With an execration, the captain grasped the beef and potatoes, and elevated them above his head—while he himself slid down the transom, and joined the medley on the floor. The steward shovelled up the fragments, and we regaled ourselves on the beef and potatoes. When night came, the captain and mate descended to the cabin in great ill humor, the mate swearing that ours was the "wettest craft" he ever sailed in, and declaring he would not embark in her again for the consideration of five dollars added to his wages. This time we contrived to hold the supper on, so that little of it escaped. I tumbled into my birth, but was so flung about from one side to the other that sleeping was not very easy. In the frequent intervals of waking, I listened to the groaning and creaking of timbers, the shouts of the men, the sullen thumps with [which] the seas struck the ship, making her shiver through her whole length, and, immediately after, the shock of the water descending in a torrent on her deck. Meanwhile, the wind howled like a wild beast—and to crown the catalogue of discomforts, my state room was so hot with a fiery stove that I would rather have been in Tartarus. I woke in the morning to another rather dismal day—but the morning after was warm and pleasant, though cloudy, and with the wind ahead. My slight sea-sickness has also left me. Today a brig—English—bore down, as if intending to speak us—but took herself off, without a word.

Saturday, Dec. 19 [Nov. 18]ᵗʰ. Until today we have been tormented with ceaseless head-winds. The captain especially has chafed incessantly, since this is his first command and he wants a quick passage for his own credit. This morning however was clear, with a respectably prosperous wind. The captain repaired to the cabin and shaved —the first time for a week—by way of celebrating our good fortune; then came up rubbing his chin and smiling with great complacency. A "school" of sperm whales are spouting a few miles off. The fogs of the Grand Banks rest on the horizon in front—but the wind is too good to suffer us to lie to and fish.

Sunday. Driving before a fair wind among the mist and haze along the south edge of the banks. Thousands of gulls, noddies and baglets are skimming over the water. We passed this morning a flock of at least five hundred of the last mentioned birds sitting on the water, filling the whole air with their rank fishy smell. A whale rose last night close to the ship, snorted and puffed for a while, then solemnly turned up his flukes into the air and settled down.

Tuesday. The captain came to my birth this morning with an announcement of another head wind. So here [we] were again, close-hauled, making constant tacks—dodging now to the north, now to the south, without gaining a league in the whole morning. Yesterday the case was different. A breeze, directly aft, carried us over the water at ten miles an hour. The ship with her studding-sails set, looked like a huge bird "predominating over" the ten million gulls that were skimming the ocean all about her.

We have a singular company on board—the three officers, "the passenger," the steward, and six men, viz., a Yankee, a Portugese, a Dane, an Englishman, a Prussian, and an old grey-haired Dutchman, the best sailor in the ship. Of the officers, the captain is a sensible gentlemanly man; the mate has rather more individuality, being, as to his outer man, excessively tall, narrow-shouldered, spindle-shanked, and lantern-jawed—with a complexion like dirty parchment. Mr. Jo[na]than Snow is from Cape Cod, a man of the sea from his youth up. When I first came on board he was evidently inclined to regard me with some dislike, as being *rich*! He constantly sighs forth a wish that he had five thousand dollars; "then ketch me going to sea again, that's all." He is rather given to polemic controversies, of which I have held several with him, on the tenets of Baptists, Unitarians, Universalists, Christians, etc., etc.! ! Of course, he imagines that men of his rank in life labor under all sorts of oppressions and injustice at the hand of the rich. Harvard College he regards with peculiar jealousy, as a nurse of aristocracy: "Ah! riches carry the day there, I guess. It's a hard thing to see merit crushed down, just for want of a thousand dollars."

Mr. Hansen, second mate, is the stoutest man on board, and has seen most service, but being, as Mr. Snow remarks, a man of no education, he has not risen very high in the service. He accompanied Wyeth's trapping party[2] to the Rocky Mts., where he was more than once nearly starved and within a hair's breadth of being shot. He speaks with great contempt of Indians, but not with quite so much virulence as I have known from some others of his stamp. He plumes himself on having killed two or three: "Oh, damn it, I'd shoot an Indian quicker than I'd shoot a dog." He is now seated at supper, amusing me and himself with some such discourse as follows:

"I've lost all my appetite, and got a horse's! Here, steward, you nigger, where be yer—fetch along that beef steak. What do [you] call this here? Well, never mind what it be; it goes down damned well, anyhow." Here he sat stuffing a minute or two in silence, with his grisly whiskers close to the table, rolling his eyes, and puffing out his ruddy cheeks. At last pausing, and laying down his knife a moment: "I've knowed the time when I could have ate a Blackfoot Indian, bones and all, and couldn't get a mouthful, noway you could fix it." Then, resuming his labors: "I tell you what, this here agrees with me. It's better than doctor stuff. Some folks are always running after the doctor, and getting sick. Eat—that's the way I do. Well! doctoring is a good thing, just like religion—to them that likes it; but damn the doctors for all me; I sha'nt die," etc., etc.

By treating Mr. Hansen with brandy and water, I have got on very good terms with him, and made him very communicative on the subject of his Oregon experiences. Would that we had a consumptive minister, with his notions of peace, philanthropy, Christian forgiveness, and so forth, on board with us! It would be sport of the first water to set Mr. Hansen talking at him, and see with what grace the holy man would listen to his backwoods ideas of retributive justice and a proper organization of society.

"Shoot him over, and that damn quick, too," is Mr. Hansen's penalty for all serious offences.

Thursday. Yesterday, Captain Fessenden was pluming himself on the remarkably fine weather and smooth seas we have lately had. He had better never have said a word. Last night, I was awakened by the voice of Mr. Snow who came into the cabin roaring after the captain, with an announcement that it was high time to take in sail, for a furious squall was coming up. The captain siezed his clothes and scrambled up stairs. Then followed the shouts, the trampling on deck, the fluttering of canvas;[3] after which sleep was out of the question, such a din did my furniture, trunks, bales, and boxes make, bounding from one side to the other of my state room; and in such an execrable style was I tossed hither and thither in my birth. As soon as it was daybreak I went on deck. Two or three sails were set—the vessel scouring along, leaning over so that her lee gunnel scooped up the water; the water in a foam, and clouds of spray flying over us, frequently as high as the main yard. The spray was driven with such force that it pricked the cheek like needles. I staid on deck two or three hours; when being throuroughly salted, I went down, changed my clothes and read *Don Quixote*, till Mr. Snow appeared at the door with: "You're the man that wants to see a gale of wind, are ye? Now's your chance; only just come up on deck." Accordingly, I went. The wind was yelling and howling in the rigging in a fashion that reminded me of a storm in a Canada forest. The ship was hove-to. One small rag of a topsail set to keep her steady—all the rest was bare poles and black wet cordage. I got hold of a rope by the mizzen mast, and looked about on a scene that it would be perfect folly to attempt to describe—though nothing more, I suppose, than an ordinary gale of wind. The sailors clung, half drowned, to whatever they could lay hold of; for the vessel was, at times, half inverted, and tons of water washed from side to side of her deck. The sea, like the sky, was of a dull gray color. The violence of the wind seemed to beat down the waves, but the sea rose in huge mis-shapen masses, marked with long diverging trains of foam as the wind flew over their surface. As for the usual horizon, it had disappeared—we seemed embedded among moving mountains. Now and then, a towering ridge of waters would heave up to windward, and bear down upon the ship, with a line of tumbling foam crowning it as it rolled on. All held their breath, and clung fast as it approached. It would strike the ship with a crash, and deluge her with water from stem to stern.[4] The wind has not yet abated. It is with much ado that I can brace myself in my seat to write.

Friday. As yesterday was Thanksgiving,[a] I may as well record how *we* fared. Our breakfast was utterly demolished, by the same catastrophe that overtook a former repast—that, namely, of being dashed in ruin upon the floor by an ill-timed lurch of the ship. We dined on a lump of ham, Cuffie being unable to purvey a more sumptuous banquet, because the seas put out the fire in his galley as fast as he kindled it. As for our supper, it was of bread, pork, and onions. Not that this is a fair sample of our bills of fare, which are usually quite as luxurious as any reasonable man need desire.

The gale abated very suddenly at eight o'clock last night. We carried sail all night, and all this forenoon, which was mild and

[a] See below, p. 113.—Ed.

pleasant, though the seas still ran very high. But the wind increased
again, sail after sail was taken in, till at twelve it became necessary
to heave-to again. Though the weather had been clear all the morning, grey clouds rose, like thunder-tops, all round the horizon and
began to overspread the sky. The wind suddenly lulled, but left the
waves huge and boisterous as ever; and the ship rose and fell, and
was flung to and fro with great violence, but in perfect silence. That
low murmuring sound, however, so often spoken of as the prelude
of a storm, but which I never happened to hear before, began to
growl like stifled thunder. The gale is now on us again. Cuffie, who
has made seven voyages to Canton, protests he never saw the like.

Sunday. Night before last was a very bad one. Being rather fatigued
by want of rest the preceding night, I slept through the worst of it;
yet when I awoke, the booming of the sea was as loud as peals of
thunder, for which I at first mistook it. The storm continued through
the day—fierce rain-squalls alternating with sunshine. It was a
noble sight when at intervals the sun broke out over the savage
waste, changing its blackness to a rich blue, almost as dark; while the
foam that flew over it seemed like whirling snow-wreaths on the
mountains. The wind being fair, we "scud" under fore and fore-top
sails, close-reefed—and flew ahead like the very devil—in the early
part of the night. At length, we were obliged to lie-to again, lest some
of the huge seas which came rolling furiously after us, should overtake
us, and sweep the deck clear of everything—men included. We were
in fact struck once or twice, in a manner too ominous of what might
happen next to be disregarded. The decks were several times buried
in water, from which the ship shook herself free with a dismal groaning and shivering. We are now close by the Azores. The gale has
subsided. Not a sail nor a spar has been carried away.

Thursday, Nov. 29[30]^{th}. This is, I believe, the true Thanksgiving
day after all—and we have fared much more suitably to the occasion
than we did a week ago. We have had, for several days, light breezes
and calms—an insufferable monotony, relieved only by the circumstance of Mr. Snow's clambering forth on the bowsprit, twining
his long legs several times round the martingale; clinging fast with

one hand, while with the other he flourished an harpoon and made an abortive attempt to strike some porpoises that were amusing themselves around the bows.

Wednesday, Dec. 6ᵗʰ. We have been tormented for ten days past with a series of accursed head winds. Here we are, within thirty-six hours' sail of Gibraltar, standing alternately north and south, with no prospect of seeing land for many days. The captain is half mad, and walks about swearing to himself in an under tone. Mr. Snow's philosophy has given way—and I never had any. Hansen alone is perfectly indifferent. He sits on deck whistling and talking over his work, without troubling himself about our whereabouts, or caring whether we are in the North Sea or at Cape Horn. The difficulty is to kill time. Recollecting my "whittling" propensities of old, I went to work at manufacturing some indescribable trinket out of a chip, to get rid of the hours till bed-time. Mr. Snow, who had just come down from his watch on deck, stood regarding me for a while with fixed attention. At length: "A phrenologist down to Brewster told me last winter I had a remarkable bump of cur'osity." After pausing a few moments for his hint to take effect, he remarked: "Well, it a'nt polite, I've heard tell, to be asking questions." And so, after another fruitless pause, he retired with unsatisfied "cur'osity" to his birth.

Thursday, Dec 7ᵗʰ. "Day after day; day after day
    "We stuck, nor breath nor motion,
    "As idle as a painted ship
    "Upon a painted ocean."
  This has been our enviable situation today. A dead calm—a stupid flapping of sails, and creaking of masts. We lay on deck, watching for hours, with the glasses, a dead fish that floated a short distance off. Mr. Snow is taken sick, and bewails dismally. The captain comes down every now and then into the cabin with: "By George, this is *too* bad! I never see the beat of this! Well, I'll have a smoke anyhow." Then he flings himself along the transom, and lighting his pipe, charged with "pig-tail," fills the cabin with its delicate odors. Breakfast, dinner, and supper are always introduced

nowadays by his exclaiming in a dolorous tone as he sinks into his seat, "By George, this is *too* bad!"

Eleven days ago, we were confident of reaching port in three days! There is a little hope, from some appearances in the sky, that there will be a change tomorrow.

Friday. The ship this morning is proceeding at the rate of about an inch an hour, with her head turned the wrong way! "A head wind and none of it!" groans the captain; "if ever I see the beat of this!" This is but the nucleus of his remarks, so to speak, which he surrounds and adorns with a host of forcible and ornamental forms of expression, which I refrain from recording. We are, however, at last warned of a change impending. The capt. beheld last night in his dreams a woman mounted astride of a white horse; an infallible sign, he says, of a gale.

Saturday. Again a calm! The captain's signs and portents have come to nought. A turtle came up at the ship's side to sleep on the quiet surface, but prudently sank back to the depths just as Mr. Hansen was lowering me by a rope to take him prisoner. A few bonetas splashed about the bows—some "rudder fish" played along side; and a pair of "gar fish" glided about in defiance of all attempts to capture them. Before noon a breeze—a favorable one—sprang up!! It bore us on a hundred miles further, but now has subsided into the old trebly accursed calm.

Monday. We lie here like a log, Gibraltar almost in sight—I could walk the distance in one day—yet not a breath of air for two days past to carry us on.

Tuesday. A light wind today, but dead ahead. More porpoises, and more fruitless attempts at harpooning, on the part of Mr. Snow. I am rapidly growing insane. My chief resource is the conversation of Mr. Hansen, who has humor, volubility, much good feeling; and too much coarse rough manhood in his nature to be often offensive in his speech. Moreover, one man may say a thing, with a very good grace, that would be insufferable from the mouth of another.[b] Witticisms

[b] Several words inked out in text.—Ed.

and stories which, uttered by Snow, would make me turn my back on the fellow with contempt and disgust, sound well enough in the frank and bold accents of Hansen.

Evening. We have beat up against the wind into full view of the Spanish coast. Right and left, from Trafalgar far beyond Cadiz, the line of rugged and steep bluffs reaches, with here and there a tower just visible with the glass. But about noon our evil genius becalmed us again! Late this afternoon I came listlessly on deck; found the sails flapping against the masts, the sea like glass, and the sky obscured by thick dull clouds. They looked of an ominous blackness in the direction of Gibraltar, and, a few miles off, the sea, in the same quarter, was dark as ink and violently agitated. There was a low moaning sound, like distant winds, as in fact it was. The blackness on the water kept approaching nearer and nearer, the noise increased; then a puff of wind struck our lazy ship, followed by another and another, till she swung heavily round, and began to rush through the water. In a moment she was plunging along in full fury. "Now," thinks the agonized reader, "we shall get to Gibraltar at last!" Not at all. The vessel's head was turned south-west. She was running away from her port! A large "shovel-nosed" shark, whom I imagine to be an incarnation of the evil spirit that has been persecuting us, followed in our wake: and thus prosperously are we advancing now, yet, strange to say, with intervals of perfect calm when the sails flap as heretofore. *Thirty days from Boston.* Old Worthington[5] promised that I should see Gibraltar in eighteen, but he is a deacon.

Wednesday. "From grave to gay; from lively to severe," from calm to tempest. A gale came roaring down the strait at about nine o'clock, struck us directly in our teeth, and forced us to close-reefed topsails again. Nevertheless, by diligent tacking and wearing we made a few miles before morning. When I came on deck, Cape Spartel, on the African coast, stretched out its lofty and black cliffs close on the right. Behind it rose, half obscured in vapors, great piles of mountains; all was clouds and darkness but one bright streak of eastern sky above and behind their summits. The sea tossed angrily, the ship careering and plunging along like an unbroken blood colt. Now, we are slowly beating up the strait, in defiance of wind and waves. At times we approach the Spanish coast, bare, rocky, and savage, with many a ruined tower among the crags; then turn away and leave it in mists and darkness behind. The town of Tarifa, renowned for the heroism of Alonzo Guzman,[6] lies about twelve miles in front, and to this point we are straining every effort to attain.

Evening. We have not yet reached Tarifa. Dozens of vessels come past us from Gibraltar, some of them of a most outlandish aspect to my eye.

Thursday. More delay and vexation. The captain has not slept for two nights, and is half worn out by fatigue and anxiety. For myself, I was so exasperated by our continued ill fortune that I could not stay below. We past Tarifa light about midnight—then were driven back four miles by a rain squall. But by nine in the morning, we had fairly entered Gibraltar Bay! "Here we are at last," thought I, and looked up with infinite satisfaction at the warlike rock which rose right above us—with a gray and savage aspect—indented all over with port-holes and scored with zigzag lines of battlements and military roads. At the bottom of the bay appeared a forest of masts. It was now our business to attain that secure haven. "There can be no difficulty there," thought I. Just then, the water at the foot of the mountain was agitated into a violent foam, while a fine spray rose from it like steam from a boiling kettle. In an instant the ship was almost laid on her beam ends by a most savage squall. She righted, to be again struck over. In the course of an hour or two, however, the crew—who worked like dogs—contrived to beat her, in the face of these paroxysms of tempest, about a mile up the bay. Mr. Hansen began to cast the sounding lead to find anchorage. "How deep?" demanded the captain, speaking in the quick tone of an harassed and anxious man. "Can't find no bottom, sir; fourteen fathom of line out." "Well, there must be bottom somewhere," responded the captain, "over with the anchor. By —— I can't stand this longer, nohow." And with a clattering and whirling, down went the anchor.

"How much cable have you let out, Mr. Snow?"

"Whole length, sir. Sixty fathom."

"She holds fast, I suppose."

"Can't tell yet, sir. Don't see how she can help it."

But she did *not* hold fast, and sixty fathoms of chain cable could not reach bottom. This was soon apparent by the rapid drifting of the vessel, toward the opposite shore of the bay. When the captain saw how the case stood, he fairly stamped on the deck with rage and mortification. The crew were set at once to the windlass, to heave the cable in. They could not start it, for two of them have been taken so sick as to be useless. Meanwhile we drifted rapidly towards the shore of Algesiras [Algeciras], opposite Gibraltar. Up went the flag, half mast, in signal of distress. The American frigate *Congress* lay under the rock, and we looked to her for help. Suddenly Mr. Hansen recollected that no boat could legally approach us, as we had not been visited by the health officer. In about an hour, however, a boat was lowered from the frigate, put off towards us, and soon came up with us, with the sailing master of the *Congress*, a midshipman, and twenty men, bringing the health officer with them. This official's examinations were soon concluded in due form, when the man-of-war's-men took us in charge, and brought us to anchor, in about five hours, by the side of their own vessel.

I was heartily tired of the *Nautilus*, and resolved to get on shore if I could before night. The capt. refused to leave his vessel. At last, about dusk, a small sail-boat came alongside with a message from the consul. I told the three rascally Spaniards on board of her to set me on shore, though I had not procured the necessary permit, determining to trust fortune and the consul to aid me in that matter. They said there was scarce time—the signal gun would be fired in half an hour, and the gates be shut. "Do your best," said I, "and I won't complain if you fail." Accordingly the little craft flew through the water, approaching the rock with long tacks, till at last we threaded the labyrinth of feluccas and a host of other strange-looking vessels, and got within ten rods of the mole. Just then the signal gun boomed from the summit of the rock—the gates closed before our eyes. I looked about me and beheld such a throng of miscreants and blackguards that I abandoned the idea that first suggested itself of sleeping in the boat on my baggage till morning. "Turn about, and back to the barque," said I. They set me again on the deck of the

Nautilus, and then the foremost came down into the cabin to settle. "How much do you want?" "*Eight dollars*, sar." I gave him a dollar and a half, which he flung down, but afterwards pocketed. A dollar was the legal price, but new comers must submit to some imposition.

Saturday. Yesterday I came ashore in the barque's boat—landed— got passport signed, and established myself at the "King's Arms." More than fifty men—I speak literally—surrounded me on the mole, arrayed in every variety of dress, jabbering every variety of language, but all entreating to be allowed to carry my baggage. I selected the most decent-looking, who was a slender built fellow, with a sickly countenance. To my utter astonishment he passed a band round my heavy trunks, swung them to his back, and set off at a "dog trot" with them up the steep streets. It needed my swiftest walk to keep pace with him. I dined at the consul's, and spent the day in exploring this singular city—the world in epitome. More of it in future. This morning I set out, in company with a midshipman, the son of Capt. Newton of the *Missouri*, to ride round the bay to the Spanish town of Algesiras. The situation of Gibraltar, as far as my words can describe it, is as follows. A long peninsula of narrow beach projects from [the] Spanish main towards Africa. At its extremity a huge mountain of rock rises, so abrupt and steep that one standing on the summit, more than a thousand feet in the air, could fling a stone down to the peaceful strip of sand below. On the southern side of this rock, where it slopes away to the water, this miracle of a town is built—fenced in on the seaside by tremendous walls, while the rock above is bored full of holes, whence project the muzzles of hundreds of cannon. This strip of sand, bearing Gibraltar on its end, forms a large bay. Algesiras is directly opposite the Rock.

The middy and I passed the British line in a few moments, and found ourselves on genuine Spanish ground. Dirty scoundrels of soldiers, with rusty firelocks, were lolling about some huts by way of guard. A long train of donkeys approached, each hidden under a pair of panniers full of charcoal. They all stopped before the guard house, where every pannier was emptied, to see that no goods were smuggled across the line. I was admiring the vigilance of the raga- muffin soldiery when we beheld a man, mounted on a splendid horse, advancing along the beach towards us. He was a noble looking fellow, arrayed in a richly embroidered dress, wrapped in the huge Spanish cloak; his horse's head, mane, and flanks were hung with tassels and spangles. He carried a carbine slung on his saddle behind him. He was a *contrabandista*—one who practised smuggling in open defiance of the law. A moment after, he was joking and laughing with the officers at the guard-house.

After three or four hours' ride, we approached the town, where more Spanish soldiers were lounging in a group by the roadside. *"Carracho! los Ingleses!"*; with that they set a dog on us; finding this of no avail, they blew their trumpets and shouted to scare our horses. We turned round, and sat laughing at them. *"Carracho! Carracho!"* and one fellow, not satisfied with this Spanish insult, made shift to exclaim "go to Hell!"; whereupon the whole took up the cry in chorus. As we rode through the narrow streets, similar maledictions were showered upon us. Boys followed us, first begging a *cuárto*, and then shouting *"Carracho."* It is a beautiful town—the houses white as snow, with bright green lattices and porticoes—the streets paved with square hewn stone, and without sidewalks. But the noblest sight was the Plaza, or public square, round which stand the public buildings. It was paved with coarse marble; a large and beautiful column rose in the centre, in the midst of a space walled in from the public. All around, by the columns of the cathedral, about the porches of the houses, were stalls of merchants; and beggars in crowds roaring in the name of the Virgin for charity. We left this hospitable town behind, galloped at full speed round the beach, passing lepers by the wayside, soldiers, donkeys, black-eyed women, hedges of aloes and groves of oranges, bare sun-burnt mountains, each crowned with its Moorish tower—vallies even now green as emeralds—and long before the evening guns fired, were within the fortifications again.

Sunday. I entered the cathedral and kneeling with the rest on the pavement, admired the noble architecture of the place; yet it looked more noble still at night, when the shadows of its huge columns and arches left it half in gloom, though a hundred tapers were burning before the shrines.

Sunday is the day to see the motley population of Gibraltar at one glance. Just without the walls is a parade large enough to hold the six regiments stationed here. This evening, according to custom, everybody was thronging up there. I established myself at the foot of a bronze statue of the Defender of Gibraltar[7]—I forget his name[e]— but there he stands towering above the trees and aloes at the summit of a hill above the parade, with the emblematic key in his hand, and with a huge cannon and a mortar on each side of him. Here I had a specimen of every nation on earth, it seemed, around me. A dozen Moors with white turbans and slippered feet lolled one side; Jews by couples in their gaberdines; the Spanish gentleman in his black cloak and sombrero—the Spanish laborer with his red cap hanging on one side of his head—the Spanish blackguard in bespangled tights and embroidered jacket. On benches among the trees officers and soldiers carried on successful love suits; on the parade below English captains were showing forth good horsemanship to the best advantage. The red coats of soldiers appeared everywhere among the trees and in the crowd below. There were women in cloaks of red and black—ladies with the mantilla and followed by the duenna—no needless precaution—and ten thousand more, soldier and civilian, bond and free, man and woman and child. Not the least singular of the group were the little black slaves belonging to the Moors, who were arrayed in a very splendid and outlandish attire; following after their masters like dogs. Bands were stationed on the parade and around a summer house among the trees. The evening gun dissolved the pageant—"God Save the Queen" rose on the air; then the crowd poured through the gates into the town.

I have seen more noble-looking men in this place than ever it was my lot to see before. The Moors, especially, are men of admirable proportions and beauty of features, both set off to the best advantage by their dress. Some of them, from the interior of Barbary, are dark as Negroes; others of a light and florid complexion. The *hamalos* or Arabian Jews who act as porters are extraordinary-looking animals. They are all less than the stature of a woman of moderate dimensions; with a leathery countenance, overgrown with sand-colored beards; a little black scull-cap; broad blue pantaloons, in the

[e] "General Eliot."—F.P.

Turkish style, which reach only to the knee, and expose the calves of their legs, swollen to treble the natural size from the nature of their labor. These fellows stand congregated in groups in the most frequented places, each with a bundle of cords over his shoulder to hold his burden.

The Barbary Jews are very different men, in all except the black scull-cap, and in a certain elongation of visage, made more remarkable by the bushy and grizzly beard. Still another animal is the Jerusalem Jew, specimens of which are rare here.

I got leave, with some difficulty, to see the excavations. They are well worth all the trouble. The solid mountain, on its steepest and boldest side, has been hollowed out into gallereies and great vaulted halls, whence cannon are pointing to all parts of the sea and land, a thousand feet below. I looked down from a porthole; on the beach, the "neutral ground" and the coast of Spain—all were spread out like a map under me. Some soldiers, like black specks of sand, on the plain below, were firing at a mark. The white smoke came from the muzzle of the musket several minutes, as it seemed to me, before the faint report reached us. I dropped a stone from the port-hole. It fell on the sand without once striking the rock in its passage.

From the excavations, I rode along a military road, near the summit of the rock, to the Signal Station. This is an old Moorish tower, with a modern guard-house near it, where a sergeant and six men are stationed. It is in the midst of the mountain—a thirty-two-pounder looks on one side toward the Mediterranean, and a small battery points toward Alge(si)siras on the other. The sergeant gave me a soldier to conduct me to St. Michael's cave. On the way, he gave chace to a young monkey among the rocks, but bruised his shins to no purpose. The rock is peopled with these gentlemen, as well as with a variety of foxes, both under the paternal care of the British government. St. Michael's cave is a vast black gulf, decked with broken stalactites, and filled with the tinkling sound of water dropping from its eaves. It has no bottom—at least none was ever found, though more than one life has been lost among its crags in the attempt. I took leave of the soldier, and followed a narrow path southward; soon reached the extremity of the rock which looks towards the African Mt. Gibil Musa, or as the English call it, Ape's Hill, on account of the baboons with which it swarms. At this point of the road, I noticed an arm-chair, carved, of massive dimensions, out of the rock; facing towards Africa—where, perhaps, the holder of this tremendous fortress might sit and overlook the passage which he commands. Half a mile further, I was on the eastern side of the rock. The path here was frequently hewn through precipices, like roads among the Alps. I saw the white breakers tumbling among the rocks below, but heard not a sound. I emerged at last on a little battlemented platform, among the cliffs. A brass howitzer and a heavy cannon lay there, pointing towards the sea. The whole scene was savage and desolate in the extreme. These grim-looking engines of war were the sole occupants of the loneliness.

I went to a diminutive theatre, in the evening, to see a play performed by the privates of an artillery company.

A "rock scorpion" carried me off to the frigates in the harbor, English and American. The reptile in question was a mixture of Genoese and French blood—spoke both languages fluently, besides English and half a score of others. In no place on earth is the gift of tongues more general than here. About twenty "scorpions"—namely, men born at the Rock—are at present drinking brandy and porter in the public room, and jabbering in twenty different languages.

Look upon this Rock as a phenomenon of nature alone; or only for the miracles of military art which it contains; or for the motley population which inhabit it; or, finally, as the scene of that bloody attack and repulse during our Revolution—in either mode of regarding it, the "Pillar of Hercules" deserves to be considered one of the wonders of the world. I was lounging this morning among the rocks toward the African side, and looking up at the battlements and the black muzzles of cannon that crowned all the highest crags, when a sentinel hastily stopped me, and said I could not pass, for they were blasting rocks in that direction. In fact, some hundred of men were at work to add new strength to a place that now might defy the whole earth.

I got shut out of the town tonight. While I was revolving what was to be done, a Highlander hailed me from the wall, asking if I would like to be admitted. I responded in the affirmative, on which a sergeant came and opened the gate. I owed my good luck to being mistaken for an midshipmen of the *Belvedere*, an English frigate.

Capt. Newton, a noble-looking officer, has just come from Granada, bringing an account which inflames my desire of seeing the place. The *Cumberland* came in yesterday.

Sunday, Dec. —— [*24*]. Got tired of Gibraltar—heard of a government steamer [*Polyphemus*][8] about to sail for Malta—embarked on board of her, abandoning my previous design of penetrating Spain immediately, because the spring will be a season far more favorable for seeing that country. I hired an *hamalo* to carry my baggage to the boat, a distance of half a mile. The little wretch shouldered it all—looking like an Atlas supporting the world—and trotted at a round pace through the streets and onward to the mole, the muscles of his bare legs gathering into solid knots with every step. He was a mass of bone and sinew. The engine snorted—the boat moved from the mole—before night the rock was out of sight. I was prepared for no very agreeable passage, knowing the *hauteur*, approaching to insolence, of a certain class of English naval officers; and was surprised as well as gratified by the polite attentions of Lt. Spark[s], the commander of the boat, with whom I spent about half the night in conversation. Unfortunately, I am the only passenger. Lt. Spark seems resolved that my voyage shall be agreeable notwithstanding—certainly, he spares no pains for my accommodation, opening his library to me—producing an endless variety of wines—doing all he can, in short, to promote my enjoyment.[9]

We have passed Cape de Got and the Sierra Nevada, which looks down on the city of Granada. The coast of Barbary is now in full sight. Today the old man mustered his sailors and marines in the cabin—a large and elegant one—and read the service of the Church, not forgetting a special prayer for the British navy, and the success of the British arms. He knew Sir John Moore,[10] Sir P. Parker,[11] and other heroes of those days—has shaken hands with Blucher[12]—has fought the French by sea and land. Beside his manifold experiences in active life, he has been a great reader—not only of English works, but of all the eminent American authors.

I left Gibraltar with some regret, taking a sorrowful farewell of the consul and his family, and of my friend the midshipman, a frank and spirited fellow, with a relishing spice of the devil in him.

Here in this old world, I seem, thank heaven, to be carried about half a century backwards in time. As far as religion is concerned, there are the ceremonies of the Catholic Church; and the English litany, with rough soldiers and sailors making the responses. A becoming horror of dissenters, especially Unitarians, prevails everywhere. No one cants here of the temperance reform, or of systems of diet—eat, drink, and be merry is the motto everywhere, and a stronger and hardier race of men than those round me now never laughed at the doctors. Above all there is no canting of peace. A wholesome system of coercion is manifest in all directions—thirty-two-pounders looking over the bows—piles of balls on deck—muskets and cutlasses hung up below—the red jackets of marines—and the honest prayer that success should crown all these warlike preparations, yesterday responded to by fifty voices. There was none of the new-fangled suspicion that such belligerent petitions might be averse to the spirit of a religion that inculcates peace as its foundation. And I firmly believe that there was as much hearty faith and worship in many of those men as in any feeble consumptive wretch at home, who when smitten on one cheek literally turns the other likewise—instead of manfully kicking the offender into the gutter.

Christmas Day. The crew have had an extra allowance of liquor. A drummer, a fiddler, and a boy with a large iron triangle sit perched on the rail, forward; while the crew, all more or less *elevated*, are dancing below, in a style that would astonish Papanti.[13] The whole deck is alive with merriment. I was talking with a young officer, when the triangle boy, a corpulent jovial-looking youth, came up at the head of a gang of followers, and said, touching his hat, "We've just had the honor to drink your health, sir,"—his companions stood grinning in the rear. The officer took the hint, grinned in his turn, and told them to go down and order a bottle of wine from the steward.

We had an admirable Christmas dinner in the cabin.[14]

Thursday. After a passage of about five days, we reached Malta. The steward waked me, with the announcement that we were in the harbor of Valetta. I came on deck—found the pale yellow walls and battlements of the "*Cité* [*Città*] *Vittoriosa*" rising all round; the harbor filled with shipping, and among the rest several huge British war-vessels, laying black and sullen, with triple tiers of guns, among the smaller craft. I bade adieu to Lt. Sparks and the rest, and went ashore in a species of gondala, multitudes of which were darting hither and thither all over the crowded harbor. Everything about this renowned city is of the same unvaried hue—all yellow except the guns on the batteries and the red-coated sentinels. The bells of St. John's Church were ringing a chime, answered from the remoter parts of the town. I landed, well drenched by a sudden shower. Calling on M. Eyrand, I found that I had the alternative of leaving town that night for Messina, or of waiting ten days. Though sorry to leave so soon a place where so much was to be seen, I had no inclination to stay longer than was enough to satisfy my curiosity. I went to the ancient palace of the knights—the governor occupies it now. The portraits of the grand masters were hung in the long and splendid galleries. In the armory stand the complete panoply and weapons of all the most distinguished of these defenders of Christendom. Banners, warlike trophies, the helmets and breastplates of several hundred men-at-arms of the order, were ranged round the walls. At the head of the hall, surrounded by a forest of weapons, stands the gigantic armor of La Valette[15] himself—a man of tremendous frame, differing in this respect from many of the less renowned brethren of the order, who seem to have been of rather small stature. The English have placed here thirty thousand muskets and other modern arms, in villanous contrast to the ancient weapons of the knights of St. John. A cannon of *ropes*, and some other pieces of artillery as well as armor and weapons, are preserved in memory of the defeat their owners—the Turks—sustained before the walls of this place.

Friday. Late last evening, I made an attempt to see the Church of St. John. It was closed. My servant pommelled the oaken door in vain. He then proceeded to sundry coffee houses in the neighborhood, hoping to find the man who had the doors in charge. Three of [or] four Maltese, all jabbering their bastard Arabic, soon aided in the search. At length the great bell began to roar from the church tower, an unequivocal evidence that somebody was there. "Gu[g]lielmo, Gulielmo," roared my troop of assistants. After a lapse of five minutes Gulielmo descended, and issued from a portal among the columns at one side, summoning me in. All was utter blackness. At length Gulielmo, a tall ghastly individual, lighted a taper—and after a moment's conference with a priest he led the way through a labyrinth of galleries into the church. Meanwhile he had provided every one of my *cortège* with a taper. We passed through a number of chapels, splendidly decorated with pictures and statues, and tombs half-illuminated by the tapers. At length we descended into a lofty vaulted chamber of massive architecture, beneath the pavement of the church. It contained the tombs of the grand-masters. The effigy of La Valette lay on the sarcophagas that contained his bones, in a deep niche. His hands were clasped—his face had an expression of deep devotion—his sword was by his side, and his helmet lay near him. Just opposite was the tomb of one who was a cardinal, and lay there in his pontifical robes, with his sword girt to his side. His hands were crossed on his broad breast. He looked like a gallant soldier, who had done good service to Christianity by dealing death to its enemies. There were more such chambers—all of costly and magnificent workmanship, and peopled with the effigies of dead knights. When we got to the body of the church I could scarcely judge of its dimensions, except by the candles which burned before the numberless altars. They glimmered faintly in the distance like points of light. The low voices of the men with me were reverberated, again and again, from the columns and the roof. Every stone of the pavement bore the name and the arms of a knight who lay below. Leaving reluctantly the church where so many brave men had kneeled to God for his blessing on their matchless enterprises, I got into a boat, and was put on board the Neapolitan steamer *Francesco Primo*, bound for Messina, where I lay an hour or two on deck, listening to the distant music of the English drums and trumpets.

As I lounged about the deck in the morning, utterly unable to hold any intercourse with any one on board except by signs, a sleek-looking fellow came up and accosted me in English. We soon got deep into conversation. My new acquaintance proved to be Guiseppe

Jackson, a Sicilian with an English grandfather, who had been a cook at the Albion, and at Murdoch's tavern[16]—had frequently been to Fresh Pond—knew some of the Cambridge students, and was now on his way to Mr. Marston's in Palermo. I was right glad to see him, cook though he was. He made me a very good interpreter. In the course of our conversation, he made some remark about "the Pope, that fool."

"What," said I, "do you speak so of the Pope? Are you not a Roman Catholic?"

"Ah! I was till I live in America. I was all in the dark—you understand what I say—till I come there. Then my eyes open; I say, dat for the Pope, and his old red cap. Ah! once I was afraid to think of him."

"You are no longer a Catholic: what religion do you believe in now?"

"Oh! no religion in particular."

I congratulated him on so happy a conversion from the error of his ways.

At breakfast—a Mediterranean breakfast of eggs, fruit, and nuts— an old man, of severe countenance and tremendous mustache, sat opposite me. We made various attempts at conversation; as neither understood the other, we had to be satisfied with reiterated bowings, and mutual attentions of various kinds, in which the old man showed himself exceedingly apt and polite. I afterwards found that he was no less a personage than il Principe Statelli, a general of the Sicilian army—but Sicilian *Principes* are apt to be humbugs.

Mount Aetna is smoking vigorously in front of us. We are skirting the shore of Sicily.

We stopped at Syracuse. A hundred boats surrounded us at once; no sooner had we got *pratique,* than we were boarded by a swarm of men, soldiers and civilians, among [whom] were conspicuous several Neapolitan officers, with grizzled moustache and a peculiarly swinish expression of countenance. Meanwhile, there was a burst of music from the town, and about a thousand men filed out from one of the gates, and fringed one of the battlements with a long line of bayonets. Not that this had any connexion with our arrival. In going ashore, a little square-built English looking man, making a low congee, presented me with a bundle of papers, which proved to be certificates of his qualifications as a guide to the curiosities of the place. Accordingly, Jack Robinson—for such was his name—and I got into a kind of ferry boat, and landed on the other side of the bay. Here we proceeded through narrow lanes, lined with aloes and prickly pears, and alive with green lizzards, till we came to a delapidated convent of Capuchins. Several of the reverend fathers were gazing from the turrets and grated windows. Half a mile further brought us into a wilderness of crags and trees. Jack knocked at a rude door at the extremity of a low arch hewn into one of the rocks, announcing himself in a loud voice as "Juan." A cadaverous, hollow-eyed Sicilian opened it—and we were in the midst of a noble garden of oranges and almonds and a host of strange unknown plants, and all shut in by perpendicular crags, near two hundred feet high, overgrown with creeping plants. In some places they would approach each other, leaving a chasm of but a few yards; then they would draw apart, and enclose an area of an acre. Here and there among the shrubbery stood a white, classic-looking cottage, or rather hut; the inmates—among whom were several very pretty girls—for the most part engaged in some domestic avocations outside. The place was full of doves, rooks, and smaller birds.

"For heaven's sake, Jack, what is this?" said I in utter astonishment.

"All made two thousand years ago! You have read of Dionysius' ear, hey? Well, he try three times before he make it—once down at the Capuchins'—once here—and once up there, where we go by and by."

Jack's residence of twenty-three years at Syracuse has greatly impaired his power of speaking English. I gathered, however, from his account that the marquis of Somebody turned to good account the abortive labors of the tyrant in this place by changing his would-be prison into a garden.

A little further on we came to the true "Ear of Dionysius" of classic renown.[d] Imagine an area of many acres, shut in by a stupendous

[d] "After travelling three months in Italy and Sicily, I have not seen a place more foreign and outlandish in its aspect than this—it took me by surprise as I saw it, when just arrived, fresh from America."—F.P.

wall of rock, hewn smoother and more regular than mason work. Dark yawning caves and passages, several by measurement a hundred feet high, lead from this tremendous prison-yard into the rock. One of them is the "ear." We entered, and groped a long distance to the end of it. I remained there, while my guide returned to the mouth. "Jack Robinson," said I in a very low whisper. "Signor Francesco," answered Jack in the same tone. The sound fell on my ear as clear and distinct as if he stood by my side. A man came and fired a pistol. I never heard a clap of thunder so tremendous or so long protracted as the roar that followed. The tearing of a sheet of thin paper was loudly reverberated again and again.

Enough of the ear; we went to the amphitheatres. There are two of them, both hewn out of the solid rock, with subterranean dens and passages for gladiators and wild beasts. It was twilight by this time. Not a tree nor a shrub was to be seen; all was bare white rock, and every rock was hewn—either into a tomb, or an acqueduct, or the foundation of a house. There was a long street, cut into the rock, which was perforated on either hand with tombs, running for rods into the hill. Returning by the larger theatre, I came of a sudden upon a low archway, green with moss, whence a stream came roaring furiously out, and boiling among the stones down into the arena of the deserted theatre. I shut my eyes, and listening to the noise, fully believed myself for the moment among the familiar forests and cataracts of New England—and almost saw the forms and faces associated with them; but when I opened my eyes, there was a filthy Sicilian wench among the rocks with a pitcher on her head, in place of my bright-eyed country women—a rascally Capuchin, instead of a stout woodsman—and there was Mt. Aetna, smoking like a lime-kiln, instead of Mt. Washington.

Next we went to a temple—I believe of Minerva—long since converted into a Christian chapel. A bearded Franciscan, in his brown cowl, led the way with a lamp of the antique form common in the Mediterranean. When he got below the surface of the ground, and showed vault after vault, of a most gloomy and massive architecture, all cold and damp as a cellar; and especially when he pointed out a granite column, to which he said that the monks were bound when condemned to the penance of flaggellation—it would have made a very fair scene for Monk Lewis.[17]

But the catacombs were the most extraordinary exhibition. The same old monk led the way with his lamp for at least quarter of a mile into the bowels of the earth. The passage was narrow and low— multitudes of others branched off on either side. Sometimes there would be a circular chamber a few yards across, with passages running from it in all directions. Jack said that they went through all Catania! I am confident that we must have passed the receptacles for a million of corpses. Some of the tombs were cut deep enough to contain twenty or more. They were empty for the most part, but I picked a bone or two from them.

There is a story of an enthusiastic schoolmaster who, with several of his pupils, got lost in this labyrinth; their remains were not found for years, they had got so deeply entangled in the maze. A subject fit for Dante; and a worthy counterpart to his Hugolino.

More fortunate than the schoolmaster, we got up to the light at last, and made a rush at full speed for the city. A sentry or two challenged us by the way, but Jack had the password. He pointed out a column of a temple of Ceres—a solitary relic—all the rest had fallen and been removed to the city, where I saw them.[e] When we were fairly within the gates, I felt myself in a starving state, and told Jack to provide a remedy. Accordingly he bought provisions, "here a little and there a little," as we went along, making his selections with great judgment. Then he introduced me into a cellar, where a crowd of red-capped ragamuffins were jabbering, who made way hastily for "Juan," who seemed well known everywhere. Juan led me to the rear, and spreading his banquet on a table, he drew a pitcher of wine from a cash [cache] and set it before me. It was the juice of the muscatelle grape, which grows here in astonishing abundance.

Jack insisting on showing me his certificates of service in the American Navy; and I being desirous of seeing how the Syracusans lived, I went home with him, and enjoyed the exhibition of his numerous progeny, who were all piled together in bed. This done, we took boat, and went off to the steamer. Jack was so well satisfied with the dollar and a half I gave him for his day's services, that he must needs salute me after the Sicilian style with a kiss on the cheek, which I submitted to. He then departed, kissing his hand as his head

[e] "There is a large temple of Minerva in the city, turned into a cathedral."—F.P.

disappeared over the ship's side—the stubborn English temper was well nigh melted away with his long sojourn among the Gentiles. He had been pressed in early youth into the navy—had served both England and America (though the latter, I believe, in the capacity of a washerman). As far as I could see, Jack was an honest man, an exceedingly *rara avis* in these quarters.

Arriving at Messina in the morning, my acquaintance the cook [Guiseppe]—an experienced traveller—was of the greatest service to me. Indeed, without his assistance, my inexperience and ignorance of the language would have put me to serious embarrassment. He showed me how to treat a Sicilian landlord, and to bribe a custom-house officer. I am indebted to him for very excellent accommodations, at a very reasonable price.

Messina, Sunday. I took my station outside one of the gates in the rear of the city, to look at the scum of humanity that came pouring out. All was filth, and age, and ruin—the walls, the tall gateway with its images and inscriptions, the hovels at the top of the wall, and in the ancient suburb, all seemed crumbling to decay. The orange and lemon groves in the ditch of the fortification were dingy and dirty—but away in the distance appeared the summits of the mountains, almost as wild and beautiful as our mountains of New England. I thought of them; and, in the revival of old feelings, half wished myself at home. I soon forgot, however, all but what was before my eyes, in watching the motley array that passed by me. Men and women, literally hung with rags, half hid in dirt, hideous with every imaginable species of deformity, and bearing on their persons a population as numerous as that of Messina itself—these formed the bulk of the throng. Priests, with their black broad-brimmed hats and their long robes—fat and good-looking men—were the next numerous class. They draw life and sustenance from these dregs of humanity—just as tall pig-weed flourishes on a dunghill. Then there were mustachoed soldiers, very different from the stately and sedate soldier of England. There were men bearing holy pictures and images—ladies in swarms, whose profession was stamped on their faces—musicians, with a troop of vagabonds in their rear. All around the gateway were the tables of butchers, fruiterers, confectioners, money changers, boot-blackers, and a throng of dirty men, women, and children. Shouts, yells, and a universal hubbub.[18]

"Dové è [Dov'è] il téatro?" enquired I, with execrable pronounciation, of a short, squalid-looking man at a street corner. "Ah! signor, I am delighted at the meeting with a gentleman of England. I shall have the honor to point out for you the way"—which he did, talking incessantly in this high flown style. "The door of the teater is not open. I think they have postponed the entertainment by the reason of the grand festival of the new year. But I shall have the honor to conduct you to the church where the grand festival is celebrated."

When we got there, I found a sight indeed worth seeing. The cathedral was in a blaze of light from many hundred candles, while all below was a black sea of heads. The priests were chanting, and the incense smoking. Every few moments, there would be a blast of trumpets and a burst of solemn music; at which every one of the thousands there knelt on the pavement, and then rose again with a deep rushing noise, produced by the simultaneous motion of such a multitude.[19]

My new acquaintance kept on talking aloud at my side throughout the whole, in spite of the hard looks of the people near us:

"The decorations of this church are very exceedingly beautiful, but I have seen it honored with a greater number of tapers. The directors of the ceremony are cautious at present. Last year, the fire *took force* on the pictures and ornaments, and the people trod on each other to get out. They trod over the ladies and the women." He said everything with a grin, as if highly amused; rolling up his large lobster eyes to my face, and rubbing the palms of his hands together. "The altar is ornamented with precious stones, which you will observe in the morning."

Here he began to translate into English, for my benefit, the *Te Domine* [*Deum*] which the priests were chanting. "Do you understand the Latin tongue, sir?" I nodded; at which he immediately repeated about half of one of the eclogues of "Virgilio," with the Italian accent. Some of the people turned round and began to talk with him, looking curiously at me meantime. "These people," he said, "regard it for a very strange thing that you should understand Latin, while you do not know the Italian tongue. They do not consider that they are two different, distinct, languages."

The service concluded with a thundering explosion of fireworks within the galleries, which filled the church with an insufferable smell of gunpowder. "Now we will hasten to go out, previously to the crowd of people." When we got into the street, I questioned this singular character, who told me that his father had taken great pains to let him have a good education. He had been to college, but now he was poor, and could not read his books. "Sir, I ask your pardon, but look at me, and you will see that I am destitute," said he, stripping open his dirty clothes to show that he had no shirt. I asked him what had brought so learned a man to such a pass. He told a story about having an office in the customs, which he had lost by being detected in some dealings with the *contrabandos*. Also he muttered something about his never drinking anything, but only taking a glass of wine with his friend. By this time his grinning mood was gone, and he had worked himself into a crying fit. Lifting his torn hat, he informed me that heaven had sent me to him, to relieve his miseries that night. Having no change with me, I was not tempted to the folly of giving it to him.[20]

Tuesday, Jan. 2nd. This morning I set out on an expedition to see a little of the country, in company with a Spanish gentleman, Don Mateo Lopez,[21] who speaks good English. We hired a carriage together, and got outside the gates by eleven, after some trouble in procuring passports. At night, we reached a little fishing town, called Giardini, not far from Aetna. The weather was beautiful; the atmosphere clear and soft. As for the scenery on the road, it was noble beyond expression. For myself, I never imagined that so much pleasure could be conveyed through the eye. The road was a sucession of beautiful scenes—of mountains and vallies on one side, and the sea on the other—but, as to the people, they are a gang of ragamuffins. The houses of the numberless dirty villages we passed are very low, with tiled roofs, grated windows—if any, at all—and built of stone or land. The narrow streets swarmed with beggars and other vermin; women spinning at the doors; jackasses of diminutive size, tottering under two barrels of water, or a man twice as large as

Joseph Thayendanegea
Portrait in oils of Joseph Brant by George Romney
(Coverdale Collection No. 2383)

themselves; loungers, in their brown capotes, grouped around the fountains. This capote gives the wearer a most monastic aspect: it has a hood attached to it, with a peaked crown, which covers the head and half the face. These disgusting holes of villages only added zest to the pleasure of the scenery, a pleasure not inferior, and not unlike that of looking upon the face of a beautiful woman. In many respects, our own scenery is far beyond it; but I cannot say that I have ever looked with more delight on any of our New England mountains and streams than upon these of Sicily. The novelty of the sight, and the ruined fortresses on the highest crags, add much to the effect.[22]

At noon of the next day, we reached Catania,[23] a large city, so old that tradition makes the Cyclops its founders. Since that time, it has passed through the hands of Greeks, Romans, Saracens, and Christians, each of whom have left oh it some trace of themselves. Every two or three centuries, Mt. Aetna knocks it to pieces, or floods it with lava. The Greek and Roman theatre is wholly buried up, except a few passages which have been excavated. There is a fountain upon which its disagreeable neighbor, in the year 1669, vomited lava to the depth of sixty feet, but a fountain is a thing of value here. A patriotic citizen, Prince Boscari, dug through the lava till he found it. It is now reached by several flights of steps, up which the women are constantly toiling with jars of water on their heads. Catania is paved and, in great part, built of lava. It is full of monks, of all orders. The Benedictines have a noble convent—and a church by far the finest I have seen. In '69 the lava *came within five yards of the church wall*, then turned aside without injuring it. On the other side it came within about three times that distance, and turned aside in like manner. It appears now like a wall of black stone.

I went to the museum of Prince Boscari, a valuable collection of antiquities, etc. In the midst of a hall, surrounded by precious fragments of statues and broken pottery, lay the skeleton of a *Chippeway birch canoe*. I welcomed it as a countryman and an old friend.

I bought some specimens of lava and amber—of a couple of rascals who asked twice their value, and abated it at once when I refused to buy.[f]

---

[f] Six and a half lines, dealing with Don Mateo Lopez's nocturnal amusements, have been inked out here.—Ed.

I went to see an opera of Bellini—a native, I have heard, of Catania. In buying tickets here, you are shown a plan of the theatre, select your seat, which is then crossed off on the paper; and receive a piece of paper like a bank bill with your number inscribed on it.[24] Lopez had a friend waiting for him here—a light-hearted and lively young Spaniard, whose youthful eccentricities sat as easily and gracefully upon him as they did awkwardly upon old Mateo. When we set out on our return, *"il mio amico,"* as Lopez called him, was rattling away incessantly, and imitating every dog, hog, or jackass we met.

We had a sort of a *calèche*. Beside the driver, a small boy ran along by our side, or clung behind, ready to do what offices might be required of him. A still smaller one was stowed away in a net, slung between the wheels, where he kept a constant eye on the baggage. The larger one employed himself in tying knots in the horses' tails as he ran along; or he would dart along the road before us, clamber on a wall, and sit till we came by; when he would spring down, with a shout, and run on again.

All around Catania is one great bed of lava. Some spots seem as if sprinkled with the refuse of a furnace: others are covered with vegetation. All the walls, all the houses, and many of the domestic utensils, such as troughs for washing, are of lava. There was an eruption of the mountain two or three weeks ago, by which more than sixty persons were killed or wounded—for, strange to say, the base of this perilous monster is covered with habitations.

At Giarri, a large place where we stopped to rest the horses, we were beset, of course, by beggars. One little rascal, about six years (years) old—whose clothes, if they answered the purposes of warmth, answered no other purpose for which clothing is intended—followed me about for half an hour, like a little dog. I could not muster sternness enough to order him away with effect—and he was too small to kick into the gutter—so he went on, begging for a *carlino* [*carlin*]. At last he began slyly to mock, for my edification, the grave countenance and stately air of Don Mateo; and did it so ludicrously that I stood laughing at him. At this he summoned a larger boy to his side, who hummed a tune, while he danced a sort of hornpipe on the pavement. I could forbear no longer, but gave him a *grano*—

about the third part of a cent. A crowd of loungers had mustered to witness the performance of this mannikin, who was about a foot and a half high. There they stood, in their brown capotes, looking gravely from out of their hoods, at the spectacle of my unparralled generosity, which was a signal for action. I was half stunned with supplications from men, women, and children; and glad, after cursing them a little, to escape into the carriage. Among the rest was a girl, most abominably ugly, who appeared to be a mute. I threw her a large copper coin—the young Spaniard added a couple more, which threw the girl into a perfect frenzy of delight. She danced about among the crowd; flinging both hands into the air—then kissing the coins, and pressing them against her breast; tossing them on the ground before her, and gathering them up again; till her ugly face seemed absolutely good looking with the excess of her pleasure.[25]

The women of this country are not handsome. You see groups of them about the stone door-ways spinning twine, with their hair drawn back in the fashion represented in the portraits of our grand-mothers.

We stopped at night at Giardini.[26] The *padrone* showed us with great complacency the register of his house, which, he said, "con-tained the recommendations of the guests who had honored him with their company." One man's "recommendations" warned all trav-ellers that the *padrone's* beds were full of fleas; another's, that nothing in the house was fit to eat, etc. The unfortunate *padrone* could not read English.

It rained in the morning. The night before had been glorious. I took my last look, I fear, of Aetna, whose immense sides were white with snow and wrapped around with clouds and smoke—the summit was just discernible among the vapors, a volume of white smoke, beautifully tinged by the setting sun slowly rolling from it. This gigantic and portentous mass towers immeasurably above the beautiful mountains that lie around it. If Aetna looked grandly that evening, they were not less beautiful in the evening shadows, with their groves of oranges, and olives, and lemons, and the dark vallies between them.

But in the morning, we could see nothing of Aetna, though we were at its base. The Spaniard and I set out to visit the ancient town of

Taormina, in the mountains above Giardini. We went on mules up a winding path, where the prospect must in clear weather have been noble. We met men, and women, and mules coming down, for Taormina is still inhabited. The chief curiosity of the place is the theatre—in very good preservation. The cicerone who showed it seemed to feel a genuine enthusiasm in his subject. The building must have been very magnificent; Greeks, Romans, and Saracens have held it; but the snails, of which I captured a fine one for a memento, are the only tenants now. Crowning a steep cliff, at an immense height above Taormina, is an old Saracen castle. This country is full of associations—of classic fable—of classic history—and of romance.

Descending—on my part, sorrowfully—we rode on toward Messina. "*Il mio amico*" could not contain the excess of his spirits. Every unfortunate Indian fig plant, with its clumsy broad plates of leaves, felt the weight of his cane, till a plant, a little tougher than the rest, jerked the instrument of destruction out of his hand. The attendant imp picked it up and restored it, but not before a cart wheel had rather impaired its symmetry. We supped together at Messina; and thus ended a most agreeable expedition. I shall not soon forget Catania, with its strange and precarious situation at the foot of the great volcano, which alternately confers blessings on it and menaces it with ruin. Aetna had given it a noble mole of lava, but has since cancelled its own gift, by a second eruption. The revenues of Catania are drawn from the snows of Aetna. Nor shall I forget its origin—back in the darkness of classic fable. The theatre, now buried under the lava, was large enough to contain the whole present population of Catania, about thirty thousand.

The church of the Benedictines is the noblest edifice I have seen. This and others not unlike it have impressed me with new ideas of the Catholic religion. Not exactly, for I reverenced it before as the religion of generations of brave and great men—but now I honor it for itself. They are mistaken who sneer at its ceremonies as a mere mechanical farce: they have a powerful and salutary effect on the mind. Those who have witnessed the services in this Benedictine church, and deny what I say, must either be singularly stupid and insensible by nature, or rendered so by prejudice.

Saturday. I recall what I said of the beauty of the Sicilian women—
so far, at least, as concerns those of high rank. This is a holy day.
They are all abroad, in carriages and on foot. One passed me in the
church of the Capuchin convent, with the black eye, the warm rich
cheek, and the bright glance that belong to southern climates, and
are beautiful beyond all else.

There were grand ceremonies in the cathedral. Five or six noblemen sat on a sort of throne which was covered with crimson silk.
They wore rich black dresses, massive gold chains on their breasts,
and the enormous ruffs of several centuries ago, making them look
as if their heads were screwed down between their shoulders, without
the intervention of a neck. A motley concourse of soldiers and women,
princes and beggars, filled the church.

Sunday. Took leave of the hospitable family of Consul Payson, with
much regret; and went off to the steamer *Palermo*, bound for Palermo.
I found her completely surrounded by boats, wedged close together—
friends were kissing their adieus, and boatmen cursing. The delicacy
of sentiment expressed in the Italian national oath is admirable—
they rival the Spaniards, in that matter—"*Arcades ambo*"; *id est*,
"blackguards both." At length visitors were warned off; the boats
dispersed, scattering from a common centre, in all directions; a man
screamed the names of the passengers, by way of roll-call; and among
the rest the illustrious one of "Signore Park-a-man"; and we got
under weigh. It was late at night. We passed the long array of bright
lights, from the fine buildings along the quay of Messina—could just
discern the mountains behind the town, indistinct in the darkness,
like thunder-clouds—left a long train of phosphoric light behind us,
as we steered down between Scylla and Charybdis—and in half an
hour were fairly out on the Sicilian Sea. The ghost of departed perils
still lingers about the scene of Ulysses' submarine adventures: an
apology for a whirlpool on one side—still bearing the name of
Scylla—and an insignificant shoal on the other. I thought, as we
passed, and the moon made a long stream of light on the water,
that it would [be] an adventure worth encountering, to be cast away in
that place—but my unwonted classical humor was of very short
duration; for, going below, I found a cabin-full of sea-sick wretches,

which attractive spectacle banished all recollection of Virgil and
Homer. I was doomed to lie all night, a witness to their evolutions;
a situation not many degrees more desirable than being yourself
a sufferer.

In the morning we were skirting the bold and wild coast of Sicily,
in a drizzling rain. We entered at length the crescent of high mountains that rise around the bay of Palermo. Midway between the horns
of this crescent, in a wide hollow between the mountains, lay the city,
with its Asiatic towers, and its two hundred thousand inhabitants.
Coming to anchor, the sea around us was absolutely *paved* with boats,
and the steamer taken by storm. After a hard fight, I rescued my
baggage, had it transported over six boats into a seventh, which last
was only a rod or two from the out-skirts of the throng—and have it
now, happily, safe in the Hotel de France.

Monday, Jan. [*15th*]. Have been a week in Palermo, and seen all
the lions, which are numerous—churches, catacombs, and mountains.
I hired Guiseppe, the cook, as a servant and a teacher of Italian,
which he is said to speak remarkably well. Palermo is under the
special protection of a saint, to whom everybody renders the devoutest
worship. It is a place as gay as any in Europe—the people moreover
have the faculty of being gay on the smallest means. Yesterday,
hundreds of tailors and shopkeepers, with an income of an hundred
and fifty piastres a year, were lounging about the fountains of the
public garden in satin and broadcloth, or prancing along the
Marina on horseback among the carriages of the nobles. The nobles
themselves do not greatly abound in wealth. As for the ladies, they
do well enough before marriage, for the sufficient reason that they
are not trusted out of their mothers' sight—but after marriage the
case is altered; insomuch that the English residents here pride themselves on keeping wholly aloof from any intercourse with the
Sicilians.[27]

The other day, I went up Monte Pellegrino, the dwelling place
of the sainted patroness of Palermo. Every year, half the city makes a
pilgrimage to the summit of this high mountain, to pay their homage,
while the whole valley below is bright with illuminations. The
mountain is very precipitous, but a road of solid mason-work has

been made, by which its perpendicular side is made accessible without the least difficulty. Our donkeys carried us up in a couple of hours. At the summit, in a great solitude of rocks and snows, we found the shrine of the saint. Santa Rosalia was the niece of William the Good, one of the Sicilian kings. She left the court in a fit of enthusiasm, and climbed to the top of this mountain, where she spent her days in a large grotto in the rock against which the present little church is built. Several centuries after, when a pestilence, wholly unmanageable by the priests, was desolating Palermo, the saint appeared in a dream to a man who inhabited a hut half way down the mountain; telling him where her bones were to be found. Accordingly they were brought from the grotto where she had died; and borne with great ceremonies to the city. The pestilence was instantly arrested.

The priests guided me through the church, into the grotto behind— a huge black den hung with broken stalactites, whence water icy cold was dropping on to the floor. The snow had found its way through a large cleft above; altogether, the habitation of the young saint wore a most sombre and cheerless aspect. The lamps were burning in a remote part of the cavern before her shrine. The priest kneeled before a grating beneath the altar, and motioned me to look in between the bars. Two or three lamps were burning there, but for some time, I could discern nothing else. At length, I could distinguish a beautiful female figure, sculptured in marble, and clothed in a robe of gold, lying with a crucifix in her hand and a scull beside her. The white transparency of the marble showed beautifully in the light of the lamps, and suited well the mild enthusiastic expression of her face. I scarce wondered at the devotion of the Palermitans. Drinking some of the water that trickled from the roof into a stone basin by the side of the altar, I left the grotto, which was as cold and chilling as a New England winter. The priest gave me a rough picture of the saint, to which I retorted with a suitable *buonamano*.[g] After taking a last look at the ancient and moss-grown church, and the black cliffs around it, I left Monte Pellegrino. As we waded through the snow down the mountain, the view of Palermo was noble. The valley was as smooth and level as the ocean, and set between the

[g] Tip.—Ed.

immense circle of snow-covered mountains, as green and bright as an emerald. The city was but a very small part—there were forests of olive-trees, and innumerable gardens, all dotted with white houses, and the palaces of the nobles. It was the king's birthday, and the city was half covered with the smoke of cannon.

The next day, I went to the Capuchin convent, where the holy fathers keep many thousand mummies, in vaulted apartments under ground. I was so edified by the interesting spectacle, that I bought a mass, for fifty cents, and appointed four o'clock the next morning to hear it performed in the sepulchres. Guiseppe waked me, and we sallied forth. Though it wanted more than two hours of daylight, many people were abroad. Fires were burning outside the *caffès* and confectioners', with ragamuffins and *filles de joie* grouped around them for the sake of the warmth. The porter made his appearance at the gate of the convent, and conducted us in, where we found five [or] six of the fathers assembled with lamps, awaiting the coming of the prior. When all was ready, we descended into the tombs. The mummies, each from his niche in the wall, grinned at us diabolically as we passed along. Several large cats, kept there for the benefit of the rats, stared at us with their green eyes, and then tramped off. When we got to the little chapel, the prior put off his coarse Capuchin dress, and arrayed himself in white robes—the curtain was drawn aside from the image of the Virgin behind the altar—the lamps lighted—and the mass performed. When all was over, one of the fathers lighted a torch to show the catacombs by its light. Coffins piled up below—men, shrunk into a mere nothing, but clothed as they used to be above ground, all ranged along the wall on either hand—a row of sculls under the cornices—this made up the spectacle, which was rather disgusting. There were one or two children, just dead, and a few men, flung down in corners, waiting for the drying process. Women are placed here, as well as men. The virgins all wear crowns of silver paper, from beneath which they grin and gape in a most alluring fashion.

I soon cried enough, and returned to the upper air. The morning mass in the church was just begun. One of the monks conducted me to an ancient apartment behind the altar: here the whole convent were kneeling, telling their beads—the faint light, their dark cowls, their beards, and their deep murmurings at their devotions made quite an impressive scene. The little church itself was half full of people, though it was not yet daylight. I looked awhile at the old pictures about the rooms and passages, then bade adieu to the fathers, who thought me mad, and departed.

The Capuchins of Monreale, four miles from Palermo, have a similar burial place. Monreale, however, is chiefly remarkable for the noble church, built in the 12th century, which is attached to the Benedictine monastery. The walls of this church are covered with mosaics representing scripture history. The monastery is a very large one. All the monks are sons, I believe, of noblemen; as is also the case with the Benedictines of Catania. Monreale is famous, moreover, for the rapacity of its inhabitants, who consider a stranger fair game. Some fellow(s) brought me specimens of the mosaic, picked from the wall of the church, which was undergoing repairs. I gave him twice their value, which he returned and demanded more. I pocketed what I had given him, and ordered the coachman to drive on, where-upon the crowd who had assembled set up a yell, and followed us with maledictions for quarter of a mile.

Palermo is full of beautiful fountains—water-gods—horses—ser-pents—fishes—every imaginable variety of figure—pouring forth the pure water of the mountains, into basins full of gold fish, or over rocks of marble covered with a growth of water-plants. Sometimes a group of water-nymphs are seen sporting together, flinging the water at each other.

The city is very regularly laid out. Two large streets cross at right angles in the centre, where is a little square, called the Quat[t]ro Cantoni, ornamented with four fountains.

I have just returned from a ride on a donkey—horses are not to be had here—about the neighborhood of the city. Guiseppe first led the way to an ancient and delapidated church at the foot of one of the mountains; a place carefully preserved in memory of the Sicilian Vespers.[28] The man, who lived in a sort of hovel under its founda-tions, had not the key. He led the way, however, up some narrow and broken stairs to a window just below the e[a]ves, from which I had a fair view down into the church—deserted, sombre, and filled with dust and decay. The slightest whisper, where I stood, was reverberated among the arches. There were two or three good pictures—a broken altar—and innumerable cobwebs. In the mountain behind this church is a grotto filled with fossil bones, which Guiseppe and the man said were the remains of giants. Doctors disagree as to the nature of these bones—some will have it that they are veritable fossils, others say that the cave was the receptacle where the animals killed in the Greek and Roman amphitheatres were flung.

Thence we proceeded to the convent of Santa Maria de Gesu. I went up to a little stone building on the summit of a rock, where was an image of the Virgin, with flowers placed before it, and an inscription promising forty days' indulgence to whoever should say three paters in that place. Without availing myself of this opportunity, I lay down in the sun on the wall, and gazed at the magnificent view of the valley of Palermo and the mountains behind. After riding about the valley all day, we returned to the city.

Tuesday. I saw today a review of several thousand Neapolitan conscripts, the only species of troops in Sicily. Ferdinand[29] sends his Neapolitans here, and keeps his Sicilians in Naples. The latter are not conscripts, but serve voluntarily. The fellows I saw were almost all slight and feeble-looking men. Many of them, in fact, were mere boys. Some of the battalions fired well, but none of the manoeuvres were executed with the precision and unity of the English soldiers. I remembered that the Neapolitans were the only nation of whom Napoleon could not make soldiers.

Wednesday. I have just arranged an expedition to Girgenti, at the southern point of the island. Travelling in Sicily is no joke, especially at this season. I engaged a man named Luigi to furnish three mules—supplies of provisions—cooking apparatus—an attendant—and thus to pilot me round the island, paying himself all tavern reckonings and *buonamano's.* For this I am to give him four dollars a day. I thus avoid all hazard of being imposed upon, or robbed, for I shall have scarce any money with me. Luigi is perfectly familiar with the island; has, moreover, the reputation of an honest man, notwithstanding which I follow Mr. Marston's advice in making him sign a written agreement. I have laid it down as an inviolable rule to look on everybody here as a rascal of the first water, till he has shown himself by undeniable evidence to be an honest man.

Guiseppe has been with me as a servant of late. The chief fault with him was his continually stopping to kiss some of his acquaintances in the street. He seems to know everybody—understands perfectly how to cheat everybody—has astonishing promptness and readiness for all kinds of service. "It is 'trange, Mist'r Park-a-man," he modestly remarked the other day, "that I cannot go nowhere, but what all the people seem to like-a me, and be good friends with me." He is vain as a turkey cock—dresses infinitely better than I ever did. He is a great coward, trembling continually with fear of robbers in all our rides. The Sicilian robbers, by the way, are a great humbug. When I engaged Guiseppe, I offered him half a dollar a day for wages. "No, Mist'r Park-a-man, I no take-a wages at all. When you go away, you make-a me a present, just as much as you like; then I feel more better." So I told him I would "make-a" him a present of half a dollar a day; which I did—a mode of remuneration more suited to Guiseppe's self-importance.

Thursday. Jan. 18ᵗʰ. All this morning Luigi Rannesi was in a fever-heat of preparation. I told him to be ready at two; he came to me at 12, announcing that all was ready; that he had engaged mules at Marineo, and that the carriage was at the door to take us there. I was not prepared for such promptitude. After some delay, I got ready, too, and we set out. Luigi, a diminutive Sicilian with a thin brown face and an air of alertness about every inch of him, began to jabber Italian with such volubility that I could not understand a word. He must needs exhibit every article of the provisions he had got ready for the journey, extolling the qualities of each—and they deserved all his praises—and always ended by pounding himself on the breast, rolling up his eyes, and exclaiming, "Do you think Luigi loves money? No! Luigi loves honor!" and then launching forth into interminable eulogiums of the country we were going to see, and the adventures we should meet there. We stopped at night at Marineo, where Luigi provided a most sumptuous dinner; talked and gesticulated, half frenzied because he found I could not understand half he said; then siezed my hand, which he dutifully kissed, and left me to my meditations. He reappeared, however, bringing a decanter of wine, and a large book of antiquities which he had brought for me to read.[30] All this was at his own expense. The terms of his bargain bound him to nothing else than to keep me alive on the road.

Early in the morning, we left Marineo—a fair sample of a Sicilian village. A group of little square, tiled-roofed, stone houses crowded close together on the side of a mountain; a castle on the eminence above, green and beautiful mountains rising everywhere around, without a tree or a shrub.[31]

We rode all day over a country of mountains, stopping at noon at a solitary inn to find some maccaroni. As we were on the point of setting out, the usual number of beggars beset us—among the most respectable was a blind fiddler and his boy, who scraped a tune on two broken violins. Luigi became excited; tumbled himself from his mule, and began a dance in a most amateur-like style to the music, in the midst of the ring of beggars. We stopped at night at a large and dirty village called Lercara [Lacara], where nothing but fleas were to be had in the enormous stone albergo.[32]

There was a storm all night. In the morning, the wind swept as cold and raw over the mountains as on a November day at home. The hazy softness of the scenery was gone—all was dark and bleak. We rode along in company with two muleteers, jabbering their unintelligible Sicilian. Some *contadini*, or field laborers, at work told us that the road had broken away in front; so we turned across the fields—which every traveller for a year or two will probably be obliged to do. After fording a stream, wading through an abyss of mud for several miles, and climbing a hill, we found an ancient pathway of stone along the side of a mountain. A headlong muddy stream was tumbling among the olives below us. The stones of the pathway were worn through with age, and kicked far and wide over the hillside by the passage of some hundred generations of mules. We soon came to the mud again; then another bridgeless stream, and another and another. One of them with its broad bed of stones—the shrunken stream rippling down in the centre—reminded me of the streams of New England—but a glance at the bare and cultivated hills—at the olive-trees in the vallies, and aloes and Indian-figs ranged along the bank, and clustered thick about the old grey house of *contadini* near the landing—was enough to dispel the illusion. The mountains closed thicker around us—grew wilder and higher, too. The weather became dark and gloomy. My mule fell and nearly flung me from the saddle— an accident which warned me to be cautious, as the miserable path frequently ran along the edge of hills where a fall would be followed by a tumble of some hundred feet into a little rocky torrent at the bottom. At length, as we were crossing a bridge at the top of [a] narrow gorge of very high and abrupt mountains, a violent wind suddenly came down the passage, bending the long tufted grass on the lower declivities—the precursor of a heavy rain-storm. But as we got out of this place we saw the cathedral dome and the tiled roofs of Castel Termini in a hollow of the mountains, far in front. After riding an hour over a stony hill-side, where our mules were nearly knocked over by the wind, we got into the ancient path, worn deep into the rock, which led up to the town. A noble diorama of stormy mountains lay on the left.

Luigi is a great antiquarian. He rakes up ancient money at every village as he goes along. His antiquarian skill is a passport to introduce him anywhere, to the nobles and princes—who are not always, however, such dignified personages as would appear from their titles. I went with him to-night to the house of a judge, who produced a bottle of *rosolio* and showed me a grotto in his garden, which he had stuck all over with specimens of the Sicily minerals. I then went with him to a *conversazione*, where some dozen people were playing cards. They looked at the *signore Americano*, as the judge introduced me to them, with great curiosity, and at last left their game and clustered round me, very curious to know something of the place I came from. I talked to them for some time in a most original style of Italian; but getting tired of being lionized in such a manner, I bade them good night and went back to the *albergo*. One of them, an officer of gendarmes, a Greek by blood, tried to talk to me in his own language, but made an entire failure. He was a broad shouldered and athletic fellow, remarkably intelligent and well informed. I told him I came from Boston, on which he asked me if it was not near Charlesto[w]n—a miracle of information for a Sicilian, with whom, as I have had occasion to observe, America from Greenland to Cape

Horn is all the same thing. He came from one of those detached Greek villages of which there are several in Sicily, established about two centuries ago [by] fugitives from the north of Greece.[33]

At the door of the inn I saw, for the first time, the national vehicle of Sicily—the *lettiga*. It is a large box, exactly like a sedan, only it is carried by mules instead of men. One strong mule goes before and one behind, while the box swings between two poles in the centre. Each mule wears gaudy trappings about the head, and a dozen large bells fastened to a triangular machine on the back. A man walks alongside, with a pole like a fishing rod to guide the mules, and another follows behind with a sumpter mule. After this fashion they proceed along paths that would break the legs of any horse in five minutes. You can hear the rattling of the bells among the mountains half a mile off.

The country inns of Sicily are notorious. This one of Castel Termini was a fair sample, though in point of dirt, fleas, etc., it fell far short of some others.[34] A Sicilian *albergo* is an ancient gloomy building of stone, like all the rest; they usually have a little sign; or at least a branch of a tree stuck at the door, by way of indicating their public character; but to look up at their half decayed walls, and the small square windows thinly distributed over the front, you would take them for dungeons. Enter, and you stumble down a stone step into the kitchen—a spacious cavern, dark as Tartarus, with a floor of earth, and seldom any windows. Water jars, harness, and outlandish-looking utensils are scattered about. Groups of idlers are crouching in the corner over a brazier of charcoal, and crucifixes and images with little lamps burning before them are hung about the walls. Close adjoining are large stone apartments for mules and asses, who have usually separate accommodations in the *albergos*, though in the private house a corner of the family room, usually the cleanest, is assigned them. Ask for *ap[p]artamenti*, and a woman leads you up a broken flight of stone steps to a room floored with a kind of cement. There is one window—one strongly secured door—a holy picture on the wall and a bed full of fleas. You can seldom get anything to eat, unless it be maccaroni. This is an inn of the interior. The others are better. I speak from the experience of three nights, and I solemnly aver that the picture is not over-colored.

I have forgotten a prominent feature of the establishment—the beggars. A decrepid beast, covered with dirt, unshaven, with bleared gummy eyes, and covered all but the face in a rotten capote, thrusts a rosary into your face, and whines out of his withered throat a petition for alms. All about the door stand groups of idlers, enveloped in the same capotes, staring and conversing listlessly. This capote covers the face exactly like the hoods of mail you see in the old editions of Tasso and Ariosto—but the face of a Sicilian is anything but martial or knightly.

Such being our nocturnal accommodations, we were glad enough to be among the mountains again. The morning was beautiful. The mule track was in many places literally paved with alabastar. We passed huge rocks of this mineral—and troughs hewn out of it, for refreshing the mules, wherever a spring came out of the hill-side. About noon we approached a deep valley, whence we heard in the stillness the loud tumbling of water—a moment after we saw a wide stream running through the meadows below us, which were covered with hundreds of the long-horned cattle of Sicily. At the height where we stood, the faint sound of their bells was like the tinkling of a brook. Descending to the river, we found waiting under the bank two men, naked below the waist. Their handsome and muscular limbs were tanned as dark as their faces by many days of exposure. Both were noble specimens of flesh and blood. One of them led the foremost mule—the other followed behind, as we crossed the ford.

The mountains around this place were very high and rich in vegetation. The sun lay on them hot and sultry—there was a haziness in the air that softened their asperities, and threw an air of quiet and drowsieness over the landscape. We soon came to a village [Carminia] on the side of a mountain. All the houses were plastered with a grey cement of gypsum—everything wore the same grey hue. As we rode up the steep street, the women were sitting in the hot sun on heaps of stone outside their doors, arranging their hair, or nursing their children; some lay stretched at full length in the sun asleep. Many were pretty—all wore the appearance of full health and vigor. They seemed like the women of earlier times—the partners of the primeval inhabitants of Sicily of whom the pastoral poets speak. On the opposite side of the valley another village lay basking in the sun, the yellow palace of its proprietor conspicuous above the grey square houses of his tenants.

I went to visit the famous sulphur works not far from these places. In the shaft I entered, the rock was solid sulphur—scarce any mixture of foreign ingredient. As we rode away, a noble prospect of volcanic mountains lay off on our right. Soon after the mule-track became a good road. A carriage from Caltanizetta passed us, belonging to some English travellers[h] who had made a wide detour for the sake of a road. We saw at last the battlements and church spires of Girgenti, crowning a high hill before us, and had occasional glimpses of the sea through the vallies. Approaching the hill, we found a deep and shadowed valley intervening. Luigi left the road and descended into it by a wretched mule-track. Flocks of goats passed on the road above us—mules and asses, loaded with their panniers, came down from the city. One of his fits of enthusiasm had taken possession of Luigi. He began to lash his mule and drive him along over mud and rocks at such a rate that I thought him mad, till he told me that it was necessary—*per bisogno*—to get to Girgenti before the Englishmen. "*Cor(r)ag[g]io*, my brave mule! *Corragio, signore*," he shouted, "we shall be the victors!" At that, he drove full speed up the steep hill toward the gate. Nothing would stop him. He leaped over ditches—scrambled through mud and stones, shouting "*corragio*" at the top of his lungs. At last an insuperable gulley brought him up short. He clapped his hand to his forehead, exclaiming "*Santissima Maria*" in a tone of wrath and despair—then recovered his spirits and dashed off in another direction. We succeeded. When we got to the top the carriage was quarter of a mile off, and Luigi shouted "*Vittoria!*" as he rode into the gate, as much elated as if [he] had accomplished some great achievement. It was a *festa* day. All the people in the crowded streets and in the little square wore white caps. They were a hardy and athletic race—their faces, their short strong necks, their broad and prominent chests, were all burnt to a dark ruddy brown. There is a strange difference in the physical character of the people in the different parts of Sicily; nor in this alone—costumes, habits, manners, domestic utensils, everything in short varies as you go from town to town. In some places, the women ride astride like men; in others, they have a kind of side-saddle. In one little village almost all the

h Named Dawson, according to Parkman's pocket notebook.—Ed.

women were exceedingly pretty, though dark as Indians. Their black hair was arranged with great neatness and care in a peculiar fashion which attracted my notice at once, since in every other place I had seen the hair was not arranged at all—and the less said or seen of it the better.[35]

Between Girgenti and the sea is the site of the ancient Agrigentum. Standing on the town wall, you can look down on immense fertile hills and plains, amid which appear the ruins of five or six temples, standing together along an abrupt ridge of land, which in one direction formed the boundary of the ancient city. I went down to the ruins, with a cicerone, of course, to plague me by his chattering. I saw all the temples—I admired and wondered, but was not exactly overpowered by enthusiasm. I bought a book to describe them; a task I leave to the more classically disposed, feeling little inclination to it myself.

Luigi brings me pockets-full of ancient money, and seems greatly astonished at my indifference. As for himself, he is rabid. He dodges into every house and shop, inquiring for *antica moneta*, stops *contadini* at work with the same question; he has scraped together an enormous bagful for which he pays scarce anything, perfectly familiar as he is with its true value, and with the *costumi del paese*, as he says, the customs of the country. His enthusiasm embraces every object, far and wide. He raves of love on the road—tells how he eloped with his wife—sings love songs; then falls into the martial vein; shouts *corragio*; defies the wind, rain, and torrents. He enters into all my plans with the most fervid zeal, leaving me nothing to do. Every night he comes up stairs, bringing all kinds of dresses and utensils of the people for me to look at. Sometimes he comes in with a handful of old coins, telling me with a chuckle that he had bought them for *pochissimo*; kissing them repeatedly in the exaltation of a good bargain. I have lived most sumptuously ever since I have been with him. He puts the whole inn into a ferment—rakes the town to find the best of everything—and waits on table with an eulogium of every dish. "Ah, *signore*," he repeats, "do you think Luigi loves money? No, Luigi loves honor." He has something to give to every beggar he meets. In short the fellow is a jewel, and shall be my particular friend henceforward.

I went with him to the house of a signor Politi, who is fairly rampant with antiquarian zeal, and deeply enamored moreover of the fine arts. The studio of this virtuoso presented a formidable display of old pictures, plaster casts, vases, fragments of statues, and a confused medley of indescribables. He was sitting at his easel copying a Madonna of Gu[i]do. Luigi pulled off his hat with great respect, advanced, and drawing an antique cameo from the multitudinous folds of his handkerchief presented it as *un picc(i)olo complimento* to signore. The virtuoso examined it through his spectacles, expressed his approval, and coolly pocketed it, leaving me in equal admiration at Luigi's making a *complimento* of such value, and at Politi's cavalier-like style of accepting it. The mystery was soon solved—it was like Turkish or Indian presents: Luigi expected as a matter of course a *complimento* in return. In fact, he retired with a handkerchief-full of antiquities. He told me he always carried something with him, *per fare un complimento* to the *signori* who honored him with their acquaintance. He knows everybody from princes to beggars.

At the English consul's, I met a blind traveller, a Mr. Hol(e)man,[36] who has been over Liberia, New Holland, and other remote regions, for the most part alone, and written seven volumes of his travels. Travelling, he told me, was a passion with him. He could not sit at home. I walked home with him through the streets, admiring his indomitable energy. I saw him the next morning sitting on his mule, with the guide he had hired—his strong frame, his manly English face, his grey beard and mustaches, and his sightless eyeballs gave him a noble appearance in the crowd of wondering Sicilians about him.

From Girgenti our course lay westward to a village called Mont' Allegro. A wretched muletrack again; a wilderness of mountains with scarce an inhabitant. There was one broad valley covered with a growth of the *jumara*—a plant of which baskets and ropes are made. It was a dark and gloomy day. Down in the bottom of the valley a herd of oxen were grazing—there was a *contadino's* hut of reeds on one of the abrupt hills near by. It was like the lodge of an Indian—the cattle were like a herd of buffalo; I could have thought myself on the prairies. But as we passed by the herd, there stood the herdsman in his shaggy breeches of goatskin, leaning on his staff—gazing at us through his tangled hair and unshorn beard. His savage dogs, wild as himself, growled loudly as we rode by. The American frontier could show no such a group.

Before night, Mont' Allegro lay before us, among mountains of alabastar, with a wide green meadow between; and a grove of orange trees at the skirts of the close compacted group of houses. A ruined Saracenic castle, and an assemblage of ancient dwellings, crowns the summit of one of the highest of the mountains. It rises before me now, as I write in the window of the *albergo*, the white rock contrasting beautifully with the thick, growth of Indian fig that springs from every crevice, from top to bottom. It is a quiet and beautiful evening. The capoted idlers in the street are talking and laughing and looking up at the stranger—the same beings that their fathers were before them centuries ago. The town is built and paved with alabastar.

Luigi came up in the evening, to hold *un discorso* with me, according to his custom. He was in his usual state of excitement. He takes a glass of wine in his hand; *"Viva l'onore, signorino mio!"* rolling up his eyes and flourishing his hands, *"Viva Bacco; viva Dio; viva il console Americano!"* and so on, the finale being a siezure and kissing of my hand; after which he enquires if I shall want him, looks about to see that all is right, kisses my hand again, and goes off.

I picked up in the morning fine specimens of alabastar—and afterwards of agates in the beds of the streams. We reached at night the city of Sciacca, handsomely drenched by a shower. In the morning I rode up the mountain behind the city to visit the convent of St. Carlogero at the summit, where are the celebrated vapor baths which Diodorus speaks of, said to have been arranged by D[a]edalus. After circling about the whitewashed walls of the convent, we entered a little dirty den for the accommodation of mules, from whence we saw the refectioner, through an opening at the head of some stone steps, cooking maccaroni for the fathers, over some little charcoal furnaces. He came down at our call, shook down his tucked-up robes, pulled his cowl over his head, and led the way to the baths. There was an immense cavern in the rock, under the walls of the convent, closed with a strong wooden door. The monk opened it, and immediately a volume of vapor came rolling out, so warm and pleasant that it was hard to leave it, though it drenched you to the skin as effectually as a shower of rain. I undressed in a sort of barn, provided for that purpose hard by, and sat quarter of an hour in the cavern on the stone benches of Dedalus. The consequence was a most profuse perspiration. There was a roaring in the remote parts of the cavern like a hidden cataract. The monk afterwards showed me a hole in side of the mountain, where a similar steam issued, with a still louder noise. When I paid the monk the usual *buonamano*, I found the holy man had cheated me by giving false money in change. The view of Sciacca on a hill by the sea, with its white battlements, its church domes, and the ruined castle of Count Perolla,[37] was very fine—its hot and sunscorched appearance was relieved by the groves of olives spreading up the sides of the hill, and over all the country.

One of Luigi's dignified acquaintances in this place was the Marchese Giacomo, a nobleman of great wealth, and a determined virtuoso. Luigi called on him with an offering of coins, and returned with an invitation to his *signore* to visit the marchese and see his pictures. He had a most admirable picture gallery—among the rest was an original of Guido. He kindly invited me to dine with him, but Luigi's care had supplied me a plentiful meal already. So much for one specimen of a Sicilian nobleman; I saw one or two more of nearly the same stamp at a *conversazione*. The next morning, I found Luigi at the *albergo* sitting over a bottle of wine with a large, fat, sleepy-looking man, in rather a dingy coat, whom on my entering, he slapped on the shoulder—"*Ecco, signore, mio amico il barone; un brav' uomo,*" etc., running on with a long string of praises of "his friend the baron," at which this extraordinary specimen of a noble kept shaking his large head in modest denial. The baron brought us a melon and some fine nuts as a present, which he did not disdain to place on the table himself. While our mules were saddling, I went with Luigi to see the domestic establishment of his friend. It was a large and reasonably clean house—some women were spinning in a spacious outer room, where some hens were cackling about the floor. The baroness received me in the inner room—the bed room. She was a stout rosy damsel, with good physical womanhood about her, and much beauty, though not over refined. She blushed, as though not used to entertaining strangers. Five or six holy pictures and little wax images with lamps burning before them were about the room. Luigi took down one picture of Santa Maria, the patroness of Sciacca, which he piously kissed and put into his pocket, observing that now we should have good weather till we got to Palermo. The baroness got me another, by way of making assurance doubly sure. Thus armed against fate we rode away. I was rather inclined to suspect a little humbug about the baron and his establishment, till I got to Palermo and I found by inquiry that noblemen of his description were very common in Sicily.

The weather was fine—the country to me uninteresting, since, though fertile, it was one great plain, on which the January sunbeams fell like scorching fire. The mules sunk to the knees in mud. The *contadini* were at work in the rich fields, slowly plodding after their long-horned cattle, sleepily holding on to the tail of their clumsy ploughs. These ploughs are worthy of all admiration, as partaking of the simplicity of primitive times. Iron seldom enters into their construction. They scratch up a little groove in the ground, without turning over the sod. The men were noble fellows; with gigantic busts, and massive limbs, and a wild untaught look. They wore the shaggy breeches of goatskin that make the people of this part of the island look like so many Robinson Crusoes.

Early in the afternoon, we approached the ruins of Selinantium [Selinus] over the fields where the Carthagenian besieging army had been encamped. The largest temple is of Jupiter—one column is standing; the rest have been levelled by the Carthaginians or by earthquakes. The stone is not of good quality, but a grey limestone, full of fossils—the relics of a yet remoter antiquity. How these sculptured rocks could have been transported is the great mystery to me, as to everyone else. The Sicilians will have it that these are houses of the giants; they may well be puzzled, since the national method of transporting building-stone is to tie it to the back of a jackass. Luigi laid a cloth on one of the flat stones, and spread a needlessly luxurious dinner of cold sole, oranges, almonds, wine, etc., which I disposed of—after which we proceeded to Castrovetrano [Castelvetrano].

The way was enlivened by the edifying singularities of the muleteer Michele, who walked along talking without intermission for an hour together, though no one listened or replied. He interrupted his discourse only to belabor his mule, and curse him in Sicilian. When we came to a steep place, he would take a firm hold of the beast's tail with one hand, while he belabored him with a rope's end that he held in the other—and thus they would scramble up together. Where the mud was more than a foot deep, Michele would place both hands on the mule's rump, and vault, with a sort of grunt, upon his back; wiggle himself about for a while to find a comfortable seat, and then burst forth with some holy canticle in praise of a saint.

Just after leaving the ruins of Selinantium, we were struggling along in the mud of a lane between rows of cork-trees and aloes, when Michele suddenly set up a yowling like a tom-cat—stopped in the midst of a note to expostulate with his mule—and then proceeded in a more dismal tone than before. Luigi clapped his hands, and shouted, *"Bravo! compare Michele; bellissima!"* at which the gratified Michele redoubled his exertions, and squalled at the top of his throat, putting his hand to the side of his mouth to increase the volume of sound. A young *contadino*, who was wading along on an ass at a little distance behind, was siezed with a fit of emulation, and set up a counter howl to one of the airs peculiar to the *contadini*. I cried *"bravo!"* to this new vocalist, while Luigi cried *"bella!"* and *"bellissima!"* to the exertions of Michele. Michele jogged along on his mule, the tassel of his woolen cap flapping; while Luigi twisted himself in his saddle to see how I relished the entertainment, remarking with a grin: *"Canta Michele!"* ("Michele is singing!")

In spite of the protection of Santissima Maria, a cold storm came up this morning, under the benign influences of which we issued from the gate of Castrovetrano. Four miles' ride brought us to the quarries of Campo Bello, whence was taken the stone of which the temples of Selinantium were built. It is a most extraordinary place. About the base of a little hill, near an old plantation of olive trees, are lying fragments of columns cut from the rock thousands of years ago. Further on are others completely carved, but not yet severed from the mother rock. The process of cutting them out was this. A circle, of the same diameter with the column wanted, was marked out on the flat rock. The workmen then hewed down into the rock, around this circle, until the column was long enough, when it was cut off and drawn out, leaving an orifice like a well. There were some where

the circle had just been traced—others where the column was standing ready to be drawn out of the hole—others where the hole was
empty, and the column was rolled down to the foot of the hill.

At Mazzara, I saw the effigy of Count Ruggeiri [Ruggiero][i] riding
over the prostrate Saracens. His tomb was in the church, but the
fathers being at table, I was much disappointed in being able to see
nothing but this effigy on the wall outside. Departed in a hard rain—
there is a gloomy satisfaction in travelling in bad weather, wholly
unconnected with the scenery or sight-seeing of any kind—we had
enough of it by the time we got to Marsala. I had ridden from sunrise to sunset without food, and felt like a starved wolf.

Marsala, as everybody knows, is famous for its wine. For travellers,
there is little to see. The fishermen here wear a hooded capote of
brown cloth, ten times coarser and thicker than a Mackinaw blanket,
and accommodating itself to the person about as well as a garment
of sheet iron. It is turnished with arms which project on each side
like the flappers of a seal, giving the wearers, who are naturally a
stout broad-shouldered race, a most gigantic appearance. The broad-
shouldered fishermen, with their ruddy visages staring listlessly out
of their formidable garments—the restless priests, with their large
three-cornered hats—the nun-like women, enveloped in their black
mantles from head to foot—the passage of mules and asses, shouldering their way through the throng—the squalls of criers and dealers
at the street corners—make altogether a lively and amusing scene in
the streets of this place.

Marsala was the ancient Sibylum. I saw the reputed tomb of the
Cumaean Sybil, under the Church of St. John.

The rocky ground around Marsala is pierced thick with narrow
passages and large subterranean chambers for an immense distance.
These caverns were made. by the removal of stone for building the
city. They are the dens of ruffians and the scum of humanity. Many
of the Sicilian cities have similar asylums for their rascals.

Morning. A gloomy and sullen day. We were riding past an old
house of *contadini*, when Luigi suddenly reined back his mule upon
mine, uttering in a whisper of consternation, *"Santissima Maria!"* I

[i] Roger of Sicily.—Ed.

looked at him, and saw that the natural ruddy brown of his thin face was changed to a most cadaverous yellow. I asked him what was the matter. He made no answer, but shouted aloud for Michele— who was a little way behind, among the trees—and then began to cross himself and mutter prayers. I could see nothing except a man with a gun, walking away from the road toward a group of a dozen *contadini,* who were standing in front of the shattered house. We had left them far behind before Luigi was so far recovered as to tell me that a man had pointed a gun at him from the bushes, but had desisted when he saw Michele. He added that next to the mountains around Palermo, this place was the most notorious for robbers in all Sicily. I do not for a moment imagine that the fellow intended us bodily harm—nothing is more likely than that he meant to exact a contribution from us—nothing more unlikely than that he meant to revive the nearly exploded custom of shooting a man first and robbing him afterwards. A simple robbery would be thought little of, while this last summary process would set the gendarmes on the tracks of the perpetrators.

We had lost the path, and got throuroughly wct through, before we reached Trapani. The fortifications of this place are tremendous. A soldier of the custom-house stopped us at the gate; a *carlin(o)* mollified him and he let us pass. We found an admirable *albergo,* and an excellent dinner.

I went out towards evening to a little gate that opened on the rocks by the sea. Some Neapolitan soldiers were standing there, looking at the breakers as they rolled in against the rock, sending the spray as high as the roofs of the houses. One of them, in answer to my inquiries, pointed out the reef of Asinello, just discernible through the mists, at half a mile's distance. This was the rock where [A]Eneas placed the green bough, when he held games in this place in honor of his father.[38] In another direction was the rock of Malo Consiglio, where the Sicilian Vespers were planned. The waves were breaking in white foam over its whole extent.

The renowned Mt. Eryx—now Mt. St. Giuliano—rises behind Trapani, next to Etna the highest mountain in Sicily. I went to the top to visit the ruined shrine of Venus—founded by Eryx—enriched by Eneas—resorted to by the old Sicanians, and in later times by the Romans. I found a walled city of six thousand inhabitants at the top. The narrow streets were almost deserted. The wind came through them as cold and sharp as on a January day at home; the citizens were wrapped in endless folds of cloth and goat skin. After traversing its whole extent, I came to the wide ditch of an old castle that stood a little above the city, over the site of the temple. The castle itself is tumbling to decay, and disgraced into a prison for captive robbers. Of the temple, there is nothing but a well and a fragment of a foundation. The scenery from this place was, however, charming beyond measure. There was a fine view, among the rest of Trapani, sweeping out into the sea in the form of a sickle, whence its ancient name, Drepanon [Drepanum]. Here Saturn dropped his sickle, after his surgical operation upon his father—or, according to the other story, here Ceres lost hers as she went to look for Proserpine. On this mountain, Hercules slew Eryx, and here was the tomb of Anchises. In after times, when Roman pilgrims came to pay their homage at the temple of their favorite goddess, a thousand fair and kind priestesses waited to welcome them. I was not so fortunate. A few crest-fallen robbers shewed me about the ruined and dingy fortress.

Descending, I stopped at the church of the famous Madonna of Trapani. A monk led me through the sacristy, and a series of chapels and passages, into the holy of holies, at the very heart of the enormous edifice. It was almost dark. Great lamps of silver swung from the roof; shadowy columns of marble, and the glittering decorations of the splendid altar were just discernible. The muleteer and guide went down on their knees, while the monk lighted the candles, drew aside the curtains, and displayed the holy image. Two angels of marble, in robes of silver, held rich lamps on either hand of the figure, which was covered from head to foot with a profusion of jewels, coral ornaments, and gold and silver watches. The effect of this little chapel, with its faint light and its magnificent decorations, was very striking. It was not at all increased by the drawing of the curtain and the revelation of the mystery behind. The lips, cheeks, and eyes of this statue were painted—an execrable practice, which ruins some of the best statues I have seen in churches.

From Trapani we rode towards the north. Met by the way a dead *contadino* riding on a mule, to which he was bound in such a manner that the body retained a position nearly upright, while the head fell forward upon the chest. The fellow was in his working dress—a remarkably large and powerful man. He was probably the victim of some quarrel. The men who rode with him seemed inclined to consider the affair as a good joke.

At twenty miles from Trapani, Luigi and I turned from the road to see the ruins of Segesta. We rode for nearly two hours over solitary and pathless hills. Two or three gigantic bulls, grazing the short reeds in the bed of a marshy brook, were the only tenants of this solitude. We entered a valley between two very abrupt mountains. The high grass swept our faces as we passed through it. Emerging, we were in the midst of an amphitheatre of high and solitary mountains. Before us on a little eminence was the temple of Segesta—the relic of a city as old as the Trojan War, and afterwards noted for its riches and its misfortunes. Agathocles[39] destroyed it, because it refused him tribute; put to death its men by torture, cut away the breasts of its women, and sold its children as slaves. He left not a wall standing, except this temple and a theatre too massive to be destroyed. I have seen nothing in art so striking and majestic as this solitary temple. Its situation apart, none of the temples of Girgenti can compare with it. Standing, as it does, a monument of the fate that overtook its builders, and in the midst of a scene so sublime by nature, the effect of its noble architecture is immeasurably increased. The city was on the mountain above. Its green side seems now more thickly spread with stones than those of its neighbors; but there is nothing to mark at a distance that a great city once stood there. Look more closely, and you find fragments of beautifully sculptured marble columns, and numberless wells filled up with stone when the city was destroyed. The theatre is at the end of the mountain, in excellent preservation.

It was near sunset when we descended from the mountain to find our way to the city. After fording a rocky stream at the bottom of the valley, we came upon the path. The attempt would be useless, or I would try to convey some idea of the scenery of this spot; it was certainly beyond any conceptions of the strongest imagination, whatever snarling cynics may say about the delusions of fancy creating beauties that never have existence. In the midst of it, a large cross, freshly cut in the bark of an olive tree, marked the scene of a recent murder. Just at sunset, we caught a parting glimpse of the melancholy temple of Segesta, standing alone among its mountains—a landscape of unmatched sublimity and beauty. I turned from it reluctantly, and rode up to the dark and dirty city.

The next day, nothing particular occurred but another ducking. We stopped at night at Partinico, a dirty village, which looked wretched and dismal in the dull rain that had set in. The *albergo* was like a deserted castle. I finished my dinner, ordered a brazier of charcoal which had no effect whatever on the atmosphere of the enormous stone-paved chamber. Placing the table in the centre, with the fire underneath, I went to work to study Italian in order to kill time. About nine o'clock the oil failed in my miserable little earthenware lamp, and I went out to order a new supply. I groped my way through two or three chambers—some damp cold passages, with a taper stuck against the wall, but saw nothing and heard nothing of inhabitants. I beat against a door with both fists till the old house echoed again—I shouted at the top of my lungs. A dead silence above and below! I groped down a flight of stone steps, till I was brought up by a strong door that evidently led to the outer air, and was secured with a number of wooden bars. I renewed my explorations above, and was rewarded at last by the sight of a light glimmering through the chink of a door. Five or six gendarmes were drinking wine within. One of them pointed out to me the lurking place of the people of the house—an enormous, cave-like kitchen, which was only to be reached by wading through the mud of the yard. About a dozen travellers were crouching here and there over braziers of charcoal, or lying on wooden benches, wrapped in cloaks. Luigi sat on a stone bench, eating maccaroni. He sprang up, the instant he saw me enter, and in half a minute the lamp was replenished.

There was a thunder-storm that night. In the morning, every mountain was white with snow. The gendarmes led out their horses, slung their carbines at their thighs, and rode off—the best looking soldiers I have seen in Sicily. We followed them, after Luigi had fought a hard battle with the landlady about the price of the lodging, and I had denied a contribution to the money-box of saint somebody, which was handed me as I was mounting. How much of the money thus received goes to the saint, may admit of some question.

An hour's ride brought us into the heart of the mountains. Meanwhile a furious snow-storm began, while we were riding up a very narrow pass between parallel mountains, by a road cut along the side of one of them. The snow obscured the summits of the mountains over our heads and the valley beneath us, where strong winds were whirling about the drifts, giving us an occasional glimpse of a muddy torrent tumbling with a loud roar among the rocks below. The snow-storm was accompanied by dull heavy peals of thunder, a novel circumstance to me. The passage was very much contracted as we approached its head. We saw there the waters of the torrent, descending in one fall from an immense rock into the gulf we had been passing. Though the passage was several miles long, we had not met a single man by the way. As we approached a little stone house, I asked Luigi what it was, but he turned round with an anxious countenance, and put his finger to his lips. We passed the place of his suspicions without interruption. Luigi drew forth and kissed his Santissima Maria di Sciacca, who, however she may have treated us in the matter of weather, certainly preserved us, as Luigi insisted, from the *briganti*. I thought to myself that I little deserved such celestial aid, as I had used my picture to light my lamp the night before. An hour more, and the broad flat valley of Palermo lay below us, green among the white mountains around it.

We turned off to the left, and after a long ride came to the monastery of San Martino, in a wild and sublime situation among mountains. The Benedictines here are all of noble blood. Everything is on a scale of magnificence and luxury—pictures, fountains, the church, the chapels, the library, the interminable galleries of the enormous building. There are no tawdry ornaments; everything is in good taste—but for ascetic privations, and mortification of the flesh, look elsewhere than at San Martino. The fathers were at table. I was served with a dinner of lampreys, and other delicacies, which a prince might have envied. There is a preserve of wild game, a formidable establishment of cooks and scullions, a beautiful *conversazione*, and billiard rooms, for the diversion of the pious devotees.

In a palace-like hall below the surface of the ground, sustained by columns and arches of the rich marbles of Sicily and lighted from above, is a noble statue of San Martino. He is a young soldier on horseback, with as little savor of the saint about him as any of his votaries in this luxurious monastery.

I have seen my last of Sicily. I bade adieu to Luigi, who insisted on my receiving a number of valuable ancient coins, and would have given me an hundred if I had let him have his own way—took leave of the Marstons and Gardiners—had my baggage carried on board the *Palmero* by three *fac[c]hini,* and followed it myself. An old monk was on board, among the crowd of nobles and exquisites, with the cord of St. Francis holding his tattered rags together. He had a little contribution box in his hand, and was gliding about in a crouching posture, with his cap in his hand, begging for his patron's benefit. He would look up into the faces of an inattentive group, with a humble and supplicating countenance, just like a starved dog expecting a piece of meat at a dinner table. A pleasant voyage and perfect safety was to be the reward of all who dropped a *grano* into the box. My heart was moved with compassion towards the old fellow, he looked so humble and so miserable. I tried to catch his eye to give him something—but my unwonted feeling of benevolence toward a Sicilian beggar was destined to bear no fruit—for just then all visitors were warned off. The old monk tumbled himself over the side into the boat of a charitable *fachino.*

The next morning the famous Bay of Naples looked wretched and dismal enough, under the influences of an easterly storm, through which Vesuvius was just visible. I went to the Hotel de Rome, an excellent house, with a restaurant beneath where you get and pay for precisely what you want, an arrangement far better than a table d'hote.

I spent the first day at the Royal Museum, where I could not determine which I liked best, the "Hercules Farnese," or the "Venus" of Praxiteles. This morning, I went to Pozzuoli in a *calèche.* Just after leaving the city, you see houses cut out, like artificial caves, in the natural rock. Not much further on, the road itself enters the rock, under which it runs for a great distance. The opening at the extremity seems like a mere point of light. This Grotto of Posilippo, as it is called, is very lofty, and wide enough to serve as one of the chief thoroughfares of Naples. It is as dark as Tartarus, and excessively damp and cold. The lamps that are kept constantly burning at intervals along the walls are a mere mockery of light. The shouts of drivers, and the heavy rolling of wheels down in this den, make a tremendous uproar, reverberated as they are by the rock above.

At Pozzuoli I selected a cicerone from fifty who beset me in the dirty street. I rode on the back of a donkey down to Lake Avernus, which lies shut in by high hills on every side; yet there was nothing very impressive or terrific about the infernal lake. Close to the bank is the Grotto of the Cumaean Sybil. The deep passages were filled with the smoke of torches, and the walls were blackened with soot. The deepest parts—the baths and chamber of the Sybil—were covered with water through which a man carried me on his back. The Sybil had a particularly modest piece of sculpture over the arch of one of her apartments. Coming to the upper air, I paid the three fellows who showed the cave what was justly due to them—they of course made a great outcry and demanded more, returning me what I had given them. They would not desist from their importunities till I brought my cane to bear a part in the conversation, which dispersed them for a while. As I rode along by the lake, I heard them coming again. This time, they brought for sale pieces of mosaic, and little bronze amulets worn by the Roman ladies, of the same delicate description as that which I had admired in the cave of the Sybil. I could only rid myself of their importunities by resorting a second time to the same summary measures. These fellows fear a cane as much as a thieving dog does.

I made the usual circuit about Baiae and Cumae, looking at all the temples. At the former place I stopped at a little *albergo*, where I got a bottle of the Falernian wine—whether the same that Horace used to drink, I cannot say, but the grape grew in the same spot. I saw Solfatara, too—a place I have long wished to visit, and which somewhat disappointed my expectations. It is the crater of an extinct volcano. The bottom is composed of a volcanic soil, with here and there an opening whence steam and sulphurous fumes issue with a roaring sound. About these orifices every stone and stick is encrusted with little crystals of sulphur. The ground sounds hollow when stamped upon. The hills around, which formed the wall of the ancient crater, are beautifully green and fertile. At every place the *custode* demands a *buonamano*, and invariably grumbles and follows begging after you, how much soever you may give him. Moreover, a troop of boys and men follow you with "antiquities"—which are manufactured in great profusion at Naples. Add to this, the beggars, most of whom pretend to be mutes, and make horrible noises in their throats to convince you of it—the boys who will wipe a spot of mud off your donkey's back, and then demand a *carline* for the service— and your insatiable cicerone—add together all these, and you have a sum of petty vexations, enough to damp any man's zeal for exploring classical localities. Fortunately I never had much to lose. I would go farther for one look into the crater of Vesuvius than to see all the ruined temples in Italy.

Among the most curious of the "sights" of today were Nero's vapor-baths—not unlike those of Sciacca, except that they consist of very long and narrow passages in the rock instead of one large cave. Seated in the entrance was a miserably emaciated old man, who stripped off his shirt, exposing his bare ribs and gaunt arms, and after lighting a torch, led the way down into one of the passages. It was so intensely hot that I told him to go back to the fresh air. When he came into the upper cave, he panted like a dog, while the perspiration ran in streams from his body. He reeled about unsteadily, and then sat down exhausted in a corner.

Friday. I went to the Lake d'Agnano, passing again through the Grotto of Posilippo. After visiting the minor lions of the place, I asked for the keeper of the Grotto del Cane, which is just on the bank. At length a fat surly old fellow, with a red cap, came slowly along, followed by two dogs. He showed none of the sharkish promptness of the other cicerones. Something had displeased him, for he was growling and swearing to himself. He said not a word when he saw me; but calling the two unhappy dogs, he made fast a cord round the neck of each, and waddled off sulkily to the cave, dragging them after him. Arrived at the cave, he bundled one of them up, holding him by all the four feet in one hand, while, with the other, he opened the door. The dog gasped and writhed about for a while, and then lay motionless, on which the old fellow drew him out by the hind leg, and tossed him on the grass. He soon recovered, ran back to the cave, smelt a little of the gas, snuffled in disgust, and ran to join his companion in demolishing a crust of bread which a boy had thrown down.

After this I went to Virgil's tomb, on the hill of Posilippo. I met a laughable adventure here. Like a genuine tourist, I thought I would take away a memento of the poet, and seeing a bush which from its position had escaped the violating hands of former travellers, I determined to get a branch of it. The tomb stands at the edge of a rock about two hundred feet high above the street; this bush was on the side of the cliff just outside an opening in the back part of the tomb. There was a stout iron bar to hold on by—no man of ordinary nerve and muscular strength would have the slightest cause of apprehension. So I told the cicerone to hold my cloak, grasped the bar, leaned from the opening, and got hold of the plant, which I was about to secure when I heard a simultaneous shout from both guides, who sprang upon me and siezed me fast.[40] I looked round at them. Both were pale as ghosts, with their mouths wide open, and eyes staring out of their heads. I asked them what the devil was the matter—they replied by siezing me by the arms and shoulders and pulling me away from the hole. I got free of them by a sudden effort, but they sprang at me again, and began to roar for help. "Oh, come this way, signore! come this way; you must not go there." I was a good deal vexed, but could not help laughing at being mistaken for a madman. I thought I would try a little intimidation, so aimed a blow with my fist at the nearest fellow's face. They dodged off a moment, but returned to the charge with faces doubly earnest and anxious, and pinioned me from behind. "Oh, signore!" they said, "we don't want money; only come up with us to the gate." I saw the folly of contending with the idea that had got possession of them, so told them I would go. Thus I went out from Virgil's tomb a prisoner. I thought my quiet compliance would have allayed their fears a little—no such thing; nothing would do but I must mount with them to the garden gate above. Half way up appeared a gang of men, rushing in hot haste to secure the madman. They were soon about me, when confiding in their numbers they loosened my arms. I was resolved not to lose my relic of Virgil, so despatched a boy to pluck a leaf from the door of the tomb, since the men would on no account suffer me to go myself. I got this memento of my adventure, and departed. I had some little suspicion that all this terror of my guides was counterfeited in order to give them a chance to pick my pockets; but all my money was safe.

I met at the house of Mr. Rogers, Mr. Theodore Parker,[41] and Mr. Farnum, from Philadelphia. I had already met Mr. Parker at the Hotel de Rome. Yesterday we went up Vesuvius together. "What stock in trade for an orthodox minister!" exclaimed Mr. Parker. The mountain is unusually active now. We stood on the edge of the great crater, which is three or four miles round and more than a thousand feet deep. In the midst of it, a great cone of lava rose up, from the top of which came smoke and fire, and every moment it would throw up showers of lava [a] quarter of a mile into the air, with a loud bellowing and an occasional shock like the report of a cannon within the mountain. The abyss that we were looking into was half filled with smoke and fumes of sulphur, which the wind drove down into it from the crater of the little mountain in the midst. The bottom was a crust of lava, full of cracks through which the liquid fire underneath was visible. What with the dismal bellowings of the mountain, the volumes of smoke, and the obscurity of the tremendous gulf below us, it was, as Mr. Parker intimated, a lively picture of Hell. We stood for a while, watching the melted lava whirling up into the air, and falling over the black sides of the cone, whose edges were continually crumbling and falling down into the crater. The grumblings and reports down in the bowels of the mountain grew louder and louder; the puffs of smoke came out thicker and thicker; till at length Mr. P. and I could endure it no longer, but determined to have a nearer view of the monster. So we scrambled down into the great crater. The bottom was so hot that it scorched our shoes. We set our canes on fire by thrusting them down into the cracks. There were numberless fissures and holes where brimstone fumes came up with a suffocating stench. We went as near as we safely could to the little mountain in the middle, which appeared at times like a fountain, flinging up showers of fire from a mouth many rods in diameter. At times, a sudden wind would come, whirling the smoke of this infernal outlet down to where we stood; which compelled us to make a prompt retreat, or else to hold the head in a crevice of the lava pavement, to avoid being suffocated. Our guides went quite near to the base of the cone, dodging the falling lava with great activity. Some of these melted masses must have weighed a ton. As they fell, they spread out over a large surface. The guide would make a sudden dash at them, detach a small portion with a pole, which he carried to a safe distance and then stamped by pressing a copper coin into it. After a while, Mr. P. and I took our part in the exercise, and secured several trophies. The floor of the great crater, on which we stood, had been a sea of melted lava only three days before.

We got some of the famous Lachrymae Christi wine at a house half way down. We reached Naples at three, where the outskirts of the town were deserted, with the exception of a few miserable old men and women sitting in the doorways. It was Sunday—the great day of the Carnival.[42] King Ferdinand, however, sets his face against the carnival, which for several years has been a mere nothing at Naples. This year, in consideration of the distress of tradesmen, he has consented, much against his inclination, to make a fool of himself. This was the day appointed for a grand masked procession, in which the king and his ministers were to pelt his subjects with sugarplums, and be pelted in return. There was a great crowd, as we entered a square upon the Toledo—the main street of Naples. While we were slowly driving through it, the head of the procession appeared. First came a dragon about fifty feet long, with his back just visible above the throng of heads, as if he was swimming in the water. He was drawn by a long train of horses. Five or six masked noblemen were on his back, pelting the crowd and the people in the galleries of the houses on each side. Then came a sort of car, full of bears, cats, and monkeys, all flinging sugar-plums. The horses of this vehicle were appropriately ridden by jackasses. Then came a long train of carriages, which we joined. The crowd was enormous. The Toledo was one wide river of heads, the procession slowly moving down on one side and returning on the other. Along the middle, a line of dragoons sat motionless, with drawn swords, on their horses. Mrs. P. was hit on the nose by a formidable sugar-plum, flung by a vigorous hand from one of the balconies. She was in great trouble, but there was no such thing as retreat. We got our full share. Mr. Farnum's dignity was disturbed—Mr. Parker had a glass of his spectacles broken—I alone escaped uninjured. At length the royal carriage appeared. Ferdinand—a gigantic man, taller and heavier than any of his subjects—was flinging sugar-plums with hearty good will, like all the rest. As they passed our carriage, the royal family greeted us with a broadside, which completed Mrs. Parker's discomposure. They threw genuine sugar-plums—the others were quite uneatable. The king wore a black silk dress which covered him from head to foot. His face was protected by a wire mask. He carried a brass machine in his hand to fling sugar-plums with. His uncle, his mother, his wife, and all his chief noblemen soon appeared, all protected by masks.

The procession passed several times up and down the Toledo, with occasional stoppages. One of these happened when the king's carriage was not far before us, while directly over against it, on the other side of the street, was a triumphal car full of noblemen. Instantly there began a battle. Ferdinand and the princes sent volley after volley against their opponents, who returned it with interest. The crowd set up a roar, and made a rush for the spoils. There was a genuine battle for the sugar-plums that fell between the two carriages—pushing, scrambling, shouting, yelling, "confusion worse confounded"; till the dignified combatants thought proper to separate.

The theatre of San Carlo here is one of the largest and finest in Europe. I liked better, however, some little boxes, scarce large enough for a hundred people, which are scattered thick along the quay, and in some of the inferior squares of the city. In these places you may see the performances of a character peculiar to the kingdom of Naples, called Pulcinella. I went tonight to the Teatro Sebeto—an establishment consisting of a pit, eight boxes, and a gallery where none but men sit. The piece was a deep tragedy, full of love, jealousy, and murder; dungeons, trap-doors, etc. Pulcinella here assumed the character of a pilgrim. He always wears a black vizard which covers his face as far as the end of his nose, leaving the lower part bare. His entrée, which was in the midst of the most tragic part, was greeted by a loud laugh. The father of the distressed lady was busy in bemoaning his afflictions on his knees, with hands clasped. Pulcinella kneeled down a little behind him, and caracatured all his motions most ludicrously. In the next scene, the distracted husband, whose lady has proved unfaithful, encounters the pilgrim and makes at him with drawn sword, taking him for the betrayer of his beloved. Pulcinella meets him with his pilgrim's staff, which he brandishes at him in a most laughable manner, turning into ridicule all his anger and distress. The audience roar with delight, but do not applaud. Pulcinella then has a scene to himself with two girls, each of whom falls in love with him, and treat[s] him to sugar-plums. Some of his evolutions are very particularly indecent. After this, he did not appear again. Tragedy resumed her reign undisturbed. After the death of the heroine, the curtain rose again for a dance, performed by several persons, who chased each other about the stage, beating each other with straps of leather, in time to the music.

Punch and Judy may be seen at any time on the quay. There are also jugglers, etc., in great abundance. Outside of all these establishments stands a soldier, with musket and bayonet, to preserve order. A whole company kept guard last night, in the porch of the theatre San Carlo, while as many more were distributed inside. Ferdinand has some fine-looking Swiss troops. There was a grand masked ball at S. Carlo last night.

I saw a funeral procession in the Toledo this afternoon. First came a large number of men in white robes, with white broad-brimmed hats, and white cloth covering their faces. The coffin, covered with gilding, was borne next, on a machine covered with gold and tinsel. Then followed a concourse of men in dingy black dresses, each of whom bore a little banner with a death's head. A soldier walked a short distance before the procession.

The men in white belonged to the company of penitents, who wish to expiate some sin they have committed. They are paid by the friends of the deceased. The money all goes to the treasury of the company. The men in black came from the king's poor-house, which contains six thousand paupers. These mourners are selected by the officers of the establishment, who receive the money. The funeral I saw was that of a man of high rank. From this downward, there is every grade of splendor and meanness, ending in the exit of some wretched *lazzaroni* who is put into a wheelbarrow and pitched head foremost into one of the pits of the Campo Santo. In some parts of Sicily, the poor are rammed by main force into a little square box, which is carried by two men to the common burial ground outside the city gates.

About sunset this evening, there was a great mustering of soldiers in the square in front of the royal palace. Among the rest, a fine body of cavalry came down the street; and some companies of the king's guard, selected for their great stature and fine appearance. There was a body of Swiss in their white uniforms. The whole open space between the elegant buildings of the square was soon filled by the soldiery and the crowd of lazy Neapolitans. It was a fine sight, as the sunlight fell on the bayonets and the helmets of the cavalry. All this was merely the preparation for a repetition of the sugar-plum farce of Sunday. It was a poor affair. I got well powdered with sugar plums, but the sight was hardly worth seeing.

The Toledo is a noble street. Every hour of the day, it is thronged with a dense crowd of men and women of every kind and degree. Carriages and carts drive along at full speed with a noise that would split the head of a nervous man. The shops are small, but elegant, and open on the street. Priests and monks, in every variety of dress— troops of military scholars, in cocked hats—straggling soldiers, mustachoed to the eyes—women in very neat and beautiful cos- tumes—criers of various commodities—and a host of well dressed men of all nations, together make up the crowd that swarms night and day in this street. The houses are very high and elegant. There are no sidewalks; woe to the absent man—he will be knocked down and run over twenty times a day, and have his pocket picked a hundred. A gayer and livelier scene could scarce be imagined.

The remoter and most obscure parts of this great city are quite as interesting. Here you may see an endless variety of costumes of the women, almost all beautiful and neat. There is something par- ticularly attractive about these women, who are seldom, however, handsome, properly speaking—but there is the devil in their bright faces and full rounded forms. Each town in the environs has its peculiar costume.

I saw Pompeii yesterday. From the nature of most of the utensils found there—which are of coarse workmanship, not unlike the pottery used here at this day—I was prepared to find a mean and sordid village. Not so, however. Many of the private houses were palaces. The temples were elegant pieces of architecture—so was the forum and the amphitheatre. We visited Herculaneum on our return. It is scarce worth seeing after Pompeii.

Pulcinella is a most original character. His ridicule does not spare the hero and heroine themselves. In a terrific scene of encantation and sorcery which I saw today, Pulcinella pretended at first to be very much frightened, but siezed an opportunity to knock over Death himself, who was rising out of a fiery pit to sieze him. He kicked a sultan in the face. He is always present in every tragic or pathetic scene, turning the whole to ridicule by his ludicrous carica- tures or his affected sympathy. He is always planning tricks to get his best friends into a scrape.

I saw him today represented by a puppet about two feet high at a little theatre on the quay, where I bought a box for two cents and a half. There was a pit that held thirty people; an orchestra of a violin and a flageolet; and one tier of five or six boxes. Everything was well encrusted with dirt. Above the stage, which a man might cross at two strides, was the classic inscription, very instructive to the audience, *"ridendo discitur."*[j] Another similar establishment had the following words on its roof, which was likewise embellished [with] a view of Mt. Olympus—*"castigat ridendo mores."*[k] Most of these little theatres are open several times a day. A man stands at the door, making the loud squeaking noise which the showmen use as the voice of Punch and Judy. This invitation is accepted by vagrant *lazzaroni*, sailors and their inamoratas, idle children and so on, who fill the place in a few minutes. The violin and flute keep them quiet till all are assembled—when the doors are closed, and the piece performed in a most business-like manner. The theatre is then

[j] "Learn by laughter."—Ed.
[k] "Correct evil ways by laughter."—Ed.

cleared, and opened again after a little breathing time is allowed to the actors. Outside of these places, Punch and Judy are screaming night and day to a ragged but picturesque crowd gathered around; beside a dozen other shows of all descriptions. Here, too, are fruit-sellers, and dealers in some very strange articles of food, which I could not master philosophy enough to taste.

There is a quarter of the city inhabited exclusively by three thousand ladies whom the policy and morality of Ferdinand keeps close prisoners—a place very edifying and curious to look at. There is another quarter, known as the "Old Town," where the streets are seldom more than ten feet wide, and often not half so large, though the ancient stone houses rise to six and eight stories. Here are shops of all kinds—small taverns—wine stands—and an endless swarm of dirty but picturesque men, women, and children. Long and low arches, so dark that lamps are kept burning there all day, connect the different parts of these streets, or lead out to the quay. Sometimes there is a wide street, or a little square, completely filled with a noisy and restless crowd of fruit- and fish-dealers, and idlers. The fruit is spread on the ground, or piled up on painted stands—the seller, man or woman, never ceases from yelling and screaming at the full stretch of lungs. There is an infinite variety of costume—from the cloak, the peaked hat, and the tight breeches of the Calabrian, to the cowl, cord, and sandals of the Franciscan friar. Near an old church, in this quarter of the city, is the square where Ma(r)saniello[43] raised his revolt—now occupied chiefly by a ragged army of dealers in cloth and old iron.

I saw, in a little "show" on the quay, a number of canary-birds who would fire cannons, pretend to be dead, come to life at the word of command; drag each other in carriages; and perform a number of other feats of the same kind. Admission, two *grani*; audience, soldiers, sailors, and *lazzaroni*, which last word means nothing more than a lazy dirty lounger about the streets.

On Saturday I left Naples for Rome in the diligence, with Mr. and Mrs. Parker. Coming to a little hill a mile from the city, the six consumptive horses attached to the ponderous machine were utterly unable to drag it up, though the postillions spattered and swore *cazzo*, and kicked their gigantic boots against the gaunt ribs of the miserable beasts, and lashed till they split their livery jackets. In vain a dozen ragamuffins tugged at the wheels—nothing would move us, till the horses were taken out and a train of oxen substituted. Then, indeed, we got slowly under weigh, when *crack* went something below—a jounce followed—a scream from Mrs. Parker—and then there was another stand-still. We had broken one of the springs. The conductor and postillions, after swearing and jabbering a full half hour, resolved to return to Naples. We did so; and got refitted in the course of three hours, when we sallied out again—came to another pause at the bottom of another hill—sent for more horses—after which we proceeded prosperously enough.

A little after midnight the summons of the conductor to alight and have our baggage searched, warned us that we(re were) were passing the dominions of King Ferdinand, and entering those of His Holiness the Pope. We rubbed our eyes, groaned, and followed our baggage to the custom house. There sat three or four officials, each of whom demanded a handsome bribe—and when this vexatious business was finished, the *facchini*, or porters, came thronging before the windows with lanterns, demanding a *buonamano*, while the postillions screamed for a *bottiglia* in the rear. This road is notorious above most others for custom-house exactions. An American, jealous of his rights as a traveller, refused a few days since to satisfy their illegal demands. His trunk was broken open in a moment, and searched to the very bottom, especial care being taken to tear and soil everything as much as possible.

When I woke at sunrise, we were passing the Pontine Marshes. It was a clear cool morning—the wide flat meadows around were white with dew; the ranges of mountains in the distance—Soracte and the rest—were enveloped in a transparent veil of mists, and hung with half-illumined clouds, dissipating slowly as the sun rose upon them.

The people in the villages were a striking contrast to the Neapolitans in dress, features, and manner. They stood gazing solemnly at us, with no trace of the gaity and vivacity of their southern neighbors. The women wore a most picturesque costume. Dozens of them passed us riding astride their donkeys, like men. At length we got a glimpse of St. Peter's. On every side of us were remains of temples, aqueducts, and tombs—Mr. Parker became inspired, and spouted Cicero and Virgil. Three young Romans followed us for a mile, running along in their rags, with their dingy peaked hats in their hands, constantly exclaiming in a wailing tone: *"Eccelenz[a], eccelenz! Povero miserabile, molto (di) fame!"*—"Your eccelency, your eccelency, I am a poor miserable devil, very hungry!"

Mrs. Parker, a pretty, timid, gentle little woman, was full of curiosity to know everything and see everything. She studied every ruin as we went along in the guide book, while Mr. P. was wrapped in his own meditations. We found a "centurion," as Mr. Parker called him, mounted at the gate, ready to escort us. We passed through the grand and imposing streets of the new city, with the soldier following behind. Mrs. Parker made a sudden exclamation "Oh, only look here: *do* tell me what this is!" Her husband burst out with rather an untheological interjection, and caught me by the shoulder, "The Coliseum!" But we had only time to look up at a mountain of gigantic arches, piled one on the other, when we were buried in the narrow streets below. The hotels were all crowded. We were fortunate enough to find rooms, but some English travellers walked the streets all night.

Monday. Today is one of the great days of the Carnival. Mr. P., with his lady and myself, went in a carriage to see the "show." The streets were crowded with maskers of all description, in carriage and on foot. A blast of trumpets from the end of the Corso was the signal for all the carriages to draw up to one side and the crowd to divide, to make way for a column of the Pope's soldiers. First came the Sappers, with beards and mustache that fell over their chests, shaggy bear-skin caps, and leather aprons. Each carried a broad axe over his shoulder, and his musket slung at his back. They were savage and martial-looking fellows. A long train of soldiers followed, with a body of cavalry bringing up the rear. So much for the Pope's summary measures for preserving order. After this, the Carnival began in earnest.

It was not the solemn sugar-plum foolery of Naples, but foolery entered into with right heartiness and goodwill. There were Devils of every description, from the imp of two feet high to a six-foot monster with horns, hoofs, and tail, and a female friend on each arm. There were harlequins with wooden swords, or with bladders tied to poles—which they beat over the heads of all they met—Pulcinellas, and an endless variety of nondescripts. Some of the carriages were triumphal cars gayly ornamented—full of maskers, men and girls, in spangled dresses. Instead of sugar-plums, they flung flowers at one another. Some of the women wore wire masks or little vizards, which left the lower part of the face bare; many, however, had no covering at all to their faces. Few had any regular beauty of features, but there was an expression of heart and spirit, and a loftiness, beside, which did not shame their birth. They flung their flowers at you with the freest and most graceful action imaginable. To battle with flowers against a laughing and conscious face—showering your ammunition thick as the carriage slowly passes the balcony— then straining your eyes to catch the last glance of the black-eyed witch and the last wave of her hand as the crowd closes around her— all this is no contemptible amusement.

The inferior class of women walked in the street, very prettily dressed in a laced jacket and a white frock that came an inch below the knee. Some were disguised as boys—some wore fierce mustache which set off well enough their spirited faces. Hundreds of men were shouting round the carriages with flowers for sale. Thus it went on for hours, till the report of a cannon gave the signal for clearing the Corso for the horse-race.

I saw Pulcinella at the theatre in the evening, in great perfection. He is *not*, then, peculiar to Naples, as somebody told me he was.

Tuesday. The last day of the Carnival[44]—a concentration of all its frolics. The Corso and the squares and streets for a great distance round were crowded with carriages and maskers again. The Corso is a noble street, of a most grand and solemn architecture, befitting Rome. Today it had little of its usual air of stately magnificence. Every window and balcony was filled with people, and hung with rich crimson hangings. The crowd shouted, laughed, and danced with redoubled vigor. The cannon fired at length. The carriages withdrew down the side streets, leaving the Corso a long perspective of gaudily attired houses and palaces, with a restless throng of fluttering plumes and spangled dresses from end to end. A body of troops marched into it again, dividing the throng to right and left, constantly dropping its rear files for sentinels as it had passed along, so that when it reached the end of the street, it had dissolved away to nothing. There was a clear space down the centre, and the people crowded on each side.

The horses were to start from the upper end of the Corso, where it expands into a square, surrounded by fine palaces and churches. The people sat on raised benches on each side of this square; a strong rope was stretched across the upper end, to restrain the horses till the signal should be given. Near this, under a canopy, sat the officers of the state.

At length a body of dragoons rode in, circling around the space, while their officer made his obeisance before the seats of the senate. They then passed out. There was a yell from the crowd without, and the horses were brought in, each by two grooms, snorting and plunging with terror. They had leaden balls, set round with needles, hung against their sides, to spur them as they ran, which they do without riders. There were large sheets of thin metal and gilded paper tied to their manes and backs. For a moment, there was an active struggle between the grooms and the frightened horses—then at a signal, down went the rope, and the horses sprang away at full speed down the Corso. The yells of the people passed down the street along with them, growing more and more faint, till they were lost entirely.

It was now almost dark. When I went back to the Corso, the street seemed on fire through its whole length, to the very roofs of the houses. The carriages had returned; the crowd were as active as a swarm of bees; thousands of wax torches were tossed about, extinguished and lighted again. This is the game with which Carnival concludes. Everybody carries a torch which he tries to keep burning, while he extinguishes his neighbor's. Flapping of handkerchiefs, flinging of flowers, blowing, and twenty other means were used to put out the lights. At every successful attempt, the man shouted: "*Senza moccolo.*" These sounds mingled into one roar which filled the street. The light of the torches glaring on the gayly dressed figures in the carriages and balconies, and then suddenly extinguished—the glittering forms of the maskers, leaping into the air to preserve their own light, or put out that of another—the shrill cries of the girls, who fought like little Amazons, and had strong arms, as I can testify —made altogether an appropriate finale to the Carnival.

There was a masked ball in the evening, where I could see nothing worth noticing.

So much for my classic "first impressions" of Rome! Yesterday was the 22ⁿᵈ of Feb.—the birthday of Washington. The Americans here must needs get up a dinner, with speeches, toasts, etc. It was like a visit home. There they sat, slight, rather pale and thin men, not like beef-fed and ruddy Englishmen; very quiet and apparently timid; speaking low to the waiters instead of roaring in the imperative tone of John Bull. There was not a shadow of that boisterous and haughty confidence of manner that you see among Englishmen— in fact most of them seemed a little green. A General Dix[45] presided and made a speech about the repudiation; the consul, Mr. Green[e][46] made another excellent speech—so did Dr. Howe.[47] Mr. Conrade of Virginia gave us a most characteristic specimen of American eloquence, and toasted "Washington and Cincinatus! Patrick Henry and Cicero!"

There are numbers of American artists here, some of them fine fellows. In fact, it (it) is some consolation, after looking at the thin faces, narrow shoulders, and awkward attitudes of the "Yankees," to remember that in genius, enterprise, and courage—nay, in bodily strength—they are a full match for the sneering Englishmen. Would that they bore themselves more boldly and confidently. But a time will come when they may meet Europeans on an equal footing.

Feb. 27ᵗʰ. A weary week of lionizing. I would not give a damn for all the churches and ruins in Rome—at least such are my sentiments at present. There is unbounded sublimity in the Coliseum by moonlight—that cannot be denied; St. Peter's, too, is a miracle in its way; but I would give them all for one ride on horseback among the Ap(p)en[n]ines. This driving all day, from morning till night, for a fortnight at a time, from church to church and ruin to ruin, keeping an account in a book of those that you have seen and those that you have not seen—it is worse than seeing nothing, and is very appro-

priately designated here "going through the mill." I met a self-
satisfied philosopher, one Mr. Smith, at Palermo, who denied the
existence of any such faculty as the imagination, and looked with
great contempt on those who could find pleasure in such a childish
amusement as looking at "old stones." "Don't tell me about your
Tarpeian rock. I've seen it, and what's more, the feller wanted I
should give him half a dollar for taking me there. 'Now look here!,'
says I, 'do you s'pose I'm going to pay you for showing me this old
pile of stones? I can see better rocks than this any day, for nothing;
so clear out!' I'll tell you the way I do," continued Mr. Smith; "I
don't go and *look* and *stare* as some people do when I get inside of a
church, but I pace off the length and breadth, and then set it down
on paper. Then, you see, I've got something that will keep!"[1]

I never thought, when I listened to these remarks of Mr. S. in
Mr. Marston's parlor at Palermo, that I should ever feel any sympathy with him; but a week of lionizing has convinced me of the
contrary. But I hope to go back among the mountains in a few days.

Yesterday I found a crowd of people in the Coliseum, attending
the company of penitents, who were clothed in a dirt-colored robe,
with cap and vizard of the same, and were parading from one to
the other of the fourteen little chapels that stand around the arena.
A cross-bearer, two lantern-bearers, and a priest led the procession.
At every chapel, they kneeled; and a prayer for deliverance from
certain evils was made by the priest, and followed by chants from the
penitents and the crowd of people around.

A Virginian named St. Ives,[48] lately converted to Catholicism, has
been trying to convert me, along with some of the Jesuits here. He
has abandoned the attempt in disgust, telling me that I have not
logic enough in me to be convinced of anything, to which I replied
by cursing logic and logicians.

I have now been three or four weeks in Rome—have been presented to his Holiness the Pope—have visited churches, convents,

---

[1] "Mr. Smith was an upstart speculator from New York, about five feet high, and
three inches broad—gulled and befooled at all hands, but fortunately about to depart
this life, for he was in consumption."—F.P.

Mr. Smith and his methods of sightseeing provide the materials of Chapter XXVIII
of *Vassall Morton*, pp. 162-66.—Ed.

cemeteries, catacombs, common sewers including the Cloaca Maxima, and ten thousand works of art. This will I say of Rome—that a place on every account more interesting—and which has a more vivifying and quickening influence on the faculties—could not be found on the face of the earth—or at least I should not wish to go to it, if it could.

It is as startling to a "son of Harvard" to see the astounding learning of these Jesuit fathers, and the appalling readiness and rapidity with [which] they pour forth their interminable streams of argument, as it would be to a Yankee parson to witness his whole congregation, with church, pulpit, and all, shut up within one of the great columns which support the dome of St. Peter's—a thing which might assuredly be done.

The Catholics here boast that their church never stood at so high and happy a point as now—converts are pouring in—wisdom and sanctity abound. There is an artist here, Overbeck,[49] from Germany, who is a man of wonderful genius. I visited his studio today. His works are scarce more than sketches with a pencil—but every face may be an hour's study, and speaks plainer than words the character of its author's mind: mild, earnest, and devout to enthusiasm. All his subjects are scriptural.

I went down to the Cloaca Maxima, which venerable common sewer still retains its ancient name, and still discharges its ancient office—as it has done for three thousand years, since Tullus Hostilius built it. The temples of Rome are turned into cattle-houses, or burnt into lime—the Forum has been a cow yard—but the Cloaca Maxima still belches out into the Tiber the accumulated filth of Rome, the only monument of the city that retains unaltered its original character. When the Tiber is high, the whole arch is concealed, but now you can easily see, by descending among some dirty houses and wading down an abyss of mud, a stream about a rod wide and of unexplorable depth slowly creeping along beneath the archway. It is best not to come too near—or scrutinize too closely into the nature of this subterranean river. There is good fishing there. The fish come up, as Juvenal says the pikes did in his day, to feed on the offal. Just below where it discharges into the river, you may see half a dozen or more large scoop-nets, arranged in the manner of a large water-wheel, so as to be turned by the force of the current and dip up any fish that may be swimming by. A fellow sits watching them, smoking his pipe, ready to take out the delicate morsel for the market. There are other flat nets, about twenty feet square, which are lowered into the muddy water horizontally by means of a frame-work of long poles; and then raised quickly up again, in the desperate hope that a fish may be passing above them. There are another kind of sportsmen about this place, and in fact all along the river, who stand on the bank with a kind of grapple made of the stem and pro-jecting branches of a small tree, cut to a proper length. This con-trivance has a long cord attached to it, coiled together on the ground like a whale-line. When they see any piece of drift wood or fragment of brush come floating down stream, they whirl the grapple once or twice round their heads, and send it flying through the air towards the valuable prize. Sometimes three or four are let fly at once for the same miserable branch of a tree—and frequently all miss, for the current runs as it used to when Horacles [Horatius] Cocles and Cloelia swam it.

The other day as I was standing in the entry of the Hotel d'Allemagne, a servant came up to me and said that my brother had been inquiring for me, and was now up stairs with another gentle-man. I told him he had mistaken the person. He asked me if I was not Mr. Parkman from America—he was sure that was my name, and he would run and call my brother now. So off he went, leaving me in some curiosity, but not without a suspicion of the truth. Sure enough, John and William Hunt[50] came down stairs, six steps at a time, and had me by the hand in a moment. The last time I had seen them was at Cambridge, when they bade us good-bye at table one morning, as they were about to sail for Europe—of course we were glad enough to meet at Rome. John was grinning from ear to ear at the idea of being taken for my brother. I went round with them to their lodgings, where I enjoyed the gratifying sight of *Peirce on Sound*, and Whately's *Logic*, which John, in an ebullition of Freshman feeling, kicked up against the ceiling. The whole family of the Hunts are here.

We rode to Tivoli—the ancient Tibur—together, the other day, with Mr. P[arker] and his lady in our company. We spent some hours in making the tour of the antiquities on jackasses—saw the villa of [H]Adrian—of Cassius—the modern villa of the dukes of Ferrara, which inspired Tasso, as well it might. Saw the cascades, too; and the temple of Vesta perched on the rock above; also scrambled down into the Grotto of Neptune—in short, finished the whole job, and persuaded the jackasses to carry us back to the village. Here we dined—the whole convoy betook themselves to their carriages, leaving my old classmate [William Hunt] and myself behind to undertake an expedition back into the country, to which I had persuaded him.

Claude Lorraine[51] chose one of the landscapes of Tivoli as the subject of one of his pictures, which I have seen, I think, in the Doria palace. What is strange enough, the finest of the cascades here is artificial—formed, like that of Terni, by turning the course of the stream over the rocks. The Anio is here conducted through a channel of very great length, cut through the heart of a mountain. You can pass from end to end by means of a narrow ledge by the side of the water, which rushes along by your side very swiftly with a loud noise, and emerging to the light, leaps over a precipice some hundred feet high into a deep valley, where it tumbles and foams among the rocks for a while; but, growing calm at length, winds prettily down among the fields and olive plantations at the bottom. Numbers of little cascades come streaming down from the mountain, and from under the arches of Mecaenas' [Maecenas'] villa to join it—so with the town on the heights above, and the Campagna like a dimly seen ocean in front, it makes, just after sunset, a landscape to which Claude Lorraine has not done justice.

We got up an illumination of the subterranean passage of the river—called the Grotto of the Syrens—by having bundles of straw set on fire, and suffered to float down on the stream. The rocks about here are recent calcarious depositions, which sometimes assume very singular forms. One of them, precisely resembling the breast of a woman, was exhibited to us as a veritable relic of Lucretia, the *"putana Romana"*—as our guide informed us she was, a version of the story quite new to us.

When we looked out in the morning and found the mountains white with snow, and the *piazza* below us wet and wretched, and the sky the color of lead, I thought my Sicilian experiences were going to be revived. But we got a couple of asses and a guide, and set out. No sooner were we outside the gate, than the clouds split apart, and scattered in all directions—the sun poured down bright and clear on the country, which looked all the fresher for the last night's storm. The road was full of knots of laughing black-haired girls— now and then a priest on a donkey would come jogging past and greet them with an expression of countenance where the temporal got the better of the spiritual.

We soon left girls and villages behind, and followed the road up the banks of the Anio, a rapid and headlong torrent. Its valley soon grew quite narrow. We came to a village at the top of a rock by the bank, containing a specimen of what our guide called Cyclopean walls, though the masses of stone were square and not polygonal.[52] Further on, we stopped in the yard of the convent of San Cosinato. It stands on the edge of the precipice, which here sinks sheer down hundreds of feet to the river. We roused up a father, who led us down the face of the rock by a zigzag path hewn into it, a work of no little danger and difficulty—the roar of the river alone was enough to startle weak nerves. To our surprise, the whole face of this rough precipice was honeycombed out into sleeping rooms and little chapels; in short, a monastery of Benedictines had burrowed into the rock and lived there. I have heard of hermits thus sequestering themselves, but a whole monastery clinging to the face of a savage precipice, above a stream like the Anio, shows an admirable example of courage and enthusiasm. Over against the rock rises a shaggy and wild mountain, and looking up the stream the valley expands into a scene of wonderful beauty. I carried away a flower as a memento of the gallant monks.

While we were stopping at a dirty *osteria* to regale the asses, Hunt and I had a tub turned bottom-upwards outside and spread our provisions upon it. Very good wine here cost three cents a quart. This *osteria* was a fair specimen of its kind. In a long dirty stone room, some muleteers and others sat drinking at venerable wooden tables—while some mules were refreshing themselves hard by. I waded along through the mud and straw of the floor to the upper end, where some olive-sticks were burning under a huge tower-like chimney. In the recess of this chimney, all round the fire, low stone seats were built; from which you could look up into the black gulf above, and see volumes of smoke lighted by the rays of sunlight that came through the lateral holes where the smoke was to have escaped. A woman discharging the maternal function, two dirty girls, two cats, and several children were grouped around this singular fireplace, all staring at the stranger in silent admiration. An old sportsman, who was drinking a flask of wine, with his dogs at his knee, in one corner, told me that the wolves had lately made an irruption, and carried off eighty sheep. Wild boars also abound here. I have seen them brought into Rome in numbers.

Leaving this place, we rode on toward Subiaco in a perfect amphitheatre of mountains. Those on the right lay in dusky shadow, for the sun was setting behind them; but on the other side the enormous bare rocks were glaring in the light, with their tops still whiter than themselves with the snow. Grey villages, with light smoke hanging over them, were scattered thinly along their sides and summits, a thousand feet in the air. The air was beautifully clear, and the afternoon still as death. Some of the distant Appenines were blue as the sky itself, and peculiarly shadowed in the oblique light.

Men and women were at work, pruning in the vineyards. The forms of the women were full and graceful, and set off to the best advantage by their costume—a tight bodice, namely, usually of a bright red or green. Their headdress is a handkerchief, folded square, and falling down behind.

We came suddenly upon Subiaco. It stood on the top of a detached rocky hill, among the mountains. Goats, cattle, trains of mules and asses, women with jars of water on their heads, old woodsmen with the heavy crooked chopping knife in their girdles and a bundle of faggots on their shoulders were coming down the different pathways from the mountains toward the gate of the town—for it was near sunset. The town was already in shadow, except the castle at the top.

All this was very well; get within the gate and the scene changed. A crowded pile of high and crumbling stone houses—streets so steep that a horse cannot ascend them, and answering the purpose of a common sewer for all the filth of the inhabitants—so narrow, too, that a strip of the red sky could scarce be seen between the tottering roofs—here was Subiaco; and not Subiaco alone, but Italian country towns in general, as far as my observation goes. The women, with their water-jars, were gathered around the town fountain—more were seated about the corners in a little public square, spinning. More still were kneeling, singing vespers, in the church. The men lounged about in red breeches, smoking and staring.

In the morning we passed down through the quarter of the black-smiths, each of whom, covered with dirt and hair, was hammering and filing in a species of narrow den under the houses. Thence, we went up to the mountains. We passed a bridge thrown over a deep and narrow ravine, where the Anio came down from the valley above. It boiled savagely down at the bottom, half obscured by the olive and laurel trees that grew thick in the crevices of the ravine. We rode for a mile up the mountain till we came to a monastery of Benedictines, under an impending rock at the top. The Anio twisted about like a white thread among the rocks directly below. It was cold as winter at that height. The porter was sitting in an old carved chair, with the brass basin under his chair, in the hands of the barber; so I called the sacristan, who showed us over the place. St. Benedict must have had a peculiar taste for wild and lonely situations. They have built the monastery over the cave where he lived from his fifteenth year. One day the devil came to tempt him in the form of a woman: the saint sprang from her embraces and threw himself upon a little thicket of briers that grew close by. They show the briers to this day, still growing in the same place! I was under strong tempta-tion to beg the fathers to let me stay in their monastery a few days—it is as strange in its interior as in its situation. Full of relics of the middle ages—and contains halls and vaults built partly by art, and partly formed by the natural rock. It seems doomed to speedy destruction. There is a deep crack in the cliff above, which leans forward, as if every moment to fall. I asked the fathers why they took no measures to secure it in its place. "Oh," they piously replied, "St. Benedict will see to that!"

Some hours after, when we had scrambled among the Appenines by a miserable mule-path, we came to a little village called Rocca di

San Stephano, where they insist that St. Stephen was stoned to death. Here was scarce a male inhabitant, except the *padrone* of the *osteria*, which consisted of one dirty and crumbling room, with a charcoal fire in the middle. Beside the *padrone*, there was a fat vender of salt and tobacco. The rest of the men were at work in the Roman Campagna, on the lands of the nobles. We spread out provisions by the fire and proceeded to eat, while the *padrone* and his friend looked on in horror and astonishment to see us carve with an old dagger, which was the only good knife we could find at Tivoli. The salt and tobacco man's wonder was still further excited by the tongue we brought with us—he had never seen such a thing, and opened his eyes as wide as his prot[r]uding cheeks would let him. We handed him a piece. He looked at it—smelt of it—laughed a sort of gurgling laugh from the depths of his vitals; then mustered his resolution and ate it. The other man hesitated. He turned his piece over and over, as if it might be poison, which, though it suited us, would not agree with a Christian constitution. He ate half at last, and kept the rest, as he said, to show to his friends.

They asked us if we were *"Inglesi?"* "No." *"Francesi?"* "No"; whereupon they looked doubtingly at each other, as if to say: "They are neither Italians, nor English, nor French—therefore they must be the devil!"

After traversing a great chestnut forest which covered the mountains far and wide, we saw a little village before us, perched on one of the highest peaks. We clambered up the steep pathway. Below and around lay in the sun a vast expanse of mountains, a panorama embracing the sea itself and the villages of the remote interior.

The battlements were ruined—the houses crumbling—the people dirty—but here we found none of the execrable inns of Sicily. The old *padrone* sat smoking at his porch, just within the gateway: off went his hat from his grey head, and with a multitude of Italian congees he ushered us into a large old house, containing long suites of rooms, some tapestried and furnished with ancient beds and chairs— others hung with blackened and dingy pictures. The *padrone* is evidently the great man of the village. Among the pictures are old portraits of knights in armor, priests, cardinals, and monks.

The beggars of Civitella call every stranger a *pittore*, because

painters are usually the only visitors of the place. Well may they
come, for the situation of Civitella is magnificent. I sat till dark on a
square Pelasgian fort, older than the Bible, watching the changes in
the scenery as the sun went down. Hunt betook himself to sketching
at once.

The old man had a fireplace not unlike a Yankee one. I spent
most of the evening trying to illuminate him on the subject of the
Indians, about whom he showed a very eager curiosity and asked
questions which showed great acuteness and some information. His
son, a stout fellow with less thirst for knowledge, stood behind,
contenting himself with remarks on the state of the paths. Two or
three priests, in their black breeches and three-cornered scrapers,
dropped in to see their friend—then came the full storm and rattle of
Italian conversation, with the true gesticulations, shrugs, exclamations, and offerings of the snuff-box.

We went next day to Palestrina, the ancient Preneste. Here we
examined the Pelasgian walls, and the ruins of the temple of Fortune,
with the extraordinary mosaic found there—and here we found
another remarkable *albergo*. It was kept by two sisters, one of whom
might be about eighteen and the other twenty, and both handsome
as the sun. They saw our admiration, which by no means displeased
them. We spent the evening before the fire talking with them,
though Hunt, who does not speak a word of Italian, kept up his
share of the conversation by signs. My Italian was not much better;
but the girls were as intelligent as they were handsome, and, I think,
as virtuous.

At six in the morning I was awakened by hearing a modest voice
below the window pronounce the word, *"Monsieur."* I looked out
and saw our guide standing below, looking patiently and pensively
up at the window, like a faithful dog—his invariable custom, for
having no means of knowing the exact hour, he usually takes his
stand under the window at least an hour before the time we tell him.
Taking leave of our handsome hostesses—who looked upon us with
some astonishment as natives of a country five thousand miles off—
we rode on to Cara. Here our good luck in *albergos* failed us. We found
rather a dirty hole, but no match for the inns of Sicily. It was a *trattoria*,
or restaurant, and therefore had a public room where a strange group

congregated in the evening before the fire. In the corner crouched two or three old crones, like living skeletons. An unshaven country-man sat on one side—fat and silent loungers from the town, with infant mustache—shabby dandies in cloaks—children and dogs, crouching together on the hearth. At a little distance, two or three thin-visaged and savage-looking *contadini* stood erect and motionless in the glare of the fire. Our guide Guiseppe sat drinking wine at the long tables ranged around the barn-like room. He had a very pretty girl to wait on him, who would come from time to time and stoop over the fire, so as to show to the best advantage her classic features and the enormous silver pin in her hair. Hunt and I sat telling each other college stories and recalling college recollections till the people had withdrawn from the room, and left us almost alone, in front of a glowing pile of half consumed embers.

The next day we went to Vellitri [Velletri] where we hired a conveyance to Rome.

Sunday, March—— [*24*] '*44*. There was High Mass at St. Peter's this afternoon. Several thousand people were in the church—hundreds of candles were burning about the altar, which was one blaze of light. By way of guarding the flesh of Christ from the too near approach of the over-pious, a line of Swiss halberdiers was drawn before the shrine, with their black hats, and the bright blades of their weapons rising above the kneeling crowd. The responses sounded through this gigantic church like a moaning of wind. There was previously the usual service in the Capella del Coro—where eunuchs supply the place of women in the choir.

Tuesday. I went off to Albano in the public carriage. In the morn-ing, I got a mule to ride up to the convent of the Passionists, at Rocca di Papa, some miles off. The Passionists are, I believe, the strictest of the orders of monks—wear hair-cloth next the skin—lash their backs with "disciplines" made of little iron chains, and mortify the flesh in various other similar ways. I had some desire to see the mode of life of these holy men, so went to ask permission of the superior to stay in the convent a few days. I bestraddled a gigantic jackass, which no sooner came to the steep part of the road, than he stopped with an expression of quiet determination. The boy cudgelled him in the rear with full force—the beast was immoveable. A man pulled him by the haltar—he grumbled his dissatisfaction and began to pull backwards, upon which I kicked him and beat him till my bones ached. He bore it for awhile—then down went his head and up flew his hind legs into the air, perpendicularly. Then he rubbed against the wall, to scrape my legs, then he reared, then twisted himself about till his head and tail were close together— then began a series of plungings and kickings that came near unseating me. The boy remarked that he was *"molto furioso,"* and ran off for another. This next one proved manageable, and climbed peacefully enough up the mountain; till reaching a wooded height, I saw Lake Albano, black as ink and set deep among the hills. The waters looked deep and sullen, as they lay directly at the foot of the steep hill, far below us. We circled half way round them among the rocks and woods till we came to the convent, which was a very large and ancient building standing alone on the rocky side of the mountain. Within, it was the gloomiest and darkest I have seen. The superior came out of his cell, like a rat out of his hole. I told him what I wanted. He said he was very sorry, etc., but the rules of his order would not allow him to receive me without a permission from his superior at Rome—which fairly defeated my purpose. Mancinelli had told me that no permission was necessary. I remounted the jackass and rode down again, thinking to go to Rome immediately, get the permission, and return next day. But the public carriage had already left Albano, and no other conveyance was to be had except at a most exorbitant price. I therefore walked out to see the Lake of Nemi. It was a most beautiful morning, and the scenery looked the brighter for the rain of the night before. The chesnuts and the elms were just budding—hundreds of spring flowers were scattered about the sides of the hills. Every place was alive with lizzards—most of whom had their tails bitten off in fights with each other. In the bottom of the wooded valley, or ravine, which separates Albano from Aricia, groups of women in their bright red national dress were washing cloths in the brook, and hanging them to dry on the branches of the olive trees.

The Lake of Nemi is like its neighbor of Albano, except that (that) it lies still deeper among the hills, and is much smaller. But when I saw it, the sun poured down bright and hot upon it and the mountains that fence it round, and puffs of wind rippled its surface—it had none of that cold and deadening aspect which Byron attributes to it, but was one of the noblest sights I have seen in Italy. One little village stands half way up one of the mountains—all the rest is a solitude of woods.

I had made my breakfast of a couple of rolls, sitting by one of the fountains by the roadside; and by the time I got back to Albano, felt a little hungry. I saw a sign over a door, *"Locanda del Americano,"* which I accepted as an invitation to enter. Neither the hostess, nor any one there, knew the origin of the name of their house—so that whether some enterprising Yankee had once actually set up a *locanda* in Albano, or whether the name was given out of pure love for the Americans, I cannot say. Americans are almost universally liked here, probably as contrasting favorably with the surly and haughty English. Talking with a priest the other day, he asked me of what nation I was—when I told him, he made a low bow and exclaimed, *"Bravo Americano!"*

This place at Albano did not, however, do the nation much credit. Wine and maccaroni were, as usual, all that could be had. Even bread had to be sent for. A dozen laborers were quarrelling over three cents worth of wine, on the question of who was to pay. This was an establishment of the middle class—the greater part are a kind of half-subterranean apartment, set round with large and dirty wine-casks, and furnished with dirtier tables and benches. Here there is a great crowd of ragamuffins, drinking and laughing—but seldom drunk—and usually attended by a very pretty girl. In Albano, nearly every other house has the green bough, or the painted door-post, or the little sign *"Spaccio di vino"*—to indicate that wine is to be sold.

Rome, Friday. Yesterday, I went to the Capuchins for permission to stay there, which was refused peremptorily; but the Passionists[m] told me to come again at night, and they would tell me if I could be admitted. I came as directed, and was shown a room in the middle of the building, which contains hundreds of chambers connected by

[m] "Their convent at Rome, beyond the Coliseum."—F.P.

long and complicated passages, hung with pictures of saints and crucifixes. The monk told me that when the bell rang, I must leave my hat, come out, and join the others—and then, displaying some lives of the saints and other holy works on the table, he left me to my meditations. The room has a hideous bleeding image of Christ, a vessel of holy-water, and a number of holy pictures—a bed—a chair —and a table. Also, hung against the wall, was a "Notice to persons withdrawn from the world for spiritual exercises, to the end that they may derive all possible profit, from their holy seclusion!" The "notice" prohibited going out of the chamber without necessity— prohibited also speaking at any time—or making any noise whatever—writing, also—and looking out of the window. It enjoined the saying of three Ave Marias, *at least*, at night—also to make your own bed, etc.

"The devil!" thought I. "Here is an adventure!" The secret of my getting in so easily was explained. There were about thirty Italians retired from the world, preparing for the General Confession[53]—and even while I was coming to this conclusion, the bell clanged along the passage, and I went out to join the rest. After climbing several dark stairs, and descending others—pulling off their scull-caps to the great images of Christ on the landing places— they got into a little chapel, and after kneeling to the altar, seated themselves. The shutters were closed, and the curtains drawn immediately after—there was a prayer with the responses—and then a sermon of an hour and a half long, in which the monk kept felicitating himself and his hearers that they were of the genuine church— little thinking that there was a black sheep among his flock. The sermon over, we filed off to our rooms. In five minutes the bell rang again for supper—then we marched off to a *conversazione* in another part of the building—where the injunction of silence was taken off. I told the directing priest that I was a Protestant—he seemed a little startled at first—then insinuated a hope that I might be reclaimed from my damnable heresy, and said that an American had been there before, who had been converted—meaning my acquaintance St. Ives. He then opened a little battery of arguments upon me—after which he left me, saying that a lay brother would make the rounds to wake us before sunrise.

The lay brother came in fact, but not before I had been waked by a howling procession of the Passionists themselves, who passed along about midnight. There was a mass, another prayer, and another endless sermon—soon after which we were summoned to coffee. I observed several of the Italians looking hard at me, as I drank a glass of water instead of coffee on account of my cursed neuralgia. Doubtless they were thinking within themselves, "How that pious man is mortifying the flesh!"

There was an hour's repose allowed—after which came another sermon in the chapel. This over, a bell rang for dinner—which was at eleven in the morning. The hall was on the lower floor—very long, high, and dark—with pannels of oak—and ugly pictures on the walls —narrow oaken tables set all round the sides of the place. The monks were all there, in their black robes, with the emblem of their order on the breast. They had thin scowling faces, as well they might, for their discipline is tremendously strict. Before each was placed an earthen bottle of wine, and a piece of bread, on the bare board. Each drew a cup, a knife, fork, and wooden spoon from a drawer under the table—the attendant lay brothers placed a bowl of singular-looking soup before each, and they eat in lugubrious silence. The superior of the order sat at the upper end of the hall—a large and powerful man, who looked sterner, if possible, than his inferiors. We who sat at another table were differently served—with rice, eggs, fish, and fruit. No one spoke; but from a pulpit above, a monk read at the top of his lungs from a book of religious precepts, in that peculiar drawling tone which the Catholics employ in their exercises. There was, apparently, little fructification in the minds of his hearers. The monks eat and scowled—the lay-men eat, and smiled at each other, exchanging looks of meaning, though not a word passed between them. There were among them men of every age, and of various condition—from the field laborer to the gentleman of good birth. The meal concluded with a prayer and the growling responses of the Passionists—who then filed off through the galleries to their dens, looking like the living originals of the black pictures that hang along the whitewashed walls.

A monk has just been here, trying to convert me, but was not so good a hand at argument, or sophistry, as the Jesuits. I told him that he could do nothing with me; but he persisted, clapping his hand on my knee and exclaiming: "Ah, *figlio*, you will be a good Catholic,

no doub !" There was a queer sort of joviality about him. He kept
offering me his snuff-box; and when he thought he had made a good
hit in argument, he would wink at me with a most comical expression, as if to say: "You see, you can't come round me with your
heresy." He gave over at the ringing of a bell which summoned us
to new readings and lecturings in the chapel, after which we were
turned out into the garden of the convent, where we lounged along
walks shaded with olives and oleanders. Padre Lucca, the directing
priest, talked over matters of faith to me. He was an exception to the
rest of the establishment—plump and well-fed, with a double chin
like a bull-frog, and a most contented and good-humored countenance. As we past the groups of Italians, they took their hats off
and kissed his hand reverently, and then immediately began to joke
and laugh with him as if he was a familiar friend—as I suppose he
was, as I have observed that many of the priests are to their parish-
ioners.

The Coliseum is close to the window of my room, with Rome
behind it—gardens in front, and endless ruins—arches—columns—
walls—and fountains—around. Now—about sunset—a hundred different church bells are ringing in the city, and the dome of St. Peter's
is red in the light of the setting sun. It is a sight that would intoxicate
an antiquary, and is pleasant enough to anybody.

After supper tonight some of the Italians in the *conversazione*
expressed great sympathy for my miserable state of heresy—one of
them, with true charity according to his light, said that he would
pray to the Virgin, who could do all things, to show me the truth.
The whole community assembled to vespers. The dark and crowded
chapel fairly shook with the din of more than a hundred manly voices
chanting the service.

There is nothing gloomy or morose in the religion of these Italians
here; no camp-meeting long faces. They talk and laugh gaily in the
intervals allowed them for conversation; but when the occasion calls
it forth, they speak of religion with an earnestness, as well as a cheerfulness, that shows that it has a hold on their hearts.

Saturday. This morning, among the rest, they went through the
Exercise of the *Via Crucis*, which consists in moving in a body around
the chapel, where are suspended pictures, fourteen in number, repre-

senting different scenes in the passion of Christ. Before each of these, they stop—the priest reads the appropriate prayer, and expressions of contrition from the book, repeats a "Pater Noster," etc.—and so they make the circuit of the whole. I saw the same ceremony on a larger scale in the Coliseum, without knowing what it was.

A thin, hollow-eyed father tried to start my heresy this morning, but was horrified at the enormity of my disbelief; and when I told him that I belonged to a Unitarian family, he rolled up his blood-shot eyes in their black sockets, and stretched his skinny neck out of his cowl, like a turtle basking on a stone in summer. He gave me a little brass medal of the Virgin, with a kind of prayer written on it. This medal he begged me to wear round my neck, and to repeat two or three "Aves" now and then. It was by this means, he said, that Ratisbon the Jew was converted not long since; who, though he wore the medal and repeated the "Aves" merely to get rid of the impor-tunities of a Catholic friend, yet nevertheless was favored with a miraculous vision of the Virgin, whereupon he fell on his knees, and was joined to the number of the Faithful. I told the monk that I would wear the medal, if he wished me to, but should not repeat the "Aves"—so I have it now round my neck, greatly to his satisfaction. Miracles, say all the Catholics here, happen frequently now-a-days. The other day, a man was raised to life who had just died in con-sumption—and now is walking the streets in complete health!

These Italians have come to the seclusion of this convent in order that their minds may not be distracted by contact with the world, and that the religious sentiments may grow up unimpeded, and receive all possible nutriment from the constant exercises in which they are engaged. It is partly, also, with the intention of preparing them for the General Confession. It is only for a few days in the year that any are here. Their "exercises" are characteristic of the Church. The forms of prayer are all written down—they read, repeat, and sing—very little time is allowed them for private examinations and meditations, and even in these they are directed by a printed card hung in each of the rooms and containing a list of the subjects on which they ought to examine themselves—together with a form of contrition to be repeated by them. The sermons and readings are full of pictures of Christ's sufferings, exhortations to virtue, etc., but contain not a syllable of doctrine. One of the first in the printed list of questions which the self-examiner is to ask himself, is· "Have I ever dared to inquire into the mysteries of the Faith?"

Sunday. This is Palm Sunday—the first day of the famous *Settimana Santa*—the Holy Week. I determined to get out of the convent and see what was going on. The day and night previous I had worn the medal, but had no vision of the Virgin—at least of Santissima Maria.[54] Padre Lucca was unfeignedly sorry to have me go with unimpaired prospects of damnation. He said he still had hopes of me, and taking the kindest leave of me, gave me a book of Catholic devotions, which I shall certainly keep in remembrance of a very excellent man. He looked at the book I had been reading the night before, and expressed his approbation. It was a life of Blessed Paul of the Cross, detailing among other matters how the apostle hated women with a holy and religious hatred, justly regarding them as types of the devil and fountains of unbounded evil to the sons of men—and how when women were near, he never raised his eyes from the ground, but continually repeated "Pater Nosters" that the malign influence might be averted.

When I got into the fresh air, I felt rather glad to be free of the gloomy galleries and cells—which nevertheless contain so much to be admired. I went to St. Peter's, where thousands of soldiers stood forming a hollow square, where a procession of bishops, cardinals, and all the high dignitaries of the Church were moving round in procession with palm-branches in their hands. The Pope was in the midst, seated on a species of canopied throne borne on the shoulders of men, with his Swiss guard round him, one of whom bore a sword whose blade—six feet long—represented flames of fire.

There was no more of this till the Wednesday after, when *Tenebrae* was sung in the Capella del Coro at St. Peter's. On the three remaining days of the week, the Church was to celebrate by appropriate ceremonies the scenes of Christ's passion. On Thursday there was High Mass in the Sistine Chapel, whence the consecrated bread, or Christ himself, was borne in solemn procession to the Pauline Chapel, the other side of the hall, where it was enclosed in a gold box, with the figure of a lamb upon it. This was to represent the burial of Christ; or rather, as they maintain, was in fact his burial. The box, called the Sepulchre, was placed in the midst of the high altar in the midst of a thousand candles which illuminated the darkened chapel, and the crowd rushed in and kneeled down before it. The cursing of Jews, heretics, etc., and the blessing of the people was the next ceremony. The Pope was borne as before on the shoulders of men to the window of the Loggia in front of the church—a cardinal came forward and damned us all in a loud voice, the people taking off their hats, and most of the heretics imitating them, in ignorance of the compliment they were receiving. There were several regiments of the Pope's army drawn up in a hollow square, in the middle of the Piazza, which was thronged with an endless multitude. Some of them had brought bags of seeds and other things, which they held over their heads to receive the benefit of the Pope's blessing. His Holiness stretched his arms towards them, and immediately the bells of the city rang by a signal, cannon fired, and then the crowd rushed at full speed up the steps, and pushed—fighting, scrambling, and laughing—through the doors to see the Pope wash the feet of thirteen Pilgrims, in imitation of the humbleness of Christ. I went up immediately to the Sala Regia, where a dense crowd was close wedged on each side of the lines of soldiers, who kept the passage open for the Pope to come out. He appeared at last, seated under his canopy, surrounded by his cardinals, bishops, and the soldiers of his Swiss guard, who to-day wore a steel helmet and cuirass. The instant he was gone, the crowd pushed furiously towards the door of the Loggia, where the Pope was to wait on the Pilgrims at table. The women screamed and fainted; the men swore. The soldiers stood composedly leaning on their muskets, unmoveable as statues. The people most distant would push—but when the[y] found themselves near the line of mustachoed guards, they recoiled. The door was thrown open at last, which redoubled the scrambling and cursing. In the Loggia, which is a lofty and richly decorated hall, a table was set, adorned with the images of the apostles, and placed so high that it could be seen above the heads of the crowd. There we stood an hour—no man could stir an inch—some grew cross—others laughed. At length there was a loud murmuring, or growling, among the crowd in the courts and staircases below. It increased every moment —the crowd in the Loggia grew restless, talked louder, and swayed to and fro. Cardinals and bishops jumped up on the seats of the table and stretched out their hands to impose silence. The Swiss, also, who had stood motionless hitherto at their stations round the hall, stirred in their corselets, and struck the butt of their halberds on the floor. At last the pilgrims,[n] dressed in white, filed in and took their stand before the table. Some looked embarrassed; some tried to keep from laughing; and others coolly surveyed the crowd. The Pope came in, surrounded by cardinals and prelates, to make an exhibition of his humbleness. He held a gold basin to each of the pilgrims, who pretended to wash his hands in it. They then took their seats. A cardinal kneeled and presented a dish to the Pope, who passed it to a pilgrim, who rose and received it, bowing with the profoundest reverence. When all were served, they began to eat, but apparently with no great relish. The Pope walked to and fro, with folded hands, looking as meek as a drowned kitten. He afterwards poured out a glass of wine apiece for the pilgrims, and then left them. The Italians seemed to regard the affair as an amusement; indeed one who stood by me said: "They expect us to feel reverence—it is impossible."

The soldiers marched to their quarters with reversed arms, in token of mourning for the death of Christ—to my thinking, one of the richest ceremonies of the day.

Two public carriages—with fourteen travellers—have been robbed by the *banditti* between here and Naples, and the travellers in one of them handsomely whipped with sticks. The reason of an attack so unusual: a jackass who was coming to Rome with several thousand francs, thought he would insure his safety on the road by hiring an escort—so he got *one* gendarme. The robbers heard of it—eight of them armed to the teeth came down from the mountains—the gendarme ran for it—the conducter lay down bellowing under the wheels—while the fellows rifled everything.

I heard it computed that there are forty thousand strangers at Rome, which must, however, be a great exaggeration. The English

n "They were no pilgrims, but priests, intended to represent the apostles."—F.P.

are the most numerous—esteemed and beloved as usual. One of them, standing in St. Peter's before the ceremony yesterday, civilly exclaimed: "How long does this damned Pope expect us to stand here waiting for him?" A priest who spoke English reminded him that since he had come to Rome, it was hoped that he would conform to the usages, or at least refrain from insulting the feelings of those around. The Englishman answered by an insolent stare; then, turning his back, he said: "The English *own* Rome!"

These ceremonies of Holy Week, about which so much is said, would not be worth seeing were it not for the crowd of people they draw together. On Good Friday, they celebrated, by anticipation, the resurrection. I was standing at the door of the Capella del Coro at St. Peter's, when Mancinelli came up and joined me. The choir were singing in a dismal and lugubrious tone—the picture behind the altar was hidden by a veil—the bishop sat with his hands before him, with his mouth pursed down, and his fat face miraculously long—all the priests looked wretched and disconsolate, as if afflicted with some awful disaster. "He is not up yet," whispered Mancinelli to me, in explanation of this dismal appearance of things. But all at once the choir came out with a grand crash—a bell began to ring— two or three cannon were fired from the Castle of St. Angelo—the priests and the bishop rolled up their eyes in an ecstasy—and the curtain was drawn aside from the picture. "He is up now," said Mancinelli. "He is just out of de tomb—now you may see how happy they all look; now de soldiers will not carry their guns upside down any more, because Christ is risen. The damn fools! Now see them all kneel—let us go away."

On Easter Sunday the Pope blessed a huge army assembled in front of the Church, for the second time. That night St. Peter's was illuminated by myriads of candles, disposed over its whole front to the very top of the cross. It was a kind of phosphorescent light— faint and beautiful. At eight o'clock all changed in a moment. Bright fires kindled in a moment over all the church and the collonnade around the piazza. St. Peter's was all at once a glare of light, and cast strong shadows among the dense crowd in front. It was a sight well worth all the rest of Holy Week.

Wolfe's Monument, c. 1830

Water color drawing by Lieutenant Colonel James Pattison Cockburn

(Coverdale Collection No. 343)

On Monday there was an exhibition of fireworks at the castle of St. Angelo, which in grandeur and magnificence more resembled an eruption of Mt. Etna than any artificial illumination I ever saw. This was the end of Holy Week.

The next day I left Rome for Florence, in the diligence—and left it with much regret and a hope to return. A young American named Marquand went with me. After two days and nights we reached Florence. A manly and soldier-like young Irish gentleman,[55] with his sister, and an old Frenchman with a lady to match and two young ladies beside, were the fellow passengers of Marquand and myself in the diligence. One of the Frenchman's convoy was an English girl, very spirited and intelligent and a Catholic—but a few years too old to make converts.

In Florence everything speaks of the middle ages and of the Medici. The Duomo is an enormous Gothic church, dark and gloomy, with stained windows. The Piazza del Granduca is surrounded by dark Gothic palaces, and has in its centre an equestrian statue of Cosmo I, returning from the conquest of Sienna. The picture galleries of the Pitti palace and of the Galleria Reale far surpass any in Rome—but there are few good statues except the "Venus de Medici" and her companions in the Tribune.

A quiet and beautiful place, full of ancient palaces and churches— the Arno dividing it in the middle, with four noble stone bridges thrown across, and a perspective of mountains and woods between the lines of fine buildings, both up and down the stream. No beggars in the streets—the people civil and goodnatured.

Sunday night thousands of people were gathered together in the Piazza Granduca, each with a lottery ticket in his or her hands, waiting for the drawing. The proceeds of this lottery go to the assigning of dowries, of ten dollars each, to poor girls who are in a hurry to get married. The people were excited, but in great good humor. This lottery was in celebration of the approaching marriage of the Grand Duke's daughter with Leopold of Bavaria, which marriage took place to-day in the Duomo. The people were *invited* by a notice at the street corners to hang tapestry from their windows

—accordingly the street glistened with red and green silk. Mr. Payson, American Consul at Messina, whom I was fortunate enough to meet here, was with me in the church. The church was illuminated, and crowded with the scum of Florence—we got wedged in the dirtiest part of it. Mr. P., who is six feet and a quarter high, saw the top of the bride's headdress. I saw nothing but a fat hog of a priest, who stood in his regimentals just within the line of soldiers before me. Before it was over, I got out. The square in front was full. I had scarce got into a breathing place when there was the rush of a signal rocket from the dome of the church; then a tremendous cannonading in the distance; then a stunning crash of musketry from two regiments drawn up close by, followed by a general start and squall from the women. I saw afterwards the bride and bridegroom, as they left the church in their splendid carriage, covered with gilding and liveried servants and drawn by six noble horses.

I went to the studio of Powers[56] the sculptor, a noble looking fellow and a wonderful artist. I have seen Florence—that is, I have had a glance at everything there, but one might stay with pleasure for months. Its peculiar architecture and its romantic situation make it striking enough at first sight, but the interest increases, instead of diminishing. It is impossible to have seen enough of its splendid picture galleries, gardens, and museums. The people, too, are as attentive and obliging as the rest of the Italians—and the town is not infected with cicerones and other beggars. There is, however, one public character, on the stage for these ten years past, who generally astonishes foreigners a little. I was sitting in a *caffè* one morning when I saw a very pretty woman, about twenty-five, with a basket of flowers on her arm, dancing about the sidewalk and distributing her flowers to every decent-looking person she met. She caught my eye fixed on her, and bounded into the *caffè* with a large bunch of flowers, which she fastened into my button hole; laughed, and ran off to repeat the same operation on somebody else. She must once have been extremely handsome—she was very good-looking still; and looked all the better for a most inimitable expression of arch impudence acquired in the course of her flower-dealing speculations, and in the other avocations which no doubt she follows. Her plan is to give flowers to all the strangers she can find, and trust to their generosity for her pay at some future day. She is sure to get twice the value of her flowers—at least if others treat her as well as I did.

On Wednesday I left Florence, unsatisfied but unable to stay longer. After all, I shall not see Granada—at least for some years; thanks to the cursed injury[57] that brought me to Europe: for as I find no great improvement, I judge it best to see what a French doctor can do for me, instead of running about Spain. I called a *facchino* to carry down my baggage to the diligence office for Milan, but was answered: "*Non si può andare, signore; bisogna aspettare, perchè è morto il nostro primo ministro dello [di] stato.*" While I was wondering what connexion the death of the first minister of state could have with the detention of my baggage, the street before the hotel door was suddenly filled with a dense crowd of people, all scrambling in the direction of the Cathedral, as if some extraordinary sight was to be seen. The throng seemed interminable—the whole length of the street was black with it—even one of the distant bridges of the Arno was covered with men, women, and children. It was late, and the diligence waits for no man; I exhorted the *facchino* to be up and doing —he expanded his hands and shrugged his shoulders, by way of expressing the helplessness of any attempt to make head against such a current; when providentially a large waggon, with two furious horses and a reck[l]ess driver, came up the street, scattering the crowd to right and left and jamming them against the sides of the houses, as it came on like a war-chariot driving through the ranks of a hostile army. The *facchino* saw his chance—made a desperate effort, and siezed the tail of the waggon fast with one hand, while he dragged his little cart of baggage with the other. Thus we got in good time to the office. I bade adieu to Mr. and Mrs. Payson, who with their daughter have just arrived from Messina, and of whose usual kindness to strangers I have certainly had my full share.

The diligence was full of Frenchmen. In one day and one night we got to Bologna. Here, in the yard of the office, among the soldiers and other officials who stood with folded arms listlessly staring at the strangers, was an animal nearly seven feet high, with a face like a large baboon. His motions, too, exactly resembled a large monkey's.

He bounded about, swinging himself up and down the diligence, tossing about heavy trunks and bales as if they were feathers, with his long muscular arms. He kept his eyes rolling about in his head, glancing at everything in the yard with an expression of infinite alacrity and anxiety; and whenever he saw anything that met his disapproval, he would jump to rectify it, with a sort of angry chattering in his throat. He was a deaf mute. I wanted my passport to be taken from the police, and applied for that purpose to the conductor of the diligence, who referred me to this human baboon. I protested against the employment of such a negotiator, but the conductor assured me that all would be safe in his hands. The animal stood by, meanwhile, attempting to express, by horrible contortions of his features, his sense of responsibility; and kept pressing his enormous skinny hand upon his heart. I gave him the commission— and in fact, when I entered the yard next morning, the first object I met was the mute bounding with a loud chattering towards me, with the passport in his hand. He took off his hat most gracefully when I gave him two *pauls* for his trouble.

Bologna is a strange-looking place. Here is none of the gaiety, the noise, the rush, and the endless variety of picturesque costume you see at Naples. The people walk gravely about their business— those of them that have any business. The streets seem, by comparison with the cities of Southern Italy, quite deserted—but the architecture is beautiful. Every sidewalk is beneath an elegant portico, supported by rows of columns—often of marble—which run the whole length of the streets and make a very fine appearance, especially when these long collonnades are lighted in the evening.

The Church of St. Petronio—a very ancient and very large Gothic building—is famous as having been the scene of Charles V's coronation. The roof is supported by innumerable lofty and slender columns—every side chapel has a splendid stained window, which sheds its peculiar light over the church. The scutcheons of noble houses—the tombs of nobles—the relics of saints—and a number of ancient pictures and effigies, give the old church an air of feudal times. The piazza in front wears an aspect in accordance with the dingy walls and heavy massive arches of the old palaces about it, and the high tower of Asinelli rising above the houses a short way off.

The next day, getting under weigh again, we passed through the duchy of Modena, and met the Duke in his carriage. In the city of Modena, I found an Italian translation of *The Last of the Mohicans*. I have seen translations of nearly all Cooper's novels, here and in Sicily.

We next entered the duchy of Parma. At the city, the diligence was to make a stay of some hours. I went out in search of a dinner, and enquired of a man, who was sitting at his shop door, if he could direct me to a *trattoria*, or restaurant. "*Signore*," he replied, "come with me, and I will show you the best *trattoria* in Parma." Passing a street or two, he opened a little door which led into a black entry, whence another smaller door conducted to a flight of stone steps. I stumbled down these steps and found myself in a twilight den with a mud floor, where a charcoal fire was burning in a corner, and two dirty blackguards were devouring something at an oak table such as you see in the lowest *osterias* and wineshops. Some hens and a few disgusting children were wandering about the floor. The *padrone*, a lubberly fellow with a red cap, emerged from a dark corner. "Would your excellency like dinner? Please step this way, and I will have it ready in a moment." On occasions of necessity, I can eat anything that a dog can, but I had no mind to banquet gratuitously on dirt; so, telling the *padrone* that his establishment was not to my taste, I went off, leaving him growling in the rear. An old soldier, who sat in a doorway with his fatigue-cap on one side of his shaggy head while he smoked his pipe and twirled his grey mustache, pointed out to me a very decent place, where I found a respectable dinner.

This finished, I proceeded to look at the town, and picked up a man who walked around with me through the whole. Among the rest I visited the beautiful garden of the Duke, which was filled with the song of birds and cooled and shaded by fountains and high trees —a most agreeable contrast to the dirt and hubbub of the city. The troops were mustering and the bands playing in the court-yards of the Duke's palace. The hall was brilliantly lighted, and centries walked to and fro within. A part of his guard were stationed at the ancient and massive gateway of the palace-yard—some talked listlessly—some slept seated on the benches—others lay stretched at full length, to get rid of time till their turn of duty should come.

Feeling inclined to imitate their example, I went to the diligence and slept there, till the harnessing of the horses and the arrival of the other passengers waked me. At ten in the evening we left Parma.

At five in the morning we were at Piacenza. Here we stopped an hour or two. Here again the striking difference between the towns of Northern and Southern Italy was manifested. The people looked as grave and solemn as the brick fronts of the palaces and churches. The town was just bestirring itself. Well dressed men were thronging to the *caffès* for breakfast—the shops were being opened, and the market people coming in with their produce. Tall *contadini* were driving flocks of goats about the street, stopping and milking one into a little tin measure whenever some housekeeper or the servant of some *caffè* came out to demand *latte fresca*.

There was an amusing concourse of market people in the public piazza, before the lofty front of the old government palace. Cheeses, meat, butter, eggs, and piles of live hens, tied neck and heels as you see them in Canada, were spread in every direction over the pavement, surrounded by sellers and purchasers, both apparently half asleep. At a little distance were two long lines of women and men, each with a basket of eggs in hand, standing immoveable with an expression of patient resignation, waiting for a purchaser. The men were little shrivelled farmers, in breeches and broad hats, with staffs in their hands and dickeys standing up erect, like diminutive Englishmen. High above this motley swarm of helpless humanity rose the statue of some great lord of the Farnese family, seated on horseback, holding his truncheon of command as if at the head of an army; and looking as if one act of his single will, or one movement of his armed hand, would be enough to annihilate the whole swarm of poor devils below him.

The fish market was under the arches, and in the enclosures of the palace. Here were gigantic eels fresh taken from the Po; pike, crawfish, and bull-frogs. These last looked exceedingly delicate, with their pantaloons taken off, and their heart and liver folded between their forepaws.

We crossed the Po by a wretched bridge of boats, and entered Lombardy and the domains of Austria. The black eagle of Austria was painted above the guard-house on the further bank, where a dozen sullen-looking soldiers loitered about. There was a barrack of them near the custom house, w[h]ere we must stop an hour and a half to be searched, and to pay the fellows for doing it. After that, we rode all day through a beautiful and fertile country, passing through Lodi, the scene of Bonaparte's victory, till at night we entered Milan, saturated with dust.

Sunday, April 21ˢᵗ. The Milan Cathedral is worthy of Rome—I like it as well as St. Peter's. Milan has a forum, an amphitheatre, and a noble triumphal arch, the last two commenced by Napoleon when he was here. I went to the top of the arch, and looking to the north, saw what seemed light streaks of cloud high in the air. As I looked at them, the idea crossed me: "Possibly they may be the Alps themselves!"—yet I thought it very unlikely they could be seen on a sultry and hazy day like this, at such a distance. I watched them for a long time—they did not change position or figure, yet to my eye— not unpracticed in observing mountains—they looked more and more like thin clouds. I inquired of a man what they were—they were in fact the Alps! He pointed out the different peaks, and the situation of the various passes. The Splügen, the highest and wildest of all, and which I mean to pass, lay hidden in black piles of clouds that rose between it and the inferior mountains around the Lake of Como.

This Triumphal Arch was designed by Napoleon as the termination of his road of the Simplon. Curse him and his roads; he should have left the Alps alone. I will steer clear of him. The country about here looks like anything but the neighbor of such a wilderness of mountains; it is as flat as the ocean, and green with rich vegetation. The forum and the Place of Arms are thickly studded with lime and horsechesnut trees, just budding in the warm spring weather; and the ditches below the ramparts of the city are bordered by elms and weeping willows. The Simplon itself, a wide level road running straight northward for the mountains, is flanked by a double line of fine trees. The whole plain of Milan is bright and beautiful in this spring weather.

As for the city, it is well enough. The people are different in appearance, in manners, in language, and in habits from the Southern Italians. The women are all out sunning themselves; whole flights of them came out of the cathedral, with little black veils flung over their heads, and mass-books in their hands. Their faces and figures are round and rich—of the fiery black eye of Rome I have seen nothing; their eyes are blue and soft, and have rather a drowsy meek expression, and they *look* excessively modest.

This morning when the whole city was quiet, the shops shut in honor of Sunday, the people issuing from the cathedral, gentlemen walking listlessly about, and porters and *contadini* sitting idle at the edge of the sidewalks, there was a group of gentlemen taking their coffee under awnings in front of each of the *caffès* in the piazza before the cathedral. This vagabond way of breakfasting and seeing the world at the same time is very agreeable. There is no place where you can be more independent than in one of these cities—when you are hungry, there is always a restaurant and a dinner at a moment's notice—when you are thirsty, there is always a *caffè* at hand. If you are sleepy, your room awaits you—a dozen sneaking waiters are ready at your bidding, and glide about like shadows to do what you may require, in hope of your shilling when you go away. But give me Ethan Crawford, or even Tom,[58] in place of the whole race of waiters and *garçons*. I would ask their pardon for putting them in the same sentence, if they were here.

Leonardo de Vinci's "Last Supper" is here—in the refectory of a suppressed convent—but miserably injured, or rather destroyed, by the damps of three centuries and a half. An old man who has charge of the place told me that he was at the Bridge of Lodi, and was a sergeant at Marengo.

A funeral procession filed into the cathedral, each priest, layman, woman, and child with an enormous wax candle in hand. The noble chapel, at the left extremity of the transept, was hung with black for the occasion; the coffin was placed in the midst; and the ceremonies were performed. The priests seemed not fairly awake—one fat bull-frog of a fellow would growl out of his throat his portion of the holy psalmody, interrupting himself in some interesting conversation with his neighbor, and resuming it again as soon as the religious office was performed. Another would gape and yawn in the midst of his musical performances—another would walk about looking at the people, or the coffin, or the kneeling women, singing meanwhile with the most supreme indifference and content on his fat countenance. I could imagine the subject of their conversation, as they walked out in a double file, leaving the coffin to the care of the proper officials, after they had grunted a concluding anthem over it: "Well, we've fixed this fellow's soul for him. It was a nasty job; but it's over now. Come, won't you take something to drink?"

I used to like priests, and take my hat off and make a low bow, half in sport and half in earnest, whenever I met them—but I have got to despise the fellows. Yet I have met admirable men among them; and have always been treated by them all with the utmost civility and attention. Civility is almost universal among these Italians—farther south, it is manifested in gesticulations, takings-off of the hat, bowings, and reiterated exclamations of *"padrone,"* which is equivalent to "your servant, sir." Here it is shown rather in deeds than in words; thank a man for any favor—he does not scrape and flourish, and say *"padrone"*—he only smiles quietly and replies *"niente fatto."*

I asked a man the way to one of the palaces this morning—nothing would satisfy him, but to go with me the whole way, which was a full mile, and when I thanked him, it was *"niente fatto"*—"I have done nothing." A ragged man with one eye knocked out, who guided me for quarter of an hour through the intricate streets, was quite angry when I offered him a *zwanziger.*

I met Marquand in a picture gallery, and was not sorry to find an acquaintance and countryman, where I supposed I was alone. We went up to the roof of the cathedral together—and saw Milan, with every street laid open to view, and the whole current of population that was circulating through them, like the skinned specimens of anatomy in the Florentine museum. Palaces, churches, and arches, and league upon league of the flat surrounding country intersected by roads, all converging to the city—all seemed to lay directly beneath. As for the church, sixty-four hundred statues, large as life, adorn its sides, roof, and the countless marble spires that rise all around you, like the masts of vessels in a crowded harbor. Thirty-six hundred statues are still to be placed in their stations—10,000 in all. All is white marble—carved everywhere into fruit and flowers.

We next went under the church to see the tomb of St. Carlo Bor[r]omeo—the richest tomb,so they told us, in the world. The coffin is of pure rock chrystal (from the Alps!) set in silver, and adorned with sixty little images of solid silver. The saint lies embalmed within, as plainly visible as if nothing intervened—clothed in his pontificals, with golden images—the votive offerings of princes—crucifixes of emeralds, and other splendid ornaments arranged about his body— *à la* Indian. The chapel is completely encased in silver, wrought to represent the events of the saint's life. I write on the Lake of Como, with three women, a boy, and four men looking over my shoulder, but they cannot read English.

I wrote the above as the lake steamer lay waiting for her passengers, as time has become a valuable commodity to me. This morning I had just time to give one parting glance at the cathedral, which, like St. Peter's, improves on acquaintance—but not to the same degree. It requires some imagination and some grasp of mind to fully comprehend St. Peter's, and great study, and, in my case, a strong effort beside. For there is no point where more than half of the church can be seen—the rest must be imagined. Not one in ten who visit St. Peter's thinks of the domes and the chapels that are hidden from his sight—they look at the great dome and the central nave, and omit to take the rest—all that lies behind the columns and between the arches—into account. But in the Milan Cathedral, you can embrace all at a glance—yet with every visit, the beauty and majesty of its hundred and sixty marble columns, of its rich tombs, its carvings, the rich fret-work of the roof and dome, and of the windows painted [with] the histories of saints, strike you with a stronger effect.

Milan has a sort of counterpart of Pulcinella, called Gerolamo; but I believe that he appears at one theatre only, which is christened after him Teatro Gerolamo. I saw an exhibition of wax figures, among which was one of a dead Christ, covered by a sheet which the showman lifted away with great respect. The spectators, who consisted of five or six young men, immediately took their hats off.

Yet, in spite of their respect for the subject on which the artist had exercised his skill, they did not refrain from making comments on the execution of the figure.

I am now at the little village of Colico, on the north extremity of the Lake of Como. Some Swiss, Bohemians, and Tyrolese are singing at the top of their voices over their wine in the room below.

I have seen nothing at home or abroad more beautiful than this lake. It reminds me of Lake George—the same extent, the same figure, the same chrystal purity of waters, the same wild and beautiful mountains on either side. But the comparison will not go farther. Here are a hundred palaces and villages scattered along the water's edge, and up the declivities. There is none of that shaggy, untamed aspect in the mountains—no piles of rocks grown over with stunted bushes, or half-decayed logs fallen along the shore. There are none of those little islands, covered with rough and mossgrown pine trees, which give a certain savage character to the beauties of Lake George. All here is like a finished picture: even the wildest rocks seem softened in the air of Italy. Give me Lake George, and the smell of the pine and fir! But now I am at the foot of the Splügen, and the Alps all around, covered with snow, their sharp summits just losing the red tinge of the evening. Not long since the lake was all in a glow; but now it is like a sheet of lead, and the western mountains have become dark as night. The path I have chosen is by far the sublimest and most savage of all; and it is little frequented. Tomorrow I shall be where I have wished to be for years.

Andeer. A village just beyond the pass, in the midst of the mountains. The Splügen itself disappointed me—scarce any part of it was superior to the Notch of the White Mountains,° which the lower parts of it greatly resemble. We were from two in the morning till four in the afternoon in getting across. Among the glaciers and endless snows at the summit it was impossible for any carriage to pass; so the horses were taken out at the Austrian government house near the top, and fastened each to a small sled. Two of the sleds carried the baggage—the other two held myself and the other

   ° Crawford Notch.—Ed.

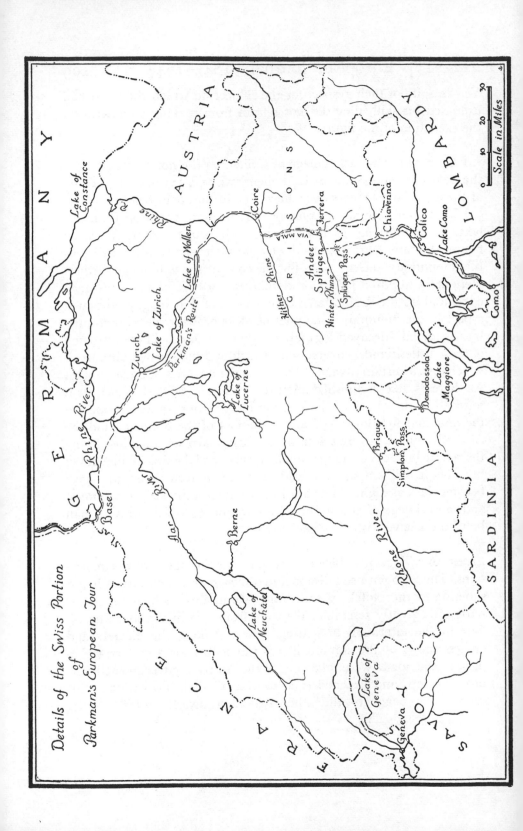

Details of the Swiss Portion
of
Parkman's European Tour

Scale in Miles

GERMANY

AUSTRIA

LOMBARDY

Lake of Constance

Rhine

Rhine

Lake of Wallen

Coire

GRISONS

VIA MALA

Ferrera

Chiavenna

Colico

Lake Como

Como

Parkman's Route

Lake of Zurich

Zurich

Lake of Zurich

Hither Rhine

Andeer

Splugen

Winter Rhine

Splugen Pass

Rhine River

Basel

Aar River

Lake of Lucerne

Domodossola

Lake Maggiore

Brigue

Simplon Pass

Berne

F R A N C E

Lake of Neuchâtel

Rhone River

SARDINIA

Lake of Geneva

Geneva

S A V O Y

traveller. The snow was fifteen or twenty feet deep in some places, and the horses waded and plunged through it as they might. The baggage was turned over two or three times, but no other accident occurred, though the horses dashed head foremost, with the sledge at their heels, down the steep descents. In fact, there is no difficulty whatever, even at this season, in making the passage; and as for the danger from avalanches—no one has been hurt by them these five years. The view was desolate and grand—one expanse of white glistening snow covering all but the pointed pinnacles at the summits, and the ragged forests of the black pine that reached up the lower declivities. Yet, as I said, I was disappointed. The road itself is so enormously high that it brings you near to the mountains' peaks, and diminishes the effect of their elevation.

But my disappointment ceased the moment we had passed the mountain. In a valley at the bottom was the village of Splügen—a contrast to the formal groups of stone houses that make up the Italian villages. It seemed like home, as we emerged from the forests of spruce and fir that covered the sides of the steep gorge where the road ran, to see before us great piles of lumber, and a wooden saw-mill, and the banks of the Rhine. The bridge, too, was of wood—so were the houses, though their projecting eaves gave them a far more picturesque aspect than belongs to a New England mountain village. The Rhine was a headlong torrent, which ran swiftly down the little valley to enter the woods and rocks again, not far below. The lower declivities of the mountains that completely surrounded this village were blackened by the heavy growth of spruce and pine, but above these woods rose gigantic peaks white with snow, that glistened with a brightness painful to the eye. In two hours we were at Andeer—a place not less wildly situated, and reached by a road winding through a succession of most savage ravines close by the Rhine, which foams and roars among the rocks and fir trees like an imprisoned wild beast.

I stopped here, and will stay here several days. Nothing could surpass the utter savageness of the scenery that you find by tracing up some of the little streams that pour down on all sides to join the Rhine; not a trace of human hand—it is as wild as the back-forests at home. The mountains too, wear the same aspect. There is one valley where a large stream comes down to join the main river, a mile from Andeer. Last night I followed it for a mile or two, back into the mountains—not Cooper himself could do it justice. The river was a hundred feet below, in a ravine, where it lashed from side to side and bounded sometimes in a fall of fifty or sixty feet—the green headlong water, the white foam, and the spray just visible through the boughs of the distorted pines that leaned over the abyss. There was in one place a peasant's hut of logs, but it seemed only to increase the sublime effect of the wilderness. I got down to the bed of the river, and leaped out to some rocks near the centre. It was nearly dark—long after sunset. What with the deafening thunder of the stream—the gloom that began to involve the shaggy branches of the yellow pines that leaned nearly across the gulf, and the stiff and upright spruces that sprang from every crevice of the rock—what with this and the savage aspect of the rocks, which were black and dripping with the spray—there was something almost appalling in the place. Above the tops of the trees, rose mountains like ours of New England, covered with fir trees wherever one could cling in the crevices of the steep cliffs. And in another direction the more distant peaks were white with snow, which retained its glistening brightness long after the moon had begun to cast a shadow.

Here was a change, with a vengeance, from the Italian beauties of the Lake of Como! I sat on the rock, fancying myself again in the American woods with an Indian companion—but as I rose to go away the hellish beating of my heart warned me that no more such expeditions were in store for me—for the present, at least—but if I do not sleep by the camp-fire again, it shall be no fault of mine.

This morning, as I got half asleep into the post-carriage at Colico, I was saluted by a *buon[o] giorno* by a small voice from a dark corner, where I discovered, by groping about, a fine boy of thirteen or fourteen, with great promise of muscles yet undeveloped. He was a young Swiss who spoke Italian; so I began to talk with him. He spoke in a frank and bold manner. I asked him if he did not mean to be a soldier. He said he should have to, for all the Swiss were obliged to serve from the age of eighteen to twenty-four[p]; but he meant to be

_p "He was mistaken—the Swiss military system resembles ours."—F.P.

an officer, because he was noble. The conductor at this moment brought a lantern to the window, which showed a handsome, Quentin Durward-like boy, but clothed in rough homespun and clouted shoes that did not look much like nobility—and reminded me of Quentin's pretensions. He had not heard of America, and inquired with great curiosity how far it was, and how long the term of military service was. I told him the period that we are expected to be in readiness, which astonished him exceedingly. *"Corpo di Bacco! Piu di quarant' anni (di) militare! Ma quell' è bello! Piu di quarant' anni (di) militare!"* He said he was a Calvinist, and that all of his religion were considered as devils—*"come diavoli"*—by the people around. He fell asleep at last, and did not wake till we stopped at Chiavenna, when he jumped up, shook himself, took his stick, and walked off to the mountains.[q]

Thursday. I spent the day yesterday in the Valley of Ferrara, one of the wildest and loneliest in the Alps, and accessible only by a bad foot-path. The river comes down at the bottom, which the sun scarcely ever touches. The mountains rise on each side many thousand feet, broken into crags and precipices, with streams falling down them in all directions, scattering into white mists before they reach the bottom. The spruce trees are sprinkled all over the cliffs, wherever there is a crevice to cling in; some gigantic pines stoop across the river, and fairly seem to quiver with the tremendous roar of the water.[59] All is solitary, and still as death except the noise of the river; yet you cannot sit on one of those rocks, and watch the green and furious water glancing between the trunks and branches below, without fancying that you hear sounds and voices about you. I never knew a place so haunted by "those airy tongues that syllable men's names."

This village of Andeer stands by the [Hinter] Rhine, in a valley where the mountains draw apart and leave a large space of fertile fields and gentle declivities. As you descend from the road to Splügen, Andeer looks almost like an American country village. There are

[q] This entry refers to an incident of Parkman's passage from Lake Como over the Splügen Pass—Ed.

barns and small houses of wood—roofed with boards, flat stones, and shingles; and, sprinkled among them, large square white houses with green blinds, which look at a distance like the buildings of a New England village. They are of stone, however, but plastered over and whitewashed. There are low walls to these villages; the little Calvinist meeting-house, something like one of ours, stands on an eminence in the midst. Beside Andeer, half a dozen others are scattered about the valley, down by the river or high up on the slopes of the mountains. You see a line of dingy wooden houses, with eaves projecting two or three feet, on almost all those declivities which the mountain forms at its base, before it rises into cliffs and inaccessible precipices. The women are all out at work in the fields, manuring them with wooden forks. Would to Heaven our women did the same, if it could make them as strong and hardy.

They speak here a German dialect, and have German faces—and here, for the first time I felt the helplessness of being without any medium of communication. A tall, stout, ruddy-cheeked mountain girl, who presided at the inn in the absence of the landlord, came up to know my commands. I tried Italian. She understood not a word; but in her zeal to serve me kept sputtering German, as if she thought to make it intelligible by repetition; so, to convince her of her mistake, I entertained her with long speeches in English, to which she listened with eyes and mouth wide open. Sometimes a bright gleam would shoot across her face, as a word similar to one of her own language struck her ear. This suggested an expedient; so I began to pronounce the English names of all the things I wanted, using all the synonyms I could think of. I thus managed to make out a very good meal, though the items of it were decided by the accidental coincidence of their names with the Swiss. When the *padrone* returned, I found that he spoke Italian, and there was an end of my difficulties for the present. The second day of my stay at Andeer, I spent in the Via Mala, a place by nature more savagely wild than the Valley of Ferrara; but not so solitary, as it is the sole outlet by which Andeer and its neighboring villages communicate with the rest of the world. But here paper fails me, and I must buy another volume!—if I can find one in Strasburg.

Strasburg, May '44. The Via Mala is a cleft in the mountains, which divides them for a mile, leaving the opposing cliffs bare and raw, as if a wedge had been driven in to split them asunder. Here the Rhine gets out from the mountains; but must force its way through a ravine, or crack, about a foot wide and, of course, immensely deep. The road that leads from the valley must take the same course, and crosses again and again the bed of the torrent, as if searching to find some means of extricating itself from the pass. Standing on one of the bridges, you may see the Rhine like a white narrow ribbon in the bottom of the dark gully, a hundred and fifty feet below. Sometimes it is buried entirely among the rocks, but you can hear its dead roaring noise; and when, after half a mile of such imprisonment, it escapes at last, it is all in a white foam. Torrents, and little streams turned all to mist as they descend from that immense height, come down the cliffs on each side to join it. Where the sun can strike them, you always see a rainbow among the scattered spray half-way down the mountain.

Four days ago I took the diligence from Andeer, and passed through this place on the way to Coire. I never left any place with more regret than these mountains. Descending into the wider valleys of the Grisons, the scenery was not less magnificent, though of a different character. At Coire, the capital of the Canton, I was reminded that I was no longer in Italy. A servant stood at the head of the stairs in the large inn there, welcoming each guest with a "good night," and ushering him into a large, low, wooden apartment, where some thirty men and women were smoking, eating, or lounging at the tables and benches. Boys stood ready to receive hats and cloaks; and waiters attended on each newcomer to know what he would have. All was ease, good-nature, and equality. The old Germans and Swiss grunted over their beer-pots, and puffed at their pipes. The young ones laughed with the servant girls. A Frenchman gulped down his bowlful of soup—sprang to the window when he heard the postillion's horn—bounded back to finish one more tumbler of wine—and then siezing his cane, dashed out in hot haste. A prim, strutting, little German student stalked to the window to watch him; pipe in hand and a complacent grin on his face; then turned to discourse in a half patronizing, half gallant way with the girl.[60]

Departed next morning for Zurich, and early in the forenoon reached the head of the Lake of Wallenstadt [Walen See]. Of the people by the way, some were Catholic, some Protestant; some spoke the German, and some the *lingua romancia*, a compound of several languages. It was a dark and cloudy day. The mountains around the lake were piles of abrupt precipices, whose tops were hidden in the clouds, and whose sides seemed alive with the numberless streams that came pouring down to the lake. Some were trickling lines of water, marking the face of the cliffs with a long dark stain; others were headlong cataracts, spouting from some cave high up among the clouds, and tumbling down the mountain, full of savage life. Others still seemed like ribbons waving in the wind from the top of a precipice. The lake itself is a black and narrow strip of water, shut close in by these tremendous rocks. The puffings of the steamboat were hoarsely reverberated from the precipices. When we reached the foot of the lake, all was bright and clear again, in seeming accordance with the change of the scenery; for I was to see no more of the Alps.

The Germans lighted their pipes with their flint and steel, and, stretching out their legs and unbuttoning their coats, disposed themselves to take their ease. Here was none of the painful dignity which an Englishman thinks it incumbent upon him to assume throughout his travels—no knee-pans aching with the strain of tight strapped pantaloons—no neck half-severed by the remorseless edge of a starched dicky.

Here began again something of Italian softness on the features of the scenery—or so at least it seemed, by contrast with the passages of the Splügen. All was cultivation and fruitfulness. The picturesque wooden cottages were more lively embellishments of the scene than the formal stone houses of Italy. But the white and neat houses of the wealthier republicans, surrounded by apple orchards and green meadows dotted by dandelions, made me fancy myself at home. Still more, when, having passed the Lake of Zurich, we approached at nightfall the town of that name. Here I could have believed myself entering an ambitious New England village—the same intermingling of white houses with blossomming apple and pear trees—the same grass-plots and wooden fences—nay, at intervals, the same old dingy barns of rough boards.

Zurich is a beautiful town; clean and neat, with all that air of newness and fresh paint that Dickens attributes to Boston.[61] Here I found myself brought to a stop, because, by the mistake of a servant, my passport had been visèd for Zurich alone, instead of Zurich and Basle. The diligence was to go in an hour. I went to the police office. Three old women were sweeping it out; and the pipes of the absent functionaries hung in a row between the windows. Remembering, however, that I was now in a republic and no longer in an Austrian state, I thought I would go on at all events, and take the chance of interruption. My passport was not even demanded of me.

In the cabriolet of the diligence were two German gentlemen, one of whom spoke several languages and English among the rest, so that I enjoyed the novelty of a companion. Waking in the morning, the sky was covered with lowering moist clouds. The glasses of the windows, too, streamed with the breath of the sleepers. It was a flat and cultivated country. Basle was just visible in front over the shoulder of the postillion. One of the Germans had shrunk down to a confused pile of legs arms and head, which latter member was tumbled over on one side, with the mouth wide open. My polyglot friend sat bolt upright in his corner, sleeping with an expression of savage determination on his mustache and compressed under lip.

At the diligence office in Basle I was nonplussed. I could not make the fat stupid-looking fellows who surrounded me understand what I wanted to be done; when the German gentleman politely offerred himself as interpreter. I went to the splendid Hotel (or rather palace) of the Three Kings, where I found a waiter who spoke a little English.

Here in Basle you find none of the palaces, and none of the dirt, of an Italian city. No soldiers, except those of the garrison of the citadel and of the gendarmerie; no beggars; no spies in the cafés; no vexatious questionings of suspicious officials; no anxious scrutiny into passports, or rummagings of baggage. The people walk about the quiet streets with solemnity on their faces, and pipes in their mouths. Fat, ruddy female faces are seen at all the windows of the steep-roofed houses, where an arrangement of mirrors enables them to see what passes below, without seeming to be on the watch.

It was Sunday, and all the shops were shut. Groups were walking quietly to church, each with a hymn-book in hand; the women arrayed in their best, with their hair braided into two long ropes behind, to which ribbons of a yard in length were attached. This ingenious contrivance, streaming out behind, gave them a most whimsical appearance. The meeting-house was large and square, and its high roof was sustained by a number of fine columns. The women occupied pews by themselves, in the middle; the men had each a kind of little stall, around the sides. The parson sailed in, in all the dignity of Geneva bands and gown, clambered into his pulpit, and with a scowling countenance opened the services. They resembled ours, with the addition of a disagreeable accompaniment to the sermon, in the shape of a man who made the rounds of the church with a bag tied to the end of a stick, in which he received the contributions of the congregation while the parson was holding forth above.

The Catholic Church holds its head scarce so high as at Rome. I saw the people coming out from mass—a stream of ugly, contented, and healthy visages. You did not see, as at Rome, a poor devil in rags, bursting with diseases and a walking menagerie of fleas, kneeling before an altar that shines with massive gold and silver, and dipping his shrivelled fingers into a font of holy water carved most exquisitely out of the richest marbles. The rough beams of this church were plainly visible—two dingy candlesticks, and some bunches of flowers, were the richest decorations of the altar—and the holy water was contained in a common copper kettle. But the people were strong, ruddy, and clean: the women looked like Amazons (though not amazonian in the etymological sense).

The Rhine divides Basle in the midst. Not the furious torrent I saw among the forests and precipices of the Rhinewald, but a broad, deep stream, whose waters make a loud rushing sound with their headlong current. The suburbs of the city are sprinkled thick with houses and orchards. Gardens are down in the ditch of the fortifications, and lime and horsechesnut trees grow on the ramparts. The fields are the resort of the people on Sunday evenings, when they come out to walk about—look at the rifle-shooting—or regale themselves on bread and cheese at benches placed outside the little inns of the suburbs. The rifle of this country is a formidable piece, carrying a ball of about twenty to the pound! Some of the German troops here in Strasburg carry them, with a short sword contrived to fit to the muzzle, by way of bayonet. After staying a day at Basle, I took the railway for Strasburg.

Passing a number of German towns, with their steep roofs half-buried in trees and the spire of the Minster rising from the midst— we got by noon to our destination. Here I staid a day, though Strasburg is an uninteresting place, with little to see; then got into the diligence for Paris. About ten o'clock, I was roused from sleep by a deafening sound of laughing, proceeding from a woman's lungs of very unusual capacities. I found that my fellow passenger had got out from the coupé, and that the conductor had introduced two women in his place. I fell back into my corner and went to sleep again; but not so soundly but that I could hear for hours an occasional remark made in the hoarse grunting voice of an old woman, and always responded to by the same shrill peal of laughter from her companion. When day dawned, I looked with some curiosity to see who my fellow travellers might be. One of them looked like a super-annuated baboon, except that she had a pair of grey mustache and a large frilled cap, which gave her such a whimsical look that I burst into a laugh. The other was about thirty—a most luxuriant specimen of womanhood. She must have weighed some three hundred pounds, though she was exceedingly well proportioned, and her features handsome. I soon, however, lost the company of this edifying pair, who got out at Nancy.

The journey to Paris occupies two days. Yesterday morning, looking from the window, I saw an ocean of housetops stretching literally to the very horizon. We entered the gate, but rode for nearly an hour through the streets before we reached the diligence office. Then I went to the Tuilleries, the Palais Royal, the Boulevard des Italiens, and the Place Vendome. "Let envious Englishmen sneer as they will," I thought, "this *is* the Athens of Modern Europe!"

I had called on my uncle, and found him not at home. He called on me with the same fortune, but left a note directing me to be at a celebrated café at a certain time, where he was to be distinguished by a white handkerchief in his hand. I found him there, and went with him to a ball at the Champs Elysées (Mabille).[62]

Bo[u]logne, May 16ᵗʰ. I have been a fortnight in Paris, and seen it as well as it can be seen in a fortnight. Under peculiarly favorable circumstances, too; for it was the great season of balls and gaieties, and I had a guide, moreover, who knows Paris from top to bottom— within and without. I like to see a thing done thouroughly. If a man has a mind to make a fool or a vagabond of himself, he can do it admirably in Paris; whereof I have seen many instances. If a man has a mind to amuse himself, there is no place like it on earth; diversions of every character, form, and degree waiting for him at every step; let him taste them—then get into the diligence and ride away—or stay, and go to the devil. You find there the same amusements variously seasoned to suit different tastes; if you have a fancy for the poetic and romantic, you can have that; but if you want to make an absolute beast of yourself, without varnish or gilding, it can be done to most admirable perfection.

I came to Bologne today; and am waiting for the boat to take me across to England. This is a dull and stupid town. The white cliffs are full in view on the horizon; but, being afflicted with a colic, I do not feel in a romantic mood; and I also hear the dinner-bell. Before midnight, however, I shall be in the "mother country."

London, May 18ᵗʰ. I approached the shores of England in a most shameful fashion. The night was dark and gloomy. Nothing was to be seen on deck but the phosphorescence on the black water, and the sparks from the chimney of the little steamer. The wind came up the straits of Dover as cold as a January northwester. I gaped, went down below, and in half a minute was sound asleep on a sofa. Two or three hours after, the captain shouted in my ear: "We are here, sir! Been here half an hour." "Here? Where is here?" said I in entire bewilderment. "Folkestone harbor, sir." The cabin lights were half burnt out, and the passengers all gone. I got up and reeled off like a drunken man to the hotel, where I went asleep again.

The next day I took the railroad for London. Heavy grey clouds seemed to rest on the very tree-tops. A tremendous wind was blowing, with an occasional puff of sleet and fine rain, sending a chill into our very bones. The passengers' noses turned blue—nobody spoke a word —two or three pulled out respirators from their pockets—and all crouched down together in the open cars, and drew cloaks and shawls close about them. Our northeasters may do their worst; they cannot match that wind.

When I got to London, I thought I had been there before. There, in flesh and blood, was the whole host of characters that figure in *Pickwick*. Every species of cockney was abroad in the dark and dingy-looking streets, all walking with their heads stuck forwards, their noses turned up, their chin pointing down, their knee joints shaking, as they shuffled along with a gait perfectly ludicrous but indescribable. The hackney coachmen and cabmen, with their peculiar phraseology; the walking advertisements, in the shape of a boy completely hidden between two placards; and a hundred others seemed so many incarnations of Dickens' characters. A strange contrast to Paris! The cities are no more alike than the "dining room" of London and the elegant restaurant of Paris—the one being a quiet, dingy establishment where each guest is put into a box, and supplied with porter, beef, potatoes, and plum-pudding. Red-faced old gentlemen of three hundred weight mix their "brandy go" and read the *Times*. In Paris the tables are set in elegant galleries and saloons, and among the trees and flowers of a garden; and here resort coats cut by the first tailors and bonnets of the latest mode, whose occupants regale their delicate tastes on the lightest and most delicious viands. The waiters spring from table to table as noiselessly as shadows, prompt at the slightest sign; a lady, elegantly attired, sits within an arbor to preside over the whole. Dine at these places—then go to a London "dining room"—swill porter and devour roast beef!

The Haymarket Theatre—a little place, very plain and simple, and scarce larger than our departed Tremont. Not like the great theatres of Rome and Naples, or the still larger La Scala at Parma. Very unlike, too, the splendid opera house at Paris, where the richness of the decorations, the beauty of the architecture, and the excellence of the performances are only equalled by the extravagance of the prices. They gave us enough of it, certainly, at the Haymarket.

The performances lasted from half past 7 till midnight. Such admirable acting I never saw before. Charles Matthews[63] was the star; and appeared in a piece of his own, in which he took occasion to vent several sarcasms against American repudiation.[64] But the drama is at its last gasp. The Haymarket alone, among all its companions, preserves unaltered its ancient character—the rest are turned to opera houses.

I went immediately to Catlin's "Indian Gallery."[65] It is in the Egyptian Hall, Picadilly. There was a crowd around the door; servants in livery waiting; men with handbills of the exhibition for sale; cabmen, boys, and pickpockets. I was rejoicing in Mr. Catlin's success, when the true point of attraction caught my eye in the shape of a full-length portrait of Major Tom Thumb,[66] the celebrated American dwarf, who it seems occupies the "Indian Gallery" for the present. I paid my shilling and went in. The little wretch was singing "Yankee Doodle" with a voice like a smothered mouse, and prancing about on a table, à la Jeffrey Hudson,[67] with a wooden sword in his hand. A great crowd of cockneys and gentlemen and ladies were contemplating his evolutions—but [as] for the "Indian Gallery," its glory had departed; it had evidently ceased to be a lion. The portraits of the chiefs, dusty and faded, hung round the walls, and above were a few hunting shirts, and a bundle or two of arrows; but the rich and invaluable collection I had seen in Boston had disappeared, and no one thought of looking at the poor remains of that great collection that were hung about the walls. Catlin had done right. He would not suffer the fruits of his six years' labor and danger to rot in the dampness to gratify a few miserable cockneys— so has packed up the best part of his trophies.

St. Paul's, which the English ridiculously compare to St. Peter's, is without exception the dirtiest and gloomiest church I have been in yet. I went up to the ball at the top of the cupola, whence the prospect is certainly a most wonderful one. I have been on mountains whence nothing could be seen but unbroken forests stretching in every direction to the horizon, and I enjoyed the sight—but to look down from St. Paul's and see tiled roofs and steeples, half hid in smoke and mist—a filthy river covered with craft running through the midst; and to hear the incessant hum and to smell the coal smoke that pollutes the air—all this is very curious and amusing for a while, but I would scarce trouble myself to look again. All was dirty and foul; the air was chilly and charged with fog and sleet, though it is the genial month of May. The smoke, that you could see streaming in the wind from ten thousand earthen chimney-pots, mingled with the vapors and obscured the prospect like a veil. It was an indistinct but limitless panorama. The taller church-spires alone rose above the cloud into a comparatively clear atmosphere; and they could be seen faintly, far off on the horizon, to show how far this wilderness of houses reached. "Now," thought I, "I have under my eye the greatest collection of blockheads and rascals, the greatest horde of pimps, prostitutes, and bullies that the earth can show." And straightway all the child's-book associations of London rose before me: the Lord Mayor's show "all so grand," and the host of narrow, stupid, beef-eating civic functionaries, and the unmatched absurdities and self-conceit of cockneyism. "Was there ever such a cursed hole?" I thought as I looked down on the smoky prospect.

You are shown a large stone vaulted room, covered with cobwebs and smoke-dust, where hang, already rotten and half dropping from their staffs, the flags that were borne at Nelson's funeral.

Walk out in the evening, and keep a yard or two behind some wretched clerk, who with nose elevated in the air, elbows stuck out at right angles, and the pewter knob of his cane playing upon his under lip, is straddling his bow legs over the sidewalk with a most majestic air. Get behind him, and you see his dignity greatly disturbed. First he glances over one of his narrow shoulders—then over the other—then he edges off to the other side of the walk, and turns his vacant lobster eyes full upon you—then he passes his hand over his coat-tail—and finally he draws forth from his pocket the object of all this solicitude in the shape of a venerable and ragged cotton handkerchief, which he holds in his hand to keep it out of harm's way. I have been thus taken for a pickpocket more than a dozen times tonight—not the less so for being respectably dressed, for these gentry are the most dashing men on the Strand.

There is an interesting mixture of vulgarity and helplessness in the swarm of ugly faces you see in the streets—meagre, feeble, ill-proportioned, or not proportioned at all, the blockheads must needs put on a game air and affect the "man of the world" in their small way. I have not met one handsome woman yet, though I have certainly walked more than fifty miles since I have been here, and have kept my eyes open. To be sure, the weather has been raw and chill enough to keep beauty at home. Elsewhere Englishmen are tall, strong, and manly; here the crowd that swarms through the streets are like the outcasts of a hospital.

I spent seven or eight days in London. On the eighth day I went up the river to Richmond in a steamboat, with a true cockney pleasure party on board whose evolutions were very entertaining. The day before, while I was in Westminster Abbey—which, by the way, is the most interesting church I ever was in—a man came up and enquired if my name was not Parkman, saying that a gentleman wished to speak to me. I did not know that I had a single acquaintance in London, and was rather astonished at finding George Atkinson[68] standing among the tombs. He was just imported by steamboat from America. He informed me, to my great surprise and admiration, that he and I had just become uncles when he left home. He went with me to visit the "industrious fleas" (not the exhibition which goes by that name in Paris!) and we made the circuit of half a dozen exhibitions together. He went with me to Richmond the next day. The river scenery of this place is beautiful—so are the fields and villages you pass on your return by land. By a miracle, the day was fine. The carriages of the nobility thronged about Hyde Park. Regent Street swarmed with thousands of people, and was filled with a heavy, stunning din from the wheels of carts, omnibusses, cabs, and carriages, careering along in both directions at full speed, but without confusion or accident. But the Strand at night is the most characteristic scene in London. The sidewalks are crowded with as dense and active a throng as in the day-time—more than half of whom are women on their nightly perambulations. The glare from the shops makes all as bright as sunlight. A watchman stands in his cloak at every corner. Strong bodies of the police are continually marching in order to and fro, with loaded clubs hung at their sides.

I got into the cars one night—having sent my trunks to Liverpool—
and found myself in the morning at Darlington, nearly three hundred
miles distant. Thence I took stage for Carlisle, famous in Border
story; having had some trouble in negotiating a passage from the
difficulty in understanding the damnable dialect of Yorkshire. It
was not long before we passed the veritable Dotheboys Hall of
Dickens, exactly answering to his description in appearance, in
situation, in all things. It is deserted utterly—*Nicholas Nickleby* ruined
not this establishment alone, but many other schools with which the
vicinity abounds, though some of these latter were in no way
objectionable.

It was not long before we passed another spot far more interesting.
As we rode out of one of the little stone villages of the country, I saw
a large ruined castle on a high rock above a clear swift stream,
shaded from the sun by beautifully wooded banks. The old coachman saw me looking earnestly at it, so twisted round his broad red
face and pointing with the butt of his whip, said "Yon's old Barnard
Castle, sir, and yon's the Tees." I burst out with an oath at being so
unexpectedly introduced to the scenery of Scott's *Rokeby*. A gentleman who had joined us at the village gave me an account of the
present proprietors, and said that he was connected with the family
of the former owners.

We dined at Penrith—resumed journey—saw off to our left the
Cumberland hills, enclosing among them the valley of St. John, the
renowned "Lakes," and the home of Wordsworth. An old farmer
who had wandered over them all, out of a very unusual admiration
of the picturesque, gave enthusiastic descriptions of their beauties—
then launched into the subject of their geological formation, whence
he diverged to geology in general—then followed a discussion on
chemistry—then on metaphysics and religion—then on the breeding
of cattle. By this time the old fellow had reached his house, and
scrambling down, lifted his dingy hat off his white eyebrows to
salute us, while we rode on to Carlisle.

I went away at four in the morning for Abbotsford. We were in
the region where one thinks of nothing but of Scott, and of the
themes which he has rendered so familiar to the whole world. The
Cheviot [Teviot River] was on our right—the Teviot [Cheviot] hills

before us. The wind came down from them raw and cold, and the whole sky was obscured with stormy clouds. I thought, as we left the town, of the burden of one of his ballads, "The sun shines fair on Carlisle walls." It was little applicable now. The ancient fortification looked [as] sullen and cheerless as tottering battlements and black crumbling walls, beneath a sky as dark and cold as themselves, could make it. I was prepared for storms and a gloomy day, but soon the clouds parted and the sun broke out clear over the landscape. The dark heathery sides of Tcviot [Cheviot]—the numberless bright, rapid streams that came from the different glens, and the woods of ash, larch, and birch that followed their course, and grew on the steeper declivities of the hills—never could have appeared to more advantage. Esk and Liddel, Yarrow, the Teviot, Minto Crag, Ettrick Forest, Branksome Castle—these and more likewise we passed before we reached the Tweed, and saw Abbotsford on its banks among the forests planted by Scott himself. I left my luggage at the inn at Galashiels, telling the landlord that I was going away, and might return at night, or might not. I visited Abbotsford, Melrose, and Dryburgh—and consider the day better spent than the whole four months I was in Sicily and Italy. I slept at Melrose, and returned to Galashiels in the morning.

Three days was all the time I had to spare for these places; but rising at six and going to bed at ten, and being on my legs during the whole interval, I managed to see almost every spot of note for eight or ten miles round. I found a little stone cottage down by the Tweed, not far from Abbotsford, where an old woman told me that, "if I wad be pleased to walk in," she could show me a room where she was accustomed to receive gentlemen in the salmon-fishing season. I came back to the house at night, and found she had arranged the room and built a fire for me, and sent for a fishing-rod and lines. The old lady had only been in [the] place about twelve years, but well remembered Sir Walter's return from the Continent and his funeral. She saw him in the carriage as they were bringing him to Abbotsford after his landing. "He was an awful dull and heavy lookin' mon, to be sic a grand writer," she said.

I asked her if she had any books in the house, on which she brought out of a closet a Testament bound up with *The Psalms of David, done into English verse, for the service of the Scottish Kirk*—also a volume of the sermons of the Reverend Simeon McCabb. She then produced a bottle of whisky, remarking, "Mayhap it wad mak ye sleep better." I rose at daylight, and fished in the Tweed for two hours, following it far up among the hills.

I like the Scotch—I like the country and everything in it. The Liverpool packet will not wait, or I should stay long here, and take a trout from every "burnie" in the Cheviot[s]. The scenery has been grossly belied by Irving and others—it is wild and beautiful—I have seen none more so. There is wood enough along the margins of the streams (which are as transparent as our own)—the tops of the hills alone are bare. The country abounds in game—pheasants, moor cock, curlew, and rabbits.

I returned to headquarters at Galashiels just in time for the Edinburgh coach; and got to the city at night, where the fine situation and magnificent architecture of the "Modern Athens" very much surprised me. The view from Calton Hill is, to my thinking, the only city view I ever saw that deserves to be called sublime. There is an amusing contrast between the old and new town—the region of the Grassmarket, and that of Moray Place and Princes Street. In point of architecture, the new town surpasses Regent Street—in point of neatness and quiet, it would be an insult to Edinburgh to make any comparison. But the old town makes the finest appearance, taken in the mass, in spite of the dirt and squalor you find there on close examination. Stand on Princes Street and look across the gulf that separates the two quarters, you see the opposite hill-side crowded with a dense mass of venerable buildings, from six to ten or twelve stories high. In this region are all the spots famous in the history of the town, and in the romances of Scott. The Castle rises, on the top of a craggy hill, far above the rest.

Sir Walter Scott is everywhere. His name is in everybody's lips, and associates itself with every spot around this place. I ask the name of such a street—such a mountain, or island, or cottage, or piece of woods—the words of the reply have been familiar to me as my own name for the last six years. The old booksellers here have all seen him—many of them had dealings with him—all speak of him alike. One of them yesterday showed me a letter written by Scott while he was collecting the *Minstrelsy*, saying that he had bought it for a great price because he was determined to have some memento of Sir Walter. They are erecting a magnificent monument to his memory on Princes Street; the more needed since his grave at Dryburgh has not even a stone to mark it.

The gentleman who showed me Scott's letter, showed me also one of Burns', or rather a fragment of one, of a very edifying nature. It was addressed to a married lady, and in a style most poetically persuasive, yet frank and bold. The end, where the enamoured poet had probably stated more clearly what he had been driving at all along, was torn off by the son of the lady. This son must have been a blockhead or a madman. He in some way got the letter into his possession, and had no scruples in selling it to a stranger, though his mother's name is written out at full upon it.

I walked up Arthur's Seat, passing the spot where Jea(n)nie Dean[s] had her interview with her sister's seducer,[69] and, when I arrived at the top, looking down on the site of her father's cottage. Under the crags here is the place where Scott and James Ballantyne[70] used to sit when boys, and read and make romances together. Edinburgh, half wrapped in smoke, lies many hundred feet below, seen beyond the ragged projecting edge of Salisbury Crag, the castle rising obscurely in the extreme distance.

In the castle are the regalia of Scotland—the crown, sword, sceptre, and jewels—the first worn by Robert the Bruce and all who succeeded him till Charles II's time. They were hidden from the light for many years. The soldier pointed out the heavy oaken chest where they lay concealed, until the Scottish nation should have forgotten its ancient independence and become content under its "annexation" to England. I remembered the scene just after the opening of the chest, when a party of *literati* and ladies were looking at these insignia of ancient glory, and one frivolous fellow lifted the crown to place it on the head of a simpering young lady. "No, by God!" exclaimed Scott, who stood by. The man blushed like scarlet and laid the crown down. There is a power in a little profanity, when it comes from a moved spirit, and is not affected, like the oaths of a consumptive apprentice with a cigar in his mouth, who lisps "Hell and Damnation" because he thinks it sounds manly.

Saw the house, just above the Canongate, where John Knox lived and preached. Even now, an image of him is stuck at the corner, in the very act of holding forth. This the people hold in great reverence. A scurvy-looking population they are. The old stone houses of High St. rise story above story to a stupendous height above them, looking more ancient and venerable than the Castle Rock. Their grey attic windows and dingy eaves look the very personifications of antiquity. The dwellings of nobles were there once, where now you find squalling town-cats and yelling children, old hags with frilled caps, ruffian men, and young ladies to correspond. Walk out of High Street to the top of Calton Hill and here you may see a magnificent specimen of *new* Edinburgh. It was designed to erect the Pantheon of Athens on this commanding height—but the men of modern Athens were too ambitious. Their funds gave out; but not till a foundation was laid, and a row of beautiful columns erected. There they stand yet; enough to display the magnificence of the design, and to excite regret that it could not be fully realised. Holyrood Palace still contains Queen Mary's bed, and specimens of tapestry worked by her hand. All is arranged as when she inhabited the room. The fatal supper-room is shown, where she sat at table with Rizzio and her guests on the night when her favorite was murdered. Darneley's armor is lying on the table. The stain of Rizzio's blood can still be seen in the floor near the door of her audience hall, where the body was found. She had a partition of wood put up, to keep the place from her sight.

The great hall of the palace, where the portraits of the Scottish kings are placed, is a gloomy and sombre room with wainscotting of some dark wood. The last of the many royal entertainments of which it has been the scene, was, I think, those balls given by the Pretender, at which Waverley acquitted himself so well.[71]

Edinburgh, altogether, is a most interesting place—not so Glasgow, where I spent a day. There is nothing there that I could find worth looking at except the Tolbooth, celebrated in *Rob Roy*. I saw in Edinburgh, by the way, the opera of *Rob Roy*, in which Mackay personated Baillie Nicol Jarvie. This performer, I think, was the original Baillie, to whom Scott sent a present and a compliment; certainly his performance was far superior to any of the rest.

The vicinity of Glasgow to the Highlands is particularly tantalising to one who has not time to go there. The steamer sailed for Liverpool on the evening of the day when I arrived. She had on board about a hundred passengers, beside seventy or eighty cattle, and a large flock of sheep. They all were taken sea-sick in the course of the voyage, and made a most curious but pitiable spectacle. I enquired for my birth, which the steward pointed out to me, and I immediately went to sleep. About midnight I heard somebody speaking to me; opened my eyes, and saw a tall thin broad-shouldered Sawney,[r] with a particularly sneaking expression of countenance, standing over me, directing me to get up as I had his birth. I told him he was mistaken, and must not disturb me; and soon dropped asleep again. Shortly after, the fellow returned with the steward, who said he had made a mistake and shown me the wrong birth: so I rolled into the next one, whence I saw Sawney by the light of the Steward's lantern tumbling himself into the one I had left, with a grunt of satisfaction at his victory. He preferred to have the birth he had engaged, though another person had slept in it, to selecting one from three or four other precisely similar which remained vacant close at hand. He spoke no word of thanks or apology, but pointed to a red-headed brat of his who was snoring like a porpoise in a birth below us. Nothing would do but the anxious father must be within arm's reach of his cub.

After a twenty-four hours' voyage, we reached Liverpool late at night. The town looked quite as dismal as I had imagined it; smoky with the chimneys of numberless iron-foundries. I found my trunks had arrived safe from London, and got an order for their delivery from the clerk of Baring Brothers, to whom I had consigned them. This order I gave to a cabman, telling him to bring the luggage to the hotel as soon as possible. He went off in hot haste, but returned in half an hour, saying that the man at the store-house refused to give them up. I was astonished and provoked; but got into the cab to see to the matter in person. When I got to the storehouse, an old

[r] Derogatory term for a Scot.—Ed.

man made his appearance, with a large bunch of keys in his hand, and inflexible obstinacy and stolidity written on his broad countenance. I produced the order, and demanded what induced him to withold the trunks. He turned over the paper three or four times, scrutinizing it in every direction; then returned it, saying doggedly, "Can't let ye have 'em." I asked him what more he would have— there was a written order for them. The old fool wriggled about and dangled his keys in evident trouble, but still replied: "Can't let ye have 'em. 'T would be much as my place is worth." Nothing would shake his stupid honesty—not even my letter of credit on the house, or the card of the Liverpool partner, Mr. Gair, which I had with me. "Oh, he didn't entertain no suspicion—not at all—he dare say all was right—but I couldn't have the trunks without the paper was signed by Mr. Gair himself." I had to send the cabman to the house of this gentleman, who was a good deal vexed at the bull-headed faithfulness of the old man. This is the only instance in the course of my journeyings where I have met with too much honesty. The matter did not end here. I had returned to the hotel, having described the two trunks to the old fellow, and told him that my name was printed on the lid of each, to which he kept replying "Oh, yes, oh, yes; there was two just such trunks in the store-room—he had been watching them for a whole week." So I thought the matter settled at last, and was writing a letter in my room when a porter entered with a box of pine boards eight feet long and four wide, beneath which he could hardly stand. "Here's the other," said the coachman, bringing in one of my trunks. "It's all right now, I s'pose, sir"; and he lifted his hat, for his remuneration. I was too much amused to be angry, and despatched him again to the storehouse, with directions to tell the old man that he was a fool. This time he brought the right trunk, which, being small, had been packed away under a desk for safe-keeping.

I was obliged to remain several days in Liverpool, and lamented the arrangement of the Glasgow steamers, which forced me to throw away, on this disgusting city, time which I might otherwise have spent in the Highlands. I was lucky enough to meet Col. Winchester with his son and Mr. Green whom I had seen at Rome. Green and I, with a young Irish friend of his, went to a *fête* at the Liverpool

Zoological Gardens, where were at least a dozen American ship-captains in the crowd. This crowd had little resemblance to the swarm of young men and grisettes at the corresponding places of entertainment at Paris. Here were other countrymen of mine, in the shape of a black bear, a cougar, and a Canada wild-cat, who were glaring through the bars of their cages in a fury at the rockets and other fire-works.

The Irishman invited us home with him to supper, where we found his brother. Like other Irish gentleman, they had not a particle of English coldness and haughty reserve—all was frankness and cordiality. Supper over, they ordered the "matarials" with which to make a pitcher of Irish punch. Green seasoned it with his dry and humorous stores, in the precise manner of Dan Slade,[72] whom he actually surpasses in stature, being six feet four inches high.

The next day we went on board the *Acadia* by the small steamer hired to take off her passengers. As we sat on deck, contemplating the destined companions of our voyage, messenger after messenger came to Green from his various acquaintances: one brought him a package of newspapers, another a bundle of letters, another a case of presents for friends, each repeating the same formula, "Would Mr. Green oblige Mr. _____ by taking charge of this little parcel?" At last a fellow came down with a large wooden box on his shoulders, full of samples of sugar, alum, salt, etc., and made the same modest request. Green had been growling and swearing for some time, as each successive bundle came in; but when he saw this approaching, he roared out—"Take it away! Pitch it overboard. Don't you see I've got enough to sink the ship alongside of me now!" The porter walked off with the box. Col. Winchester was quite exempt from this species of nuisance; but as we were leaving the wharf, a small active-looking man hastily shouldered through the crowd, siezed his hand, and proffered for his acceptance a thin volume of poems—a production of the donor's deceased wife—which he ventured to hope might afford amusement and consolation to the Colonel during the hours of sea-sickness. The present was understood to be from the daughter of the defunct poetess. A note from her was enclosed in the volume. The Col. showed it to me—the whole composition was extraordinary, but I only remember the conclusion:

". . . we part, I fear, for many months; but that Heaven may bless you and yours, will ever, sir, be the ardent wish of one whose pride it is to enrol herself,

"With respect and affection
"On the long catalogue of your friends

_____ W___"

We soon got on board of the *Acadia,* and watched the smoky city, half concealed behind a forest of masts. The spectacle was ugly enough; but not uninteresting, as this was the last we were to see of European cities. In two hours more we got under weigh—were saluted from a fort not far down the Mersey, and replied from two brass guns, to the consternation of the ladies.

It was two days before we passed Cape Clear. Head winds, and a sea not smooth. Our sixty-five passengers kept below for the most part, for the sight of dinner had become an abomination. There was nothing but groanings and vociferations, through the long ranges of state-rooms. The poems failed to console the Colonel, who was terribly sick.

There were on board English, Irish, Scotch, French, Germans, and Americans, beside half a dozen Canadians. In a week, the general sickness nearly disappeared. The table is set five times a day, beside which many of the passengers manage to keep eating in the intervals, for anything is to be had when called for—by the terms of the engagement. Those who are disposed for more intellectual enjoyment play cards, or gather round the chimney on the upper deck to dispute on the merits of their respective countries.

The English gather into a knot by themselves. They sit in a group near the captain, discussing the quality of their wine, or talking on military matters, as they are chiefly Canada officers. The "damned Yankees" are scattered everywhere about the tables, and of every grade and character, from gentlemen down to some vulgar and conceited travelling-agent from New York. When evening comes, the din of conversation and laughter begins. Everyone has his punch, his wine, or his porter, and joins a group according to his taste. The Bishop of Newfoundland, who is on his way out, betakes himself to the study of a volume relating to his interesting diocese. The Englishmen gather and talk of their wine again, casting from time to time contemptuous glances over their shoulders at the noisy groups of Americans, Scotch, and Irish. One of them usually retires by himself to the farthest corner of the room, where the tables are quite empty, where he drinks his bottle of wine, neither looking to the right hand nor to the left. He always appears in full dress, with startched dickey erect, threatening to saw his ears off. Occasionally he will honor the Bishop's chaplain with an intimation that his company will be agreeable, and the pair drink the wine together.

In calm weather, when the upper deck is dry, Green comes up with a Scotch plaid round his shoulders and propping his head against the mast, flings out his legs to an incredible distance, and reads the *Mysteries of Paris*—a needless task with him, by the way, for he is tolerably initiated into *les vrais Mystères*. Col. W. comes up also, and wrapping himself in his cloak, lies down likewise. His son joins the party. Then merchants, travelling gentlemen, agents—in short a fair representation of the Yankee Nation—gather round and assume the same comfortable but inelegant attitude. Meanwhile the officers have been perambulating the deck, head erect, shoulders back, with a measured tread of dignity, and a look of supreme contempt for all the world. When they approach the Americans, their [there] is a perceptible rising of the chin, and a redoubled stiffness of carriage. Their eyes seem to be bent on vacuity, but they will glance down an instant disdainfully at the variety of uncouth attitudes of the group—then as they turn away, one will curl his lip and whisper to the other. Green bawls out to the Colonel's son: "Billy, you don't understand how to be comfortable. Here, let me show you the way to enjoy yourself like an American and a freeman" —so he lifts one of his long legs up to Billy's head, and reaches the other out to the railing of the deck. "Well, I swow!" says another, "you do things first rate, I calculate, and no mistake. *We* don't live under a despotic government, I guess!"—and this man tries to emulate Green by stretching both feet across his neighbor's lap. "Yes," says the next man, "Freedom's the word—to all but the niggers! I wish we kept those cattle in the north—a good thing to exercise a man on, of a cold morning, and give him an appetite for breakfast. I'd lash mine till they roared again." "I'd roast mine alive," says another, taking out a pen-knife to pick his teeth, "if they didn't behave." "I'd raise a breed for the doctors," adds another, "they sell well, and it don't cost anything to raise them, because the thinner the body is, you know, the better it is to dissect."

All this being uttered in a loud voice, the Englishmen could not help hearing. Unlike some of their countrymen, they began at last to "smell a rat"—so, casting a look of disdainful ire on the grave countenances of the Americans, they descended with stately steps, to the lower deck.

I knew a young American in Paris who was possessed with the same hatred against Englishmen which the buccaneer Morgan is said to have felt against Spaniards. Walking with him in the street, if an Englishman happened to pass, his face would change suddenly; he would turn round and follow the man with his eyes, as if he were a mortal enemy. He used to insult them, and play tricks on them, on every occasion. The masked balls, especially, gave him ample opportunities; and he particularly delighted in manoevring to turn them to ridicule before their partners, or to get their partners away from them—and then he would assail them with sneers and jests which would have got him into a scrape at any other place than a masked ball.

On Saturday evening the different nations separate, and remain till late drinking the customary toast of "Sweethearts and Wives." On Sunday the Bishop of Newfoundland preaches us sermons which the meanest Freshman in Harvard ought to have been ashamed to have written. The Bishop (who—with reverence to his lordship be it said— seems not to be gifted with any extraordinary share of common sense, whatever his spiritual gifts may be) takes great delight in lengthening out his precious liturgy as far as possible, repeating the creed, and the prayers for the government and the Royal Family several times. He does not deign to regard the two-thirds of his auditors, who are neither British subjects nor Episcopalians.

His lordship is a great enemy of the Temperance reform, and relates with great satisfaction the story of a pewter mug which was presented him by the "publicans," for preaching a sermon against it. It is a sin, he says, to teach men to do for their worldly interest that which they ought to do purely for the glory of God. It may, he says, produce results apparently good, but it "implants a bad principle"— and the evil effects are at some future day to be made manifest.

One evening we saw an iceberg in the distance. A double watch was set all night, and one or two passengers were nervous enough to sit up in dread of a catastrophe. None occurred; the sea was perfectly calm in the morning, with no ice in sight; the ship moving steadily on at the rate of eleven knots. Hitherto we had made an average course of no more than six knots, on account of the rough sea and constant head winds.

The sea has now been calm for several days. I came on deck this morning[s] and smelt the land breeze; half an hour after, the coast of Nova Scotia was visible, but fogs and cloud soon sank upon it, and shut it from sight. We are now too far distant from any part of the shore to discern it by the ordinary laws of vision; yet you can see distinctly from the deck a long line of high lands, with forests and patches of open soil. As the state of the atmosphere changes, and its refractive power becomes greater or less, this false coast rises higher above the horizon, or sinks down below it.

[s] *"June 17th."*—F.P.

Appendix
European Notebook

Polyphemus. There is a man on deck, with a face dark as a Negro or mulatto, yet features unlike those races and very powerful—a beetling brow, shaggy with hair, a swelling nostril, black strong beard—and an expression as fierce and savage as I ever saw. He stands with folded arms, a strange contrast to the light hair, florid faces, and military stiffness of the Marines.

Lt. Sp[arks] still nourished a strong dislike against the French—the embers of natural hatred still-born. He expressively calls them "tiger-monkeys."

Speaking of English leniency towards colonists, he mentions, as an instance of forbearance, that the English religion has been *forced* upon none of them, but they have been suffered to enjoy their own.

Christmas Day. The men dancing on deck, to the sound of a drum, a violin, and a fiddle, the musicians perched on the rail. All more or less "excited." A group approached a young midshipman with whom I was talking. "We've had the honor to drink your health, sir," said a fat drummer boy, touching his hat, while his companions were grinning in the rear. The midshipman stop'd a moment, blushed, hesitated, then told them to go and get another bottle of wine from the steward. All are in high enjoyment.

We had an excellent Christmas dinner. The swarthy Maltese officer was, even at table, a butt for his companions, especially the officer who the other day insolently shrugged his shoulders as I past.

After dinner we adjourned to the gun-room and played cards, this quiet personage called the Dr. taking a rather unwilling and indifferent part.

The officer aforementioned was half "slewed," flung the furniture and plates carelessly about, and designated everything as "bloody."

Messina. A broad long street along the water—with stone buildings, many of them exceedingly large and beautiful, on one side—the shops on the other. Shops and stores of all kinds on the ground story of the buildings, all with wide open fronts crowded with merchandise. Splendidly tinselled liquor shops, with here and there a padre for a customer—barber's shops with the row of basins in front—tobacco shops—exchange—cobbler's shops. The broad street full of people. "Boot blacks" waiting for a job at the sides and corners—butchers, fruiterers, money changers thronging around the bases of the columns where an arch opens into the back of the town, exposing a long perspective of narrow crowded streets. Capuchins in their brown garb—priests with their looped-up hats—and embryo priests on a smaller scale. Criers and hawkers; soldiers moustachioed, with the broad white belt across their grey surtouts. Men carrying sacred pictures and images—a madonna or some saint, by the way, is stuck at every corner.

"*Dové è il téatro?*" I enquired of a fellow at the corner of the street. "Ah! *signore*, I am delighted at de meeting with an Englishman. I shall have de honor to show you to the teater. This is the night of the grand festival through the countries of the Catholic religion. . . . Ah! the door of the teater is closed, dey have postponed the entertainment. But I shall have the honor to show you the church where they celebrate at present the grand festival of the new year."

We went there—the cathedral was a blaze of light—all the floor was a black sea of heads—the priests were chanting, and incense burning—a flourish of trumpets—a burst of solemn music, and the throng bowed down as the host was elevated.

"Thee, God, we praise," said my acquaintance who stood at my side, looking up into my face with his large grey eyes—and translating the *Te Domine* for my benefit. "The decorations of this church, sir, are very exceedingly beautiful, but I have seen it honored with a greater number of tapers. They are cautious at present. Last year the fire took force on the pictures and ornaments and the people trod on each other to get out, the women, and the ladies, and the men." All this he said with a grin, as if highly amused, rubbing the palms of his hands together. The people all looked towards us.

"The altar is adorned with precious stones, which you will observe in the morning. Do you understand the Latin tongue, sir?" Then he began to repeat with Italian accent several lines from the eclogues of "Virgilio." Several of the people turned round or talked with him in Italian, looking curiously at me. "Those people," he said, turning to me, "consider it to be for a very strange thing that you should understand Latin, while you are ignorant of Italian. They have not reflected that these are two different languages."

Here, with a crash of fireworks in the galleries, the service concluded. "Now we will hasten out, previously to the rush of the crowd. Take care of your pockets, sir. There are very nimble fingers here."

When we got out, I questioned this singular character. He said his father was in good circumstances, and had taken great pains to give him an education—sending him to college. But now he was poor and had no shirt—"Sir, I ask your pardon, but look here"—and he stripped himself to show the truth of what he said. He could not read his books now, and he had a family at home.

I asked him how he had fallen so low. He told some story about having an office in the customs and being caught dealing with the *contrabandos*— and of drinking a glass of wine with his friends.

By this time he had worked himself up into a crying fit. Lifting up his ragged hat, he said he thought heaven had sent the English gentleman to relieve him—but having nothing less than a dollar, I left him.

Have just arrived at Giardini—stand in the window of the *albergo*— filled with admiration at the singular beauty of the scenery. Had no idea that so much pleasure could be conveyed through the eye.

"Recommendations" at Giardini.

Road to Catania. Etna, in clouds, snow, and smoke. Beggars. Lava. At Catania, visited the convent of the Benedictines which so narrowly escaped destruction in [16]69. The Boscari Museum; and fountain. The Greek theatre. Went in the evening to the opera—one of Bellini's, said to be a native of Catania. Lopez and a young Frenchman my companions, the latter an admirable example of the national liveliness and light-heartedness. In buying pit tickets for the theatre here, you are shown a plan of the theatre—select an unoccupied seat, which is numbered—and a paper ticket given you, corresponding to the number.

Etna had an eruption two or three weeks since—more than sixty killed and wounded.

Sicily is called by Mrs. Starke "the birth place of pastoral poetry"—for Theocritus was buried there. It is well fitted to be.

Returning, were accompanied by a singular looking boy, who ran behind, or clung on, ready to help in emergencies. Everybody here rides mules; the rider often the biggest of the two. The brown capote of the country is worthy of notice. I tasted the Indian fig at Giarri, where we stopped. Beset there by beggars, one of whom, a little boy, trotted after me wherever I went, danced a kind of hornpipe, and made most ludicrous signs and grimaces. Also a mute girl. The old blind beggars by the roadside the most disgusting. Etna looked most grandly, in clouds and smoke. The smaller and nearer mts. were a noble spectacle at sunset.

*Giardini. Thursday, Jan. 5[4]*th. The people about here seem chiefly engaged in weaving, spinning, dying cloth, and fishing. Their plows are not very unlike the Spanish. They drive their oxen with a rope round the horns like reins. About the church-porches groups are basking in the sun and picking vermin from one another's heads.

Every house, as far as I know, has a holy picture, with a lamp before it. Dined at Mr. Gardiner's. Greatly edified by Mr. B[rown]'s conversation.

The two captains at Mr. Marston's. Silence of Capt. *Emily*, interpreted into deep thinking and observation; the frankness, good nature, and heartiness of Capt. *Cecilia*, with his conversation: "Now I can't get along without tobacco, nohow. Some say it's a nasty trick to be chawing of it all the time, but I—," etc.

The English invalid gentleman.

The legs, heads, and arms of wax, hung up in the churches—given in commemoration of vows by the sick afflicted in any of those members.

Mr. Brown—his table talk—his conversations with Miss ———— at the theatre, explaining the formation of the thighs of women as distinguished from those of men—making constant *double-entendres*—very plain ones. A gay bachelor.

The people here paint crosses against such walls as they do not wish defiled.

Mr. Smith, the invalid, at the Marstons'—his notions of antiquities.

Books and pictures are exposed for sale on the sidewalks—scriveners sit in the frequented places, ready to write letters. The shops are all open in front—the signs are carved with images, for the benefit of those who cannot read. Hosts of foppishly dressed and sickly looking men beset the streets. The carriages of the nobility, with liveried servants, roll through the streets. The little painted mule carts—the mule with a high-peaked and gaudily ornamented saddle—are seen everywhere. Indian figs, corn, beans, chesnuts, oranges, and sweetmeats are sold at the street corners. The confectioners usually have a little fountain, in the form of a bird pouring a small stream of water from its beak.

Giuseppe—his . . . .

Stockings	1	Shirts	5
Dickey	1	Drawers	1
Handks.	4	Towels	2

Village ten miles from Palermo. Some of the people wear leggings of thick fur—and of leather. "*Viva la divina providenza*" inscribed over the wine shops. Mules, asses, and sheep kept in the house.

A Silician Town. A great cluster of square-shaped, tiled-roofed houses, in a hollow among green and beautiful mts.—an old castle on an eminence above—green and cultivated fields around. Enter it and you must pass through narrow and muddy streets; the houses of stone sometimes plastered and whitewashed, with strong grated windows and open doors. Old women sit spinning; ragamuffins lounge in their capotes; mules and ass-carts, soldiers and priests, pass you. Here and there is a fountain, green and mossy, with groups of boys and women filling jars and little casks. Holy pictures and images in niches. The Piazza with its loftier houses—its *albergos*—its throngs of idlers around the provision stalls—and the church with the solemn-looking capoted loungers on its steps.

Village of M[arineo]. Luigi is a diminutive Sicilian, thin and spare, full of shrugs, and gestures, and exclamations. In the carriage he began to talk with the greatest vivacity, gesticulating and rolling his eyes, half frenzied by desire to be intelligible. He has provided a most excellent dinner here, where we stop till tomorrow, when we change the carriage for mules. I went to the house of our muleteer's brother and was treated with nuts. Luigi says he will be my Italian master—talked and gesticulated —kissed my hand—and after arranging all things, went off. He has brought excellent provisions—wine—and a large book of antiquities for me to read.

Staleles: salt-cellars. Greeks: Calabrians.

Friday. Left the town on mules—changed them for a carriage. The scenery very beautiful. Luigi talkative and lively as ever. When we stopped to lunch, a blind man came up and began to play on a violin, accompanied by another. Luigi jumped out and began to dance in a most amateur-like style to the music. An ugly beggar woman, who stood by, tossed her child in time with the musicians, hoping probably to win a *carlin*[*o*] in consideration of her part in the performance. When we reached a village, we found nothing to eat either in the *albergo* or the town, and had to depend upon Luigi's preparations. A large and dirty village. A floor of earth to my room. Costumes vary in different parts of Sicily, as do dialects. We passed warm baths—great houses for the *contadini*—and straw huts for the same. Luigi found a friend—his "Don Juanino mio." Stone here supplies the place of wood in architecture. Troughs—all of stone. Natural fountains have stone troughs hollowed out of the living rock beneath, for the mules, etc. Flax and grain of various kinds—spinning still the occupation of the women. The black-capoted and staring idlers, grouped around the huge stone stables beneath my room, make a strange appearance.

Morning, La Cara. A throng of men and cattle in the stable below, mules going out with their panniers and their tails knotted; others being equipped.

Began on foot. Walked on over a bad road in company with two muleteers talking their villanous patois, of which I understood not a word. It was like a New England November—the wind came cold and sharp over the mountains. The mules overtook us, and we mounted. We had not gone far, when some *contadini* told us that the road was broken away. We turned back—waded through a vast slough of mud in the bottom of a valley—then followed a narrow and broken pathway of stones along the side of a hill, while a swollen stream roared along among the olive-trees below. After this we found no road at all—or where there was one, it was a gulf of mud. We forded a dozen streams—one of them in its broad bed of stones, with the water rippling in a narrow stream down the centre, closely resembled ours—but the illusion was dispelled by a glance at the bare and smooth hills, with olives and Indian figs, and the stone house of refuge with tiled roofs, not far from the landing place.

My mule did not behave himself. He had a propensity for stumbling in dangerous places—would also turn longing glances at the fair ones of his race, and make a horrible noise meanwhile. When fairly in among the mts., it began to rain. A violent wind, too, sprang up as we crossed a little bridge at the bottom of a narrow gorge, where a stream came down from the mountains.

We soon after saw Castel Termini on the side of a hill in front. After riding an hour over a stony and barren hill-side in the rain and wind, which were excessively cold, we got to the town. The scenery about here might be beautiful in fair weather; it was gloomy and savage then. We approached the town by a path a yard wide—which by the use of ages had become worn deep in the soil so that to a spectator at a distance we should have seemed half buried. The town is a fine one; very clean. The usual crowd collected at the *albergo* to see us. I dined and (and) went out with Luigi, who show'd some antique coins, and a beautiful grotto adorned with Sicilian minerals. A broad-shouldered Greek, a non-commissioned officer in the Neapolitan gendarmes, attempted a conversation in his own language with me, but without success. The judge showed me into a *converzatione* where a dozen or more people were playing cards. They stared at me with great curiosity, and finally left their game and gathered round me in a ring, very curious to know something of the place I came from. I talked as I could with my limited stock of Italian. They asked me what province I came from; I told them Massachusetts, at which they paused in astonishment, and then muttered *"Cattivissima parola!"* The Greek alone succeeded in pronouncing it. I got tired of being an object of curiosity to so many, bade them good night, and went to the inn.

Yankee curiosity is nothing to the curiosity of these people.

Left the inn in the morning and rode over a country of mountains by a mule-track, literally paved with alabastar in some places. Saw a *lettiga*. Approaching a deep valley, we heard the noise of water at the bottom, and saw a wide and turbid stream that we must cross. The broad meadows below us were dotted with hundreds of the long-horned oxen of Sicily, each with a bell round its neck, which sounded at that height like the tinkling of a stream. The mountains lay still in the hot sunshine, softened by a sort of sleepy haze. When we got down to the bank, we found there two men naked from the waist downwards, whose muscular and handsome limbs were tanned as black as their faces by constant exposure. One went before our mules—the other brought up the rear. The water was up to the horses' bellies, but we got through dry. Stopping now and then to water the horses at alabastar troughs cut at the bottom of springs, we reached the village of Carmina at noon. It was excessively hot, and sultry as we entered the town and climbed the steep street. All the houses were plastered up with a gray cement of gypsum—everything was of the same gray hue but the brown roofs. The women sat on stone benches outside their doors, with loose hair and a primitive dress, combing their hair or caressing their children. Some basked at full length on the ground. Many were pretty, though the full vigor and health on their sunburnt cheeks were the chief part of their attractions. All was rude and primitive. Capoted starers and Neapolitan soldiers were congregated in the piazza before the ancient church. Opposite this village—on the other side of the valley—another similar village lay basking in the sun, with the yellow palace of its proprietor conspicuous above the grey houses. There was no *albergo* here. Luigi took possession of a private house, where he produced dinner. Some fellows then guided me to the sulphur mines just back of the village.

As we rode away, we had from the hill-top a glorious spectacle of ——— and mountains. We rode until late in the afternoon, when we saw Girgenti crowning a steep hill in front, and caught glimpses of the sea through the vallies. It was near sunset—the scenes we past were rich and beautiful beyond expression. Flocks of goats were driven past us; mules and asses with their panniers came down from the city. We left the road, and crossing a little mule path, descended into a deep and shadowy valley, on the opposite side of which rose the hill on which the city stands. Luigi was in a great excitement to be there before the Dawsons. *"Corragio, my brave mule; corragio, signore, we shall be victors."* He went on driving his mule at full speed up the steep hill; making short cuts; leaping dangerous gullies, in neck or nothing style, till he got to the top; and shouted, *"Vittoria!"* as he rode into the gate, as much elated as if he had accomplished some great enterprise.

"Ecco mi pronto; sono Luigi! Viva l'onore!"

The women of Cara—they reminded me of the women of Virgil's ecclogues, the wives of the primitive inhabitants of Italy. There was health and strength and good physical womanhood about them. There were the affections of a Roman—strong and unpolished: some fondled their children; some caressed their husbands; some hugged and kissed pet dogs—fit mates all for the wild foresters and mountaineers of whom the pastoral poets speak.

A Sicilian inn. An old house of stone, like all the rest. A den below, with a mud floor—filled with water jars, harness, stone troughs, and a thousand strange utensils of cookery—all handsomely encrusted with dirt. A dirty image of the Virgin on the wall, with a lamp before it. Dirty loungers crouching over braziers of charcoal—this in the kitchen, all as dark as Tartarus. Close adjoining to it, on the same floor, are great stone apartments for the mules and asses, who in the good inns are usually accommodated with separate apartments, though in private houses a corner of the family room, always the cleanest, is assigned to them. Ask for *apartamenti,* and you are conducted up flights of dilapidated stone steps to a room floored with cement as hard as stone—with plastered walls garnished with a crucifix or a holy picture—one strongly secured window—and a bed whereof you are never allowed to be the sole tenant, for a regiment of fleas is always quartered upon you. The only kind of fire is one of charcoal in a brazier. As to food, it cannot be had. I speak from the experience of three nights, and I solemnly aver that the picture is not over colored.

It is an amusing sight to see the mules and asses go out from their quarters in the morning. The mule I have ridden is young and inexperienced—though a wretched mule, he has sympathy with his kind.

A prominent feature of a *locanda* I have for[gotten]—it is the beggars.

A filthy and wretched beast, all tatters and rags, unshaven, with bleared gummy eyes and a crouching posture, stands covered all but the face in a rotten brown capote at the door—thrusts forth a rosary in your face, and mutters a petition for alms. Some of them have a cylindrical box with an image of the Savior on the cross painted on it, which they hold out to receive your gift. Luigi takes off his hat to the image, but declines any more substantial token of respect. These are professed beggars—only one form of the nuisance. Each man, woman, or child about the place occasionally practices the trade.

Morning, Monday. Visited the old temples of Agrigentum on the hill below Girgenti—tombs, temples, roads, *fascinae*, etc. I had rather see Mt. Washington, notwithstanding dear Miss Prentiss' predictions.

Luigi has provided an excellent dinner—his zeal is most admirable. He comes in: "Ah, *signor*, do you think I love money? No, Luigi loves honor," slapping himself on the breast and rolling up his eyes. He is perfectly rabid with enthusiasm in everything—raves of love on the road— tells stories of his elopement with his wife—sings songs—shouts "*Corragio*" —says, assuming a most heroic attitude on his mule's back, "*Il vento—il [la] neve—il pioggia—li fiume—tutto fa niente, corragio, signore*"; and then breaks out into a song. He is mad after antiquities—comes up to tell me that he can buy *antiqua moneta* at Girgenti for *pochissimo*. He enters into my plans with most fervid zeal, leaving me almost nothing to do. Wherever we stop, he first provides dinner—waits on table with an eulogium on every dish, and a list, daily repeated, of the provisions he has provided— then reappears, bring *molte cose de curiose* in the shape of vases and domestic utensils. I hint at anything to be done—he pounds his breast, and exclaims: "*Ecco mi pronto; sono Luigi!* All is safe under the care of Luigi; do not trouble yourself, *signore*."

This ebullition of zeal in all things is curious enough at times—last night in his fiery charge up the mountain, with his whole soul set on vanquishing the Dawsons. We came to a ditch which he could not pass— he struck his forehead—exclaimed, "*Maria Santissima!*"—then recovering his spirits, roared "*Corragio*," and dashed off, mad with eagerness, in another direction. This sort of enthusiasm seems common enough here. There is a Signor Politi, half rampant about antiquities—he and Luigi boil over together, and aggravate each other's madness.

Luigi says he always brings with him some antiquities *per fare complimenti* to his acquaintances—for which he receives other *complimenti* in return—an interchange of civilities very characteristic of this excitable

people, with their huggings, kissings, and swearings of eternal friendship.
The blind traveller, Mr. Oldham(?) [Holman].

Went to see Signore Politi—got his antiquities of Sicily and saw the
works of Signore Fennimore Coopero, translated. Visited the Duomo—
gathered curiosities—descended to the port, five miles distant, and thence
proceeded to Mont'Allegro. When half way there, a large town lay
before us among the mts.—Siculiana—built of alabastar; the people were
different in costume from others—some of the women wore their hair
arranged in a very beautiful manner. The occupants of the crowded
doorways were, however, engaged in spinning like the rest. The women
here in Sicily ride astride the mule, like the men.

We proceeded thence by a mule path through a country of rocky and
broken mts., with an occasional view of the sea betwixt them. The
valleys we traversed were full of sheep. Our mules waded frequently to
their knees in mud. Late in the afternoon we saw Mt. Allegro—a village
wildly and beautifully situated at the base of mts. of alabastar—the
summit of one of them, just above, is crowned with a ruined castle and an
assemblage of ancient dwellings. It rises before me now as I write at the
window of the *locanda*—the white rock contrasted with the thick growth
of Indian fig that springs from every crevice, from top to bottom. It is
a quiet and beautiful evening. The usual groups of idlers in the streets are
talking and laughing—the same beings that their fathers were before
them, six centuries ago. The approach to this place, which is almost
surrounded by a belt of orange groves, is over rocks of alabastar, in which
the constant passage of mules and asses has worn a deep narrow channel.

Luigi excited. He sat by the table with a glass of wine, gesticulating,
rolling up his eyes, opening and shutting his mouth: *"Viva l'onore! signorino
mio, viva Bacco—viva Dio—viva il console Americano";* then he kisses the
buttons of his coat, which have the American eagles; then seizes my hand
and kisses that.

Morning. Picked up beautiful specimans of alabastar. *Afternoon.*—of agates
and jaspers. It rained—the country uninteresting—the mules slipping in
the mud—reached Sciacca, a town of more than 20,000 inhabitants.
Found rooms, after some difficulty.

Morning. At Sciacca are vapor baths—arranged by Dedalus, but now the
property of Santo Carlogio—at the summit of a high mt. a few miles from
town. I rode up there in the morning, came to the convent of the St. at
the top where, circling around the whitewashed wall, we came to a

diminutive stable, where through an opening at the head of a flight of stairs we beheld the refectioner engaged, with gown tucked up, in the operations of his office. He conducted me to the baths—a great cavern under the convent, secured by a strong door. I undressed in an apartment opposite, and staid quarter of an hour in the cavern, where a stream of vapor, with a roaring down in the bowels of the mt. like a waterfall, filled the whole place and brought on a most active perspiration. My cicerone, who staid there, discoursed meanwhile on their antiquity, till I cried enough, made a dash for the room, where he rubbed me down with a towel. Not that the towel was supplied by the fathers. The holy father then led me to a hole in the mt. below, where a similar steam issued, with a still louder noise. The view of Sciacca on the little hill below—with its white battlements, ruined castle, and numerous churches—was very fine. Descending, bought pots and kettles, etc.; saw the castle and the tomb of its ancient master, Ct. P———; the Carmelite church, which was a gift of his to the monks. He was a grandson of Roger, the expeller of the Saracens. The fathers were at dinner—one of them, however, showed me the church, and faintly refused my *bonamano*, as the rules of his order dictated; he took it, however, on my holding it forth again.

Accounts of European Journey

	Drafts
Mr. Sprague	£13 in sovereigns
Mr. Payson	$20 sp. in Spanish dollars
—Do.—	Piasts. 30 in Piastres
Mr. Gardiner	Piasts. 80
Do.	Piasts. 70
Booth and Jean	Psts. 100
Do.	Sp. dolls. 50 in Spanish dlls.
Freeborn	Sp. dls. 60
Do.	Sp. dls. 20
	Sp. dls. 40
Du Fresne	Tus. dls. 100—each Tuscan do.——=Sp. dlls. 1.05
Ulrich	Francs 200
Hottinguer	Francs 1200
Baring Brs.	£ 70.1.6

```
  200                           13
 1200                           70.1.6
 ————                          ————————
 1400 francs                   £83.1.6
```

```
        30   Payson    50
       150   Gardiner  60 ⎫
       100   R.J.J.    20 ⎬ = 120          83
       ———   piastres  40 ⎭                 5
       280             ————                ———
                       170                 415
                                           450
     1400 francs                           500
      280 piastres                        ————
      170 Sp. dols.                        1365
       83.1.6 £.s.d.
           80
           70
          100
           50
           60
           20
           40
```

Expenditures

Gibralter   £ 6   in sovereigns

Passage to M. £ 13   in sovereigns

Malta and ⎰ £ 4   in sovereigns
Syracuse   ⎱ Doubl. ½   in 1 quarter and 2 eighth doub.

Messina ⎧ Doubl. ⅛   in eighth doub.
⎨ Sp. $ 16   in Spanish dollars
⎩ Piastres 14

Palermo   ⎧ Piastres 96
and journey ⎨ Sp. $ 4
to Girgenti ⎩ Doubl. ¼

Luigi's services began at noon, Thursday, Jan. 18th.

Crucifixes, pictures, images suspended in churches by the sick.

11 piastres to sundries

$\frac{5}{18}$ Giuseppe

20   Luigi

D. 16.75 = 1	1st	Thursday		
½D. 8.37½ = ½	2nd	Luigi		[?]
D. 16.75 = 1	3rd	15½		31C
	4th–8th = 13 pieces	$\frac{4\frac{1}{4}}{}$	31	24 5
3	9th	60	2	7
3	10th	2		84
4	11th	$\frac{62}{}$		
		3		
		$\overline{65\frac{7}{8}}$		
		65.10½		

Boston & Berkshire Journal
1844

Introduction

IN THE course of his European travels Parkman had not lost his love for the New England countryside; and as soon as he could get away from home after his return, he made an expedition to the Berkshire Hills in western Massachusetts. The record of this journey is of particular interest, for it shows him observing his country and his people with eyes freshened by European travel. He was awakened to a new appreciation of America; and he liked his land none the less for having seen others. The opening pages of this Berkshire journal offer more of Parkman's conclusions about Europe than the European journal itself. His observations of the New England scene are sharper and more objective than before he went abroad, and they reveal a greater maturity. In short, travel was beginning to make him a citizen of the world.

The journal opens with an account of the Fourth of July celebration at Concord, which is followed by the record of an excursion to Nahant. Then, scrawling a note on the flyleaf of his little notebook that he must be at Cambridge on the third Wednesday of August— for his graduation from Harvard—Parkman set off westward for a few weeks among those Berkshire Hills which had aroused his interest two years before, when he was bound for Lake George. He had historical research in mind, for the region was rich in legends and traditions of its frontier days, which figure considerably in *A Half-Century of Conflict* and *Montcalm and Wolfe;* but Parkman was also anxious to refresh himself with a few weeks of outdoor life. He traveled light, with a knapsack containing "three shirts, two stockings, flannel drawers, fishing apparatus, powder and shot, and *History of B[erkshire]*." Passing westward by Springfield, Cabotville, Chester Factory, and Lee, he came at last to Stockbridge, perhaps the most charming of the old New England towns. Here he gathered a great store of memories from ancient village notables. Then he turned southward to Great Barrington and Mount Washington, the most isolated settlement in Massachusetts; then northward to Lebanon Springs, over the New York line, where he witnessed a mass meeting of the Anti-Rent Rebellion. Finally he came to North Adams and Williamstown, once the frontier outposts of Massachusetts and consequently full of interest to him. He had a long interview with General Epaphras Hoyt, the antiquarian and historian of the French and Indian War; and learned much of Major Robert Rogers, Sir William Johnson, General Israel Putnam, Montcalm, the partisan Marin, Baron Dieskau, and other great figures in his drama. For the rest the notebook is crammed with references to books, magazines, papers, maps, and a long précis of Dieskau's own account of his defeat at Lake George in 1755. History had resumed its unrelenting hold on Parkman.

The record of this journey is contained in a small green leather notebook, 4 by 2½ inches. The penciled writing is badly smudged on the opening and concluding pages, and is sometimes indecipherable. There is much greater use of a personal shorthand, involving many abbreviations, than in any of the earlier journals.[1]

1844

July 4th, [*18*]*44.* The Celebration at Concord. The admirable good-humor of the people in the cars, during some very vexatious delays, was remarkable.

Some young men sung songs and amused themselves with jokes, among whom my former schoolmate was conspicuous. In spite of the coldness attributed to the Am[erican] character, he seemed to play the *rowdey* with all his heart, and as if he considered it the height of glory.

The cheerfulness, the spirit of accommodation and politeness, was extraordinary. Perfect order, in the most difficult evolutions of the day. An hundred soldiers would not in Europe have ensured such quiet and unanimity. Some young men exhibited a good deal of humor, and of knowledge, in their observations, and I remembered that this is *our lowest class.* This orderly, enthusiastic, and intelligent body is the nearest approach to the peasantry of Europe. If we have not the courtly polish of the European upper circles, the absence of their stupid and brutal peasantry is a fair offset.

The girls came in throngs to the road as the train passed, to be greeted with cheers. And in Concord, when the procession passed the groups of women in the windows and balconies, there was the same cheering.

I saw two drunken men. One, at the dinner, was immediately pushed out with expressions of vexation and contempt. He made long speeches at the door to the crowd. A tall, thin, black-browed Yankee had pushed him out, and was disposed to assume the bully over him; but finding his position in that capacity rather absurd, he began to change his bullyism into a half-amused air and tone.

"Now, don't ye be provoking me to strike ye," he said, "'cause if I should, I should make a leetle daylight shine through you in no time"—turning with a triumphant consciousness of superiority to the bystanders, to see how they would be amused by his treatment of the drunken man.

An old farmer exhibited a sprightliness not very common among Yankees. He danced about with great activity, giving his advice aloud on all topics in a humorous strain—when the train was coming slowly up, he shouted out: "Fetch a log there, and block the team."

Students of H[arvard] do not on all occasions appear much better than their less favored countrymen, either in point of gentlemanly and *distingué* appearance or in conversation.

The rooms of Jonas and Levi, with their jack-at-all-trades knick-knacks—bugs, pictures, guns, skeletons of fish and mice, etc., etc. Levi's manufacture of wreaths for his sisters and friends. The simplicity and absence of forms—what Englishman would call the *provincialism* of society here. A species of family—admits familiarities which could not be borne elsewhere.

The discussion on Fourierism,[2] etc., of the she-philosophers of W[est] Roxbury. Their speculations, and the whole atmosphere of that haunt of *new philosophy*, were very striking and amusing after seeing the manners of Paris and London—the entertainments and pleasures and the workings of passions which they in their retirement seem scarce to dream of.

Monday, July——. "Old Snow"[3]—his careless abandonment—his tobacco chewing—his admiration of George[4]—his hatreds—his indifference and laziness—his want of foresight—his violent expressions of friendship.

A ship without a rudder—a good fellow, but on the way to wreck and worthlessness.

England has her hedges and her smooth green hills, robed with a spirit of power and worth, strengthened and sanctioned by ages—but give me the rocky hill-side, the shaggy cedar and shrub-oak—the wide reach of uncultivated landscape—the fiery glare of the sun among the evening clouds, fling[ing] over all its wild and ruddy light. All is new—all is rough—no charm of a familiar country.

Fierce savages have roamed like beasts amid its rugged scenery—
there was a day of struggle, and they have past away, and a race of
indomitable men have supplanted them. The day of struggle was
short, yet its scenes of fear and blood are not without a horrid
romance; and well does the rugged landscape recall them to mind.

The spring at the granite ledge near Pine Hill. "It's chockfull of
animils"—a host of frogs leaped in. "Is the water good?" I asked.
"Well, I guess it ain't the best that ever was," etc.

Nahant, July 17ᵗʰ. The company on board the steamboat—difference in silence and intelligence from a cockny party. The man with
the model of a bee-hive from Ohio. His dry sarcastic replies. "Why,
what hurt do the millers do?" asked a man, with reference to a sort
of trap to catch bee-moths.

"Hurt! Why, when they've killed about nine-tenths of the bees
in the United States, and spoilt every hive in Ohio state, I should
think they might be doing hurt, shouldn't you?"

The travelled fool, setting his name in the bar-book as "———
———, *Cosmopolite*."

He finds some improvements here "very creditable to the town"—
of which he is a native. He imitates English dress and manners.

The dinner party was various and far from *distingué*.

At Whitney's another class yet of people were assembled—
awkward heroes of the counter, bashful boys, and corresponding
young ladies—they drive off in waggons to fish. The old fisherman,
when I paid him for a rod and declined to take change, simply and
gruffly said "thank yer" as he walked off.

59 & 51 Pine St, N. Y.   J. G. W. Shea[5]

"Have your ever seen any about here?"—"No, not about here,
I ha'nt." Q. Had he anywhere?

Roland Green,[6] Mansfield—his family have relics of the Indians.
House before you come to the R. R., left hand.

The disagreeable, whining manner of some vulgar Yankee girls.

John Norton's Captivity[7]—taken at a fort in Adams, 1746.

"A thousand associations throng on us at their name. The breezes of the Tweed are an atmosphere of poetry and song, chivalry and romance. They kindle the spirit of the enthousiast into flame—the dullest feels that wonder and romance are around him—thus have the deeds and the fancies of ages charmed that spot. And now turn thence to our dark unstoried woods! The poetic spark grows dull and dies, for there is nothing to fan it into life.

"For a thousand ages her trees rose, flourished, and fell. In the autumn the vast continent glared at once with yellow and red and green; and when winter came, the ice of her waters groaned and cracked to the solitudes; and in the spring her savage streams burst their fetters, and bore down the refuse of the wilderness. It was half a world consecrated to the operations of Nature!"

Springfield.   The independent Yankee whom I spoke to about his failure to call me. In Job's language, he "stood right up to it," giving shot for shot. No English cringing.

The landlord—no bowing.

Montague[8]—grape shot dug up.

Cabotville.   The Negro family, who sell "refreshments beer & cake." The old man, the boy with the pears and water-melons, and the woman with the money-box.

The landlord of Chester Factory, sitting cross-legged on his chair, took no notice of me as I came in; but on my asking if the landlord was in, he said, "Yes, here I be."

Parties—dances—ministers.

The stage and driver from Ches[ter] Fac[tory]. A fellow with hollow eyes, and peculiar sullenness and discontent on his features. He had travelled all over the State, sometimes driving, and sometimes singing at cows[a]—but usually following his inclinations. Nothing pleased him. He hated the country, the road, and everything else. He had engaged on it for a year, but intended to get away at the first opportunity. He hated hard labor, and set such a value on his services that he refused to be coachman to a southern gent. who offered him $15 when he demanded $25. He intended never to marry, but liked "training with the girls." We past the house of a man who was rich for the country, having about $20,000. "I suppose he likes this place," said the driver, looking up with contemptuous discontent, and giving his horses a switch under the bellies. He says he could be rich in a month, if he chose to try, but he "always wanted to take comfort, and have nothing to think on when even'g came. Working in the day-time was enough for him."

There are occasional dances in the villages. The Methodist ministers are changed every two years. Beside their salary, they receive contributions and presents. The people are in the habit of coming to tea, sending or bringing the materials to the minister's house.

The driver turned to me with a surly envy, and said he guessed I "warn't used to hard labor." The lazy rascal envies all who can live without labor. As we were driving on, I remarked on the beauty of the road. "*Humph!* Wouldn't you like to live here?" I enquired who were the occupants of a certain house. "Paddies"—with exquisite surly indifference. "Where does that road lead?"—"Don't know," in the same tone.

Clark[9]—Watchmaker, West Stockbridge

An American landlord does not trouble himself to welcome his guests. He lets them enter his house, and sits by quite indifferent. He seems rather to consider himself as conferring an obligation in anything that he may do for them.

Lee is full of factory girls. The very devil beset me there. I never

[a] As a cattle drover.—Ed.

suffered so much from certain longings which I resolved not to gratify, and which got me into such a nervous state that I scarcely slept all night.

Stockbridge. Maple and beech have followed the fir of the original growth. The railroad has lessened the value of land by the influx of western produce. These towns never sent produce to Boston and do not now—the expense of the R.R. transportation is too great.

Stockbridge. An old man at the church told me that the original meeting-house where Sergeant[10] preached stood on the green in front. About half a mile off is the site of the church of 1784 where, in the mound on which it was built, were found a number of Indian bodies. An old man, present when the grave was opened, said that they were heaped confusedly together, without instruments of any kind with them. Perhaps they were flung there by the whites after Wolcott's [Talcot's] fight in [King] Philip's War.[11] The Stockbridge Indians had a burying ground, the care of which they consigned, on leaving the place, to old Mr. Partridge,[12] who keeps it carefully for them. It is in the village, and seems to contain a large number of bodies.

The old Negro[13] at the church. He remembered all about the Indians and exchanged recollections with the old man aforesaid. He had been a soldier in W's [Washington's] army. He had four children in the churchyard, he said with a solemn countenance, but "These are my children," he added, stretching his cane over a host of little boys. "Ah, how much we are consarned to fetch them up well and virtuous," etc. He was very philosophical, and every remark carried the old patriarch into lengthy orations on virtue and temperance. He looked on himself as father to all Stockbridge.

Agrippa Hull—the "African Prince."

The "full-blooded Yankee girl," of whom I asked the way to Monument Mt. "She'd been up there going arter the cows." Bold, lively, and talkative. "Would she go and show me the way?" "Well, that *would* be rather curious!"

The group by the road-side—the beautiful girl with her hand in that of the man on horseback, and her friend sitting close by on the bank.

Mrs. Stephen Jones[14]

Went up Monument Mt.

House of Jones.[15] His kindness and obliging disposition. He had two large bowls of ash knots—a beautiful material—made by the Indians. The largest is used only for making wedding-cake. Also a mortar, of a piece of the trunk of a maple, made by the Indians for his grandfather. The pestle was of stone. The conch which was used to call the Indians to church now calls his household to dinner. His brother, Mr. Stephen Jones, is a great geologist, and very talkative. I got of him a chisel and two arrowheads.

Dr. Partridge. The old man was in his laboratory, bedroom, etc. among his old tables, book-cases, etc., with shelves of medicines, and scales suspended hard by. He is about 94,[16] and remembered Williams[17] well, who he describes as a large stout man, who used often to visit his father, and taken him on his knee. And once went out the door and blew a trumpet to amuse him. He says he remembers the face as if he saw it yesterday, especially the swelling of the ruddy cheeks.

His father, Colonel Partridge,[18] was in the service, and despised Abercrombie [Abercromby][19] as a coward. The Dr. remembers seeing a thousand of Abercrombie's Highlanders at Hatfield, or some other town where they were billetted. Abercrombie was always trembling with fear of Indians, and sending out scouts about camp. When Howe[20] fell, Partridge, the Dr. says, was at his side; and his lordship said: "This army has no leader, and is defeated."

On one occasion Abercrombie ordered 800 rangers to be detached. Partridge, or some other officer, drew them up in a cornfield, directing the short men to stand on the hills and the tall ones in the hollows. The British officers were struck with admiration at the uniform height of the men.

When A. was about to sail down the lake, he ordered the rangers to stay behind to protect the embarcation[b]; when it was finished, they received immediate orders to pull forwards to the head of the column. They did so, and left the army behind; stopped at an island where they caught fish and made a meal; and then pulled on to the foot of the lake, keeping under the eastern shore till they reached the outlet. Here they landed, and concealed themselves at its south side. When the army appeared and attempted to land, the French opposed them. The rangers, taking deliberate aim from their ambush, fired on their flank, and in the doctor's expression "killed half the regiment."[c] [21]

Amherst[22] he considers a very different man from A[bercromby]. When he had landed and sat down before Ti[conderoga], he offered a great reward to any spy who should explore the works. Three men at length offered themselves: an Indian, a half breed, and an Irish ranger named Morrison,[23] who died in Stockbridge and from whom the Dr. got the story. Amherst reminded them of the peril of the service, but they resolved to venture; and passing down the outlet in the breech-clouts of Indians, they landed under the walls. Passing on in a violent rain, they found the first sentry in his box. Him the Indian killed and scalped; and directing Morrison to remain there, the other two proceeded. They served another sentry in the same manner, till they arrived to where there was a flag, with another sentry, who was also killed. They then withdrew, and had only reached the beach when they heard the drums beat to relieve the sentinels. Morrison could not run as well as the others; so they siezed hold of him to help him, and dragging him behind, they got into the woods and hid. They soon heard guns fired, as the relief guard came to the first sentry box, followed soon by two other successive discharges, as the other dead bodies were discovered; and they heard noise and firing for some time in the direction of the fort. When they came to camp, the Indian showed the scalp to Amherst, who refused to believe on such evidence that they had gone so far into the works, on which the Indian unfolded from his body the flag which he had taken on killing the third sentry—indisputable evidence. The general

---

[b] "Partridge used to describe the embarcation as he then witnessed it as superb."—F. P.

[c] "On his father's authority.—F.P."

Major Robert Rogers, 1776
Engraving by Martin Will
(Coverdale Collection No. 2280)

ordered some rum, and promised the reward in the morning. In the night the fort was evacuated. Morrison took credit to himself as the cause, and old Dr. P., admitting his claim, promised him doctoring gratis in consideration of his service to the country.[d]

The Dr. tells some familiar anecdotes of Williams, and says that Kunkapot[24] and some other Indians accompanied him to the war. He remembered nothing of the affair of William Henry.[25]

Great Barrington. On entering the bar-room, an old man with a sunburnt wrinkled face and no teeth, a little straw hat set on one side of his gray head—and who was sitting on a chair leaning his elbows on his knees and straddling his legs apart—thus addressed me: "Hullo! hullo!! What's agoin' on, now? Ye ain't off to the wars aready, be ye? Ther' ain't no war now as I knows on, though there's agoin' to be one afore long, as damned bloody as ever was fit this side o' hell!" He proceeded to inform me that he was an old soldier, and always fought on the side of Liberty. He swore like a trooper at every sentence. He cursed the temperance reform which has run mad all over Berkshire.[26]

Someone speaking of a girl's uncle—"Uncle, is it; uncle ain't the (the) thing. You must look farder up"—and then laughed between his toothless gums. "The' ain't none o' them thing now-a-days, now the temperance folks says you mustn't," remarked a man. "You mustn't," said the old farmer, "G–d d–m you mustn't."

He then began to to speak of some of his neighbors, one of whom he mentioned as "that G–d damnedest sneakingest, nastiest puppy that ever went this side of Hell!" Another he likened to a "sheep's cod dried"; another was "not fit to carry guts to a bear." His features were remarkably bold and well formed, but thoroughly Yankee, as also were his positions. "That d——d rascal's brother," said he, pointing to a man near him, "played me the meanest trick you ever seed," etc. The man was rather amused.

The old Dr. at Stockbridge told me that when Williams went to the war, he told a girl of the village that if she would mourn eleven months for him in case of his death, he would leave her a great part

[d] "Rather doubtful, like the rest of the old man's stories."—F.P.

of his property. The girl replied that she would put on mourning for no one but her husband. It afterwards appeared that she was engaged to a young man of the place.

The Dr. was fond of dwelling on Abercrombie's failings. Once, he says, his father's rangers fired their guns in the woods about camp. "'What, what,' says the general"—thus he tells the story— "'we shall have the Indians on us if you let your men go on so.' 'Your lordship,' says he, 'don't know nothing about our kind of fighting. We fire our guns off for the Indians to hear, and when we see them coming, we shoot 'em!'"

Stopped to get a dinner at a house in Mt. Washington. One was provided, such as it was. The old woman was very kind. Speaking of the difficulty of finding the way to the falls, she said in the peculiar whining tone, "Well, I should think the folks at the house might accommodate a stranger with somebody to show the way." "Well," replied the daughter, "I guess they a'nt got nobody that's big enough."

Bash-a-bish lower Fall [*Bish-Bash Falls*]. A noble spectacle. Rocks covered with pine, maple, yellow birch, and hemlock sweep round in a semi-circular form, the water plunging through a crevice in the middle.

The cliffs stretch away above, thick-set with vegetation—you see but a small patch of sky from the deep gorge. The basin at the foot of the fall is filled with foam, and the stream escapes downward in a deep gulf, full of rocks and shadowed by the trees of the opposite mountain declivity.

An old Indian told Murray° that the word *Taconic*, applied to the mountain, was derived from the following circumstance. A stream of water in the west of Berkshire flows out and forms a pond on a level with its outlet. In the summer the pond grows less by evaporation; and the Indians, imagining that the water had run back into the mountain by the passage whence it issued, called the place "Taconic." The word means "run out and run in" or something similar; and is pronounced "Ta-con-nic."

° See below.—Ed.

Mt. Washington. As I rested by the road, a little boy came up with a kettle full of vinegar in his hand. He said he lived near the head of the falls. But was going to move soon, and go off he did not know where, but "Mr. Jenkins said it was a great ways." I showed him how to fire my gun, which very much pleased [him]. After clambering up the steep path for a mile or more, we reached the top; and the path led on into a very wild and narrow valley, with a house at the foot of it. The brook ran down through the middle, till it flung itself over the cliffs at the foot, some hundred feet down, into the deep gorge we had just come up. The mountains of this little valley were very steep, and drew nearer to each other as we proceeded up the brook. There was a delapidated barn, some old potato fields, etc., but the woods of birch and maple came close down on each side, and all was wild enough. At length a high dam and a mill appeared up stream, and a new log-house on the other side among the pine trees. We came opposite to it, where, though drift-rotten logs enough were laying about, there was no means to pass the stream. A woman[f] came down to the other side and tried to lay a plank across, but without success, so I waded through with the little boy. The woman immediately began to apologize for her bare feet, saying that she had mistaken me for her cousin, and was so glad to see an acquaintance in that place that [she] had "ran right down to see." She showed me her house, which was remarkably neat, with a little sheltered porch before it, and a rude garden fenced with the outside slabs of boards from the mill. There were plenty of ducks and geese about. She did not wish to give me lodging as she was alone, her husband being gone; but she sent "Abel" to the spring for water, killed a duck, and gave me an excellent supper. "I warn't never rich," she said, "but I a'nt always lived in a log hut." The place she stigmatized as a "Hell on earth," which she was going to leave as soon as possible. She described her terror when, sitting alone, she hears the footstep of a man about the house. Once, she says, she thought nothing of it; but now, in that lonely place, it frightens her. A wild cat from the mountains has invested the house, and stolen her ducks and hens. She has seen it; and one night, hearing the hens cackling, she went out, though in great terror, and made a fire to keep it off.

[f] Mrs. Comstock. See below.—Ed.

I went to Mr. Murray's—the other house—to spend the night. His wife was Dutch. He is a broken tradesman. His house is neatly plastered; and he, the picture of ill-health and leanness, sat smoking his pipe, and talking slowly between the whiffs. The room where I slept contained various relics of departed prosperity. A handsomely curtained bed—images and french toys on the mantel. A table with books, vases, pamphlets, and a *basket of cards* upon it. His girls' dresses were hung up around, with a few maps, etc. The furniture, though a little old, evidently belonged to his better days; and these various articles contrasted queerly with the hearth of rough stones, and the rude whitewashed fireplace, filled by way of ornament with pine and hemlock boughs.

Murray is a broken man every way—duns are frequently upon him, Mrs. Comstock says, but he says that he is pleased with that place, because it is *"retired."* He has had enough of company, and wants to be by himself, and his wife echoes his words. "Well," says Mrs. C. in a true woman's strain, "I should think Mrs. Murray might wait till she *feels* what she says, and not pretend to be so Christain like and humble, when we all know she don't like the mounting no more than I do."

I breakfasted with Mrs. C. in the morning, who on my departure refused to take any remuneration, which I was obliged to throw into the form of a gift to her little boy; and took my leave of this very kind and hospitable woman.

The falls from the top of the rock are an extraordinarily fine scene—almost as fine below and seem to me one of the finest scenes in N. E. [New England].

The rainy day—the scene of mountain and vapors from Scott's field at the top of the ascent.

The hearty, horse-swapping, thumping young Dutchman, who would be damned if he cared for anything if he could only swap off his old waggons for Jim Pray's colt.

The crouching, cadaverous, lank old man, with the opium for his rheumatic wife, and the long string of misfortunes.

Mr. Tuttle's private tavern, with the store. His "woman."

Widow Evans, Pownal, near Rev. Grand.

A man at Lebanon Springs, not far from the lower tavern, says that he has some journals of his father, which contain, for what he knows to the contrary, notes of his services in Rogers' Rangers[27] when a young man. The man is grandson of the W[idow] Evans above.

The Patroon's (or the "Patteroon's") tenure is in peril.[28] The tenants refuse to pay rent. I went to Stephentown to see the gathering for resistance. All along the road occurred boards with "Down with the rent"—and flags in the village and the gathering place, which was on a hill at a mean tavern surrounded by a group of houses. The assembly was of the very lowest kind. The barroom full to suffocation, and vilely perfumed. One old man sat and talked for a long time. He had been with Indians, and kept remarking on their good qualities; which remarks were received with great applause. The chief actors were to appear in the disguise of Indians. There was another old fellow who had been with the Indians and kept constantly talking of their friendship for him, perfuming all near with the stench of his filthy, rotten teeth. Another fellow had been at Plattsburg,[29] and distinguished himself by the vileness of his appearance and conversation. Another old fool, with a battered straw hat, and a dirty shirt for his only upper garment, kept retailing his grievances, lashing himself into enthusiasm and exclaiming "Down with the rent!" The "Indians" at length appeared, and went through some meaningless manoevres. A hole in a block of cast iron was charged with powder, and a plug being driven hard into it, it was repeatedly fired. After a while, it was attempted to come to business. A few of the more decent squatted themselves on the bank of grass before the platform erected for the directors, but were listless and inattentive while the directors, who managed the whole affair, nominated deputies from the different districts to arrange the matter. Those loudest in their noise were not of the number on the bank. The voice of the old man with the straw hat could be heard declaiming, and sharply exclaiming, "Down with the rent!" while the rest were eating or watching the clumsy and absurd movements of the "Indians."

The other towns of the Patroon's domain have also revolted; and his feudal tenure, so strangely out of place in America, has probably lived its time.

I have never seen a viler concourse in America.

Captain Edmund Badger,[30] North Adams
W's [William's] Will[31]

Family of Col. Jones[32]

Dr. Robbins—"Pastor of a church in Rochester, Mass."—author of the Address.

The "Hopper." A great mountain rises before me, covered with trees—birch, beech and fir; and near the top and down its sides light vapors are resting among the tree tops—now sinking below them, now rising up and obscuring them; sometimes a line of firs will be relieved against the white cloud, turning nearly black by the contrast. A ridge beyond is black with firs, with a few light green birches dotted among them and a rough, bare avalanche slide. They are stiff and erect all along the top of the ridge.

The clouds rise upward from the forest like smoke from firs below. The shadows of the clouds pass over it—now it is dark and now light—now the brightness is on the wet smooth stones of the slide. The clouds move rapidly overhead, and the weather grows clearer. The stream makes a loud noise below. The hillside where I sit is scattered with the remains of large pines—lying with their branches tangled and twisted together—and numberless dead ones stand erect, burnt about the roots by fire. The living pines above raise their arms out towards the light—opposite the declivity they stand on.

The little brown wren hopping among the fallen pine trees.

Ft. Massachusetts.[33] It stood on wide green meadows, surrounded on every side by hills. The Hoosic on the other, some 6 or 8 hundred yds. distant, with a high forest-covered hill—a ridge of Saddle Mt., I think, beyond. Wooded hills on the other side, sloping down to the meadow, less distant. In front and behind, as I stand, distant, undulating hills. The crows caw loudly among the woods. Under an apple tree is a broken head-stone with a fragment of inscription, where the bones of the officer who was shot—bones now in the W [Williams] college—were found. The bullet was in the spine.

It is a beautiful situation, this fine day.

French hatchets have been found here, beside Indian weapons of stone.

Horse radish planted by the soldiers grows here quite abundantly. I got a hatchet and gouge from Capt. B[adger].

The Irish Priest—with his jovial conversation and hints about a mitre. The surly boy of a driver.

The number of geologists among the old farmers of the country. The country Professor Hopkins,[34] Stephen Jones, Capt. Badger, etc. Geology seems a science of peculiar attraction to this class of people all the world over—witness the old farmer whom I met in England.

Boston Telegraph, Sept 9th, 1824: Col. Williams' legacies.

Capt. E. Badger at North Adams showed me a copy of the will of Col. W.—the final will made at Albany. The original is in the Hampshire [County] offices.

Capt. B., an old member of legislature, a great geologist, has been about with me, discoursing on marble quarries, manufactories, etc., with his old hat pulled down over his eyebrows, his dingy coat hung on his shoulders, and his cane in his hand. He is, of course, practical in all his views of things. He has a number of stones in an old kettle which constitutes his collection. He was very obliging and talkative.

Col. W. had a house in Stockbridge, as appears by the will, but the Capt. says he lived at Deerfield—perhaps he meant Hatfield.[35]

The old Capt. returned tonight, bringing me some little bits of crystal, and a fragment of jasper which he had smoothed on a grindstone. He was much pleased, evidently, at my listening to his geological remarks, which are none of the most profound. He makes some queer assertion, to which I venture to dissent; he then makes some preposterous argument, winking on me with one eye in the triumph of success. An idea once in his head, it monopolises it wholly. Everything is the work of "iron." Every phenomenon is caused by "petunse."

He showed me a common stone in the street, which he said he could at any time polish and get $10 for it.

American Medical Biographies.[36] They will contain a valuable letter from the brother of Col. W.

Stephens [Stevens] writing a hist. of Putnam.[37]

Dr. Williams[38] of Deerfield has letters of Col. W. and his b[rothe]r, the Dr., of the greatest interest.

Moulin
Molang } ? [Marin][39]

Rogers[40] born at Methuen, Mass.

Father killed while hunting a bear. Rogers himself was a hunter and a wanderer from his youth up.

Old General Hoyt[41]—unquestionable authority—says that a man at Deerfield named Catlin, in the rangers, told him that he was conducting a train of waggons to Abercrombie's army at the lake. Between Ft. Ed[ward] and Bloody Pond, he saw a crow picking the dung in the road, which ran through a low swampy place. He was in front of the wagons, and thinking no danger, thought he would shoot the crow. So bending under the bushes, he crept along the side of the road to get a shot. The crow would not suffer him to approach, but flying up and re-alighting, drew him on some distance from his men, and at length flew away. He was now on a rising ground again, when a tremendous yell and fire of musketry burst forth below him. The train, in the low part of the road, were fired on by a party who did not touch him, although he had passed close to the muzzles of their guns. He immediately escaped to the station at Half-Way Brook, but most of his men were killed.[42]

Stephens [Stevens] at Cambridge has plans of Johnson's and W [Williams'] battle grounds,[43] and a minute account of Montcalm's descent by a Jesuit[44] who accompanied the expedition.

General Hoyt has journals, letters, etc., of great interest, and a *complete unpublished life of Rogers.*

Nil desperandum.

Rogers' Rock was the scene of the great winter fight where the two officers were lost on the ice.[45] So says the General.

Was Putnam's fight with Molang [Marin] the narrows of S[ou]th Bay (1) or the narrows nearer Whitehall (2)[46]? Hoyt says that an old man found a sword and a gun, much decayed, in a species of cave near the latter place. H. asked for the sword. "It made me a damned good carving knife," said the man, who had cut it in two for this purpose.

The two girls on the road from N. Adams. One of them was a mixture of all the mean qualities of her sex, with none of the nobler. She was full of the pettiest envy, spite, jealousy, and malice, singularly impudent and indelicate.

"Should have given ye a pie today, but ain't got no *timber* to make 'em."

Gen. Hoyt has plans of Montcalm's siege[47]—perhaps also Stephens.

I had a talk of four or five hours with the old General, and took tea with him.

Williams' *Hist. of Vermont*[48] and Thompson's hist.[49]

Hendrick[50] rode a little pony.

Hoyt's *I[ndian] wars*[51]
Gentleman's Magazine—By means of Index

Maps: "Province of Quebec according to Proclamation of '63"—Various maps of Canada—"Province of N. E."[52]

Wynnes' B[ritish] Empire in America[53]

Rogers' Concise Account of North America[54]—Proposed to be continued by a volume with map. Does such a vol. exist?

State histories

The Contest in America. Relation of the F[rench] & E[nglish] colonies. London, 1757.[55]

Barber's Hist. and Antiquities of N. E.[56] contains an account of Dieskau's fight taken from Dwight's Travels.[57]

On the border of a swamp—a bright warm afternoon—with my rifle. There is a brisk breeze. The wind involves together the upper boughs of a hickory and a cedar, and the bare blind top of the latter grunts a sound, as if some animal were in the branches.

A high detached rock at the bottom of a shaggy, woody hill at the edge of a swamp. It is half buried among cedars, hickory, saplings, etc. The dry swamp is full of little bushes; and a wood of swamp-maples, rising from among the shrubs and undergrowth border it—bright in the sunlight, while the swamp and the wooded hollow in front are in the shadow of the hill behind. The distant pine-trees on the rising ground in front are also bright, but the shadow has almost reached themselves.

Dwight's Travels—account of Gen. Lyman, Vol. 1, Letter XXXI.

Account of and reflexions on Crown Pt. (Vol. 2, p. 447), with other matters of local history through the volumes.

"Two Journies to Lake George," with accounts of its battles (Vol. 3, p. 337, etc.).

"The Iroquois"—with poor list of authorities (Vol. 4, p. 186).

Camp Meeting, Saturday Evening, Aug 24; there will be a steamboat at 10 o'clock.

Mrs. Upham's—one day

4410-4414—Maps of B. & Fr. settlements [17]55

"Carte de l'Amérique Septentrionale"—the French claims. 4415

Fr. Claims in 1720—Map 4416

Br. Claims 1715—4419. This old map has a small colored picture of Niagara, with an inscription remarking "some make this Water Fall be half a league, while others reckon it to be no more than a hundred Fathom." In the foreground a colony of beavers dragging building materials on their tails.

Br. dominions by the treaty of [17]63—4421

Large maps of the N. E. states and other parts of N. America, 1776—4403.

Large maps of Pensylvania in the same volume (?)

Turn over: *Topographie Générale de L'Amérique Septentrionale et Indes Occidentales, ou recueil de toutes les cartes marines ou autres arpentages particuliers et plans de cette Partie de Monde.* Londres, 1768. No. 4394

Ms. containing invaluable plans and maps and among the rest Braddock—Bat. of Lake George—Bouquet's fights—Little Meadows —Plan of Du Quesne—line of march to its attack—Ticonderoga and Aber.'s [Abercromby's] attack—New York—a small but minute map of the lakes with surrounding country—Shegnekto Bay and Ft. Lawrence—Louisburg—Montreal—Quebec. English attack (several maps)

Murray's *Travels*[58] and novel.

Campaigns of '55-'56. Winslow's MS. journal[59] in Mass. Hist. Soc. Library.

Letters from officers in the State House.[60]

Part of Montcalm letters in England.[61]

Sir W. Johnson papers were at Albany, the possession of a family named Cooper, Sparks thinks, but Stone got them.[62]

Dieskau's letters in Sp[ar]ks'.[63] library.

There is a Jesuit account of Montcalm's descent on W[illiam] H[cnry]—the priest was in the expedition.[64]

A pamphlet accompanied the map of the Bat. of Lake George— but Sparks has not been able to find it.[65]

M. W. F. [Monday, Wednesday, Friday] 10–11. Introduction first on Friday

---

The following are notes taken from a Fr. manuscript, supposed to be written by Dieskau when he had returned to France. This is the supposition of Sparks, who copied the MS. from the F[rench] War dept.[66]

Dieskau was to attack *Chouayen* [Oswego] with 4,000 men and 12 cannon. 2,000 had gone to [Fort] Frontenac, where was the rendevous; when news came from Varin,[67] Commissary of Marine at St. John's, that Johnson was within (in) two days' march of Fort Frédéric(k) [Crown Point], with 3,000 men.

The Gov.-General,[68] at this, would have Johnson opposed at all events, though Dieskau urged that, though the news were true, the possession of Ft. Frédéric was by no means the possession of Montreal —for Ft. St. John's and Chambley would remain to be taken, to say nothing of the difficulties of the country. But the Gov.-Gen. was resolved to opp[ose] Johnson—so D. set out, and reaching Ft. Fred., found Varin's story false. He had 3,000 men. At Ft. F., D. learnt that J. was at St. Sacrement [Lake George] with 3,000 also—that he was building a fort to ensure his retreat, and that all his supplies were drawn from Ft. Edward, which he heard was ill fortified, with 500 wretched levies camped round it. He resolved to make himself master of the Ft. and so cut off J.'s supplies. The first day he got to Carillon [Ticonderoga], whence he marched with 1,500 men, leaving the other half of his army, part at Carillon and part at *les deux rochers* [Twin Rocks], to secure a retreat in case of need. He took 8 days' provision for his meditated *coup de main*. The night of the 4th day, he camped in the woods a league from Ft. E[dward]. Here he mustered a council of I's. [Indians] and told them his plan. They demanded time to deliberate it. Two hours after, the Algonquin, Nepissingues [Nipissing], and Abenaki chiefs came and said that, for their part, they were willing, but the Iroquois (300 in number) had refused, and, they being the superior, the other tribes must follow them. He sent for the Iroquois chfs.; [told them] that he only wanted them to make a false attack—the reglrs. and Canadians would fight—they should be safe; but they said they would not attack the E[nglish] on their own ground, refusing absolutely.

He said it was shameful to turn back with nothing done, on which they offered to go against J.'s army, which they said was not on English ground. So at daybreak they marched up the road from Ft. E. in three columns, C[anadian]s. on the right, Inds. left, reglrs. centre.

A prisoner told them that 1,000 men were within half a league. He sent Canadians 300 paces in advance in ambush, keeping reglrs. behind, so that the disposition had the figure of a *cul-de-sac*.

D. thought he should take all the E[nglish].; but some Indians, "more curious than the rest," looked up and saw that the E. had with them "un corps d'Agniere [Agniers]."[69] These told the rest, on which the Iroquois fired in the air to warn the E. The attack then began, but the Iroquois alone would not fight.

They followed the E. to the fort, where the Indians first, and then the Canadians, refused to obey, though D. told them the regs. should bear the brunt of the cannon which so much frightened them. Urging them on, D. was wounded at one moment by two shots in the leg, and one in the knee, exposing himself too much. He fell near a tree and was helped behind it by Montreuil,[70] second in command, whom D. ordered to take the command and, if necessary, to order a retreat, but to send two men to take care of him. M. left him reluctantly, and soon sent 2 Canadians. One was shot and fell across D.'s legs, the other went to find assistance—but soon D. heard the retreat beating, but saw nothing, being in a hollow place with his back against a tree. Half an hour after, he saw a soldier aiming at him from behind a tree, close before him; to whom he signed not to fire, but was shot through the body. The sold. leaped out, exclaiming in F. "*Rendez-vous!*" D. demanded why he fired at a wounded wretch like him. The s. said he might have pistols—and that he was a F. deserter—deserted 10 yrs. before. Others came up and D. was carried to J.'s tent.

Indians soon came rushing in, frantically demanding D. to be burnt, but J. pacified them and sent them off, telling D. that he was safe.

The I.'s came again with the same demand, but J. pacified them, and they gave their hands to D. D. wished to go to another tent, but J. said he must wait till the I.'s were asleep as they would fall on him. He went to a Col.'s tent with a guard of 50 men. An Indian came in, in the night, apparently unarmed, and the sentinel let him pass, but he drew a sword from under his cloak and would have killed D., had not the Col. sprung between.

9 days after, D. was sent to Albany to the house of Johnson, and 4 weeks after to New York.

A letter of Dieskau to Doriel[71] at Montreal:

Of D[ieskau]'s original army 700 were regulars, 1,600 Canadiens, 700 Indians—in all, 3,000. He had all along suspected the Iroquois of the Sault and of the deux Montagnes—300 in all.

27th August one Boileau, Canadian, told him that 3,000 E. were camped near the house of Lydius, where a fort was begun.[72]

The Abenakis brought him a prisoner, who told him that 500 men were at Edward, the main army at Lydius' house. He took with him 600 Indians, 600 Canadians, and 200 regulars.

He was to have reached and attacked Edward on the 4th night, but the Iroquois guides misled him and brought him to the road a league off, too late.

Here he took a courier and some prisoners.

Marching toward the lake, his scouts told him of W.'s [Williams'] detachment—a prisoner confirmed the news. "1,000 men or more, going to the succor of the fort."

He ordered his savages to be ready to take them *behind*.

The Iroquois at the left treasonably showed themselves.

D. wished to enter the camp pell mell. But the Iroquois gathered together, and would not advance; the Abenakis followed their example; and the Canadians were discouraged.

The regulars were almost all killed.

———

Turner's Falls

Indian Orchard Falls, Springfield

Leyden Glen

Cascade in Leverett

Bash-pish Falls, Mt. Washington, ascend the rock above the upper Fall.

Gorge and Falls in Royalston

Road from Will[iamstown] through New Ashford

Saddle Mt. & the Hopper, Williamstown Bridge, N. A. [North Adams].

Monument Mt.

Town of Mt. Washington, by way of Egremont, Bashapish falls.

Sugar-Loaf Mt, Deerfield. Bloody Brook (from Williamston to Hancock "an interesting excursion")

Westfield River following the Pontoosuc turnpike

The defile of Deerfield River between Shelburne and Conway[g]

Analysis of C. Disignate Introduc.: America in a state of transition. Her original state—her present—England's present—we look to the future, her future—no romance of warlike achievement—all peace and utilitarianism—Indian wars—even now.

The child's journey, his associations—true elements of the romantic —but age dispels the fanciful illusion—too close a view. The heroes of our old wars, the farmers, etc., of our day. Matter of fact, universally prevalent. The traveller's attempt to find a hero. Abandons America in despair.

Every possible thing done to ruin the face of nature—but unsucessful. Instance.

The traveller in Europe. Art, nature, history combine.

In America Art has done her best to destroy nature, association nothing. Her former state. Her present matter of fact aspects illustrated.

The battle ground of the North—her history—her matter of fact struggles.

Essentials of poetical war-fare. The Spanish guerrilla—the revolutionary soldier.

Obscure recesses of other countries contain men untouched by civilization—the Welsh—the Highlander—the American backwoodsman.

Traveller abandons the search for the poetical.

America's remaining beauty. Her wildness. Her associations—the scenes that encounter the traveller.

Lake George and its heroes.

[g] Evidently Parkman listed in advance of his excursion the beauty spots of central and western Massachusetts.—Ed.

Old Northwest Journal
& Pontiac Notes
1844-45

Introduction

THIS notebook is something of a grab bag, with a curiously assorted collection of contents which mirrors Parkman's diverse interests at this period. References to historical books and documents predominate; then there are brief sketches of Parkman's forays and excursions when the Dane Law School (forerunner of the Harvard Law School) weighed too heavily upon him. There are vivid bits of autobiography concerning the misunderstood lover, amusingly irreverent accounts of Millerite and Fourierite meetings, and thumbnail pictures of various Bostonians and Harvard men. These sketches of character and incident were part of Parkman's apprenticeship to the writer's trade, and they are sharp and promising. The main portion of the notebook is an account of a journey to the Old Northwest in July and August 1845, a research trip centered on Pontiac's conspiracy, the subject of Parkman's first historical work, published six years later.

The aim of Parkman's *History of the Conspiracy of Pontiac* was "to portray the American forest and the American Indian at the moment when both received their final doom," as the author put it in his preface. The British conquest of Canada in 1759-60 upset the balance of power in America. "Could the French have maintained their ground, the ruin of the Indian tribes might long have been postponed; but the victory of Quebec was the signal for their swift decline. Thenceforth they were destined to melt and vanish before the advancing waves of Anglo-American power, which now rolled westward unchecked and unopposed. They saw the danger, and, led by a great and daring champion, struggled fiercely to avoid it." This champion was Pontiac, chief of the Ottawas, one of the greatest of Indians, who almost brought about a great coalition of all the tribes against the whites. Since his mother was an Ojibwa, he was able to form by 1755 a loose confederacy of the Ottawas, Ojibwas, and Potawatomies. He was an ally of the French, and probably saw service with them at Braddock's defeat in 1755 and at Quebec in 1759. He knew that the policy of the British, who were interested in settlement and hence in exterminating or driving out the Indians, was very different from that of the fur-trading French, who made allies and converts of the savages. After the conquest of Canada, the French traders and hunters of the Great Lakes encouraged the uneasy Indians with vague promises of help from France if they would war against the English. In the winter of 1762-63 Pontiac organized a simultaneous assault on all the British outposts from Fort Niagara to Mackinaw on the Lakes, and from Fort Presqu'ile down along the Alleghany frontier. Though the main attacks on Fort Pitt and Detroit failed in the summer of 1763, nearly every minor fort was captured, and the English suffered great losses in men and property. Then the great conspiracy petered out, as one tribe after another was forced to make treaties with the English. Pontiac himself made peace in 1766, through the efforts of Sir William Johnson. Two years later he was murdered at Cahokia near St. Louis by an Indian who had been bribed by an English trader.

Parkman's journey in search of Pontiac material took him first to New York and Philadelphia, and then, with Simon Stevens as his guide, to the old Alleghany frontier: Lancaster, Harrisburg, Williamsport, Trout Run; then north to Buffalo by Tioga Creek, and Seneca Lake, and then along the Great Lakes to Detroit, Mackinaw, and Sault Ste. Marie—the focal points of the Old Northwest. Lieutenant Henry Whiting showed Parkman about Mackinaw, the strategic center of the Lakes, and introduced him to Robert Stuart, the fur trader of Astoria fame. At the Soo, in the absence of the Indian agent H. R. Schoolcraft, Parkman checked that authority's statements with missionary, trader, and savage. He continued on to Palmer (St. Clair), Michigan, to sift six trunks of papers belonging to Lieutenant McDougall, Pontiac's prisoner during the siege of Detroit. On his return trip he crossed over into Canada to seek out descendants of Baby and Campeau, the early French traders at Detroit; and then went back down Lake Erie, taking careful topographical notes as he went. At Niagara he stopped to inspect the battle sites and to marvel at the cataract, and then continued eastward by train, stopping at Onondaga to visit the home of the Five Nations. After fruitless attempts to elicit historical information through gifts of cheap cigars to the stolid descendants of the Iroquois, he continued on down the Mohawk Valley, the scene of many a border fray. Reaching the Hudson, he returned to Boston by way of the steamer from New York, just in time for the Commencement festivities at Harvard. The trip had added much to Parkman's historical lore, and notably had given him a fuller acquaintance with the Indians than he had previously had.

The journal indicates Parkman's state of mind at this period. At his father's insistence he was studying law under Judges Story and Greenleaf; for it was one of the three professions open to a Boston gentleman of his position, and he had no inclination toward medicine or the ministry. Indeed, he had none toward the law; but since his father refused to take his literary ambitions seriously, it was the least of three evils, since it left him some leisure to pursue his own chosen path. Most of his energy was devoted to historical studies, and references to this avocation far outnumber legal notes in his notebooks of this period. There is a despairing note in this one that "according to Burke, more Blackstones were sold in the Colonies than in England," which indicates how unwilling an apprentice Parkman was to the law. His discontent and frustration are echoed in the ruthless sketches of friends, companions, and casual acquaintances. Parkman was dissatisfied with his own life and hence had little use for his fellows. Only the few purple passages devoted to nature are free of the acid which flowed all too freely from his pen at this period, and at least one of these is haunted by a brooding melancholy.

The accounts, reckoned to the last half-cent, which fill a good portion of this notebook, are given in the appendix. They indicate how little capital was involved in Parkman's historical investigations, and how his money went for historical books and copying fees, rather than for personal comforts or pleasures.

This notebook covers from September 13, 1844 to the latter part of August 1845. It is contained in a black leather pocket notebook, 5x3 inches, and in two improvised supplements; for at Mackinaw Parkman had exhausted his writing space, and wrote the rest of the journal, largely in pencil, on two large sheets of paper, folded and stitched into such form that they could be slipped into a pocket of the original notebook. Further notes on the law school, and on the Northwest and Pontiac, will be found in the 1846 Account Book, page 484.

The front end papers of the notebook contain some scribbled notes of names of books and authorities, and sources of reference material. Among those which can be deciphered are those of Gallatin,[1] the Philadelphia Society, the City Library, the Historical Society, Conyngham,[2] Ingraham, G. W. Baker,[3] Miller of 114 Cherry St., *Wars of North West*, Stone's *Red Jacket*,[4] Baumgarten's (?) *American Archaeologia*, Atwater's *Antiquities*,[5] Mr. Van Cleve (?) of Ohio ("is an investigator of antiquities"), and Stephens [Stevens][6] of 19 West Strand. There is also a note: "Read Dryden's Prose."

1844-1845

Sept. 13 [*1844*]. Muster at Concord—on a hill, with the tents with provisions for the companies on one side, and the booths, peddlers, oyster stalls, bookstalls, etc., on the other. Several companies of rangers in frocks and with rifles. The tall artillery sentinel—the gambling at the tavern, the congregation in the barroom. George P.'s [Parkman's][7] follies.

That remarkable constraint [to] which the presence of a person of inferior sense, acuteness, and energy will sometimes subject one far his superior.

A letter from Orne [Orme] describing the battle of the Monongahela. Winslow, p. 136.[8]

Another letter: The inhabitants of Nova Scotia, on whose quiet remaining on the soil, one of the French claims was founded—they remained, probably, on sufference, though they refused the oath of allegiance, except on condition that they should not be compelled to bear arms.

Winslow's Nova Scotia Journal—His Journal at Lake George.[9] Trumbull's Papers,[10] Mass. Hist. Soc.

Sunday, Sept 21. Some men are fools—utter and inexpressible fools. I went over to Dr. B[igelow]'s[11] last night to call on Miss———— [Prentiss?][12] Heaven knows I am quite indifferent to her charms, and called merely out of politeness, not caring to have her think I slighted her. But the Dr., in the contemptible suspicion that he is full of, chose to interpret other-wise. William Train was there, whom

I allowed to converse with Miss. P. while I talked with the Dr.'s lady. The Dr. watched me, though I was not aware of it at the time, till happening to rise to take a bottle of Cologne, out of a mere whim, and applying some of it to my handkerchief; the idiot made a remark, in a meaning tone about "*long walks* in the evening" injuring me. He soon after asked me to take a glass of wine, saying that it would make me *feel better*. He whispered in my ear that Train *would go soon*, and I better stay. What could I do or say? I longed to tell him the true state of my feelings, and above all what I thought of his suspicious impertinence. I left the house vexed beyond measure at being pitied as a jealous lover, when one object of my indifference to Miss ——— that evening was to prove, to her and the rest, how free I was from the influence of her attractions. Is it not hard for a man of sense to penetrate all the depths of a blockhead's folly? and to know what interpretation such a fellow will put on his conduct? I sent him a letter which I think will trouble not a little his jealous and suspicious temper.

Sept. 23. Watertown Miller[ite] Meeting,[13] which I went to with White.[14] At a private house. A dozen or so of men and oldish women were seated silently about the room. We sat down, and for a long time the silence was interrupted only by sighs and groans. At length a big stout fellow struck up a hymn, which was fervently sung by all. Then they dropped on their knees, while another prayed aloud in a hasty and earnest manner, responded to by sighs, exclamations, and cries of "Amen." Several other prayers were made. One large, broadfaced, stupid fellow was a long time getting under weigh, but grew at last very loud and fervent. A woman joined immediately in a voice still more rapid. Then there was silence. All rose from their knees. A moment after, the large man by the table rose slowly, and fixing his eyes on vacuity, exclaimed: "How bright the vision! Oh, how long shall this bright hour delay?" I at first thought this a burst of enthusiasm—it was no such thing, but a quotation from Dr. Watts.[15] The fellow went on with more quotations, gathered from far and near, describing the glories of heaven, etc. There was a good deal of spiritual pride about this man. He evidently thought himself a full match for any clergyman at expounding scripture, and gifted with a large share of grace. I set him down as a vain, proud fanatic, of a cold nature. Of course he was speaking from the immediate impulse of the holy spirit within him, and his discourse was rambling and bungling enough. He said he once went out West; and described, *à la* Yankee, the difficulties he encountered, and drew a parellel between his journey and the Christian heavenly journey. He then spoke of Christ, giving a sketch of his life, and remarking that though he might have "associated with the popularest men of his time," he preferred persecutions. He said that all true Christians must be persecuted; as he told a minister at Boston, if they were not persecuted they were not Christians.

"Well, now, I tell you what it is, brothers, and sisters, and *friends*, these here ministers, the (the) popularest men of their day, ain't Christians," etc. He thought that a "blazing stake would be set up here in Watertown, to persecute the true believers—yes, I do, and that are within three months, too."

The enthusiasm of the poor devils is exalted amazingly by the tricks played on them. He exposed their doctrine—Christ was to take the form of flesh—heaven was to be "located" on earth—and then he drew a bungling picture of the heaven.

Several speakers followed him. One woman modestly remarked that it was easy to endure the cross and the stake, and such like great evils, but it tried the Christian's soul when it came to parting with little ornaments and dresses. The Bible champion corrected some of her quotations as she went on. When she sat down, he said that for "them that hadn't got grace inside of 'em it *was* hard, as sister Stone said, to part with little worldly trifles   but if one has truly got the spirit of God, and is persecuted and shunned and despised of men, he don't want no more to do with them things. If a man or a woman sticks to his jewels, it's a sign he han't got grace, but goes by rule, like them that preach in meeting off of notes," etc., etc., etc.

With screams, ejaculations, and prayers, the meeting was going on when we left.

Nothing is more cheerful and bright than the clear sunny days of autumn, when the woods have changed—but it is a dull and chilling sky—all is cold and cheerless. Blue jays are screaming and occasionally a squirrel chirrups. The shrubs have grown dark and dull with last night's frost, and the cold puffs of air shake them in a melancholy manner. The pines along the edge of the clearing, the piles of wood—the rocky hill with its various colored shrubbery, and rough and broken growth of wood along its top—all wear the same gloomy aspect. A white spot on the dull sheet of cloud marks where the sun should be.

The Methodists have bishops and a sort of hierarchy. There are conferences to settle the affairs of the church, appoint ministers, pay them, etc. The great annual conference at Baltimore confirms and rejects the acts of the rest. Though the salary of the ministers is not paid by the parishes, they meet great hospitality and attention, and want for nothing during their stay.

More Blackstones were sold in the Colonies than in England, says Burke.

Money more than their just proportion paid by the Colonies for the last two F[rench] wars.

The Assemblies had always *paid* the Governors, and civil officers. Assemblies expected to provide a civil list on the arrival of each governor. This practise discontinued—Governors paid annually.

Folsom family,[16] Exeter, N.H., descendants of the officer in the War. The editor of the *News Letter*[17] will probably know about it.

"*Cornwallis*"[18] at Brighton, Oct. 18, '44. I was there before the militia had gone off. Some had the large skirted coats of revolutionary officers; some wore battered helmets; some three-cornered hats; some nothing. They had every variety of weapon, from blunderbuss to rusty saw; and were of all ages and sizes. A more ragamuffin assemblage I never saw.

"Officers to the front," exclaimed the general on his horse. The long line of ragamuffins, who stood leaning on their rifles or muskets in every variety of outlandish costume, looked as if they had never an officer among them. But at the word a number of fellows straddled out from the line—with yellow breeches and red coats; or with false beards and dirty shirts; armed with axes, swords, or guns. These marched up to the front and faced gravely towards the general. "*Gentleman* officers," he began, etc.

The address over, the officers withdrew, and the music struck up, at which the whole line of ragamuffins got under way, and marched straggling off the ground, just as the sun went down.

In the space in front of the tavern was the usual congregation of idlers and loafers—with a gang of Indians firing their guns and yelling close by.

*Nov. 3*rd. The family of ————. He himself is a generous, open, hospitable, kind-tempered man of vulgar birth and education who has got an enormous fortune. His delight is in liberality, and he scatters money like water. His lady—a very dull and vulgar personage—is chiefly solicitous to make a display of the "tasty" and "genteel." They have a score of half-gentleman hangers-on around them. The house is furnished with an elegance that would better befit a palace. ———— has brought from Europe a splendid collection of pictures, which he has not the cultivation to appreciate, but delights to listen to their praises. He has statues, splendid articles of *bijouterie* from Paris, some of which are most antirepublican in character, and piled together with a profusion akin to that of a warehouse. The damask curtains, the artificial flowers, the wax-candles, and the numberless and regal ornaments give his rooms a most remarkable aspect.

His children, who play at whist with the aforesaid hangers-on all evening, are much petted, and provided with lapdogs. ————, his son, educated in Paris, is particularly weak and senseless, placing the height of human glory in dissipation, in which he has of course indulged, though scarce sixteen. The mother and children are, indeed, all very weak and ill-informed, but the cordial hospitality and kindness of———— may make up for all, though [he] is quite in want of tact and discrimination, as might be expected.

————

Where in America is to be found that spirit of sport and bluff hearty enjoyment, that is seen in English country gentlemen and others? Business here absorbs everything, and renders people incapable of every other *pleasure*.

Officers of the army and navy are sometimes an exception. There is an old retired navy surgeon at Medford,[19] who lives with his dogs and his guns like an English squire, enjoying himself in the same hearty manner. Business, too, swallows much that is noble. The somewhat chivalrous sentiments, the reference of all things to the standard of a gentleman's honor, a certain nobleness (though it may be joined with debauchery and blackguardism) is found among the officers of armies.

Our business men, on the other hand, have narrowed away all this. Thoughts bent on practical gains are not pleasant to contemplate, no matter how much virtue may accompany them.

Old Mr. Blanchard, who, though past eighty, toothless and grey, stumped about with more than the vivacity of a boy. He was all liveliness and excitement. Some one offended him. "Damn you," shouted the old man, thumping down his cane, and shaking his fist. A general laugh followed, at which he stumped off elbowing among the crowd, shaking his head in wrath. A moment more found him all light and cheerfulness again, amusing a group of bystanders with jokes and stories.

The theological discussion at the Medford barroom, between Wait the blacksmith, James the Irishman, and the Whig who had been invited to drink a glass of champaign with Dudley Hall.[20]

Jan. 8th, '*45*. One of the most amusing characters of "our table"[a] is Bigelow,[21] a man so nervous and excitable that he has no self restraint, and is constantly advancing strange propositions with a most absolute air. This morning, he was inveighing bitterly against the "aristocracy" of the cadets,[22] but his more usual expression is that of the most unmitigated contempt for "clod-hoppers." Tonight he pitched upon "counter-jumpers" as the subjects of his animadversion, roundly declaring, rolling back his head and bringing his fist

[a] At a law school eating club.—Ed.

down upon the table, that there was not a respectable "counter-jumper" in Boston. Cobb[23] remarked that Mr. Lawrence[24] had extolled to him the character of that respectable class, on which Russell[25] remarked that Mr. Bigelow's acquaintances were probably from the inferior ranks of counter-jumpers. "That's a damned imputation! I defy any man here to say that I ever associated with counter-jumpers—least of all, Mr. Russell, those whom it is your pleasure to denominate, in so highflown and grandiloquent a style, the *lower ranks* of counter-jumpers," etc.

Fitchburg, Jan. 18. A bad inn. Sitting in public-room with an old woman, an(d) old man, and Joe [Peabody].[26] Landlord came in with a quantity of wood, which he put on the fire. He wished to make excuse for the tardiness of his preparations for supper, which he did thus: "Well, I never see nothing to beat this!" "What's to pay?" said I. "What's to pay! Why there's them damned boys won't stir nor do nothing! Here I've been a slaving this fortnight, and them lazy cusses, sitting on their arses. I won't stand it—nohow. They pretend to do work, do they—they *shall* do work, I guess they'll find that out, pretty quick. I guess their wages 'll feel it; if they don't, I'm mistaken. I'll tell 'em what it is to be hiring out and then not doing work, arter all," etc.

S[now] and his family[27] on the hill.

Sunday. This morning all the trees were crusted with the sleet of night before last. Every little twig was cased in crystal, and the green spires of the pines which showed through the coating of ice, were like diverging bundles of pea-green icecles. The sun rising behind a wooded hill made a most gorgeous appearance. All seemed studded with diamonds.

Mahon's, *Eng[land]*, IV.[28]

Coll[ection] of Extracts,[29] Series of Letters on the Scheme of Invasion in '59.

Harrison, *Ind. Life.*[30]

Lee, *Britain, Cocking's War*, a poem.

W's [Williams'] *Vermont*[31]
Romans' *Florida*[32]
Catalogue, Worcester Lib'y[33]
There is a printed journal mentioned in Worcester Cat. of service on the Lakes in '63 or '64.[34]
Filson's *Kentucky*.[35]
Hudson's Bay Compy: Ellis[36] and Dobson [Dobbs],[37] etc.
The Importance of Gaining and Preserving the Friendship of the B[ritish] Interest Considered, 1751.
Waldegrave's *Memoirs*.[38] Sermon on Death of Titcomb
Pickering's *Wyoming*.[39]
Guizot, *Cours d'Histoire Moderne*.[40]
Dryden—Pope—Bolinbroke—Swift's *John Bull* and *Martinus Scriblerus*[41]

The two deaf and dumb men in the public-room of the Elm Hotel. The old stage-agent playing chess, with the man looking over his shoulder.

The Senate Chamber[b]—the thin, large-nosed man, who tried to know everybody—took the Prex's cloak, with an "how-de-do, Mr. Quincy,"[42] and whom the Pres., with his usual felicity of manner, cut. The mean-looking man who sat listening with his mouth open.

The Penobscot Squaw at Roxbury: "You come up here to see; not for buy. You must give something." A large woman with quite expressive features.

March 10. The trees this morning were covered in every twig with feathery chrystals of snow, which gave them a beautiful appearance.
"Pride goeth before destruction and a haughty spirit before a fall" —think of that!

Lyman[43]—his silence, his oaths, his indecencies, and filthy habits.
P———, his white coat at class supper—his squirt, and his . . . .

Sunday. March 15[16]. The caterpillars of the willow just diverging
    [b] At the State House in Boston.—Ed.

from the bud. The long, stiff, awkward young shoots of Sumach. The beaded ends of the young maple-twigs. Q. Are the bright-red forked shrubs maples?

The crust of ice with the water run away from beneath.

J——y. His vanity and love of display, joined with energy, combine to make a fool of him. He affects the man of the world—goes always in full dress, and though he has no sportsmanlike propensities, keeps a breed of dogs about him, and affects the connoiseur: also a fine equipage. He is foolishly proud of money and his supposed rank in society, and lets drop no opportunity of showing his superiority. From constantly pushing himself into the foremost place, and affecting to command everywhere, he has raised a host of enemies. His vanity impels him to lie enormously. I suspect him of not being remarkably brave, though I should never have made the remark but for some boastful lies he has lately been telling about a street battle with some fellows who insulted him. He is hospitable and bountiful through ostentation.

March 16 [*17*]. The Navy Club[44] paraded today in a variety of costumes. The "Lord High" had an old Continental uniform; the drum-major flamed in red, the drum was carried by Dunlap,[45] who was plainly conscious of the dignity of the place. The band wore a variety of uniforms. The standard was borne by Grey [Gray],[46] who came little short of nine feet high, measured to the top of his plume. The "Rear-Admiral"—"the laziest fellow in the class"—walked behind in a Turkish dress, with two Negroes to carry a chair for him to sit in, and another with his pipe and handkerchief. The "digs" all wore square caps. The doctor was admirable, and had a whole hospital of bones and skulls hanging about him. The chaplain, too, was done to the life: he had a Bible in his hand, which on examination proved a cigar-box. One of the "Horse marines" was mounted.

Is a man a coward, because he feels less than himself in a crowd?

Lyman's freaks; his disgusting habits at table; windows broken and he will not mend them; goes to Brooks'[47] room, looks into his drawers —"Hulloa, you've got some gingerbread!"; invites himself to spend the evening there; stays till morning, and sleeps standing against the wall, like a horse!!

The theological controversy at Mrs. Sanders'.[48] Brooks is a good-natured, thoughtless, careless fellow, without either application, ambition, or any settled principle. He thought church-going was "horrid"—"such a damned bore to sit under a sermon 40 minutes—ministers ought to know better, damned if they hadn't," etc.

Ritchie[49] seriously and fervently upheld the Church of England, which seems in his eyes the receptacle of all holy and eccellent things, while J. Peabody laughed at B.'s random heedless remarks, at the same time taking an occasional part in the discussion like one who had deep feelings on religious subjects—perhaps he thinks he has. J. G. also came in with his silly boyish observations, but was immediately snubbed. "Oh, *there!* that's enough," said Brooks, "stop now, that's good fellows—nothing I hate like talking religion, because it never comes to good—you can't convince one another—here, Watch, come here, old boy, and get your supper!"

Halkett,[50] *Historical Notes respecting the Inds. of N[orth] A[merica] with Remarks on the attempts made to Convert and Civilize Them* (by John Halkett, Esq., 8vo., pp. 480, London, 1825) contains notes and references to authorities.

Letters in Pa. arranged by John Jordan, Jr. 91 South 3rd St. Member Hist. Soc., Philadelphia.

Letters of Bouquet, etc.

John Sonntag Havil[l]and

Bro(a)dhead[51]

Birbeck [Birkbeck][52]

Travels through that part of America previously called Louisiana. By Mr. Bossu, Captain in French Marines, *translated from the French by John Reinhold Forster,*[53] *F.A.S. Illustrated with notes relative chiefly to Natural History, to which is added by the Translator a systematic Catalogue of all the known plants in N. America,* etc., etc. (London, 1771).

Read Rich's *Catalogue*[54]—Cat. Phil. L'by.

Hartford Hist. Soc. Newspapers. New London Papers, in Mr.

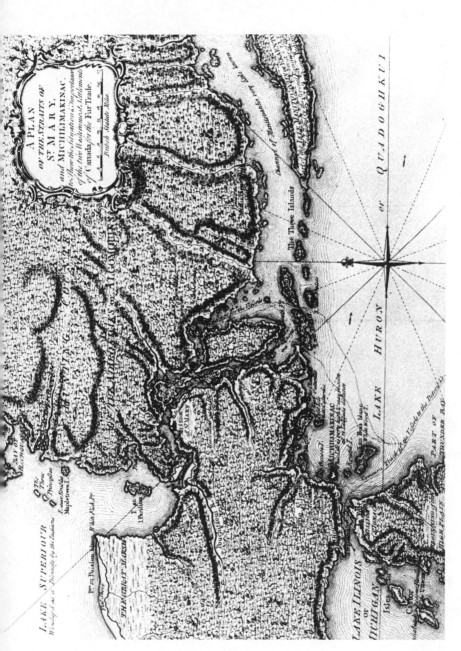

A Plan of the Straits of St. Mary and Michilimackinac
Engraved map
(Coverdale Collection No. 210)

Green's (Samuel?) hand. Putnam's letter originally published in a New London Paper?

Quebec Hist. Soc.[55]

Rich's *Catalogue*

Pouchot *sur la dernière guerre de l'Amérique.*[56] Very good.

Force[57] has authorities for Pontiac's notes of hand.

Lanman[58]

Little P.—about 13 years old—talks as if he were 50. "I do not think that seventeen is an appropriate age for entering college. The boy is too unexperienced. I agree entirely with my father that eighteen is preferable," etc., etc.

Brooks: "Law! Damn it, I never knew anything like it. Why, I can't take up a book without it puts me to sleep. I don't know what in the devil made me take Law—it's horrid! Greenleaf[59] met my father the other day and told him I was making fine progress; what does he know about it. Father swallowed it all; I wish Greenleaf would hold his tongue; I swear, it's horrid."

Law School Debating Soc. Batchelder[60] brought in numerous books from whence he read for three quarters of an hour, and made beside a most loose and ridiculous speech. He seems an instance of a man who is suspicious and timid, from *running* or *snubbing*, in private conversation, but will talk on forever, feeling a perfect independence in the debating club, where no one interferes with him.

Lee [Lea][61] of Louisiana spoke in the negative of the question which was that of nullification.

Hoadly [Hoadley][62] of Ohio, whom I have often remarked for a wretchedly sickly and feeble-looking person, spoke in the affirmative. His voice was like a lion's; and a supernatural energy seemed to animate his yellow, faded features, and give them an expression of fierce resolution.

Hooper[63] of South Ca. also spoke in the aff. He is a very gentlemanly southerner; pale, long-haired, well formed, and well-dressed; apparently haughty, proud, and aristocratic. He spoke with great fluency and not without taste; and was eminently courteous and stately in his manner.

Thayer[64] of Mass. took a *common-sense view* of the matter—every one of that assembly were *presumed to know* various things which he mentioned; the members of the convention were "*at least* men of ordinary abilities," etc.—a weak Yankee.

Ap. 23. D.D.S. [Daniel Denison Slade][65] on Fresh Pond—cross, childish, self-willed. He likes people whom he can direct, and who always yield to his selfish will. He is anxious to be treated with courtesy and consideration, yet is himself often very offency by his childish obstinacy and self-will.

Promised land of Canaan, to which the Israelites were entitled by right, but which was occupied by barbarous nations ordered to possess it. Application of this as a figure representing the kingdom of heaven—obstacles interposing to prevent attaining it—nevertheless sure. 1st-2nd Distrust of merits—2nd Distrust of power—3rd Worldiness—4th Fear of men, etc.

"They exchange opinions casually, and these are final. Councils generally deliberate upon what has been beforehand pretty well settled." [pp.] 27, 100.

Acct. of Chipawas by Cass.[66] Religious advantages, etc., [p.] 101. Pride in the *totem*: he is jealous of its honor and will avenge for insult offer(r)ed to it, [p.] 102; different totems different in political influence.

May 30, 1845. A great meeting of the Fourierites in Tremont Chapel. Most of them were rather a mean set of fellows—several foreigners—plenty of women, none pretty—there was most cordial shaking of hands and mutual congratulations before the meeting began. A dirty old man, four feet high, filthy with tobacco, came and sat down by me and was very enthusiastic. He thought Mr. Ripley, who made the opening speech, "one of the greatest men our country can produce." Ripley was followed by a stout old man, in a sack, who had previously been busy among the audience, welcoming, shaking hands, etc. He spoke with his hands in his pocket, and gave nothing but statistics, in a very dry, uninteresting manner. It surprised me to see these old fellows, who looked like anything but enthusiasts, attached to the cause. Horace Grant [Greeley]—the editor from N. Y.—spoke in a very weak, indecisive manner, seeming afraid of himself and his audience. He, however, gave some remarkable details of the working of the "present system of society" as illustrated by the working classes of N. Y.

Brisbane and Dana followed in a pair of windy speeches, and Channing was beginning a *ditto* when I came away. They say that there is a system of laws by which the world is to be governed "harmoniously," and that they have discovered those laws. F. Cabot was there, looking much more like a lunatic or a beast than a man.[67]

The Foot Race, June 17. There was not much excitement or enthusiasm. Thimblerig, etc., was going on. Among the characters most worthy of notice was the spectral puppy on horseback, with a patch over his eye, and the "special constable"—a perfect specimen of Yankeeism, with all its oddities and humors, internal and external.

Withers' *Cronicles of Border Warfare* (Clarksburg, Va., 1831).[68]
Doddridge's *Notes on the Ind. Wars* (Wellsburg[h], Va., 1824).[69]

Shallus's *Tables*, Hv'd [Harvard] L'by.

Napier's *History of the Conquest of Scinde*[70]
"Wiandots: by the Delawares called Delanatinos"—*Ettwein.*[71]
"The Six Nations[72] called the Mohicans, Delawares, and all the N. England savages, *Agozhaganta*"—Ettwein.
Toganawita—Mohawk. Otatscheehte—Oneida. Tatotarko—Onondaga. Tagahajon—Cayuga. Caniadario—Sataga-ranjes—Seneker. Six Nats.—Aquanophionihaga.—Ettewein (comp. the *printed* work—there may be mistakes in transcription!).
Delawares—Wapanachti. Oucheporiais—Chippeways. Chawainon —Shawnese [Shawnees]. Redmond Conyngham—Lancaster.

Prov[incial] Rec[ord] Bk., S[tate] P[aper?] 426, Colonial Recs.[73]
Plan of F[ort] Duquesne at Lancaster
1. Lancaster *Intelligencer*, 1843[74]

2. Chief Justice [J. B.] Gibson, Carlisle or Harrisburg, for Armstrong.[75]

3. Loudin's Work [Fort Loudon]—Carlisle

4. J. Francis Fisher,[76] Philadel., for admission to Phil[osophical] Soc., etc.

5. Plans of Ft. Pitt in Phil. Soc.?

6. James Ross at Pittsburg.[77]

7. Delaware *Register*. Wilmington.

8. Historical Coll. by Sherman Day.[78]

9. Bradstreet[79]—see notes to Letters of Junius.

Bouquet's[80] character—he employed Capt. Jack Smith and others.

The girl at table, who, probably afraid of being vulgar, made no answer when I offered to hand her what she was looking at with evident longing.

N. Y. [*New York*], *July 10.* The woman at Union Park who had dreamed of chairs, and after, on another night, of glass tumblers; and as she looked on the workmen at the fountain, felt a presentiment that she was destined to make her bread by means of it—so she bought chairs and a pitcher and glasses for water and lets them out for the people, as in the Champs Elysées. She also remarked upon the girls who made the park a place of assignation—spoke of the inconstancy natural to mankind—and was plainly up to snuff.

7535—*An Historical Review of Penna. from Its Origin, founded on authentic documents.*[81]

Chronicon Ephratense[82] (Lancaster, 1786), in German, but probably contains something.

Logan MSS., Vol. 3: a paper on Paxton Boys[83]—a paper on Ind. grievances, etc.

Ed. Shippen M.S. Col. [James] Bird's [Burd's], with Miss [Mrs.] Thom[p]son—Stevens[84]

Lancaster, Pa. A town of 9,000 inhabs.—laid out in a singular form, the main streets crossing each other thus:

The people chiefly Dutch—among them a number of Mennonists,[85] with long hair and beard. All the people here are as strong and hardy as any men I ever saw—seem to take life easily—have open and hearty manners, but are represented by Stephens [Stevens] as particularly close and miserly—as ignorant and stupid also, knowing nothing beyond their farms, and in the management of these following the manner of their forefathers. The land here is very rich, producing excellent wheat—there are a number of very rich people living in a plain manner here. Lancaster City is said to be the richest in the States. According to Stephens, this little place contains four distinct and separated circles of society.

Rode out to Paradise, to visit Mr. Redmond Conyngham.[86] Passed not many miles from the establishment of the "protestant monks" at Ephrata. Country rich and not very hilly—houses small, but many of them well built of stone, with very large and queerly shaped barns of the same, or on the poorer establishments of squared logs.

At Paradise stopped at the fine, old, whitewashed stone house of Mr. Whitmer, who came out, dressed like an ordinary laborer, and gave us a hearty Dutch welcome, inviting us to pass the night, which we promised to do. I was presented to his wife and daughter, who sat in the "stoup," after which the old gentleman hoped we would spare him the trouble of "bucking up"—he being evidently too lazy. We found his house stored with marine and mineral curiosities, etc.; he being a virtuoso after his fashion, and—a miracle for a Dutchman —a dabbler in science!

Going to Mr. Conyngham's who gave me much information on the Inds., we returned and found two young ladies, who quite deserved the title, invited to meet us. Having taken supper, during which the old gent. thrust in his head, and with a hearty grin, exclaimed ironically to his daughter who poured out the tea, "Hulloa, Laura, don't these fellers mean to be done eating pretty soon—they'll starve us out of house and home." Having taken supper we took a walk with the girls by the side of Peckway Creek—a small and not very clear stream, close by the house. Our apartment was quite sumptuously furnished—Stephens says the old man is worth $40,000—but S. exaggerates.

Found my classmate Baker[87] a schoolmaster here.

Returned to Lancaster in the morning—visited the famous jail[88] —explored the yard and the rooms—the *reputed* scene of the massacre. The prisoners are sometimes afraid to enter No. 13 or 14—which tradition points out (falsely?) as the place—no blood visible!

July 18. Came to Harrisburg. Walked at evening by the Susquehanna—a most broad and majestic stream—full of islands—with a fine prospect of mountains beyond—waters that ripple over a stony bottom, making a deep low murmuring. It is low at this season— though very wide, it seems not from the shore to have the majesty of *depth*, as the lines and streaks on its surface extend apparently from one shore to the other.

I saw a group of Dutchmen playing a game, something like quoits, with iron rings. Their faces bore no stamp of Yankee care and thought—they and the women were as stout specimens of flesh and blood as could be desired—a remarkable contrast to the puny Philadelphians.

July [?]. Canal Boat from Harrisburg to Williamsport. This is a new mode of travelling to me.

The old Baltimorean and his daughter, with the foreigner—the thin, meagre fop who said he looked like Tyler[89]—and a host of countrymen on board. The country beautiful, but not wild—the river very low.

At Harrisburg, locofocoism[90] has, of course, the ascendancy; consequently dinners are eat with a dispatch truly astonishing. Several men in the offices were true representatives of their party—blackguards of the first water, though one or two were quite gentlemanly men.

July [?]. From Williamsport, I came to Trout Run by a most wretched Rail Road. Trout Run is a little tavern among very wild mountains, not far from Lycoming Creek. Great Island, the scene of Armstrong's exped[ition], is about 26 miles above Williamsport— at least I am told so. The river there is said to be flanked by high hills, as it is below with wide intervals. The mountains on the south side of the river, near Wmsport, are called Laurel Rock.

Between Trout Run and a place called Blockhouse—*i.e.*, "Log-house"—the mountains are exceedingly wild and high, and without clearings—the chief one is called Laurel Hill.

A low and disagreeable set of fellows in the stage.

Dined at Blossberg, a mining place—very small—very rough— very dirty—and very disagreeable. It rained—went on thence by a wretched Railroad to Corning. Beyond Blossberg, the settlements are principally Yankee, along Tioga Creek.

A drunken, swearing puppy in the cars first amused and then disgusted me. Such a railroad I never saw before. Stopped at night at Corning, a new and flourishing place, and in the morning came to Seneca Lake, and took steamboat at Jefferson, ₁(t) town at its head.

Buffalo. Saw several Senecas[91] in the street.

The Detroit steamer was crowded—among the rest, a host of Norwegian emigrants—very diminutive—very ugly—very stupid and brutal in appearance—and very dirty. They appear to me less intelligent and as ignorant as the Indians. Besides these, a motley swarm of passengers of all nations.[92]

The shores of the lake consist of banks covered with trees, with now and then some land a little higher visible behind—but all is in general low and monotonous. A slight wind—yet the waves beat loudly on the shore

The group of Inds. at Detroit: the little squaw—the old one with her continual grin—the old man with his nose poxed away—and the rest. They had got a kettle of rum and were drinking it. They were miserably weak and slender. Evidently, their only enjoyments were eating and drinking. They laughed and were very happy over their liquor.

Hog Island has a border of marsh on the east side—so have the eastern and much of the western shores as you approach Lake Sinclair [St. Clair]. Flat, usually marshy ground in front—a line of forest behind—is the general appearance of the country. Isle à la Pêche is small, low, and in part marshy. Presqu'ile is a rising ground at the edge of the water, with marsh behind. The land in general is flat as a map.

The lands around the outlet of St. Clair River are very low— here the river splits into a multitude of ramifications, amongst flat marshy islands, interspersed with tracts of wood. The waters rise to the very brim, and seem ready to pour themselves upon the shore. On Lake St. Clair, a faint narrow line of distant woods, resting on the waters, divide the lake from the sky on the horizon. It is said that the waters never rise. No hills are visible—nothing but smooth green marsh, forests and the abundant waters.

Going towards Lake Huron, the banks become higher. Along the east shore is a thick group of trees, where a tribe of Inds. live, scattered along the bank in little log houses. Fort Gratiot,[93] a stockade work, stands close by the outlet of the lake. At the outlet the land is low and flat.

The western shore of Huron, near the outlet, at sunset—it presents nothing but a uniform dark line of forests, with a splendid display of purple and golden clouds behind, and the leaden colored waves below tinged with the evening colors. The woods stretched away into nothingness on each side.[c]

Thunder Bay. The land becomes a little higher before reaching Thunder Bay—though the Capt. says that it bears the same uniform flat appearance from this place to the Sinclair. The lands deep in Thunder Bay seem low and flat in the distance. Several islands are about its mouth, shaggy with firs. They tell me that thunder is very common here.

[c] Pp. 108-50 of the notebook consist of accounts and bibliographical references. This material is given in the Appendix to this journal.—Ed.

Mackinaw.[94] Approach from the low extensive island of Bois Blanc on the right—the main shore just visible on the north—another little island between Bois Blanc and Mackinaw.

The place is a picture of an ancient Canadian settlement—the little houses in Canadian style—some of them log, with roofs thatched with bark—the picket fences, of rough sharpened stakes, that surround them all—the canoes and Ind. huts on the shore give them a wild and picturesque air. Wild-looking half-breeds in abundance— a group of squaws and children, wrapped in their blankets, sat on the steps of a store—one little Canadian, three-quarters savage, had a red shawl tied round his head, red leggins, gay moccasins, and a blanket coat—another, who looked out from between his straight black locks with a wild and particularly vile expression, was staring at the steamer.

Sunday. This morning, before breakfast, walked round the shore. The lake beautifully clear—banks of limestone frequently jutting in rough spires, feathered with shrubs, from the midst of a thick growth of arbor-vitae, birch, and maple, etc., that cover the steep and high banks; while white and waterworn masses are strewn along the water's edge. The shore is most beautiful. Saw the "arched rock"— then walked over the island, which is covered with a thick growth, chiefly maple.

Capt. Martin Scott[95] inspecting his men on the parade.

Lieut. Whiting[96] showed me the "Sugar loaf," which is truly remarkable—an abrupt spire starting up ninety feet from the midst of the woods. Near at hand, is Fort Holmes,[97] on the highest point of land, commanding the present fort—and close to this, on the descent below, is the "Scull-rock" where Henry[98] hid.

The houses are chiefly thatched with elm bark—the sides of many are also covered with it, though they are for the most part of squared and whitewashed logs.

Lieut. W. gives the Canadians the following character: good natured—jovial—lazy, as far as regular work is concerned, but extravagantly fond of wandering about, fishing, etc.

The Ind. trade here is chiefly managed by pedlars who go into the Ind. country on their own account—the fir [fur] companies are used up[99]—Mackinaw is no longer an outfitting place—the voyageurs' occupation's gone.

Various deposits of sculls and bones have been found in different parts of the island, among the rocks.[d]

Scull Rock. The cave was once two or three feet deeper than at present—it was filled up by the Ind. boys at the Mission, each of whom as he visited the place, threw a stone in. Capt. Scott remembers to have seen bones there.

Passage to the Sault. Coast as far as the Detour low, wild, and covered with firs. The same around the Detour. Passage wide in many places and dotted with fir-covered islands—all wild, forlorn, and desolate—trees hung with mosses—many of them dead and leafless.

Farther on, the distant coasts and islands presented a strange appearance—by an optical illusion, they assumed the appearance of basaltic formations—then low and dimly seen islands would swell up into high peaks—then the top would be apparently detached and lifted like a cover from the base. Blue and distant coasts would alternately rise above and sink below the horizon; and on a long point that thrust itself out against the horizon, a few detached trees, and ragged firs, swelled up like the spires of a city, and soon after seemed pillars supporting a canopy over the land. Day a little obscured by piles of fleecy clouds.

We took the "Montreal Channel," that being the most picturesque. For a long time the shores were wide stretched apart. They gradually approached.

On a green beach connecting a rocky island with the shore, were the skeletons of what the pilot, Mr. Peck, called a Chippewa[100] encampment. Some of the poles were arranged in the peaked, some in the round form. On this place are the graves of the band. Peck say[s] he has known food placed on them at intervals for twenty years.

The channel grew narrower, and was filled with wild rocky

---

[d] At this point Parkman had filled up his notebook, and so continued his narrative on a sheet of paper headed "Journal of Part of Journey in August '45—No. 1. Commenced at Mackinaw, Aug. — 1845."—Ed.

islands—the bare rock sloped upward from the water, or rose sheer in precipices. The islands were shaggy with a growth of firs, large and small, dead and living—the channels between deep and black—opposing shores often abrupt and high, and covered with the rough and savage growth of firs. Some rocky and mossy promontories were almost bare—here and there rose a wild and battered tree from a crevice—shrubs were scattered around among dead trees standing and prostrate. Such was the passage for a long way, seeming narrow from the multitude of islands.

They tell me that there is good land inland, especially on St. Joseph's Island.

Met Mr. and Mrs. Arnold of New Bedford, with Miss Chandler and James Lawrence.[101]

The channel soon widens, and loses some of its picturesque character, though some highlands and precipices appear(s). Two Ind. lodges of bark on the shore. Suddenly we turned into a narrow winding passage where, toward evening, the scene was as wild and beautiful as any I ever saw. This was not many miles from the Sault.

At the Sault, everything full of copper speculators.[102] Found, with the party aforesaid, lodging at the Baptist Mission house—Mr. Bingham's.[103] Conversed with him on the Inds.—hope he is not a fair specimen of Ind. missionaries; he is stupid and ignorant, and said to have no influence. Protestant missionaries generally are said to be without power or respect.

Ft. Brady[104]—a square stockade with block-houses at two corners.

The inhabs. of the Sault are chiefly Canadian and half-breeds—always dancing and merrymaking—who live in houses resembling those at Mackinaw.

Ind. lodges, some round, some peaked, on the bank of the rapids. All Ojibway. Lodges covered with *pukivi*[e] mats and birch bark, the former very thick and warm. Saw Ind. fishing in the rapids.

Mr. Arnold failed in his attempt to get the ladies a paddle down the rapid. Lawrence and I went down together. A half-breed, educated at the Mission at Mackinaw, and named Joseph [Gurnae] directed the canoe. (The Chippewa birches are all large—they have small wooden canoes.)

[e] Bark.—Ed.

Joseph was remarkably intelligent. I afterwards conversed with him. All the Inds., he said, knew of Manabosho, and he mentioned several of his exploits, as recorded by Schoolcraft[105]—also those of Paupukeewis, whose name he mentioned with a laugh. He spoke of fasts, love philters (which he said were universally in the hands of the young women), charms, etc., etc. He evidently believed much of them himself, and cautioned me against ever letting an Ind. girl, to whom I might become attached, get possession of one of my hairs, as she would then have it in her power to do me mischief. He boasted to have once defeated a spell cast on a man by a conjuror.

Mr. and Mrs. Jones, copper-speculators grown elevated by prospects of wealth. The latter coolly introduced herself at Bingham's —on scarce any pretext—to Mrs. Arnold, and then presented her husband. She has been up to Copper Harbor, an exploit which increases her self confidence and complacency. She gives her opinion as to where *forts* should be built, etc.

We returned to Mackinaw by the Channel we came by—scenery appearing no less fine than before.

Whiting introduced me to Mr. Robert Stewart [Stuart][106] of Astoria memory. Mr. S. thinks Tanner's book[107] of much value, and that T., who at the time of dictating it had recently become a member of the church, told nothing but what he *believed* to be true—that however his superstition and savage imagination sometimes deceived —that he had been in the custom of telling stories till he believed them himself. Mr. S. said he had seen an Ind. who was convinced that he had changed himself into a rattlesnake, etc. He thinks highly of Tanner's native powers of mind and courage.

Mr. S. thinks that Schoolcraft's *Algic Researches* are a superstructure of falsehood on a true foundation—that having once caught the tone and spirit of the tales, he multiplied them *ad libitum*—though he thinks that many of them are genuine.[108]

Capt. Martin Scott, being bent on getting up a picnic, seemed little inclined to fulfil his promise of sending me to Old Mackinaw with a crew of his soldiers; so Whiting found an old Canadian, François Lacroix, who with his two sons carried us over in a fishing boat. The distance is about eight miles. We explored the ruins of the fort[109] (see *Miscellanies*), made a dinner there, and returned. The old

Canadian and his sons rowed with a quick easy stroke that carried us rapidly; yet before we left the land, the thunder was growling from a huge pile of black clouds to the southwards; and before we were half over, a long flash leaped from the edge of a black curtain of thunder cloud down to the dark waters at the horizon, and then

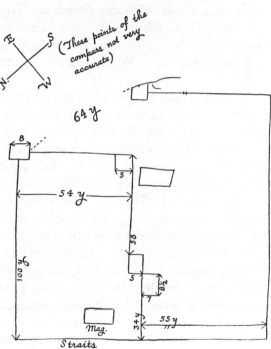

Old Fort Mackinaw
plan taken by Lieut. Whiting

(These points of the compass not very accurate)

the thunder bellowed over the waste. The shore of Michigan was obscured by white mists and rain—then Bois Blanc grew dim also—the old fort too was veiled, and it evidently rained there, though away to the north the long undulating shore of Pt. St. Ignace was easily seen, and the nearer white cliffs and green shrubbery of Mackinaw. At last the drops fell fast upon us—another thunder clap bellowed over the water—old François laughed and put on his *chapeau*, and we pulled hard for the town. As we skirted the shore, the Canadians stood at the doors of their huts in the rain looking at us. Passing between an old wreck and the shore, the swells, which run high in the straits, nearly capsized Whiting, who stood in the boat. At length, we gained the beach—the boat was hauled up—and we found the picnic party had abandoned their purpose, though the storm was passing and a fine *arc-en-ciel*, as François said, rested on the water to the southwards.

Mackinaw seems to have been a great resort of Inds. I saw this morning at the fort, a box of bones found in various caves and crevices about the island. Some were discovered yesterday by a soldier who took refuge from the rain under a rock. A large number have been got from the cave Whiting and I visited day before yesterday.

Last night the Inds. in the lodges on the beach got drunk. I heard them singing for a long time in a mournful, maudlin fashion, repeating the same words, and varying the song with what seemed to be boasts or narratives of exploits. The same monotonous music rose from half a dozen lodges that stood in a line together.

This morning I found a group sitting among the ruins of a hut, which they seemed to have pulled down about their ears. They were still drunk, singing and laughing. One of them was a remarkably handsome squaw, with a good-looking young man, with his leggins and bare thighs, at her side. There was another drunken fellow coiled up singing on the ground. Then a tall, thin, savage-looking old fellow came along and seated himself in the midst. They turned rum out of a bottle into the cover of a tin pail, and tried to drink it raw, keeping up a constant laughing and maudlin merriment.

At another lodge, a squaw was making very neat mats out of rushes—much finer and neater than the *pukivi* mats.

Mr. Turner, the sportsman and boon companion at Mackinaw.

Palmer, Michigan, Sunday. Attended church—orthodox—clergyman a vile-looking fellow, tall and sallow, with a loud voice and a bad obtrusive face. A very pretty face in the choir. People really good-looking and strong. A severe thunder-storm came up, which detained the little congregation singing psalms for some time after service.

Reflected this morning on the disadvantage of republican governments, being led thereto by Backus's aspirations after a despotism!

The intelligent fellow with whom I conversed at Brown's Tavern, Palmer, and who told me so much of mines and steamboats.

The women at work making carpets in the large room of Whitman's house, where I spent a disagreeable day in overhauling *six trunks* of old McDougall's [M'Dougal's] papers.[110] They worked on in a dismal silence—not a word spoken. I found a fine engraving of General Washington in the trunk, which I gave to the elder woman, who declared she would not take a dollar for it: another woman came in, who, smitten with jealousy, tried to get a gift or a swap of it, but it would not do.

The dyspeptic man who insisted on helping himself to such morsels as suited him (with his own knife and fork). He had nursed himself till he had reached a state of egotistic selfishness.

The Canadian gentleman on board the steamer *Red-Jacket*, between Detroit and Palmer. Mr. Rice, the trader, lumberer, etc., who told his story of being left on an island in Thunder Bay—and of his hospitable reception by an Indian when he reached the shore. He said that this island, which he had set on fire in order to get a good crop of grass, burnt for several months, as the soil is, as he says, "sulphur rock."

As you approach the opening of Detroit River on leaving Lake St. Clair, Presqu'ile, projecting before Hog Island, seems like another island. Hog Island is covered with a thick growth of trees, but is bordered by much low, level, and grassy land.

M. François Baby[111] and his establishment at Windsor. A fine old brick house; the porch, the shrubbery, and the hall have a waste and picturesque air—books, guns, neglected tables, old clocks, chests of drawers, and garments and Indian equipments flung around. The little Negro girl, and the strange-looking half-breed, who were sunning themselves among the hens and hogs in the back yard.

Went to Sandwich. The old Canadian houses often have little square porches in front. Here men ride always at a canter, as far as my observation goes.

Canoes are often made of a peculiar shape of a bent log,[f] the hinder

f A very rough sketch of a canoe occurs here in the journal.—Ed.

end being elevated and squared—sometimes both ends are high and sharp, like the elegant log canoes of the St. Lawrence, but not so well made. The large Chippeway canoe is the perfection of the thing. The Chippeways use a small log canoe for hunting, etc. They have no small bark canoes. A Mackinaw boat is unique—it is a hugely magnified and elaborated skiff, moved by oars that are secured by leather thongs fastened to a single pin by way of rowlock, as also are the oars of the fishing skiffs at Mackinaw.

The old Huron church, just above Sandwich, is a most venerable and delapidated structure, with the green in front and the old buildings round. Here were congregated a host of little Canadian waggons, with corresponding horses. The people seem to have caught English manners, and their French complaisance has disappeared.

There are some English cottages. I stopped at one, mistaking it for Mr. Askin's.[112] The owner was an officer—his sword hung with his garments in the hall, and hard by was his gun and fishing rod. A fine pair of antlers lay on the window-sill of a little projecting room that seemed his study. So much for English tastes.

Mr. Askin(s), a little, dried-up, *distingué* man, received me with great courtesy, and expressed much interest in my objects. His mother was a Campeau. He talked incessantly, though almost unintelligibly from his front teeth being knocked out, and finally ushered me from the door with a profusion of compliments, etc.

The opposite shores are low, but beautiful—no high land in sight, but a line of woods rises behind the buildings and scattered Canadian cottages with a beautiful effect.

Below Detroit, the shores grow lower still. Fighting Island is almost without trees at present, its upper parts are elevated some feet above the water with here and there a clump of bushes or a tall tree; but as you go down, it changes to a complete marsh, beyond which the other arm of the river may be seen, and puddles of glistening water vary the surface of the rank grass. Turkey Island is all marsh. The shores in this part present the same uniform marshy appearance, and are almost level with the water, with which they seem imperceptibly to mingle, as the strong grass grows thinner along their edges.

Bois Blanc near Malden is raised some feet above the water.

Aug. 16. North shore of Erie, near Point Stanley. The bank is high and steep, and composed of earth work by the water and quite raw, with the forest along the top.

Sometimes the section of a ravine appears, filled with trees, seeming like a notch cut in the shore. In a wider and very pretty opening stands Port Stanley. East of this, the bank is high for many miles, but gradually becomes lower, and fifty or sixty miles further on, it is almost level with the water, at Long Point. Long Pt. is extremely low and flat. On the other side, about Erie, the land seems quite high, but where the opposite shores converge towards Buffalo, they are neither of them very high.

Conversed with an old emigrant from the north of England, who spoke highly of the advantages of Canada, and the yet greater advantages of the States.

The scene on landing at the Quay at Buffalo—it surpassed anything I ever yet saw for hubbub and noise.

Niagara, Aug. 17. The Cataract is a bloated noisy house—a set of well-dressed blackguards predominated at table. One fellow—very good-looking—I particularly noticed. He sent the waiter with a bottle of champagne to a friend of his at another table, who coolly helped himself, and then proceeded to fill the glasses of some ladies near him out of his friend's bottle. At this the latter's face became heavily overshadowed; he reddened with vexation, played uneasily with knife and fork, and turning to a neighbor remarked that he "always knew ——— for a damn mean fellow, but that was a little *too* sneaking." So he bowed across the table and sipped his glass with great gravity. When the bottle which had got into such dangerous hands was returned to him, his face wonderfully brightened. Poor fellow! He had come with a half year's clerk's salary to be gay and live fast for a week at Niagara; it was hard that his earning should be drank up in that unceremonious fashion.

Niagara. I have looked at the great cataract, but do not feel in the temper to appreciate it or embrace its grandeur. An old woman, who, for the pure love of talking and an itching to speak to everyone, several times addressed me with questions about she knew not what, filled me with sensations of particular contempt, instead of amusing me as they would have done, had not my stomach been disordered. I sat down near the rapids. "What's all this, but a little water and foam?" thought I. "What a pack of damned fools," was my internal commentary on every group that passed—and some of them deserved it. But, thank Heaven, I have partially recovered my good-humor, can sympathize with the species, and to some degree feel the sublimity of the Great Cataract.

How many of the visitors here deserve to look on it? I saw in the tower a motherly dame and her daughters, amid the foam and thunder and the tremendous pouring of the waters. "Oh, ma!" (half whispered), "He's looking at us! There, I've torn my sash; I must go home and pin it up, etc." Old Niagara pours bellowing on forever, as it has poured since the beginning of time, and generation after generation of poor little devils of human beings play their little pranks and think their little thoughts around him. He roars on undisturbed, while age after age of the manikins look at him, patronize him with their praises, and go to the devil before his eyes. What does he care for their pranks, their praises, or their fault-finding? His tremendous face never changes; his tremendous voice never wavers; one century finds him as the last did, in his unchanging power and majesty.[113]

Aug. 18th. Visited the Devil's Hole. A violent rain. It is the very place for an Ind. massacre.[114] The great cliffs that flank the river are here notched away, leaving an immense, deep gully withdrawn back from the river, with sheer, savage lime-stone fencing it on three sides, and the furious river on the other. Stand on the "Platform Rock" and look down into the gulf upon a mass of vegetation—bass-wood—white cedar (*arbor vitae*)—ash—sumach—iron-wood, rising together in the abyss, with now a savage, bristling spruce or hemlock shooting up above the rest. The man measured the height from the Platform—his line lodged at seventy feet, but it must be nearly twice as deep, measured from the centre of the gulf upwards. The old road, he says, followed the edge of the precipices somewhat thus[g]—the men that were precipitated must have fallen eighty feet or more into this

[g] A very rough pencil sketch has been omitted here.—Ed.

rocky and wooded den. Bloody Run dribbles downward near the platform, and is large enough to carry a mill in spring. According to the man, the attack was made just above or at the upper corner of the Hole. Here, on one side, is a hollow, probably filled with dense bushes in 1763, while on the other a hill rises, whence a rush could be made with great effect. Behind this hill is a ravine, the mouth of which is plainly visible a few rods down the road, and below the Hole. The man says that the foundation of a blockhouse is visible on the hill above the Hole.

The view from the Platform up and down the river, raging between its precipitous banks and compressed to a width of from 50 to 30 rods, is most extraordinary.

We descended among the rocks and dripping woods through the Hole to the bank. The surges run six or eight feet high—the channel seems filled with great rocks, though it must be extremely deep. The waters boil up from the bottom like a chauldron.

The man says that all that changes the height of the water are the winds of Lake Erie. He has known them to rise and fall from this cause, 9 feet. Indeed, the bushes have been swept away some height above the present level all along the banks. He has known the ice piled and frozen together the whole way across. The Falls themselves struck me less than these scenes.

The view from above the Whirlpool is no less magnificent—and that from Bellevue, including the distant cataract, is more sublime and beautiful than anything I ever saw. When the sun broke suddenly out upon the face of the Fall, and brightened the white and gushing foam, the Torrent fairly seemed to laugh.

The loafer near me at table. The poor devil was out of his element. He could not conceive why it was that the waiters were so attentive to his neighbors, while he was quite neglected. He sat embarassed and disconsolate, siezing upon, as a forlorn hope, every dish that happened to come within reach. At length, a waiter siezed upon a knife that lay by his plate and transferred it to some more favored individual, whose demands were imperative. When next the waiter passed, the neglected one said, "Now bring that knife back again, if you've mind to." Pitying his helplessness, I offered him dishes, for which I got no other acknowledgement than an instant siezure of the proffered viands, or a decisive "No!"

Went behind the "sheet," under the guidance of a nigger—an opposition. "They are generally reckoned the Seven Wonders of the World, sir!" he remarked, speaking of the Falls. "What a *preliminacament* a man would be, sir, on that 'ere rock, sir, wouldn't he?"

The world cannot match the view from the Table Rock.

I saw an old, withered, hollow-eyed, straight-backed Yankee peering at the Falls with a critical scrutiny, as if he was judging of the goodness of a bank note.

The view from the Lewisto(w)n railroad—the original of Bartlett's picture, "Forest on Lake Ontario."[115] River at Lewiston—the abrupt rocks here cease, though the banks are still high. The river wide deep and tranquil; headland after headland give it a very picturesque appearance. The rapids begin immediately above Lewiston.

Fort Niagara[116] stands on the point that projects from the shore at the outlet of Ontario. Behind it stretches away even now a great level forest, apparently unbroken, the same seen from the railroad. About this point, and all along the lake for a great distance, the land is quite flat and wooded, with abrupt raw banks of earth along the water. Looking back after passing the Fort, you see it standing on its point of land, with the more distant shore on the other side, the outlet stretched out like a promontory behind.

About Oswego, land rolling and in part wooded—forming a beautiful and graceful shore. The morning mist hung around it when I saw it. Entering the river, a hill on the right, another on the left, where the present fort stands.

Though now dammed up, the river was once stoney and rapid. In some places the banks are still high and wooded with chesnut, maple, beech, hemlock, pine, etc.

Passed Lake Salina—country undulating—farther south, hilly. Saw the large salt works about the salt springs near the Lake, mentioned by Bartram.[117] Lake itself fresh.

At Syracuse, took a horse and rode to Onondaga Castle, about nine miles distant. Descended into the valley at near sunset. Scenes formed by the wooded hills far and near, the rich flats bordered and dotted by trees, and the little stream Onondaga, very beautiful and romantic. Bartram's description will answer for the present day, except that there are many frame houses, possibly more cultivated land, and a frame council house in place of that seen by B. The smokes and houses may be seen far up on the borders of the woods— many good cornfields along the hills and intersecting the patches of woods—rich hay in the interval[e] meadow, through which among rich groves of trees winds the Onondaga, small and choked up, as described by Bartram.

I treated a man to cigars—he showed me the council-house, where by the way they are to celebrate the Green Corn Dance on Monday. (They have many dances in the course of the year.) It was a long, plain, one-story building, containing only one large room, with a fire-place at each end, benches placed around, a brass horn to convoke the people, and a large turtle-shell rattle to keep time to the dance.

I got the Inds. into excellent humor by presents of cigars and pipes. They are to hold a general council of the Six Nations at Tonawanda in the Fall.

They are the worst people in the world to extract information from: the eternal grunted "yas" of acquiescence follows every question you may ask, without distinction.

Pro[nounced] "Onondawga."

One old fellow whom I conversed with seemed to remember the council-house described by Bartram, with the partitions in it. It is impossible to say, however, whether he really did so. The present council-house, he told me, was erected eight years ago.

(Examine Barber's *N. Y. Hist. Coll.*[118] for an acct. of Onondaga.)

Fort Stanwix[119] stood in the midst of a very level country—the Mohawk is here quite small.

At Oneida, I saw several Indians (examine Barber's *H. Coll.*).

German Flats are a level and beautiful interval.

The Valley of the Mohawk has no pretension to sublimity. Its hills are not high, but the river winds like a snake in the interval between, with trees fringing its banks, forming a rich and picturesque landscape. (I am getting a stronger relish for quiet beauties.)

The lawyer with the sharp nose, thin face, and small mouth. His vehement narratives about himself, and the singular contortions of countenance with which he enforced them.

The noisy and vulgar party of girls, who sat on the backs of the seats and filled the cars with their cackling. The old fool of a woman, their mother, who rivalled the accomplishments of her daughter. Is not a *half*-educated, vulgar, weak woman a disgusting animal? Where there is no education at all, and no pretension, the matter is all very well—where high education and good sense are united, it is very well indeed—but the half-and-half genteel—damn them!

The fury of the man who saw the cars run over and kill a man and woman at Schenectady—his exclamations and threats against a man whom he took for one of the company. "I accuse you for a murderer!" Clenching his fists: "By G— I'll have the law on you. I want to know who you are. I want to know if you are a gentleman," etc.

The drunken fellow, who said he was wounded at Texas,[120] on board the steamer.

Appendix

Accounts
Previous Expenditures

Omnibus	.15
Brandy, etc.	.08
Cars from Medford	.15

(Received from C. in payment of debt: .75; carried over to account of funds on opposite page[below]).

Joseph Gurnae, Sault St. Marie

Funds at starting, Tuesday, July 8, 1845: $103.17[h]

July 8:	Cravat	.75
"	Shave	.06
"	Cider	.04
"	Ticket to N. Y.	2.00
"	Supper on board	.50
July 9:	Ale	.06
"	Boots	.12½
"	Porter	.11
		3.64

"	Carriage to Astor H[ouse]	.50
"	Baths	.25
"	Carriage	.50
"	Soda & Omnibus	.18
"	Waiter	.18
July 10:	Soda, etc.	.18
"	Porter	.06
"	Astor House	3.50

[h] "A bill of credit for $100. more."—F. P.

317

July 10:	Carriage & Porter	.37½
"	Passage to Philadel.	4.00
"	Supper	.50
"	Cab	.50
"	Waiter	.25
July 11:	Ale	.06
"	Tanner's *Am[erican Trav[els]*	1.50
"	Soda & Omnibus	.09
"	Bath	.35
		12.97

July 12:	Sundries	.18
"	Colombia H'se	3.63
"	Waiters	.70
"	Congress Water	.12
"	Dinner & Tea	.55
"	Bath	.25
July 13:	Breakfast	.15
"	Servant	.05
"	Soda	.06
"	Dinner	.35
"	Bath	.12½
July 14:	Breakfast	.28
"	Dinner	.58
"	Supper	.35
July 15:	Breakfast	.15
"	Sundries	.12
"	Dinner	.45
		8.54

"	City Lib'y	.25
"	Bath	.25
"	Tea	.20
July 16:	Breakfast	.15
"	Bath	.25
"	Franklin House	4.25
"	Waiter and Porter	.75
"	Soda	.18
"	To Lancaster	2.52
"	Porter	.12½

July 16:	Sundries		.25
July 17:	Books		4.00
"	Hotel and chaise		4.75
"	Lancaster *Intelligencer*		2.50
July 18:	To Harrisburg		1.50
"	Breakfast, etc.		.63

$100.00	$54.	$22.67
44.	20.	13.
56	34.	8.50
		$43.67

Papers copied	5.00
Hotel	6.95
Porter, etc.	.25
Boots	.12
Fare to Williamsport	3.62
Supper and fare to Trout Run	$1.00
Fare to Blossberg	1.50
Lodging at Trout Run	.50
Fare to Corning	1.50
Dinner	.25
Salts	.06
Lodging and Fare to Seneca Lake	1.50
Passage across	1.50
" to Rochester	2.00
Lodging and Porter	1.12
To Buffalo	2.50
Dinner & Tea	1.00
Bath, etc.	.37
Fare to Detroit	7.00
Cider	.12
Shoes cleaned	.12
Map of Michigan	2.00
Sundries	.25
Hotel at Detroit	6.22
Passage to Mackinaw	7.00
Lodging at "	2.70
Passage to the Sault	5.00
Lodging	.50

Canoe down the Sault	1.00
Ale and porter	.50
Passage from Sault	5.00
Key to Valise	.37
Boat to Old Mackinaw	2.00
Lodging at Mackinaw	3.00
Passage to Palmer	6.00
Shoes blacked & Cider	.18
Lodging at Newport	.87½
Supper at Palmer	.25
Porter	.12
Ale	.06
Passage to Detroit	1.25
Porter	.25
Daguerreotype	3.37½
Postage	.26
Tracing paper	.37½
Map of Wayne City	.50
Rhubarb	.06
Trip to Windsor	.15
Hotel	4.87
Steamboat *London*	6.00
Porter and Brandy	.30
Guide to Niagara	.25
Fare to Niag. (steamer)	.75
Porters	.37
Ferry to Am[erican] Side	.12
Goat Is[land] Bridge	.25
Bath	.25
Waiter	.12½
Man at Devil's Hole	.50
Driver	.25
Man at Whirlpool	.25
Buggy to Devil's Hole	1.00
Ind. chisel	.25
Brandy	.06
Ferry	.30
Museum	.25
Going under Falls	.50
Cane	.50

Ind. Curiosities	2.00
Hotel bill	4.87½
Porter and waiter	.37½
Fare to Syracuse	5.00
Breakfast	.50
Boots cleaned	.12
Cigars, etc., for Inds.	.30
Horse to Onondaga	1.00
Hotel at Syracuse	1.50
Porter	.25
Fare to Albany	5.50
Dinner	.25
Hotel at Albany	1.50
Sundries	.37½
Fare to N. Y.	1.50
Dinner	1.37
Omnibus	.12½
Lodging	.50
Breakfast	.30
Carriage	.37
Porter	.12
To Boston	2.00
Nigger	.12½
Supper	.25
Carriage	.25
Sundries	.37
Carriage	.25
Lodging at Pavilion	.50
Carriage (on Father's acct.)	2.00
Omnibus	.15
Stage	.25
Postage, etc.	.12½
Cars	.15
Boots cleaned	.10
H[asty] P[udding] Supper	3.00

(Owe to Rice for furniture removed 1.50—.75 for lamp, oil, etc., sold him)

Owe Wyman .75 for horse

　　” Clapp[i] 　” 　” 　”

[i] "Began with Clapp. Sept. 1."—F. P.

Owe Clapp .75 for horse
Rcd. from Mother   .25
Omnibus   .15
Class Supper   3.55
Big Bear   .50
Joseph   1.00
Cars (on mother's acct.)   .15
Dinner   .31½
Stage to Medford   .18¾
  ,,   ,,   ,,   .18¾
Omnibus   .15
Stage   .18
Dinner   .44
Hornden's Ex[press]   1.25
                      _____

4   1.00   .25
37½   2.12   .50
8   2.50   1.37½
               6.12   .65

1.00 ⎫
2.62 ⎬ ½
2.50 ⎭
 .12½   Miss Adams
3.50   Seignourry C. Carol
 .46   Miss Wood
 .12½   Phillomine Seeds
 .62½
 .62½   Miss Hall: Bryant
2.02
3.00
 .25
 .37½
 .12½
 .50

Historical Notes

Trumbull [Papers], II:
P. 30, Whitehall, Jan. 27, 1763
P. 44, St. James's, Oct. 19, 1763
P. 45. Norwalk, Conn. Nov. 10, '63

McKenney's *Memoirs*[121]—soon to be published
Dryden
Look up Military—Colonial
Franklin's *Hist. Rev[iew] of Pennsylvania.*[122]
Marshall's *Kentucky*[123]
Jefferson's *Notes on V[irgini]a*[124]
Chapman[125]
Jenessies—Senecas

Letters, '56-74, in State House (?). Page 415.
Letter from Ft. Pownal, Capt. Goldthwaite, to the hunters on Quontabagook Pond, warning them to leave it, as the I's [Indians] were dissatisfied. March 24, '64.
Journals, Page 328.
Acct. of C[row]n Pt.
Elinor Noble—page 330 and Military, May 16, '62.
Page 343. Letter from Capt. Goldthwaite, at Ft. Pownal, Me. Insolence of Inds. Sept., '67
Indian '57.—'75, let.[p] 295
A letter from Johnson, dated April 25, '64. An expedition against the enemy. 200 houses burnt.
Page 289. From Capt. Goldthwait, Penobscot Inds. discontented. Page 292.
Goldthwait. Penobscots. They had been infected. P. 294
Col. Lithgow to Dr. Gardiner, *Penobs.*

Oct. 7, '63. A Royal Proclamation about the I[ndian] trade.[126]
Van Schaack's *Reminiscences*[127]
Putnam's letter, *Conn. Courant*, '64.
A View of the Causes and Consequences of the Am. Rev.
A Second Letter to a friend on Dieskau's fight.[128] Boston, '55
General Review, '52
Martial Review by Boyce *excellent.*

N. Y. Hist. [Soc.] *Coll.*, vol. III, for character of Rogers.

Mrs. Coghlan, *Memoirs*[129]—a daughter of Major Moncrieffe.

Border Life, Lancaster, Pa.

London Mag[azine] for '63, etc., a Rev[iew] of the War.

Authorities on the Indians (from Bancroft):
Le Jeune. Chateaubriand—read it—6th vol. Joutel. Lafit[e]au. Brainerd. Marest. Le Clercq. St. [Mother] Mary of the Incarnation. Le Caron [Lecaron]. Benjamin Constant (ninth). Creuxius. Alloüez. Jarvis [Jogues] (in N. Y. Hist. Coll.). Purchas. Bernard Romans. Brebeuf. Du Pratz, *Hist. Louisiana.* Mackenzie.[130]

Acadia and Ft. W[illiam] H[enry] Hist. Worcester. Alloüez, Le Jeune, and Brebeuf—see *Relation de la N. France.* Le Clercq, *Rel. de la Gaspésie.*

Book of Collections in [Mass.] Hist. [Society] Lib'y, '20-'61. P. 172: Proceedings of Albany Congress, July, '54. Mass. Gen[eral] Court. Act for levying soldiers, April 5. Letters of Bollan to Hse. of Reps. and to W. Pitt, '57-'58. List of provincials who deserted from Ft. Cumb[erland], Chignecto, with a vessel. (This collection is principally of letters on domestic and church matters).

Col. Israel Williams Papers,[131] '56-80. This contains a great many letters, official and otherwise, chiefly details of the war. Burk to Williams; important details of Put[nam] and others July 2, '57, p. 29. Summons to aid of William Henry, p. 30. Alarm of the country at its capture, p. 41. Lt. Pierce's scout afterward, p. 42—Whiting to Williams.

Univ. Magazine[132]
Smith's *Journal*[133]
Sullivan's *Maine*[134]
Williams' life[135]
Belknap[136]
Peter Williamson[137]
Withers[138] (for Braddock, etc.)
Uni[versal?] Museum
Haz[ard] *Pa. Reg.*[139]
Gordon[140]. Entick[141]
Burk[e].[142] Churchman[143]
Heckewelder's *Narrative*[144]
Wright's *Hist.*[145]
Price[146]
Withers.[147] Humphreys[148]
Gibson's *Journal of Siege of Louisburg*[149]
Smith's N[ew] J[ersey][150]

Apx. [Appendix] of Dogsby's *An. Reg.*
Marston
Niles' Reg.[151]
Hewat[t].[152] Reissel.
Trumbull[153]
Wynne
Indian Miscellany
For Devil's Hole Massacre see *Ind. Miscel.—Bk. of Inds.*[154]—*An. Reg.*—
Maude's *Visit to Niagara.*[155] Mante.[156]

Lettre d'un François à un Hollandois au sujet des Differends entre la France,
etc., 1755.
Lettre d'un Anglois contenant un rélation authentique of F. and E. negotiations
at opening of the War, 1756.
*Raisons que prouvent qu'il est impossible que les deux nations Angloise et Françoise
puissent vivre en paix,* 1670
De Lisle's "Carte de Nouvelles Découvertes."
Rélation de la Louisiane[157]
Bradbury's (*Travels?*)[158]
An Essay on the Government of the Colonies (said to be partial).
Coxe's *Carolina*[159]
Keith's *Virginia*[160] (1738).
Virginia and Carolio (1471 Liby.), containing a satirical poem on southern
manners, etc. A very curious old collection, 1610.
Journal in N. Y., 1701
Louisiana. Père Vivier's letter, *Lettres Edifiantes*, v. 28.

Mémoir[e]s sur le Acadie

Loudon, etc. See Franklin's life by Sparks. Braddock, etc.—d[itt]o————.
Oct. 14th, 1755. Rogers' scout, State House "Letters," 1755-'56, No. 25.
Letters of the '56 Campaigns in abundance.
Oct. 3rd, 56. E[nglish] Fugitives from Canada arrive at No. 4, with
news of Oswego. See 1755-'56, No. 483.
July 11th, '56. Descent on Ft. Hoosuck. No. 375.

Ohio Defeat, Boston, '55.
A Reminiscence of Oswego.
New American Mag., 1759-60, by Sylvanus Americanus. Pa. Liby.
Mémoire[s] sur le Canada.[161] 3 vols. on the War

Martel's *Mémoire dans l'Affaire du Canada*, 1763.
Shirley's Statement, Mante (?)
Cape Breton—1760[162]—a large volume.
Porcupine's Works.[163] A MS. Journal of a soldier in '55 Battle.

Mr. Officer—Winwatts ⎫
Judge Reed   ⎬ Carlisle
Hepburn   ⎭

M. W. F. [Monday, Wednesday, Friday]—Greenleaf
Tues. T. S. [Thursday, Saturday]—Story. 10–11 o'clock.
Story on Bailments, Tuesday from 10–11.
Blackstone on Wednesday, 11–12, 2nd and 3rd Sections especially.

Historic Authorities to be Consulted

Winslow's *Journal*,[164] Mass. Hist. Library
Philadelphia *Gazette*.
Cole's charges against Lyman.
Letters of Officers in the state house, by means of Dr. Palfrey[165]
A Letter to the People of England on the present Situation and Conduct of National Affairs. It contains charges against the ministry.
Bradford's *Am. Avt.* [*Advertizer*]

"The Indians of the different States, and a collection of anecdotes, etc., illustrating Indian manners." The whole a mere compilation. Barber, p. 69.[166]

Loskeil's *Hist. of Missions*[167]—an acc[ount] of I's [Indians].
Dieskau—Hoyt's *I[ndian] wars*
Smith's *Discourses on Public Occasions in America.* Frontiers of Pa., etc. '54–'63

The Iroquois—attempts to convert them. Humphrey's *Accnt. of Soc[iety] for Propagtn. of Gospel in Fgn. Parts.*[168]

Barton's *New Views*, a comparison of Indian Tribes.

Contest in America,[169] an acct. of the relative situation of the two colonies—causes of the war—and the most expedient measures to be taken, 1757.

True and Impartial State of the Province of Pensylvania—Its Govr., proprietaries, Assemblies, etc., etc., 1759.

Smith's *Hist. of N. Y.*[170] contains a sketch of Oswego, and descriptions of fur-trade—social character, &c., 1757.

Cooper's Sermon before the General Court on the Reduction of Quebec.[171]

Loskeil contains an acct. of Christian Inds. on the frontier in '50-64.

"English Discoveries in the Ohio Valley, '44-'74."[172] *N[orth] A[merican] Review*, vol. 49, p. 69.
General Sketch of Canada Gov. etc.[173] *N. A. Rev.*, [vol.] 46, p. 409.
American Magasine, '57-'58[174]
Contest in America by Mitchel[l].

Drake's *Chronological collection* mentions facts with the authorities, 1757. Price.[175] *Martin's Magazine*, '55, '56, etc.
Wright[176] contains Abercrombie's official letters.
There is a journal of Bradstreet's expedition against Frontenac by one of the volunteers.[177]
Col. Grant's expedition. Trumbull's *Connect[icut]*.[178] Burk's *Va.*—Cuming's *Tour*—Palmer's *Travs.*—Gordon's *Pa.*—Wynne—Knox—Holmes—*Life Arthur Lee*—Withers—Hazard's *Pa. Reg.*, VIII, 141—Mant[e].[179]

Montcalm's Jesuit paper is in the last edition of the *Lettres Edifiantes*.[180]

Cherokee War. Simms' *Life of Marion*[181]

Heriot's *Canada*[182] (description).
Athenaeum[183]

Elder
Miner[184]
Lee—Baker
Stephens [Stevens] and brother
Newton   *trio—famous*
Lee the Doctor   *laid* down

Baker's name ⎫
P. O.   ⎬ Cambridge
Room   ⎭

W. S. Pearce—Corner of Court St. and Tremont Row.

Indian regard for flags of truce.
1688, 1st F[rench] War: 74 years of war; 34 of active hostilities.
'88 K[ing] William's
Queen Ann[e]'s War
Spanish [Succession]
Old French

G. W. Baker   Postage [?]
                                  Toll   [?]
                                    Books $3\frac{1}{2}$

Militia systems except *in Pa.* $\frac{1}{4}$ of colonists trained to arms. Their intelligence.

1690—Phipps' Expedition against Penobscot, etc., Quebec. Both Colonies left alone. Ryswick.

Phipps and Fletcher try to obtain command of the militia. Assemblies decided to have full power over the militia. *Volunteers* out of states. Requisitions to Govrs., for assemblies raised by offs. and given to E. officer in chief. 1 year

---

1710. Q. Ann[e]'s War—felt at the South. *Utrecht, 1713*—Nova Scotia gained.

Sp[anish Succession] War—Aix-la-Chapelle.

O[ld] F[rench] War. 1st American Dispute. There were causes in Europe.

English Monopolies—Companies—Colony Companies

Va. tobacco—King James—to be landed in England.

Restrictions long limited to Va.—prohibitions of foreign trade. Foundation of N[avigation] Act. Carrying trade by Englishmen; imports and exports to sent but to E[ngland]. European commodities to be landed in E.

Timber, N. E. fish, etc., bounty.

Selfish policy of England.

Internal trade and trade to the W. I[ndies] islands—restrictions. Customs houses established by British law.

Resistance of Mass. Assembly and others to N[avigation] Act. They had not been consulted, nor were they represented.

Attempts to crush Colonial Manufactures

Smith's *Wealth of Nations*—Colonies

Whitman,   Sanderson
　　Palmer   between 4th

Prov. Recs.

Stephens ⎫
Stevens ⎬Tremont Row.

Notes

I. 1841 JOURNAL

[1] James Monroe Tower (1823-?) of New York was attached to Parkman's class of 1844 at Harvard during their sophomore year.

[2] Dr. Daniel Denison Slade (1823-96) of Boston was a classmate and lifelong friend of Parkman, and a favorite cómpanion on tramping and hunting excursions during their college years. Slade was known to his fellows as "The Chieftain," while Parkman's college nickname was "The Loquacious." Slade studied medicine and became professor of applied zoology at Harvard in 1871. He was a pallbearer at Parkman's funeral.

[3] Parkman and Slade traveled sixty-eight miles on the Boston & Maine to Dover.

[4] Alton, New Hampshire, is twenty-eight miles from Dover.

[5] Washington Irving (1783-1859), author of *The Alhambra* and at this period the dean of American letters, was a favorite with Parkman, both in youth and later life, because of Parkman's historical interests. Irving's *Tour of the Prairies* (1835), *Astoria* (1836), and *Captain Bonneville* (1837) may well have inspired Parkman's Oregon Trail trip of 1846.

[6] Red Hill towers some two thousand feet above the head of Lake Winnipesaukee. S. A. Drake, in his *History of the White Mountains* (New York, 1881), comments: "This eminence would be called a mountain anywhere else. Its altitude is inconsiderable, but its situation at the head of the lake, on its very borders, is highly favorable to a commanding prospect. . . ." (pp. 14-15)

[7] Parkman seemingly visited Lake Winnipesaukee and the White Mountains in 1838 with his father, but there is no known account of this journey.

[8] There are innumerable variants of this romantic tale. See B. G. Willey, *Incidents in White Mountain History* (Boston, 1856) 54, 271-76.

[9] Abel Crawford (1765-1851), who married the daughter of Captain Rosebrook and was the father of Tom and Ethan Allen Crawford, long kept a tavern, the Mt. Crawford House, at the southern end of the Notch

of the White Mountains. Later the Notch was named after his family, who did so much to make the region accessible to visitors.

Abel Crawford was the first guide to the White Mountains. At seventy-five, he rode the first horse to reach the summit of Mt. Washington, over the trail cut by his sons. He represented the district in the state legislature during the last five or six years of his life.

[10] From 1829 to 1852, Thomas J. Crawford kept the Notch House, which had been built in 1828 by his father Abel and his brother Ethan at the northern entrance of the Notch. It was long the center for excursions on the western side of the White Mountains and is not far from the present Crawford House. In 1840, Tom Crawford improved the footpath to Mt. Washington, which had been cut by Abel and Ethan in 1819, into a bridle path. This is now the foot trail known as the Crawford Path.

[11] The Willey House, for some time the only stopping place for travelers between Abel Crawford's and Captain Rosebrook's at Fabyan's, a distance of thirteen miles, was built by Leavitt Hill in 1792 and occupied by his brother Henry for some years after the opening of the turnpike through the Notch in 1803, being kept for part of the time as a tavern.

Later abandoned, it was occupied by Samuel Willey, Jr. (1788-1826) in October 1825. On the night of August 28, 1826, Willey, his wife, five children, and two hired men met death from tremendous landslides, which left untouched the house from which they had fled at the moment of danger. Hawthorne's story "The Ambitious Guest" is based upon this Willey Disaster, one of the most famous New England tragedies. A brother of the victim, the Reverend Benjamin G. Willey, gives a very detailed version of the story in his *Incidents in White Mountain History*, pp. 110-40.

[12] Professor Benjamin Silliman (1779-1864), Yale geologist and chemist, made the geological survey of Connecticut, the first of its kind in the United States. After taking law and medical degrees at home and traveling abroad, he published *A Tour to Quebec in the Autumn of 1819* (New Haven, 1820). Two years earlier he had founded the *American Journal of Sciences and Arts*, better known as *Silliman's Journal*, in whose number for April 1829 (No. 15, 217-22), he gives an account of his visit to Crawford Notch in May of the preceding year. But Parkman may have been thinking of Dr. Oliver Hubbard's ascent of the Willey Gorge in 1837, described in the same journal (Vol. 34, I, 105-24), where this Dartmouth professor says his "ascent was impeded by a perpendicular front six feet high."

[13] The first bridle path on the mountains was made by Ethan Crawford in 1821. A path from the Notch House to the summit of Mt. Washington

was opened by Tom Crawford in 1840. Another bridle path, following nearly the same course as the cog railroad, was opened by Horace Fabyan after 1840. The bridle paths were abandoned after the opening of the Carriage Road, on the eastern side of the mountains, in 1861.

[14] Miss Pamela Prentiss (1821-?) of Keene, to whom Parkman paid his attentions two years later during a winter vacation spent in Keene, visiting his classmates George Silsbee Hale and Horatio J. Perry, is probably the original of the intrepid heroine of his novel *Vassall Morton*.

[15] Probably Mt. Willard, which stands nearly 2,800 feet high in the jaws of Crawford Notch, which it commands.

[16] George Blankern Cary (1824-46), Parkman's brilliant and frivolous classmate and clubmate at Harvard, died of pneumonia caught after a Boston ball while still in law school.

Henry Tuke Parker (1824-90), a classmate of Parkman both in college and law school, lived in London for many years, where he was a corresponding member of the Massachusetts Historical Society and London agent of the Boston Public Library. He distributed the American Relief Fund to the French after the Franco-Prussian War.

Edward Wheelwright (1824-1900), Parkman's college and law school friend, pallbearer, and first biographer, was an artist, man of letters, and antiquarian. He was art critic for the *Atlantic Monthly* from 1876 to 1879, and as class secretary he prepared biographical accounts of members of the Harvard class of 1844. His "Memoir of Francis Parkman," *Publications of Colonial Society of Massachusetts*, I, 304-5 (1894), is the best of the early biographic accounts.

[17] The Basin, a mile from the Franconia Flume, is now regarded as quite as much of a spectacle as the Flume itself.

[18] Fifield's tavern was called the Notch House.

[19] John Prentiss (1778-1873) of Keene, the founder of the *New Hampshire Sentinel*, state senator, and a successful publisher of school texts, was the father of the girl who attracted Parkman's attention at Crawford Notch by her fortitude.

[20] James Annance of St. Francis, Quebec, attended Dartmouth 1831-34, but did not graduate. He is quoted as having said of Dartmouth that it "spoiled a great many good Indians and made very poor white men." He became the best-known hunter and guide in northern New Hampshire and Vermont. An Indian called "Old Louis" Annance, a Congregationalist, was well known about Moosehead Lake, where he came in the early 1850's. He supposedly met Thoreau in 1857 at Northeast Carry. Whether or not James and "Old Louis" were the same man is a question. The St.

Francis Indians may have adopted the French-Canadian custom of bestowing double- or triple-barreled Christian names, on which there were many variations in English.

[21] Dr. Charles T. Jackson (1805-80), geologist and chemist, studied medicine in Paris and Vienna after graduating from the Harvard Medical School in 1829. He patented in 1835 a telegraphic apparatus similar to Morse's, and in the following year decided to devote himself to chemistry and mineralogy. In 1837 he surveyed the public lands of Maine and Massachusetts, and became the Maine state geologist, publishing reports 1837-39. In 1838 he made a similar survey of Rhode Island, and from 1840 to 1847 he conducted the New Hampshire state survey. In 1846 he patented his discovery of guncotton; and in the same year he discovered anesthesia and suggested its properties and applications to his pupil Dr. W. T. H. Morton. His claim to the latter discovery was recognized by the French Academy and Jackson was awarded a prize for observations and experiments, while Morton was given a similar award for introducing ether into medical practice in 1848.

[22] Moses B. Williams, a former pupil of Dr. Jackson, was his field assistant during the second year of the New Hampshire survey. Williams had spent the summer of 1840 measuring sectional profiles across the state and the following winter in laboratory research. Jackson pays tribute to Williams' volunteer service in his introductions to the 1841 and 1844 *Reports*.

[23] Baltimore was a publishing center in the 1830's and 40's, with Edgar Allan Poe as one of its notable editors.

[24] Captain James F. Bragg was the leading man of the tiny first settlement of Errol, New Hampshire, which was brought into existence by lumbering operations. The first town meeting was held in his house in 1831, and he long served as selectman. The town numbered only thirty-eight inhabitants in 1871, half a century after its settlement.

[25] No Bennet is mentioned in such fragmentary accounts of the early days of Errol as exist, but a Bennett Brook is shown on the topographical map, below Wilson Mills.

[26] Joshua Lombard is not referred to in the early accounts of Errol. Parkman corrected the spelling of the name in the 1842 Journal.

[27] Captain Wilson, like Captain Bragg, gave his name to the place where he settled, now known as Wilson Mills, Maine.

[28] Jerome, the nephew of James Annance, evidently lacked both the intelligence and the education of his uncle, although he appears to have been a pupil of Peter Masta, who walked three hundred miles from his

home on the St. Lawrence in order to attend Dartmouth, and upon his return taught at the St. Francis reservation.

29 Mettallic, or Mettallak, was the son of a chief whose tribe dwelt on the upper Androscoggin. Some sickness gradually killed off the tribe, until only Metallak and his wife and children remained. His daughter married a St. Francis Indian, and his beloved wife died some time later. Mettallak put her body in his canoe and buried her on a small island in Lake Umbagog, where he mourned for three days and nights. After that, he lived alone, the last survivor of his people, fishing and hunting and acting as guide to the region. He had lost one eye in early life, and the other was put out one day when he fell against the stub of a tree. In 1846 he was found wandering blind through the forest by two hunters, who led him to Stewartstown, New Hampshire, where he spent his few remaining years as a public charge.

30 By way of the fifteen miles of the Nashua & Lowell and the twenty-six miles of the Boston & Lowell. In the early days of rail transportation, New England was covered with a network of small roads, usually originating locally and constructed on strongly individualistic lines, with a fine disregard for their eventual place in a larger scheme.

II. 1842 JOURNAL

1 The Boston & Albany was only completed in 1839, so the journey between the two cities by train was still regarded as a novel experience.

2 Henry Orne White (1824-87) was a member of the class of 1843 at Harvard. His lack of interest in historical matters made him an unsatisfactory companion for Parkman, as the latter indicated in a letter of September 30, 1892 to Abbé Raymond Casgrain about this trip: "White did not sympathize with my ideas, and was sometimes rather disgusted at my persistency in searching after localities for which he did not care a pin." White's lack of endurance and his proneness to discouragement when things were going badly were still more serious liabilities on the wilderness part of this expedition.

3 Fort Edward is near Glens Falls, New York, on the upper Hudson. A stockade fort was first built on this site—long known as the Great Carrying Place because it was the chief portage on the Hudson–Lake George–Lake Champlain–Richelieu water route—by Colonel Francis Nicholson

in 1790 and was named after him. Another fort, first known as Lydius after a Dutch settler and later as Fort Edward after the Duke of York, was built here by General Phineas Lyman of Connecticut in 1755, and was sometimes called Lyman's Fort. Its occupation by General Webb halted Montcalm after the French capture of William Henry in 1757. Fort Edward was also the goal of Marin's French and Indian raid earlier in the same summer. See *Half-Century*, I, 140; and *Montcalm and Wolfe*, II, 173, 205-7.

⁴ Parkman first visited London two years later, but he was familiar with Dickens' accounts of it.

⁵ Union College, which grew out of the Schenectady Academy (1784), was chartered in 1795.

⁶ Saratoga Springs was a favorite summer camping ground of the Iroquois, particularly the Mohawks, who were attracted to the place by the medicinal springs long before white men visited the region. The district was the scene of several conflicts between the French and English and their Indian allies. In 1693 a French expedition was defeated by Governor Benjamin Fletcher and Peter Schuyler. In 1745 the settlers were massacred by French and Indian raiders. The battle of Saratoga during the Revolution was fought about five miles southeast of the present village. The first lodging house for visitors to the springs, a log cabin, was built in 1771, and by 1830 the place had become one of the most popular American resorts.

⁷ In Fenimore Cooper's *The Last of the Mohicans* (Ch. 6-9) Hawkeye, Uncas, and Chingachgook hide Cora, Alice, Duncan Heywood, and David in these caverns while fleeing from the Mingoes. Cooper was Parkman's favorite novelist.

⁸ The skirmish of Rocky Brook, which is referred to in the text, took place on the morning of September 6, 1755, when the French and Indians under Baron Dieskau and Le Gardeur de St. Pierre ambushed a portion of Sir William Johnson's forces, under the command of Colonel Ephraim Williams and Lieutenant Colonel Whiting. After the initial French success in this skirmish, they were defeated at Lake George by Johnson, and Dieskau was wounded and taken prisoner.

⁹ Colonel Ephraim Williams (1714/5-55), who came to Stockbridge, Massachusetts, with his family in 1737 from the Connecticut Valley, commanded the line of frontier outposts known as the Massachusetts Forts, which ran from Fort Dummer in Vermont to Fort Massachusetts near Williamstown, where he usually resided. In 1755 he commanded the 3rd Massachusetts in Johnson's army, and headed the detachment

sent out from the main camp at Lake George to intercept Dieskau's lines of communication with South Bay. Early in the engagement at Rocky Brook he was shot through the head, when he mounted a rock to reconnoiter. He was buried near the spot where he fell, at the foot of a huge pine beside the military road linking the lake and Fort Edward. His grave was later marked with a boulder inscribed E.W. 1755. He made provision in his will for a free school at Williamstown, which in 1793 became the college called after him. There is a tablet to his memory in the Williams Chapel. See *Montcalm and Wolfe*, I, 301-4, 309-15.

[10] Sir William Johnson (1715-74), who was born in Ireland, came to America in 1738 to take charge of the New York estates of his uncle, Admiral Sir Peter Warren. He was appointed Indian agent in 1744 and obtained remarkable influence over the Iroquois. In 1755 he became Superintendent of Indian Affairs, and was also made major general in command of the expedition against Fort Frédéric (Crown Point). Braddock's ill-fated march against Fort Duquesne and Shirley's expedition against Fort Niagara were part of the three fold plan of this campaign. Johnson intended to build a fort at the head of Lake George, proceed up the lake and capture Carillon (Ticonderoga), and there await the rest of his army before attacking Fort Frédéric. But news of Dieskau's flanking attack by South Bay on Fort Edward forced him to give battle at Lake George on September 5. For his victory he received the thanks of Parliament, a baronetcy, and £5,000. He has been criticized for not following up his success and moving against Carillon and Fort Frédéric as originally planned, but it was late in the season and his army had been rudely handled before it won its triumph. See *Montcalm and Wolfe*, I, 296-329.

[11] Captain William McGinnis (?-1755) of Schenectady commanded the detachment from Fort Edward which encountered French stragglers at Bloody Pond, after the battle at the lake. During this final action of September 5, 1755, McGinnis was hit in the head by a ricocheting ball, but continued in command until the end of the fray. He died two days later. See *Montcalm and Wolfe*, I, 319-20.

[12] Bloody Pond, two and a half or three miles south of Johnson's camp at Lake George, was the place where two hundred men from Fort Edward under Captains Folsom and McGinnis fell upon the French and Indian stragglers and drove them to their boats at South Bay, after capturing their baggage and ammunition. The name of the pond commemorates the unceremonious burial in its waters of the victims of the fray.

[13] The first fortification at the head of Lake George, consisting of embankments of gravel surmounted by logs, was built by Sir William

Johnson in 1755 and named by him after the commander in chief, the Duke of Cumberland, younger son of George II, the victor of Culloden and the loser of Fontenoy. The site was an unfortunate choice, being swampy and easily commanded from the surrounding hills. The fort was captured by Montcalm on August 9, 1757, and most of its garrison were massacred by his Indians, who refused to abide by the terms of capitulation. The French burned the fort, which had been greatly strengthened since 1755, and stripped it of munitions and supplies.

[14] The Marquis de Montcalm (1712-59), who came to America as commander in chief in 1756, sent Rigaud de Vaudreuil to reconnoiter William Henry in March 1757, and then himself besieged it in form in the following August with 8,000 men. Landing at Artillery Cove on August 3, he opened trenches and parallels, and bombarded the fort, which surrendered six days later. His lines ran from Artillery Cove to within a few hundred yards of the fort, around the southwest corner of the lake. See the plan, "Siege of Fort William Henry, 1757," in *Montcalm and Wolfe*, II, 183.

[15] Fort George, a short distance southeast of William Henry, was surveyed by General James Abercromby and his engineer Montresor in 1758, but was not built until the following year under Amherst. It was solidly constructed of masonry on the hill which had formed part of Johnson's camp in 1755 and of a division of Munro's forces in 1757. The capture in 1759 of Carillon and Fort Frédéric on Lake Champlain eliminated its usefulness, and only one bastion was completed.

[16] William Caldwell was the son of General James Caldwell, an Albany merchant, who acquired 1,595 acres of upstate New York land in 1787.

[17] The legend of treasure buried at William Henry, probably at the time of its surrender to Montcalm in 1757, is referred to in Hoyt's *Antiquarian Researches*, which is quoted in Van Rensselaer, *Battle of Lake George*, 69.

[18] This was probably one of the trenches of Montcalm's siege works. See *Montcalm and Wolfe*, II, 192 & n.

[19] General James Abercromby (1706-81), called "Nambycromby" by the provincials for his excessive caution which bordered on poltroonry, came to America in 1756 and superseded Shirley and Webb in command of the army, being supplanted in turn by the Earl of Loudoun. In 1757 he commanded the second brigade in the Louisbourg Expedition, and in 1758 he became commander in chief on Loudoun's recall. He led the unsuccessful expedition of that year against Carillon (Ticonderoga), with Lord George Howe as his second-in-command. After the latter's death at

Trout Brook the campaign became a dismal failure, with Montcalm hopelessly outwitting Abercromby. After his disastrous attack on Carillon, Abercromby retreated to the head of Lake George, and burned his boats in the general panic.

[20] These batteries may have been part of Montcalm's siege works.

[21] In Cooper's *The Last of the Mohicans*, Chapter XX, Hawkeye, Uncas, and Chingachcook are pursued by the French Indians while conveying Colonel Munro and Duncan Heyward up the lake.

[22] Ethan Allen (1737/8-89), Revolutionary soldier and author, was born in Litchfield, Connecticut. He served at William Henry in 1757, and in 1769 became a resident in the New Hampshire Grants, as Vermont was then called. In 1770 he organized the Green Mountain Boys, whose "colonel commandant" he became. Acting on Connecticut orders, he captured Ticonderoga on May 10, 1775. In September, while serving with the American army of invasion in Canada, he was captured in a brash attempt to take Montreal by surprise. He was a prisoner in Quebec, England, and New York for the next two years, before being exchanged. Washington gave him the brevet rank of colonel on his release. After the fall of 1778 he was immersed in Vermont politics and commanded the militia in border warfare with the New York settlers. With his brother Ira, he negotiated with Governor Haldimand of Canada to make Vermont a British province rather than an American state. Aside from controversial works on political subjects, his claim to authorship rests on *Reason, the Only Oracle of Man* (Bennington, 1784), a curious deist production. He became one of the great folk heroes of the Revolution.

[23] Parkman's enthusiasm for historic spots here led him into rhetorical excess. Sabbath Day Point was merely the scene of the ambush of Colonel Parker's scouts by the partisan Corbière and his Indians on July 26, 1757, and a stopping place of Abercromby's army on July 5, 1758 as it moved against Ticonderoga.

[24] Captain Samuel Patchin was among the first settlers on Lake George, making his home on Sabbath Day Point. The veteran was fond of his liquor, and one winter day tried to sail a sled load of grist over the ice to the mill at Bolton. Relying too much on the local name of the sleigh—a "jumper"—he came to grief on Vicar's Island over which he had tried to jump his load.

[25] French Canadians, some of whom had served with the American invaders of Canada in 1775-76, began to settle about Lake Champlain after the American Revolution under land grants from Congress. More

drifted south after the Papineau Rebellion of 1837, which centered in the Richelieu district along the outlet of the lake.

26 "Judge" Nathaniel Garfield's tavern was on or near the site of the Phoenix Hotel at Hague. He is said to have had "an intimate acquaintance with every deer on the hill-sides and every trout in the waters." His courtesy title was due to the fact that he was town supervisor for many years.

27 Naumkeag was the Indian name of Salem, Massachusetts, and these bills were doubtless issued by a Salem bank. In 1842, that city was just beginning to lose its commercial importance as a great shipping center.

28 Rogers Rock, or Bald Mountain, near the foot of Lake George, was so called because of "an unsupported tradition that he escaped [from Captain Hebecourt's ambush of March 1758] by sliding on his snowshoes down a precipice of Rogers Rock." (*Montcalm and Wolfe*, II, 220 n.)

29 Colonel John Butler (1728-96), the hated Tory from Connecticut and the Mohawk Valley, served under Sir William Johnson in the 1755 expedition against Carillon, in the Niagara campaign of 1759, and in the Montreal expedition of the following year. He was also with Abercromby at Carillon and with Bradstreet at Fort Frontenac. During the Revolution he was the commander of Butler's Rangers, who displayed great cruelty in their raids on their former neighbors of the Mohawk settlements, notably at Wyoming. His son Walter, who was even more cordially hated than his father, was responsible for the Cherry Valley massacre. After the war the elder Butler was appointed Superintendent of Indian Affairs for British North America, with headquarters on the Niagara peninsula.

30 Joseph Brant (1742-1807), or Thayendanegea, a Mohawk chief whose sister was Sir William Johnson's mistress, commanded the British Indians under St. Leger and raided the Mohawk Valley and northern Pennsylvania with the Tories of John Butler and John Johnson during the Revolution. He was at Oriskany in 1777 and at Cherry Valley in the following year, but is believed to have had no part in the Wyoming massacre. He was rewarded for his services with a colonel's commission in the British Army.

31 Fort Stanwix on the Mohawk guarded the portage from Wood Creek and Lake Oneida. An old blockhouse known at Fort Williams stood near this place until 1756, when it was destroyed by General Webb in his panic after Montcalm's capture of Oswego. The new fort was built by General Stanwix in 1758. It was unsuccessfully besieged by St. Leger in 1777. Its site is now occupied by the city of Rome, New York.

[32] Fort Anne, named after Queen Anne, was built by Colonel Nicholson in 1709 to protect the route from Fort Edward on the Hudson to South Bay on Lake Champlain. It was later destroyed by the French, but subsequently rebuilt. Robert Rogers fought the French and Indians under Marin near by in 1758. The fort was captured by Burgoyne in 1777 and by Major Carleton in 1780.

[33] Sir John Johnson (1742-1830), a son of Sir William Johnson, was made a major general of the New York militia in 1774, but served with the British in the Revolution. He was St. Leger's second-in-command against Arnold in 1777, the year after he fled to Canada, and twice raided his old domain of the Mohawk Valley in 1780. He became Superintendent of Indian Affairs in 1783, thus succeeding his cousin Guy Johnson and his father in that office. He lived in Montreal during the latter part of his life.

[34] A. Loring Cushing was a prominent Boston lawyer of the day.

[35] William Caldwell owned almost all the town of Lake George, then named after him. He lived near the site of the Mansion House and built as an office the stone edifice now used as the post office.

[36] "Old Dick," who was also known as the "Old Man of the Fort," came originally from Massachusetts, but spent forty-five of his seventy-six years about Lake George. He worked at odd jobs on shore and on the lake boats, but his chief interest was in rattlesnakes, then plentiful about Black Mountain and Cobble Hill. He is supposed to have been able to extract the fangs of the snakes, which he sold and exhibited on the boats. His snake box was thus inscribed: "In this box a Rattell Snaick Hoo was Kecht on Black mountaing. He is seven years old last July. Admittance sixpence site. Children half price, or notten."

[37] Parkman refers to the abatis constructed across the peninsula of Ticonderoga, along the ridge about half a mile from the fort, in 1758, at the suggestion of a French officer named Guges. This position broke Abercromby's attack.

[38] Amherst began to besiege Ticonderoga in form on June 22, 1759, but on June 23 the French commander Bourlamaque retired to Ile-aux-Noix on the Richelieu, leaving Captain Hebecourt to blow up the fort on June 26. See *Montcalm and Wolfe*, III, 79-82.

[39] Ticonderoga, known to the French as Carillon, was built by Chartier de Lotbinière in 1755-56 on a promontory overlooking the junction of the outlet between Lake George and Lake Champlain. It was the key to the Hudson–Champlain–Richelieu invasion route, and the chief French outpost against British attacks on Canada. Abercromby was badly beaten by Montcalm in his attempt against it in 1758, while in the following year

it fell with ease to Amherst, Bourlamaque having been ordered by Vaudreuil to retreat rather than risk his whole army. Ethan Allen captured the fortress by surprise in 1775, thus opening the way for the American invasion of Canada by way of Champlain and the Richelieu. It was recaptured by Burgoyne in 1777 and remained British until the close of the Revolution. Under the peace treaty it became the property of the United States. Parkman thus describes the fort, basing his account on De Lotbinière's report to the minister, October 31, 1756: "It stood on the crown of the promontory, and was a square with four bastions, a ditch, blown in some parts out of the solid rock, bomb-proofs, barracks of stone, and a system of exterior defences as yet only begun. The rampart consisted of two parallel walls ten feet apart, built of the trunks of trees, and held together by transverse logs dovetailed at both ends, the space between being filled with earth and gravel well packed." (*Montcalm and Wolfe*, II, 64-5.) Only one bastion was destroyed by the slow match left burning in the magazine when Hebecourt retired from the fort. After years of the vandalism described in Parkman's notes, the site and its ruins were acquired by a conscientious and historically minded proprietor, who was largely responsible for the restoration of the fortress to its former impressiveness. Ticonderoga is now a public park and museum.

[40] Steam navigation on Lake Champlain was opened in 1809 by the *Vermont*, built at Burlington in the preceding year and the world's second successful steamboat. The *Burlington* (built in 1837) and the *Whitehall* (1838), of the Champlain Transportation Company, maintained a service between Whitehall, at the head of Lake Champlain, and St. John's on the Richelieu. The *Burlington* evoked one of Charles Dickens' few favorable *American Notes*, in the same year that Parkman sailed up the lake: "There is one American boat—the vessel which carried us on Lake Champlain from St. John's to Whitehall—which I praise very highly, but no more than it deserves, when I say that it is superior even to that on which we went from Queenston to Toronto or to that on which we travelled from the latter place to Kingston, or, I have no doubt, I may add, to any other in the world. This steamboat, which is called the *Burlington*, is a perfectly exquisite achievement of neatness, elegance, and order. The decks are drawing rooms; the cabins are boudoirs, choicely furnished and adorned with prints, pictures, and musical instruments; every nook and corner of the vessel is a perfect curiosity of graceful comfort and beautiful contrivance." (*American Notes*, Ch. XV.)

In 1909 the *Burlington* and *Whitehall* were still in existence at the graveyard for outworn ships at Shelburne Harbor. With the development of the railroads in the 1850's, the passenger traffic on the lake soon degenerated largely into excursions.

[41] The University of Vermont at Burlington was founded in 1791. At the time Parkman visited it, the university's faculty boasted six members, of whom the most notable was the classicist and philosopher Joseph Torrey. There was a prevailing climate of theological controversy about the institution at this period, though it was nonsectarian.

[42] Camel's Hump, known as Camel's Rump in the pre-Victorian era and as Lion Couchant to the French, is the third highest peak in the Green Mountains, its 4,088 feet being surpassed by Mt. Mansfield's 4,364 and Killington's 4,241. It would seem that Parkman confused Camel's Hump and Mansfield, for Mansfield lies to the left of one approaching the mountains from Burlington, with Camel's Hump to the right, south of the gap in the range formed by the Winooski Valley.

[43] Tension between the United States and Great Britain had been prevalent along the Canadian border since 1837 because of boundary disputes, such as the War of Pork and Beans between Maine and New Brunswick in 1839, and the Indian Stream Republic incident in New Hampshire. The Webster-Ashburton treaty of August 9, 1842 settled these boundary questions.

[44] Paul Chase of Stanstead was probably one of the Yankees who had migrated over the border from New England after the Townships were opened for settlement in 1792. The name is common in New Hampshire and Vermont.

[45] William Miller (1782-1849), the Prophet of the Second Coming of Christ in 1843 or 1844, was born in Pittsfield, Massachusetts; brought up in Poultney, Vermont; served as an officer in the War of 1812; and became a Baptist preacher in Low Hampton, New York. About 1831, after fourteen years of intensive self-study of the Bible and elaborate mathematical calculations based upon the prophecies of Daniel, he began to preach that the year 1843 would usher in the millennium. His doctrine found ready acceptance in a New England fermenting with new sects and theological debate as the old Calvinistic system broke up. First farmers, then tradespeople and members of every class, were numbered among his followers, who probably never exceeded fifty thousand convinced believers. Three other Second Adventists flourished at this period: Joseph Wolff of Palestine and England, who set the date at 1847; Harriet Livermore of Massachusetts, whose views coincided with Wolff and who on four different occasions preached the approach of the Second Coming in the House of Representatives at Washington; and Lady Hester Stanhope, who installed

herself upon Mount Lebanon in Syria in order to be ready for the Advent, in anticipation of which she kept two white Arab horses ready, one for our Lord and the other for herself. The years 1842 and 1843 were marked by a feverish agitation among the Millerites, who were particularly numerous in New England, but the failure of the Advent to materialize on Miller's schedule rapidly broke up the sect.

[46] Peter Barnes came to Pittsburg, New Hampshire, from Corinth, Vermont, in 1822.

[47] James Abbot of Pittsburg, New Hampshire, was probably a son of the Elisha Abbot who was one of the group of Corinth settlers who came in 1822. His political views were exceptional for this region, for in the 1841 election for governor, Pittsburg tallied 51 Democrat and only 8 Free Soil Whig votes.

[48] William Henry Harrison (1773-1841) was elected to the presidency on the Whig ticket in 1840, after what is known as the "log cabin and hard cider campaign" because Harrison made the most of his frontier background. Harrison died one month after his inauguration.

[49] John Tyler (1790-1862), in his early career a Democrat of the Calhoun school, was nominated for the vice-presidency on the Whig ticket in 1839 and was elected with Harrison. Upon Harrison's death, soon after the inauguration, Tyler succeeded to the presidency. Harrison's cabinet resigned, with the exception of Daniel Webster who was then engaged in negotiations with Lord Ashburton for the settlement of the Canadian boundary dispute, when Tyler vetoed the "fiscal corporation" bill. He had the support of neither party and faced the opposition of a Congress controlled by Henry Clay. In 1844, Tyler was an irregular Democratic candidate for a second term, thus confirming Abbot's suspicion that he was not a true Whig.

[50] Parkman evidently did not regard this verbal tradition as trustworthy, for it does not figure in his account of the William Henry massacre in either *Pontiac* or *Montcalm and Wolfe*.

[51] The first settlements in the Connecticut Lakes region were made in the 1820's.

[52] The lunge is a fish usually found farther north than the Connecticut Lakes in North America.

[53] Ebenezer Oakes, the tavern keeper at Franconia, was a member of the family which operated the Franconia ironworks.

[54] Gurnsey, or Guernsey, was a pioneer settler in the Franconia region. His wife is credited with the discovery of the Flume, while out fishing.

[55] Captain Artemas Knight was one of the founders of Franconia in

1774, and the new keeper of the tavern at Lincoln may have been one of his three sons. This house was three-quarters of a mile from the Pool and one of the earliest inns, if not the first, in the Notch.

⁵⁶ The Reverend George Punchard (1806-80), who graduated from Dartmouth in 1826 and from the Andover Theological Seminary in 1829, was ordained at Plymouth in 1830 as a Congregational minister. After suffering throat trouble, he entered journalism, founding the *Daily Evening Traveller* and editing it from 1845 to 1857, and again after 1867. During the interim he was secretary of the New England branch of the American Tract Society. He was the author of the five-volume *View of Congregationalism* (1841-80).

III. 1843 NOTEBOOK

¹ Giles F. Yates of Schenectady, New York, was the son of Robert Yates (1738-1801), the Revolutionary patriot and jurist whose notes on the Federal Convention, *Secret Proceedings and Debates*, were published by his widow in 1821. A brother, John Van Ness Yates (1779-1839), edited and continued William Smith's *History of New York*. Albany, 1814. *Bib. Can.* 267.

² The Reverend John Williams (1817-99), who later became president of Trinity College, Hartford, and Episcopalian bishop of Connecticut, was rector of St. George's Church, Schenectady, from 1842 to 1848. He was the son of Ephraim Williams (1760-1835) of Old Deerfield, Massachusetts, who edited Volume I of the *Massachusetts Reports*; the grandson of Dr. Thomas Williams, Sir William Johnson's physician; and the great nephew of Colonel Ephraim Williams (1714/15-1755), the defender of the frontier in the French and Indian War. He was educated at Harvard and Trinity, and became professor of history and literature at the latter institution, so his interests were akin to those of Parkman.

³ Clermont is ten miles south of Hudson, New York.

⁴ The Palatine settlers of the Mohawk Valley were tenants of Sir William Johnson. Fonda was named after Lieutenant Jelles Fonda, a scout with Johnson at Lake George in 1755 and at Oswego in 1757.

⁵ Père Isaac Jogues, S.J., (1607-46) escaped from the Iroquois in 1642 through the aid of the Dutch of Rensselaerswyck (Albany). See his letters to Lalement dated August 30, 1643 and January 6, 1644, in Vimont's

Relation of 1642-43, Ch. XIV (Thwaites, XXV, 92-9); also Lalement's *Relation of 1647*, Ch. VII (Thwaites, XXXI, 92-9). The old Dutchman of the story Parkman heard may be Dominie Johannes Megapolensis (1603-1670), who was born a Catholic but became the Reformed Dutch minister of the place until 1649 and afterwards pastor of what was later known as the Collegiate Reformed Church of New York (Thwaites, XXV, 288 note 4). Père Jogues was sent home to France after reaching New Amsterdam (New York) in 1643; but returned to Canada in the following year, and in June 1646 came to Fort Orange (Albany) as ambassador to the Iroquois.

Schenectady was burned by the French and Indians under Le Moyne de Ste. Hélène and D'Ailleboust de Mantet on the night of February 8, 1690. No Jesuit accompanied the expedition. The house of John Sander Glen (known as "Captain Sander," a name rendered by the French as "Cendre," "Condre," and "Coudre") was alone spared because of his kindness to French prisoners (E. B. O'Callaghan, *Doc. Hist. of N. Y.*, I, 285-312; Parkman, *Frontenac*, 225-27).

It is probable that Parkman's informant confused the two local legends and linked them together to make a better story.

[6] Joseph Brant, or Thayendanegea (1742-1807) was a Mohawk chief and one of the most notable figures of his race. His sister Molly's relationship with Sir William Johnson helped him to rise to the leadership of his people. At the age of thirteen he fought under Sir William at Lake George in 1755; and later was sent through Johnson's interest to Moor's School, Lebanon, Connecticut, where Eleazar Wheelock began his educational work with the Indians. Brant fought with the whites against Pontiac in 1763; and served as secretary to Guy Johnson, who succeeded his uncle as Superintendent of Indian Affairs in 1774. During the Revolution Brant won the Iroquois to the British interest, and for his efforts was rewarded with a colonel's commission in the British Army. He went to London in 1775 and was presented at Court, entertained by Boswell, and painted by Romney. He commanded the Indians under St. Leger, and with the Tories of Butler and Johnson harried the Mohawk Valley, southern New York, and northern Pennsylvania. He was at Oriskany in 1777 and Cherry Valley in 1778, but is believed to have had no part in the Wyoming massacre of the following year. He frustrated Red Jacket's attempt to win a separate peace for the Mohawks from the Colonies, and got Canadian land grants for them from Sir Frederick Haldimand. On a second visit to England in 1785-86, he secured indemnities from the British govern-

ment for the losses suffered by the Mohawks during the Revolution. He died in Ontario, where he made his home after the Revolution.

[7] The place where the Mohawks burned their prisoners at the stake. Prisoners were always brought home for this purpose by the Iroquois after a war party.

[8] Fort George was constructed as a permanent fortification in masonry by Amherst in 1759; but its site had been occupied by part of Johnson's armed camp in 1755, by part of Munro's forces in 1757, and by Abercromby in the following year. The lines were traced by Abercromby and his engineer Montresor in June 1759, and the works were completed within a month; but the fall of Ticonderoga eliminated the fort's usefulness. During the Revolution it was held by the Americans, except for brief occupations by Burgoyne in 1777 and Carleton in 1780.

[9] The Soeurs Grises, or Gray Nuns (Soeurs de la Charité de l'Hôpital-Général), are an order founded at Montreal in 1737 by Madame d'Youville. They devote themselves to the care of the old and infirm and of abandoned children, to hospital work and the visiting of the sick and poor, and to conducting orphanages, insane asylums, and institutions for the blind. The order has run the General Hospital at Montreal since 1747.

[10] Parkman visited the third Cathedral of Montreal, built in 1825 by Bishop Lartigue at the corner of St. Catherine and St. Denis streets. This church was completely destroyed by fire in 1852, when a conflagration laid waste most of the city.

[11] The 71st Highland Light Infantry was one of the famous regiments of the British Army, having served with distinction in the Peninsula campaigns and at Waterloo. In 1843 the service battalion had its depot in Montreal, while the reserve battalion was in garrison at Chambly. Lieutenant Augustus Terrick Hamilton, an officer of this regiment, did a fine series of drawings of Montreal and Chambly.

[12] The 89th Regiment of Foot had served at Niagara in the War of 1812. Lieutenant George F. Ruxton, author of *Life in the Far West*, served in this regiment.

[13] The 43rd Monmouthshire Light Infantry had a distinguished record in the Peninsula campaigns during the Napoleonic Wars.

[14] The fort at St. John's, on the Richelieu River, after having been burned by the French in 1759, was rebuilt by the English ten years later. Under the gallant Major Preston, it finally surrendered to Montgomery's American army of invasion in 1775, after a siege of forty-five days. Between 1778 and 1784, £24,000 were spent on restoring the fortifications, but by 1804 they were again ruinous.

[15] This fort at Ile-aux-Noix on the Richelieu was constructed at the time of the War of 1812, but it saw little service and never underwent a baptism of fire.

[16] The Hope Gate, named after Sir Henry Hope (?-1789), lieutenant governor of Quebec from 1785 until his death, was built in 1786, ten years after Montgomery's assault. It was altered during the reconstruction of the fortifications in 1823-32, strengthened in 1840, and demolished in 1874.

[17] Richard Montgomery (1736-75), an Irishman who long served in the British Army—he was with Wolfe at Louisburg in 1758 and at Ticonderoga and Crown Point under Amherst in the following year—settled in New York, married the daughter of Robert Livingston, and was named one of the colony's eight brigadier generals under Major General Philip Schuyler. In 1775, while Arnold led 1,000 men against Quebec by way of the Kennebec and the Chaudière, Montgomery, under Schuyler, headed another army of 1,300 which advanced by the Hudson–Champlain–Richelieu route against Montreal. Schuyler fell sick and Montgomery was given the chief command. After taking the forts at Ile-aux-Noix, Chambly, and St. John's, whose capture resulted in the capitulation of Montreal, Montgomery joined forces with Arnold at Pointe-aux-Trembles on the St. Lawrence, above Quebec. After a siege of twenty-five days, a double assault was planned for the night of December 30, with Arnold leading one party by the Saut-au-Matelot and Montgomery another by Près-de-Ville, at the foot of Cape Diamond. The plan called for a juncture of the two parties after they had won the Lower Town, and a subsequent joint attack on the Upper Town by the Côte-de-la-Montagne. But Montgomery was killed at the head of his force while attempting to surprise the battery which commanded the passage under the Cape. By his friend Guy Carleton's orders, Montgomery was buried with military honors under one of the bastions of Fort St. Louis, not far from the present St. Louis Gate. His remains were removed to St. Paul's churchyard, New York City, in 1818, but memorial plaques mark both his death place and his temporary grave in Quebec.

[18] The Wolfe and Montcalm Monument stands in the Governor's Garden, adjoining the Chateau Frontenac and facing Dufferin Terrace. Lord Dalhousie laid the cornerstone on November 15, 1827, and the monument was completed on September 8, 1828, the day of his departure from Canada. A competition was held for the best inscription, and the prize medal was won by J. Charlton Fisher, LL.D., with the admirably concise text noted by Parkman.

19 Wolfe's Monument stands near the Provincial Museum, in the center of a *rond-point*, in Battlefields Park. It is a plain round column, surmounted by a sword and helmet. A plate attached to the base reads:

Here Died
WOLFE
Victorious
Sept. 13
1759

Until Lord Aylmer raised a monument here at his own expense in 1832, neither the scene of Wolfe's victory nor that of his death was commemorated fittingly, though a simple memorial was built by the army in 1759 on this site. Aylmer's monument was replaced in 1849 by the officers of the garrison. The crown piece and inscription of the 1849 monument are preserved in the present one, which was set up in 1913 by the National Battlefields Commission.

20 Frances (Moore) Brooke (1724-89), *The History of Emily Montague* (London, 1769. *Bib. Can.* 425.) This romantic novel, in the style of Richardson, is dedicated to Guy Carleton. The first Canadian novel, it depicts the scenery and social life of Quebec. The author, whose husband was garrison chaplain from 1760 to 1768, spent five years in Quebec, and had a good eye for scenery and character. She was also no stranger to psychology.

21 The reference is probably to Charles Butler's *The Book of the Roman Catholic Church* (London, 1825), a reply to Robert Southey's anti-Catholic *Book of the Church*.

22 See note 9, 1841 Journal, p. 330.

23 Ethan Allen Crawford (1792-1846), known as "The Giant of the Hills" for his great height and strength, cut the first paths up the mountains in 1819 and 1821. He was nearly seven feet tall, and the tales of his feats are reminiscent of Paul Bunyan. He frequently carried weary excursionists home on his back from the mountains, and is supposed to have mastered a bear with no weapon but his bare hands. Guildhall was his birthplace and the former home of his maternal grandfather, Captain Eleazar Rosebrook.

24 Dennison conducted a tavern at the Rosebrook house, near Fabyan's.

25 See note 10, 1841 Journal, p. 331.

26 The Aroostuck expedition arose out of a boundary dispute, sometimes known as the War of Pork and Beans. In 1838-39 the boundary between

Maine and New Brunswick was in question. Maine erected forts along the line she claimed; Congress authorized the President to resist any attempt of Great Britain to enforce exclusive jurisdiction over the disputed territory; and open conflict seemed imminent. Fortunately the level-headed General Winfield Scott was given command on the frontier, and on March 21, 1839, he arranged a truce and joint occupancy of the region until a satisfactory settlement should be reached. A compromise, allowing each party less than it had claimed, was attained in the Webster-Ashburton Treaty of 1842.

[27] The theologically-minded Russell came from Bethlehem (founded in 1790 as Lord's Hill).

[28] Daniel Pierce Thompson (1795-1868), *The Green Mountain Boys: a Historical Tale of the Early Settlement of Vermont* (Montpelier, 1839).

[29] Knapp had taken over the Notch House at Franconia, which Parkman had found deserted in 1842 and which had been kept by Fifield in 1841.

[30] Center Harbor, on Lake Winnipesaukee, was one of the chief gateways to the White Mountains, since roads led thence to both Crawford and Franconia notches. It was a favorite resort of the Abenakis, who feared the mountains and usually camped to the south of them. Ossipee and Fryeburg are rich in Indian burial mounds, in which some relics have been found.

[31] Charles Fenno Hoffman (1806-84), editor, poet, and novelist, began his journalistic career by writing for the New York *American*, which he later edited with Charles King. He was editor of the *Knickerbocker Magazine* (to which Parkman later contributed) for a few months in 1833; then left on a tour of the Northwest by horseback. His travel letters, first published in the *American*, were collected in the two volumes of *A Winter in the West* (1835). His "Scenes and Sources of the Hudson" were collected in *Wild Scenes in Forest and Prairie* (London, 1839; New York, 1843). He also wrote an undistinguished novel, *Greyslaer, a Romance of the Mohawk* (1839). At this period, his interests were close to those of Parkman.

[32] George Barstow (1812-83), *The History of New Hampshire from Its Discovery* (Concord, 1842).

[33] William Dunlap (1766-1839), *History of the New Netherlands, Province of New York, & State of New York to the Adoption of the Federal Constitution* (New York, 1839-40). Dunlap's best-known works are his history of the New York stage and his diary.

[34] John Milton Whiton, *Sketches of the History of New Hampshire* (Concord, 1834).

35 Paugus, war chief of the Pequawkets, a tribe of the Abenakis, organized the famous ambush of Captain John Lovewell's party. Paugus was killed in the fight at Lovewell's Pond on May 8, 1725, by either Ensign Seth Wyman of Woburn or John Chamberlain, the honor being disputed. Cf. *Half-Century*, I, 256-71.

36 There were several guidebooks entitled the *Northern Traveller* in circulation at this period. Theodore Dwight (1796-1866) published one in 1825 which was reprinted four times by 1841. *The Northern Traveller and Northern Tour; with the Routes to the Springs, Niagara & Quebec, and the Coal Mines of Pennsylvania; also the Tour of New England* was published at New York in 1831.

37 Probably Thomas Starr King (1824-64), Unitarian clergyman, lecturer, and writer, who was a great lover of the White Mountains, which he celebrated in 1860 in his classic *The White Hills*. In 1843 he had just finished three years as a schoolteacher in Charlestown and Medford (the home of Parkman's maternal relatives), and had taken a job as bookkeeper in the Charlestown Navy Yard, which gave him more time for his studies. Three years later he became a minister in Boston, and soon rivaled Henry Ward Beecher as a lyceum lecturer.

38 Lucy Howe Crawford (1799-1869), *The History of the White Mountains from the First Settlement of Upper Coos and Pequaket* (White Hills [Portland], 1846).

39 Timothy Nash and Benjamin Sawyer were hunters who in 1771 "discovered" the passage through the White Mountains, doubtless long known to the Indians. In 1773 they received from Governor John Wentworth as reward a grant of 2,184 acres to the west of the range, but they did not long retain control of this enormous property. A route through the mountains to Portland was very important for the development of northern New Hampshire and Vermont at this period; hence the magnificence of their reward.

40 Captain Eleazar Rosebrook (1747-1817), a native of Massachusetts, early settled in the north country, first at Lancaster and later at Colebrook, then thirty miles beyond the last settlements. He once traveled eighty miles on foot in order to get a bag of salt at Haverhill, which he carried home on his back through the trackless wilds. Later he lived at Guildhall, Vermont, where his family stayed while he served in the Revolution. In 1792 he sold this farm and became the first settler in Nash and Sawyer's Location. He built his house on the Giant's Grave (at Fabyan's) where he also had saw and grist mills. He opened the first hotel for summer

visitors in 1803. In 1817, Captain Rosebrook left his property to his grandson Ethan Allen Crawford, who had served as his hired man.

[41] An account of the disaster appears in note 11, 1841 Journal, p. 331.

[42] Susannah Willard Johnson Hastings (1730-1810). *The Captivity of Mrs. Johnson* (Windsor, Vermont, 1807.) (Cf. *Bib. Can.* 320.) Mrs. Johnson, a native of Charlestown, New Hampshire—then known as "No. 4" from its place in the chain of frontier forts—was captured in an Indian raid on the village in 1754, carried overland to Lake Champlain, and thence to Montreal and Quebec, finally returning home by way of London. Her book is a colorful epic of the French and Indian War, though the story doubtless gained in vividness during the long period that elapsed between the events and their chronicling.

[43] A Meserve was one of the first settlers of Jackson, New Hampshire, in 1790. Stephen Meserve of Bartlett represented that town and Jackson in the state legislature.

[44] Captain Samuel Willey (1754?-1844), the father of the victim of the landslide, was one of the first settlers of Upper Bartlett, and later lived in North Conway. He came from Lee, Massachusetts in 1777. Another son, the Reverend Benjamin G. Willey (?-1867), was the author of the best early book on the White Mountains (*Incidents in White Mountain History*, Boston, 1857).

[45] Colonel Joseph Whipple of Jefferson, New Hampshire, whose farm was near the mill on the Cherry Mountain road, owned most of the good land north of the mountains in the early days of settlement. He came from Portsmouth in 1772. He was a paternalistic landlord, and on his annual visits to Portsmouth acted as agent for most of the inhabitants of the region. Willey gives a different version of the corn story (*Incidents*, 71), saying that it was a famine year and that the colonel refused to sell grain to any save his neighbors, for fear that they should suffer. The "Indians" were from Bartlett, thirty miles away. Willey also has a happy ending for the Tory raid story. After his escape, the colonel "went directly to a meadow, where he had men to work, and, ordering each man to seize a stake from the fence and shoulder it as he would a gun, soon presented himself again to the Indians, who were already in search of him. Seeing him in the distance, as they supposed at the head of a large company of armed men, they hastily seized what plunder they could lay hands on, and fled." (*Incidents*, 72.)

[46] John Josselyn (1638-75). *New Englands Rarities Discovered* (London, 1672); *An Account of Two Voyages to New England* (London, 1674). Josselyn's observations on nature are to be found in *New Englands Rarities* (Transac-

tions of American Antiquarian Society, IV). The *Voyages* was reprinted in *Massachusetts Historical Society Collections*, Series 3, Vol. III (1833). A famous passage describes the view from Mt. Washington: "The country beyond these hills, northward, is daunting terrible; being full of rocky hills, as thick as mole-hills in a meadow, and clothed with infinite thick woods."

[47] See note 35, of this journal, p. 350.

[48] "About 1827, such of the Wolfe papers as had descended from General Warde, the executor of Wolfe's mother, to his nephew, Admiral George Warde, were placed in Robert Southey's hands, but a life of Wolfe which he had designed was not prepared, and the papers were lost sign of until they appeared as lots 531-32 of the Catalogue of the Dawson Turner Sale in 1858 . . ." (J. Winsor, *Narr. & Crit. Hist. of America*, V, 602, n. 4.)

[49] This was Parkman's favorite sister Caroline, who acted as his amanuensis and copyist during his early labors on *The Oregon Trail* and *The Conspiracy of Pontiac*, and who married the Rev. Dr. John Cordner of Montreal in 1852. Like her brother, she was troubled with weakness of sight, and underwent the attentions of the noted oculist, Dr. S. R. Elliott of Staten Island, a year before he did.

[50] The Penobscot mission village of Panawariské was above Bangor, at or near the mouth of the Passadumkeag River. After Colonel Westbrook burned it in 1723, the village was re-established nearer Bangor, a little below Old Town. This settlement became the nucleus of the reservation which Parkman visited, and which still exists. Cf. *Half-Century*, I, 244-45, 254.

[51] The Lord's Supper was probably a cyclorama, a popular form of traveling show at this period.

[52] The Caughnawaga Mission for the Iroquois was established by the Jesuits in 1667 on the south shore of the St. Lawrence at the mouth of the St. Jacques River, in the seigneury of Laprairie, near Montreal. It is still in existence as a reservation, not far from the original site opposite Lachine and once more under the direction of the Jesuits. Cf. E. J. Devine, S.J., *Historic Caughnawaga* (Montreal, 1922).

[53] Castine, Maine, at the mouth of the Penobscot, is named after the Baron de St. Castin (1650-1712), who established himself in a fort called Pentagoet at that place and took an Abenaki wife. He and his sons had great influence over the Indians.

[54] This account of the Mohawk raid on the Penobscots is mentioned in *Pontiac*, I, 10 n.

IV. EUROPEAN JOURNAL

[1] George Borrow's *The Bible in Spain* was first published in 1843. Since Parkman had a vague plan of wandering through Spain, to which he later refers in the journal, it was not surprising that he should be reading Borrow and *Don Quixote* on the voyage to Europe.

[2] Nathaniel Jarvis Wyeth (1802-56) of Cambridge, Mass., led a fur-trading party into the Oregon country in 1832 and again in 1834. In the latter year he was accompanied from the Missouri to Fort Hall by the first Oregon missionaries, Jason and Daniel Lee. An account of Wyeth's first journey by his cousin John B. Wyeth, *Oregon: or a Short History of a Long Journey* (Cambridge, 1833) is one of the early classics of Western history, although Nathaniel called it a book "of *little lies* told for gain." John Kirk Townsend's account of the second journey, *Narrative of a Journey Across the Rocky Mountains . . . in 1834* (Philadelphia, 1839) was also doubtless familiar to Parkman, as references in this journal and that kept on his Oregon Trail trip indicate. Wyeth's own account of his experiences was not printed until 1899 (G. E. Young, Ed., "Correspondence and Journals of Captain Nathaniel J. Wyeth," *Sources of History of Oregon*, I, 3-6, [Eugene, O., 1899]).

[3] Cf. *Vassall Morton*, p. 394.

[4] This description of the gale is taken over word for word in *Vassall Morton*, pp. 395-96.

[5] Probably William F. Worthington of William Worthington and Co., merchants, of 20 Central Wharf, Boston, who either owned or chartered the *Nautilus*. The small merchant vessels of the eastern seaboard were very active in the Mediterranean trade at this period.

[6] Don Alonzo Perez de Guzman (1256-1309), known as "*El Bueno*," defended Tarifa in 1296 and allowed the besiegers to kill his son, whom they held captive, rather than surrender the town. The Duke of Medina-Sidonia, the commander of the Spanish Armada, prided himself on his descent from Don Alonzo.

[7] Sir George Augustus Eliott (1717-90), later Lord Heathfield, commanded Gibraltar during the four years' siege which was begun in 1789 by the Spanish and French.

[8] See Appendix to this journal, p. 237.

[9] See Appendix to this journal, p. 237.

[10] Sir John Moore (1761-1809) was mortally wounded at Corunna

353

during the Napoleonic Wars. The familiar poem by Charles Wolfe about his burial in the ramparts has immortalized his name.

[11] Admiral Sir Peter Parker (1761-1811) was Nelson's first patron.

[12] Prince Gerhard von Blücher (1742-1819) was Wellington's trump card at Waterloo.

[13] Lorenzo Papanti of 21 Tremont Row, Boston, was the best known dancing master of the day in that city.

[14] See the Appendix to this journal, p. 237.

[15] Jehan Parisot de la Valette, Grand Master of the Knights of St. John, defended Malta in the great siege of 1565, which checked the advance of Mohammedan power in southern and western Europe. Under him the order reached its highest fame. He refused a cardinal's hat, preferring independence, and made Valletta the best fortified place in the world.

[16] The Albion on Tremont Street and Murdoch's Tavern were famous Boston eating and drinking places of the day.

[17] Matthew Gregory Lewis (1775-1818) was known as "Monk" Lewis for his celebrated romance, *Ambrosio or the Monk*.

[18] See the Appendix to this journal, p. 237-38.

[19] See the Appendix to this journal, p. 238.

[20] See the Appendix to this journal, p. 238-39.

[21] Don Mateo Lopez' card was found in Parkman's pocket notebook.

[22] See the Appendix to this journal, p. 240.

[23] See the Appendix to this journal, p. 239.

[24] See the Appendix to this journal, p. 239.

[25] See the Appendix to this journal, p. 239-40.

[26] See the Appendix to this journal, p. 239.

[27] See the Appendix to this journal, p. 240.

[28] The Sicilian Vespers were the massacres of the French at Palermo and elsewhere in 1282, as a result of the conspiracy of the Sicilians with the Greek emperor Michael Palaeologus and King Pedro of Aragon against the Angevin dynasty.

[29] King Ferdinand II of Naples and the Two Sicilies used the jealousy between the two parts of his kingdom to advantage in the revolutionary agitation of 1847.

[30] See the Appendix to this journal, p. 241.

[31] See the Appendix to this journal, p. 241.

[32] See the Appendix to this journal, p. 241-42.

[33] See the Appendix to this journal, p. 242-43.

[34] See the Appendix to this journal, p. 244.

[35] See the Appendix to this journal, p. 245.

[36] James Holman (1786-1857) became blind at the age of twenty-five, after serving in the British Navy. He then traveled widely, describing his journeys in three books: *Narrative of a Journey* . . . *1819-21* (London, 1822), *Travels in Russia, Siberia, Poland, Austria, etc.* (London, 1825), and *Voyage Round the World* (London, 1834-35).

[37] Count Perolla was the grandson of Count Roger, the Norman who drove the Saracens out of Sicily.

[38] *Aeneid*, Book V.

[39] Agathocles, the greatest of the early rulers of Sicily, was tyrant of Syracuse and eastern Sicily (317-301 B.C.). He waged a long war with Hamilcar of Carthage; and in quelling a revolt led by Syracuse's rival Acragas, he laid Segasta waste.

[40] This incident serves as an episode in *Vassall Morton*, pp. 115-16.

[41] Theodore Parker (1810-60) was the great Unitarian preacher of his day. He was a man of great erudition and later advised Parkman in his first historical work.

[42] Carnival was a period of from three to ten days of merrymaking, just before the beginning of Lent. The custom is probably a survival of the Roman Saturnalia, and Rome was the headquarters of it, although all the principal Italian cities had carnivals. The throwing of sweetmeats and flowers was the result of the reform by Pope Sixtus V of the old custom of throwing dirt, dust, and flour.

[43] Masaniello led a revolt at Naples in 1647 against Spanish rule.

[44] Shrove Tuesday.

[45] John Adams Dix (1798-1879) served in the War of 1812 and was adjutant general of New York in 1830. He soon became a prominent leader of the Democratic Party, and was a member of the "Albany Regency," which controled the party from 1820 to 1850. From 1841-43 he was editor of *The Northern Light*, an Albany literary and scientific journal.

[46] George Washington Greene (1811-83), a grandson of General Nathaniel Greene of Revolutionary War fame, was the American Consul at Rome from 1837 to 1845, when he returned to America. In later life he was a teacher and historian.

[47] Samuel Gridley Howe (1801-76), who had taken part in the Greek Revolution and founded the Perkins Institute for the Blind in Boston, was traveling in Europe in 1844 on a prolonged tour of philanthropic institutions. He was accompanied by his wife, Julia Ward Howe, later the author of "The Battle Hymn of the Republic," whom he had married in the previous year.

⁴⁸ A fuller account of the Virginian St. Ives is given in Parkman's article, "A Convent at Rome," (*Harper's Magazine*, August 1890 [LXXXI, 448-54]), which was based on this journal.

⁴⁹ Johann Friedrich Overbeck (1789-1869), the German painter, was a leader in the nineteenth-century revival of Christian art. He went to Rome in 1810, and for the rest of his life it was the center of his labors.

⁵⁰ William Morris Hunt (1824-79), the painter, was Parkman's classmate at Harvard, but had been suspended for inattention to his studies. His brother John was a freshman at Harvard. The Hunt family decided to remain in Europe, where William studied painting for ten years, before he returned home to become the apostle of the Barbizon School and the dean of the Boston art world. When Parkman encountered him, Hunt had already begun to study in Rome with Henry Kirk Brown, the American sculptor.

⁵¹ Claude of Lorraine or Claude Gelée (1600-82), the great French landscape painter. His works in the Altieri and Colonna palaces at Rome were probably fresh in Parkman's memory.

⁵² Cyclopean masonry, the chief survival of the prehistoric period in Italy, is characterized by polygonal stones set in irregular courses.

⁵³ By "General Confession" Parkman probably meant the obligation of all Catholics to confess and to receive Holy Communion at Eastertime.

⁵⁴ Cf. *Jesuits*, I, 197 n. 2.

⁵⁵ Probably Mr. William English of Castlerock, Dublin, whose card was found in Parkman's pocket notebook.

⁵⁶ Hiram Powers (1805-73), the American sculptor, settled in Florence in 1837. His "Greek Slave," completed in 1843, made his reputation as one of the leading artists of the day.

⁵⁷ The disorder that brought Parkman to Europe is described by Edward Wheelwright, one of his Harvard classmates, as "heart-strain" brought on by overexertion in the college gymnasium. A mule-back tour through rugged Sicily and rambles in the Alps were hardly calculated to help a bad heart. It is possible that the doctors told Parkman to go easy because of his heart, when they really wanted him to relax because of the nervous hypertension from which he undoubtedly suffered at this period.

⁵⁸ Ethan and Tom Crawford, the giant sons of old Abel Crawford, kept taverns in the White Mountains which Parkman had frequented in 1841-43.

⁵⁹ Cf. *Vassall Morton*, p. 244.

⁶⁰ Cf. *Vassall Morton*, p. 194.

⁶¹ *American Notes*, Ch. III.

[62] The Jardin Mabille was one of the most notorious pleasure-places in the Paris of the period. Parkman seems to have had a very knowing uncle.

[63] Charles Matthews (1803-78) was one of the most famous English actors of his day. He played at the Haymarket during much of 1843 and 1844.

[64] The repudiation of foreign debts in the great financial panic of 1837 made as many enemies for the United States as did insistence on the payment of the war debts of 1914-18.

[65] Catlin's "Indian Gallery," first shown in New York in 1837 and in London in 1839, did much to arouse the interest of both Americans and Europeans in the Far West. George Catlin spent six years painting the Indians and collecting this valuable mass of relics in the West and South. Many of his paintings were reproduced in lithograph in his *North American Indian Portfolio* (London, 1844), and have found a permanent home in the National Museum at Washington, D. C.

[66] Tom Thumb, later known as "General," was one of a celebrated line of dwarfs who have gone by this name.

[67] The dwarf Jeffrey Hudson (1619-82) was a favorite of Henrietta Maria, wife of Charles I of England. He saw service against Cromwell in the Rebellion.

[68] George Atkinson was a brother of William P. Atkinson, Parkman's brother-in-law.

[69] In Scott's *The Heart of Midlothian*.

[70] James Ballantyne printed Scott's first book, the *Minstrelsy*, in 1802; and later was his partner, first as a printer and then as a publisher. The collapse of the Ballantyne firm involved Scott in bankrupcy, out of which he struggled through his writing.

[71] In *Waverly*.

[72] Daniel Denison Slade, Parkman's companion on his first excursion in the White Mountains in 1841.

V. BOSTON & BERKSHIRE JOURNAL

[1] The front end papers of this notebook contain a note to "Pay Pratt"; and some scribbled names, mostly of Harvard classmates; and the note "Third Wednesday of August be at Cambridge." This was Parkman's

graduation day, as commencement was then held in the autumn. The rear end papers contain some illegible law and sermon notes, and the following list of equipment for his Berkshire expedition:

		three shirts
shoes		two stockings
waistcoats	Knapsack to contain	flannel drawers
card for gun		fishing apparatus
knapsack		Powder & shot
		Hist. of B[erkshire]

There is also a list of names: "Hall, Hamilton, Trollope, Cooper's *Works*, Bird's *Works*, *Green Mt. Boy*, Leatsfield, Miss Leslie—Pencil sketch."

2 In 1840 Albert Brisbane, the father of the late Arthur Brisbane of the Hearst press, published *The Social Destiny of Man*, a book which introduced the social ideas of Charles Fourier to an America already interested in Robert Owen's ideas of association. In April 1841 George Ripley, who had recently resigned from the Unitarian ministry, launched the Brook Farm experiment at West Roxbury, which Emerson referred to as "a French Revolution in small and an Age of Reason in a patty pan." By 1844 Brook Farm had become a Fourier phalanx, with a membership of about a hundred.

3 Parkman's classmate, Charles B. Snow of Fitchburg, Mass.

4 George Blankern Cary (1824-46), a brilliant figure of Parkman's class at college.

5 John (Dawson) Gilmary Shea (1824-92), after studying law and being admitted to the New York bar in 1846, entered the Jesuit novitiate in 1848 and spent six years in the order, being closely associated with Père Félix Martin, the historian and first rector of St. Mary's College, Montreal. Soon after leaving the Society of Jesus, Shea began a systematic study of the Indian missions in America. He won notice with his *Discovery and Exploration of the Mississippi Valley*. In 1854 he published his *History of Catholic Missions, 1529-1824* which brought him into correspondence with Parkman and in 1857 he initiated his series of Crémoisy reprints of early voyages. He was considered the best-informed American on Indian questions of his day.

6 Rolland Green of Mansfield, Massachusetts?

7 John Norton (1716-78), *The Redeemed Captive, Being a narrative of the taking and carrying into captivity of The Reverend Mr. John Norton When Fort Massachusetts Surrendered . . . August 20, 1746* (Boston, 1748). *Bib. Can.* 203.

8 Montague City is on the east bank of the Connecticut River, opposite

Greenfield and near Turner's Falls, Massachusetts, where Captain Turner killed 300 Nipmucks in 1676.

[9] Probably Horace T. Clark (1823-?), who is listed in the West Stockbridge records as a "machinist."

[10] John Sergeant (1710-49) of Newark, New Jersey, abandoned his tutorship at Yale to become the first missionary to the Stockbridge Indians in 1734. He was ordained at Deerfield in the following year. His first church stood on the green, "a few rods north-east of the present South Church," and was opened on Thanksgiving Day, 1739. Sergeant gave himself so zealously to the task of educating and converting the Indians that he came to an early death. He was much loved by his flock.

[11] During King Philip's War (1675-76), Major Talcot of Connecticut and some Stockbridge Indians defeated two hundred hostile savages on the Housatonic, midway between Westfield and Albany.

[12] Dr. Oliver Partridge (1757-1848), who was born in Hatfield, came to Stockbridge as a young man. He was a son of Colonel Oliver Partridge, the sheriff of Hatfield.

[13] Agrippa Hull (1759-1848), a resident of Stockbridge from childhood. He served over six years in the Revolution, four of them as Kosciusko's body servant. He was long in the service of Judge Sedgwick. In later life he was one of the noted characters of the village.

[14] Mrs. Stephen Jones was the widow of the son of Captain Josiah Jones (1725-?), who was referred to by the Stockbridge Indians as "Good man, always kind to Indian." When the tribe left Stockbridge for the West, they gave the Captain the old conch shell which had always been used to call them to the mission church.

[15] A grandson of Captain Jones.

[16] Actually Dr. Partridge was eighty-seven in 1844.

[17] Colonel Ephraim Williams (1715-55) early went to sea and visited England, Spain, and Holland, but abandoned the sailor's life at the request of his father, who had removed from Hatfield to Stockbridge in 1737. The son acquired considerable land holdings and represented the town in the General Court, before returning to Hatfield in 1748 to serve as deputy sheriff under Colonel Oliver Partridge. In 1746 he was given charge of the line of frontier forts running from Fort Dummer on the Connecticut River to Fort Massachusetts near Williamstown. Since he was engaged in preparing an invasion of Canada to check the French and Indian raids, he was not at the latter place when it was attacked by Rigaud de Vaudreuil in 1746; but successfully defended it against a second attack in 1748. He was promoted from captain to major, and at

the end of the War of the Austrian Succession settled again in Hatfield. In 1755 Williams commanded a regiment in Sir William Johnson's army and was killed at Rocky Brook. Cf. *Half-Century*, II, 232, 241-42; *Montcalm and Wolfe*, I, 301-14.

[18] Colonel Oliver Partridge of Hatfield was sheriff in peacetime and soldier in wartime.

[19] General James Abercromby (1706-81) became British commander in chief in North America in 1758; and led the unsuccessful expedition against Ticonderoga in that year, which ended in Montcalm's great victory of Carillon. Most of the colonial officers regarded his Scottish caution as cowardice.

[20] Brigadier General George Augustus, Viscount Howe (1724-58) came to Halifax in 1757 as commander of the 60th Regiment, and was transferred in the same year to command the 55th. He was Abercromby's second-in-command on the expedition against Ticonderoga in 1758; and was killed in a preliminary skirmish on July 8, near the junction of Trout Brook with the outlet of Lake George, by the French advance party under Langy and Trepezec. (See *Montcalm and Wolfe*, II, 295-304.) He was a brother of General William Howe and Admiral Lord Howe of Revolutionary War fame.

[21] Cf. *Montcalm and Wolfe*, II, 300-4.

[22] Major General Jeffery, Baron Amherst (1717-97), a former aide-de-camp of the Duke of Cumberland in the German campaigns, came to America in 1758; and with Admiral Boscawen captured Louisbourg in that year. He was colonel of the Royal American Regiment and succeeded Abercromby after the latter's recall. Amherst captured Ticonderoga and Crown Point in 1759; in the following year he moved against Montreal down the St. Lawrence from Lake Ontario, while Brigadier Haviland proceeded by Lake Champlain, and Brigadier James Murray came up from Quebec. Amherst was thus responsible for the final capitulation of Canada on September 8, 1760. He was appointed commander in chief and governor general in North America in 1761.

[23] No Morrison from Stockbridge is listed among Rogers' Rangers.

[24] Captain John Konkapot, the leader of the Stockbridge Indians, sold a good part of the Berkshire Hills country to Connecticut Valley proprietors in 1724, "in consideration of £450, 3 barrels of cider, and 30 quarts of rum." Konkapot lived on the east side of the Great Barrington road, a few rods north of the brook still called after him. Under missionary pressure he evinced some desire to become a Christian; but objected that if he did so, his people might discard him, and also that "the conversation

of the Christians about him was even worse than that of the heathen."
Konkapot, who was given a captain's commission by Governor Jonathan
Belcher, was nonetheless instrumental in the establishment of the mission
at Stockbridge, which he befriended. He and his family were the first
Stockbridge Indians baptized by Sergeant in 1735.

[25] Parkman probably refers to the massacre of Lieutenant Colonel
Monro's garrison at William Henry in 1757 by Montcalm's Indians. Cf.
Montcalm and Wolfe, II, 184-203.

[26] An auxiliary of the American Temperance Society, formed in 1826,
was established shortly after the original society was formed at Stockbridge.
It was particularly flourishing from 1840 to 1843, with a total abstinence
program.

[27] Rogers' Rangers were organized by Major Robert Rogers from among
the frontiersmen and hunters of New England for service during the
Seven Years' War. Their most famous engagements were on Lake George
and Lake Champlain; and their most notable achievement was the
destruction of the Indian village of St. Francis on the river of the same
name near the St. Lawrence, which had served as headquarters for many
of the French and Indian raids on the New England settlements.

[28] The anti-rent agitation in New York began during the first term of
William H. Seward as governor (1838-40). Its center was the Hudson
River counties, where most of the land was included in the vast estates
of Rensselaerswyck, Livingston, Scarsdale, Phillipse, Pelham, and Van
Cortland manors, under the leasehold system with perpetual leases, leases
for 99 years, or leases for one to three lives. Feudal dues and alienation
fines were part of the system. The agitation reached its climax in 1845,
when the anti-rent associations elected Governor John Young, who was
favorable to their cause, and were responsible for the calling of the
constitutional convention of 1846, which abolished feudal tenure and
destroyed the leasehold system, thus breaking up the great estates.
Fenimore Cooper wrote three anti-rent novels: *Satanstoe* (1845), *The Chain-
bearer* (1845), and *The Redskins* (1846).

[29] Plattsburg, New York, on the west shore of Lake Champlain, was the
headquarters of the American Army on the northern frontier in the War of
1812. On September 11, 1814 the British fleet was defeated by Commodore
Macdonough in Plattsburg Bay.

[30] "Captain" Edmund Badger of North Adams, Massachusetts was
honorably discharged from the U. S. Army in 1815 as a first lieutenant.
Like other retired officers, he seems to have risen in rank after the days
of his active service.

[31] Colonel Ephraim Williams (1714/5-55) of Stockbridge and Hatfield made a will at Albany on July 22, 1755, in which he provided for a free school in Williamstown, near where he had been stationed at Fort Massachusetts. This school was incorporated in 1785, and in 1793 became Williams College.

[32] Since no Jones of Stockbridge was an officer in the Revolution or War of 1812, the reference is probably to Captain Josiah Jones (1725-?).

[33] Fort Massachusetts was the most exposed of the line of frontier posts built to defend the New England settlements against the French and Indian raids. Colonel Ephraim Williams usually made his headquarters there, after he was placed in charge of the forts; but he was absent when the place was attacked in 1746 and its garrison of fifty was overcome by Rigaud de Vaudreuil's force. In 1748 he successfully defended the fort against another assault.

[34] This "country Professor" was Albert Hopkins (1807-72), the astronomer, who was a resident of Stockbridge and an early graduate of Williams. He returned to Williams to teach mathematics and natural history in 1829. In 1834 he went to Europe to purchase apparatus for the college, and upon his return built with his own means the first astronomical observatory in an American university. A great botanist and a pioneer in the organization of field trips for students of the natural sciences, he was a correspondent of the Royal Astronomical Society of London, and a brother of Mark Hopkins, the famous president of Williams.

[35] Colonel Ephraim Williams divided his time between Stockbridge and Hatfield.

[36] Stephen W. Williams (1790-1855), *American Medical Biographies* (Greenfield, Massachusetts, 1845). Dr. Thomas Williams, brother of Colonel Williams, was appointed a surgeon in the army raised for the Canada expedition in 1744, and also for the line of frontier forts commanded by his brother. He was a member of his brother's staff at Bloody Brook, and dressed Dieskau's wounds.

[37] A life of Israel Putnam by Oliver W. B. Peabody was published in Sparks' *Library of American Biography*, Series I, Vol. 7. The "Stephens" of Parkman's note may be either Henry Stevens (1819-86), then at the Harvard law school, who went to London in the following year and became a famous bookseller and authority on Americana and Canadiana, or his brother Simon, with whom Parkman visited the Pennsylvania frontier in 1845. Henry Stevens had spent his college holidays ransacking New England and the Middle Atlantic states for material for Peter Force's *American Archives*, so he is probably referred to here.

[38] Dr. Stephen W. Williams (1790-1855) carried on researches into local history, botany, and chemistry, as well as his medical practice. He wrote many papers for the New York Historical Society and the Massachusetts Medical Society. His memoirs of medical men were collected in *American Medical Biographies* and two years later he published a family history.

[39] The "Molang" of Humphreys' account of Israel Putnam was Marin, the famous leader of French and Indian raids, who was defeated by Putnam and Rogers near Fort Anne in 1758. Cf. *Montcalm and Wolfe*, II, 329-34.

[40] Robert Rogers (1731/2-95), the famous partisan, was born at Methuen, Massachusetts, but grew up on his father's farm near Concord, New Hampshire.

[41] Major General Epaphras Hoyt (1765-1850) of Deerfield, Massachusetts, was at various times postmaster, justice of the peace, register of deeds for Franklin County, high sheriff, member of the constitutional convention of 1820, and a ranking officer of the state militia. He wrote extensively for *Silliman's Journal*, and his *Treatise on the Military Art* (1798) went through several editions. His *Antiquarian Researches* (1824) was his best-known work. He never published the copious notes on the Indian wars and Burgoyne's campaign, which were his chief concern for some years before his death.

[42] This story of the ranger at Bloody Pond was not used by Parkman in the histories.

[43] Either Henry or Simon Stevens may have had Samuel Blodget's "A Prospective Plan of the Battle Near Lake George," which was published at Boston soon after the battle in 1755.

[44] This account of Montcalm's advance against William Henry in 1757, by Père Roubaud, S.J., missionary to the St. Francis Indians, is found in *Lettres Edifiantes et Curieuses*, VI, 189 (1810). Parkman uses it largely in *Montcalm and Wolfe*, II, 168-203.

[45] The two officers were Captain Pringle and Lieutenant Roche. See *Montcalm and Wolfe*, II, 215-20.

[46] Cf. note 39.

[47] Possibly Engineer Lieutenant Thérbu's map, "Attaques du Fort William-Henri."

[48] Samuel Williams (1743-1817), *The natural and civil history of Vermont* (Walpole, New Hampshire, 1794).

[49] Zadock Thompson (1796-1856), *History of Vermont, natural, civil, and statistical* (Burlington, Vermont, 1842).

[50] Hendrick, chief of the Mohawks with Johnson at Lake George in

1755, was killed in Dieskau's ambush of Colonel Williams at Bloody Pond. He was one of Parkman's Indian heroes, and one of the horses on the Oregon Trail trip was named after him.

[51] Epaphras Hoyt (1765-1850), *Antiquarian Researches, comprising a History of the Indian wars in the country bordering the Connecticut River* (Greenfield, Massachusetts, 1824).

[52] These maps were doubtless in the Harvard Library. It has not been possible to identify them without full titles.

[53] John Huddlestone Wynne (1743-88), *The History of the British Empire in America* (London, 1769).

[54] Robert Rogers (1731-95), *A Concise Account of North America* (London, 1765). Rogers' *Journals* were also published at London in the same year, and this may be the book Parkman had in mind.

[55] John Mitchell (?-1768), *The Contest in America between Great Britain and France* (London, 1757).

[56] John Warner Barber (1798-1885), *The History and Antiquities of New England, New York, and New Jersey* (Worcester, 1841).

[57] Timothy Dwight (1752-1817), president of Yale, traveled widely through New England and New York from 1796 to 1815. His *Travels* were published in 1821-22 at New Haven.

[58] Sir Charles Augustus Murray (1806-95), *Travels in North America* (New York, 1839).

[59] Colonel John Winslow's *Journal* and *Letterbook* are invaluable sources on the expulsion of the Acadians in 1755. Parkman used them in *Montcalm and Wolfe*, I, 243-95.

[60] The Massachusetts Archives, in the State House at Boston, are rich in manuscript material on the French and Indian Wars.

[61] The reference may be to the renegade Roubaud's forgeries, which he placed in the hands of the King when he went to England, and which were partially printed at London in 1777. See *Montcalm and Wolfe*, III, 170-1 n.

[62] General John Taylor Cooper presented a large collection of Johnson MSS. to the New York state library; and W. L. Stone (1793-1844) procured many more from the Johnson family in England and other sources. These have been printed by the State of New York in nine volumes (Albany, 1921-39).

[63] Jared Sparks was Parkman's historical mentor and adviser at Harvard.

[64] Roubaud's account, in *Lettres Edifiantes et Curieuses*, VI, 189.

[65] Soon after the battle at Lake George in 1755, Samuel Blodget published at Boston *A Prospective Plan of the Bat⁺ˡe Near Lake George, with an*

Explanation thereof, containing a full, though short, History of that important Affair, by Samuel Blodget, occasionally at the Camp when the Battle was fought. This is reproduced in E. B. O'Callaghan, *A Documentary History of New York,* IV. The "Explanation" is only found complete in the original. Cf. *Montcalm and Wolfe,* I, 328-29 n.

[66] Dieskau's account of the battle of Lake George has been printed in O'Callaghan, *Documents relating to the Colonial History of New York,* X, 316-8. Cf. *Montcalm and Wolfe,* I, 307-29.

[67] Jean Victor Varin de La Marre was Commissaire de la Marine at Quebec 1734-47 and at Montreal 1747-54. He served as substitute for the Intendant Bigot, in whose fraudulent operations he was involved after 1749.

[68] Pierre de Rigaud, Marquis de Vaudreuil, was the last French governor of Canada.

[69] The Agniers were the Mohawks, a tribe of the Iroquois Confederacy. They generally fought for the English in the French and Indian War.

[70] The Chevalier de Montreuil served as adjutant general in Canada from 1754 to 1758. He later played a part in the defense of Quebec in 1759 as a major general.

[71] Doreil was Commissaire de la Guerre with Vaudreuil in 1755 and 1757.

[72] Fort Edward on the Hudson was first known as Fort Lydius, after a Dutch resident of the place.

VI. OLD NORTHWEST JOURNAL & PONTIAC NOTES

[1] Albert Gallatin (1761-1849), Swiss-born American statesman and scholar, abandoned public life in 1827 and settled in New York City, where he devoted himself to science and literature. In 1836 he published, in the second volume of the *Transactions* of the American Antiquarian Society, his notable *Synopsis of the Indian Tribes within the United States East of the Rocky Mountains and in the British and Russian Possessions in North America.* In 1842 he founded the American Ethnological Society with H. R. Schoolcraft, John R. Bartlett, Branz Mayer, and E. G. Squier, all of whom became correspondents of Parkman. In 1843 Gallatin was president of the New York Historical Society, to which Parkman was elected as an honorary

member four years later, on the strength of *The Oregon Trail*. In *Pontiac* (9 n.) Parkman refers to a conversation with Gallatin.

2 Evidently Parkman planned to visit the chief Philadelphia libraries, and to consult Redmond Conyngham of Paradise, Pennsylvania, a member of the state legislature and a historical amateur who published documents on the Pennsylvania part of Pontiac's conspiracy in the Lancaster *Intelligencer*.

3 George Washington Baker (?-1895) was a member of the class of 1844 at Harvard.

4 William Leete Stone (1793-1844), *Life and Times of Sa-go-ye-wat-ha, or Red Jacket* (New York, 1841).

5 Caleb Atwater, "Description of the Antiquities Discovered in Ohio and other Western States," in *Archaeologia Americana*, I (Worcester, 1820).

6 Probably Parkman's correspondent Simon Stevens, a brother of Henry Stevens; the latter was the famous bookseller and bibliographer, who at this time was combing attics for old books as the agent of James Lenox of New York, whose collection formed the nucleus of the New York Public Library.

7 George Parkman (1823-1908), Harvard 1844 and Dane Law School 1846, was Parkman's cousin. He was the son of the Dr. Parkman who was murdered by Dr. John Webster in the Medical School Laboratory at Harvard.

8 This letter of Captain Orme, Braddock's aide-de-camp, dated July 18, 1755, is cited in *Pontiac*, I, 118.

9 Colonel John Winslow (1702-74), a descendent of the early governors of Plymouth, Massachusetts, served in the expeditions against Crown Point and the Kennebec, but is best known for his connection with the deportation of the Acadians in 1755. His journals are in the possession of the Massachusetts Historical Society. They were extensively used by Parkman in *Montcalm and Wolfe*, I, 243-95.

10 The Jonathan Trumbull Papers, formerly in the Massachusetts Historical Society (portions published in M. H. S. *Collections*, Series 5, IX & X) consist of twenty-eight folios and two quartos of miscellaneous papers, dating from 1750 to 1783. They are now in the Connecticut Archives at Hartford.

11 Dr. Jacob Bigelow (1786-1879), Rumford Professor and Professor of Materia Medica at Harvard, was a prominent Boston physician and an amateur botanist of some note. He shared Parkman's love for the White Mountains, and made several botanical expeditions there as a young man,

Notes—Old Northwest Journal 367

while preparing his *Florula Bostoniensis*. Parkman married his daughter Catherine Scollay Bigelow in May 1850.

[12] Parkman's early attachment to Miss Pamela Prentiss of Keene, New Hampshire, was evidently waning. Cf. 1841 Journal, p. 12-17.

[13] The Millerites were disciples of William Miller (1782-1849), leader of the Second Adventists in America. From 1831 onward Miller preached the Second Coming of Christ in 1843, and when the Advent failed to materialize on schedule, set the date for the following year. The Millerite meetings were a notable feature of New England life during 1843-44. Parkman had already encountered some members of the sect on the Vermont frontier. Cf. 1842 Journal, p. 66.

[14] Henry Orne White (1824-87), Harvard 1843, was Parkman's companion on his 1842 excursion to Lake George and northern New England.

[15] Dr. Isaac Watts (1674-1748), the noted English divine and writer of hymns.

[16] The Folsoms of Exeter, New Hampshire, were descendents of that Captain Folsom who shared with Captain McGinnis the command of the scouting party to Fort Lyman, at Bloody Pond in 1755. Cf. *Montcalm and Wolfe*, I, 320.

[17] The Boston *News Letter* (1704-75), modeled on the London *Gazette* and one of the longest-lived newspapers of the eighteenth century, had several later namesakes.

[18] Such historical pageants as this were popular in the United States up to World War I.

[19] Medford, Massachusetts, was the home of Parkman's mother. In his youth he frequently visited his grandfather Hall's farm there.

[20] Dudley Hall was probably one of Parkman's Medford cousins.

[21] Samuel Cutler Bigelow (?-1904), a Williams graduate of 1845.

[22] The First Corps of Cadets was Boston's crack milita outfit. At this period each American city had at least one such socially notable military unit.

[23] Moses Gill Cobb (?-1903), Harvard 1845.

[24] Abbott Lawrence, the magnate of the Lowell cotton mills, was the prophet of commercial Boston at this period.

[25] Thomas Hastings Russell (?-1911), Harvard 1843.

[26] Joseph Peabody (?-1905) of Salem was a great college friend of Parkman.

[27] Charles H. B. Snow (?-1875), Parkman's college classmate, belonged to one of the old Fitchburg families who lived on the hill overlooking the mills.

[28] Philip Stanhope, Viscount Mahon (1805-75), *History of England from the Peace of Utrecht to the Peace of Versailles, 1713-83* (London, 1836-54). Mahon became involved in a controversy with Parkman's historical master, Jared Sparks, over the latter's editing of *Washington's Writings* (Boston, 1837).

[29] This *Collection of Extracts*, frequently referred to by Parkman, may have been Jared Sparks' compendium of European documents, made during his studies in the French and English archives.

[30] William Henry Harrison's "Discourse on the Aborigines of the Ohio Valley, in which the Opinions of its Conquest in the Seventeenth Century, by the Iroquois or Six Nations, supported by . . . Colden . . . Pownall . . . Franklin . . . Clinton . . . and Haywood . . ., are Examined and Contested" was printed in the first volume of the Ohio Historical and Philosophical Society's *Transactions* (1839).

[31] Samuel Williams (1743-1817), *The Natural and Civil History of Vermont* (Walpole, New Hampshire, 1794).

[32] Bernard Romans (*c.* 1720-84), *A Concise Natural History of East and West Florida* (New York, 1775).

[33] The Catalogue of the Worcester Library was published in 1836-37.

[34] Captain Morris kept a journal of his embassy to the Illinois in 1764, which was printed in *Miscellanies in Prose and Verse* (1791). Cf. *Pontiac*, II, 208 n.

[35] John Filson (1747?-88), *The Discovery, Settlement, and Present State of Kentucky.* (New York, 1793).

[36] Henry Ellis (1721-1806), *A Voyage to Hudson's-Bay . . . in the Years 1746 and 1747* (London, 1748). *Bib. Can.* 207.

[37] Arthur Dobbs (1689-1765), *An Account of the Countries adjoining to Hudson's Bay* (London, 1744). *Bib. Can.* 193.

[38] James, second Earl Waldegrave (1715-63), *Memoirs* (London, 1821). Waldegrave was an intimate friend of George II, and for a time "governor" or tutor of George III. In 1755-57 he negotiated on the part of the king with Newcastle, Devonshire, Pitt, and Fox about the formation of a ministry.

[39] Timothy Pickering, *A Letter from Colonel Pickering, containing a Narrative of the Outrage committed on him at Wyoming, with an Account of the Controversies respecting the Lands claimed by the states of Pennsylvania and Connecticut, which led to that Event* (Salem, 1819).

[40] François Pierre Guillaume Guizot (1787-1874), *Cours d'histoire moderne* (Paris, 1829-32).

[41] Jonathan Swift (1667-1745) was a kinsman of Dryden, the bosom

friend of Bolinbroke, and with Pope and Arbuthnot established the Scriblerus Club, writing parts of both *Martin Scriblerus* and *John Bull*.

42 Josiah Quincy (1772-1864) was president of Harvard from 1829 to 1845. He was also active in Federalist politics.

43 George Theodore Lyman (?-1908) did not graduate from the law school.

44 The Navy Club seems to have been a Harvard social organization.

45 Robert Hartly Dunlap (?-1847) was a graduate of Bowdoin in 1842.

46 George Gray (?-1850) graduated from Harvard in 1845.

47 Francis Brooks (?-1891).

48 Mrs. Sanders' was one of the numerous Cambridge boardinghouses of the period.

49 Harrison Ritchie graduated from Harvard in 1845.

50 John Halkett (1768-1852) was Lord Selkirk's brother-in-law and supported him in his dispute with the North-West Company. Halkett also wrote the *Statement respecting the Earl of Selkirk's Settlement of Kildonan, upon the Red River* (London, 1816).

51 Jordan and Havilland were pillars of the Pennsylvania Historical Society, whom Parkman consulted about the Alleghany frontier. John Romeyn Brodhead (1814-73), while attached to the American Legation at The Hague, became interested in the early Dutch history of New York. Governor Seward appointed him agent of the state to procure materials bearing on its early history. Brodhead spent four years in the Dutch, French, and English archives; and returned home with eighty volumes of copied documents. These were edited by E. B. O'Callaghan and B. Fenn, and published as *Documents Relating to the Colonial History of New York* (Albany, 1856-86).

52 Morris Birkbeck, the English associationist, founded the colony of New Albion, Illinois, in 1817. His *Notes on a Journey in America* (London, 1818) would have interested Parkman.

53 Forster was also the translator of Peter Kalm's *Travels*.

54 Rich's *Bibliotheca Americana* (London, 1832-44) was the best bibliography of Americana before Sabin's monumental work.

55 The Quebec Literary and Historical Society was founded in 1824 through the influence and generosity of Lord Dalhousie, then governor general. The library was started in 1828 and now includes a valuable collection of Canadiana, both French and English. The society's series of *Transactions* (1829-1924) and *Historical Documents* (1838-1906) are full of important historical materials. For a fuller account of the society's history and activities, see *Centenary Volume, 1824-1924* (Quebec, 1924);

for a calendar of its publications, see Colonel William Wood's *Index* (Quebec, 1924).

[56] Pierre Pouchot (1712-69), *Mémoires sur la dernière guerre de l'Amérique, 1755-60* (Yverdon, 1781). Cf. *Bib. Can.* 330.

[57] Peter Force (1790-1868), *American Archives* (Washington, 1837-53). But in *Pontiac*, I, 265, Parkman gives Robert Rogers as his authority on this point.

[58] James H. Lanman, *History of Michigan* (New York, 1839).

[59] Judge Simon Greenleaf (1783-1853), Royall Professor of Law from 1833 to 1846 and Dane Professor from 1846 to 1848, was Judge Story's great colleague at the Dane Law School, the precursor of the Harvard Law School. Greenleaf was noted for the thoroughness of his legal knowledge.

[60] Eugene Batchelder (?-1878) left law school before graduation.

[61] John B. Lea (?-1846) was a graduate of Princeton in 1843.

[62] George Hoadley graduated from Western Reserve in 1844.

[63] Charles Edward Hooper (?-1914).

[64] Andrew Eliot Thayer (?-1873) graduated from Harvard in 1842.

[65] Daniel Denison Slade (1823-1896) was Parkman's companion on his 1841 journey.

[66] Lewis Cass (1782-1866), *et al.*, *Historical and Scientific Sketches of Michigan* (Detroit, 1834). Cass was the first governor of the territory of Michigan, and did some admirable pioneer work on the history of the region. His collection of documents bearing on the siege of Detroit proved of great value to Parkman for *Pontiac*. Schoolcraft, Henry Whiting, and John Biddle also collaborated on this volume. General Cass wrote many articles on the Indians in the *North American Review*.

[67] The Fourierites, as the Brook Farmers were called because of their adoption of the ideas of Charles Fourier, were viewed with alarm by right-thinking Bostonians of the day. In 1841 Emerson noted: "The view taken of Transcendentalism in State Street is that it threatens to invalidate contracts." George Ripley, who had earlier resigned from the Unitarian ministry, launched the Brook Farm experiment in community living in April 1841. Horace Greeley, editor of the New York *Tribune*, was drawn into the movement through the enthusiasm of his collaborator, Albert Brisbane, who had introduced Fourier's ideas to America with *The Social Destiny of Man* (Philadelphia, 1840). Charles Dana, later editor of the New York *Sun*, was one of the early members of the community. The Reverend William Henry Channing longed to join the group, but yielded

to his wife's opposition. 1845 saw the highwater mark of the movement, which shortly after dissolved.

[68] Alexander Scott Withers' *Chronicles of Border Warfare* (Clarksburg, Virginia, 1831), a valuable collection of legends of the frontier, was edited and annotated by R. G. Thwaites in 1895.

[69] Joseph Doddridge, *Notes on the Settlement and Indian Wars of the Western Parts of Virginia and Pennsylvania, 1763-83* (Wellsburgh, Virginia, 1824).

[70] Sir William Francis Napier (1785-1860), *History of the Conquest of Scinde* (London, 1845). Napier's *War in the Peninsula* (1824-40) has established his fame as the greatest British military historian.

[71] Bishop John Ettwein (1721-1802) compiled a dictionary and phrase-book of the Delaware tongue. In 1788 he wrote an account of the traditions and language of this tribe, which was published by the Pennsylvania Historical Society in its 1845-47 series of *Bulletins*, after Jared Sparks had found the MS. among Washington's papers. Parkman evidently used Sparks' transcript.

[72] The Iroquois Confederacy, originally known as the Five Nations, became the Six Nations after the Tuscaroras joined the Mohawks, Oneidas, Onondagas, Cayugas, and Senecas.

[73] The *Colonial Records of Pennsylvania, 1683-1736*, were printed at Philadelphia in three volumes in 1837-40. In 1852 these three volumes were reprinted and thirteen more added, covering up to 1790.

[74] Matthew Smith's account of his massacre of the Conestogas was published in the Lancaster *Intelligencer* for 1843. See *Pontiac*, II, 131.

[75] Colonel Armstrong destroyed an Indian village at Great Island on the west branch of the Susquehanna in October 1763. See *Pontiac*, II, 108-9.

[76] J. Francis Fisher (1807-73) of Philadelphia was a well-to-do lawyer who never practiced his profession. He was very active in the Pennsylvania Historical Society from 1828 to 1865, and his own special interest was in the early history of the state. Parkman saw him to get admission to the Philosophical Society.

[77] James Ross (1762-1847) of Pittsburgh, lawyer, land speculator, and U. S. Senator, was a staunch Federalist, and hence known to Parkman.

[78] Sherman Day, *Historical Collections of the State of Pennsylvania* (Philadelphia, 1843).

[79] Colonel John Bradstreet (c. 1711-74), an Englishman or Nova Scotian, distinguished himself at the attack on Louisbourg in 1745 which owed its origin partly to him. He defended Oswego and captured Fort Frontenac in 1758. In 1764 he was sent to punish the Western Indians for their part in Pontiac's uprising. See *Pontiac*, II, 174 *ff.*

[80] Colonel Henry Bouquet (1719-66), a Swiss professional soldier, came to America with Haldimand in 1754, when the latter took command of the second battalion of the Royal Americans at Philadelphia. In 1758 Bouquet marched with General Forbes against Fort Pitt, which he commanded until 1762. In the following year he returned and raised the siege. After Bushy Run he organized an expedition into the Indian country, which penetrated to the Delaware towns and resulted in a treaty of peace. Bouquet did not have the usual British officer's contempt for Indian methods in warfare, which he adopted. Captain James Smith, having been a captive among the Indians for some years, trained his men to fight Indian fashion.

[81] *An Historical Review of the Constitution and Government of Pennsylvania, from its origin . . . founded on authentic documents* (London, 1759). This work is generally attributed to Benjamin Franklin, though disowned by him in a letter of September 27, 1760 to David Hume. It was published at Franklin's expense. See P. L. Ford, *Franklin Bibliography* 109-11.

[82] Brother Lenneck (?-1767) *Chronicon ephratense* (Lancaster, 1786). An English version of this history of the "Protestant monks" was published at Lancaster in 1889.

[83] The Logan MSS. were deposited in the Pennsylvania Historical Society in 1840. The Paxton Boys were the Pennsylvania settlers who banded together to repress Indian outrages on the frontier in 1763. Cf. *Pontiac*, II, 130-67; 392-404.

[84] The Edward Shippen MSS. are quoted in *Pontiac*, II, 136 n., and Appendix E. The Burd MSS. were given to the Pennsylvania Historical Society by Mrs. Thompson of Thompsonville, Pennsylvania, and form part of the Shippen Papers. They include Colonel James Burd's letter-book, 1756-58, and two volumes of military papers, 1755-95.

[85] The Mennonites, so called after their leader Menno Simons (1492-1559), originated in Zurich in 1523 among the Anabaptists. Their strongholds were long in Holland, Germany, and France, but intolerance toward their beliefs in all European countries but Holland drove many of them to America. Their first colony was established at Germantown, Pennsylvania, in 1683; and by the middle of the eighteenth century Lancaster County was a Mennonite stronghold, as it remains today.

[86] Redmond Conyngham of Paradise, an antiquarian, employed himself in collecting documents on the Paxton Men, which he published in the Lancaster *Intelligencer*, and which are used largely by Parkman in *Pontiac*, II, Ch. 24-5.

[87] George Washington Baker, Harvard 1844.

[88] For an account of the massacre of the Indians in the Lancaster jail, see *Pontiac*, II, 133-38.

[89] John Tyler (1790-1862), tenth president of the United States (1841-45).

[90] Locofocoism was a left-wing movement within Jacksonian democracy of the 1830's, so called because its adherents relit with locofoco matches the gas which the Tammany Democrats had turned out in the hall where both groups assembled in 1835. As a Whig, Parkman had no use for the extremists of a party which he regarded with horror for its levelling tendencies.

[91] The Senecas were one of the Six Nations of the Iroquois Confederacy, and eventually the most important tribe. Their home was in western New York, between Seneca Lake and the Genesee River. The majority of the tribe still lives on reservations in this region.

[92] Norwegian emigrants came to the United States as a result of the struggle during the 1820's and 1830's between the peasantry and the old ruling class. Immigration from Europe to the Great Lakes region began in the 1830's, and in 1845 immigrant vessels sailed three times a day westward from Buffalo.

[93] Fort Gratiot was built in 1814 on the site of old Fort Joseph.

[94] Mackinaw (Michilimackinac) was the great Western center of the fur trade, a role for which its geographical position at the crossroads of the Lakes admirably suited it in the days of canoe and bateau transport. The Mackinac Company was organized about 1784. It operated from Cahokia to the sources of the Mississippi, and from northern Illinois into Spanish Louisiana, west of the Missouri. In 1811 John Jacob Astor bought out the Canadian company and merged it with the Southwest Company, which became the American Fur Company in 1816. The first trading post was established at Michilimackinac in 1668, while the Jesuit mission of St. Ignace dates from 1670. Mackinaw was the chief rendezvous of the winterers in the heyday of the Hudson's Bay Company, and the field headquarters of northern division of the American Fur Company.

[95] Captain Martin Scott (?-1847), a Vermonter who had served as a lieutenant in the War of 1812 and subsequently in the Fifth Infantry, was breveted major in May 1846, for gallantry at Palo Alto and Resaca de la Palma, and lieutenant colonel that fall for his conduct at Monterrey. He was killed the following year at Molino del Rey.

[96] Lieutenant Henry Whiting (?-1851) of New York served in the Fifth Infantry from 1840 to March 26, 1846, when he resigned. He had collaborated with General Cass in studying the early history of the region.

[97] Fort Holmes, or George, was built by the British after their capture of Mackinaw Island in the War of 1812. After the recovery of the place by the United States, the fort was named after Major Andrew Holmes, who was killed in the American assault of August 4, 1814.

[98] Alexander Henry (1739-1824), a pioneer fur trader of the Northwest, came to Montreal with Amherst's army in 1760, and in the following year reached Michilimackinac with a fur-trading permit. His experiences in the West for the next sixteen years are described in his *Travels and Adventures in Canada and the Indian Territories* (New York, 1809). Henry's account of the massacre in 1763 is the chief source of Parkman's account in *Pontiac*, I, 351-75, which describes his taking refuge in the Skull Rock cave. Henry returned to Montreal in 1776, and became a dormant partner in the North-West Company.

[99] The fur trade of the old Northwest, after a century of French exploitation and a century of cutthroat competition among the Hudson's Bay Company, the North-West Company, and the X Y Company, was finished as far as large-scale operations were concerned by the middle of the nineteenth century. Beaver, the most profitable fur, was becoming scarce; and the development of modern felting methods by hatters had eliminated the great demand for it. The American Fur Company, whose main business was now in buffalo robes rather than in beaver, wound up its operations at Mackinaw in 1842. With the growth of steam navigation and the railroads, the voyageurs who had carried trade goods from Montreal to the Western posts and returned with cargoes of fur, became victims of technological unemployment.

[100] The Chippewas or Ojibwas were a large tribe of Algonkin stock who occupied the country around lakes Huron and Superior. They were allied with the Ottawas and Potawatomies, and their language was long used for trade and diplomacy by the other tribes of the Great Lakes. Their myths were the basis of H. R. Schoolcraft's *Algic Researches* (1839), upon which Longfellow founded *Hiawatha*.

[101] James Lawrence (?-1875) graduated from Harvard in 1840 and was an overseer of the university from 1866 to 1870.

[102] The Lake Superior copper boom began in 1844 when mines were put into production, after the geologist Douglas Houghton had revealed the presence of the precious metal in his report of 1841.

[103] Abel Bingham was one of the missionaries who made their headquarters at the Soo, where the Indian agent for the Lake Superior tribes resided.

[104] Fort Brady was built by the Americans on the south side of the strait between Lake Superior and Lake Huron.

[105] Henry Rowe Schoolcraft (1795-1864), Indian agent for Lake Superior, recorded the Algonkin legends in his *Algic Researches* (1839) and *Oneota* (1844-5). His work is no longer taken seriously by anthropologists, but was widely hailed at the time. Robert Stuart's comments recorded by Parkman and the latter's reviews in the *North American* for July 1865 and July 1866 (CI, 28-64 & CIII, 1-18) were dissenting opinions.

[106] Robert Stuart (1784-1848), a Scot educated in Paris, came to Montreal in 1806 to join his uncle David, who was in the fur trade. Both joined Astor's Pacific Fur Company and sailed in the *Tonquin* for the Columbia River in 1810. Robert Stuart returned in 1812 with the Astorian overland party to St. Louis and New York. After 1819 he represented Astor at Mackinaw as manager of the Northern Department of the American Fur Company. He retired in 1833 and made his home in Detroit. Parkman was fortunate to catch him on a visit to his old headquarters. This encounter doubtless played a part in determining Parkman to make the Oregon Trail trip in the following year.

[107] John Tanner (1780?-1847), *A Narrative of the Captivity and Adventures of John Tanner, U. S. interpreter at the Saut de Ste. Marie, during thirty years' residence among the Indians in the interior of North America* (New York, 1830). *Bib. Can.* 1612. Tanner was captured by the Indians in Ohio in 1790, and fought, hunted, and traded with them in the Middle West until 1820. His narrative ends about 1830.

[108] Parkman adopted this opinion in an article in the *North American* for July 1865 (CI, 28-64).

[109] P. J. B. F. X. Le Gardeur de Repentigny built a fort on the southern shore of the strait in 1751, which was destroyed by fire in 1762. In 1780 Major Sinclair, the British commander, moved the fort and village from the south shore to the island. The North-West Company's post on the north shore was burned by the Americans in 1814. Parkman probably visited the south shore ruins.

[110] Lieutenant M'Dougal was captured while on an embassy to Pontiac in the spring of 1763. His son's papers, "which were very voluminous and contained various notes concerning the Indian war," came into the possession of a Mr. Whitman of Palmer, Michigan, "who permitted such of them as related to the subjects in question to be copied by the writer" (*Pontiac*, I, 263 n.).

[111] François Baby, Jr. of Windsor, Ontario, was the grandson of Jacques Duperron Baby (1731-89), the Detroit trader who was a friend of Pontiac

and aided Major Gladwin's garrison with supplies during the siege of Detroit in 1763. See *Pontiac*, I, 269 n.

[112] John Askin (1738-1815) of Albany was a trader at Detroit and Mackinaw after 1762. In 1772 he married Marie Barthe, whose mother was a member of the Campeau family, and in 1796 he moved to Windsor when the Americans took over Detroit. His son Charles lived in Windsor from 1812 to 1862, and was probably Parkman's informant.

[113] Beginning of "Journal of Part of Journey in Aug. '45—No. 2."

[114] On September 13, 1763 a British wagon train from Fort Schlosser was ambushed by the Indians at the Devil's Hole. See *Pontiac*, II, 82-5.

[115] William Henry Bartlett (1809-54), an English artist, traveled widely through the United States and Canada in the late 1830's, making drawings for the well-known engravings of *Canadian Scenery* (1840) and *American Scenery*.

[116] Fort Niagara stood at the mouth of the Niagara River, on the American side. The first fortification on the spot, built by La Salle in 1678, was burned two years later. Chaussegros de Léry built a fort in stone in 1726, which replaced the blockhouse of 1721. The fort was rebuilt again in 1749, but was captured by Sir William Johnson ten years later. Like the other frontier outposts which were important in the Indian trade, it was not surrendered to the United States until 1796. During the War of 1812 it was the American base of operations for the Niagara campaign, until its capture by Colonel Murray in 1813. It was restored to the United States by the Treaty of Ghent.

[117] John Bartram (1699-1777), *Observations on the Inhabitants, Climate, Soil, Rivers, Productions, Animals, and other matters worthy of Notice* (London, 1751). *Bib. Can.* 186. Bartram's description of the long house of the Iroquois— the council chamber of the Five Nations—at Onondaga, which he visited in 1743, is quoted in *Pontiac*, I, 20-1 n. Onondaga was the capitol of the Iroquois Confederacy, and is still a reservation.

[118] John Warner Barber (1798-1885), *The History and Antiquities of New England, New York, and New Jersey. Collected and compiled from authentic sources* (Worcester, 1841).

[119] Fort Stanwix on the Mohawk River guarded the portage from Wood Creek and Lake Oneida. It was built by General Stanwix in 1758, and was unsuccessfully besieged by St. Leger in 1777. Its site is now covered by the city of Rome, New York.

[120] Texas revolted from Mexico in 1835-36, and was admitted to the United States in March 1845. Since fighting in the Mexican War did not

begin until the spring of the following year, Parkman's "drunken fellow" must have seen service against Santa Anna in the revolt ten years before.

121 Thomas Loraine McKenney (1785-1859), *Memoirs, official and personal* (New York, 1846). Cf. *Bib. Can.* 998.

122 [Benjamin Franklin (1706-90)?], *An Historical Account of the Constitution and Government of Pennsylvania* (London, 1759).

123 Humphrey Marshall, *History of Kentucky* (Frankfort, Ky., 1824).

124 Thomas Jefferson, *Notes on the State of Virginia* (Paris, 1782).

125 Probably Thomas Jefferson Chapman, *The French in the Alleghany Valley* (Cleveland, 1887). Studies collected from historical magazines.

126 The Proclamation of 1763 prohibited the intrusion of settlers upon the Indian reserve of the Ohio Valley and adjacent regions.

127 Henry Crugar Van Schaack, *Life of Peter Van Schaack* (New York, 1842). Van Schaack's Onondaga campaign was a phase of General Sullivan's expedition against the Six Nations in 1779.

128 Charles Chauncy (1705-87), *A Second Letter to a Friend* (Boston, 1755). *Bib. Can.* 234. Chauncy was pastor of the First Church. This letter is also attributed to Timothy Walker. See *Montcalm and Wolfe*, I, 328 n.

129 Margaret Moncrieffe Coghlan, *Memoirs* (London, 1794).

130 Paul Lejeune, S.J. (1591-1664), *Jesuit Relations, 1632-40*.

François, Vicomte de Chateaubriand (1768-1848), *Travels in America & Italy* (London, 1828).

Henri Joutel (1640-1735), *Journal du dernier voyage de M. de la Salle* (Paris, 1713).

Joseph-Henri Lafiteau, S.J. (1681-1740), *Moeurs des Sauvages Américains* (Paris, 1724).

Jonathan Edwards (1703-58), *Memoirs of David Brainerd* (Boston, 1749).

Gabriel Marest, S.J. (1662-1714), "Lettre au Père de Lamberville," *Lettres Edifiantes et Curieuses*, X, 268-327 (Paris, 1732).

Chréstien Leclercq (1641-95?), *Premier établissement de la foi dans la Nouvelle France* (Paris, 1691); *Nouvelle relation de la Gaspésie* (Paris, 1691).

Marie de l'Incarnation (1599-1672). *Lettres* (Paris, 1681).

Joseph Lecaron, S.J. (1586-1632), *Relation de 1624*.

Benjamin Constant, *Oeuvres*, IX.

Creuxius [François Ducreux (1596-1666)], *Historia canadensis* (Paris, 1664).

Claude Alloüez, S.J. (1622-89), "La continuation de ses voyages [Marquette]," in Thevenot, *Récueil des voyages* (Paris, 1681).

Isaac Jogues, S.J. (1607-46), "Papers," New York Historical Society *Collections*, II Series, 3.

Samuel Purchas (1575?-1626), *Purchas, His Pilgrimes*, III & IV (London, 1625-6).

Bernard Romans (1720-84), *A Concise Natural History of East & West Florida* (New York, 1775).

Jean de Brébeuf, S.J. (1593-1649). See Rageneau, *Relation des Hurons, 1649.*

LePage du Pratz, *History of Louisiana* (London, 1763).

Sir Alexander MacKenzie (1755-1820), *Voyages, 1789-93* (London, 1801).

131 The Colonel Israel Williams Papers in the Massachusetts Historical Society consist of two volumes of letters and papers (1730-80), dealing with the French and Indian Wars, together with letters from Governor Hutchinson and material concerning the founding of Williams College.

132 The *Universal Magazine* was published in London in the 1730's.

133 Colonel James Smith, *Account of the Remarkable Occurences in the Life and Travels of Colonel James Smith during his Captivity with the Indians, 1755-59* (Lexington, Kentucky, 1799).

134 James Sullivan, *History of the District of Maine* (Boston, 1795).

135 John Williams, *Biographical Memoir of the Rev. John Williams; with Papers relating to the Early Indian Wars in Deerfield* (Greenfield, Massachusetts, 1837).

136 Jeremy Belknap, *History of New Hampshire* (Philadelphia and Boston, 1784-92).

137 Peter Williamson (1730-99), *French and Indian Cruelty* (Glasgow, 1758); *Occasional Reflections on the Importance of the War in America* (London, 1758).

138 Alexander Scott Withers, *Chronicles of Border Warfare* (Clarksburgh, Virginia, 1831).

139 Samuel Hazard (1784-1870), *Hazard's Register of Pennsylvania* (Philadelphia, 1828-36).

140 Thomas F. Gordon, *History of Pennsylvania to 1776* (Philadelphia, 1829).

141 John Entick, *et al.*, *General History of the Late War in Europe, Asia, Africa, and America* (London, 1763-64).

142 Edmund Burke, *Account of the European Settlements in America* (London, 1757).

143 Joseph White, *An Account of the Gospel Labours and Christian Experiences*

... *of John Churchman, late of Nottingham, in Pennsylvania* (Philadelphia, 1781).

[144] John Heckewelder, *Narrative of the Mission of the United Brethren among the Delaware and Mohegan Indians, 1740-1808* (Philadelphia, 1820).

[145] John Wright, *A Compleat History of the Late War* (Dublin, 1763).

[146] Richard Price, *Observations on the Nature of Civil Liberty, the Principles of Government, and the Justice and Policy of the War with America* (London, 1776).

[147] See note 138.

[148] Colonel David Humphreys, *Essay on the Life of the Honorable Major-General Israel Putnam* (Hartford, 1788).

[149] James Gibson, *A Journal of the Late Siege* (London, 1745).

[150] Samuel Smith, *History of the colony of Nova Caesaria, or New Jersey, to 1721* (Burlington, New Jersey, 1765).

[151] *Niles' Register* (Baltimore, 1811-49).

[152] Alexander Hewatt, *Historical Account of the Rise and Progress of the Colonies of South Carolina and Georgia* (London, 1779).

[153] Henry Trumbull, *History of the Indian Wars* (Boston, 1841).

[154] Samuel G. Drake (1798-1875), *The Book of Indians* (Boston, 1841).

[155] John Maude, *Visit to the Falls of Niagara* (London, 1826).

[156] Thomas Mante, *History of the Late War in America* (London, 1772).

[157] Henri de Tonti (1650-1704), *Relation de la Louisiane* (Amsterdam, 1720).

[158] *Bradbury's Transcript Copy of the Early Court Records and other Important Documents pertaining to the Settlement (of Maine), 1636-1686* (Portland, 1843-45).

[159] Daniel Coxe, *Description de la Carolana*. In Margry, *Découvertes & établissements*.

[160] Sir William Keith, *History of Virginia* (London, 1738).

[161] *Mémoires sur le Canada, depuis 1749 jusqu'à 1760* (Quebec, 1838). *Bib. Can.* 326.

[162] Thomas Pichon (1700-81), *Lettres et mémoires pour servir à l'histoire ... du Cap-Breton* (La Haye, 1760).

[163] William Cobbett, *Porcupine's Works: a Faithful Picture of the United States of America ... 1783-1801* (London, 1801).

[164] Colonel Winslow's *Journal of the Expulsion of the Acadians*, long preserved in the Massachusetts Historical Society, was printed by the Nova Scotian Historical Society in Vol. 3 of their *Transactions*.

[165] John Gorham Palfrey (1796-1881) was a Unitarian clergyman who devoted much of his life to education and history. He was a classmate of Jared Sparks at Harvard and shared his love of early colonial history.

Palfrey wrote much for the *North American Review*, substituting for Sparks as editor in 1825 and acquiring control of it in 1835. He edited the magazine from that year to 1843, when it passed into the hands of Francis Bowen. Palfrey's *History of New England* (1858-75) incorporates much of his historical labors and is a monument to his scholarship.

[166] John Warner Barber, *Connecticut Historical Collections* (New Haven, 1836).

[167] Georg Heinrich Loskeil, *History of the Mission of the United Brethren among the Indians in North America* (London, 1794).

[168] David Humphreys, *An Historical Account of the Incorporated Society for the Propagation of the Gospel in Foreign Parts* (London, 1730).

[169] John Mitchell, *The Contest in America between Great Britain and France* (London, 1757). *Bib. Can.* 264.

[170] William Smith (1728-93), *The History of the Province of New York* (London, 1757).

[171] In *Montcalm and Wolfe*, II, 337-38, Parkman cites Jonathan Mayhew's sermon rather than Cooper's.

[172] J. H. Perkins, "English Discoveries in the Ohio Valley, 1744-74," *North American Review*, XLIX, 69, is a review of Captain Jonathan Carver's *Travels* (1780) and his *Travels in Wisconsin* (1838).

[173] J. H. Lanman, "General Sketch of Canadian Government," *North American Review*, XLVI, 409, is a review of John McGregor's *British America* (1833) and Schoolcraft's *Narrative of an Expedition to Itasca Lake* (1834).

[174] The *American Magazine, or Monthly Chronicle for the British Colonies*, was published in Philadelphia by William Bradford in 1757-58. The Rev. William Smith was the chief editor.

[175] See note 146.

[176] John Wright's *A Compleat History of the Late War* (Dublin, 1763) contains Abercromby's official letters.

[177] *Impartial Account of Lieutenant-Colonel Bradstreet's Expedition, by a Volunteer* (London, 1759). Cited in *Montcalm and Wolfe*, II, 135 n.

[178] Benjamin Trumbull, *Complete History of Connecticut* (New Haven, 1818).

[179] John Daly Burk, *History of Virginia* (Petersburg, Virginia, 1804-5).

F. Cuming, *Sketches of a Tour to the Western Country* (Pittsburgh, 1810).

J. Palmer, *Journal of Travels in 1817* (London, 1818).

Thomas F. Gordon, *History of Pennsylvania to 1776* (Philadelphia, 1829).

John Huddlestone Wynne, *A General History of the British Empire in America* (London, 1770).

John Knox, *An historical journal of the campaigns in North America* (London, 1769).

Abiel Holmes, *Annals of America*, 1492-1826 (Cambridge, 1829).

Richard Henry Lee, *Life of Arthur Lee* (Boston, 1829).

Alexander Scott Withers, *Chronicles of Border Warfare* (Clarksburgh, 1831).

Samuel Hazard, *Register of Pennsylvania* (Philadelphia, 1828-36).

Thomas Mante, *History of the Late War in North America* (London, 1772).

[180] *Lettres Edifiantes et Curieuses* (Lyon, 1819).

[181] William Gilmore Simms, *Life of Francis Marion* (New York, 1844).

[182] George Heriot (1766-1844), *Travels through the Canadas* (London, 1807).

[183] The Boston Athenaeum, a private library rich in historical materials.

[184] Charles Miner, *History of Wyoming* (Philadelphia, 1845).

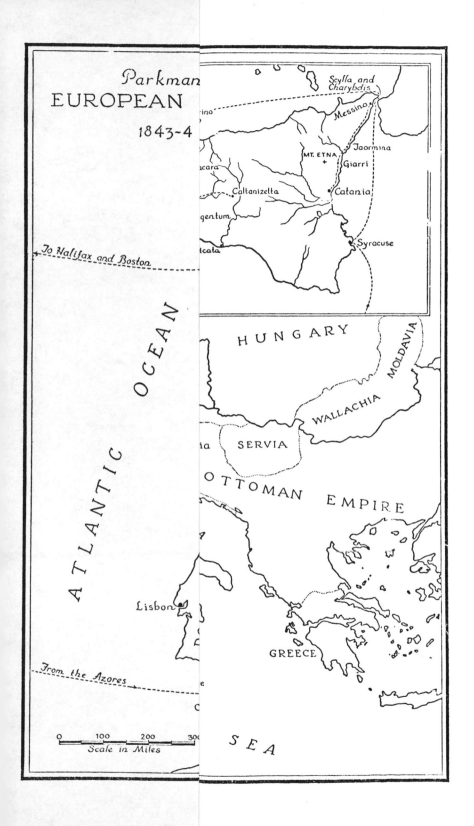

Parkman's
EUROPEAN
1843-4

Scylla and Charybdis
Messina
Jaormina
MT. ETNA
Giarri
Catania
Caltanizetta
Syracuse
gentum
cata

To Halifax and Boston

OCEAN

HUNGARY

MOLDAVIA

WALLACHIA

SERVIA

ATLANTIC

OTTOMAN EMPIRE

Lisbon

From the Azores

GREECE

0   100   200   300
Scale in Miles

SEA

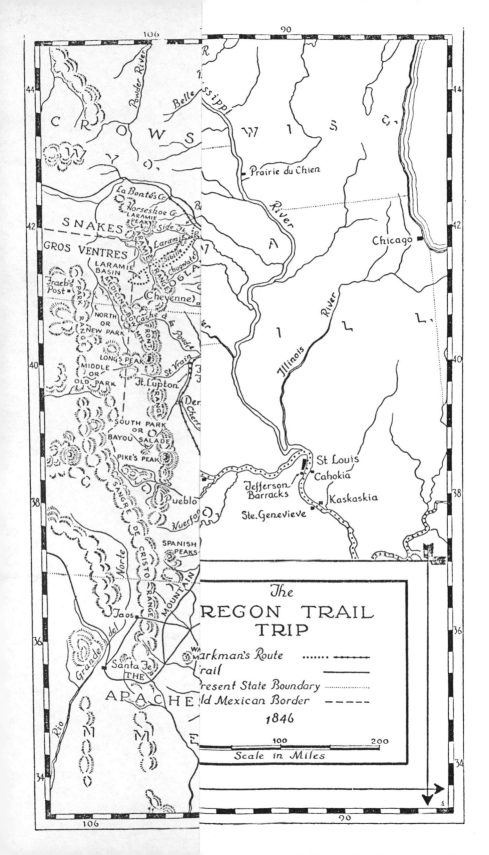

The

OREGON TRAIL TRIP

Parkman's Route	·······— — —
Trail	———————
Present State Boundary	·················
Old Mexican Border	— — — —

1846

Scale in Miles

THE
JOURNALS
OF
FRANCIS PARKMAN

———

VOLUME II

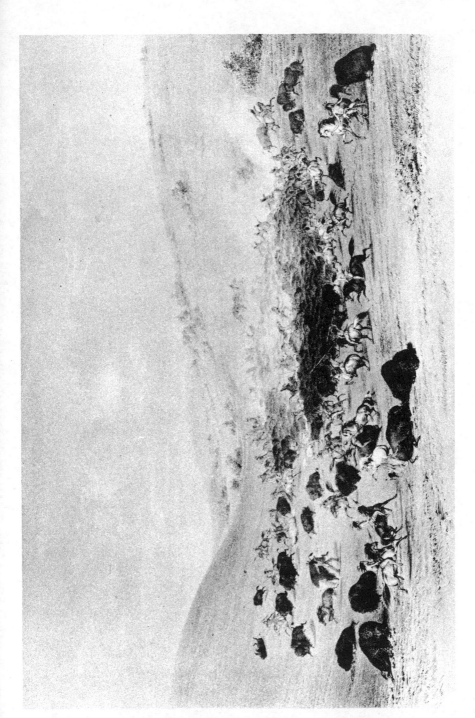

Buffalo Hunt—Surround, 1832

One of George Catlin's paintings of life in the Far West from the lithograph by McGahey

THE

JOURNALS

OF

FRANCIS PARKMAN

Edited by MASON WADE

Author of

FRANCIS PARKMAN: HEROIC HISTORIAN

ILLUSTRATED

VOLUME II

NEW YORK AND LONDON

HARPER & BROTHERS PUBLISHERS

MCMXLVII

KRAUS REPRINT CO.
New York
1969

TABLE OF CONTENTS

VOLUME II

LIST OF ILLUSTRATIONS

VOLUME II

The Oregon Trail Journal
1846

Introduction

PARKMAN'S Oregon Trail trip was the greatest of the journeys that he undertook in preparation for his lifework, and the diary kept on that arduous expedition is the most notable of all his journals. Its importance is twofold: it casts an invaluable light on *France and England in North America* as the chief source of Parkman's understanding of the Indians, the third party in the great struggle for the continent; and it is a major document of Western history, for 1846 was a vital year in the development of the West and Parkman was thrown into the company of many of the great men and movements of the time. Alone among the journals, this informal record is more important than the book for which it furnished the raw material, since *The Oregon Trail* was diluted triply by the circumstances of its composition, and for all its reputation is inferior to the notes upon which it was based.

It must not be forgotten that *The Oregon Trail* was Parkman's first book, begun when he was only twenty-three and finished, under singular difficulties, three years later. In a new preface, written a quarter of a century after the book first appeared in 1849, Parkman discounted the dangers he had run with these words: "My business was observation, and I was willing to pay dearly for the opportunity of exercising it." He did pay dearly for the knowledge he obtained, for he went back to Boston from the West a sick man. It seems clear that the journey brought about the breakdown of a constitution already strained by unwise attempts to strengthen it. The summer in the West was intended as rest and recreation from too much study, for Parkman had supplemented his law studies with extensive historical research. He returned home with his already strained sight weakened still further by exposure to the pitiless glare of the sun and to the harsh alkali dust of the Plains. He had acquired an impaired digestion and the insomnia to which he was to be a lifelong victim; and he had further advanced the arthritis that later crippled him and prevented him from ever again leading the strenuous outdoor life he loved so well. Most serious of all was an obscure mental disorder, which Parkman thought was brought on by this general collapse of his health, but may have been the basic trouble of which the other ailments were merely symptoms. In its train came hypochondria, which haunts the book, while the journal possesses an entirely different spirit. But just as a starvation diet and the exercise of the strong will which was his greatest asset had brought Parkman through the onslaughts of illness on the journey, when "a horse, a rifle, a pair of pistols, and a red shirt might have offered temptations too strong for aboriginal virtue" had he yielded to invalidism, so upon his return home he conquered his "Enemy" by acting on his favorite principle that "to tame the devil, it is best to take him by the horns." Condemned by baffled doctors to complete repose and unable to use his eyes in the historical work he yearned to do, he wrote *The Oregon Trail* by dictation, a procedure of which he soon caught the knack and which he found as "easy as lying."

The journal lost much, however, in the process of thus being transmuted into book form. Parkman was forced to rely upon others to act as amanuenses and to revise his work. His companion on the journey, Quincy Adams Shaw—who significantly bore a triply sacrosanct Boston name—was one of the cousins who read the notebooks aloud to Parkman as he underwent medical treatment at Staten Island, Catskill, and at the Brattleboro Spa, and then took down the version which he dictated after recasting the narrative in his head. Shaw made the Oregon Trail trip for sport, adventure, and his health, while Parkman went chiefly as a student; and doubtless Shaw's outlook helped to shape the book into an adventure story, "A Summer's Journey Out of Bounds," as the original subtitle runs, and into the record of "a tour of curiosity and amusement," as it is described on the opening page: "The restlessness, the love of wilds and hatred of cities, natural perhaps in early years to every unperverted son of Adam, was not our only motive for undertaking the present journey. My companion hoped to shake off the effects of a disorder that had impaired a constitution originally hardy and robust; and I was anxious to pursue some enquiries relative to the character and usages of the remote Indian tribes, being already familiar with many of the border tribes."—*The California and Oregon Trail* (New York, 1849), Ch. II. Much valuable material about the Indians and about the fur traders, soldiers, emigrants, mountain men, and sportsmen they encountered thus was lost; and also most of the immediacy and vigor of the original notes. Parkman had yet to shed the rhetorical impedimenta with which Harvard had encumbered his style; and he was self-consciously trying to be literary, under the romantic influence of his own literary idols, Byron and Cooper, and those of Gaylord Clark, in whose *Knickerbocker Magazine* the first version of *The Oregon Trail* appeared as a serial from February 1847 to February 1849, complete with Byronic epigraphs. Still more of the original quality was lost by the editing of Charles Eliot Norton, who revised the *Knickerbocker* version for book publication in accordance with the literary amenities as then understood by right-thinking Bostonians. On September 12, 1848, Parkman, beset by illness, accepted Norton's offer to read proofs for him, though it is evident that he was critical of Norton's style, for in the same letter he urged his friend to "put a little pepper and allspice" into a contribution to the *North American*: "It will not harm its respectability, and perhaps will make it more welcome to the taste of some of its readers." But Norton was constitutionally incapable of taking this injunction to heart, and *The Oregon Trail* as we know it was carefully bowdlerized of much anthropological data and many insights into Western life which seemed too crude to his delicate taste. Harvard's future professor of fine arts was not the best imaginable editor for one of the great firsthand records of the West, though Norton did a service to history by correcting some of Parkman's remarkable distortions of French names.

What happened is best illustrated by examples, aside from the many minor changes occasioned by Norton's low shock-point, which toned down or omitted Parkman's references to the prevalence of heavy drinking and loose sexual behavior in the West. But more serious than this bowdlerizing was the attempt to make literature out of history, at the expense of the latter, for which Parkman himself must bear the ultimate blame. In the journal Parkman thus described his impression of the American Fur Company upon his arrival at Fort Laramie:

Fort Laramie, June 16th. Prices are most extortionate. Sugar, two dollars a cup—5-cent tobacco at $1.50—bullets at $.75 a pound, etc. American Fur Cmp'y. exceedingly disliked in this country—it suppresses all opposition, and keeping these enormous prices, keeps its men in necessaries on these terms.

In the book this vivid picture of fur trade practices became merely:

Fort Laramie is one of the posts established by the "American Fur Company," which well nigh monopolizes the Indian trade of this region. Here its officials rule with an absolute sway . . .

Again, the journal offers this incisive account of Parkman's second visit to Fort Bernard, where an emigrant party has just arrived:

June 28th. Yesterday rode down with Paul Dorion, who wished to swap a wild horse, to Richard's fort. Found there Russel's or Boggs' comp'y., engaged in drinking and refitting, and a host of Canadians besides. Russel drunk as a pigeon—some fine-looking Kentucky men—some of D. Boone's grandchildren—Ewing, Jacobs, and others with them—altogether more educated men than any I have seen. A motley crew assembled in Richard's rooms—squaws, children, Spaniards, French, and emigrants. Emigrants mean to sell liquor to the Miniconques, who will be up here tomorrow, and after having come all the way from the Missouri to go to the war, will no doubt break up, if this is done. Paul very much displeased, as well as the Canadians.

In the book this became:

Two large villages of a band of Dakotah had come three hundred miles from the Missouri, to join in the war, and they were expected to reach Richard's that morning. There was as yet no sign of their approach; so pushing through a noisy, drunken crowd, I entered an apartment of logs and mud, the largest in the fort: it was full of men of various races and complexions, all more or less drunk. A company of California emigrants, it seemed, had made the discovery at this late day that they had encumbered themselves with too many supplies for their journey. A part, therefore, they had thrown away, or sold at great loss to the traders; but had determined to get rid of their very copious stock of Missouri whiskey, by drinking it on the spot. Here were maudlin squaws stretched on piles of buffalo-robes; squalid Mexicans, armed with bows and arrows; Indians sedately drunk; long-haired Canadians and trappers, and American backwoodsmen in brown homespun, the well-beloved pistol and bowie-knife displayed openly at their sides. In the middle of the room a tall, lank man, with a dingy broadcloth coat, was haranguing the company in the style of the stump orator. With one hand he sawed the air, and with the other clutched firmly a brown jug of whiskey, which he applied every moment to his lips, forgetting that he had drained the contents long ago. Richard formally introduced me to this personage, who was no less a man than Colonel R———, once the leader of the party. Instantly the colonel, seizing me, in the absence of buttons, by the leather fringes of my frock, began to define his position. His men, he said, had mutinied and deposed him; but he still exercised over them the influence of a superior mind; in all but the name he was yet their chief. As the colonel spoke, I looked round on the wild assemblage, and could not help thinking that he was but ill fitted to conduct such men across the deserts to California. Conspicuous among the rest were three tall young men, grandsons of Daniel Boone. They had clearly inherited the adventurous character of that prince of pioneers; but I saw no sign of the quiet and tranquil spirit that so remarkably distinguished him.

In the journal Parkman gives this sharply-drawn picture of Smoke's village of Sioux fording Laramie Creek:

This morning, Smoke's village appeared on the opposite bank, and crossed on their wild, thin, little horses. Men and boys, naked and dashing eagerly through the water—horses with lodge poles dragging through squaws and children, and sometimes a litter of puppies—gaily-attired squaws, leading the horses of their lords—dogs with their burdens attached swimming among the horses and mules—dogs barking, horses breaking loose, children laughing and shouting—squaws thrusting into the ground the lance and shield of the master of the lodge—naked and splendidly formed men passing and repassing through the swift water.

In the book the sharpness of impression is lost amid too much detail and a certain romanticization, in the approved manner of Cooper and Irving, which Parkman later condemned:

The stream is wide, and was then between three and four feet deep, with a very swift current. For several rods the water was alive with dogs, horses, and Indians. The long poles used in pitching the lodges are carried by the horses, fastened by the heavier end, two or three on each side, to a rude sort of pack-saddle, while the other end drags on the ground. About a foot behind the horse, a kind of large basket or pannier is suspended between the poles, and firmly lashed in its place. On the back of the horse are piled various articles of luggage; the basket also is well filled with domestic utensils, or, quite as often, with a litter of puppies, a brood of small children, or a superannuated old man. Numbers of these curious vehicles, *traineaux*, or, as the Canadians call them, *travaux*, were now splashing together through the stream. Among them swam countless dogs, often burdened with miniature *traineaux*; and dashing forward on horseback through the throng came the warriors, the slender figure of some lynx-eyed boy clinging fast behind them. The women sat perched on the pack-saddles, adding not a little to the load of the already over-burdened horses. The confusion was prodigious. The dogs yelled and howled in chorus; the puppies in the *traineaux* set up a dismal whine, as the water invaded their comfortable retreat; the little black-eyed children, from one year of age upward, clung fast with both hands to the edge of their basket, and looked in alarm at the water rushing so near them, sputtering and making wry mouths as it splashed against their faces. Some of the dogs, encumbered by their load, were carried down by the current, yelping piteously; and the old squaws would rush into the water, seize their favorites by the neck, and drag them out. As each horse gained the bank, he scrambled up as he could. Stray horses and colts came among the rest, often breaking away at full speed through the crowd, followed by old hags, screaming after their fashion on all occasions of excitement. Buxom young squaws, blooming in all the charms of vermilion, stood here and there on the bank, holding aloft their master's lance, as a signal to collect the scattered portions of his household.

So much for the literary consequences of the way in which *The Oregon Trail* was written. Much more important was the loss of historical information of considerable importance. Until the journals came to light, it was impossible to make a satisfactory itinerary and chronology of Parkman's trip, for many of the essential details of the journey were omitted in the book version. It was also impossible to identify many of the people that he met; and it so happens that though Parkman was far more interested in Indians than in whites or halfbreeds, he met an extraordinary number of Western notables.

The Oregon Trail has often been criticized on the grounds of how much Parkman missed, as well as of how much he reported. The journal proves that he missed less than has been assumed on the basis of the omissions that his friends led him to make in both the magazine and book versions. Neither Shaw nor Norton saw the value of many a note on the Indians which later served Parkman well, and neither was concerned with the making of the West.

Parkman's primary purpose in taking the Oregon Trail trip was to study the Indian. This he made clear in his foreword to the first edition:

The journey which the following narrative describes was undertaken on the writer's part with a view of studying the manners and characters of Indians in their primitive state. Although in the chapters which relate to them, he has only attempted to sketch those features of their wild and picturesque life which fell, in the present instance, under his own eye, yet in doing so he has constantly aimed to leave an impression correct as far as it goes. In justifying his claim to accuracy on this point, it is hardly necessary to advert to the representations given by poets and novelists, which, for the most part, are mere creatures of fancy. The Indian is certainly entitled to high rank among savages, but his good qualities are not those of an Uncas or an Oudalissa.

During his college years Parkman had formed the intention of writing the history of the American forest and of the American Indian. The Appalachian forest, the scene of that Old French War which he at first thought would be the focal point of the history he proposed to write, was now thoroughly familiar to him; but in the East the Indian had died out, or had been hopelessly corrupted by white civilization, or had been transferred to Western reservations. Parkman's earlier encounters with the Abenakis of the Penobscot, with the Iroquois of the Mohawk, and with the Ojibwas of the Great Lakes, had not given him the knowledge of primitive savage life which he required. Only in the West could that knowledge still be obtained; for beyond the western boundary of Missouri, then the frontier of the United States, the remnants of the Eastern Indians had recently been settled on reservations; while on the Plains and in the Rockies the Western Indians lived much as they always had done, still little affected by casual contact with mountain man and fur trader and emigrant. The culture of the Plains Indian was very different from that of the forest-dweller of the East, but his psychology was much the same, and Parkman used his acquaintance with the Sioux to unlock many an Iroquois mystery. He was fortunate in going West when he did, at almost the last moment suitable for his purpose; for the opening of the West had begun, and with the rising tide of emigration and the establishment of fixed trading posts in the mountains the doom of the savage and of his ancient way of life was assured.

In his great triangular sweep through the prairies and the plains, Parkman had an opportunity to observe many different Indian tribes at first hand. His route took him across the prairie and the plains from Westport (Kansas City) to Fort Laramie in eastern Wyoming, along the first part of the Oregon Trail; then he spent some weeks hunting with a Sioux village beyond the Laramie Mountains in the Laramie Basin, and in the eastern foothills of the Medicine Bow Mountains. Returning to Fort Laramie, he traveled southward along the Front Range of the Rockies to the Pueblo and Bent's Fort on the Arkansas (near La Junta, Colorado) by one of the oldest Indian trade routes, which crossed the sites of Cheyenne and Denver. Then he turned eastward, following the Mountain Route and then the main Santa Fe Trail across the plains to his starting point, leaving the Arkansas at the Big Bend, Kansas, and crossing the prairies to Westport by way of Council Grove. On the steamer from St. Louis, where he had met Shaw and acquired part of his outfit, to Westport, the jumping-off place for his prairie journey, Parkman encountered the degenerate Kansas or Caws, who had become thieves and beggars. About Westport and near-by Independence, he found the missionized Shawnees and Delawares, Eastern Indians recently installed on reservations. The Shawnees had become farmers and half-civilized, under the influence of their Methodist Mission; but the Delawares were the Indian Ishmaels of the Plains, extremely useful to the whites as scouts and hunters, since their hand was against that of every other Indian. Near Fort Leavenworth he saw the semicivilized Kickapoos, whose white trader kept both a loaded revolver and the poems of John Milton close at hand.

With considerable good fortune Parkman passed scatheless through the country of the Pawnees along the Platte, for they had become master thieves and cattle lifters on the Oregon road which to their surprise was being thrust through their ancient homeland. The region about Fort Laramie had long been a neutral ground, where buffalo and trade goods lured each summer both the Sioux (whom Parkman calls the Dakotas) and their enemies the Shoshones (Snakes) and the Crows; though when Parkman came upon the scene, the Sioux had for some years been trying to make Laramie Plains their own. While hunting with the Sioux to the west of Fort Laramie—Parkman's Black Hills are the fir-covered Laramie Mountains, not the Black Hills of Dakota—he feared an onslaught of the Gros Ventres, who had allied themselves to the Blackfeet of the Rockies and were the toughest fighters and raiders of the region. The far more powerful and populous Sioux told him tall tales of their enemies' prowess. Turning southward to Pueblo and Bent's Fort, he encountered stray Cheyennes, whose center was the latter establishment, after the trader William Bent married Owl Woman of their tribe. On his way back to Westport along the much-traveled Santa Fe Trail, Parkman missed the Comanches, the cruelest and most murderous of the Plains Indians; but he did encounter the southern Arapahos, no less dangerous than their northern relatives but somewhat intimidated when he met them by the passage of the Army of the West on its way to Santa Fe. Here Parkman also fell in with the southern Pawnees. Any of these tribes would have cheerfully wiped out or "counted coup" on so small a party as Parkman's, or at best would have as cheerfully robbed it. But Parkman had great good fortune in what was an extremely foolhardy adventure.

Parkman and Shaw ran a very real risk of death because of their dislike for the company of fellow travelers; and only luck and the wisdom of their guide, Henry Chatillon, a master mountain man, brought them through unscathed. To be sure, the Pawnees were more interested in robbing the whites than in killing them. But the theft of weapons, provisions, and horses on the Plains often meant merely a less merciful death than that from arrow, gun, spear, or knife. Chatillon would never have led so small a party into the Indian country, and must have thought that Parkman and Shaw planned to join an emigrant train. But they had no love for the "offscourings of the frontier," and when they reached the Forks of the Platte they parted with their British companions, reducing their number to four. Again, they set off southward from Fort Laramie without companions for the most dangerous part of their journey. And at Bent's Fort, instead of waiting for the formation of a regular party, they merely picked up casual reinforcements and set out for home. The Arapahos and Comanches had richly earned a reputation as violent and dangerous—they were true "hostiles," in the phrase of the trails. The Sioux were as yet well disposed towards the whites, but Parkman might have been casually killed while in their company with but two other white men, if it had not been for Henry Chatillon's high standing with the tribe, into which he had married.

Parkman had two further assets for his firsthand study of the Indians. In St. Louis, before setting out on his trip, he had talked at length with Thomas Fitzpatrick, one of the greatest of the mountain men, who probably knew the Western Indians as well as anyone. And then, as they pushed westward across the prairie and into the true High Plains, beyond the 98° meridian, Parkman found that Henry Chatillon was an encyclopedia of Indian information. These circumstances made Parkman's encounters with stray individuals or small groups of various tribes more profitable than they would otherwise have been; for Fitzpatrick had provided him with a general frame of reference, based on a rich experience of the whole West, while Chatillon fitted additional pieces into it and helped Parkman to interpret what he saw. It was from Fitzpatrick and his old companion Jedidiah Smith that Albert Gallatin, the pioneer of American ethnography, had gathered many of the basic concepts of his *Synopsis of the Indian Tribes within the United States* (1836).

But Parkman's great and unique experience in the West, which he owed to the fact that Chatillon was the son-in-law of an Oglala chief, was that of living with the Sioux as they pursued their normal life. His three weeks with the Sioux village in the foothills of the Rockies made him the first American man of letters to possess any real firsthand understanding of the Indian. Washington Irving's *Astoria* and *Captain Bonneville* are remarkable recreations of the experience of other men, but Irving's *Tour of the Prairies* is no *Oregon Trail*. Parkman destroyed Fenimore Cooper's highly romantic concept of the Noble Savage—one who had lived with the Dakota Sioux had few illusions about Indian nobility of character—and enriched American literature with the most lifelike Indians it was to know for years to come, although Parkman's Indians are a little too inevitably "snake-eyed" or "lynx-eyed" for the less romantic modern ethnologist. How revolutionary the Indians of *The Oregon Trail* were in the literary world of the day is indicated by the fact that Herman Melville was thoroughly upset by Parkman's view of them as not much better than brutes, and publicly informed him that "Xavier and Elliott despised not the savages; and had Newton and Milton dwelt among them, they would not have done so."* To Francis Bowen of the *North American*, Parkman's encounters with the Indians figured merely among "the other incidents which usually lend variety and interest to a journey to the Rocky Mountains" in these "pleasing and truthful sketches." Bowen found Parkman's book far superior to Edwin Bryant's *What I Saw in California*, but quite obviously it did not evoke in him the same enthusiasm as Irving's *Tour*, in which he found the "finest qualities of Addison and Goldsmith, without the free language of the one or the shallow judgment of the other."† In 1849 the East wanted from the·West either elegant romance or information useful to the prospective gold miner, and it ignored Lewis Garrard's *Wah-To-Yah and the Taos Trail*, a better job of writing than Parkman's far more celebrated book, but too truthful and uncouth for the taste of the times in its lively picture of the West.

Parkman's experience on the Oregon Trail trip served him well in dealing with the past in which the Indian had played so great a role; the basis of many a statement in the histories may be found in some incident or observation recorded in the Oregon Trail journal. The Sioux might well be called the Iroquois of the West, and as such they were particularly apt subjects for Parkman's study. They were the most typical of the Plains Indians, and one of the best tribes, though inferior both physically and mentally to the Crows and Cheyennes, and mentally to the Arapahos. Thanks to their primary

* Unsigned review of *The California and Oregon Trail* in *The Literary World*, IV, 113 (March 31, 1849), 291. I am indebted to Mr. Bernard DeVoto for calling this review to my attention.

† *North American Review*, LXIX (July, 1849), 175.

importance to the fur trade and their stubborn resistance to white encroachment after 1865, they became for most Americans the symbol of the Indian. A Sioux was the model for the Indian-head nickel, and the Sioux war bonnet has been thrust by artists upon many an Indian who never saw such a headdress.

The Sioux confederated better than any other Indians except the Iroquois, and matched them in their belligerency and bravery. In their gradual progress from their original home in the forests about the Lake of the Woods to the Plains, they conquered or drove out every nation they encountered, except the Ojibwas, who forced that southwestward movement when their European weapons, provided by French and English traders, proved superior to the Sioux bows and arrows. The Sioux, like the Iroquois, were a confederation of tribes, made up in their case of seven main divisions, each divided into bands and sub-bands. Four of these main divisions, grouped under the name of Santee, lagged behind in the great migration and centered in Minnesota; while the Yankton, Yanktonai, and Teton divisions pushed on west of the Missouri and adopted the cultural characteristics of the Plains Indians.

The Oglalas, with whom Parkman sojourned, were the principal band of the Teton Sioux. Their 5,000 souls made up half the nation, though they constituted only one of its seven divisions. The Oglalas led the southwestward movement in the late seventeenth and eighteenth centuries; they were the first of the Sioux to cross the Missouri, about 1750, and the first to reach the Black Hills of South Dakota, about 1775. After crossing the Missouri, they began to use horses and to hunt buffalo, which they followed westward in many small bands; from this, they derived their name of Scattered or Divided People. They pushed the northern Cheyennes and the Kiowas out of the Black Hills, and by the end of the century they were waging war on the Arikaras to the north, the Kiowas and the Crows to the west, and the Omahas and Poncas to the south. In 1795 they had a great struggle with the Cheyennes, to whom they later showed more tolerance than to any other Algonkin tribe.

Parkman was familiar with Jonathan Carver's description of the River Bands of the Sioux, whom the latter had found in 1766 near the Ste. Croix River of Minnesota. These laggards in their nation's migration fought with the British in the American Revolution and the War of 1812, while their Western kinsmen gradually gave up the practice of wintering east of the Missouri and formed new ties with the St. Louis French, with whom they traded at the mouth of the Bad River. From 1785 to 1820 the Oglalas had no less than three wars with the Crows, whom they cut off from the East and from British traders at the Mandan and Hidsata Villages on the Upper Missouri. Consequently a north-south trade developed along the Front Range of the Rockies about 1815, when the Kiowas began trading horses and Spanish goods with the Crows at Horse Creek on the North Platte.

During the first quarter of the nineteenth century the Oglalas continued to roam the Black Hills north of the Bad River, trading with the St. Louis French and becoming friendly with them, though not above raiding traders bound upstream, as in the case of the Astorians in 1811. In 1823 they aided Colonel Henry Leavenworth's expedition against the Arikaras of the Missouri villages, who had attacked W. H. Ashley's fur brigade, but the Sioux were not impressed by their first contact with the U. S. Army, which to their disgust refused to wage war in the ruthless Indian style. In 1823, when they signed a treaty with the Americans who had gradually taken over the Teton fur trade from the French, the Oglalas numbered 1,500, of whom 300 were warriors. One of their three sub-bands was then headed by Bull Bear (Mato-Tatanyka), who later became the head chief of the Oglalas. In 1832 they were visited by the artist George Catlin, who mentions Parkman's acquaintance, the Whirlwind, in his *Manners, Customs, and Institutions of the North American Indians* (London, 1841), a book with which Parkman was familiar. About 1835 half the Oglalas were grouped into four sub-bands under Bull Bear, known as Bear People, while the other half of the tribe, known as Smoke People, followed Chief Smoke. As the American Fur Company's monopoly of the Oglala trade broke down, they moved southward toward the Platte, drawn by the liquor which was the most effective weapon in these fur trade wars.

They first came to Laramie Creek in 1834, lured to Fort William by John Sabille and C. E. Gilpin, traders for Sublette & Campbell, who sought to break up the practical monopoly of the American

Fur Company's Oglala Post, conducted by Thomas L. Sarpy on the South Fork of the Cheyenne, near Rapid Creek. This move brought them into conflict with their old enemies the Pawnees, with whom Bull Bear quarreled over the buffalo hunting—the best within five hundred miles—near the forks of the Platte, which marked the western boundary of the Pawnee country. By 1840 Bull Bear's warriors were hunting west of the Laramie Mountains, while Smoke's took over the Platte Forks range. The two Oglala bands came into frequent contact, for the fine horses which Smoke's people obtained from the south were an attraction to Bull Bear's followers. Both bands were on good terms with the whites, but had formed different alliances among the neighboring tribes whose war and hunting parties frequented Laramie Plains, long a crossroads of Indian trade. The northern Arapahos and Cheyennes, whose territory lay to the south of Laramie, were well disposed towards Bull Bear's people, while the Crows to the north were their bitter enemies. Another trade war flooded the region with liquor in 1841, and in November of that year Bull Bear was killed in Smoke's camp on the Chugwater during a drunken brawl. The Oglalas then split into two factions, a division which endured for forty years, despite the unifying effect of growing anti-white feeling as the swelling tide of emigrants spoiled the grass, timber, and game of the Sioux' favorite hunting grounds. The Grattan massacre at Fort Laramie in 1854 was a forerunner of the trouble to come, and after 1865 the Sioux were the terror of the expanding frontier. General Custer was sent out against them in 1876, when the invasion of the Black Hills in Dakota by gold seekers brought them out on the warpath. After the massacre of his command, the Sioux were gradually forced northward into Canada, where many of their descendents remain today, reunited with the remnants of the western divisions of their people.

Parkman was fortunate in meeting the Sioux just before they turned against the whites, though they were in social anarchy as a result of the fur trade wars and Bull Bear's murder. He was still more fortunate in that his guide Henry Chatillon was married to Bear Robe, Bull Bear's daughter, and thus was allied to the great leader of the Oglalas, for whom no real successor had yet been found and whose prestige still was great. Though personal fitness and popularity determined chieftainship more often than heredity, where descent did operate among the Sioux, it was from father to son; and the elder Bull Bear's fame had been great enough to overcome his son's lack of qualifications for leadership. In any case, among the Teton Sioux the authority of the chief was limited by the band council, without whom, as Parkman observed, little or nothing could be accomplished. War parties were commonly recruited by individual warriors, such as the Whirlwind, who had the reputation of being successful leaders. The dispersion of the Sioux into small bands made it difficult for them to muster a large war party for action against another tribe, as Parkman saw when the grand alliance of the Oglalas and the Miniconjous against the Snakes fell through. The only unity of the seven divisions of the Sioux was in language and in the fact that they did not commonly wage war upon each other. Even the Teton Sioux were united solely by a common dialect and by the Plains culture which set them apart from their Santee kinsmen, who still followed the forest way of life.

The chief characteristics of the Teton Sioux culture were their utter dependence upon the buffalo, which not only supplied their food but their clothing, shelter, and utensils of all kinds; their use of the horse and the *tepi*; their custom of using "soldiers" to maintain order in camp and in the cooperative buffalo hunt; and their cult of the sun dance. They used the short bow, which held its own for buffalo hunting on horseback, as Parkman bears witness, until the invention of the repeating rifle in the 1870's. They practiced little agriculture, and made no pottery or textiles. The Crows were better workmen than the Sioux, and the Nez Percés made better bows. Like almost all the Plains tribes, the Sioux used the *travois* (from the French *travail à cheval*), an A-shaped frame of poles bound together by sinews and drawn first by dogs and later by horses. They made little use of wild seeds and grass in their diet, but their development of pemmican, sun-dried buffalo meat packed in fat and sometimes flavored with pounded wild cherry stones, gave them a balanced diet ideally adapted to their life. They were among the few Plains Indians to eat dog, and, as Parkman discovered to the alarm of an already queasy stomach, a dog feast had ritualistic significance for them. Their use of the by-products of the buffalo—skin, bones, hair, horns, and sinew—was often ingenious; but their whole culture depended too much upon this one beast, and when it failed them, they were doomed. While the buffalo roamed the Plains in thousands, the Sioux squandered their only resource; and only when the whites had driven it into extinction did they realize that they, too, were threatened with a like fate. Then they turned and fought the new-comers who had destroyed the source of their civilization. In the 1840's the Sioux were slow to recognize that they were being exposed to a new form of the white encroachment which had forced them from their original home in Canada. It was fortunate for Parkman's purpose that this was so, and that the Sioux were as yet unwilling to go on the warpath against the whites, as the southern Arapahos did that very summer and as the Cheyennes soon would.

It is clear that Parkman had an invaluable opportunity to study the Indian way of life. It is also clear, from both the journal and the book based upon it, that at twenty-three he was not equipped to make the most of that opportunity. Bred in a romantic conception of the savage which is clearly reflected in his frontier tales for the *Knickerbocker* in 1845, he was too shocked by the contrast of the reality with his concept to appreciate fully what he saw. Ethnology was an infant science in America in 1846, and Parkman had hardly begun to think in its terms. The journal is full of vivid impressions of Sioux life, but little deep penetration of Indian thinking is evident. Parkman's understanding of the Indian grew with the years, as he pieced together what he had observed with the findings of later students. In 1846 he was too much under the influence of Henry Rowe Schoolcraft, then considered the leading authority on the Indians, and too full of enthusiasm for that worthy's romantic fictionalization of Indian thought. By 1851, when he opened *The Conspiracy of Pontiac* with a long chapter on the Eastern Indians, he had become familiar with sounder authorities, and had had the opportunity to reconsider his own observations in the light of their views. Fifteen years later, when writing *The Jesuits in North America*, his understanding of the Indian had matured, and he used his knowledge of the Sioux to good advantage in dealing with the Iroquois and Hurons. As student and critic he had closely followed the great advances during his lifetime in Indian studies, keeping in touch with men such as Adolph Bandelier, Lewis H. Morgan, E. G. Squier, and John Bourke who were carrying on investigation in the field. Notes which had meant little to him as he scribbled them in the Oregon Trail journal now took on new significance as he turned over the faded pages; and they formed the basis of many a conclusion advanced in the later histories. But the journal remains the best measure of Parkman's youthful understanding of the Indian and the West.

It is also one of the great historical records of our national past, for, aside from its bearing on Parkman's work, the Oregon Trail Journal is an invaluable document of Western history. The same good fortune which had lavishly endowed Parkman with a great Boston name, social position, means, and the best education his environment afforded, also gave him the most ample opportunities to witness history in the making that any young historian could imagine. In 1845 at Mackinaw he had encountered Robert Stuart, an old Astorian; and in New York before setting out for the West, Parkman met Ramsay Crooks, another original Astorian who since 1822 had been administrative head of John Jacob Astor's American Fur Company, and was given all the aid and advice that master of the fur trade could supply. He also had an interview with Schoolcraft. Then he passed westward along the old Alleghany frontier and down the Ohio with the trickles of the westward movement which united at St. Louis to form a great stream. In the old metropolis of the West he had discussions with Pierre Chouteau and Pascal Cerré, patriarchs of the Western fur trade, and with Thomas Fitzpatrick, who soon was to become the first Indian agent for the Plains tribes. At Westport he joined forces with a party of three Britishers, supposedly traveling for sport and adventure, but probably not uninterested in the threat that the swelling Oregon emigration represented to Britain's claims in that disputed region, where Joint Occupancy by the two countries was about to be terminated. One of them, Romaine, had accompanied the Jesuit missionary Father De Smet into the buffalo country with Bidwell's historic Oregon party of 1841, while another, Captain Chandler, had seen service in Canada and may have been one of the British agents who abounded in the West as American war talk over the Oregon question rose ever higher. In Westport Parkman also encountered Daniel Boone's grandsons, who were following the family tradition of ever looking to the West; and Passed Midshipman Woodworth, who was carrying dispatches to the Columbia River, notifying the Oregon settlers that Joint Occupancy was about to be terminated. This hotheaded young officer on leave, drunk on the potent brew of Manifest Destiny, was talking loudly of his plan to raise a body of volunteers and capture Santa Fe—a little matter soon to be taken care of by the trader James Magoffin at President Polk's request. At Fort Leavenworth Parkman dined with Colonel Stephen Watts Kearny, who in the previous year had marched his dragoons over much the same route as his guest was to follow, in order to quiet the Indians by a show of force; and that very summer was to lead the Army of the West to Santa Fe and California. On the Oregon Trail Parkman met the ill-fated Donner Party, one of the chief groups of the emigration in that year, and some of the notables of the California uprising which brought the flag to the Pacific. At the Pueblo and on the Santa Fe Trail he encountered some of the forerunners of the Mormon migration, searching for a New Jerusalem free from the persecution of the Gentiles. At Fort Laramie he swapped horses and stories with Paul Dorion, the grandson of the half-breed voyageur who had accompanied Lewis and Clark as far as the South Mandan Villages and who had shared the rigors of Wilson Hunt's journey to found Astoria. He met many of the leading mountain men and traders: Louis Vasquez, Jim Bridger's partner; Pierre Papin, the famous *bourgeois* of Fort Laramie; Jim Clyman, returning disgruntled from the Oregon settlements; Sublette, Sabille, Richard, Bissonnette, Robidoux, and many more. Returning by the Santa Fe Trail, he saw the rear guard of the Army of the West on the march, in the form of Sterling Price's Missouri Volunteers and Andrew Jackson Smith's Mormon Battalion, and he met Marcellin St. Vrain, of the great Southwestern firm of Bent & St. Vrain. He was one year ahead of the great rush to Oregon, of the Mormon trek to Salt Lake, and of the first great swelling of the emigrant tide to California. But while Parkman was on the trail the destiny of the West was being fixed in an American pattern: Frémont was declaring the Bear Flag Republic and preparing the annexation of California, while Zachary Taylor was advancing into Mexico and winning the victories of Palo Alto, Resaca de la Palma, and Monterrey, which paved the way for the collapse of Mexican power in the Southwest in the following year.

But the significance of most of this was missed by the young Bostonian who had long suffered, as one of his Harvard classmates put it, from "Injuns on the brain." He lived so much in the past that he ignored too much of the present, though there is more of the pageant of the West in 1846 in the Journal than in *The Oregon Trail*, which Parkman first conceived merely as a record of adventure rather than as the history which he later saw it truly was. By force of environment and heredity he was blind to the profound social forces at work in the West; by tradition and taste he was contemptuous of the masses, and so he found the company of foreigners more congenial than that of the men who were making America out of the wilderness. He had only amused contempt for the democratic spirit of the emigrants and for the Jacksonianism of the West; he had no understanding of the forces behind the westward movement, which upon reflection he likened to the savage hordes of Huns who swarmed over Europe in the last days of Rome. The Mormons were mere miserable fanatics, "a very dangerous body of men," in his eyes. The easy friendliness of the West grated on his Bostonian reticence, and he was happier with the Indians and with the French-Canadian halfbreeds, to whom he could adopt a superior attitude, than with his fellow Anglo-Americans, who would not tolerate such an attitude. This was all very well for his basic purpose, since it made him concentrate his attention on the savages and leave us this invaluable record of their primitive life; but the missed opportunities are such as to make the Western historian weep, and to add *The Oregon Trail* to the long list of unfinished masterpieces of American literature. Fortunately, some measure of the great book that never was written can be recovered from this journal.

The diary of the Oregon Trail trip is written in pencil on the blue paper of three small notebooks, 4 by $6\frac{1}{4}$ inches, with leather spines and marbled boards. The first volume carries Parkman from New York to Fort Laramie; the second is chiefly devoted to his stay with the Sioux in the Laramie and Medicine Bow Mountains, though it continues the record until the Pueblo and Bent's Fort were reached on the southward leg of the journey; and the third, very scrappy and sketchy because of Parkman's illness and weariness, covers the eastward journey along the Santa Fe Trail to Westport. The route followed by Parkman is shown in as much detail as possible on the endpaper map in this volume, while a chronological itinerary of the trip is provided. There is also another small leather pocket notebook, which contains 1845 law school notes, references to historical books and papers, a diary of a brief historical research trip to New York, Philadelphia, and Baltimore in January 1846; some notes on the early part of the Oregon Trail trip, and accounts of the expenses of the expedition. This notebook is printed as an appendix. In a pocket of this notebook were found the passport issued to Parkman and Shaw by Pierre Chouteau, Jr. & Company, the successors of the American Fur Company as the overlords of the West—and some weather-worn calling cards. No Boston gentleman could go adventuring among the Indians and mountain men without such tokens of gentility!

1846

Volume I

New York,[1] *March 29*[th], *1846.* I met at Mr. Bellows'[2] a Mr. Kay,[3] a Philadelphia bookseller, a man who, though successful in his calling and very conversant in his business, is one of the Fourierites—a queer combination of worldly shrewdness with transcendental flightiness. His face bespoke it all—it was thin and sallow, and comical in the extreme. He exposed the secrets of the bookselling trade, which he thought the most trickish going.

The little, contemptible faces—the thin, weak, tottering figures—that one meets here on Broadway, are disgusting. One feels savage with human nature.

March 31st. Saw Mr. Schoolcraft.[4] Indian phlegm and apparent immobility may, in part, arise from temperament, but it is also the result of long training. If the child cries, or becomes angry, the mother says, "You will never be a warrior." Under such influences he grows up, accustomed not to suppress the emotion, but to conceal it. The man is encased in this impenetrable exterior—within he may be full of hatred, malice, and suspicion, but none of this appears. He is a statue!

He lives in constant fear. The world, to him, is full of spirits—or of the Great Spirit manifested in a thousand forms. He is surrounded with evil and with good—every voice of nature has its hidden meaning to his ear.

March 31. Mr. Stoddard, the cracked man, who copied my papers, and then tore them.[5]

Harrisburg,[6] *April 1.* The bridge swept away—the fields strewn with logs and debris of the woods by the freshet. The river swollen, but already much subsided—it was calm but swift, and dimpled with eddies. Looked at it at sunset—rafts and canoes floating rapidly down—flat boats passing the ferry with Conestoga waggons—a beautiful scene at that hour.

Man lounging by the river bank. Is it not true, that the lower you descend in education and social position, the more vicious men become?

Carlisle,[7] *April 2ⁿᵈ.* Crossed the Susquehanna in a flat boat filled with quiet, stupid, stout Dutch—men, women, and pretty girls. Some old, octogenarian veterans, and two young, fat dandies with checked breeches and frogged wrappers. The whole was a striking contrast to a corresponding group of Yankees. In the wretched cars, too, the same phlegm and stolidity were apparent—their minds were gone to sleep.

Carlisle is eighteen miles from Harrisburg. As you go to it, the Blue Mts. sweep away on the right—behind them is Sherman's Valley, with —— Gap opening into it. Opposite is a corresponding range, called also, I believe, the Blue Mts. You are traversing Cumberland Valley—level and rich.

The ancient barracks of Carlisle stand in the midst of broad meadows—overlooked from far off by the Blue Mts; and not far distant is the town.

The same range, sweeping southwardly, makes a lofty wall across the west—not enough to exclude the savages who prowled around the place in 1763. Around these barracks Bouquet's[8] army was encamped, and behind those hills lay the scene of their dangerous enterprise!

Carlisle, April 3ʳᵈ. Mr. Officer *versus* Waldstein, the German optician. Officer wished to bargain for a pair of spectacle glasses: A cheap article was the thing for him. Damn it, he had been a dealer himself, and had put in many hundreds, yes and thousands, too, of glasses. He was an impertinent, obtrusive fellow, always talking, and seemed to take pleasure in exposing his own meanness.

The population here is said to be chiefly of English and Irish descent. The men at the tavern seem to be chiefly lawyers, and are of decent appearance.

Chambersburg, April 3ʳᵈ. Shippensburg is situated in a country less level than that around Carlisle. The Southern Blue Ridge is nearer, while the northern presents a wide gap. The country is broken into low hills, and continues so to Chambersburg. The day was beautiful.

Pittsburg[h], April 6ᵗʰ. Left Chambersburg in a shamefully crowded coach at 12 o'clock at night. Soon reached Loudon among hills, at the ascent of Cove Mountain. The morning rose beautifully among the mountains. Were passing Cove Mt. Cove Valley near at hand. Tuscarora Mt. on the right—a long range. Soon came upon Sidling Hill. These mts. are not high and run in long parallel ranges. Juniata Crossings, where the bridge passes the Rayston Branch of Juniata. Bloody Run, the scene of Col. Smith's[9] exploit, in a valley beyond Sidling Hill. Bedford, in a valley at the foot of Wills Mt. Dunnings Creek near by.

Passed the Alleganey—the woods quite leafless and lighted by the slant sun. Late in the night reached Ligonier. This was, I suppose, the identical road cut to meet Braddock's road in 1755, and the same by which Bouquet passed.[10] Leaving Greensburg, we came in a few hours to a very rough, hilly country—no mountains. It was a succession of hills and hollows, like waves. Bushy Run was not far on the right, in a deep hollow. Very few people had heard of the battle, and no one could show the scene of it.[11] Turtle Creek was about eight miles farther, and the latter place is some 13 or 14 from Pittsburg. It runs through a very deep hollow, across which the road passes, descending and ascending the banks. A bad place for an Indian surprise. Thence to Pittsburg, the road was more level, till at length the town appeared, on its peninsula, surrounded by the river bluffs.

Steamboat, Ohio River. Yesterday visited Braddock's Field. It is as described by Sparks.[12] B. crossed at a riffle, called Braddock's Riffle, several hundred rods below (above ?)—marched first over flat, and then gently sloping ground to the foot of a knoll, where there is a spring at which the men stopped to drink. The ascent to this knoll is steep; marching up, the army found itself between the two ravines mentioned by Sparks. These flank the knoll or hill—the one on the left is comparatively shallow, with gently sloping sides, but that on the right is a deep, abrupt trench, and from this, as the bullets indicate, the heaviest fire proceeded. The army could scarce have advanced from between these fatal ravines, for beyond the knoll the ground rises into very abrupt hills. A sword was, however, found not long ago, high up the slope of one of these. Bones are still easily to be seen on the field. Returning, I rode down the beautiful shore of the Monongahela—spring was just advancing.

The man who showed me the field could not be persuaded to take any recompense.

Visited, with Mr. Biddle,[13] Bouquet's redoubt, and saw the scanty remnant of the pavement of Fort Pitt.[14]

Grant's Hill is very near the extremity of the peninsula, on the Monongahela side. Where Ft. Du Quesne[15] stood was quite level— but some distance behind, the country rises into hills—and the opposite shores of both rivers presenting lofty declivities, the situation of the town is very fine. The Ohio, too, is flanked by lofty eminences.

The physique of the Pennsylvania country people is very fine, but they strike me as dull and stupid. One of the stage-drivers completely realized my idea of an Indian trader—bluff, boisterous, profane, and coarse. As I watched him, I could not help recurring to certain female friends, and wondering how beings so opposite in all points of person and character could belong to the same species.

"Human nature is the same everywhere"—so says everybody, but does not education make most essential distinctions? Take a Wordsworth, for instance, and how little will you find in him in common with the brutish clods who were my fellow passengers across the Alleghanies. Or take any ordinary man of high education, and what sympathies can he have with such?

Read some good history of Penna. and observe out of what combination of nations and religions the present population sprang.

"La Belle Riviere"[16] deserves its name. High up, the shores are hilly and picturesque—below, the country is more level.

April 9th. My careless, frank, lighthearted New York acquaintance, P. M.

The man who, on some delay occurring, saluted me with: "I shan't see my wife tonight," this being our first acquaintance. Poor fellow—he was neglected in his youth, and though of a susceptible turn of mind, had—according to his own account—plunged into every kind of excess. About six years ago, he "got religion"—and he lately married. His constitution is injured by hardships when an engineer on a railroad, and he seems of a melancholy temperament; but is most frank and unreserved in his disclosures. He is on his way to see his new wife in Cincinnati.

A precious set of gamblers and ragamuffins cn board.

April 10. Passed the rapids at Louisville in the steamboat.

The English reserve or "offishness" seems to be no part of the western character—though I have had no opportunity of observing a gentleman of high standing. I observe this trait in myself—today, for instance, when a young fellow expressed satisfaction that he should accompany me to St. Louis, I felt rather inclined to shake him off, though he had made himself agreeable enough.

My acquaintance, P. M., for whose extensive travels I found it hard to account, is a lecturer on Gouraud's system of Mnemotechny[17] —for which his agreeable person and manner well qualify him.

Spring is beautifully awakening as we descend the Ohio—a hundred shades of green are budding out along the steep declivities; and around the scattered houses are peach trees in rich bloom. It is pleasant to look upon all this, after contemplating the deformity of minds and manners that prevails hereabouts.

April 11th. Passed the site of Fort Mass[i]ac,[18] situated on low, wet land. The banks of the Ohio grow more low as we descend, and now the forests rise from the very margin of the water—it is a wide expanse, with here and there an island.

At night, at Paduca[h], three flat-boats of West Virginian emigrants came on board—they had built their flatboats on Holston River, near which they lived, and had been from the 1st of March descending to the mouth of the Tennessee. The boats were like floating houses—the same, probably, with those originally used in navigating the Ohio. The men were good-looking and hardy, though not so large as the West Pennsylvanians. Some were dressed in red rifle-frocks, and they tell me that Indian leggings are still occasionally used in the Valley. All their domestic implements had an old-fashioned air: chairs with bottoms of ash-slivers—gourd dippers—kettles—anvil—bellows—old bureaus—clothing—bedding—frying pans, etc., etc., were rapidly passed into the steamer. Several old, long-barrelled, flint-locked rifles followed. Conversing with the men, I found them intelligent and open, though apparently not much educated. They were going to Iowa.

We are on the Mississipi, with its rapid muddy current, and low, forest-covered banks.

The men of the emigrant party are manly, open, and agreeable in their manners—with none of the contracted, reserved manner that is common in New Englanders. Neither have the women, who are remarkably good-looking, any of that detestable, starched, lacka-daisical expression common in vulgar Yankee women.

The true philosophy of life is to sieze with a ready and strong hand upon all the good in it, and to bear its inevitable evils as calmly and carelessly as may be.

St. Louis, April 15th. A crowd was gathered round the door of the Planters' Hotel,[19] and in the midst stood Henry Clay,[20] talking and shaking hands with any who chose. As he passed away, he asked an old man for a pinch of snuff, at which the mob was gratified, and the old man, striking his cane on the bricks, declared emphatically that Clay was the greatest man in the nation, and that it was a burning shame he was not in the presidential chair. So much for the arts by which politicians—even the best of them—thrive.

April 16th, St. Louis. Quin[21] not yet arrived. Infinite difficulty from contradictory accounts of the Indian country. I went over to Cahokia yesterday—in the midst of a beautiful level country, part forest, part prairie, the whole just awakening into life and bloom. A warm spring day. Herds of wild ponies running about. The forests here are not like ours—they are of a generous and luxuriant growth, and just now fragrant with a multitude of buds and blossoms, and full of the song of birds. They are fettered and interlaced by grape-vines that overrun the whole, like so many serpents.

Cahokia is all French—French houses, with their far-projecting eaves and porches—little French horses—and a little French inn. Madame Jarrot's[22] house is the chief establishment of the place. Calling on the old lady for historic information, I entered a large hall, with a floor of polished oak—oak panels—a large fire-place, and two stair-ways in the rear leading up to the chambers. This hall was the reception room—the only part of the house I saw—but it smacked sufficiently of the Olden Time.

Passed Midshipman Woodward [Woodworth][23] is here (St. Louis), on his way with despatches to Columbia River. He has a wild plan of raising a body of men, and *taking Santa Fe.*

Apr. 19th. How infinite is the diversity of human character! Old M. Cerré[24] of nearly eighty—lively, bright, and active—the old man goes about rejoicing in his own superiority to age—wrapped up in himself, unobservant, impenetrable, impassive. His companion was the reverse—young, silent through bashfulness, observing all, feeling all, and constantly in hostility to external influences—though resolute and determined, acting ever under the burden of constitutional diffidence. How hostile is such a quality to a commanding character. It is the mind as it stamps its character on the bearing and manner, that carries weight—the bold, unhesitating, confident expression has authority—not the forced, sharp, painful expression of resolution, struggling against diffidence. Some men have a sort of power from their very vanity—they are too dull, too impassive to feel a repressing influence from other minds—and thinking themselves the greatest men on earth, they assume a port and voice that imposes a sort of respect. Others there are who, with many of the internal qualities of command, can never assume its outward features—and fail in consequence.

How wide and deep and infinitely various is human nature!—and now the contemplation of it grows more absorbing as its features disclose themselves to view.

Pontiac,[25] says tradition, was killed near Cahokia.[26]

April 20th. Yesterday I went over to the Cahokia side—a beautiful Sunday afternoon. Numbers were passing over for amusement. A lank, half-idiot German was strolling up the banks of the muddy creek, just beyond the landing, with a long spear catching frogs; and two boys were laughing at his ineffectual attempts. I walked up its banks into the woods—it was nothing like our swift and clear mountain waters—all was teeming with life, animal and vegetable, just awakening in the warm spring sunshine. The creek was slow and sluggish—a haunt, in the season, for fever and ague—the luxuriant woods overshadowed it, interlaced with vines like snakes, and all bursting into leaf and flower—full, too, of birds, who would come down to splash and wash themselves in the water—and fragrant with the fresh smell of young leaves and blossoms. The pool was full of frogs and great turtles, sitting on logs, and among slime—now and then a water-snake, with his head lifted high, would writhe his way across—and as you passed by some sheltered cove, the whole water would be alive with minute fishes, skipping out of it in their terror.

The country overflows with game. In returning, I saw on board the boat some twenty sportsmen. Some had a dozen or two of duck slung together—others as many fish as they could carry—perch, bream, gar-fish, buffaloes, cat-fish, etc. The sportsmen were chiefly Germans. No wonder that the French at the old settlements led a merry life of it.

Old Mr. Thomas Fitzpatric[k],[27] the well-know[n] hunter and frontiersman, wrote to Lieut. Abert,[28] of the Topog. Engineers, a letter expressing his opinion of the origin of the western tribes—the following is its substance:

There are two great roots from which all the Indians of the territory east of the Rocky Mts. are derived, "with the exception of a few tribes which have no resemblance whatever to the others, and are the Pawnis [Pawnees], Ari(c)karas, Mandan, Chiennes [Cheyennes], and Kiawas [Kiowas]. These tribes, I think, have originally belonged to the extreme southern parts of the union, or far in Mexico."

Of the Inds. derived from the two roots spoken of, some of those of the first and most numerous stock are the Sioux, Kanzas [Kansas], Osages, Otoes, Iaways [Iowas], Mahas [Omahas], Punkas [Poncas], Saxes [Sauks], and Foxes, "and besides these, there are numbers of others that have a close affinity to them."

"The other root is the Ir(r)oquois, to which belongs the Shawnees, Delawares, Chippewas, Tuscaroras, Mohawks, and indeed, all the N. York and Canadian Inds., together with those bordering on the Lakes, etc."

The Crow language is a dialect of the Sioux.

The Camanches [Comanches] properly belong among the Shoshome [Shoshone] or Snake Inds., as their language is exactly the same; "and with them I would also place the Otaws [Utahs], Ponacs [Bannocks], Sandpitch [Sanpets], Pintas [Pintos], Tinpana [Timpaivats], Utas [Utes], together with all the very numerous small tribes in the great desert west of the Salt Lake, and lying between the Columbia on the North and the Colorado on the south, all of which belong to the Shoshome nation."

On the north fork of the Columbia, the tribes differ entirely in language and character from the above. They are, the Cotonary [Kutenais], Flathead, Collespillum [Kalispels] or Pond de Veil [Pend d'Oreilles], Spogan [Spokan], Nez Percé, Kinsé, Wallowalla [Walla Walla], "and many smaller tribes, all of which speak a similar language, but so harsh and guttural that few of our people have made any progress in attaining it."

The Chinooks belong to the coast Indians, "who differ very much in language and appearance from those of the interior, and, I believe, ought rather to be classed with the Islanders of the Pacific than with any of the inland tribes."[29]

The date of the above is from St. Louis, Feb. 5, 1846.

April 22nd. Rode out to Jefferson Barracks.[30] A beautiful April day— a mingling of clouds, showers, and sunshine, in which the landscape looked most fresh and verdant. This was not a forest country, though there are fine oak-openings at intervals; and across the Mississipi is one great ocean of woods. From the hill overlooking Vuides Pouches [Vide Poche][31] the scene was lovely—the French settlers plant fruit-trees everywhere amongst their picturesque-looking houses, and these were all in bloom. The French are content to live by the produce of their little gardens, knowing nothing and caring nothing for the world beyond their little village. Returning, we were overtaken by a tremendous but momentary shower.

Mr. Fitzpatrick speaks of the high discipline he has seen on war-parties. The chief's authority is absolute. Among the Crows,[32] where he thinks that the government and discipline are better than else-where, this is particularly the case. He has seen the young men erect the chief's lodge for him, cut off the choicest parts of the meat and bring them to him, waiting till he had eaten before they satisfied their own appetite. Boys, even the sons of the highest chief, will attach themselves to a distinguished war-leader and consider them-selves honored in discharging the meanest offices for him. This con-tinues till they have themselves made some *coup* in war, when the apprenticeship ceases. He thinks that the warlike spirit is the stimu-lant that saves the Indian from utter abasement, and mentions, in proof, the wretches whom he met near the Great Salt Lake, who were without this motive.

There is no *permanent* aristocracy—the meanest man may raise himself by talent, and the highest born sink into insignificance from the want of it.

The power of the peace-chiefs arises from their influence over their "soldiers" or counsellors (*comites*).

He thinks them *not* brave—though he mentions some extraor-dinary instances of courage—as that of a Crow whose favorite horse was stolen by a Blackfoot. The Crow went into the B. village where his enemy was sitting at evening before his lodge, with the horse at his side. He was singing his songs, and playing with the haltar which he held in his hand. The Crow took it from him, tied it round the horses' nose, mounted him and rode off, the B. thinking all the while that it was one of the young men of the village who wished to prove the merits of the horse.

Mr. F. is staggered by some of their *medecine* feats. There was a very famous medecine man in a Crow village, who, on going on a war-party, had fasted, retired, sung his songs, etc.; and prophesied that if within two days it rained the party would be unsuccessful, but that otherwise they would return in triumph. They departed—the weather was then fair and had long been so—but on the afternoon of the second day, a tremendous thunder-storm came suddenly up. All the village was instantly in the greatest commotion. The storm passed, and a horseman was seen approaching. He was the *only survivor* of the party.

April 25th, St. Louis. I have seen a strange variety of characters— Dixon, the nonentity—Ewing, the impulsive, unobserving ardent Kentuckian, who lays open his character to everyone, and sees nothing of those about him—the quiet, sedate, and manly Jacob(s), his companion. These two are going to California.[33]

April 27th, St. Louis. Rode out at the eleventh hour to see old Pierre Chouteau[34]—three miles from St. Louis. Found his old, picturesque, French house in the middle of the woods—neat Negro-houses, with verandahs—bird cages hung in the porch—chickens chirping about the neat yards. The old man was not well—and could not tell me much. He, however, described Pondiac [Pontiac] as a man six feet high, of very commanding appearance, and, whenever he saw him, splendidly dressed.[35] He used to come to St. Louis on visits.

His son, Liguest P. Chouteau,[36] told me the following, as coming from his father. Pondiac held a high command among Montcalm's Indians.

He was killed at Cahokia, at the instigation of the English. The Spaniards requested his body, and buried it at St. Louis. Mr. L. P. C. promises to look into the church records for the mention of it.[37]

April 27[8]th. On board steamer *Radnor.* All our equipments embarked. A number of Kanza[s] or Caw Indians on board. Their gravity seem[s] to me rather *vacant* than *dignified.* When they speak, their gestures are lively and natural.[38]

April 29th. On board the boat are a party of Baltimoreans—flash genteel—very showily attired in "genteel undress," though bound for California. They make a great noise at table, and are waited on by the Negroes with great attention and admiration. Also a vulgar New Yorker, with the moustache and the air of a Frenchman, bound for Santa Fe.

The Mississipi is channelled through a rich alluvial soil, giving away and caving in every moment. The small creeks, swollen by the rain, pour down a torrent of muddy waters, trees, and refuse that sweep under the banks at the rate of four miles an hour.

Entered the Missouri in a dreary rain.

The weather is now clear—the banks are loaded with a luxuriant growth of cottonwood, elm, etc. At one of the landings was a grove of trees six feet through, that would have been a noble ornament for a park. Snags are frequent.

A young man on board from St. Louis, bound for Santa Fe, has one brother on the Atlantic, another on the Pacific, and a third on the Mississipi, while he is going to the [Rio Grande] del Norte. So much for American wandering.

Rocky limestone bluffs, with here and there lofty and noble forests.

The river changes constantly—young forests are springing up— old ones are swept away—an old tree completely enveloped in young grape leaves. Sand-bars and new channels constantly forming.

April 31st. The wretched Caw Indians on board were hired, for a pint of whiskey, to sing. The chief, a mean-looking old fellow, expecting a friend at Jefferson, painted, took his sword, and wrapped his blanket about him. In this attire he went ashore, and saluted his acquaintance—a white man—with great cordiality. One of the others indulged in a little fooling with a fat Negro, who danced while the Indian sang.

Henry Chatillon[39] mentions an Ogillalah [Oglala] chief of great authority, who made nothing of killing his subjects. In a drunken revel he would place his robe in the midst of them, and not one, even then, would dare to disturb it, for fear of the consequence. He was killed, not long ago, by the friends of some of his victims.

May 1st. The Indians are playing cards about the deck. They have a paper for begging, and one of them sat on the deck collecting contributions yesterday.

May 2ⁿᵈ. The landing at Independence[40]—the storehouses—the Santa Fe waggons—the groups of piratical-looking Mexicans, employees of the Santa Fe traders, with their broad, peaked hats—the men with their rifles seated on a log, ready for Oregon. Among the waggons behind, some of the Mexicans were encamped. The Baltimoreans got shamefully drunk, and one of them, an exquisite in full dress, tumbled into the water.

Speyer,[41] the Santa Fe trader, has an immense number of goods on board.

Walked a mile or two into the woods at evening—had felt a little "hipped."[a] The reawakening of old thoughts and feelings, recurring along with the whole train of subsequent observations and experiences, is very agreeable. I felt as I had felt many years before, but I was no longer the same man, either in knowledge or in character.

C. W. of St. Louis, who harnessed his mule into his waggons, and drove off for Santa Fe, bent on seeing. He seemed about eighteen years old, open, enterprising, and thoughtless. He will come back a full-grown man.

Westport, Mo., April [May] 5ᵗʰ. Rode to the village of Westport[42] from the landing, where we put up at the solid log house of Col. Chick.[43] A beautiful morning. Hipped and wavering. The Indians passed us, travelling towards their homes. Mules and horses in abundance.

Rode from Westport to find the Sac [Sauk][44] encampment. They had gone—but we had a sight of the great green ocean of the prairies; for the forest terminates at this place, where also is the boundary of the State of Missouri.

A lofty forest, all fresh and verdant in the spring—then a tract of shrubbery and crab-trees full of fragrant blossoms—and then the great level expanse of prairie. The Kansas Inds., arriving again at their native haunts, stopped and sat in a circle on the grass to have a talk. Shawnees dressed in shirts and handkerchiefs passed us on horseback. Their reserve, together with that of the Del[aware]s and Wyandots, is near here.[45] They are farmers, and demi-civilised. The Dels. have the reputation of being very brave and enterprising, and are called "Grandfather." They are constantly wandering and fight-

[a] Depressed.—Ed.

ing in the direction of the Mts. The Wyandots are considered very intelligent.

The emigrants, encamped at some distance, are choosing officers. W[oodworth] seems to be making a fool of himself. We have joined Chandler's party.[46] Bought an excellent horse, for which I paid too much.[b]

Col. C[hick] is an excellent old man, and his house stands nobly on the bluff above the river. The weather is beautiful—the scenery noble—we are in the very region of enterprise—all promises well.

April [May] 6th. Yesterday rode on Hendrick across the Kanzas River to visit the Wyandots, lately removed from Sandusky. The ground but partially cleared—a trader lives amongst them, who conducted us to a school, kept up by the tribe out of their annuities. They are called "Uncle" by the other nations, and have not the wandering propensities of the Dels. and Shaws., their neighbors.

Bought two mules[c] today at Wes[t]port, and rode over on Pontiac from Kanzas to bring them down. Quin and I each took one, by a haltar twisted round the pommel of the saddle. The thunder had growled incessantly all the afternoon. Just after we set out, a terrific storm began. The lightning was very bright, and followed on the instant by crashing peals of thunder, louder than I ever heard. The woods were half obscured by the torrents of rain, which swelled the brooks so rapidly that passing was difficult in one or two place[s]. We drove on our horses—the mules trotted behind—and we scoured along rapidly, till at last we saw the logs of Col. Chick's house and barn up the side of the hill, and rode to the primitive little stable, completely drenched.

The freshness and fragrance of the crab-tree groves along the edge of the prairie, just before the storm came on, was delightful. I rode Pontiac at a gallop among the paths and openings, exalting in the possession of a fine buffalo horse.

May 7th. Rode by vile roads, through the woods, to Independence. The clouds in this region are afflicted with an incontinence of water

b $60.—1846 Account Book.
c For $75.—1846 Account Book.

—constant alternations of showers and sunshine—everything wet, bright, and fresh. Plenty of small game and gorgeous birds. At Independence, every store is adapted to furnish outfits—the public houses were full of Santa Fe men and emigrants. Mules, horses, and waggons at every corner. Groups of hardy-looking men about the stores, and Santa Fe and emigrant waggons standing in the fields around. While I was at the Noland House,[47] the last arrival of emigrants came down the street with about twenty waggons, having just broken up their camp near Independence and set out for the great rendezvous about 15 miles beyond Westport. What is remarkable, this body,[48] as well as a very large portion of the emigrants, were from the extreme western states—N. England sends but a small proportion, but they are better furnished than the rest. Some of these ox-wagons contained large families of children, peeping from under the covering. One remarkably pretty little girl was seated on horseback, holding a parasol over her head to keep off the rain. All looked well—but what a journey before them! The men were hardy and good-looking. As I passed the waggons, I observed three old men, with their whips in their hands, discussing some point of theology— though this is hardly the disposition of the mass of the emigrants.

I rode to Westport with that singular character, Lieut. Woodworth. He is a great busybody, and ambitious of taking a command among the emigrants. He tells me that great dissentions prevail in their camp—that no organisation had taken place, no regular meetings been held—though this is to be done on Saturday and Sunday, and the column to get under weigh on Monday.

Woodworth parades a revolver in his belt, which he insists is necessary—and it may be a prudent precaution, for this place seems full of desperadoes—all arms are loaded, as I have had occasion to observe. Life is held in little esteem.

This place, Westport, is the extreme frontier, and bears all its characteristics.

As we rode home, we met a man itching for Oregon, but restrained by his wife—at McGee's[49] at Westport, there was a restless fellow who had wandered westwards from N. Y. [New York] in search of work, which he had not found; and now he was for Oregon, working his passage as he could not supply himself with provisions.

Met at McGee's Parks, the chief of the Shawnees, who keeps a store here—a fine-looking man, scarcely distinguishable from a white. He was educated by Cass.[50] He told me the story of the wanderings of the Shawnees, and of their being attacked by the Senecas, whom they at last completely defeated. The Senecas then employed the Wyandots to attack them, as they passed down the Ohio; but the latter, instead of this, made a treaty with them. The Wyandots kept the council fire of the western Inds.

Everybody here is full of praises of the courage of the Delawares. They are by far greater wanderers and hunters than any of the other half-civilised tribes. In small parties they spend years among the most remote and hostile tribes—they will fight with a courage like desperation, and, it is said, completely awed the Spaniards at Santa Fe.

Plenty of vagabond Inds. are about here, trading at the different stores, and getting drunk.

I saw many at the store of Mr. Boone,[51] a grandson of Daniel.

May 9th. After great trouble yesterday with one of our mules, bought of Fogel [Vogel],[52] who played the deuce in the cart, and had to be changed—we got under weigh. Left Westport this morning —the cart stuck several times in the mud, and delayed us much. We passed out through the Shawnee country. Stopped at noon to eat and rest animals by the side of a creek. An old Caw Ind. in full paint came riding up, gave his hand, and sat down to smoke.

Presently the whole tribe passed along on their way to Westport, on miserable little horses. Some were in full costume, but the greater part were ragged vagabonds, with bad or vacant faces, and a very mean appearance. They crowded around, men, women, and children, the first offering their hands as they came up. Many had bows and arrows—all were adorned with wampum or beads, and often a snake skin. In the beautiful country we had passed, Shawnees were constantly riding by on a canter, upon little stubborn ponies, and with their calico shirts fluttering in the wind.

Not far from where we met the Caws, there was a religious meeting of the Shawnees. Most of those present were good-looking—much more robust than the Caws, and well-dressed in the English fashion. The place was the Methodist meeting house.

We traveled a few hours and encamped by the Caw River. The horses, not used to hobbles, were in a great quandary. A vagabond Caw sat sometime by our camp, talking by signs, and expecting some food. This river is the boundary line of the Dels. and Shawnees.

The vexations and deprivations of such a journey do indeed resolve a man into his first elements—and bring out all his nature.

May 10th. Left camp and crossed the Kanzas by the Ferry,[53] after much difficulty. The cart had to be unloaded and so carried up the steep road. Travelled only eight miles and encamped in a beautiful prairie—abundance of flowers—the borders of the beautiful oak-openings we had traversed—the shrubbery along the course of a little stream—the occasional rich and sunlit groves—and the emerald swells of the vast plain, made a beautiful scene.

This was a part of the Delaware country. Many of the tribe have been killed in their incessant wars and wanderings. I hear but one opinion expressed of their extraordinary bravery and enterprise. One of them brought us in some eggs, and lay for some time talking by our camp. He had heard of the Dels. being made women by the Six Nations.

The horses gave great trouble in hobbling.

May 11th. A beautiful day. Travelled slowly through the country of the Delawares. Fine, swelling prairies. Stopped for nooning at a creek in a wooded bottom, turned the horses loose, lunched in the shade, bathed, and conversed. Resumed our course—very hot—lines of beautiful woods ran along the bottoms, intersecting our road, with invariably a stream running through them—a most grateful refreshment in the heat. At one of these places we met a party of Del. Inds. —men, women, and children—returning on their ponies from a trapping expedition. This tribe is constantly diminishing from the numbers that are killed in their wanderings.

Soon after, the white walls of Leavenworth[54] appeared in the distance, and in a level meadow by a wooded stream we saw the horses and tents of our English friends—a welcome sight.

May 12th. Still at camp. Rode to Fort L. and saw Col. Kearn(e)y.[55]
Then, with Q., went over to Kickapoos,[56] four miles. All half-
civ[ilized] Ind. villages in wooded countries are the same thing—
straggling paths through woods and underbrush, with here and there
a log house—a creek winding through the midst. Inds. are most
provoking beings. We addressed one who was lying at full length in
the sun before his house—he would not give the least sign of recognis-
ing our presence. We got from the rest nothing but silence, hesitation,
or false directions. Pottawattamies [Pottowatomies][57] in a neighboring settlement, with their *pukivi*[d] lodges. Some of the scenery—the
rich, sunlit, swelling prairies with bordering hills and groves—was
very beautiful.

Returning, we stopped at the trader's. Plenty of Inds. around with
their little scraggy ponies—he characterises them as ungrateful—the
more they get, the more they expect, and become suspicious in the
extreme. We were hot and tired; and the trader showed us into a
neat, dark, and cool parlor, where he gave us iced claret and an
excellent lunch—a most welcome refreshment. His mistress, a yellow
woman, brimful of merriment, entertained us with her conversation.

Stopped at the Fort—sat down to the Col.'s table with Romain[e][58]
and the Capt.[59]—the last Madeira, the last fruits that we shall enjoy
for a long time. This over, rode to camp with Romain.

May 13th. Broke up camp at the meadow. Travelled several miles,
and took the wrong turning to the road—none of the party had been
on this route before—the ordinary emigrant route is farther south.
Their [the Englishmen's] waggon stuck badly in the mud several
times and had to be unloaded. At last we found ourselves *close by the
Kickapoo trader's*. Struck off on a bye road—wandered over wide
prairies for a long time, and at last struck the trail of two companies
of dragoons who went out yesterday to build a new fort up the
Missouri.[60] This was the right path. Nooned and passed on. Noble,
swelling prairies varied with wooded declivities, groves, and scattered
trees. Riding at the head of the line and looking back, our straggling
line of horsemen and animals stretched over the plain for a mile or
more, and on the horison the white waggons were slowly moving

d Bark.—Ed.

along. We have 23 horses and mules. A severe thunder-storm at camp. The Capt. very solicitous about his horses, moving about morning and night in an old plaid to watch them. Wolves seen at evening on the prairie. The thunder and the wolves, who approached at night, frightened the horses. Pondiac and several others broke their haltars.

*May 14*th. Great trouble at a stream. Waggon stuck. As we were on the [point of] departure after nooning, Pondiac stepped down to drink, and then trotted off on the back trail for the settlements. I followed, impeded by gun and accoutrements. He led me a chace of about 5 miles to the wooded creek where the waggon [had stuck?] —for mile after mile of beautiful prairie, swell after swell, he kept trotting on before me—sometimes I would be close upon him, and then he would start again. Tried to head him but in vain. Nearly caught him at a stream where he stopped to drink—slid from my horse but my rifle bothered me—Hendrick darted back, and I could not catch the trail rope. He stopped again at the creek aforesaid— slid down and got the rope—a joyful moment. Had much trouble in getting the reluctant brutes back to camp, which meanwhile had moved on some miles. At last, saw on the green swell of a hill, beyond a line of woods, the white tents and the band of horses in the meadow below.

*May 15*th. After riding all the morning, we came to what we thought was Clough Creek, the place where the old dragoon trail[61] of last year diverges to the left and leaves the new trail we have followed. No such divergency appeared. The Capt. and I went forwards as "videttes"—waited long for the party by a creek, and saw them coming at last with four dragoons. They told us we had passed the place where we should have diverged a day and a half ago—that our present road led to the Iowa village, and thence to the emigrants' road to St. Joseph's.[62] So we determined to keep on. This morning, fired at a wolf among the horses, and missed.

*Sunday, May 16*th. Advanced as far as a deep creek, where we had great trouble with the waggons. Nooned here—a beautiful spot, where in the woods about the stream was a variety of birds. S[haw] and I set out in advance to find the Iowa village, but without success. Struck the St. Joseph's trail. Followed it for many miles over a vast, swelling prairie with scarcely any trees in sight, where the advanced waggon looked like a mere speck on the green surface. Camped on a spot occupied about a week since by the Mormons,[63] whose cattle had eaten the grass close. Up to this time, our progress has been very slow—about thirty miles in three days. This Mormon trail is much better than the previous ones.

May 17th. Rode for nearly twenty miles before we nooned. The heat was intense. Stripped off all superfluous clothing. Very few camping places; and at these the Mormon cattle had eaten the grass. Rode on—the expanse of prairie stretched for mile after mile without tree or bush—we ascended swell after swell and could see nothing but the vast, green level. At last, turned aside from the road to a clump of trees in the distance. Camped, and Q. and I tried a bath. The water was the same that we have had lately, only worse—quite warm and full of frogs and snakes—no current, but plenty of weeds and mud. We struggled through bushes, reeds, and mud till we came to a nasty pool, rich in mud, insects and reptiles, where we washed as we could. Dor-bugs swarmed in the prairie and camp.

May 18th. This morning all the horses ran off for at least a mile, and gave us great trouble to head them back. Both Pondiac and Hendrick broke their hobbles. Nooned at an old encampment of the Mormons. Prairie without a tree for many miles—a good road, but no place to camp. Travelled about twenty miles, and then our party turned off to a piece of woods some distance from the road. The Englishmen kept on—the devil knows where. Their hunter, Sorel,[64] had kept in advance about a mile, and they followed. Sorel is dissatisfied about something.

May 19th. The Englishmen were encamped about half a mile in advance. We advanced—passed a beautifully wooded stream, which we supposed to be the Little Nemaha[65]—kept on till we had made about ten miles, and nooned. The Englishmen, as usual, were impatient to get on the moment they had snatched a dinner—we chose to remain, as our mules were much tired. So the parties were again separated. Romaine, virtually the leader of the other party, seems jealous of his authority and desirous of having all his own way. Capt. C. and his brother are of a different stamp—very good-natured, sociable fellows.[66] We let them move on and followed at our leisure. Came to camp alongside of them, having made about twenty miles (as we did yesterday).

May 20ᵗʰ. Last night, were awakened by tremendous peals of thunder, quite different from any in our part of the country—beginning with a tremendous burst, they ran reverberating around the whole firmament. The rain that followed was like a cataract, and beat through the tent in a thick drizzle, wetting everything. The lightning was very intense and brilliant. Lay by today until afternoon, when the restlessness of Romaine impelled his party to move. We, against our judgment, consented to follow, not caring to appear obstinate—so broke up camp and moved off. Intensely sultry and oppressive, and when the sun came out it was terribly hot. The sky was hung with clouds, and thunder muttered incessantly. As we rode on, things grew worse, till the whole prairie and the grove grew almost black in the stormy shadow, and the lightning kept flashing vividly. The masses of cloud in front grew blacker and more ragged—the thunder more and more threatening—till both horses and men took alarm, and we all rushed forward in a medley, running or gallopping, and the muleteers lashing and shouting. We wheeled round behind a line of trees—tore off our saddles—hobbled the frightened brutes—seized the tent and thrust the pole into the ground. No sooner was this done than a sharp flash and a crashing peal came upon us, and the rain descended like a torrent.

We do not know our exact position, but we are on the Mormon trail, and probably within ten days of the Platte.

Henry says that at Laramie, a common clay pipe sells for half a dollar—a three-bit calico shirt for four dollars—a pair of the very coarsest pantaloons for ten dollars—a gallon of whiskey for thirty-five dollars, etc.[67]

The trading companies have their head quarters, whence single traders are sent out to winter in the several Indian villages, where they are usually received in the chief's lodge, and treated with great distinction.[68]

May 21st. It kept raining over night, and in the morning the road was in a wretched state. Sultry and showery all the morning. At noon, the road being a little improved, we set out. It still threatened rain. We passed the recent grave of one of the Mormons, who had been buried near the road. The other party were in advance, and discovered a cow, straggled, no doubt, from the Mormons. They gave chace and drove her back on the road, where we headed her, and various awkward attempts were made to noose her. After a while, she was let alone and gently driven along before us by the Captain. This would have done very well, had not a tremendous gust of rain come down suddenly upon us. The horses all turned tail to it, and stood stock still; and the cow ran off, back on the road. A rifle ball was sent after her ineffectually; and the Captain, in defiance of the storm, cocking one of his huge buffalo pistols, galloped off in pursuit, and both soon vanished in the diagonal sheets of rain. Presently he and the cow appeared looming through the storm, the Capt. shouting to us that he had shot her. He rode behind her, driving her along, which was very easy as she was shot through the body. As we approached the woods where we were to encamp, something was seen that looked like a tent, on which the cow was allowed to fall into the rear, for fear of lighting on her owner; but the alarm proving false, she was driven to camp, and at last finished by Romaine, who shot two bullets into the poor devil. We feasted on her at night.

May 22nd. Left camp and found the road very muddy from last night's rain. The road was still over the open prairie, with here and there a little wood about the streams. Our cart got through some of these with difficulty, and the waggon was soon "stalled" and had to be unladen—this happened several times, and the other party were so much detained that only the Capt., who was in advance, came to nooning with us. All this day we had milk from the dead cow's udders—and at this nooning-place, we found *another cow*, which we also milked and drove on with us. Camped by a beautiful stream, unknown, but supposed to be the Little Vermillon,[69] and I enjoyed a most delightful bath in a deep, clear pool, surrounded by beautiful woods, full of birds, and at that time lighted by the setting sun.

Pondiac will scarcely eat, he is so annoyed by his hobbles—the horses around the camp all night after salt, of which we had given them a little. Made eighteen or twenty miles today—cannot tell where we are, as not one of the party has been on the route.

Henry says that there is a great difference in point of *virtue*, between the women of different [tribes]—that many of them are very debauched, while the Sioux (among whom, however, he has a squaw) are comparatively very chaste. He mentions a custom among them of a woman's giving a feast, at which females are invited who, laying their hands on a gun or some similar implement, are required to declare whether or not they have been guilty of any breach of chastity. This solemn form of declaration seems tantamount to an oath. He saw a young Sioux girl cry all night because, as she stepped out, a young man took an indelicate liberty with her person.[70]

I am more and more convinced of the differences between tribes.

May 23rd. Leaving camp this morning, we had gone but a mile or two, Boisverd[71] driving the cow along, when we came to a muddy gully where our cart passed, but the waggon stuck as usual. Then came, as a matter of course, the curses, shouts, and blows of their muleteer Wright;[72] but all in vain, and the waggon had to be unloaded. A mile or two more, and we came to a belt of woods, and the long-looked-for Big Blue.[73] It was so high with the late rains—though subsiding rapidly—that we had to raft across. Romaine, with his usual activity, waded across to ascertain the depth. Plenty of wood grew on the banks, and in an hour or two the raft was made, the Canadians working like dogs in the water and out of it. Romaine was, as usual, noisy and obstrusive, offending the men by assuming the direction of affairs of which he knew nothing.[74] The fellow over-boils with conceit. Got across, after a fatiguing work—dined, and advanced about five miles. Coming to camp by a creek, we saw waggons ascending a distant swell.

Delorier [Deslauriers] was particularly active and talkative at his work—he is a true specimen of Jean Baptiste.[75]

Henry mentions the singular ceremony of the white robe. The possessor of a white buffalo robe gives a feast, at which he gives away all his possessions to his very lodge—his horses, arms, food, and all. This ceremony entitles him to much respect, and he is usually amply remunerated in a few days by those to whom he has given his property.[76]

The *medicines* of the various tribes differ. A red-headed wood-pecker is great medicine with the Sioux—a rattle-snake with the Caws, etc. The Caws I saw wore snake-skins.[77]

The custom prevails among the Sioux of a son-in-law not speaking to his mother-in-law, who never enters his lodge. He veils his face when she passes. A squaw does not mention her husband by name, but as the *father of her child* (naming him). How shall we account for these extraordinary customs?

A widow has her season of mourning, during which she gashes her legs frightfully.[78]

May 24th. We have struck upon the old Oregon Trail, just beyond the Big Blue, about seven days from the Platte. The waggons we saw were part of an emigrant party, under a man named Keatley [Kearsley].[79] They encamped about a mile from us behind a swell in the prairie. The Capt. paid them a visit, and reported that the women were damned ugly. Kearsley and another man came to see us in the morning. We had advanced a few miles when we saw a long line of specks upon the level edge of the prairie; and when we approached, we discerned about twenty waggons, followed by a crowd of cattle. This was the advanced party—the rest were at the Big Blue, where they were delayed by a woman in child-bed. They stopped a few miles farther to breakfast, where we passed them. They were from the western states. Kearsley had complained of want of subordination among his party, who were not very amenable to discipline or the regulations they themselves had made. Romaine stayed behind to get his horse shod, and witnessed a grand break-up among them. The Capt. [of the train] threw up his authority, such was the hurly-burly—women crying—men disputing—some for delay—some for hurry—some afraid of the Inds. Four waggons joined us—Romaine urged them, and thereby offended us. Kearsley is of the party.

Advanced twenty-five miles to Turkey Creek. Several more waggons are just now in sight.

The great Sioux chief Bull Bear,[80] whom H. described as possessed of such authority and power, and commanding such dread in the village, was unable to restrain his party from attacking Frapp [Fraeb].[81] Comp[are] this with what Fitzpatrick says of the discipline of war-parties.

May 25th. One advantage arises from the emigrants—they give us milk. Put Hendrick into the cart. Soon came to an infernal gully— mud four or five feet deep—waggon stuck—oxen of the emigrants drew it out, though the mud came to bottom of waggon. Hendrick would not pull—oxen put to cart, and drew it out. Pondiac and Hendrick both came down floundering in attempting to cross. Emigrants' waggons themselves had great difficulty. Passed on to Elm Creek—a deep, rocky stream. Axle of waggon broke short in crossing, and we stayed for a new one to be put on. Proceeded after this delay—emigrants ahead. Overtaken by a thunderstorm and well drenched. Put up the tent in the mud, and the fury of the wind nearly threw it down. Cleared up beautifully towards evening.

The four emigrant waggons are farther on.

May 26th. Nooned on Black Walnut Creek. Put Pond. in harness. Afternoon, not well—sat slouching on horse, indulging an epicurian reverie—intensely hot—dreamed of a cool mountain spring, in a *forest* country—two bottles of Champagne cooling in it, and cut-glass tumblers, full of the sparkling liquor.[82] A wide expanse of perfectly flat prairie—rode over it hour after hour—saw wolves—and where they had dug up a recent grave. Turkey buzzards and frequent carcases of cattle; camped on Wyatt's Creek. Twenty miles or so.

May 27th. Are doubtful where we are. Set out from camp, and travelled eight or ten miles. Henry went forward with S.'s gun to shoot a prairie hen—came gallopping back to say that he had seen antelope and borrow my rifle. His hasty approach made some of the party think the Pawnees were on us. He could not kill any, but found some curlew eggs. Nooned on a nameless creek and set out again— bad rain, like last night—evening cleared up beautifully—we suppose ourselves on the Little Blue. Mules suffer much.

Among the Sioux, a species of penance, or act to secure the favor of the manito[u], is to fasten a buffalo's skull to a hole through the sinews of the back, and to run until it tears out—or rots away (comp. Mandans).[83]

May 28th. Wolves all night. Camped on Little Blue. Saw wolves and two antelopes in the morning. Grave of a child 4 yrs. old—May 1845.[84]
Henry hunted in vain for antelopes. Nooned on Little Blue. Made a very long afternoon march—hour after hour over a perfect level— not very well. Sorel wounded an antelope. After twelve miles riding, approached Little Blue again. Immense masses of blue, lurid clouds in the west shadowed the green prairie, and the sun glared through purple and crimson. As we drew near the valley of the stream, a furious wind, presaging a storm, struck us. We galloped down in the face of it—horses snorting with fear. Rode to the ground—up went the tent and on came the storm.

May 29th. Left camp—saw plenty of antelopes and fired at one across the river. Kept along the Little Blue, and just before nooning had great trouble in crossing a tributary creek [Pawnee Creek?]. As we (we) were dining, Henry brought in a fine antelope—a very welcome acquisition as our bacon is almost gone. Afternoon— more antelope and turkeys. Scenery very beautiful and prairie- like. The Capt. very merry, riding off in all directions and run- ning a wolf over the prairie. Bones of game scattered in all directions, indicating a surround.[85] Moved rapidly and merrily —camped on a beautiful plain, hard by the woods that fringe the Little Blue. Flowers—prairie peas—*pommes blanches*.[86]
Mounted guard for the first time last night—three hours. Middle

watch to me and Delorier tonight. Delorier is a true Canadian—all his acts and thoughts are subject to the will of his *bourgeois* [boss].

Met yesterday in a rough meadow by the Little Blue two Delaware Inds. returning from a hunt—one of them a remarkably handsome fellow.

May 30th. Made a very hard day's work—came more than thirty miles from the Blue to the Platte. We had all along mistaken our route, thinking that we were less advanced than in fact we were. Soon after leaving the Blue, saw two men, Turner and another, come back from the emigrants[87] in search of an ox. They set us right, telling us we were 26 miles from the river. Just before seeing us, they had met six Pawnees, who wanted to change horses, and laid hand on the bridle of one of them, till threatened with a pistol—the only weapon they had. They told this to Sorel, and then foolishly continued their journey. Nooned early at a bad creek. Antelopes. A level plain—the low, blue line of the Platte Buttes in the distance. Badger holes. Towards sunset, drew near the Buttes—a range of low, broken, sandy hills—and after a long and gradual ascent, saw the Platte from the summit—apparently one vast, level plain, fringed with a distant line of forest—the river ran invisible in sluices through the plain, with here and there a patch of woods like an island. Camped late—an emigrant came to us, on his way to look for Turner—he told us that Robinson's party were encamped three miles off—that the four waggons that had joined us, and got ahead a few days ago, were in advance—and that a large hunting-party of Pawnees were encamped close to them.

This afternoon, passed a very large Pawnee trail, and a small foot-trail recently travelled.

May 31st. Early this morning, the Pawnees, about 30 in number, passed a short distance from our camp—a hunting-party—no women, these being probably planting corn at the village. Rather mean-looking fellows, each with a bow and arrows—led horses, loaded with dry meat. The chief walked behind—I gave him a piece of tobacco, which very much pleased him.

When three or four miles from camp, overtook the emigrants—

Robinson's party of about 40 waggons—who had just set out. Turner had got in safe. One fellow had inscribed his waggon "54°48′"[88]—a mean set, chiefly from the east. A very cold, raw, disagreeable day, with a violent freezing wind, which benumbed us—rain soon followed, which wet us through. Keathley [Kearsley], with the 4 waggons that had joined us, was ahead about a mile. Disorder in both these parties.

Went twelve miles and camped—miserably cold and dismal—wet through, with no means of getting dry—a set, cold rain. Wrapped ourselves up as we could and went to sleep in the tent, while the emigrants kept on.

The Pawnees say that buffalo are two days ahead.

June 1. The emigrants were encamped a mile ahead of us. Started early and passed them. Weather clear, but astonishingly cold and bitter. Road through the flat bottom of the Platte, with the low line of sand buttes just visible on right and left. Keathly's four waggons which had joined us, and left us when the axle broke, were ahead—soon came up to them. At nooning, the weather changed—the sky was filled with dark windy clouds, and sharp, cold gusts of rain kept coming on. We started, however, again passing Keathly, who had kept on, and travelling always in the face of an infernal bitter driving mixture of icy wind and sleet. Once it came so furiously, driving in horizontal lines, that all the animals turned tail to it and could not be moved—cart, waggon and all turned about. With Pontiac in the cart, we came 25 miles, and camped near Plum Creek.

There are plenty of emigrants ahead. Among the different bands that we have passed, there is considerable hostility and jealousy, on account of camping places, etc.

June 2nd. Soon after leaving camp, saw in the prairie a little mound of earth with a buffalo skull on top, and two horse skulls with other bones at the sides. Henry thought that it was a place where the Pawnees had buried a favorite horse. Passed a large village of prairie dogs. The 4 emigrant waggons keep along with us. Many antelopes—three of them killed. Buffalo wallows, and fresh traces of the animals. A broad, level bottom, with lines of low buttes on each

side. Nooned early, and set out again very soon, much to *our* dissatisfaction. Q.'s wilfulness is roused, and he wishes to push on alone
to Laramie. Travelled long over the level bottom—no wood—nothing but musquitoes, mud, buffalo-wallows, and their dung. Camped
on this flat. The weather is become warm.

June 3rd. Cold and gusty again. Travelled slowly for 10 miles over a
most monotonous plain. After nooning, Henry went off to look for
buffalo. I gave him Pont. to ride, and accompanied him on Hendrick. Passing towards the hills, we saw on the intervening flat plenty
of wolves and antelopes, and at last H. discerned a black speck
slowly ascending one of the distant hills. It was a buffalo cow, and
we set of [f] at a gallop after her—the wind blew directly towards her,
but as we entered the hills, we saw several buffalo in a distant ravine,
who scented us and began to ascend the hills in Indian file, appearing
and disappearing in the gorges. Presently more and more appeared,
but all, getting wind of us, got in motion. Henry's blood was up.
We spurred along through ravines, and getting to leeward, managed
to approach one little herd of cows. I held the horses—Henry crept
over the hill and fired. I saw the buffalo come running down the
hollow, and soon perceived that we had shot one. Skinned and cut
her up, and then saw another herd, at which Henry again fired and
brought down another cow. By the time we had finished dissecting
her, a devil of a cold, penetrating, driving storm of sleet came upon
us, and as, with the meat at our saddles, we rode from the hills and
over the prairie to find the camp, we were well drenched. An infernal
storm—temperature about 32°. Rode through a village of prairie
dogs, and envied the little varmints their snug habitations. At camp,
learned that Sorel and others had been unsuccessfully chasing them.

June 4th. This morning rode off towards the hills with Q. and the
Capt. to look for buffalo—no success. Returning, met Henry on his
little poney Wyandot; he came to say that 11 boats were coming
down the river from Laramie. Gave my letter to Q. to be delivered,
and rode back two or three miles after the waggons to get a letter H.
had given me, intended for Papin,[89] the *bourgeois* of the boats. On
my return, found the boats lashed to the bank waiting—flat-bottomed

—with 110 packs each—one month from Laramie—aground every day, for the Platte is now low, and is very shallow and swift at best. The crews were a wild-looking set—the oarsmen were Spaniards [Mexicans]—with them were traders, F[rench] and American, some attired in buckskin, fancifully slashed and garnished, and with hair glued up in Ind. fashion. Papin a rough-looking fellow, reclining on the leather covering that was thrown over the packs.

I saw Woodworth here—his party are close behind.

Papin reports that the Mormons are a few miles ahead—that the Pawnees have taken 10 of their horses, and whipped one of their men into camp—that the Sioux have been out in force, and driven off the buffalo—all this alarms the Capt. exceedingly.

In the afternoon, made 10 miles or so and encamped on a beautiful spot. Hills not unlike those of Sicily.[90]

Henry says that (that) the Pawnees are much more subordinate to their chiefs than the Sioux—that a chief of the former can with impunity whip one of the young men, but that if a Sioux chief does it, he is sure to have some of his horses killed. The Crows are under better regulation than the Sioux. Observe how this is in the Sioux village, and comp. with Murray's acct. of Pawnees.[91]

June 5th. Shaw and Henry went off for buffalo. H. killed two bulls. The Capt. very nervous and old-womanish at nooning—he did not like the looks of the hills, which were at least half a mile off—there might be Inds. there, ready to pounce on the horses. In the afternoon, rode among the hills—plenty of antelope—lay on the barren ridge of one of them, and contrasted my present situation with my situation in the convent at Rome.[92]

June 6th. Emigrants' cattle all driven off by the wolves for many miles—their guard having fallen asleep. This detained us; and Q. and I, with Henry, went off to run buffalo. Rode 6 miles—saw a herd of bulls and several of cows—set after the former full-drive. Could not bring Pont. close up—wounded, but killed none. Q. shot one. Got separated from the others—rode for hours westwardly over the prairie—saw the hills dotted with thousands of buffalo. Antelopes

—prairie-dogs—burrowing owls—wild geese—wolves, etc. Finding my course wrong, followed a buffalo-track northward, and about noon came out on the road. Awkward feeling, being lost on the prairie. Waggons not yet come—rode east eight miles and met them. At the same time saw H. and Q. coming down from the hills. They had been looking for me 3 hours. Camp near Side Fork.[93] Only *bois de vache*.[e] Very much fatigued, having ridden some forty miles.

June 7th. Nothing special occurred. Walked all day along South Fork—no wood in sight—all prairie, and distant hills. The lagging pace of the emigrants—the folly of Romaine—and the old womanism of the Capt. combine to disgust us. We are resolved to push on alone, as soon as we have crossed the South Fork, which will probably be tomorrow. Saw rattlesnakes and other curious snakes.

June 8th. Sorel, Romaine, and two of the emigrants went off yesterday morning for buffalo, and did not return at night. At nooning yesterday, four men came to us from the Mormon (?) party ahead, saying that, a few days since, ten of their horses had been run off in broad daylight by several hundred Indians, at whom they had fired, and that lately they had lost a hundred and twenty-three cattle, of which they were then in search. Some of our emigrants also thought they had seen Indians when after their cattle—so that there was some anxiety as to the four men. The Capt. declares, "It is a serious business, travelling through this cursed wilderness." This morning, we set out to cross the South Fork, intending to wait there for them.

Approaching the ford,[f] we saw the party of emigrants encamped opposite—they have not cattle enough to carry them on, and are in great trouble. Nooned and made the fording—a picturesque scene— river half a mile wide and no where more than three feet deep— swift and sandy—had some little trouble. On the farther bank were collected a crowd of the emigrants—rather mean-looking fellows, much less respectable than those with us. Romaine and the rest

---

[e] "*Bois de vache*" or "buffalo chips", sun-dried buffalo dung, was the standard fuel on the treeless prairies.—Ed.

[f] Lower California Crossing, near Brulé, Neb.—Ed.

came in just before, having followed the buffalo too far, and camped. The Capt.'s eternal motto: "Anything for a quiet life."

June 9th. Nothing worth note. Advanced about 16 miles. Tomorrow we shall push on alone.

June 10th. The Capt. last night sat with a group of the emigrants, telling his peculiarly elegant stories, to the great edification of the audience. Bade adieu this morning to him and the rest. He considers our leaving "an extraordinary proceeding"—and seems to look on us as deserting them in a dangerous crisis. They seem to have thought that we were obliged to remain with them for protection. They say their party ought to be *larger*. Wright, the muleteer, plainly hopes in his heart that our horses may be stolen. Travelled fast—passed round the head of Ash Hollow[94] and the other ravines—nooned by a mud puddle—and in the afternoon descended from the sand hills by an abominable sandy trail to the North Fork [of the Platte]. Road here not much better—sand—sand—sand; recent marks of a large party on the road. Travelled late—Quin hurt by a kick from Hendrick—came up with the emigrants camped in a circle—fires, tents, and waggons outside—horses within. The bottom covered with their cattle. They visited us at camp—a very good set of men, chiefly Missourians. Extinguished fire, and went to sleep.

June 11th. Set out early, and dragged some ten miles through an abominable sandy trail along the Platte. Scenery monotonous to the last degree. Very hot—the sand flies outrageous. Nooned on a pleasant spot and lay sleeping some three or four hours, when Henry awakened us with the announcement that people were coming. They were the van of the emigrants—first came a girl and a young man, on horseback, the former holding a parasol—then appeared the line of waggons, coming over the sand hills. We saddled in a trice, pushed ahead, and kept on. The girl and her beau apparently found something very agreeable in each other's company, for they kept more than a mile in advance of their party, which H. considered very imprudent, as the Sioux might be about. Distanced them, and camped by a *clear, swift stream*. Nothing but *bois de vache* ("prairie chips") for several days.

June 12ᵗʰ. Rode to Lawrence Fork[95] and nooned. Passing on, saw in the distance a half-subterranean house which Frédéric[96] had made to winter in, in charge of some furs to be sent down in the spring. What a devil of a solitary time! Chimney Rock[97] in sight. Henry entertained us with accts. of his adventures at one of the *blows-out* given by the bourgeois at the Yellow Stone, when the traders come in the spring. It was very characteristic. This is the custom at all the forts.[98] Overtook a company of emigrants, Americans and foreigners, encamped with whom were five men from Laramie,[99] going down. Crept into one of the waggons—wrote letters—and gave them to these people. Then advanced to Roubideau's [Robidoux's] party,[100] camped a mile or two in advance. Camped by them.

A Sioux received a present from another, who expected to get his favorite mule in return. The Sioux gave it accordingly, which so aggrieved the squaw who had been accustomed to ride it (the previous present being a dress for another of his squaws) that the two women fell fighting. The Sioux flogged them both; but being unable to separate them, and exceedingly exasperated at losing the mule, he grew so furious that he went out and vented his passion by killing seven of his horses. What a bump of destructiveness! This is the sort of passion that often drives an Ind. to his exploits of desperate courage.

H. says that the Crows are not jealous like the Sioux—that among the latter, the owner of a good horse often has him killed by some envious neighbor, which is not the case among the Crows.

The Oregon men returning to the settlements—the vulgar-looking fellow in the white shirt and broad-cloth pants, who gave us the acct. of the Oregon settlements and govnt. [government].[101] His companions around their campfire. What a character of independence and self-reliance such a life gives a man!

June 13ᵗʰ. Roubideau left the emigrants and joined us. Travelled 8 miles & nooned on Platte—then came 15 or 16 farther and camped by the spring at Scott['s] Bluff.[102] All these bluffs are singular and fantastic formations—abrupt, scored with wooded ravines, and wrought by storms into the semblance of lines of buildings. Midway on one of them gushes the spring, in the midst of wild roses, currants, cherries, and a hundred trees; and cuts for itself a devious and wooded ravine across the smooth plain below. Stood among the fresh wild roses and recalled old and delightful associations.

Henry tells a story of an attempt to murder the men at the Blackfoot fort, eight years ago, by the Gros Ventres for the sake of liquor—betrayed by a squaw.

Sometimes among the Sioux a peculiar cap is placed by a medicine man on the head of a chief or warrior in a war party, thus binding him either to be killed or to make a *coup*.[103]

A war party turned back because they saw the spirits of the dead casting rocks at them.

A feast is often given to a dead chief—the pipe is offered him, and food buried for his use.

Some Inds. give themselves out to be invulnerable.

Roubideau says that the Navaho(e)s near Santa Fe make glazed pottery and beautiful ponchos.

The Apaches,[104] in the White Mts., steal the cattle, dresses, women, etc., of the Spaniards, and defy them in the midst of their towns. The latter hired an American[105] to protect them, who raised a band of Dels., Shaws., and Americans, and chastised them.

June 14th. A fellow who had been back to look for stray cattle, remained and camped with us—a true specimen of the raw, noisy, western way. "Hullo, boys, where do you water your horses?"—this was his style of address. We put up no tent—after dark, it suddenly rained—we set up the tent in pitch darkness, and huddled into it as we could.

In the morning, H. and I rode on in advance. H. saw an Ind. village in motion over a distant bluff. Soon an Ind. came gallopping up. It proved to be Smoke's village.[106] Some of them soon joined us, and rode or walked along with us. Passed two [parties of] emigrants, who in the night had camped just in advance of us—chiefly from Missouri, and many of them singularly rude and intrusive. Forded Horse Creek[107]—found the Inds.—twenty lodges—ready to camp. Old Smoke on the bank, with his white horse, his pack horse with

Saint Louis, 25 April 1846

To any person or persons in
our employ in the Indian Country, —

This will be presented by
our friends Mr. F. Parkman and Mr. Quincy A. Shaw, who
visit the interior of the country for their pleasure & amusement,
and whom we beg to recommend to your kind & friendly attention —

If these Gentlemen shall be in need of anything in the
way of supplies &c. you will oblige us by furnishing them to
the extent of their wants, as also to render them any & every
aid in your power, of which they may stand in need

Very truly yours &c

P. Chouteau Jur & Co,
Jno C Clapp

Signature of Mr F. Parkman — F. Parkman
    do   Quincy A. Shaw — Quincy A. Shaw

Oregon Trail Passport
Issued by John Clapp of Pierre Chouteau, Jr. & Company, St. Louis, to Parkman and Shaw
(Parkman Papers, Massachusetts Historical Society)

the lodge poles, and his finely caparisoned mule. Nooned here, and feasted the Inds. on sweetened tea, buffalo meat, and biscuit—then passed the pipe. Emigrants passed on to get rid of Inds. Camped ten miles further on.

The camp was a picturesque scene. The squaws put up temporary sun shades, and scattered their packs and utensils about—the boys splashed in the river—the horses were picketed around. The shield and three poles hung up for each lodge—medicine—Smoke's was pure white. One old fat man[108] rode along with us, professing great friendship for the whites, and boasting what he would do against the Crows, a party of whom are out.

June 15th. Camped on a very pretty bottom on the Platte. Rode over the sand as far as a little, unfinished log fort, in the midst of a steril[e] prairie, built by Sapi [Sarpy][109]—log houses in form of a square, facing inwards—two Sioux lodges in the open area—*corale* behind, and plenty of shaggy little ponies feeding on the bottom. The *bourgeois* Richard received us politely, and ushered us into a log room, with a rock fireplace, and hung with rifles and their equipments, *fanfaron* bridles, garnished buckskin dresses, smoking apparatus, bows & quivers, etc. The men lounging around on robes— passed the pipe—an Ind. seated in the corner—Reynard [Reynal?][g] filling the pipe in the chimney corner—a voyageur, with hair glued in Ind. fashion, lounging on a bedstead.

Nooned by the Platte, having invited our entertainers to a cup of coffee. Previously we arranged our toilets, washing in the mud of the Platte, which, from its late rising, was perfectly opaque. Gave our feast under a cotton wood tree, and rode towards the fort. Laramie Mt. [Peak], Sybil [Sabille] & Adams's deserted fort,[110] and finally Laramie[111] appeared, as the prospect opened among the hills. Rode past the fort, reconnoitred from the walls, and passing the highest ford of L[aramie] Fork [River], were received at the gate by Boudeau [Bordeaux],[112] the *bourgeois*. Leading our horses into the area, we found Inds.—men, women, and children—standing around, voyageurs and trappers—the surrounding apartments occupied by the squaws and children of the traders. Fort divided into two areas—

[g] See below.—Ed.

one used as a *corale*—two bastions or *clay* [*adobe*] *blockhouses*—another blockhouse over main entrance. They gave us a large apartment, where we spread our blankets on the floor. From a sort of balcony we saw our horses and carts brought in, and witnessed a picturesque frontier scene. Conversed and smoked in the windy porch. Horses made a great row in the *corale*. At night the Inds. set up their songs. At the burial place are several Inds. laid on scaffolds, and a circle of buffalo skulls below. Vaskis [Vasquez], Cimoneau, Mont[h]alon, Knight,[113] and other traders and hunters are here.

Roubideau says that twenty Iroquois warriors, from Canada, were not many years since on the Upper Missouri, and were braver and more enterprising than any other of the Inds.[114]

Volume II

[The front end papers of the second notebook contain these jottings:

"Jack and the Captain (!)."

"An Indian's character is more rigid and inflexible than that of other savages. A Polynesian will become a good sailor, a good servant, or a good farmer. An Ind. is fit for nothing but his own mode of life. Neither has a Polynesian the same dark, sinistre, and uncertain character. Once received into his village and you are safe."—Ed.]

Fort Laramie, June 16th. Prices are most extortionate. Sugar, two dollars a cup—5-cent tobacco at $1.50—bullets at $.75 a pound, etc. American Fur Cmp'y. exceedingly disliked in this country—it suppresses all opposition, and keeping up these enormous prices, pays its men in necessaries on these terms.[115]

The fort has a double gate at the main entrance under the blockhouse. When there was danger from the Inds. the inner gate was closed; the Inds., admitted to the space between, traded through an open window or orifice, opening from a large room now used as the blacksmith's shop.

Lodged in Papin's room and visited now and then by Inds., the fathers or brothers of the whitemen's squaws,[116] who are lodged in the fort, and furnished with meat at the company's expense.

This morning, Smoke's village appeared on the opposite bank, and crossed on their wild, thin, little horses. Men and boys, naked and dashing eagerly through the water—horses with lodge poles dragging through squaws and children, and sometimes a litter of puppies— gaily attired squaws, leading the horses of their lords—dogs with their burdens attached swimming among the horses and mules— dogs barking, horses breaking loose, children laughing and shouting —squaws thrusting into the ground the lance and shield of the master of the lodge—naked and splendidly formed men passing and repassing through the swift water.

They held a kind of council in the fort. Smoke presided, but he had another man to speak for him, and ask for presents, and when these were placed on the floor before him, they were distributed under his eye, by one of the "soldiers."[117] Several of the warriors had their faces blackened, in token of having killed Pawnees, or at least of having been on the war-party when they were killed.

Some who visited us kept looking, with great curiousity, at the circus pictures that Finch[118] has nailed up in the room.

At their camp in the even'g, the girls and children, with a couple of young men, amused themselves with a dance, where there was as much merriment and fooling as could be desired.

The emigrants' party passed the upper ford, and a troop of women came into the fort, invading our room without scruple or reserve. Yankee curiosity and questioning is nothing to those of these people.

A Sioux of mean family can seldom become a chief—a chief generally arises out of large families, where the number of relatives who can back him in a quarrel and support him by their influence, gives him weight and authority.

June 17th. Emigrants asking questions and peering all about the Fort. Q. went to one of them and asked him to sell lead—the fellow pondered with fixed eyes and compressed lips for awhile—haggled for quarter of an hour—decided to let it go at .16 a lb.—went off to get it, and did not return.

A man came up to me and said that he had 30 lbs. of lead, which he did not want and meant to throw away if he could not sell. Offered him .10 a lb. which he at once took up, and set off for his lead. He did not return, and when I found him sitting on the pole of his waggon, and asked him where his lead was, he said he had con-cluded he could not spare it. Such is the indecision of these people, and their fear of being overreached.

Most of them are from Missouri—coming in companies from the different counties. The bad climate seems to have been the motive that has induced many of them to set out.

They gave a feast to the Inds. this evening. They were seated in a ring, Smoke and his chief men at the head, then the young men, the old squaws, the young squaws, the children, each in their place— two or three dandies stood around outside, too bashful, perhaps, to set in the circle, The feast was distributed by the "soldiers." Pre-viously the women had danced in a circle, singing a song in which the exploits of the Sioux over the Pawness were boasted of.

An old Brulé came to visit H. He was miserably dressed, for the Crows had lately killed his son, and in his mourning he had given away all his possessions.

The Capt. and his party have just arrived.

June 18ᵗʰ. Gave a small present to the old Brulé—this morning, he comes to ask for more. Another Ind., who was present when we gave it, was very jealous, and soon came to say that his flag was torn, and he wanted some thread to mend it.

The old Brulé had with him some rude pictures of horses, as medicine to catch wild horses.

The Sioux women are more virtuous than the Crows, etc. A girl of respectable family can only be had on condition of taking her as a squaw—there are plenty of prostitutes, who are despised.

They are strangely jealous and indignant—their appetite for presents is insatiable—the more that is given to them, the more they expect.

Smoke's lodge, and his squaw and daughter with sore eyes. The lodge of Jack Hill's[119] father-in-law, and his dandy son.

Old Lalamie[120] had two mules, and his son wanted a horse of the Englishmen. The old man did not wish to part with the mules, but finally consented to, for fear his son would kill them out of spite.

Dandies, in full dress, are lounging about in all directions. Nothing is so striking as the indolence and inaction of the Indians. They merely vegetate.

June 19ᵗʰ. The begging dance—monotonous enough—in the area of the fort. Led by three dandies, the young squaws moved round singing in a circle. Mont[h]alon brought out the presents and placed them in the middle—and here the characteristic self-restraint of the Inds. was apparent. The squaws did not rush forwards to look, but stood quite quietly, and looked on with apparent indifference and without showing any jealousy while one of the young men distributed them.

Bordeaux laughs very much at the suspicion and distrust of the emigrants, who are constantly asking questions, and then refusing to credit the answers.

Gifts pass here as freely as the winds. Visit a trader, and his last cup of coffee and sugar, his last pound of flour, are brought out for your entertainment; and if you admire anything that he has, he gives it to you. Little thanks expected or given on either side.

June 20ᵗʰ. Old Smoke had a fat puppy killed and put into the kettle for us this morning. It was excellent. H. sent a messenger for his squaw's lodge to join us, and crossing Laramie, we set out to encamp at the mouth of Chugwater. Swapped Pondiac for Paul Dorion's[121] little mare.

Our party consisted of ourselves and followers, with an additional hand named Raymond[122]; Raynale [Reynal],[123] the trader at the village we mean to visit; his squaw; and her two nephews, brothers of the messenger H. had sent. We made rather a wild-looking band. Raynale's squaw's property fastened by the lodgepole arrangement[124] to a mule—herself riding a handsomely caparisoned mule, and her

Ind. nephews galloping about on their horses, in full equipment of bows and arrows, etc.

Travelled seven miles and came upon some wild and beautiful bottoms of the Laramie, where we encamped. Abundance of strange flowers and minerals.

June 21ˢᵗ. Rode to Chugwater, about 10 miles, country arid and desolate, broken with precipitous buttes—Black Hills[125] in the distance—wild sage, absanth,[126] wild tanzy, and a variety of strange plants. Here and there the pickets of a deserted wintering-house. One of the restless Indians ran a large wolf into the river. Camped by its wooded banks, near a prairie-dog village.

Raynale speaks of the legendary tales of the Sioux—of their mystic associations, in one of which there are tricks played with fire.[127]

That species of desperation in which an Ind. upon whom fortune frowns resolves to throw away his body, rushing desperately upon any danger that offers. If he comes off successful, he gains great honor.[128]

To show his bravery, an Ind. rushed up to a grizzly bear and struck him three times on the head with his bow.[h] Such acts are common.

The terrible penance to gain success in war, etc.—remaining for days, starving, with buffalo skulls fastened to cords run through the sinews of the back.[129] The animal that is dreamed of when in this state is the guardian spirit.

The initiatory fast prevails among the Sioux.[130]

One wishing to be a chief feasts the nation and gives away all he has in presents. The *war bonnet* is put on him, by which he is doomed to *count a coup* or be killed.[131] This is the test of his fitness for the office.

Raynale says as follows: The Sioux are subdivided into several bands—each band has one or more head men who direct it; for instance the Ogalallahs [Oglalas] have the Man Afraid of his Horses, the Yellow Thunder, the Panther Runner, the Whirlwind, etc., as

[h] "Counted coup."—Ed.

headmen—their influence is great, both in war and peace, and was gained by descent and personal merit.

On the great war exped[ition] now preparing against the Crows, they are directors. Messengers were sent from one band, determined on war, to another, with tobacco and scarlet cloth—stating the design and the time and place of rendezvous. A council was called by the chief to whom the messenger came, who stated the intention of it, and when it was approved a similar message was sent back to express concurrence. Thus the general agreement was made to meet at La Bonté's Camp.[132]

There will be no great head chief of the exped. Each band acts under its own headman, and the result will be division. The Whirlwind was prime mover of the thing, to avenge the death of his son killed by the Snakes, whose scalp we saw at the fort[133] with tobacco attached to signify a wish of peace. Will not the Whirlwind and his band leave the rest to make war on the Snakes?

The most efficient executive functionaries of the Inds. are the "soldiers." They are appointed in a council, called, probably by one of the chiefs for the purpose—an old man rises and mentions some young one brave and meritorious enough for the office, who is called out and invested with it. They are very necessary—the[y] direct the place to encamp—they direct the movements of a "surround" and prevent the buffalo from being frightened by vagrant hunters. In old Bull Bear's day these things were all well regulated, but now all is loose among the Ogalallahs.

Bull Bear, a wise as well as brave chief, used to call together his young men when he had any design in view, and ask if they thought it a good plan. No one ever dissented. Like all the chiefs, he was very profuse in presents.

On a surround, those who first come up to the game take what they choose of the meat—all are entitled to a share, whether hunters or not. This is all that prevents many from starving. So much for generosity and public spirit.

During the war ceremonies a ring is formed, and the old men call out those young warriors whom they think most deserving for their bravery. This public acknowledgment is considered a great honor.

On a large tree near our camp, the bark is cut off for the space of a foot square, and marked with 14 pipes and 14 straight marks, to indicate that a band of Crows had come down and struck *coups*.

June 23rd. Still at the camp at mouth of Chugwater. One of the two young Inds., His Horses,[134] is sent to find Henry's squaw's lodge and bring news of the movements of the Inds. Some danger from war-parties of Crows. Q. and I rode to the beautiful bottoms of Laramie not far up. Arid prairie around. Prickly pear, and another cactus, with a beautiful red blossom.

Reverence for age. A boy veils his face before an old man. The "dandies" at the fort were ashamed to sit and smoke with their elders—and at the feast, several stood outside the ring, apparently unwilling to sit down.

Bull Bear's son aspires to emulate his father's power. His chance is good, for besides his bravery and resolute character, he has more than 30 brothers. Henry, his brother-in-law, is told that he need fear nothing, for nobody will dare to touch him, since he has so many relations growing up around him. Family connexions are evidently a great source of power.

Bull Bear's connexions were numerous and powerful. Smoke and he once quarrelled. Bull Bear ran for his gun and bow, and Smoke withdrew to his lodge. Bull Bear challenged him to come out, but Smoke, fearing the vengeance of his enemy's relatives in case he should kill him, remained quiet, on which Bull Bear shot three of his horses.

This quarrel was brought to an end by Smoke's procuring Bull Bear's death, since which there has been a constant feud between the relatives of each, patched up last year by the traders, but still rankling.

One of Henry's brothers-in-law nearly fell a victim—four of Smoke's nephews entered the room where he was, *standing before them with his face covered*. H. protected him.

June 25th. Yesterday and today still at camp. Two antelopes killed. Rode to the fort this morning—saw a band of 200 elk—found Smoke's village gone over the Platte, where many hundred lodges are. Plenty of Ill. and Michigan emigrants. Returning, found His Horses with a young son of Bull Bear—they say that Tunica's[135] village is four days distant, and that the lodge of Henry's squaw will be here day after tomorrow.

June 26. Not to lay idle at camp, rode again to the Fort. Bought flour, bacon, etc., of the Company. Emigrants crossing the river, and thronging into the fort—a part of Russel[l]'s comp'y,[136] which becoming dissatisfied with their pragmatic, stump-orator leader, has split into half a dozen pieces. Passed along the line of waggons, conversing with the women, etc. These people are very ignorant, and suspicious for this reason—no wonder—they are grossly imposed on at the store.

A few lodges at the fort—Old Lamalamie's among them. He offered me his niece for a horse. Paul [Dorion] is here. The Miniconques[137] are a day or two below. Tunica came in with one of his head men, and confirms the accts. brought by His Horses. The great mass of the Inds. are hunting across the Platte.

The emigrants had a ball in the fort—in this room—the other night. Such belles! One woman, of more than suspected chastity, is left at the Fort; and Bordeaux is fool enough to receive her.

May[138]—his nervous fiery temper, and his acct. of the French in the country.

*June 28*th. Yesterday rode down with Paul Dorion, who wished to swap a wild horse, to Richard's fort. Found there Russel's or Boggs' comp'y, engaged in drinking and refitting, and a host of Canadians besides. Russel drunk as a pigeon—some fine-looking Kentucky men —some of D[aniel] Boone's grandchildren—Ewing, Jacob(s), and others with them—altogether more educated men than any I have seen. A motley crew assembled in Richard's rooms—squaws, children, Spaniards, French, and emigrants. Emigrants mean to sell liquor to the Miniconques, who will be up here tomorrow, and after having come all the way from the Missouri to go to the war, will no doubt break up if this is done. Paul very much displeased, as well as the Canadians.[139]

Returning to the Fort, met a party going to the settlements[140]—

to whom Montalon *had not given my letters*. Sent them by that good fellow Tucker.[141] People at the fort a set of mean swindlers, as witness my purchase of the bacon, and their treatment of the emigrants.

News of two traders killed by Arapaho(e)s—one just going up told me, remarking that he was bound to meet the same fate.[142]

Started late in the afternoon—lost my way—wounded one antelope and killed another, and, long after dark, saw the glimmering of the camp-fire on the bottom. Q. and Henry were gone to bury the latter's squaw, who is just dead.[143] Reynal had heard guns in the course of the day, and was in some apprehension.

Today lay at camp.

Tunica, in order to excite the war, had to give away all his horses and property. He was bent on avenging his son's death—his messengers, bearing the tobacco and cloth, were admitted into the councils, where they stated his designs, and how much he would give that village if it would concur in them. The old men consulted—the tobacco was smoked, and the engagement thus ratified on both sides —hence this extensive combination, which so many causes may still defeat.

Henry says that the relations of his squaw are determined to kill a horse and bury it with her, because, as she was very lame, she would be left on the prairie without the means of travelling to the land of spirits. Q. says that the relations have cut their hair off, and the women cried incessantly. He spent the night in a lodge with about 20 of them—strict silence for hours, the faces just discernable by the fire.

June 29th. Q. and H. came in yesterday, saying that the squaw was about to be buried. A young Ind. with an extraordinary name, importing that his propensities were the reverse of amorous, came with his squaw and child to camp, on his way to the fort, where he means to leave the squaw in charge of Bisson[n]ette,[144] while he goes to war. His medicine, on the strength of which he has counted two *coups*, is to light the pipe whenever it is passed round. This morning, he went off. His domestic drudge packed the horses, and arranged all their paraphernalia while he stood looking on, and then jerking himself into his saddle, he went off at a trot, leaving her to follow.

July 2nd. A most weary series of delays, arising from the utter uncertainty of the Indians' movements. Day before yesterday, a party of trappers[145] came from the fort, in order to give their horses a chance to fatten before entering on their dangerous and uncertain expedition. Their hunts occupy but two months or more—spring and fall—and for the rest of the time, they are idling about the forts or on the prairie, eating, drinking, or sleeping.

They brought news of Bisonnette's arrival, and we allowed Henry to go down and see him. They also said that Bordeaux and another man had quarrelled at the fort, and B. had shown himself a coward—which I can easily believe.[146]

Tunica, after all his pain and preparations, has, it seems, been dissuaded from going to war by Bordeaux, who represented that he would destroy all his horses. So much for Indian constancy—in fact they are the most uncertain people living—their resolutions no more to be trusted than those of children. An old Ind. came here yesterday with this news.

This morning, Q., Reynal, and I rode out to meet Tunica's village—met an Ind. who said their *plan of movement was changed.* He came to camp with us—sat in Reynal's lodge, blackguarding. Soon after, young Bull Bear, with his brother, and one or two more, besides women and children, came to camp. We feasted them.

The utter laziness of an Ind.'s life. It is scarce tolerable to us, and yet is theirs from year's end to year's end. Bull Bear, a young chief, famous for his intrepidity, ambition, and activity, lies kicking his heels by the fire like the rest.

A certain ceremony, it seems, is necessary to constitute a chief—as a preliminary, he *gives away all that he possesses.*

Is an Ind. desirous to become a chief—is he mourning for a dead relative—is he making the medicine ceremony of the white robe—in all these cases, he *gives away all that he has.*

An Ind. becomes great by such exploits as stealing other men's wives, and refusing to make any present in compensation. The Mad

Wolf, Bull Bear's brother, now with us, had often done this. It is a great proof of bravery, thus setting the husband at defiance. If the husband claims a present, and it is given, the merit of the thing is gone.[147] So much for the regulation of Indian society.

An old squaw in one of the lodges is the very picture of one of Macbeth's witches. Plenty of fine children are playing about. Squaws laughing and blackguarding with one another.

July 3rd. Tunica's village here at last. Bull Bear and several of his brothers came yesterday. Today the whole village appeared, straggling down the swell of the prairie, and encamped within a quarter of a mile. Our camp was soon thronged with anxious expectants of a feast—doomed to disappointment. They sat round while we eat, looking on with eager eyes, staring fixidly at us. Tent thronged with smokers.

Afternoon visited several lodges with H. & Q. and got a pipe of Tunica.

Old Bourne [Borgne],[148] brother to the elder Bull Bear, lay sick in his lodge—one of his squaws was nearly blind—what a wretched condition is that of a sick or superannuated Ind.! Mad Wolf,[149] a young aspirant, sat on the other side of the lodge. The woman with the sore eyes was one of Q's patients,[150] and groaned fearfully under his treatment. Her sister, who assisted, was laughing heartily all the time—so much for the affection and tenderness experienced by the sick in an Indian lodge.

Last night the village resounded with the howlings of the women, who were crying for H.'s squaw—though the sick are neglected, the dead are grieved for.

Criers are old men, much respected, chosen in a council.

An Ind. gift is like a Turkish—it is revoked unless an equivalent is given.

They are singularly jealous—feed one, and the others look on with very dark eyes.

The women are full of jokes and raillery.

In one lodge were two Shienne [Cheyenne] strangers, who occupied the place of honor at the top of the lodge.

An old man sent to invite us to a dog-feast—the dish was placed before us—we eat what we wished—then took away what we thought proper, and passed the rest to our host and his family, who had looked on meanwhile.

The old joker, who kept up a constant stream of raillery—especially about the women, declaring in their presence that he had lain with them, at which they laughed, without the slightest inclination to blush. Reynal says, and indeed it is very observable, that *anything* may be said without making a girl blush; but that liberties cannot be taken with a young girl's person without exciting her shame.[151]

They keep up a constant stream of raillery and blackguarding.

All is still uncertain about the war—some of the Inds. are for going and some for returning—it is even doubtful if any of them go to the rendezvous at La Bonté's Camp. The present intention—if so it can be called—of Tunica's village is to hunt back of Laramie Mt. and then go to war. Some of the warriors are preparing their dresses against this contingency.

July 4th. This afternoon three Inds. came to camp, bringing on a mule a wretchedly emaciated Negro. He was out 33 days ago with Richard on Horse Creek—the oxen ran off—he went to look for them, and had been wandering in circles and starving every since, without gun, knife, moccasins, or any knowledge of the country or its productions. We seated him in the midst of a circle of trappers, squaws, and children—the wretch could scarcely speak. The men considered his escape almost miraculous.

Rouleau and other trappers told stories of their own hardships.

The squaws are constantly laughing. It is astonishing, what abominable indecencies the best of the Inds. will utter in presence of the women, who laugh heartily.

Old Borne thinks he shall get well—he is very thankful to Q.

An opposition doctor was howling and rattling over a sick child in an adjoin[in]g lodge.

A broken-down old man, in one of the lodges, kept telling of his past greatness and his friendship for the whites.

July 6[5]*th*. Moved camp to-day, with the village, to the Forks [of Laramie Creek]—a picturesque sight. A few old men went ahead and sat down, when they wished the line to stop—and when they stopped in the bottom, the camp was formed in a circle round them.

We had, it seems, a narrow escape a few days ago. The tracks seen on [the] Chug[water] by Reynal and H. proved to be a party of Crows, as the Sioux have just found some bones and corpses flung from their scaffolds. They were some thirty in number, and probably missed our camp in the morning fog.

Saw the dance of the Strong Hearts in the village this morning— great frolic and buffoonery.[152]

This afternoon, a war parade in full dress—sat in the shade of Reynal's lodge and looked at it—listened to the constant joking and trickery of the squaws—tasted sundry messes of *pommes blanches* and venison placed before us—saw a domestic quarrel, where the rebellious squaw pulled down the lodge, packed her horse, and rode off, while the husband looked quietly on. The warriors were in full dress—a miserable old squaw squalled after them from a lodge door, exciting them to glorious exploits—as one of them rode from the ring, a crier proclaimed his name, and published his renown before the whole village.

Soon after the ceremony, an old man walked round, shouting the name of one who had feasted him, and thanking him before the village.

There seems to be good discipline on matters of war, even among the Sioux. The society of Strong Hearts has soldiers, who compel attendance on such ceremonies as this, the penalty being the cutting to pieces of the recusant's lodge. The war-dance once danced, the recruit is enlisted, and subject to the regulations of the soc.

Bull Bear, being in mourning, did not join the band.

July 6*th*. Shot a war-eagle, which was siezed upon by the Inds. before I could get up to it.

Left the village, and with the trappers went over to Bitter Cotton Wood Creek,[153] to meet Bissonnette and go with him to La Bonté's. In the afternoon, reached the rendez-vous where we were to lay and wait one day for B. Waited accordingly through the 7*th* July.

An Ind.'s meanest trait is his unsatiable appetite for food and presents. They are irrepressible beggars, and at meals, no matter how slender the repast may be, chiefs and warriors surround us with eager eyes to wait for a portion, and this although their bellies may be full to bursting. If one wishes to see an Ind. village, send a notice that you will feast, and they will come a two days' journey for the sake of your cup of coffee. What a life! where the excitement of an enjoyment so trifling can tempt them to such pains-taking. In fact, the greater part of a trapper's or an Ind's life is mere vacancy— lying about, as I am now, with nothing to do or think of.

Yesterday, July 6ᵗʰ. While we were nooning, a party of emigrants appeared, on which two Inds. attached to the lodge of Moran's [Morin's?] squaw, who is along with us, went off to get a treat. The whole line of emigrants stopped nearly an hour, made them coffee and gave them bread—such is their timidity and perplexity, and want of management and regulation. The Inds. are getting more and more importunate in their demands upon them.

Today, 7ᵗʰ. Rouleau and the one-eyed Canadian [Séraphin] set out on their trapping exped. to the Mts.

Chatron and a party came from the fort and reported that B. will not be here till tomorrow.

July 9ᵗʰ. Yesterday, Bissonnette not arriving, rode in intense heat to a beautiful camp on Horse Shoe Creek—swift water, limpid as crystal. Today came to La Bonté's Camp on the Platte—no Inds.— no buffalo—but plenty of flies. Camp is the laziest place on earth. The family of Moran's squaw is along with [him]. Her brother, a lazy good for-nothing fellow, sits under a shade of robes apart, cooing with his new squaw (yesterday they had a long ramble in the bushes together). Her father, an old, lean, mean-looking medicine-man, sits perched on the limb of a dead tree like a turkey buzzard, apparently looking out. His medicine-bag and apparatus is hung over the little sunshade of robes that he has made. There are plenty of children about the lodge. Moran's friend Jeangras [Gingras] brought in an antelope at about 4 o'clock—it was instantly cooked, and all fell to eating. The utter laziness of Indian life!

Jeangras met a party of emigrants, from whom some trapper from the fort stole a woman, as they were camped night before last. He approached with two horses—met the fair one at the edge of the camp—mounted her, and vanished.

July 10th. There will probably be no muster of Inds. at La Bonté's— there are no buffalo. Spent an abominably lazy day; and, as Q. is averse to returning to Tunica's village, resolved to go alone, that my object may not be wholly defeated. This afternoon, Q. rode to our last camp to see if there were any signs of Bissonnette.

July 11th. Q. did not return till near daylight, when he came in on foot, having lost his horse Sorel. I set out as soon as possible, taking Raymond with me, and a little flour and tea, with a haunch of antelope. Henry went to look for Q.'s horse, while Q. remained to accompany the cart on its proposed movement to Horse Shoe Creek.

Steered about south. Prairie scorched and arid—broken with vile ravines and buttes—plenty of agate, jasper, etc.—gigantic grass-hoppers and crickets—scorched pines along the sides of the ravines— a good place for grizzly bears. Nooned on Horse Shoe Creek, and striking the Oregon trail, reached at night our former camp on Bitter Cotton-Wood.

July 12th. Raymond saw an antelope, and went to shoot it. The animals were hobbled, but, tormented by the flies, ran suddenly off, Paul Dorion's mare breaking her hobbles. I followed in vain. Raymond, returning, ran up the high butte, and saw them careering over the prairie. He followed, and did not return for about four hours, when he came in with them, having followed them to the Side [North] Fork of Laramie—ten or twelve miles. He had had no water, and that which he drank on returning was immediately vomited.

His appetite was gone, but I made him some tea and let him rest. In his eager pursuit, he left his rifle on the ground, and we had much difficulty in finding it in the afternoon. I had good reason to be anxious during his absence, as I did not know exactly where Q. was encamped, and every day's delay made it more difficult to find the Ind. village. Camped on Side Fork of Laramie.

July 13ᵗʰ. Breakfasted on the remaining one of a pair of curlew I shot. Struck across for Laramie Creek, to find the trail of the village. Raymond got sight of an antelope down a ravine—fired, and broke his shoulder—my mare easily overtook her. Came to Laramie, and saw the print of a moccasin—crossed to a little, sandy creek, running into it from the south, where tracks of men and horses were very distinct and thickened as we proceeded, till after an hour's search we came upon one of their camps—several days old. Our search was rendered much more difficult by the furious storm of yesterday afternoon, which, descending from Laramie Mt., drove us for shelter to the depths of a dry ravine, where we crouched for an hour or more, but ill protected.

Nooned, and set out on the trail—it led towards the mts., but such was the nature of the arid, barren, stoney ground, that only here and there the faint trace of a lodge-pole was visible, as it passed over some ant-hill, or clump of prickly-pear—or sometimes a stone would be turned over by the kick of a horse. Intensely hot. Followed slowly all the afternoon, losing the trail repeatedly. Saw a heavy smoke rising from a valley this side Laramie Mt. Lost the trail at last, and encamped in a hollow bottom, where Laramie comes swiftly out of the hills, and where our fire would be invisible.

July 14ᵗʰ. Following a creek that flows from the south into Laramie, we found the traces of lodge-poles again, but soon lost them. Not long after, we found them again, and a camp, where by the number of fires we saw that we were on the trail of only part of the village. Traced it up a bare and scorching valley of the mts. where we led our animals. Descending, we came to a succession of little grassey and well watered nooks among these black and desolate hills, and presently came upon another camp. Not long after, with a dreary interval of hot and barren prairie, we came to a succession of defiles among fine abrupt mts., like the Dixville Pass.[154] Bare cliffs above— beautiful woods below—a clear stream glancing in their shadows over a bed of rock—and all alive with birds like Mt. Auburn.[155] It was a place to repay a week's travel. After twelve miles' riding we found another camp and nooned there. Several rude little forts, some twelve feet square, of interlaced logs and branches, marked the warlike character of the region. In the afternoon we ascended a narrow and most romantic pass—the stream in its bed of rocks by our sides, a dense foliage around us, and lofty beetling cliffs above. Larkspur and a sort of aster were among the numberless flowers— pleasant mementos of civilization in such a wilderness. In a basin among rugged hills, at the head of the pass, the Inds. had encamped again, and a little farther on we did the same. (Absanth everywhere.) Just emerging from the hills, saw several bulls on a distant butte.

July 15th. Started, and soon got on a prairie where the traces were totally lost—a wide stony expanse, tracked with buffalo. Medicine Bow Mts. in the distance. After some weary and anxious hours, found the lodge-pole marks, again to lose them. They pointed, however, towards the head of Laramie Creek, and thither we resolved to push. A number of little lakes, where wolves, antelopes, and large plover were congregated. Tried in vain to kill some, our meat being nearly gone. Were fast approaching a region quite dangerous on acct. of Snakes, Gros Ventres, and Arapahoes.[156] Raymond advised return. Resolved to advance till night, and soon after, ascending a butte, saw the circle of lodges, with the bands of horse, close by the bare banks of Laramie. Thanked God that my enterprise was not defeated. Groups stood in front of the lodges as we descended, and we presently saw Reynal coming to meet us. He quartered me upon Big Crow, the village having disagreed and split up, Tunica going one way and Bad Wound another.[157] Invited to plenty of feasts, as the village was full of meat, and soon after was seated in R.'s lodge, with a large group, discussing the cause of thunder, a storm having just risen.

The Sioux, like the northern tribes, say that the thunder is a bird flying over the firmament, and that once an old man saw it descend and flap its wings on a lake which caused the lightning.[158]

This ev'ng, two young men, desirous of raising a war-party, went round the village crying to the Great Spirit to give them success in killing their enemies and stealing horses. Next morning, one of them was on a distant butte, crying in the same manner.

The firelight scene in the lodge at night.

The squaws played ball before dark, and various games of hazard were going on—these, together with smoking and eating, pass away an Ind.'s time.

Heap of Hail[159] and his friend and crony.

July 16th. Today, gave them a feast—dog, tea, and bread. My host, the Big Crow, issued the invitations—a slender banquet for more than 20 guests, but nothing gratifies an Ind. like giving him a morsel of food, especially that which the whites use. Old Red Water,[160] the fast friend and imitator of the whites, spoke at some length, expressing his gratitude. I answered, Reynal interpreting. Feast distributed by soldiers chosen for such purposes, whose awards, says R., never give dissatisfaction. R., on the instigation of the Eagle Feather, took the occasion of this meeting to enforce the expediency of moving tomorrow after the buffalo; Eagle Feather seconded him, and remarked that since Bull Bear's death, there had been nothing but divisions and separations among them—they were a body without a head. Others gave their opinion, but there was no decision—a completer democracy never subsisted. When all was eaten, Red Water sang his song of thanks, made another speech, and then intimated that the company ought to leave breathing room to the whites—on which they went out. This was a soldier feast.

Old Red Water says that the large crickets so common about here, when taken in the hand, always twist their long horns, when asked, in the direction of the buffalo. This was told them by their great grandfather, and the name by which they call crickets means: "Those that show where the buffalo are."[161]

The conversation in the lodge at night—one man would keep on in a lively strain with much gesticulation for an hour together, the others not interrupting; and then another would take up the conversation. When the chief men sat down to smoke today (17th) during the march, the conversation was very gay and lively. In the evening, the squaws amused themselves with plenty of lively and vociferous games.

Big Crow, my host, took out his medicine bags and had a smoke, in ceremony, over them.

Reynal—his insatiable avidity to get hold of whatever he sees.

July 17th. Moved camp, though very slowly and in disorder. Old Redwater in a loud voice upbraided the village for their want of promptitude and having *two hearts*. The chief men marched before, as usual. Camped on a fine spring, ten miles off.

Redwater's voice soon heard in the village, proclaiming a feast that he was giving.

Old Redwater's tale, told with great animation and gesticulation: When he was very young, he was hunting beaver with three others, and he crept alone into the lodge, with a rope. When he had crept a great distance, passing several very small dark holes, he crawled into a place where it was very dark and slimy, and he felt very sleepy (here the dumb show became very expressive). Presently, he saw something white and indistinct—for some time he was so sleepy that he could make out nothing, but at last he discerned two white men and two white women. Just then he heard his companions singing outside, and feeling alarmed, he succeeded after a long while in crawling out. It felt very cold. His companions had thought him dead. He went to the place over that where he saw the four whites, and, beating with his foot, made a hole. Soon a beaver came out, which they caught, and then three more.

The old man says he has always considered the beavers and the whites the wisest of all animals; and he is now certain that they are the same.[162]

The boys playing at evn'g outside the village. Every little fellow has his bow and arrow, and they show great skill in knocking down small birds with them.

July 18th. Made two moves today, to get near the buffalo. In camping, each lodge has its appropriate place relatively to the others. At even'g, two bulls came directly upon the village and were killed within a few rods of it, by two men laying in wait. In the morning, His Horses killed a bull, which was at once surrounded and butchered, and much of it eaten raw. Some of the boys killed a fine prairie-cock. It was resolved on the march to cache the meat, and advance tomorrow to where the buffalo are, to surround.

The woman, with her legs gashed, howling through the camp, mourning for her son, killed a year ago. Her lodge was full of cries and songs of mourning.

The little Gros Ventre prisoner adopted into old Red Water's family.

Old R. W.'s unwillingness to tell his tales—he says it is against his medicine, for they are about to go to war, and it is not good to talk much at that time.

A young man of considerable repute is getting up the warparty. He called me to a feast today, and begged a little powder.

Eagle Feather came to me this morning to make me a present of an old waistcoat—his object was to get one of my shirts. A woman presented me a dish of *wasna* or pemmican,[163] expecting a knife in return. To give nothing for nothing is the Indian maxim.

July 19ᵗʰ. The meat being cached, the village began to move about 11 o'clock and advanced about twelve miles, encamping on a stream of which they did not know the name. Their course is westward; and they are very apprehensive on acct. of the Snakes, who they fear will attack them.

The young man[164] who feasts me so often, and asks for the paper of recommendation. He is at the head of the war scheme, and his equipment—war-bonnet, shield, bow and arrows, shirt, robe, and pipe—are very complete and elegant.

Raynal is absurdly offended, because I required Raimond to take care of the horses, instead of going to help him cache his meat.

July 20ᵗʰ. Made a short and early move. No sooner were we camped, higher up on the creek, than all the men and most of the boys set out after the buffalo, on account of which this westward move had

been made. It is time to provide new lodge-skins. Most of them led
their buffalo horses, and rode inferior animals—a wild, helter-
skelter, hurrying group. No soldiers for the buffalo have been
appointed, the village being so small. One or two young men rode
forwards occasionally, and one or two old ones assumed the direction.
After twelve miles riding, seeing only scattered bulls, some bands of
cows appeared. The Inds. separated. Followed the largest party.
Bulls wading hastily across a sandy creek. A general break-away
after the band of cows on the other side. Soon plenty were down, and
the whole scattering far and wide. Too languid to hunt with spirit,
and my horse very sick. Wounded two cows, but lost them. Came
back to where Big Crow was butchering, and his son eating raw
meat, in which I joined and found the liver excellent. A tiresome ride
back—at length saw the group of lodges, bereft of warriors, on the
green bottom of the creek. Laid down on a robe, while the women
and children discussed the raw meat we brought.

When the Big Crow came in, his squaw brought him water, pulled
off his moccasins, and brought him a dish of meat. The village was
soon filled with meat. Groups were gorging themselves around all
the lodges—eating was the engrossing occupation of the time, and
the result was that all night vomitings and retchings could be heard
among the children of the lodges around. Old Red Water (Mene-
Shula [Seela]), though over sixty, drove an arrow clean through a
cow, and talked with great glee and animation of his exploit.

The Big Crow (Kongratonka [Kongra-Tonga]), my host, showed
me his wounds, of which he has many. He has killed fourteen men;
and dwells with great satisfaction on the capture of a Utah, whom he
took prisoner; and, with the other Sioux, scalped alive, cut the
tendons of his wrist, and flung, still living, into a great fire.

The Inds. are much afraid of the Snakes and Utahs, and reproved
Raimond for going out without his rifle today.

July 21ˢᵗ. Today the squaws are busy upon the robes.

No family here lays by fresh meat for its own use—if a man gets
half a buffalo, he is sure to be eased of it before night, by a congregation of hungry relatives and friends.

Kongratonka's medicine is to sing in the night, which he never
fails to do, to my great annoyance.

The White Shield, the young brave who is raising the war-party, lurks around our lodge about meal times, expecting his share like the meanest of the village.

July 23rd. Yesterday went out with Raimond to hunt. Wounded an antelope, and fired some six or eight ineffectual bullets into a bull. In the morning Reynal said he had dreamed of strangers arriving, and it happened that his dream coincided with that of a young Ind. Both were strong in faith, and the latter went out on discovery. By a singular coincidence he met Saraphin [Séraphin] and Rouleau, who, having trapped in the [Laramie] Mts., were coming to the village. They are bound to the Rocky Mts., trapping.

All the Inds. here try to dissuade them, saying that, since the death of Boot and May, the Arapahos have grown very audacious, having got over their first terror, and call the whites dogs, saying that none of them shall leave their country alive. They laugh at the government and the dragoons. The trappers are resolved to go on. There is considerable danger in the immediate vicinity of the camp, from the Snakes. Today the Inds. are out on another surround. The camp is full of meat drying on scaffolds, and the squaws are working like dogs at cleaning the robes.

Rouleau describes the fight in which Bull Bear was killed. The determined bravery and obstinate will of the chief are remarkable. He speaks of a Brulé chief of similar character—in such terror was he held that his will was absolute law. There was in this village a young half-breed, killed last fall, so dreaded that he could strike with impunity the considerable men of the village. There seems to have been in these modern Pontiacs an impetuous force of mind that entitles them all to be called great.

One day it stormed furiously. Something had displeased the Brulé chief. "*I am mad*," said he to R. "I will make the village move." His squaw levelled his lodge, and no sooner was this done than the rest were down also—such was the force of his example.

Crying is the commonest thing in the world. Tonight an old squaw's horse foundered in the surround, and her lamentations were audible from her lodge for hours. I have often seen squaws crying on the way from camp to camp.

The White Shield came and sat before Reynal's lodge. He had a bad sore throat, which he bore with anything but stoicism. He seemed depressed to the last degree.

R. says that they bear *wounds* with the greatest fortitude, but yield at once to a stroke of sickness. The White Shield said he meant to have gone to war tomorrow—that his brother was killed last summer, and he must avenge him or die—that ten young men would follow him. His preparations are complete; and his sickness makes him very despondent. I hear the medicine drum at this moment—he is probably under medical treatment.

July 24ᵗʰ. Skins enough have now been obtained for the lodges—they are all stretched on the ground, and the squaws labor like dogs over them.

Rouleau and Saraphin set off this morning on their dangerous exped. Rouleau says if he only had one more horse he would not go—this is his present necessity for continuing his dangerous trapper life. He whistles, sings, and laughs with the utmost gaiety, and rides off with as careless a heart as if bound back to the Fort.

July 26ᵗʰ. Night before last, the White Shield put on his full war-dress; and, mounting his horse, paraded around the village, crying for success to the Great Spirit. Here and there, an old woman set up a song of glorification and encouragement. He was a very splendid and chivalrous-looking figure; but he is a notorious beggar, like the rest. Next day, he was still quite sick—the long projected war-party fell through, the warriors alleging a want of powder and arrows.

Yesterday, the skins being nearly prepared and the camp insufferably dirty, moved in the afternoon to our last camp higher up the creek, with the intention of getting the cached meat, and cutting lodge-poles in the hills.

Scarcely arrived—old men and warriors seated smoking in the middle—squaws unpacking horses and dogs—when a quarrel arose. There are in the village three of the broken and dispersed band of the Arrow Breakers—they undertook to sieze upon a horse belonging to a brave killed not long since. A brother of the deceased took the horse away from them, on which they shot him. There was a rush from all parts of the village—guns and arrows were siezed and discharged, some taking one side, some another. Some squaws set up a howling for the slaughtered horse—other ran to a place of safety with their children—and other siezed on the weapons. A fight was threatened, but it ended in smoke—soon all was quiet. (For the true cause of the quarrel, see *post.*)

When the pipe is passed from left to right, it is medicine.

All the evening, the village was filled with the mourning songs of squaws who lost relatives last year.

Immediately after the quarrel, an old squaw sang out the name of the man who had rescued the horse—the Tall Bear—in honor of his bravery.

Today moved nearer the Mts. and encamped.

During the quarrel, old Red Water, old as he is, rushed out of his lodge, gun and bow in hand, with the upmost vehemence, but tripped and lay sprawling on the ground.

The great number of societies, with their peculiar ceremonies and discipline.

July 27th. Last night there was a festive meeting (?) with songs, etc., in one of the principal lodges.

Moved camp to the Mts. to cut lodge-poles. Camped in the valley of a clear, cool creek—boys wandering about the rugged and broken mts., killing prairie-cocks, or perching themselves on tall rocks and looking down on the straggling array. Men cutting *shongsasa*[i] among the bushes. Raimond and I looked in vain for a beaver-lodge.

Camped in a narrow, grassy spot, hollowed among the rough hills —a most picturesque scene. Lodges no sooner up than, with characteristic hurry, forth poured half the population to get the lodge-poles, trotting, running, and scrambling on their horses, with dogs, colts, and all, along a rude, narrow valley. Squaws in full attire, twinkling with their ornaments and laughing. Two deer sprang up— Reynal fired—jumped from my horse to do the same—instantly the whole helter-skelter procession was sweeping by me. A suitable place

---

[i] "Shongsha" or "kinnikinnick" was red-willow or dogwood bark, arrowroot, or some other herb used to eke out tobacco, which was expensive and scarce among the Indians.—Ed.

found, squaws and men were all at work. Left the two men, and wandered up the mts. A hunter's paradise—signs of game incredibly thick—cold streams—rocks, pine, and spruce—all had the air of my old friends, the mts. of N. E. [New England]. Strawberries—larkspur—robins—bumble-bees. Mts. very abrupt, precipitous, and broken. Saw beaver dams in returning. Sat down in the lodge to a hearty meal of buffalo meat, purveyed by Red Water in the absence of my host, his son.

On arriving at our present camp, several women set up mourning songs for relatives killed in war, and whom they had last parted from at this spot last summer.

July 28th. Set out with Reynal on a hunt. Rode over mountain after mountain—wild and picturesque, but no game but two deer in the distance. Emerging upon the prairies, saw three bulls—gave chace—old mule took fright and threw me—could not approach—circled back to village over craggy mts.

A great variety of games and exercises among the Ind. children.

Reynal's "old woman" gave a feast to the squaws—consisting of dry bull-meat, lumps of fat, flour, and corn-meal, boiled in a kettle together. The object was (she always has some such object) to procure their assistance in preparing her lodge-skins.[165]

Camp full of new lodge-poles—men and women at work trimming them. Others gathering *shongsasa* by the brook.

July 29th. Climbed a high rocky Mt. a few miles from camp. On the way, in woody ravines where little streams came down, cold as ice, among the stones and moss, and everywhere about the rocks were scattered the Ind. boys, looking after berries or small game. They destroy all that comes to hand—young rabbits, ducks, prairie cocks—every thing; and this is their education. A savage prospect from the summit—lodges in the green valley like a circle of white specks.

Dozed away the afternoon in Raynal's lodge, thinking of things past and meditating on things to come. Here one feels overcome with an irresistable laziness—he cannot even muse consecutively.

At evening, Heap of Hail appeared with the skin and liver of an

elk. He is very ambitious, and always after game; while his elder
brother lazily struts about.

As the pipe passed the circle around the fire in the evening, there
was plenty of that obscene conversation that seems to make up the
sum of Ind. wit, and which very much amuses the squaws. The Inds.
are a very licentious set.

July 30ᵗʰ. Broke up camp, and moved round to the pass through
the Mts.—about twelve miles, to where we encamped on a bottom in
the midst of them. On the way passed the site of a camp, whence last
year the war-party that was defeated set out. The relatives of the
slain immediately raised the mourning song, and the half-breed
Shienne, one of whose relations was killed, gave away on the spot two
horses. He will receive their value back again. After camping,
nothing was heard but shouts of praise and thanks.

Just before reaching the ground, a large flock of sheepʲ seen on
the mts. Drove up with Raimond, to look after them—plenty of Inds.
in pursuit. Tied animals and scrambled over rocks and ravines till
tired of the work. Returning, saw the camp just forming in the plain
below, and heard the occasional shots of the Inds. who had so per-
plexed the poor animals as to bring several within range of their
wretched guns. Reynal and Raimond followed one they had
wounded, and pelted her to death with stones in a ravine. Meat
tough and old. Several more frightened flocks, appeared on the
mts. in full sight from camp.

July 31ˢᵗ. As the camp broke up this morning, set out with Raimond
among the hills for a hunt. Killed an antelope. The White Shield
followed, for a share in the spoils. Arrived in camp in time to join
the circle of old smokers in the middle. A noble spring of water not
far distant—a great basin of rocks, fringed by soft [ferns?]—water
like crystal, many feet deep, and cold as ice. Escaping, soaking
through the soil or creeping almost invisibly down the grassy ravine,
it formed many rods below another basin, still larger and deeper—

ʲ Probably these were antelope, known as "goats," rather than the bighorns called
"sheep."—Ed.

equally clear, but not so cool—a natural bathing-tub and a luxurious refreshment in the intense heat.

Aug. 1ˢᵗ. Fairly among the mts. Rich, grassy valley—plenty of gooseberries and currants—dark pine mts.—an opening dell that tempted me to ride up into it, and here in the cool pine woods I recalled old feelings, and old and well remembered poetry. Climbed a steep hill—on the left, the mts. and the black pine forests—far down, the bare hills, and threading the valley below came the long, straggling procession of Inds.

They soon camped in a grassy nook, where crowded together—dogs and horses, men, women, and children—the sight was most picturesque. The men sat smoking—the women worked at the lodges—the children and young men climbed the steep rocks, or straggled among the pine-covered hills around the place. Droves of horses were driven to water—girls with spoons and buffalo paunches went down to a deep dell for water. Heat intense—sat on a shady rock and watched the scene. Climbed at sunset a high hill and looked over the mts. and pine forests. All night, the Inds. were playing at a great gambling game.

Aug. 2ⁿᵈ. Set out early, after a dog-breakfast, to take leave of the Inds. and meet S[haw] according to agreement at the fort. Looked back down the dell at the camp in full hubbub of preparation for departure, thinking it my last look. Heap of Hail accompanied us, to show us the way through the mts. Had not ridden long through the pine glades in the cool of the morning, when we raised a black-tailed deer. R. wounded at 200 yds.—I broke shoulder at 300,[166] and the young Ind. followed him into a deep dell and finished him. Butchering delayed us, and we joined the Ind. line of march. They were straggling down a deep and narrow gorge—rocks and pines—a confused, noisy, and wild procession. The mts. in front were all on fire, and have been so for weeks—a boundless and cloudlike volume of smoke obscured the whole landscape in front, except here and there the jutting ridges of bold cliffs and bristling pines, or the paler outline of more distant heights, just visible through the veil. High and stern crags on every side. But soon we descended into a milder region—one of vallies and little streams where plenty of wild fruit grew, which the children gathered.

Emerged from the mts. and camped on the scorching prairie. Hot as the devil. Employed myself in thrusting head, arms, and feet into deep, delicious "holes" of water, and watching the little fishes gliding in them—then smoked—then ate—then waited impatiently till the horses were brought up; and R. and I, taking final leave, set out for the fort, accompanied by a young Ind. Camped on Chugwater. The Ind. was afraid to stop at a spot I proposed on Laramie, because two dead men were buried there.

Aug. 3rd. Setting out before daybreak, reached the fort early, and found all there, Shaw having been there a fortnight. A civilized breakfast not to be sneezed at!

Aug. 4th. There is an old Ind. at the fort, badly wounded, who is always singing to cure himself. His "medicine," which he always resorts to when in pain, is to hand some bystander a cup of water and let him drink it.

Rouville[167] and his animated rattling conversation.

In the afternoon set out with Rouville, a trapper, and his Pah Utah squaw towards the camp of Bissonnette, on our way to Bent's [Fort]. Camped on a little run, ten miles—plenty of wild cherries.

Aug. 5th. Camped at noon on a stream perfectly dry, where we had to scratch holes in the sand for water. Traversed "Goshen's Hole"— a damned dry place, full of ravines—saw bear tracks, and camped very late.

Rouville's acct. of old Borne's life—told him by the old man. Old B. was eighteen when he dreamed of an interview with a grizzly bear—the *war-spirit* of the Inds. as the *antelope* is the *peace-spirit*. He saw the bear eating; and, waiting till he had appeased his hunger, went up to him. The bear told him it was time for him to think of going to war, but he must not do as the other Inds. did—he must fight openly, and not commit useless barbarities.

Next day he set out, went to the Black Hills, and soon discovered

a Crow, before the latter observed him. As he was on the point of
firing, he recalled the white bear's injunction, refrained, and called
out to his enemy to step forwards and fight. They grappled—the
Crow fell wounded. B. was on the point of despatching him, when
he begged to speak a few words—he told B. that too much ambition
was the cause of his present fate—that he had killed thirty-six Sioux,
and now fell a victim to his desire to kill more—that he (B.) was a
brave and good young man—that he had better renounce ambition
and be content with a peaceful life. So old Borne has led a peaceful
though honored life, very different from that of his fierce and
ambitious brother, Bull Bear.

The Inds. shoot at the clouds to scare away the thunder. They
think it an enemy, and turn out to fight it. So in case of an eclipse.

The Frenchmen—Rouville and Delorier—an amusing contrast to
the Yankee temperament.

Aug. 6ᵗʰ. Advanced to Little Horse Creek and nooned. Tracks of
bear. Afternoon reached Horse Creek, where was encamped Bissonnette, N. Sibille [Sabille],[168] and their party, along with some 40
Sioux lodges—Tunica's—and several Shienne.

Horse-races in the evening; Paul Dorion—the *ci-devant* circus rider;
Rouville, Antoine,[169] and the Canadians; the swarm of Inds. on
horse and foot.

Ind. Outrages: The Pawnees—their alarm—stopping Finch—
alarm subsides—killed Bradley with an arrow in June—stopped
Bissonnette June 4ᵗʰ—tried to rob Turner—steal horses—whip an
emigrant into camp. Told Rouville that they would rob and kill
every white who passed through their lands.

Sioux told Rouville that the Pawnees had been committing outrages for years and no dragoons had come, and now *they* meant to do
the same. But few of them saw the dragoons, being afraid to come,
then dissatisfied at getting no presents. Never so turbulent as this
year. Declare that if the emigrants continued to pass through, they
would rob them and kill them if they resisted. Broke up the pots and
pans of the emigrants who feasted them. Robbed Sublette[170] and Red-

dick, and fired upon them. Robbed Bonn[e]y.[171] Robbed a party of eight waggons at Independence Creek in July.

Arapahos killed Boot and May this spring. Alarmed at first—afterwards grow insolent and declare that no whites shall ever leave their country. Trappers—Rouleau and Saraphin—dissuasions of the Inds. at the village.

Cayou, 52 Green St, St. Louis

Sibille told me the following story, told him by a young Shienne, very fond of talking with the whites about religion.

In a band of the Shiennes was a young man who always painted in a peculiar manner, and enjoyed much respect and influence. Once the band met on the prairie another young man, resembling in paint and in all respects the former, who advanced and demanded who he was, and why he imitated his paint. The latter, who was a divinity, embraced him, and directed that he should follow him, while the band stopped. Leading him into a deep dell, he entered the waters of a spring, where the young man followed. Presently after, they emerged, the young man bearing two dishes of boiled corn given him by the spirit, who told him to distribute two kernels to each person to eat. He then asked if they liked them—they said "yes," on which again disappearing in the spring with the young man, he came back with two dishes of seed corn. This he gave to the Shienne, telling them to plant it at the time the grass was springing up, and return after several moons.

Thus the Great Spirit gave corn to the Shiennes.

An Ind., when sick or wounded, feels obliged to imitate the movements of the animal whom he has as his guardian spirit. A wounded Sioux, sought for some days by his companions, was found in a deep hollow, scratching and growling like a bear.

Ind. speeches always prepared beforehand. Bissonnette once caught the Sioux *rehearsing* the speech they were to make to Col. Kearney on the visit they expected from him this summer.[172] One of them personated their American father.

Bissonnette's feast—coffee—corn boiled with grease—a huge kettle of pounded cherries, grease, and flour.

First a speech from him telling them to make more robes than they had made last winter. A reply from the orator, followed by a broad intimation that they had now better begin to eat—at which an old "soldier" poured out the coffee, which was at once gulped down. Then the corn preparation was devoured—then the other mixture.

Lomalomie, the "Hog"—the sick Tunica, gorging like the rest—the Shienne guests, served by the soldier with a treble share—the Crow prisoner. Pipe circulating constantly. Concluding speech of thanks from the orator.

Aug. 7ᵗʰ & 8ᵗʰ. Lay at Camp. Evening of the 8ᵗʰ, a dance of the Strong Hearts, Shienne and Sioux. This society extends through the Shienne and Sioux—Bissonnette does not know if it exists in other nations. The same is the case with other societies—the Hawk—Short Hairs, etc. Each has some animal as a guardian spirit, that of the Strong Hearts being the fox, whose movements they imitate in their very curious dance. They passed round to all the principal lodges, dancing at each, the object being a present—a begging dance. The object of all these societies, says B., is warlike.

The Stabber, a Missouri Ind., comes from the Arkansas, and brings vague reports of troops passing up, and of a victory over the Spaniards.[173] He tells his story as vaguely and unconnectedly as a child.

A Shienne came to B., saying he would like to swap a fine horse of his. He postponed the bargain day after day, coming every day to eat at B.'s lodge, till at last it appeared that this was his sole object in proposing the swap!

Bull Bear comes to see Henry. He seems to be a true friend, and regularly places himself in our tent as our "soldier."

The War-Whistle, not used by the chief as a signal, but blown by the young men during the fight. It is a "medicine" instrument, and is blown by the Inds. while undergoing the penance of the buffalo skulls.[174] A society among the Ponkas [Poncas] and Omahas, called the Thunder-Fighters, during a thunder-storm sit on a hill, whistling to the storm to frighten it.

The true cause of the quarrel I saw at the Ind. village[k] (related by Bull Bear) was as follows. A horse was given, with the usual expectation of another one, to which the giver had taken a fancy, being given in his place. This not being done, the giver tried to take back his gift, upon which the "givee" fired an arrow into the animal, and hence the quarrel.

The gross indecency of many Indian names, even of the most distinguished men.

Aug. 9ᵗʰ. The Inds. and Bissonnette moving, we made a move in the afternoon, and after passing through a region of wild cherries (on which, in the dearth of meat, the Inds. have been living for some time) we came to a very pleasant camp on Spring Creek.

Aug. 10ᵗʰ. Travelled all day—nooned on Pole Creek, which was nearly dry, and camped on a little stream beyond.

Aug. 11ᵗʰ. This morning the horses ran back to Pole Creek, which caused delay. We, however, stopping now and then for a smoke on the road, came to Crow Creek, and nooned. A hot and level prairie. Camped on a brook running into Crow Creek.

Aug. 12ᵗʰ. A long day's journey. Nooned low down on Crow Creek. Travelled till near sunset, and finding the creek dry, had to keep on to the mouth of Cache à la Poudre, which we reached at nine o'clock.

The Sioux, Crows, Arapahos, according to Henry, have every year or thereabouts medicine ceremonies, similar to the Mandans.
There is a "squaw" feast, where the married women come forwards and swear to their virtue and fidelity.[175]

Aug. 13ᵗʰ. Yesterday, towards evening, saw the very high Mt. called Vaskiss's [Vasquez] Peak [Longs Peak?]. This morning the air was not clear enough to distinguish it. Crossed the South Fork [of the Platte]—killed an immense rattlesnake—rode some ten or twelve

[k] Cf. pp. 462-63.—Ed.

miles—and nooned close to St. Vrain's Fort. Deserted—entered it—two bastions—built of *"doughbies"* ["dobies" or adobes]—fast tumbling in ruins—fine situation. Rode on five or six miles and camped on South Fork, not far from Vaskiss's Fort. Saw fresh trail of an Ind. village this morning.

Aug. 14ᵗʰ. Very dry, hot, and smoky. Passed Upton's [Lupton's] deserted fort,[176] six or seven miles from Vaskiss's. Nooned on the Fork. Made a long day's march, and camped on the Fork, where the road leaves it and crosses to Cherry Creek.[177] Saw a last night's camp of a large village—probably Arapaho.

Aug. 15ᵗʰ. A long morning's march brought us to Cherry Creek, over a very hot and dry prairie. Weather too smoky to see the mts. Creek dry—camp of Mormon emigrants, who passed this way with Richard a few week[s] ago.[178] Cherries—plums—black currents—and gooseberries. No water in creek—dug holes and got some. Camped at night on the creek.

Aug. 16ᵗʰ. Today, nooned on Cherry Creek. Camped upon it where the road leaves it to cross over the waters of the Arkansas. A hilly country, full of pines. Rained in the night, and we had to put up the tent in the dark.

Aug. 17ᵗʰ. Weather cloudy, but more clear than before, and Pike's Peak was visible, with snow on the top. Henry killed a straggling bull, too rank and tough to eat. Rode about a dozen miles, and nooned on the head of Kiowa, where, the animals looking ill, we stopped the rest of the day.

Aug. 18ᵗʰ. Nooned on Black Squirrel Creek after traversing a fine piece of pine woods. In the afternoon, a thunder-storm gathered upon the mountains. Pike's Peak and the rest were as black as ink. We caught the edge of the storm, but it had passed by the time we arrived at Jamie's Camp,[179] where several little streams were tumbling down to the bottom in waterfalls. Before night, the black shroud was lifted from the mts. and a bright sunset greeted us.

Aug. 19th. As we left camp, there was promise of a warm and clear day, but white wreaths of cloud soon gathered about the mts., reminding one of Byron's description of Luli and Pargo. The white snow patches—the ravines and the black forests were obscured and revealed by turns—it was a sublime and beautiful sight.

Presently the weather grew clear, and we reached the stream of the Fontaine qui Bouille, in time to noon there.

In the afternoon a tremendous storm of thunder, rain, and hail, beginning on the mts., overtook us and drenched us well. The sun presently broke above the mts.—a beautiful [sight], and when the storm passed two fine rainbows appeared, relieved against the thick black and purple of the clouds. Camped lower down Fontaine qui Bouille.

[*Aug.*] *20th*. Made about 12 miles this morning and nooned as before. In the afternoon soon saw the valley of the Arkansas and, soon after, the cornfields and the low mud wall of the Lower Pueblo.[180]

The Crows choose "comrades" from among the whites and each other, and treat them with disinterested liberality. The Sioux pretend to do the same, but (in the case of the whites, at least) they expect a return, with interest, for their gifts, which are otherwise revoked.[181]

The stab given to my mule is a specimen of a Sioux's revenge.

The Pueblo is in a beautiful bottom. Found Richard there, being prevented by the war from going to Taos till the troops make a way. News of the victory at Metamoras [Matamoras]—of Kearney's march to Santa Fe—and of the road below being full of troops.

The Pueblo built like a rude trading fort. But two or three men and a few Spanish women there. Richard entertained us hospitably in the little mud room, the best in the fort, and gave us a good supper on the floor.[1]

The Mormons that came across with him are on the other side

---

[1] At this point the journal begins to use only one side of the page. Parkman's failing health is indicated by the paucity and terseness of the remaining notes, except when the fever of the buffalo hunt revived him.—Ed.

encamped for the winter, and perhaps longer, and on the 21st we rode over to see them. Found them at work upon their log-houses, but they suspended their labors to talk with us. Some of them completely imbued with the true fanatic spirit—ripe for anything—a very dangerous body of men. One of them had been wounded by a grizzly bear in coming here. A great many more are said to be on their way up the Arkansas.

The barefaced rascal, Bonny.

[*Aug.*] *22nd, 23rd, 24th.* Spent these three days in riding down the Arkansas from Pueblo to Bent's Fort.[182]

[*Aug.*] *25th.* Near noon, encamped within a few miles of Bent's. All the grass about here eaten by the animals of the Mormon emigrants and the troops. Visited the fort in the afternoon. Holt[183] was in charge, the rest being absent. Several sick officers and soldiers, the troops having suffered much in coming up from the heat and the excessive use of water. The military ardor of the invalids[184] had chiefly evaporated. Simpson—Lt. Abbot, of the dragoons—Forrest, who is to go down with us. A man on the road told us that the Spaniards would evacuate Santa Fe without fighting.[185] Papers at the Fort, with accounts of the Matamoras victory. A very hot day— the area of the Fort burning hot.

[*Aug.*] *26th.* Sent on Delorier with the cart, to encamp a few miles below the fort, while we staid and dined there. A volunteer named Hodgman,[186] who has been at the fort sick with a brain-fever—a very "slow coach"—is to go down with us, as also two men from California, Munro[e][187] and the sailor Ben.[188] A homesick emigrant, turning back from Bridger's Fort,[189] is with them. The commissary officer at the fort furnishes Hodgman with provisions, but no gun. Holt and young St. Vrain[190] treated us very hospitably. The Bents[191] are both absent. Yesterday, 40 waggons of supplies for the Santa Fe exped. came up in very poor plight.

Several Shienne lodges are a mile or two below the Fort, the main body of the nation being on Dry Creek after buffalo.

[*Aug.*] *27ᵗʰ*. Left camp, rode about 12 miles, and nooned. Hodgman had trouble with his new mule. Ben very ready and active.

Afternoon, camped some eight miles below nooning place. Henry and Ellis, or rather H. alone, caught three stray dragoon horses, in very low condition and bitten by the wolves. The worst of them was taken by Ellis, we retaining the others.

[*Aug.*] *28ᵗʰ*. Made a morning march of 15 miles, one of our new auxiliaries in the cart. Camped on Arkansas—H. killed a crane and a fawn. Mexican *soap plant*—tarantula—lizards—very hot.

Hodgman, good-natured but helpless, has been clerk on Mississipi steamboats for eight years—has rubbed through the world for thirty—and is a boy yet. How much a man may see without learning! Ben, the sailor—his stories of California horses and horsemen.

Afternoon, made a good march. River always near.

[*Aug.*] *29ᵗʰ*. Nooned on Arkansas. Afternoon, met a train of Santa Fe waggons, belonging to McLaughlin [Magoffin][192]—news that the buffalo were within a day and a half—the Arapaho village, just this side. Also of Pawnees on the road. They killed Swan. He was buried, but they dug him up and scalped him. McL. saw his remains, mangled by the wolves, and reburied them.

[*Aug.*] *30ᵗʰ*. Afternoon, met a train of government waggons. They say that the road is dangerous. They themselves were alarmed, and had made a halt of some time, a few days back. Raw, smock-faced boys, and of a sickly appearance. By a ready lie Hodgman procured "sick rations" from Coates, the master driver. They told us that the Pawnees had tried to steal horses from Ewing's[193] party, and that Ewing had fired at and killed one as he approached. Advise us to make our best speed between the Caches and the Pawnee Fork. Buffalo near.

Aug. 31ˢᵗ. This afternoon, saw the Arapaho village on the other side of the river. Crossed over with Henry and Q. Hodgman, thinking the whole party were going, was clamorous for my pistols, and wished to put on his cap and uniform coat, to strike terror.

Some young men who were guarding their numerous horses went with us. Village all in a stench with meat. Squaws busy with skins. Sat before one of the chief lodges, holding our horses fast, and the curious crowd soon gathered around. Bad faces—savage and sinister. In complexion form, size, and feature inferior to the Sioux. Their faces formed a complete wall around us. Distributed a few presents—traded a shield, trail-ropes, etc.—took out some awls, and had the women called to receive them. They came screaming with delight—very ugly and dirty, like the men. The whole village, lodges and all, were in keeping with the inhabitants. Near sunset, rode through the long grass and across the Arkansas to camp, where a few Inds. had arrived before us. Hodgman was engaged in trading a robe with them, and behaved so ridiculously, or rather insanely, that he amused us all. Jim^m made great fun of him. H. traded one of the horses we found for a mule.

At night the wolves set up a most mournful and discordant howling which lasted all night. There was little sleep in camp—the men were anxious for the horses—H. was sick—Hodgman was fidgetty and restless—and I was kept awake by the burning pain of my poison[194]—the horses, too, tramped incessantly through the camp. Hodgman woke me out of a nap with a story that he had seen an Ind. in a white robe drive off three horses, which were just out of sight. Went out to see, and on the way he talked so vaguely and strangely that I perceived the fever had not left his brain. It was, I suppose, nothing but his fright.

Sept. 1. Began to see plenty of bulls. Q. and I each killed one. Wolf tracks astonishingly numerous. Nooned on Arkansas, and as we rested after dinner, saw a large band of Arapahos full drive after a herd of cows across the river. Saddled horses and rode through the sands and shallow water in time to see the ground strewed with carcases, and the process of butchery began.

We had not gone a mile, when the prairie in front was literally black with buffalo.[195] Q. and I put after them, driving them up the hills on the right. The mare brought me upon the rear of a large herd. In the clouds of dust I could scarcely see a yard, and dashed

---

^m The sailor, previously mentioned as Ben, is hereafter referred to as Jim.—Ed.

on almost blind, amidst the trampling of the fugitives. Their rumps became gradually visible, as they shouldered along, but I could not urge the mare amongst them. Suddenly down went buffalo after buffalo, in dust and confusion, into an invisible ravine some dozen feet deep, and down in the midst of them plunged the mare. I was almost thrown, but she scrambled up the opposite side. As the dust cleared, I fired—the wounded beast soon dropped behind—I plied him with shot after shot, and killed—not a cow—but a yearling bull!

Tonight, the bellowing of the bulls supplied the place of the howling of wolves.

Sept. 2. Advanced among the buffalo a dozen miles or so and camped. H. killed four cows. We are to dry some meat here for the journey. Had met by the way some trading waggons; and after dinner two companies of Munroe and Platte City mounted volunteers, bound for California, came up, and some of them gathered around us—most unmilitary-looking fellows.

Saw this morning an old bull stuck in a quagmire. . . .[n]

Volume III

Sept. 3rd. H. killed yesterday four cows, and today meat is drying all round our camp. Hodgman is taken with an astonishing flow of spirits and rattles away in the most amusing fashion. Shot an old bull in the back, as he came up from the river—his death-agonies were terrific. Shot another in the afternoon. H. killed a number of cows, and Q., who was with him, by laying behind one of them killed 5 bulls as they approached. A long line of buffalo stretched over the prairie beyond the river. The roaring and fighting of the bulls were incessant. Very hot in the day, but cloudy at night. Put up the tent, but about 9 o'clock a furious tornado came up, with driving rain; down went the tent upon us all; we held it up as we

[n] Three lines illegible here, because of smudging or erasure.—Ed.

could, and got completely drenched, bedding and all. Hodgman kept on singing and rattling away, but the predicament was uncomfortable enough.

Sept. 4th. Still at camp, drying meat. Clouds of turkey-buzzards, hawks, and crows, with here and there an eagle, around the carcases. Wolves in abundance—they are fighting and howling all night.

Sept. 5th. At camp. Hodgman is very amusing—he has seen a great deal of *life* and dissipation.

[*Sept.*] *6th*. Left camp and made half a day's journey, when we stopped to dry meat. No sooner had we left camp than it was thronged with wolves and clouds of buzzards. Henry killed several cows when we stopped. I shot some bulls back upon the prairie. Mounted guard.

[*Sept.*] *7th.*° A beautiful day. Fired at bulls as we rode along. Hodgman ran one at a slow lope! At noon I shot one; and in the afternoon Q. and I ran some.

[*Sept.*] *8th.*° Cold and dreary.
    On the 6th two companies of volunteers of Price's rgt.[196] came up to our camp—a set of undisciplined ragamuffins.

[*Sept.*] *7th* (see above).

[*Sept.*] *8th*. Cold and raw. Nooned on Arkansas. More of Price's regt. came up—St. Louis county—much less raw in appearance than the former. They had lost horses, and bought some of us. Their questioning was most pertinacious and tedious. Our amusement is plaguing Hodgman, whose good-nature is unperturbable—equal to his gluttony and helplessness. In the afternoon, picked up three stray horses of the volunteers, saddles and all! We are within 50 miles of Pawnee Fork.

    ° These entries for September 7 and 8 were crossed out, as Parkman had missed a day, of which the record follows.—Ed.

[*Sept.*] *9ᵗʰ*. Picked up three more horses. Met at noon a train of trading waggons, and got information as to the road. Saw several Pawnee forts, and passed a large Indian trail. In the afternoon, we left the main road along Arkansas, and took the "Ridge Road"¹⁹⁷ —made ten miles and camped on Coon Creek. No wood. Severe gusts of rain at night.

[*Sept.*] *10ᵗʰ*. The traders yesterday told us that we should find plenty of water, but we rode some 25 miles without seeing a drop. Very warm. At length met a company of Price's regt. straggling along in their usual manner. We had just discovered some water, or rather mud, in a ravine two miles from the road. We told the soldiers of this, and they told us in return that there was good water three or four miles farther on. Capt. Garrison, the commissary, was of the party.

Rode on, and as we descended the hollow where the water lay, saw the opposite swell covered with waggons and footmen, and the water itself surrounded by white tents, cattle, and waggons drawn up in order. These were other companies of Price's regt., the Mormon battallion¹⁹⁸ commanded by Col. Smith, and waggons of Mormon emigrants. There is, it seems, a general movement of the Mormons to California. The battallion consists of 500 men, who have volunteered as soldiers, taking this method of emigrating. We encamped lower down the little stream, and were soon surrounded by the inquisitive throng.

Yesterday afternoon, all our American horses were reclaimed by the rightful owners, to the great dissatisfaction of the finders, especially Jim, who parted very reluctantly with his mare.

[*Sept.*] *11ᵗʰ*. Advanced 15 miles to a creek three miles from Pawnee Fork, where we spent the day to recruit the animals. Here we began to see signs of the settlements. There were fine ash and elm trees along the creek.

[*Sept.*] *12ᵗʰ*. Crossed Pawnee Fork—a stream running in a deep channel—plenty of trees—prickly-pear fruit.

Picked up three stray mules. Crossed towards Walnut Creek—made about half way, and turned aside to encamp on Arkansas. About dark, 28 gov'nt waggons came up and formed their *coral* on the road. Hodgman, as usual, rode out on a begging expedition, but upon his hailing the waggons from afar off with "Camp, ahoy!" he was frightened almost to death at seeing the whole force turn out and level their guns at him. They thought he was a band of Inds. raising the war-whoop—were as frightened as he—and came very near shooting him. He behaves on all occasions very foolishly and childishly.

[*Sept.*] *13th*. Met this morning another train of waggons. Nooned on Walnut Creek, where we found grapes, and another trace of the settlements in the shape of walnut trees. Camped on the Big Bend of Arkansas, where the road leaves the river.[199] A train of Sutler's waggons came up.

[*Sept.*] *14th*. Moved across to Cow Creek—16 or 18 miles. H. and I left the line to hunt—chased several bands all in vain, on account of the perverse vigilance of the bulls. Very hot—no water—we were very thirsty, and drank mud-puddles. Approaching Cow Creek and in sight of our camp, saw a band of cows. I held the horses in a ravine—H. approached. He had just got within shot, when a tremendous rattle of musketry came from the bushes on the creek, and out rushed a dozen fellows, belonging to a train of gov'nt waggons that was approaching in the distance. Off ran the cows. We found on the creek plenty of plums and grapes, besides the welcome novelty of a spring of water.

The waggoners proved a very disorderly set, and quite set at defiance the authority of Brown, the master waggoner.

[*Sept.*] *15th*. Advanced to Owl Creek and nooned. Camped on Little Arkansas. Rain at night.

[*Sept.*] *16th*. My 23rd birthday. Nooned at a mudpuddle. Hodgman afflicted with a variety of complaints. Ellis impudent to S. and effectually silenced.

Munroe gives me an acct. of California. Tells a story of a Sioux medicine chief who, Decius-like, sacrificed himself in battle to secure victory to his followers.

[*Sept.*] *17ᵗʰ*. Last night camped on one of the Turkey Creeks. Ceased to keep guard. H. saw signs of Kanzas Inds. Met waggons. The usual questioning. Dead cattle and broken waggons along the road. Prairie hens. Camped on Cotton Wood Creek, where we arrived late. Character of the Prairie entirely changed—green and rich. The Creek a pretty and well timbered stream.

[*Sept.*] *18ᵗʰ*. Nooned, after a long morning, on Lost Spring, where, as last night, we enjoyed the novelty of good water. Moved only two miles in the afternoon, and camped on a mudpuddle. We had brought water to drink with us. Met waggons. Animals getting poor and weak. Rouge's [Hodgman's] feet very sore. Munroe, Jim, and Ellis went ahead, and we saw no more of them.

[*Sept.*] *19ᵗʰ*. Nooned at the beautiful Diamond Spring. Met waggons, *three weeks* from Fort Leavenworth.[200] Camped at Rock Creek. A beautiful sunset. Made only 17 miles.

[*Sept.*] *20ᵗʰ*. Came at noon to Council Grove—beautiful meadows and woods. Here was a blacksmith's shop, and a train of waggons repairing. Passing through the luxuriant woods at this place was a foretaste of the settlements. Nooned two miles farther on at the excellent spring called Big John. More woods, and more waggons. The men, like the volunteers, well tired of their trip. Camped on one of the Beaver Creeks, and met another train, conducted by an old man of seventy.

[*Sept.*] *21ˢᵗ*. Camped at Dragoon Creek, after travelling 21 miles. Met waggons. "Whar are ye from? Californy?" "No." "Santy Fee?" "No, the Mountains." "What yer been doing thar? Tradin'?," "No." "Trappin'?" "No." "Huntin'?" "No." "Emigratin'?" "No." "What *have* ye been doing then, God damn ye?" (Very loud, as we were by this time almost out of hearing.)

[*Sept.*] *22ⁿᵈ*. Nooned at the Hundred and Ten. Made a late camp, having come nearly 30 miles with our jaded animals, at Rock Creek. Here we found Messrs. Folger, Lee, and Upton, connected with Bent & St. Vrain, whose waggons were encamped a few miles behind.[201]

[*Sept.*] *23ʳᵈ*. Met Bent's train this morning. St. Vrain was there, as also a brother of Catlin's friend, Joe Chadwick.[202] Nooned at a spring by the roadside. It rained at night. Camped near waggons.

[*Sept.*] *24ᵗʰ*. Hodgman left us. Nooned at a puddle. Met wagons. Camped at another puddle, 30 miles from Westport.

[*Sept.*] *25ᵗʰ*. Nooned at Elm Grove, where we met some men sent to hurry on the tardy waggoners. With them, were a Sac Ind. and a number of squaws—the round faces and flattish features of these Inds. were characteristic of the Algonkin stock, and quite different from the Sioux. Camped at a stream about 12 miles from Westport. Here was a party of traders with their waggons. A cold night.

[*Sept.*] *26ᵗʰ*. Met Maj. Doroughty[203] on his way to look after the waggons. Soon began to see Shawnee farms. A beautiful country; the foliage just touched with the hues of autumn. Neat houses— fields of corn and grain—pastures with cattle—and a glorious day after the dreary rain of yesterday—combined to make the ride agreeable. Saw the Shawnee mission—passed the borders of the forest country where in place of the blossoms of last spring was now hanging fruit hardly less fragrant—and at length saw Westport. Met Jim and Munroe. Sold off our outfit, and in the afternoon rode to Kanzas, Delorier on his gaunt yellow horse, in tip-top spirits. Pawpaws. Slept under Col. Chick's roof.

[*Sept.*] *27ᵗʰ*. Sunday—remained at the Col.'s.

[*Sept.*] *28ᵗʰ*. Went over to "Wyandot City"—the payment for improvements on their lands in Ohio was going on.[204] A throng of sickly faces about the building—very few full-blooded Inds. A few were adorned with plumes and gewgaws, and had their faces stained with pokeberries. There are men among them, it is said, of considerable education.

Oct. 1st. Stuck on a sandbar in the river. There is a gang of slaves below. Two of them are chained together. Another fellow, with an immense mouth, is beating the banjo, and a dance is going on with the utmost merriment. None are more gay and active then the two fellows chained together. They seem never to have known a care. Nothing is on their faces but careless, thoughtless enjoyment. Is it not safe to conclude them to be an inferior race?

> "The mind is its own place and of itself
> Can make a Heaven of Hell, a Hell of Heaven!"

Appendix: Account Book, Historical Notes, and Chronological Itinerary of Oregon Trail Trip

[St. Louis]

[J. B.] Clapp,[205] 62 St. Ch[arle]s north of ———
[M. S.] Cerré, 36 Pine St.
At Wiggins', Main St., near Market

[Cambridge]

Commons, up to Nov. 3 ——— 5
                         1

[Philadelphia]

Feb. 15
[F. J.] Fisher—85 Front St.
Pine Ids Sch 8th
[J. S.] Hav[iland]—196 Spruce
White, Walnut St. bet. 4th & 5th
Mrs. Richard [Biddle?]

[St. Louis]

Campbell[206] & Fitzpatrick, Main St. 3rd House above Bank
Corner of Morgan and 7th, Waggon Murffit

[Baltimore]

Brantz L. Mayer[207]—82 St. Paul St., office at 10 o'clock
Burnap, 49 N. Calvert St.

Eliot & Swartout

10th Peters

[Law School]

Omit Estates Tail
do ——— after possibility
Copyholds
Statute Merchant, [staple?,] Elegit
Advowsons, Tithes, Commons
Offices, Dignities, Franchises
Escheat
Not read Vol. 5—except Private Acts and King's Grants & Recoveries

---

Sept. 28, '45

Preface to Pope's *Iliad*

Blackstone
Lieber on Property & Labor
Law of real property—3rd vol. of Kent.
Tenures—Wright on tenderers—Dalrymple on Feuds
Sullivan's Dig.—Lomax's Digest. Woodson
Estates for Life—Bisset's
Roper—Merchand & [?]
Bacon's Abridg.—Estates for years
Woodfalls on Landlord and tenant. Comyn, do.
Bacon on Statute of Uses—Chief Justice Gilbert, do.
Powell on morgages by ——— Cornish on morgages—Patch, do.
Gilbert on rents
Angell on adverse enjoyment
Angell on limitations
Alienation
Shepherd's precedent of a deed.
Shepherd's Touchstone—on conveyancing.
Barton—Preston—on conveyancing—Perkins, do.
Powell on divises. Wigram [?] on wills.
Feuds. Dalrymple on feuds—Cruise on Real properties
Leges Barbarorum
Executory Devises
Hawley v. Northampton, 8 Mass.
Forfeiture for treason abolished by U. S. statute—and by the statutes of *some* of the States.
International boundary by rivers—Dunlap v. Stetson—Mason's Rep. Maine and Mass. claim the marsh for 100 yds. from the shore.

Historical Notes

Arbuth. *John Bull;* Addison on Italy.

Read John Ledyard's remarks on different nations of savages—see his *Life* towards the end *passim*.[208]

Write for *Del[aware] Reg.*

For notice of Amherst see *Gent.'s Mag.*, Sept. 1797, "Annual Necrology 1797-98." Chalmer's *Biog. Dict.*, Collin's *Peerage.*

Burnap, Baltimore. Furness

Mr. P. A. Remsen's—two miles from B[altimore] on Hookstown road, a little beyond first gate (Draper's Address)

[New York]

Call on [J. R.] Brodhead[209]

Leave letters

Knickerbocker [Magazine].[210] Hist. Soc.

[Ramsay] Crooks[211]—Univ. Pl., between Eleventh & Twelfth

John R. Bartlett

[Law School]

Studies Parallel to Cruise

Law of Real Property—Wright on Tenures—Lomax's Dig.

Coke, Lit.; Life, Bisset

Parke on Dower

Comyn's Landlord and Tenant

Uses & T

Bacon

Cornish—Saunders

Fletcher

Mortgages

Patch—Coats—Rand's Powell

Remainders

Farn

Common

Abner—Woolwich

Gilbert

Prescription

Best on presumptive

Deeds

Shepherd's Touchstone

Watkins—Preston
Cornish—Perkins
Devises
Jarman—Foxhead
Ram—Wigram
Art. on Consuls—*Hunt's Merchants' Mag.*—late no. (English Consuls)[212]

Historical Notes

"Young Bolton," a clergyman, who, says Morris, is writing a history of Westchester C'nt'y.

The extracts from E[nglish] newspapers down to 1800 mentioned by Brodhead as being in the N. Y. Hist. L'b'ry.

There is also there a set of *St. James' Cron[icle]* '63 '64.

Simms, *Schoharie County and Border Wars of N. Y.*, contains a sketch of Devil's Hole Fight, etc.

The Clinton Papers—in Mrs. Beekman's possession, N. Y.

The map in the Hist. Soc. L'b'y.—Sullivan's march.

Mrs. [W. L.] Stone has, says Moore, two trunks full of Johnson papers, belonging to an Eng. or Irish family—she proposes to write J's life.

Oneota

Whitehead's *History of N. Jersey*

Enquire of the Rutherford family.

"   of Mr. King, co-editor of the *Courier*, N. Y.

Mrs. Stone is a sister of Dr. Wayland.

Gordon—Trenton

Fenno Hoffman, N. Y.

Write to R. Conyngham—Stevens—Shippen and Burd papers in possession of Mrs. Thompson.

Write to Chs. Miner about the Elder papers still in his hands.

The Armstrong papers now at Carlisle—to be sent to the Hist. Soc.

Write to Mr. Biddle of Pittsburg. J. W. Biddle.

Bouquet letters in the Fisher family.

Francis papers in the ——— family

Lee papers on the Inds.

Minutes of the Friendly Ass.

Peter's papers

Mr. Smith

J. W. Biddle, Pittsburgh.

St. John de Crèvecœur's work—Bouquet—Phil. Soc. Lib'y

Watson's *Annals of Phil[adelphia]* for acct. of Friendly. Ass.

C. A. Poulson, Jr. Philad[ia]

John Penington, Bookseller

St. Clair Papers in Philadel. mentioned by [L. H.] Draper

Foulke family—the son at Kittunning, father near Freeport. Bouquet MS.

J. N. Whiting, Bookseller, Columbus, write for Hist. Soc. *Coll.* of Ohio part Second, Vol. I.

Hist. of Indiana by John B. Dillon at Indianapolis

Brown's *Hist. Illinois* (F[rench] settlers, etc.)

Patterson's *Hist. of the Backwoods*

American Pioneer 2 vols.—John S. Williams, Cincinati (descrip. & plan of Ft. Pitt)

Ind. Wars of the United States by Moore. Philad[ia], Gorton, 56 N. 3rd St. 1843

Wm. Leaner & Son, Bookseller, Batavia, N. Y. (write for Mary Jennison)

Washington Papers in Congress—examine them carefully.

"Address delivered before the Vincennes Hist. Soc." By Judge Law. (Send for it.)

Hon. John Law, Vincennes (ask concerning the Hist. Coll. there).

Col. John Johnston, Piqua, Miami County, Ohio. (He has been Ind. agent, and can give traditions of Pontiac.)

Hon. Nathaniel Pope, Kaskaskia.

Rev. John M. Peck, 31 N. 6th St., Philad[ia] (till 1st May—then Rock Spring, Illinois) (Enquire of Pontiac War.)

Campbell's *Bushy Run?*

Get for Draper, Hutchins. Send Whiting's *Discourse.*

Cresap Papers mentioned by Mr. Brantz Mayer as to be sent to Baltimore Hist. Soc.

(Copy for Mr. Mayer the poem on Maryland in H[vd] L'b'y. For Fisher, copy Hamilton's letter.

Ask Mead where Hutchin's Papers are.

An old Seneca, named Blacksnake, 96 yrs old, living at Allegania settlement, 30 miles from Buffalo, was at the Devil's Hole massacre, and tells the story.

Notes

Jan. 15 [1846]. The Swiss on the Sound Steamer—he was from Splügen —had walked with his box of watches and trinkets on his shoulders, all over Germany, Austria, etc. What chiefly displeased him in America was the treatment of women, who in his country, he says, are served in the same way as men, and he could see no reason why it should not be so.

Jan. 17. The black barber at whose shop I waited on Sat. night. "Coffee" said that he was a conglomerate of Caffer [Kaffir] and Moorish blood on his father's side—and Indian, white, and Negro, on his mother's. He had been a traveller—had laid up a few dollars, and, instead of trying to multiply them, had taken the whim of seeing the world.

April 17. Tradition here (St. Louis) says that Pontiac was killed in a drunken fray *near Cahokia.*

Letter to Pliny Miles, care of Chs. A. Hough, Baltimore, Md.

Baptiste Vallée of St. Geneviève must have seen Pontiac.
Mr. Lignest P. Chouteau tells me, as coming from his father, that Pondiac had a high command over the Inds. in Montcalm's army—that the English hired an Indian to kill him at Cahokia—that the Spanish requested his body, and buried it at St. Louis.
Old Mr. Chouteau speaks of him as six feet high, of very commanding appearance, and when he saw him, very splendidly dressed.

Opium and Brandy (Diarrhea)
Ipecac—vomit
Sup. Carb. Soda—acidity
Rhubarb and aniseed (costiveness)

Sandford's *Hist. of the Indians.*
Hildreth of Marietta (says [N. B.] Craig) has the St. Clair papers. He is writing a history of Ohio or the Reserve, and has in press a Hist. of Va.

Blister once a week—in front of ear—behind—and on back of neck.
1st ointment for a month.
2nd do., six weeks, applied every other day.

Proceedings, N. Y. Hist. Soc., 1844—p. 77 Schoolcraft's *Indian Names of New York*
Consult Edwin James[213]
Dobson's *Annals of the War* (Old F[rench])

Some Acct. of the N. A[merican] Inds., their Genius, Character, Customs and, Disposition towards the F. and E. Nations, 8 vo. 1754.

The Country of the Confederate Inds. 1760 (Evans' Analysis of his Map).

Benjamin P. Poore, No. 5 Rue Chananielles, Faubourg St. Germain [Paris]

John F. Watson, Germantown

Rev. John F. Schermerhorn (from near Albany) has some of Johnson's letters.

For Wayland: No competent person would undertake it. Money or affection for the deceased would be the only motives.

[W. L.] Stone's plan could not be strictly carried out by me—I have not his resources of recollection, etc.—the work would be meagre.[214]

Notes on the North West & Pontiac

Alfred Elwyn, M.D., Walnut St., East Schuykil 8th, Philada.

Mem. of Heckewelder, just published

Edward Armstrong

John Jordan, Jr.

R. L. Dickson, No. 59 South 3rd St., Phila.

Miss Mary Heckewelder, Bethlehem, Northampton Co., Pa. Inquire for the Heckewelder MS. relating to Bouquet's exped. *Jordan*.

Samuel Brenizer, Harrisburg

Richard Biddle, Esq. Pittsburg. (Mr. Reed)

Look up the Cn. Pt. [Crown Point] orderly books and the Letters for J. Sonntag Havilland (copy)

Neville B. Craig, Pittsburg, (ed. of *Olden Time*)

John Jay Smith, Librarian, Philada. L'by.

William B. Reed, Atty & Councillor, Philada.

Write to Watson (See *Annals*, V. 2, p. —) F. appreciation.

Write to Robert (?) Clark, son of the late Gen. Wm. Clark, St. Louis, enquiring of his father's papers.

Keep an eye on McKenney's lost trunk of papers, deposited at the Washington House—it contained the original papers of his accts. in the *Tour*, etc.

Write to Trowbridge, Detroit.

Shawnese = Chasuanous (*Am. State Papers*)

Jouett's "Report, containing the Descrip. of Detroit," is in *Am. St. Papers*, Vol. V.

Indian Affairs, Vol. I, 758, also, *Public Lands*, Vol. I, p. 190.

Cagnawagas = Kaughnawaugas = Caunawagas

"Conferences at Burlington and Easton 1758." Appendix to Smith's N. Jersey

Franklin's *Hist. Review of the Govn't of P*ᵃ.

Gordon's *Gazetteer of P*ᵃ.

Barton's *Views*

Volney's *View*

Douglass's *Summary* } Inds.

Chalmer's *Collection of Treaties*

Geo. H. Moore, Historical Rooms, University, N. York

Giles F. Yates, ask Schoolcraft, Schenectady

N. Y.: [G. H.] Moore—Allen—Crooks—flask—cotton.

Phil.: Elwyn—Fisher (Peters, McMurtrie), Poulson, Reed, Jordan (Bird [Burd] papers)—Frémont—ticket—map.

Harrisburg: Craig—Brenizer—return papers.

Hildreth of Marietta (says Craig) has the St. Clair papers.

Oregon Trail Accounts
Travelling Expenses March 28, 1846

March 28:	Fare to N. Y.	$ 5.
	Tea on board	.50
M. 29:	Sundries	1.00
31:	Bill at Astor	4.75
"	Porter, etc.	.75
"	Fare to Phil.	4.00
"	Copying MSS.	4.50
Apr. 1ˢᵗ:	Fare to Pittsburg	11.00
"	Book from Penington	.75
"	Bill at Jones	2.25
"	Porter, etc.	.50
"	Drinking flask	1.25
"	Porter	.12½
Ap. 2:	Brenizer, copying	25.00
Ap. 6:	Meals on road	2.00
"	*Olden Time*	2.00
"	Dinner, etc.	.66
"	Map of R[iver] Ohio	.25
Ap. 7:	Hotel Bill—Pittsburg	4.81
"	*Am. Pioneer*	4.00
"	Fare to Cincinnati	5.00

Ap. 7:	Sundries	.25
9:	Boots cleaned	.12½
"	Hotel at Cin.	.75
"	Porter	.25
"	Johnston's *Articles*	1.00
10:	Fare to St. Louis	6.00
"	Writing apparatus	1.00
"	Sundries	.25
13:	"	.25
" 13[14?]:	Porter	.25
"	*Desc. of St. Louis*	.50
"	Bath	.25
"	Hunting knife	2.25
"	Swab-stick	.50
15:	Concert	1.00
"	Postage	.10
"	Horse & Ferry, etc.	1.40
17:	Vest	5.20
"	Sundries	.30
20:	Hat	1.25
"	Suspenders	.25
"	Goggles	1.75
"	Pistols	14.00
"	Bath	.25
"	Cape	.20
22:	Horse hire	.50
"	Gun repaired	1.57½
"	Collar	.20
"	Sundries	.20
24:	Shirts	3.00
"	Saddle bag	2.50
"	Spurs	.75
25:	Bullets, etc.	.75
"	Pistols repaired	1.00
"	Pencil for F.	3.00
	Cr. Shaw to Holster & Guncase	5.00
26:	Exchange	1.50
"	Veil, etc.	.82
"	Horse	40.00
27:	Sundries	1.75

May :	Horse Prov., etc.		3.00
„	Carriage of horse		5.00
„	Moccasins, etc.		1.10
4:	Horse		60.00

Accts. in Common with Shaw

	Paid by	
	S[haw]	P[arkman]
Powder (¼ keg)		1.75
Hooks & lines, Caps, etc.	2.85	
Powder horns	1.50	
Tobacco	6.25	
Shot, Caps, etc.		
Water-proof cloth	3.15	
Blankets & powder	20.50	
Bread	7.42	
Tent equipments	5.00	
Shot	.62	
Ind. presents	*75.11	
Harness		65.48
Groceries	16.75	
	139.15	67.23
Spy Glass		7.00
Patent pencils		.50
Porter		.50
Basins		.50
Cart	43.00	
Tent	20.23	
Drayage	1.50	
Ribbons, needles, etc.	2.85	
Fare etc. to Westp[ort]		32.00
Sundries		2.00
Waggon hire, etc.		4.00
Buckskin		.80
*Henry	10.00	
De Lorier		20.00
Sundries		4.25
Sundries		5.00
	77.58	76.55

	S.	P.
Horse for Henry	38.00	
Col. Chick's Bill		8.00
Lead	.50	
Henry's Saddle		2.75
Horses shod		$1.87\frac{1}{2}$
Pots & pans		$6.12\frac{1}{2}$
Mule—to Henry's Acct.	15.00	20.00
Sundries		2.25
Bacon, etc.		9.92
Delaware Ferry		2.00
Mules		75.00

     *Paid Henry on joint acct.
      Ind. presents—23.82 (Shaw)
      Advance wages— $10.00 (Shaw)
      Mule—30 (check on C[houteau] & V[allée])
        " 5 (P.)

	53.50	127.92

Paid Delorier advance wages 20.00 (P.)
Engaged Raymond June—on leaving Ft. Laramie for Chugwater Camp.
Advanced Raymond $3.00 price of shirt at Laramie (pd. from draft on Fur comp'y)

Advanced Raymond, Taylor's work	.75
Exchange for rifle	10.00
Bill at Planters'	25.00

Bought on Credit at Fort Laramie, June 28

Sundries	29.95
12 lb. Flour (.25 pr. lb.)	3.00
1 Shirt for Raymond	3.00
42 lb. Bacon (.$13\frac{1}{2}$ cts.)	5.25

    Henry bought on our acct. July 2nd of Richard and Bissonnette:

70 lbs. flour (.15 pr. lb.)	10.50
(he bought also 25 lbs. for himself)	
10 lbs. coffee & sugar—1.00 per lb.	10.00
8 lbs. bacon (.10 pr. lb.)	.80

Bt. [Bought]—Ft. Laramie
$105.50

Common ac.	49.50

Q.A.S.	49.50
F. P.	$ 6.50
Q.A.S.	10.00

Ft. Bent

Common Acct.	43.00
F. P.	6.00
Raimond's wages	38.00

Receipts

P.	$47.00
S.	35.00
Common	66.00
P.	

Historical Notes

Armstrong family: The Col. had two sons—of the[m] the youngest, Genl. A., has a son living near Baltimore—others, one of them called Koskiusko, in N. Y.

Dr. A., of Carlisle, thinks the family papers in their hands.

Baird of Reading (formerly of Carlisle) has collected materials for a history of Cumberland Cnty.

Expenses

Jan. 16, 1846:	Fare to N. Y.	$5.00
	Dinner	.50
	Carriage	.25
	N. B. Always take a driver's card.	
	Supper	.25
17:	Breakfast	.25
	Omnibus, etc.	.16¾
	,,	.12½
18:	Breakfast	.25
	Din[n]er—Astor House	1.00
	Tea	.25
19:	Breakfast	.25
	Dinner (at Florence's)	.67½
	Tea	.25
	Omnibus	.25

Jan. 20:	Lodging: (at the Globe—room without fare—3 days and one night—three shirts washed)	3.00
	Breakfast (Globe restaurant)	.37½
	Porters and boots	.37½
	(N.B. employ a porter in preference to a carriage for baggage)	
	Fare to Trenton	2.50
	Porter at T.	.25
	Dinner & Tea	1.00
	Fare to Phil.	.75
	Porter	.25
	Ale	.06½
	Roger's *N. America*	1.25
22:	Bill at Sanderson's: ($2. per day—every fire .50!—candle .12—lunch for two .50)	4.83
	Waiter	.25
	Beggar	.18
	Museum	.25
	Ale	.12½
26:	Bill at Washington House: $2 pr. day	10.00
	Waiter and porter	.50
	Fare to Baltimore	4.00
	Sundries	.12½
27:	Chaise to Draper's	2.00
	Hist. of Backwoods	1.00
28:	Breakfast: (Tea, eggs, rolls, & toast—at lunch room under hotel)	.25
	Bootblack	.10
	Ale	.12
29:	Breakfast, etc.	.37
	Umbrella	.75
	Chocolate, etc.	.18
	Ale	.12
30:	Breakfast	.25
	Dinner	.75
	Copying	1.50
	Tea	.25
31:	Breakfast	.25
	Dinner	.75
	Chocolate	.12½

Feb. 3:	Bill at Barnum's	14.83
	Waiters, porters, etc.	.75
	Fare to Harrisburg	.03
	Bill at Buchler's	1.25
	Fare to Philada.	4.00
	Omnibuses	.42
4:	Books	1.50
5:	Copying	5.00
7:	Bill at W. House	6.75
	Waiter	.25
	Carriage	.50
	Fare to N. Y.	4.00

(Always ask for a porter's card—see your baggage
ticketed in person and get the number of the car
that contains it)

10:	Omnibuses	.30
	Ale	.12½
11:	*Oneota*	1.25
	Omnibus	.30
	Museum	.25
12:	Omnibus	.18

HENRY CHATILLON

FRANCIS PARKMAN

Howland & Aspenwall, South St. [N. Y.]
Crooks, 30 Ann St. [N. Y.]
Hayes & Barber, Market St.
Comstock, Main St.

Tow—cooking implements
Flour?—Bacon—tongues—cups and plates—spoons—tea—matches—
flint & steel—patches—salt and pepper: 5 lbs., 2 lbs.—axe—bullets for gun.
R——— Powder, 17 Levee Smith & B., Enfield, Conn.

Paid Henry on joint account by Q. A. S.: $33.82—(paid along with
Ind. present acct.)

Baird, Reading, Penna.
Miss Lyons, Lancaster
Mr. G. Lyons,   Cross corner of ——— and Paine St.

Mr. T. Green[?]

Genl. J. A. Armstrong, eminently notable general, for patriotism, valour, and piety, departed this life 9th March 1795, aged 77

[The following appear to be catch lines to material dealing with the Paxton Boys and the Carlisle massacre—Ed.]

In my last
Besides this tribe
Whilst these precautions
Whether this butchery
Whilst they were upon their march
In the morning
Notwithstanding
The day passing over
Before I proceed
The persons in arms
About 11 o'clock
In the afternoon
Night
The weather now clear
The following day
It was now hoped
The Paxton chiefs
think it is now
P. S. I should take it
Struck the Dog
Aug. 19th

CHRONOLOGICAL ITINERARY OF OREGON TRAIL TRIP

March 28.	Left Boston.
March 29.	In New York City, consulting authorities.
March 30.	In New York City, consulting authorities.
March 31.	To Philadelphia.
April 1.	Left Philadelphia for Pittsburgh. Reached Harrisburg.
April 2.	Carlisle.
April 3.	Chambersburg.
April 6.	Pittsburgh.
April 7.	Visited Braddock's Field and site of Fort Pitt.
April 8.	Took steamboat down Ohio.
April 9.	Cincinnati.
April 10.	Louisville.
April 11.	Fort Massiac. Paducah.
April 13.	St. Louis. Shaw did not join Parkman here until after the 16th.
April 15.	Cahokia. Visited Madame Jarrot. Met Midshipman Woodworth.
April 19.	Cahokia. Visited P. L. Cerré. Quotes Thomas Fitzpatrick's letter to Lt. Abert.
April 22.	Jefferson Barracks. Reports meeting with Fitzpatrick.
April 25.	St. Louis. Met Dixon, Ewing, and Jacob.
April 27.	Met Pierre Chouteau, Sr., and Lignest P. Chouteau. Parkman, Shaw, and guide Chatillon took steamer *Radnor* for Kansas Landing [Westport].
April 29.	Entered Missouri River.
April 31 [May 1?]	Jefferson City.
May 2.	Reached Independence Landing at sunset. Walked about camp of Santa Fe traders and Oregon emigrants.
May [3].	Reached Kansas Landing. Put up at Colonel Chick's.
May 5 [4].	Rode to Westport and to Sauk encampment on prairie. Joined Chandler's party and bought horse.
May 5.	Rode across the Kansas to visit the Wyandots.
May 6.	Bought two mules at Westport, and led them to Kansas Landing.

May 7.   Rode to Independence. Emigrant party from western states setting out for rendezvous on prairie. Rode back to Westport with Woodworth. Emigrant train to be organized on 9th or 10th and set out on 11th. Met Shawnee Chief Parks at McGee's in Westport and visited Boone's store.

May 8.   Chandler's party set off. Parkman's delayed by balky mule.

May 9.   Parkman, Shaw, Chatillon, and *engagé* Delorier left Westport. Passed Shawnee Mission. Camped on the Kansas.

May 10.   Crossed Kansas on ferry [Lower Delaware Crossing]. Camped 8 miles beyond, on Delaware reservation.

May 11.   Joined Chandler's party [Captain Chandler, Jack Chandler, Romaine, Sorel, Boisvert, and Wright] at Fort Leavenworth.

May 12.   Visited Colonel Kearny at fort, and Kickapoo village. Lunched with trader and returned to fort. Entertained by Kearny.

May 13.   Left Leavenworth with Britishers and lost trail within a few miles. Ended up at Kickapoo trader's and then followed fresh dragoon trail. Thunderstorm at night.

May 14.   Wagon stuck in creek after nooning. Pontiac ran off on back trail in afternoon.

May 15.   Nooned on Clough Creek (?). Met four dragoons, who told them that they had missed last year's dragoon trail a day and a half back, and were on way to Iowa Village and St. Joseph's Trail. Decided to keep on.

May 16.   Nooned on deep creek. Struck St. Joseph's Trail. Camped on week-old camp site of "Mormons." 30 miles in last three days.

May 17.   Twenty miles before nooning. Bath in pool full of snakes and insects. Dorbugs infested camp.

May 18.   Horses ran off before start. Nooned on old "Mormon" campsite. Trail better and prairie treeless.

May 19.   Crossed Little Nemaha (?) and nooned after 10 miles. Trouble with Britishers last night and today about camping and nooning places. Camped together that night, having done 20 miles in day. Violent thunderstorm.

May 20.   Camped in shelter of line of trees as bad storm broke.

"On the Mormon trail and probably within ten days of the Platte."

May 21. Set out at noon, after storm had ended. Passed recent grave. Picked up stray cow.

May 22. Trouble with wagons on muddy prairie. Picked up another cow at nooning. Camped on Little Vermillion (?). Made 18 or 20 miles.

May 23. Reached Big Blue. Rafted across. Camped on creek, 5 miles beyond. Emigrant wagons in sight. Captain visited them in evening.

May 24. Struck Oregon Trail beyond Big Blue, seven days from Platte. Kearsley, captain of emigrant train, came to their camp in morning. Passed 20 wagons of advance guard of train in morning. Romaine invited Kearsley and 4 wagons to join Parkman's party, after break-up of train. Advanced 25 miles to Turkey Creek. More wagons in sight.

May 25. Broke axle of wagon at Elm Creek and emigrants went on ahead.

May 26. Nooned on Black Walnut Creek. Camped on Wyeth's Creek, after 20 miles.

May 27. Nooned on nameless creek and camped on Little Blue (?).

May 28. Grave of 4 year-old child, "May 1845." Nooned on Little Blue. Camped on same stream after doing 12 miles in afternoon. First night-guard. Two Delawares.

May 29. Kept along Little Blue, and camped on it.

May 30. Thirty miles from Little Blue to Platte. Met Turner and another emigrant, just stopped by 6 Pawnees. At camp, emigrant from Robinson's party came in looking for Turner. Large party of Pawnees ahead. Parkman had crossed large Pawnee trail in afternoon.

May 31. Met hunting party of Pawnees in morning. Overtook Robinson's party of 40 wagons bound for Oregon. Camped after 12 miles. Emigrants went on.

June 1. Passed Robinson's party again. Caught up with Kearsley's wagons, passed them, and camped on Plum Creek after 25 miles.

June 2. Pawnee horse grave. In company with Kearsley. Shaw wanted to separate from Chandler's party. Camped on flat by Platte.

June 3.   Ten miles in morning over plain. First buffalo hunting in afternoon.

June 4.   Met Papin and boats from Laramie. Saw Woodworth, with party close behind. Buffalo hunt in morning, 10 miles in afternoon. Camped amid hills.

June 5.   Buffalo hunt. Emigrants' cattle driven off by wolves that night.

June 6.   Thus detained, went buffalo hunting. Parkman got lost. Camped near Side Fork [South Platte].

June 7.   Followed South Fork. Parkman and Shaw decided to part company with emigrants and Chandler's party after crossing South Fork. Four emigrants from party ahead, in search of 123 cattle and horses run off by large Indian party. Sorel, Romain, and two emigrants did not return at night from buffalo hunt.

June 8.   Crossed South Fork. Stranded emigrant party on north side. Romaine and others returned.

June 9.   Advanced 16 miles.

June 10.   Parted with Chandler's party. Passed around head of Ash Hollow and camped on North Fork [North Platte]. Camped by emigrant corral [Missouri party].

June 11.   Ten miles in morning. Overtaken by emigrants at nooning, pushed on, and camped by clear, swift stream. No wood for several days.

June 12.   Nooned on Lawrence Fork. Saw Frédéric's wintering place. Chimney Rock in sight. Overtook emigrant party of Americans and foreigners, with whom 5 eastbound men from Laramie were encamped. Camped by Robidoux' party, a mile or two ahead.

June 13.   Joined by Robidoux. Nooned after 8 miles on Platte. Camped by spring at Scott's Bluff after 15 or 16 miles. Joined by western emigrant at camp.

June 14.   Met Smoke's village in morning. Passed two emigrant parties from Missouri. Nooned on Horse Creek with Smoke's village. Camped ten miles farther on.

June 15.   Visited Richard at Fort Bernard. Met Reynal. Nooned by Platte, entertaining Richard. Passed Sabille and Adam's deserted fort. Received at gate of Fort Laramie by Bordeaux. Vasquez, Simoneau, Monthalon, Knight, etc., at fort.

June 16.   Fort Laramie. Smoke's village arrived in morning. Visited
            Indian camp in evening. Emigrants arrived.

June 17.   Fort Laramie. Emigrants gave feast for Indians. Chandler's
            party arrived.

June 18.   Fort Laramie. Shaw treated sore eyes of Smoke's squaw
            and daughter.

June 19.   Fort Laramie. Indian begging dance.

June 20.   Fort Laramie. Smoke gave Parkman puppy feast at
            noon. Chatillon sent for his squaw Bear Robe to join
            party. Parkman swapped Pontiac for Paul Dorion's mare
            Pauline. Parkman, Shaw, Chatillon, Delorier, Ray-
            mond, and Reynal, his squaw, and her two nephews
            set out for Chugwater. Camped seven miles from fort
            on "wild and beautiful bottoms of the Laramie."

June 21.   Rode 10 miles to Chugwater, camped by its mouth.

June 23.   Chugwater. One of Reynal's nephews, His Horses, sent
            to find Bear Robe's lodge and get news of war-party
            rendezvous at La Bonté's Creek.

June 24.   Chugwater.

June 25.   Chugwater. Rode to Fort Laramie. Smoke's village gone
            north of Platte. Illinois and Michigan emigrants at
            fort. His Horses returned with son of Bull Bear. Tunica's
            [Whirlwind's] village 4 days off and Bear Robe due on
            27th.

June 26.   Chugwater. Rode to Fort Laramie for supplies. Part of
            Russell's company arriving there. Tunica arrived.
            Minniconjous a day or two away. Recent emigrant ball
            at fort.

June 27.   Chugwater. Rode to Fort Bernard with Paul Dorion.
            Found Russell's or Bogg's party, the Boones, Ewing,
            Jacob. Sent letter east by Tucker. Returned to camp
            and found Shaw and Chatillon gone to bury Bear Robe.
            Reynal in alarm about Indian raid.

June 28.   Chugwater. Shaw and Chatillon return. Indian at camp,
            on way to leave squaw with Bissonnette while on war
            party.

June 29.   Chugwater. Indian left for Fort Laramie.

June 30.   Chugwater. Trappers from fort arrived, and reported
            arrival of Bissonnette.

July 1.	Chugwater. Henry went to see him. Tunica talked out of war by Bordeaux.
July 2.	Chugwater. Shaw, Parkman, and Reynal rode out in search of Tunica. Met Indian who tells them plans changed and returns to camp with them. Young Bull Bear, his brother, and several others came to camp.
July 3.	Chugwater. Tunica's village arrived and camped near by. Parkman visited camp and was given a pipe by Tunica. Met Old Borgne and Mad Wolf. Mourning for Bear Robe. Given dog feast. Tunica's village abandoned rendezvous at La Bonté's and planned hunt beyond Laramie Mountains and then war party.
July 4.	Chugwater. Three Indians arrived, with rescued Negro Jack.
July (5).	Moved camp to Forks [of Laramie]. Strong Heart Dance. War parade.
July 6.	Shot a war eagle. Left Indian village with trappers for Bitter Cottonwood Creek to meet Bissonnette and accompany him to La Bonté's. Emigrants feast Indians.
July 7.	Waited at Bitter Cottonwood for Bissonnette. Rouleau and Séraphin set out to trap in mountains. Chatron and party arrived from fort with news that Bissonnette will arrive on 8th.
July 8.	Rode to Horseshoe Creek, since Bissonnette did not arrive.
July 9.	Rode to La Bonté's on Platte. No Indians or buffalo. Morin, his squaw, and her brother in camp, as well as her father, a medicine man. Gingras also.
July 10.	Abandoned hope of Indian rendezvous at La Bonté's. Shaw went to Horseshoe Creek in search of Bissonnette.
July 11.	Shaw returned near daybreak, having lost his horse. Parkman and Raymond set out in pursuit of Tunica's village; Chatillon in search of Shaw's horse. Shaw to accompany Delorier and the cart to Horseshoe Creek. Parkman headed south, nooned on Horseshoe Creek, and followed Oregon Trail to Bitter Cottonwood Creek.
July 12.	Animals ran off ten or twelve miles to Side Fork of Laramie [North Laramie]. Camped there.
July 13.	Headed for Laramie Creek. Found tracks on tributary southern creek [Sibille?]. Nooned and headed for mountains. Laramie Peak in sight. Camped where Laramie comes out of hills.

July 14.   Followed southern tributary of Laramie. Then on Indian trail up into "bare and scorching valley" of mountains. Descended into grassy parks amid hills. Crossed bare prairie and followed defiles, like Dixville Notch, beneath bare cliffs. Nooned after 12 miles. Indian forts. Climbed narrow pass and camped beyond its head. Buffalo in sight on distant butte as they emerged from hills.

July 15.   Stony Prairie. Medicine Bow Mts. in distance. Trail led towards head of Laramie Creek. Little lakes. Approaching Snake and Arapaho country, according to Raymond. Found Reynal and Indian village on banks of Laramie.

July 16.   Feasted Indians.

July 17.   Moved camp westward. Camped on fine spring, 10 miles off.

July 18.   Made two moves westward in search of buffalo. First buffalo killed.

July 19.   Meat cached and camp moved 12 miles westward to unknown stream [Rock Creek?].

July 20.   Moved short distance higher up creek. Buffalo surround. Sioux on guard against Snakes and Utes.

July 21.   Robe-making.

July 22.   Parkman and Raymond went out hunting antelope. Séraphin and Rouleau arrived from Laramie Hills, headed for Rockies [Medicine Bow]. Indians out on another surround, though in great fear of Snakes.

July 23.   White Shield uncertain about war party because of sore throat.

July 24.   Squaws still making robes and lodge covers. Rouleau and Séraphin left. White Shield did war dance.

July 25.   War party abandoned. Moved to last camp on creek to collect cached meat, and then to cut lodge poles in Laramie Mountains. Indian quarrel. Squaws mourned dead of last year.

July 26.   Moved nearer mountains [Laramie Hills]. Ceremony in lodge.

July 27.   Moved. to mountains. Camped in valley of "clear, cool creek." Shongsha cut. Parkman wandered among mountains like those of New England, while Indians cut lodge poles. Much game, pine and spruce forest,

	rocky and precipitous mountains. Mourning for warriors last seen at this spot last summer.
July 28.	Parkman went hunting with Raymond in mountains. Descended to prairie and saw buffalo. Circled back to village over mountains.
July 29.	Climbed high, rocky mountain a few miles from camp, crossing wooded ravines with small, icy streams. Heap of Hail killed elk.
July 30.	Broke camp and moved "round" to the pass through the mountains, about 12 miles. Passed campsite of last year's war party. Hunted mountain sheep near camp.
July 31.	Parkman and Raymond went hunting in hills and rejoined Indians at camp near crystal spring amid great basin of rocks.
August 1.	In mountains, following grassy valley amid pine-covered hills. Camped in grassy nook.
August 2.	Left Indians and set out for fort, with Heap of Hail as guide. Delayed by butchering black-tailed deer and rejoined Indians as they descended rocky gorge. Mountains in front on fire. Descended into milder region of valleys and streams, and emerged on prairie. Left Indians and camped on Chugwater.
August 3.	Reached Fort Laramie in morning. Rejoined Shaw, Chatillon, and Delorier.
August 4.	Parkman's party of five set out for Bent's Fort, accompanied by Rouville and his Ute squaw, bound for Bissonnette's camp. Camped after ten miles.
August 5.	Nooned on dry stream. Crossed Goshen's Hole and camped late.
August 6.	Nooned on Little Horse Creek. In afternoon reached Horse Creek, where Bissonnette, N. Sabille, and party, and 40 lodges of Tunica's Sioux village and several Cheyennes were encamped. Horse races, with Paul Dorion, Rouville, Antoine, and other French Canadians. Bissonnette feasted Indians.
August 7.	At camp.
August 8.	At camp. Dance of Strong Hearts. The Stabber arrived with news of Army of the West on the Arkansas and of victory of Matamoras. Young Bull Bear took Parkman's party under his protection.

August 9.   Indians and Bissonnette moved. Parkman and party continued to Spring Creek.

August 10.   Nooned on Pole Creek and camped on little stream beyond.

August 11.   Delayed by horses running back to Pole Creek. Nooned on Crow Creek and camped on tributary.

August 12.   Nooned low down on Crow Creek, and camped at 9 P.M. at mouth of the Cache à la Poudre. Saw Vasquez [Longs?] Peak.

August 13.   Crossed South Fork [of Platte] and nooned near St. Vrain's Fort, after 10 or 12 miles. Rode on 5 or 6 miles and camped near Vasquez' Fort. Fresh Indian trail.

August 14.   Passed Fort Lupton, 6 or 7 miles on. Nooned on the Fork. Camped on it, where trail left it to cross over to Cherry Creek.

August 15.   Nooned and camped on Cherry Creek. Campsite of Mormons guided by Richard.

August 16.   Nooned on Cherry Creek and camped on it where trail left to cross over to the Arkansas.

August 17.   Pikes Peak in sight. Rode 12 miles and nooned at head of Kiowa Creek. Camped there because of sick horses.

August 18.   Nooned on Black Squirrel Creek. Storm over Pikes Peak. Camped at Jamie's [James'?] Camp.

August 19.   Nooned on Fontaine Qui Bouille and camped lower down it.

August 20.   Made 12 miles in morning, nooned on Fontaine Qui Bouille. In afternoon saw Arkansas Valley and reached Lower Pueblo. Richard there. News of Matamoras, Kearny's march to Santa Fe, and of troops on Santa Fe Trial.

August 21.   Rode across Arkansas to see Mormons. Met Bonney.

August 22-24.   From Pueblo to Bent's Fort along Arkansas.

August 25.   Nooned a few miles from Bent's, grass being exhausted about fort by Mormons and troops. Visited fort in afternoon. Received by Holt. Invalid soldiers. Simpson, Lt. Abbott of 1st Dragoons, Forrest. Rumor of capitulation of Santa Fe.

August 26.   Delorier sent on with cart to camp a few miles below fort, while Parkman dined there. Hodgman, Munroe, Ben the sailor [Jim Gurney], and homesick emigrant [Ellis]

	join party; Raymond paid off. Both Bents absent. Forty supply wagons arrived. Cheyenne lodges near fort, but most of nation on Dry Creek after buffalo.
August 27.	Left camp and nooned after 12 miles. Camped after eight miles more. Three stray dragoon horses caught.
August 28.	Fifteen miles in morning. Camped on Arkansas, after "good march."
August 29.	Nooned on Arkansas. Met Magoffin's wagons. Buffalo reported a day and a half below, with Arapahos this side of them. Also Pawnees on trail, who had killed Swan, whom Magoffin reburied.
August 30.	Met government wagon train under Coates. Trail reported dangerous. Ewing's brush with Pawnees, who tried to steal his horses. Parkman urged to hurry between the Caches and Pawnee Fork.
August 31.	Saw Arapahos on south bank and crossed over to visit them in afternoon. Camped on north bank at night. Many wolves.
September 1.	Plenty of buffalo bulls. Nooned on Arkansas and afterwards saw Arapahos pursuing band of cows across the river. Rode across and found prairie black with buffalo. Parkman got caught in stampeded herd.
September 2.	Advanced a dozen miles among buffalo and camped. Met traders' wagons and two companies of Munroe and Platte City mounted volunteers. Hunted buffalo for supplies for homeward journey.
September 3.	More hunting and meat-drying.
September 4.	Still at camp, meat-drying.
September 5.	Still at camp, meat-drying.
September 6.	Set out and made half a day's journey. Encountered companies of Price's volunteers.
September 7.	Ran and shot buffalo as they traveled.
September 8.	Nooned on Arkansas. More of Price's regiment. Picked up three stray volunteer horses. Fifty miles from Pawnee Fork.
September 9.	Picked up three more stray horses. At noon met trading wagons. Saw Pawnee forts and passed large Indian trail. In afternoon left the Arkansas and took Ridge Road. Camped after ten miles on Coon Creek.
September 10.	Twenty-five miles without water. Met company of Price's,

with Captain Garrison, the commissary. Camped on little stream near more of Price's and the Mormon Battalion. Horses reclaimed by soldiers.

September 11. Advanced 15 miles to creek three miles from Pawnee Fork and camped. First ash and elm trees.

September 12. Crossed Pawnee Fork and camped on Arkansas, halfway to Walnut Creek. Train of 28 army wagons.

September 13. Met another train in morning. Nooned on Walnut Creek. Camped on Big Bend of Arkansas where trail left river. Train of Sutler's wagons.

September 14. To Cow Creek, 16 or 18 miles. Buffalo hunting. Plums and grapes. Army wagon train under Brown.

September 15. Nooned on Owl Creek and camped on little Arkansas.

September 16. Camped on one of the Turkey Creeks. Stopped keeping guard.

September 17. Camped late on Cottonwood Creek, after entering true prairies. Trail littered with dead cattle and broken wagons.

September 18. Nooned on Lost Spring, and camped 2 miles beyond. Met wagons. Munroe, Jim (Gurney), and Ellis went on ahead.

September 19. Nooned at Diamond Spring. Met wagon train three weeks from Leavenworth. Camped on Rock Creek after doing 17 miles.

September 20: Reached Council Grove at noon. Nooned at Big John Spring, two miles beyond. Camped on one of Beaver Creeks, after meeting many wagons.

September 21. Camped on Dragoon Creek after 21 miles.

September 22. Nooned at the 110, and camped at Rock Creek, after doing 30 miles, with Folger, Lee, and Upton of Bent & St. Vrain.

September 23. Met Bent's train, with [Marcellin] St. Vrain and Chadwick.

September 24. Hodgman left for Ft. Leavenworth. Camped 30 miles from Westport.

September 25. Nooned at Elm Grove. Met Sauk Indians. Camped on stream 12 miles from Westport, with party of traders.

September 26. Met Major Dougherty. Passed Shawnee settlements and mission, and entered forest country. Met Jim [Gurney] and Munroe in Westport, where Parkman and Shaw sold their outfit. In afternoon rode to Kansas Landing and put up at Col. Chick's. Delorier lived at Kansas.

September 27. Spent this Sunday at the Colonel's.

September 28. Went over to Wyandot City to seek payment for the Ohio lands.

October 1.   Stuck on sandbar in river.

October ?   Reached St. Louis, where Parkman and Shaw said farewell to Chatillon.

1856 & 1866 Notebook

French Colonization

Introduction

THIS apparently rather uninteresting record of references to authorities, books, and documents, relieved by thumbnail sketches of historic places in Canada, is far more important than it looks, for here is an early measure of Parkman's thoroughness as a historian and of the wide range of his research. Nine years before he published the first volume of *France and England in North America*, he knew most of the sources and many of the pioneers of the history of New France. Barred by illness from travel, after the publication in 1851 of *Pontiac*, his first historical work, he put in five years of concentrated study and carried on a vast correspondence with workers in the field that preoccupied him. Finally, in October and November 1856, during a brief interlude of comparative good health in the long period of physical and mental suffering which plagued Parkman from 1852 to 1862, he was able to make a brief excursion to Quebec, Montreal, and the Ottawa Valley to consult books, authorities, and the scenes of the great history which he had undertaken after publishing *The Conspiracy of Pontiac*.

The task was difficult enough in itself—"Go to work at consulting fifteen hundred books in five different languages with the help of a schoolgirl who hardly knows English, and you will find it a bore," Parkman wrote to his friend E. G. Squier on September 17, 1851— but the young historian was also beset by difficulties quite apart from the task. His eyes were so sensitive that they could not support sunlight, so that his work had to be carried on largely with the aid of others. But still worse was the mental disorder which he thus describes:

"Between 1852 and 1860 this cerebral rebellion passed through great and seemingly capricious fluctuations. It had its ebbs and floods. Slight and sometimes imperceptible causes would produce an access which sometimes lasted with little respite for months. When it was in its milder moods, I used the opportunity to collect material and prepare ground for the future work, should work ever become practicable. When it was at its worst, the condition was not enviable. I could neither listen to reading nor engage in conversation, even of the lightest. Sleep was difficult, and was often banished entirely for one or two nights during which the brain was apt to be in a state of abnormal activity which had to be repressed at any cost, since thought produced the intensest torture. The effort required to keep the irritated organ quiet was so fatiguing that I occasionally rose and spent hours in the open air, where I found distraction and relief in watching the policemen and the tramps on the Malls of Boston Common, at the risk of passing for a tramp myself. Towards the end of the night this cerebral excitation would seem to tire itself out, and give place to a condition of weight and oppression much easier to bear."—Letter to Martin Brimmer, 1886.

Under such handicaps Parkman ransacked the libraries of the Boston Athenaeum and Harvard College, and through correspondence sought the advice and help of other historical workers. The necessary books were rare and hard to come by; the essential documents were scattered among the disordered archives of Paris and public and private collections in France, England, and Canada. The collection of materials proved "abundantly irksome and laborious," but Parkman was considerably aided by the little group of historical pioneers in this neglected field. Among the most helpful was George Bancroft, then the dean of American historians. Another friendly fellow-worker was Dr. Edmund Bailey O'Callaghan, the Irish physician and politician, who made a new career for himself as the state archivist of New York after being exiled from Canada for his part in the Papineau Rebellion of 1837. His *Documentary History of New York* was of great value to Parkman, and probably Parkman owed the idea of visiting Papineau at Montebello to the latter's old lieutenant. John Gilmary Shea, the first American Catholic historian of note, also proved a most useful correspondent, since he was in close touch with the clerical historians in Canada, where he had spent some years in the Jesuit novitiate. Through Shea or others, Parkman was soon in correspondence with Abbé Ferland of Laval University, Père Félix Martin of St. Mary's College, Montreal, and other Canadian historians, and with Jacques Viger of Montreal and Georges-Barthélemi Faribault of Quebec, among the antiquarians. From this nucleus his circle of correspondents broadened out as his researches opened up new paths of enquiry. This correspondence is singularly rich in historical interest, for the field was almost untouched; and here are the eager reports of pioneers working from many different points of view. Through the exchange of letters, Parkman's correspondents became his friends; and when a brief interlude of good health enabled him to go to Canada, they showed him their treasures of books and documents and offered advice with the freedom of old acquaintances.

After his return home, the work went on as health permitted. In 1862 illness was banished for a period, and by 1864 Parkman was able to complete the first volume in his proposed series, *The Pioneers of New France*, as well as to report the following progress on the great task he had set himself:

"At present the work, or rather the series of separate works, stands as follows. Most of the material is collected or within reach. Another volume, on the Jesuits in North America, is one-third written. Another on the French explorers of the Great West is half written, while a third, devoted to the checkered career of Louis de Buade, Comte de Frontenac, is partially arranged for composition. Each work is designed to be a unit in itself, independent of the rest, but the whole, taken as a series, will form a connected history of France in the New World.

"How far, by a process combining the slowness of the tortoise with the uncertainty of the hare, an undertaking of close and extended research can be advanced, is a question to solve which there is no aid from precedent, since it does not appear that an attempt, under similar circumstances, has hitherto been made."—Letter to George Ellis, 1864.

In 1866 Parkman revisited Quebec and Montreal, renewing his friendships of ten years before and making new ones. His circle of acquaintance was soon to become larger in Quebec than in Boston; and in Montreal his favorite sister Caroline, now married to the Reverend John Cordner of the Unitarian Church of the Messiah, made him welcome in her home. Some of the following notes were clearly made on this later visit, although this notebook has previously been dated 1856. The references to *La Revue Canadienne* (founded 1863) and *Le Foyer Canadien* (founded 1866) are sufficient to indicate that there were later entries.

The present notebook is largely a collection of references to books, papers, and works in progress. These are not without interest, since the value of many Canadian primary sources depends upon the edition used. There are also some revealing stories about historians, and some accounts of the religious institutions so foreign to Parkman and so important in his history. The vivid shorthand notes on the localities visited form the basis of the famous descriptions in the later histories. Parkman was adept at catching in a few words a striking likeness of the scene before him, and sometimes these rough sketches are more effective than the more labored purple patches of which they were the source.

This notebook, which contains both the record of the 1856 journey and notes made as late as ten years after, is bound in brown pigskin and measures $3\frac{3}{4}$ by 6 inches. The writing is in ink and very legible. The front cover bears the inscription "French Colonization" in ink.

1856 & 1866

[On the inside front cover and flyleaf are written three tentative titles: "France in the New World: a history of French Dominion (Power) in N. America; its rise, growth & fall," "France in the New World: a history of French Colonisation in North America," and "French Colonial Empire in North America: its Rise, Progress and Fall."[1]]

M. Faillon is preparing an account at length of the settlement of Montreal[2]—consult his previous books.

Catalogue of the Bibliothèque Impériale (Royale) now being prepared.[3]

Papers Collected by Hon. L. J. Papineau[4]

Cass's Papers on Detroit[5]

Gayarré's Papers[6]

French's　　" 　[7]

In hands of J. G. Shea: Chaumonot's Autobiography—Perrot's Memoirs—Dablon's Relations 1672-3, 1673-9—Chronicle of the New Orleans Ursulines.[8]

MSS. at Rome—see Bancroft's note Aug. 9, '56.[9]

Biddle papers—Bancroft.[10]

Garneau examined the notarial registers of some 600 marriages at Quebec, where the place of birth of both parties is given. The result was that the emigrants came from many provinces, Normandy & the Isle of France (chiefly Paris) predominating. Many from Poitou, many from Brittany, a few from Burgundy—but chiefly the coast provinces from Flanders to Spain.[11]

Perrot, *Moeurs des Sauvages* is to be published.[12]

———

Montcalm—saw his skull at the Ursulines, where he was buried in their chapel—(see the Ursuline nun)—a chapel with plain white walls, now hung with good pictures—a very handsome altar with ancient tapestry-work, gilded oak carvings, etc.—a large grating on one side, a pulpit on the other.[13]

Lorette—near the foot of a range of hills. Here the St. Charles foams over a broad rock, and rages along a wooded ravine. Below, stretches a vast level towards Quebec, once carpeted with forest. Lorette was once the advanced station of civilization. Saw Chaumonot's virgin.[14]

Cap Rouge. The shores of the St. Lawrence fall away gradually as one sails up. Near Montreal, a broad watery expanse—low lines of shore studded with habitans' cottages and trees, chiefly poplar.

C. P. Drolet,[15] Admiralty Court, Court House, Quebec.

Charles Panet, Jr.,[16] Student at Law, care Messrs. Lelièvre & Angers, Advocates, Quebec.

N. Fages,[17] Notary, Quebec.

Th. Sterry Hunt,[18] Esq., Montreal.

Very Rev. C. F. Cazeau,[19] Grand Vicar of Quebec.

Hon. Henry Black,[20] Quebec.

G. B. Faribault,[21] Esq., Quebec.

Rev. F. Martin,[22] S. J., Prest. [President], St. Mary's College, Montreal.

M. le Commandeur J. Viger,[23] 24 Notre-Dame St., Montreal.

Hon. L. J. Papineau,[24] Monte Bello, Petite Nation, River Ottawa. See a few pages farther

---

St. Anne [-de-Bellevue]. A narrow & swift current between the Point & Isle Perrot—then widens to the lake of 2 Mountains.

The Mission[a]—small houses & hovels along the shore—above, among the spruce & other trees, a great tract of sand.

The Calvary with its stations.

The river is a broad expanse as far as the Long Sault, where it narrows. A portage of 14 miles. Above, steamboat again to Petite Nation. Hilly picturesque shores.

Passed the night at the inn—the day at M. Papineau's. Above, to Ottawa. The shores rather low & tame. A little above Mr. P.'s,

* At Oka, on the Lake of Two Mountains.—Ed.

View of Montreal, 1830
Engraving by W. L. Leney after drawing by R. A. Sproule
(Coverdale Collection No. 112)

View of Quebec, 1850
Lithograph by T. Picken after a drawing by Captain B. Beaufoy
(Coverdale Collection No. 179)

is the spot where a detachment of soldiers was stationed to intercept traders going up without license.

At the Chaudière, the river foams over vast sheets & ledges of rock in horizontal strata, and falls boiling into two great chasms—then rushes down, on the left bank, between a rocky island and the shore.

Tanner[25] is of little acct. Alegambe[26] is valuable (a copy in N. Y. Hist. Soc.). (No.)

At M. Viger's is a portrait of Champlain[27] & of Mme. C. in his "Album"[28] (doubtful).

Also of Charlevoix[29]—a fine manly face.
   "   of Lafit[e]au[30]—young & good-looking.
   "   of Piquet[31]—lively—vivacious—full of health & vigor.
   "   of Crespel[32]—a sullen-looking monk.
   "   of La Corne,[33] uncle or great-uncle to M. Viger.

Also an illuminated drawing of a banner on which were embroidered the articles of covenant between a band of Iroq.—joining Picquet's mission of La Présentation—and the French. The banner itself is still in existence at Montreal. The cross, the emblems of the Virgin & the Savior, the *fleurs de Lys*, and the Iroq. totems, are all embroidered, and linked together by strings of wampum-beads wrought into the silk—the whole edged with a gold fringe; and on the reverse the covenant is written in French.

Notre Dame des Neiges was on the site of the Priests' farm. Some of the bastions still stand.

At Caughnawaga are the remains of a stone fort,[34] on the river.

At St. Anne's, a strong current. Five or six wooded islands just above.

At the Mission of 2 Mts.[35] is the original portrait of Picquet—very good pictures in the church.

I heard the squaws, wrapped in blankets like so many blue spectres, sing in the church. Their voices were strangely high-pitched.

Hospital Genl. at Quebec[36]—St. Vallier's[37] tomb, & picture.
Soeurs de la Congrégation,[38] & their school.

Visited the Soeurs de la Congrégation—teachers of children of all ages.

The Soeurs de la Charité[39] (Madame Youville). They receive the aged, infirm, & disabled.

The Bon Pasteur,[40] a new sisterhood, in part a Magdalen asylum.

The Hôtel Dieu,[41] a hospital.

The Ursulines,[42] a school.

At Charle[s]bourg, the farms were laid out in wedge-form, diverging from a common centre.[b] Each man built his house near the centre, and the houses, being contiguous, together formed a polygonal fort, with a common area in the middle. The farms still retain the wedge form, and the point of junction is called the *fort*, though the building has disappeared.[43]

Marie de l'Incarnation's *Lettres*[44] are in [the] Bishop's Library, Quebec.

Hon. J. Fraser, Quebec, has a copy.

Also, Rev. Mr. Plante,[45] Hospital Genl.

Charlevoix's *Life of Marie de l'Incarnation*[46] is in possession of the priest of Lorette (ask Mr. Black) and of Mr. Plante. Said to be now reprinting at Paris.

Mr. Faribault, Mr. Plante & Mr. Viger have La Tour [Latour].[47]

Juchereau,[48] 2 copies, in Seminary Library, Quebec.

Mr. Plante has Ragueneau's Life of Mère Augustin[49] (said to be only a leaf or two, and valueless).

On crossing the bridge of the St. Charles, one finds a level country, and shores easy of access but for the shallow extending out to the channel, where the water deepens very suddenly. The shore rises & grows abrupt as you approach Montmorenci.

Above Quebec, Cape Diamond forms a bold, precipitous height shouldering out into the river. As you go towards Wolfe's Cove, there are places where it is perfectly easy to walk down to the river, and which, except for the forces of the current, would have offered but slight natural obstacles to landing.

---

[b] A rough pencil sketch has been omitted here.—Ed.

The list of docs. on Louisiana which Margry offered me at $500. is in the hands of Govnt. at New Orleans—a copy.[50]

In the Bibliothèque Impériale, a MS. vol. of *Alphonse de Saintonge* [*Alfonce Santongeois*],[51] said to contain details of the first exploration of the Saguenay (note in "Catalogue of Library of M. Puibusque,[52] sold 1864"). (No.)[53]

Monsieur Pierre Margry,[54] Conservateur-adjoint des Archives de la Marine, Ministère de la Marine, Paris.

Penecaut, MS.[55] alluded to by Charlevoix. There is a copy in Canada. Shea will perhaps get a copy from it.

Hon. P. J. O. Chauveau,[56] etc., etc., etc., Montreal.

Canada, Documents Divers,[57] MS. in fol[io] in Bibliothèque Provinciale Canadienne (Faillon).

La Bibliothèque Canadienne (a collection, historical, literary & scientific).[58]

La Revue Canadienne (begun in 1863).[59]

Owen, *Exploration of Iowa & Wisconsin* (govt.)[60]

Munsell Series—Explorations of the Mississippi, St. Cosme, Guigues, etc.[61]

M. l'abbé H. R. Casgrain,[62] Quebec, has letters of Baby[63] ([concerning] Pontiac), his great-grandfather—also can point out various docs. on Canadian Hist. Offers aid. He is now President of the *Foyer Canadien*[64] (Mar. 1866).

Johnstone, *A Dialogue in Hades*[65] (Wolfe, Montcalm). (Montreal, Dawson, 1866)

De Gaspé, Philippe-A., *Mémoires*[66] (Ottawa, 1866, Desbarats). (Manners in Canada in the writer's youth.)

Vétromile, *The Abenakis & their History* (N. Y., 1866).[67]

M. Maurault has now (Oct. 1866) in press a history of the Abenakis.[68] He is missionary at Lake St. Francis.

First Paris Notebook

1869

Introduction

IN OCTOBER 1868, after enjoying reasonably good health for some seven years, Parkman suffered a return of what he called "The Enemy"—the cerebral confusion which made work impossible, except for the briefest periods. Since the attack, which was the worst since 1858, showed little sign of ceasing in the following month, he decided to spend the winter in Paris, hoping that the change of scene would benefit him and that the French doctors, then the leading specialists in nervous disorders, might be able to offer him some aid. It was not only the pursuit of health that took him to Paris. He was then engaged upon the volume which was called *The Discovery of the Great West* when it first appeared in the fall of 1869, and was published after 1879 as *La Salle and the Discovery of the Great West*. For this work he needed the use of the great collection of La Salle material which M. Pierre Margry, director of the Archives de la Marine et des Colonies, had amassed during a quarter-century of research. After surveying the Paris archives, Abbé Casgrain had reported to Parkman that Margry was *"très avare de ces richesses, qui sont grandes"*; and Parkman went to France prepared to offer Margry a large sum for the use of his collection.

But Pierre Margry was a jealous guardian of the riches entrusted to his care, if not a wholly scrupulous one. His years in the archives had given him an unsurpassed knowledge of their contents. He knew them not only as a curator but as a researcher, for General Lewis Cass had employed him to collect documents on the old Northwest; John Romeyn Brodhead had found him helpful in selecting material dealing with the early history of New York; and the Canadian government had commissioned him to select and arrange two series of colonial papers. This work, in addition to his official duties, had given him what he viewed as a vested right to the public documents entrusted to his care; and he kept his collection inaccessible to other scholars until he achieved his aim of publishing the results of his researches. In 1869 Parkman succeeded in winning Margry's friendship, but not the use of his great collection. This notebook contains the record of Parkman's conversations with Margry in January, February, and March 1869, in which the latter offers a few hints and urges his own theory that the Jesuits sabotaged La Salle's expedition to the mouth of the Mississippi. For the rest Parkman had to dig for himself in the Bibliothèque Impériale (formerly Royale, and soon to be Nationale), the Archives de la Guerre, and the Depôt des Cartes de la Guerre. At Margry's suggestion, he also hunted out the current Marquis de Montcalm, who proved most helpful and put him on the track of the Montcalm Papers purchased by Sir Thomas Phillips a few years before and of relevant material in the British Museum, which Parkman inspected in March before returning home. But Margry himself remained deaf to Parkman's pleas for the use of the La Salle material, and held up the latter's work for ten years by doing so. Nevertheless Parkman did not question Margry's private right to public documents; he became his friend and lifelong correspondent; and eventually he made it possible for Margry to reap a second crop from his labor by arranging for the publication of the collection under an appropriation by Congress as *Découvertes et Etablissements des Français dans l'Ouest et dans le Sud de l'Amérique Septentrionale, 1614-1754* (Paris, 1879-1888). Before leaving Paris, Parkman also commissioned Margry to supervise the copying of a vast mass of documents which formed the raw material of later books in his epic of New France.

Paris helped to rout "The Enemy," and Parkman led anything but an invalid's life during his stay. In addition to the historical investigations noted in the journal, he formed friendships with Count Adolph de Circourt, who was a friend of the George Ticknors; Count Jules Marcou, the translator of Bancroft; and General Dix, the American Minister. He wrote his sister: "If I accepted invitations, which I do not, I should have the run of the Faubourg St. Germain. I have just declined an invitation from the Prince de Broglie to dine." He saw the sights of Paris from Versailles to the sewers, and took pleasure in random walks about the city when his mental state prevented him from working in the archives.

Margry's influence on Parkman is historically important. After the publication, late in 1869, of *The Discovery of the Great West,* John Gilmary Shea protested that his friend "had been led too far by Margry, who is of the modern French school continually yelping at the Jesuits." The Puritan Parkman, amusingly enough, assured the Catholic Shea that Margry was "a most zealous Catholic." But Margry's letter to Sainte-Beuve (for text, see note 39), in reply to the latter's request for information about Parkman's *Jesuits,* supports Shea's opinion. Margry was so zealous a Catholic that he thought the militantly Protestant Parkman had been led up the historical garden path by the clerical historians of Canada. The book which raised the ultramontane storm against Parkman in Quebec was too Catholic for Margry's taste. The truth of the matter seems to be that Parkman was affected for the rest of his life by the growing anti-clericalism of France through his correspondence with Margry, and on the other hand was subject to the Catholic influence of his other great historical correspondent, Abbé Casgrain.

The record of this historian's holiday in the Paris archives is contained in a small black leather notebook, $5\frac{1}{2}$ inches by $3\frac{1}{4}$, which opens at the end. The text is largely in ink, with some passages in pencil.

1869

Paris, Jan[uary] 1869. 21 Boulevard St. Michel.[1] Portrait of Mad[ame] de Frontenac (Versailles 3508), young, blooming, handsome, with helmet, plume & shield; see catalogue of Versailles (apparently as Minerva).[2]

Plaster bust of Montcalm, Galerie des Batailles, Versailles. Better than any other representation of him I have seen.[3]

Picture of La Salle's exped. 1684, "La Salle découvre La Louisiane," Salles des Marins, Versailles. A deep bay—low shores, all lighted by a warm sunset—on the right, marshes with rank tropical vegetation and trunks of fallen trees—Indians gazing at the ships or pushing canoes into the water. The *Joly* in the foreground—a boat's crew about to land—on the left, more distant, another vessel—in the distance the *Aimable*, stranded.

Margry, 23 Jan. La Salle was the name of an estate near Rouen, belonging to the Caveliers.

Joutel was the son of a gardener of La Salle's uncle.

Margry says that his book was composed by Michel who accompanied La Salle on his first exped., the material being furnished by Joutel (see Joutel's title page).[4]

Acte de naissance de La Salle,[5] *registres de l'état civil, Paroisse Saint-Herbland, Rouen.*

"*Le vingt-deuxième jour de novembre, 1643, a été baptisé, Robert Cavelier, fils de honorable homme Jean Cavelier, et de Catherine Geest; ses parrain et marraine, honorables personnes Nicolas Geest et Marguerite Morice,*" discovered by Margry in 1847.

Margry in *Revue de Rouen,* 1847: "Réné-Robert Cavelier, sieur de La Salle."

"*La Salle partit pour le Canada en 1666 âgé d'environ 22 ans*"—baptised

22 Nov., 1643 in the church of Saint-Herbland—*"ses parents étaient merciers-grossiers."*

26 Jan. Margry says that he has the letters of La Salle on which the *Relation des Découvertes* is founded.[6] That this is the official account but that the letters are full of La Salle's personality—complaints against Jesuits—his troubles from his rivals—pecuniary distress—the embarassments caused him by the weakness of his brother (who at one time tried to persuade him to marry). He alludes to the charges of harshness brought against him and defends himself, but adds that indeed *he will have no blasphemers in his camp: "Je suis Chrétien."*

Margry insists that it was N. Perrot the voyageur who tried to poison La Salle.[7]

He says that he has positive proof of the treachery of Beaujeu, and that he was in league with the Jesuits.[8]

Margry says that all the papers of Frontenac's time, and sometime later, have been sent (copies) to New York or Canada, with the exception of those of La Motte Cadillac and the foundation of Detroit, wh[ich] are retained for publication. There must be also other exceptions—certainly the La Salle papers.[9]

Jan. 27. Margry says to-day that though the papers on Detroit are not in the government collection of Canada, they are among those copied for Cass and also for Papineau.[10]

He says that the Montcalm letters, found in Quebec after the capture, are at the Depôt de la Guerre [War Office] of England. These, he says, have been chiefly published by Dussieux.[11]

There is another collection in England in the hands of a person whose name he does not remember, but thinks he can find it out.[12]

Perhaps, he adds, there are papers in the hands of the Marquis de Montcalm at Montpellier.[13]

Frontenac's dispatch, 1672. The part about the Jesuits is written in cipher (figures) with the explanation interlined in another hand.[14]

30 Jan. Margry read a paper from his collection by which it appears that the father of Joutel received from Henri Cavelier, La Salle's uncle, who employed him as a gardener, 50 francs a year, equivalent perhaps to 300 now.

Young Cavelier, La Salle's nephew, who was with him on his last voyage, died a few years after, an officer in a regiment.

The La Salle who wrote the letter preserved in Thomassy[15] was no relation to the Caveliers, but the son of a naval official at Toulon.

The concluding part of La Salle's letter to the Minister from St. Bernard's Bay, 4 mars, 1685,[16] partly printed in Thomassy, accuses the *"capitaine"* of the *Aimable* of having purposely wrecked her & says that he (La Salle) was convinced of his treachery before leaving St. Domingo. He adds that it is his purpose to retire within the mouth of the river (supposed[ly] the western mouth of the Mississippi) to avoid the notice of the Spaniards—that he proposes a journey to the Illinois—that if he does not hear when there that peace has been published in Canada, he will proceed to the mines of St. Barbe— that though his soldiers are wretched, he can still succeed, his chief reliance being on Inds., who only want to feel that they are supported by F[rench] soldiers, and will never know whether the soldiers are good or not.

A map (Margry), bearing the name *"Minuty del."* & entitled: *"Plan de l'Entrée du Lac où on a laissé M*. de la Salle."*[17]

minuty del.

A   Camp of La Salle
B C Indian huts
D Aimable wrecked   The Joly is represented not far
E La Belle   from shore.

Margry: A map (a mere sketch) of Raudin on which is laid down "*Rivière de la Divine ou l'Outrelaise.*"[18]

On another map of Raudin, the Mississippi is called "Buade" (1688?)[19]

A very curious map of Le Sueur of the Upper Mississippi.[20] Great detail—names of all the Sioux nations.

Several curious maps of La Verandrye [Vérendrye], one of them made up from Indian maps.[21]

Margry: By a letter from a Jesuit to Margry, it appears that La Salle must have been 16 years old before he could enter the novitiate. Then 2 years, and afterwards teaching in the schools.

Map, MS: "Route que firent les Espagnols pour venir enlever les François restés à la Baye St. Bernard ou St. Louis après la perte du vaisseau de M^r. de la Salle, en 1689."[22]

By this it appears that they passed from C[o]ahuila by the [Rio Grande] del Norte, the upper Nueces, the "Hendo" [Hondo, or Rio Frio], the de Leon [San Antonio], the Guadalupe. After crossing the del Norte their line of march west marked out.

La Hontan's "*Rivière longue*"[23]

Route marked east & west from "*Chacagou*" down "*R[ivière] à la Roche*" to the Mississippi.

"*Tabula Novae Franciae Anno 1660*" (Creuxius)[24]

Bib[liothèque] Imp[ériale]: Duval, 1677: "*Village avec palissades attaqué par Champlain*"[25]—about midway between the Oswego and the Genessee. This map is very much behind its time and is founded partly on Champlain. The Lakes all wrong.

Cornelli, "*Partie occidentale du Canada ou de la Nouvelle France 1688.*"[26] Lakes laid down with great accuracy (like Fran(c)quelin). Upper Mississippi after Hennepin. As far south as 34°.

Bib. Imp.: Vaugondy, Canada (1756?) (Argenson, secretaire d'Etat)[27]

Nolin, "*Canada et La Louisiane, 1756* [28]

"*Canada et La Louisiane.*" Le Rouge, 1755[29]

Bellin, 1745[30]

"*Partie de la N. France.*" Jaillot, 1685.[31] Hudson's Bay & forts on it, etc.

Bib. Imp.: Ms. map of Pierre Raffeix, S.J.[32] Indicates voyage of
La Salle 1679, who, he says, writes that he went to the sea in 1681.
A better way, says the Jesuit, would be from L. Erie by the Ohio.
Marks out Du Luth's course & says he rescued Hennepin.

"Canada, Louisiane et Terres Angloises," D'Anville, 1755 (very
large).[33]

"*Amérique Septentrionale*," D'Anville, 1746.[34]

"*L'Amérique Septentrionale*," Bellin, 1755.[35]

Popple's Map, (old F[rench] war)[36]

Le Marquis de Montcalm, 27 Rue Casimir-Périer, Paris. He has
a fine portrait of his ancestor, also a miniature taken at an earlier
age, and an old engraving, not very good, from the portrait.

For genealogy of Montcalm see *Armorial de la Noblesse de Languedoc*,
par La Roque, Firmin Didot, 1860.

M. de Montcalm says that the Marquis his ancestor was of short
stature and rather fat. He kept aloof from court intrigue. His mother,
Mad. de St. Véran, a *femme maîtresse*, urged him to go to America, &
it was her influence that induced him to take the command.[37]

Feb. 25. Margry says that Sir Thomas Phillips is the person in
England who has the Montcalm Papers; and that a catalogue of the
Phillips collections exists, and is probably to be seen at the British
Museum.[38]

Margry read me his letter to Ste.-Beuve about the "Jesuits."[39] He
insists that I have not exposed their political character—that they
controlled the Co. of the Hundred Associates, and held the colony
in a subjection so irksome that it could not long be tolerated—that
they constantly tried to make the governor their instrument—in
short, to absorb everything. He says that he has a document, of date
subsequent to 1660 (1663?) "very damaging for them." I do not find
that he has anything earlier, though he says that this doc. refers back
as far as 1642.

It might be added to the text that the "Northern Paraguay"
could not long have endured, as the growth of political and commercial interests must sooner or later have subverted the Jesuit
empire.

Feb. 27. Several small *bouches à feu* of the 14th century at the Musée d'Artillerie, in general principle of construction like that found at Ottawa,[40] but the tube is of 3 or more staves, instead of one piece lapped and welded. Made of wrought iron, and not much larger than the Ottawa piece. See cat. of Museum, No. 1-5.

The Marquis de Montcalm says that, soon before the battle of the plains of Abraham, Montcalm heard of the death of one of his daughters—which one he could not learn—and that his distress almost overcame him.[41]

Archives de la Guerre. The papers here on America do not antedate Louis XV. Abundance on the war of 1755-63.[42]

I was shown only 1 letter—"Talon au Ministre, 19 Oct. 1667"— of the reign of Louis XIV.

Légende de la carte:[a] *"Canada (carte des limites du) avec les colonies anglaises depuis les montagnes de la Virginie jusqu'à la ville des 3 Rivières sur le fleuve S[t]. Laurent. Echelle d'environ 4,5 lignes pour une lieue."*[43]

Cette carte est un essai fait sur les limites en 1758—elle n'est nullement curieuse. MS.

La carte est classée aux Archives des Cartes du Dépôt de la Guerre, à Paris, sous le classement 7—b. 59. La carte est manuscrite.

"Le port de Louisbourg, dans l'isle Royale, représenté de basse mer."[44]

L'Isle royale, au Sud de laquelle est ce port, forme avec l'Isle de terre neuve l'entrée du golfe de S[t]. Laurent, d'où les vaisseaux montent le fleuve jusqu'à Québec dans le Canada. Carte dessinée avec soin. MS. Classé à 7-B-64.

A large MS. map of Detroit (1796?), colored, with a picture of the fort and town of Detroit.[45] This map is in great detail, very large, and well executed.

The above are in the Dépôt des Cartes de la Guerre, which contains little else besides printed maps which may be found elsewhere.

Several maps of Vaugondy, time of Old French War.[46]

The following is the title of the Detroit Map: *"Plan topographique*

[a] This and the following entry are in the handwriting of Pierre Margry.—Ed.

du Détroit et des eaux qui forment la jonction du lac Erié avec le lac St. Clair, dressé pour l'intelligence des voyages du Général Callot dans cette partie du continent en 1796." Carte MS. *classée à 7-6, 61.* (Dépôt de la Guerre— Archives des Cartes.) Settlements extended as far up as Lake St. Clair on west side, and as far down as middle of Turkey Island on east side.

The MS. maps are in the Dépôt des Cartes de la Marine, 13, Rue de l'Université.

Mar. 7. Margry says that Beaujeu had an understanding with the Jesuits to defeat La Salle's plans, as, he thinks, may be inferred from the following:

1ˢᵗ. Beaujeu says in a letter to Seignelay, that since La Salle *knew that his wife was devoted to the Jesuits,* he has been very cold and reserved. Hence Beaujeu was in relations with the Jesuits.

2ⁿᵈ. Beaujeu's separations from La S. in the Gulf was clearly intentional, and his refusal to return in search of the river was grounded on false pretences, for M. says that he has evidence that, after leaving La Salle, he *did* return, find the Mississippi, and take its latitude & longitude, after wh[ich] he sailed for France, leaving the colonists and La Salle to their fate. La Salle, as M. thinks, had given him the latitude of the river.

3ʳᵈ. That there was a plot on the part of the Jesuits was shown by the behavior of Alloüez when Joutel saw him at St. Louis, and his agitation when told that La Salle was approaching

4ᵗʰ. The Jesuits, after La Salle's death, hastened to enter upon the field which he had occupied, and undertook to discover and possess the Mississippi, completing the work of La Salle (see the memoir in my possession).[47]

P. S., Mar. 8. The evidence alluded to by M. as to Beaujeu's return to find the Mississippi is that of a manuscript map wh[ich] he showed me. Here is laid down the mouth of the Mississippi "as described by M. de La Salle," but on the *back of the map,* immediately under this part of it, is another representation of the mouth of the Missisippi, with the words, *"Embouchure du Mississippi telle que nous l'avons trouvée."*[48]

La Salle had a triple aim, the discovery of the western passage to

D'Anville's Canada, Louisiane et Terres Angloises, 1755

(Coverdale Collection No. 592)

China—the opening of an interior commerce—and action against the Spaniards by war in time of war and by *contraband trade* (Margry) in time of peace.

Frontenac was needy. La S., to gain his aid in his schemes, approached him on this weak side. F. had no money to give—therefore, unlike all others whom La S. induced to aid him, he lost nothing—but he gave his influence and authority as capital. La S., a man of broad views and not mercenary, was forced to use the greed of others as a means of success. His associates hoped for large profits. Thus alone he could raise money.

Early in his career La S., having no money, was forced to look to his brother for supplies. Hence his enemies were always trying to discredit him with the priest. La S. complains much of him for trying to direct him & meddling in his affairs. Once, when he wished to marry a young demoiselle of Canada, his brother annoyed him greatly by his interference.[49]

The Marquis de Montcalm says that Montcalm was so abandoned in Canada that he was forced to make great outlays on his own credit—that his family paid after his death a hundred thousand francs to his creditors, for debts contracted in Canada, and that the family was so reduced in means that his three surviving daughters had only 1,000 francs a year.[50]

9 March. The Marquis de Montcalm says that 5 or 6 years ago a collection of papers on the Canadian war and his family (autographs) was sold in Paris & bought by an Englishman.

Q. Sir Thomas Phillips?

Sir Thomas Phillips, Bart., Thirlestane House, Cheltenham

11 March. British Museum: *Lettres de Monsieur le Marquis de Montcalm Gouverneur Général en Canada à Messieurs de Berryer & de la Molé écrites dans les années 1757, 1758, 1759, avec une version Anglaise.* (*Londres, J. Almon, 1777*) 8 vo. Title of translation: Letters from the Marquis de Montcalm & Messieurs, etc. (1777). 28 pp. of the French, each opposite a page of the version bearing the same number.[51]

There are but 3 letters of Montcalm:

1st to Berryer, 4 April 1757, enclosing a long letter from S. J., dated Boston, 4 Jan. 1757.

2nd to Montreal, 1 Oct. 1758.

3rd Quebec, 24 Aug. 1759. This is the famous letter of wh. I have a copy.

All relate to political affairs of Eng. colonies.

Mt. Desert Notebook
1870

Introduction

THIS notebook stands alone among the later journals, for it is the commonplace book of Parkman the poet rather than of Parkman the historian. Parkman was first drawn as a young man to poetry, but after a few ventures in the ballad form on themes from colonial history, he decided, in his own words, to "confine his homage to the Muse of History, as being less apt than her wayward sisters to requite his devotion with a mortifying rebuff." But like many another literary man he wrote better prose for having once written verse, and many pages of the great history are almost lyrical. Nature always evoked the poetic mood in Parkman, and when at forty-seven he spent a few weeks with a college friend, Judge Horace Gray, at Mount Desert and Grand Manan Island, off the Maine coast, the glories of September called forth these vivid prose poems devoted to sea and shore, which rank among his best pictures of the nature which he loved so well. Evidently he could not resist paying a visit to his old haunts in New Hampshire on his way back to Boston; for the final entry in the notebook is a description of the scene about Center Harbor on Lake Winnipesaukee, when the frosts of early October had set the forest afire with scarlet and crimson and gold.

Since this 1870 notebook is devoted to literary sketches, it will not be amiss to consider here Parkman's style. He was trained by William Russell at the Chauncy Hall School and by Edward Tyrrel Channing at Harvard in the old rhetoric based upon classical models; and he never lost his fondness for the periodic sentence, with one clause balanced against another and the whole piling up to a formal conclusion, reminiscent of the great classical orations. Byron, Cooper, and Scott, his favorite authors, taught him how to describe action in words, and also gave him a certain tendency to wordiness and to formal rather than familiar language. Byron encouraged his native romanticism and lyricism. His wide reading for professional purposes among the early chroniclers—Hakluyt and Purchas and the authors of the *Jesuit Relations* were among his favorites—clearly affected his stylistic development, and he gained from them an appreciation of the rhetorical force of simplicity, which was a valuable antidote to the early Augustan influences upon his writing. From them, too, he probably learned the great Elizabethan trick of using the well-worn word in such a way that it took on all the vigor and force that it had held at first; and also acquired the habit of using a slightly archaic idiom, appropriate to accounts of an almost forgotten past.

Parkman's great weaknesses as a writer were to strain too hard for rhetorical effects and to allow his sentences to become of unwieldy length and congested with unnecessary words, with a consequent loss of the simplicity and vigor so necessary to good narrative. It is difficult to explain the first tendency entirely: his early training had much to do with it, but there seems to have been a natural instinct for the phrase that is just a shade too high, just as his ear was naturally faulty. The second weakness undoubtedly can be explained by the methods of mental composition that were forced upon him by the condition of his sight: the writer who is unable to revise a dictated draft with pencil or pen habitually falls into this fault. In later years the improved condition of Parkman's eyes allowed him to edit his own work carefully, to its notable benefit. In the earlier period, when this process was not possible, there is an interesting difference in style between the advance chapters of *The Pioneers* which appeared in the *Atlantic* and the final version in book form: a great gain in clarity and simplicity has been achieved by the pruning away of unnecessary epithets. This revision seems to have been the work of Charles Folsom, a friend of Jared Sparks, who served as librarian of both Harvard and the Boston Athenaeum, and who is thanked by Parkman in the preface to the book for his "skillful and friendly criticism."

In the present notebook (in printing which all variants have been preserved) there is abundant evidence of Parkman's talent for self-criticism, as well as of his methods of composition. First he struggled for perfection of phrase, and when that was attained, he had little difficulty in constructing sentences which have something of the finality and inevitability of the classics. He relied too much upon adjectives for the modern taste, but this was perhaps unavoidable in descriptive writing. But there can be no question of his flair for language and of his literary power; he was no mere phrasemaker, unable to sustain a theme for more than a few notes, but rather the capable composer of historical operas, who could carry an epic drama along on a high level, punctuated by brilliant arias which are the purple patches of the anthologies. He is certainly the greatest writer among American historians, and consequently these sketches which illustrate his methods of composition are of major interest.* They are also more perfect poems than any he wrote in his poetic youth.

These notes are written in pencil on the pages of an orange paper-covered account book, $3\frac{5}{8}$ by $5\frac{3}{4}$ inches.

* Similar sketches of Acadia occur in the 1871 & 1873 Notebook, pp. 551-53.—Ed.

1870

Mt. Desert,[1] *Sept[ember] 1870.* ~~The lifeless water~~

~~—The forest, black in sunset shadow,~~

The pale dull blue of the lifeless waters; the forest black in sunset shadow, tracing its ridgy line against the sky, and, above, one small cloud-speck, bathed by the vanished sun in opalescent fire, floating in the rosy crystal of the west.

The forest, where sunbeams stream aslant among the deep-green verdure of the hemlocks, and athwart the white gleaming stems of the slender birch trees; and the tall spruces rear aloft thin tall and tapering spires, high in the illumined air.

~~—where breakers surge and pound against the adamantine granite~~

Under a leaden sky, the island rocks rest sombre and cold upon the leaden water, as strong men, under the clouds of an inexorable dreary destiny, bide their hour in still and stern endurance.

~~Betwixt. The~~

Towering, and ledge above ledge, half seen ~~athwart~~ betwixt the restless plumage of the birches—dark sheets of sun-scorched rock, where in rift or crevice, and every point of vantage, clings a hardy population of storm-defying trees.

Cliff and ~~rock~~ crag and long black reef, where ~~in crested ranks~~ the ~~fierce~~ crested breakers charge headlong against the adamantine granite, to be dashed ~~back~~ to a chaos of creamy foam, tossed on high in clouds of shining spray, and poured back in snowy cascades from the impassive rock.

The low hanging clouds—the streaked and mottled surface of the gray torpid sea pitted ~~with~~ by restless rain drops—the dark coast line of islands whose tops are veiled in ~~mist~~ fog—the wet rocks & the spectral host of fir-trees half wrapped in fleeing mists.

~~Under the keen wind sunlight and the keener wind,~~ The white topped waves flash and foam under the keen sunlight and the keener wind; the island rocks are dim with ~~bounding~~ silvery spray, ~~and~~ all the vast reach of iron-bound coast is edged with creamy foam, and breakers leap madly aloft as if to scale their craggy barrier.

Where vast crags cast their shadows on the deep blue sea that surges at their base.

The cliffs of the Grand Menan[2] are much higher than those of Great Head, and extend for miles with scarcely a break. Cape Split & Cape Blomidon (Bay of Fundy) are also greatly superior.

Pemaquid[3] may be easily reached from Bath.

Katahdin[4] is now very accessible.

~~The breathless water is like a sea of glass~~
~~The quivering mirror of the (breathless) glassy water.~~
~~Pale sunbeams chase each other along the rocks.~~

Soame's Sound. Reflected from the quivering mirror of the glassy water, pale sunbeams chase each other along the bordering rocks, carpeted with ~~juni~~ trailing juniper and plumed with ferns. The leaves of the poplar and the birch hang ~~unstirred~~ motionless in the breathless air, and in the dry top ~~arms~~ of the dead pine an eagle sits basking, his white head gleaming in the sunlight.

Sunrise, Sept. 10. The low murmuring of the tranquil sea; shores and islands painted in shadow against the ~~glowing~~ rosy east; the light that glistens on the wet black ledges, the brown waste of lank sea-weeds, and ~~the~~ pools left by the receding tide; the moon that pales from gold to pallid silver before the advancing dawn, and the mountains that, dusky and cool, ~~lie~~ sit waiting for the sunrise.

Deep mountain gorges where brooks plunge and gurgle in the damp and silence; where ~~the~~ firs and ~~the~~ hemlocks, anchored in the rifted rocks, cast funereal shadows, and corpses of fallen trees lie mouldering, swathed in green winding sheets of moss.

~~Where~~ The mountain rears its bluff bold front, where knarled spruce trees, ~~stretch their shaggy~~ grisly with pendant mosses, stretch thin shaggy arms against the storms.

Senter [Center] Harbor,[5] *Oct. 7.* The ~~rocky~~ verge of some sunny cliff, where birch trees shake thin gilded leaves, and ~~the~~ crickets chirp from among the crisp mosses— ~~far~~ below the forest ~~stretches~~ lies outspread for many a league, a carpet of red & russet, green & gold, with far mountain ranges dark with evergreen, and lakes of lustrous blue, ~~and~~ where islands float in hazy light.

Acadian Notebook
1871 & 1873

Introduction

IN THE summer of 1871 Parkman first visited Acadia, which he saw again in 1873 and in 1879, and whose history he chronicled in *Montcalm and Wolfe* (1884), *A Half-Century of Conflict* (1892), and the revised edition of *The Old Regime* (1893). A note to this last edition, sent to press only a few months before Parkman's death, indicates that his original intention had been to take up the subject in the first edition (1874): "I was unable to gain access to certain indispensable papers relating to the rival claimants to Acadia— Latour and D'Aulnay—and therefore deferred all attempts to treat that subject." Twenty-two years having passed and the papers having come to hand, Parkman supplied the three missing chapters by adding a new first section, "The Feudal Chiefs of Acadia," which covered Acadian history from 1604 to 1710 and was chiefly devoted to the struggle between the rival seigneurs Latour and D'Aulnay for control of the rich fur trade of the region.

Parkman's Acadian history was written backwards; for he discussed the final phase in *Montcalm and Wolfe*, and the middle period in *A Half-Century*, the last volume of the series to be written, though not the last in chronological order. This odd procedure was demanded by the fact that the necessary source materials were long lacking. The ancient bitterness over the deportation of the Acadians in 1755 was fanned up once more in the 1880's by a controversy among the historians concerned with the question, and by Longfellow's sentimentalization of the matter in *Evangeline*. Parkman's two Acadian chapters in *Montcalm and Wolfe* involved him in a long feud with Abbé Casgrain and Philip Smith, who were backed by Rameau de St. Père and Edouard Richard, as Parkman was backed by Sir Adams Archibald, William Kingsford, and George Stewart, Jr. Parkman had based his work upon documents edited by Thomas

Akins of the Nova Scotia Archives. Casgrain demonstrated that Akins had tampered with the evidence, and expounded his case at length in *Un Pèlerinage au Pays d'Evangéline* (1889), and in three volumes of new documents, *Collection des documents inédits* (1888-90). Parkman reviewed *Un Pèlerinage* condescendingly for the *Nation* (March 14, 1889—XLVIII, 232-3), remarking that the Abbé "has chosen to make the question a national and religious one." Of course the question *was* essentially a national and religious one, which accounts for the bitterness which its discussion evokes. In such circumstances Casgrain's emotional temperament was apt to lead him astray, but so was Parkman's growing bias in his closing years against Catholicism and its clergy. It is unfortunate that Parkman came to treat one of the most difficult problems of his subject only when his zest for research and his passion for objectivity had been somewhat dulled by a lifetime of unrewarded labor. Casgrain really had the better of the controversy, and Parkman was doubtless glad to bury the hatchet in his last few years. The modern view is that Parkman was led astray by insufficient and altered evidence.

On his trip to Acadia in July and August 1871, Parkman went first to Annapolis, Nova Scotia, then north to the Minas Basin, and then across the Bay of Fundy to St. John, New Brunswick. After going up the river to Fredericton, he returned home by way of Bar Harbor. In November of the same year he paid a flying visit to Quebec. In August 1873, after visiting Abbé Casgrain's old family home at Rivière-Ouelle on the lower St. Lawrence, opposite the mouth of the Saguenay, Parkman returned to Nova Scotia, visiting Annapolis, and then crossed the Bay of Fundy to St. John, returning home by way of Eastport and Portland, Maine.

The record of these early visits to Acadia is contained in a maroon leather notebook, $6\frac{3}{4}$ inches by $3\frac{7}{8}$, which opens at the end rather than the side, and from which seven pages, either cut or torn out, are missing. Parkman sometimes removed such field notes to insert them in books which concerned the subject. Three loose pages from another notebook, $6\frac{5}{8}$ inches by 4, held together in a blue paper wrapper marked "Acadia, local notes, 1873," contain the record of the 1873 journey.

1871 & 1873

[Two pages have been cut out.—Ed.]

Annapolis, 26ᵗʰ July. The site of the fort perfectly apparent on approaching the shore from the direction of Digby Gut[1]—a rising ground between Annapolis River on the left & Allen's River, also called Lequille River, on the right.[2] A blockhouse to guard the bridge across the ditch at the entrance, a range of barracks, a magazine, & two wells are the principal remains besides the earthworks, which are very strong, though almost exclusively directed to defend the water side, the rear being made very difficult of access by the two rivers.[a] There is also an arched covered way from the body of the work to a strong exterior work, facing the basin and showing the remains of a battery. Other exterior works command the meadows bordering the Lequille. There are remains of *chevaux de frize*[b] all along the water. The magazine seems to be French. The cream-colored limestone with which it is arched is said by Judge C.[3] of this place to have been brought from France.

Remains of French occupancy are said by Judge C. to have been found about 3 miles up the Lequille.[4] There seems to be none near the town.

There is a Micmac town on Bear River,[5] towards Digby, and a F[rench] Acadian settlement at Clare near St. Mary's Bay.[6] There are none here or in the direction of Minas Basin.[7]

[A page torn out here—Ed.]

Lyon's Cove, near Cape Blomidon,[8] 28 July. Large rich meadows along

[a] "There was a garrison here within 18 or 20 years."—F.P.
[b] Sharp-pointed stake barricade.—Ed.

549

Annapolis River, separated from the Bay by North Mt., which extends from Digby Gut to this place, and forms the heights at the Gut, wh[ich] is less than half a mile wide. Current extremely swift, Annapolis Basin being like a great mill-pond. Tide rises 36 feet. Goat Island in the basin said to be the site of Sir Wm. Alexander's settlement.[9] Heights about the Gut covered with forests, except some cliffs on the outside.

The part of North Mt. about Blomidon, and apparently the rest also, is a red sandstone, which forms cliffs along all this part of Minas Basin. It is very friable & rapidly disintegrated by wet & frost, changing into a rich red soil which is washed by the tide over the meadows, and, when the salt water is diked out, makes them extremely fertile.[c] This is the character of the meadows of Grand Pré and the neighborhood, which is reclaimed by dikes. Several streams, as the Avon, Habitant, Perreau [Perrot],[10] etc., run up into the country, with fertile diked lands about them, all formed of this red soil. No French left about here. The river Gaspereau,[11] which enters the basin between this place & Grand Pré, is full of mill privileges: the F. are said to have had more than 20 mills on it.

Sunrise at Lyon's Cove. Tide out, leaving a broad expanse of red beach between the steep red cliffs & the water. Blomidon is of this red rock,[12] but the upper part is covered with wood.

Last evening the North Mt. was covered with sea fog from the Bay.

On the way from Lyon's Cove to Canning, a fine view of the country between the N[orth] Mt. & the South Mt., extending from Minas Basin towards Annapolis.

From Blomidon one sees Grand Pré and the Minas Basin from a height said to be about 450 ft. Could not get down to edge of cliffs, which are said to be 150 ft. perpendicular.

Grand Pré is described as a vast expanse of rich grass land, reclaimed by dikes.

[Page headed "Digby Gut, Sat. 29 July" cut out.—Ed.]

[c] "Every spring, the rock, as far as the frost penetrates, falls from the face of these red cliffs and is quickly changed to soil."—F.P.

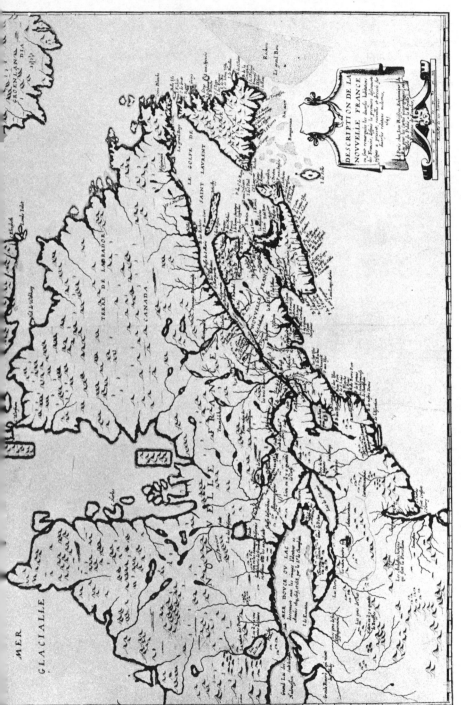

Boisseau's Description de la Nouvelle France, 1643
One of the oldest and rarest maps of Canada
(Coverdale Collection No. 1675)

The country around Grand Lake, from wh. the Jemsec [Jemseg][13] flows, is said to be hilly.

Nashwaak River, the site of the fort attacked by Church,[14] is just opposite Fredericton. Somewhat low flat shores here.

River St. John, below Fredericton, 31 July, morning. Warm drizzling rain.
The distant hills lie pale & faint, & along the dim shores, the elm trees loom like dark phantoms through the dull grey mists.

St. John, 1 Aug. "Fort La Tour" is on the site of Carleton, just opposite Navy Island. A few traces of earth works visible among the mean houses which occupy the ground. It is generally known as the "Old Fort."[15]

The rapids are a short distance above. Below them, the tide rises *27 feet*—above them, *18 inches*. Hence there is a fall of $25\frac{1}{2}$ feet. At high water the rapid is effaced and vessels go up & down with ease! Steep limestone rocks, forming a narrow passage, spanned by the suspension bridge.

Above are the narrows where the river runs between rocky heights, feathered with evergreens, then expands into Grand Bay, to which the Long Reach succeeds. The steep rocks here turn to undulating hills. Nerepis River, where is said to have been a F. Fort,[16] enters on the left as you ascend. Above the Long Reach, a rich farm country—at first upland, but above the Jemsec it takes the character of broad meadows of the richest kind, which continue above Fredericton.

2 Aug. Sea, off St. John. The dull grey sky, the dull grey sea; the dark waste of ridgy forests; the mists that float around the brows of cold stern cliffs; the reefs & rocks that lie in sullen slumber on the leaden waters. Now the fog rolls in and all is veiled from sight, till the seamed & scarred front of some grisly headland, crowned with bristling firs, looms grimly through the mists.[d]

[Two pages missing; the second headed "Bar Harbor."—Ed.]

d Last sentence was crossed out.—Ed.

Quebec, Nov., 1871. Height of citadel 350 feet (P. L. Morin)[17]
Rock an argillaceous limestone (Sterry Hunt)[18]

Quebec, Nov. 4, [18]71.

[Page and a half missing.—Ed.]

St. Lawrence, near Saguenay, after a shower. The setting sun, half sunk behind the hills of Tadoussac, bathes with soft golden fire the fleecy clouds that hang above the west, pours floods of level radiance athwart the falling drops, and paints a mighty rainbow against the grey eastern sky.

Acadia
Local Notes, 1873

Aug. 9, 1873. Approaching entrance of Annapolis Basin.
Dark mountain ridges rise above the faint blue haze that slumbers on the sparkling sea.
The entrance. Where the fierce tide surges between opposing walls of verdent forest and weather-beaten rock.
Annapolis Basin, tide out, shores near Goat Island. Vast beds of oozy mud, studded with brown rocks and patched with stranded seaweeds, where the blue heron stalks in the shallow pools, and flocks of crows feed on the countless shell-fish.

The tide rises about 40 feet at Digby. Rode in a wagon thence to Annapolis. Views of Basin & shores very fine. There is a small Indian settlement on Bear River. The French in Digby [Annapolis] county[19] are said to form more than a third of the population—descendants of the Acadians.

As Gray[20] and I smoked our cigars on the rampart of the old fort at Annapolis, the moon rose full, among small dense clouds drifting before a strong wind. They took strange reptile-like forms, with silvered edges and black bodies, and seemed to devour & disgorge the moon by turns. The effect was so weird that the legal mind of Gray was moved to wonder and admiration.

Aug. 11. Sea, near the coast between St. John & Eastport. The north is thick with mustering clouds whose fleecy mists hang lowering above the shadowed forests and the sombre sea.

Aug. 12. Morning, entrance of Portland Harbor. Under the flush of dawn, dark reefs & islands slumbering on the glazed and quivering sea.

Second Paris Notebook
1872

Introduction

IN THE autmn of 1872 Parkman returned once more to Paris, to resume the research he had begun in 1869. During the troubled years of the Franco-Prussian War and the Commune, he had worried over the fate of the archives so necessary to his work; but the tides of war and revolution had washed over them without harm. Once more he laid siege to Pierre Margry, who proved somewhat more helpful and listed references to La Salle material in his own cramped hand in Parkman's notebook. Parkman also met Gabriel Gravier, the great Rouen authority on La Salle, and Henry Harrisse, whose knowledge of Canadiana and Americana was unmatched. Harrisse—whose *Notes pour servir à l'histoire, à la bibliographie et à la cartographie de la Nouvelle-France et des pays adjacents, 1545-1700* (Paris, 1872) remains a standard work today—had formed a collection of manuscripts and printed maps of Canada, which passed into the hands of Samuel L. M. Barlow of New York soon after Parkman was in Paris. This notebook is devoted mainly to references to maps, plans, and documents inspected by Parkman under the guidance of Margry and Harrisse.

Parkman's acquaintance with Margry had ripened into friendship through correspondence, and the latter produced a long birthday ode in honor of the American historian who had hymned "*les beaux actes de notre histoire.*" But Margry was still unwilling to let Parkman use his La Salle collection; and Parkman found that many essential documents had been withdrawn from the archives by the collector-curator. The best that Parkman could obtain from Margry was authorization to offer the rights of publication to the former's Boston publishers. But when Parkman returned home, he found Boston in flames; and since the business section of the city was nearly wiped out by the great fire of November 17, no Boston firm was inclined to

557

undertake what at best would be a bit of philanthropic publishing. Parkman went to work creating a lobby for a Congressional appropriation for the publication of Margry's documents, with the help of O. H. Marshall and Charles Whittlesey. Eventually the lobby included Senator George Frisbie Hoar, General James Garfield, and William Dean Howells among its members; and its efforts were crowned with success and the publication in 1878 of the first three volumes of the *Découvertes et établissements des Français*.

Only in one respect was Parkman's Paris stay wholly unrewarding. He had hoped to find materials of interest in the archives of St. Sulpice and among the papers of Abbé Etienne Michel Faillon, who had died in 1870 soon after publishing his *Histoire de la colonie française en Canada* (Montreal, 1865-66). Abbé Casgrain had arranged with Abbé Villeneuve, the superior of the Montreal Sulpicians, that his friend should be well received when he visited St. Sulpice in Paris, but Parkman found "nothing of much account" in their archives and little to his purpose in Faillon's papers, which are now preserved in Montreal.

The terse record of this September and October stay in Paris is found in a black cloth clasped notebook, opening at the end and measuring 5¾ inches by 3. The notes are in pencil.

1872

Paris, Sept. 19, 1872. "*Epures de De Lisle*"[1] 13 (17) Rue de l'Université, Archives du 4me étage

Alcan, Rue St. André des Arts, no. 53, is about to publish an *étude* on the Cramoisys in 2 vols.[2]

Papers on La Roche [Le Rocher], containing testimony of the returned colonists, at Rouen. Ask Gravier (Harrisse).[3]

---

17 Rue de l'Université, "Grandes Archives," No. 122-143 (Amérique Septentrionale): Le Gardeur, La Verandrye, Carton 5, No. 18.[4]

Bibliothèque du Depôt des Cartes, Recueil A. Du L'hut? 33e.[5]

Amérique Septentr[ionale], Canada No. 35. Franquelin?[6]

Amérique Septentr., Cartes anciennes, Recueil B. Franklin [Franquelin] Maps.[7]

9 a.b.c.d.e. Picture of Quebec.[8]

10. Quebec (earlier).[9]

D. Joliet–Franklin map.[10]

14. Beautiful Map[11]—Varennes de la Veranderie

Carton 5, No. 17

    " " No. 19[a]

    " " No. 18[12]

Joliet, *Labrador*. Carton 5, No. 15.[13]

Quebec, picture[14b] (1695-9?). Chateau St. Louis: 2 *étages*, gallery below. Redoubt on Cap Diamond. Recollets', Jesuits', Cathedral (tall steeples), Ursulines', seminary, where now they stand. *Evê(s)ché*, top of Mountain St. Projecting battery in river just below chateau. In river, Algonquin, Abenaquis, & Ottawa canoes, the two former

---

a "Oldest 1716."—F.P.

b "La Potherie's picture is founded on this."—F.P.

thus: [with rounded bow and stern]; the latter thus: [with pointed bow and stern].[c] A map of the river attached. Nearly all the settlements above 3 Rivers have small forts. Those below rarely have them (marked 9a by Harrisse).

Another drawing (10a Harrisse) (No. 240)[15] evidently earlier,[d] gives only a platform in place of the battery, a *buste du Roy* a little below, near the shore. Cemetery below *evêché*. No redoubt on Cape Diamond. A windmill above the town. Steeple of cathedral unfinished.

Another drawing of Quebec is attached to the great map of Franquelin 1699 (12 Harrisse, No. 259 of his catalogue).[16] Vol. no. 4042, Am[érique] Sept[entrionalle], cartes anciennes. P.S. The picture marked 9a by Harrisse is that used by La Potherie as the foundation of his engraving of Quebec.

Names of the Great-West:
Mamtoumie (Jesuits)
Frontenacie (Raudin)
Colbertie
La Louisiane[e] (La Salle)

A great number of maps and sketches of Franquelin are preserved in the Dep[ôt] des Cartes de la Marine. Nearly all bear, distinctly and more or less completely, the features of the great map of 1684, which is more complete and elaborate than any. That of 1683 (Harrisse No. 219)[17] is very handsomely executed but lacks the lower parts of the Mississippi.

Document in wh[ich] the Recollets demand the expulsion of protestants from Canada (Harrisse No. 421).[18]

Depêche de Richelieu urging restitution of Canada, 1629. (Harrisse No. 443).[19]

Jesuit fur-trade. *Ibid.*, No. 501.[20]

The name of Louisiane is mentioned in the act of concession of Bellisle to La Forest, *10 Juin 1679*. (Harrisse No. 150)[21]

[c] Two very rough sketches in the text have been omitted.—Ed.
[d] "Harrisse gives date 1689."—F.P.
[e] "See Harrisse [p.] 201."—F.P.

The *MS. Joutel* is probably at the Depôt des Cartes, though "mislaid."[22]

Expédition contre les Iroquois en 1695. M. De Frontenac représenté porté dans un canot.[f]

Bibliot[hèque] Nat.? Lorsque j'ai consulté, il y avoit un Portefeuille, Intitulé "Amérique Septentrionale Canada, Etats Unis, Mexique"[f]

La Pièce indiquée plus Haut peut Etre dans un autre portefeuille, je ne m'en souviens plus.[f] Not found (Sept. 24).

Brienne papers, Brit[ish] Museum, contain, says Faillon, a great deal on Canadian Missions (Har[r]isse).[23]

Jesuit collections, Rue des Postes.

Ask Father Tailhan, Missions étrangères, rue de Sèvres.[24]

Engraving of Frontenac, at *Bib. Nat.?* (Margry)

Archives, Dep. des Cartes Marines.

"A correct Plan of the Environs of Quebec, 1759" (engraved) detail of fortifications. Archives, Dep. des Cartes[25]

"*Carte des Environs de Québec, par Villeneuve 1688*"[26] (great detail), lines of settlements, more or less continuous, radiate from Quebec along the St. Louis & St. John's roads to Cap Rouge & Ganderville; up the St. Chs. [Charles] to Old Lorette, and down the shore to the church of Ange Gardien, where the map ends. Numerous houses at Charlesbourg, Bourg Royal (Talon), and Grand & Petit St. Bernard.

Others on Isle of Orleans, and about the church of Point Levi[s]. A few scattered along south shore. Beauport forms a considerable village. Between these lines spreads what seems to be forest. Near Charlesbourg are the Déserts Grand St. Joseph and Petit St. Antoine, the latter near the site of Jeune Lorette (falls of St. Chs.).

"*Carte des Environs of Quebec 1685.*" Villeneuve (5 feet square).[27]

Archives, Dep. des Cartes de la Marine: "Véritable plan de Québec fait in 1663."[28] 17 scattered houses extend along St. Louis St. The *maison* of Jesuits, thus:

[f] In Pierre Margry's handwriting.—Ed.

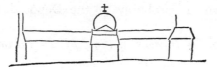

Lower town, scattered houses.

A plan of New York by Franquelin, 1693. Also coasts of N. E. [New England].[29]

An article on Canadian society, Frontenac, and *la comédie* by P. M. [Pierre Margry] in *Annales des Voyages*, Jan. 1844. P. M. has a paper about this affair by La Motte Cadillac.

P.S. Margry promises a copy of the passage from La Motte Cadillac. An extract is printed in the *Annales*, as above.

Dep. des Cartes de la Marine: "Partie de l'Amérique Sept., etc., etc.," par J. B. L. Franquelin, Geogr. du Roi 1699" (M.S.?)[30] Drawing of Quebec, cartouche. Extreme right, distant tower of hospital, mountains beyond. Nearer, towards the left, by the St. Chs., the tall, slender spire of the Hôtel-Dieu. On the rock, the Seminary, with its wall and trees of garden. Next, the Cathedral: tall square tower, surmounted by cross & weather cock. Close beyond, the more slender spire of the Jesuits. Then the trees of the garden of the Ursulines and their massive convent, with its short spire. Next, and nearer, the Recollets, a spire surmounted by cross & weather cock. In front, the Chateau, with its gallery resting on a solid wall & buttresses at edge of rock. One range of large windows above, & a double roof with windows, thus:

The magazine and garden on the left at foot of slope of Cape Diamond. A windmill beyond them. Lower town, many closely built houses—a straggling line up Mountain St. Short tapering spire of N. D. [Notre Dame] des Victoires. *Evê(s)ché* and burial ground near top of ascent. In the earlier drawing (10 Harrisse),[31] not only is the spire of the cathedral unfinished, but the garden of the chateau, and the line of palisades and towers or blockhouses wh[ich] border it in the map of 1699 are omitted. Neither does the Recollet church appear at all. The *Evêché* is different and much smaller. This map must be between 1680 & 1690.[g]

The map marked 9 by Harrise is also of 1699 (Fonville).[32]

Mad[ame] de Frontenac. De Lude [Luth] gave her rooms at the Arsenal. This does not imply, as has been said, that she was *entretenue* by him. He was governor of the Arsenal and apartments in it were granted, to a recent period, to such persons as had the influence to secure such a favor.[33] (P.M. [Pierre Margry])

Oct. 6. At St. Sulpice I was shown 4 Ms. vols., as all that Abbé Faillon had left. Notes from *greffe* of Montreal, etc., etc. Nothing of much account.[34]

Dep. des Cartes, *"Fortifications des Colonies,"* 359, 369.[35] Plans of Quebec.

Over library, Dep. des Cartes

D'Avezac,[36] 42 Rue de Bace

The publisher Teschner (?) has a MS., in a vol. of autographs, of a young man named, I think, La Salle, in one of the expeds. of Cavelier de la Salle. Margry has tried to get a copy of it, but says he has failed. About 40 pages.

Probably the author of the letter of 3 sept. 1698, cited by Thomassy.[37]

La Salle Docs. formerly in Dépôt de la Marine, 13 Rue de l'Université.

Archives scientifiques (Notes of Harrisse).

Canada, etc. Carton 64, no. 1: *"Mémoires, lettres et notes sur le Canada*

[g] 1689—Ed.

et sur quelques parties de l'Amérique Septentrionale (1541 à 1732)."—
"Délivré au Ministère."

Carton 67, No. 1: *"Cahier contenant relation du voyage de M. de la Salle dans le nord de l'Amérique Septentrionale pour y faire un établissement dans la partie qu'il en avait auparavant découverte (1684 à 1687).—Prêté le 26 juin '69 à M. Margry."*

Carton 67², no. 1: *"Cahier contenant lettres de M. M. Delasalle et de Tonty par lesquelles on donne la description de l'embouchure du fleuve Mississipy (1685-1686). Prêté le 26 juin '69 à M. Margry."*[38]

Dép. de la Marine, Archives scientifiques, Carton 67², no. 15: "Rapport que fait le Sʳ de la Salle écrivain dans la Marine de ce qu'il sait de la découverte de la partie septentrionale de l'Amérique qui a esté faite par ordre du Roy sur le commandement du Sʳ de la Salle depuis 1678 jusqu'en 1685."

Toulon, 3 sept., 1698. 6 pp.[39]

Mr. Saml. L. M. Barlow,[40] 1 Madison Avenue, N.Y.

Maps of M. Harrisse are to be sent to him; send to him for permission to see them.

Clerembault, Purse.

The *Fond[s] Clerembault*[41] at Bib. Nat. may contain papers on Frontenac.

Henry Harrisse, 30 Rue de Cambacérès. (Send *Pontiac* & *Oregon Trail*)

John Meredith Read Jr, Consul Gen. U.S., Rue de Chateaudun. Send *Pontiac* & *Oregon T.*

Pierre Margry: Send new ed. *Pontiac* and *Oregon Trail.*

D'Avesac, 42 Rue du Bac—send *Great West.*

Mrs. W. F. Wharton, Barningham Rectory, Barnard Castle—*Oregon Trail.*

1878 Notebook

Lake George, Ticonderoga & Quebec

Introduction

IN NOVEMBER 1878 Parkman visited Lake George, Ticonderoga, and Quebec, in order to re-examine the battlefields of the Seven Years' War, which he was to chronicle in *Montcalm and Wolfe*, published six years later. The ground was already familiar to him from many visits, but with typical thoroughness he covered it once more to fix the scenes of action firmly in his mind, jotting down notes on distances and the terrain about the ruins of the old forts. Such fieldwork as this accounts for much of the extraordinary vividness of Parkman's descriptions. At Quebec he sought out rare books and documents which could contribute to his purpose, benefiting as usual from the suggestions of his great Canadian friends and fellow workers, Sir James Macpherson Le Moine and Abbé Henri-Raymond Casgrain. And at the request of Le Moine, while at Montreal on his way home, he wrote a letter encouraging the Quebec Literary and Historical Society to continue its archival work of collecting and publishing historical documents. Until 1924 this society, of which Parkman became an honorary member, carried on the work now done by the Provincial Archives of Quebec, as well as functioning as a private library.

By 1878 Parkman was a familiar figure in Quebec, and shortly after this visit he attained unwelcome notoriety there. Le Moine announced his coming in a letter to the editor of *Le Journal de Québec*, comparing him to Garneau, Ferland, Faillon, and Laverdière as a great historian of the Canadian past, and proposing that he be honored by the Literary and Historical Society and the Institut Canadien. Jules-Paul Tardivel, no friend of Le Moine and an ultramontane journalist of the most intransigent type, replied with a bitter attack on Parkman as a Protestant American who had undertaken to write the history of a French and Catholic country, and, "not understanding the glorious destiny of the French-Canadian people," had failed to write a single page which might be dignified with the name of history. Tardivel thought that Parkman's writings insulted his race and his religion, and belittled them in the eyes of the world. This onslaught, and the storm of journalistic controversy which followed, prevented Laval University from awarding Parkman its honorary degree of *docteur-ès-lettres*, as planned at the instigation of Abbé Casgrain, Dr. La Rue, and other French-Canadian friends of Parkman in Quebec. McGill University, the stronghold of the Protestant English Canadians in Montreal, soon after gave Parkman its honorary doctorate; and by accepting this degree Parkman convinced the Quebec ultramontanes that he was on the side of the enemy. The incident doubtless served to strengthen his anti-Catholic basis.

This brief record of Parkman's 1878 journey is found in a small red leather notebook, 3⅜ by 5¼ inches. It is written in pencil, and the writing has become smudged. The notebook is marked "Lake George–Quebec 1878" in ink on the front cover.

1878

Ticonderoga. Tuesday. F[rench] lines[1] are 800 or 1,000 yards from fort.[a]

2 Redoubts near R.R. tunnel to protect heights in rear of F. left, which could easily be climbed at this point without exposure to cannons of fort.

In front of the works, the land slopes away gently like an immense glacis; opposite the flanks, it is more broken.[b]

Behind the lines, the ground slopes towards the fort.

A redou[b]t on left rear of F., opposite to the two on right rear, to protect the ascent from the valley of the stream, which, after passing a rocky promontory nearly opposite F. left, runs through marshes which make landing from boats very difficult or impossible. This side much less exposed than the other to flank attack.

Fort to Falls = 2 miles.

Rapids, 1 mile long.

Upper fall, head of rapids, to landing, 1 mile.

Between landing & mountain on left side, $\frac{1}{2}$ mile of rich meadow. This continues till near head of rapids, where the ground becomes broken & hilly, but rich & capable of bearing heavy forests. Upper fall very beautiful—a sheet of foam over steep sloping ledges.

An Ind. path led over back part of Mt. Defiance to L. Champlain.[2] The gap through wh[ich] it runs is visible from near landing place, i.e., old steamboat landing.

There is a path just below Rogers' Slide by wh. valley of Trout

[a] A very rough sketch by Parkman of the right front of the French lines has been omitted.—Ed.

[b] "Especially on the left flank of the F., where an enemy could in some places approach to within fifty yards without exposure to fire. The works here are very elaborate & strong."—F. P.

Brook, now called Lord Howe's Brook,[3] may be reached. It may also be reached by Hague.

Head of Lake George,[4] Friday, Oct. 3[d]. Johnson's position seems to have been about 300 yards from lake, between the hill & an extensive swampy hollow, full of young trees, on the right, his front being not more than 150 to 200 yards. A shallow ravine, running down to the lake, intersects the position and soon branches into two. The ground in front is broken, and slopes somewhat towards the camp. Bullets in abundance are found in the fields within musket shot of this supposed line.

The low rocky hill on the left is crowned by the ruins of Fort George,[5] chiefly stone laid in mortar. The work is small, but the walls are of very considerable height & thickness.

Some apparent remains of the old road, where it turns from the present road to Ft. W[m]. Henry are distinguishable, but are soon lost in ploughed fields. It might run about 100 to 200 yards in front of Johnson's supposed line, or perhaps much nearer, and even into the camp,[6] in wh. case, the F. must have left it and filed to the right as they approached.

The forked ravine wh. intersects J's camp, is prolonged into a hollow now filled with trees & bushes, and wh. seems to have been directly in his front, within easy range of shot. The general slope of the land in this direction is, however, upward.

From Artillery Cove a marshy ravine runs back from the lake, with good camping ground on the north side.

Levy's [Lévis'] camp was on a level plateau towards the west mountain.[7]

A small sluggish brook, running through a marshy hollow, enters the lake between Caldwell and grounds of W[m]. Henry.

Oct. 4. R. G. Bradley & Co., Hundred Island House, Lake George.

Whitehall is opposite Bolton. The head of South Bay may be reached over a low ridge of mountains, or a high gorge 10 or 12 miles from the head of the lake. The distance over is 5 or 6 miles. Why did not Johnson send a party this way to destroy Dieskau's

PLAN DU FORT CARILLON

Echelle

Rer St Frideric

ATTAQUES DES RETRANCHEMENS DEVANT LE FORT CARILLON
en Amérique
par les anglais commandés par le général Abercrombie contre les français
aux ordres du Marquis de Montcalm le 8 Juillet 1758.

RENVOIS.

A Le fort Carillon. B Retranchemens, que les français ont commencé à faire le 7.e Juillet, au matin. C Camp de l'armée française, où elle se rendit le 6 & resta sous les armes pendant la nuit du 7 au 8. Le 8 à la pointe du jour elle prit la position D en ordre de bataille derrière les retranchemens. E Les grénadiers & les piquets pour reserve derrière chaque bataillon. F Colonnes des anglais, qui attaquent les retranchemens à midi & demie. G Pelotons de troupes legères & provincia- les fusillant entre ces colonnes. H Les canadiens sortent du retranchement, & attaquent une colonne anglaise en flanc. I Chaloupes des anglais, qui parurent pendant l'attaque, & furent repoussées par l'artillerie du fort. K Retraite des colonnes anglaises dans leur premier camp près des moulins à scier vers sept heures du soir; leur troupes legeres couvrirent cette retraite par leur feu prolongé jusques dans la nuit. L Position des Français après la retraite des anglais. M Batteries redoutes & retranchemens, que les français établirent après le combat.

C. P. S. C. M.

Plan du Fort Carillon (Ticonderoga), 1758
Line engraving by Contgen after Engineer Lieutenant Therbu
(Coverdale Collection No. 1796)

boats & provisions? The stream that enters the head of South Bay is rapid and rocky—not navigable. The road thence to Brown's,[8] four miles from Caldwell, is about 15 miles, behind the mountains on east of L. George, and round the end of French Mt. At Brown's the road from South Bay & Fort Ann[e] joins the plank road to Caldwell.[c]

The principal cross street in the village of Caldwell [Lake George], nearly opposite the Lake House and in the midst of the ground covered by the siege lines, is called Montcalm Street.

Uncommon brilliancy of swamp maples in swamp by W[m]. Henry[9]—orange, claret, & gold.

7 Oct. W[m]. Henry to Brown's, 4 miles. *Ib[id]* to Bloody Pond, 2 miles. Height of land just south of the pond, which is a mere pool without outlet or inlet. Valley rugged & broken, between French Mt. & West Mt.

Drove to Fort Anne, 16 miles from W[m]. Henry[10]; 12 from Brown's. South Bay, 19 from W[m]. Henry, 15 from Brown's. Turned E[ast] round end of French Mt.; then N[orth] along E[ast] side. Sandy, hilly, country. Mountains in front & on left.

South Bay is surrounded by mountains. The stream[11] at its head is navigable for small boats for a little distance & then becomes rocky.

Fort Ann[e].[12] The fort stood on a knoll on Half Way Brook, near its junction with Wood Creek,[13] overlooking wide meadows, bordered by rocky hills.

Wood Creek writhes through meadows between low hills.

Oct. 8. Soon after leaving Whitehall, the entrance of S[outh] Bay appears on the left, and part of the bay is seen, with mountains sloping on all sides.

Lake Champlain is here, and for some distance below, only a few rods wide. The channel runs through inundated meadow, with rank grass growing in the water.[14] Rocky hills on each side. "The Two Rocks" are high cliffs, crowned with wood, between which the lake runs at one point. Then the marsh begins again. A few miles above

---

[c] A rough pencil sketch by Parkman of Fort William Henry has been omitted.—Ed.

[below] Ticonderoga, the lake widens to a gunshot across and sometimes more.

Quebec, 12 Nov. Memoirs of Laterrière[15] contains matters of interest on condition of Canada just after conquest.

Mère de Ste. Hélène wrote *Hist. de l'Hôtel-Dieu* from dictation of Mère Juchereau (Casgrain).[16]

Papers of Judge Ne[i]lson.[17]

Papers of Seminary.[18]

Maples Leaves: 1873,[19] "Fraser's Highlanders at Quebec," (good) p. 141.

Buttes à Neveu,[20] where the Martello towers stand.

Ruisseau St. Denis—the name of the stream in Wolfe's Ravine.[21]

Did Stobo or De Vitry guide Wolfe's men up the height?[22]

MSS. of Abbé Bois[23] of Maskinongé—probably a great deal about the war.

"*Siège de Québec en 1759, copié d'après un MS. apporté de Londres par l'hon. D.-B. Viger.*"[24]

1834-5 (Hartwell Lby [Library]) Have I got this? (Yes)

Hon. George Baby[25]—Ottawa—a great collector of autographs—has 10 or 12 original letters of Montcalm.

Send M. Bédard[d26] the paper Mandement mentioned in *Frontenac,* p. 330, note.

Send Le Moyne [Le Moine][27] the pamphlet on the false letter of Montcalm.

Bédard's *table* of Reg[istres] du Conseil Souv[erain] will be printed in 3 months, up to 1700.

"*Résumé des Evénements les Plus Remarquables des Annales du Monastère des Dames Ursulines de Québec*" (in Beatson).[28] Montcalm died in Chateau St. Louis, 14 Sept. Buried same evening by torch light, not in hole made by a bomb, but in a grave.[29] Nobody could be found to make a bier, so M. was buried in a box made of old boards.[e]

Candiac is near Nîmes.

---

[d] "T. P. Bédard, Parlement, Q."—F.P.

[e] "From Beatson."—F. P.

Gleig, *Lives of Eminent British Military Commanders*[30] (Montcalm & Wolfe).

"Plan of the Town & Basin of Quebec and part of the adjacent country, shewing the principal encampments & works of the British army commanded by Maj. Gen. . . . ."[31] (have it)

Write to J. M. Le Moine about importance of collecting maps & docs. relating to 1759—Quebec Hist. Soc.[32]

Ask J.M.L. about the pamphlet on Siege of Quebec wh. I have not got.

Send *Frontenac* to Mr. Marmette,[33] Treasury Dept., Quebec.

Rev. Thomas Hamel,[34] Rector of Laval University, Quebec.

Paul	3 yrs.
Marie Luce	6 " ·
Marie Louise	13 "

children of Dr. H. La Rue,[35] cor[ner] St. Ann[e] & St. Ursule sts.

Write to J. M. Le Moine about publication of Index to Registers, which Bedard is making.

Hon. F. G. Baby, Joliette, 10 autograph letters of Montcalm. Has a large coll[ection] of autographs.

The height of the plateau above Wolfe's Cove is about 200 feet, by measurements of Royal Engineers.

The Ruisseau St. Denis runs down to the cove through a huge ravine, & a few rods from its mouth leaps down a rock of considerable height; whence it runs to the St. Lawrence. The local tradition—probably correct—is that the grenadiers climbed into this ravine and then, turning to the right, scaled its side at two points to the plateau above. Vergor's[36] post was then but a few rods before them.

1879 & 1885 Notebook

Quebec & Acadia,
Carolina & Florida

Introduction

IN AUGUST 1879 Parkman returned once more to Quebec. Since the cover of his notebook lists the children of his good friend Dr. Hubert La Rue, it is probable that he stayed at the latter's home in St. Louis Street, where he was a welcome guest on his Canadian visits. Dr. La Rue was one of the leading members of the Laval faculty, whose manifold interests embraced medicine, the physical sciences, agriculture, and folklore. He found relief from his intellectual labors in managing the family farm on the Ile d'Orléans near Quebec. A farmer friend of his once called at his town house while he was entertaining Parkman and other distinguished guests; the farmer wished to go away when he found that his friend was engaged, but Dr. La Rue insisted on making him, as the best Canadian of them all, join the company.

This notebook also contains a long précis of the journal of Louis Franquet, a royal engineer who was set out from France to inspect the fortifications of Louisbourg, Acadia, and New France in 1750-51 and 1752-53. His *Voyages et mémoires sur le Canada*, published by the Institut Canadien of Quebec in 1889 from an Ottawa copy of the original in the Archives de la Ministère de la Guerre, Paris, (Bib. Can. 229) affords a richly detailed picture of New France in 1752. Parkman, with his mind already at work on the problems afforded by the tale he was to tell in *Montcalm and Wolfe* (1884), also examined the battlefields on the Plains of Abraham where the fate of New France was settled in 1759.

Equipped with letters to Acadian curés from his friends at the Séminaire de Québec, Parkman set out for Nova Scotia, Cape Breton Island, and New Brunswick, where he carefully examined once more the chief scenes of the long struggle between French and English for possession of this gateway to the New World. He visited

Louisbourg, Beauséjour, Fort Lawrence, Port Royal, and St. John's, in preparation for writing the Acadian chapters of *Montcalm and Wolfe* (IV, VIII, and XIX) and of the later *Half-Century of Conflict* (VI, VII, IX, X, XIX-XXII), which were to involve him in one of the greatest controversies of his career, the long feud with Philip Smith, Abbé Casgrain, and Edouard Richard over the thorny Acadian question, which Parkman finally summed up thus: "The truth is that the treatment of the Acadians was a scandal on both sides."

In March 1885 Parkman spent two weeks visiting the sites of the early French Huguenot settlements at Port Royal (Beaufort, South Carolina) and the River of May (the St. John's River, Florida), whose brief history he had chronicled in his first link in the chain of histories, *The Pioneers*. A revised edition of this book was in prospect, and with his conscience troubling him for having once written without going over the ground involved—that had been impossible at the time, because of the Civil War—Parkman took this opportunity to acquire "a more exact knowledge of the localities connected with the French occupation of that region," as he put it in his preface dated the following September. The New Englander reveled in his first taste of the tropics, and the lushness of the Floridian flora delighted the eye of Harvard's first professor of horticulture. Parkman was an impassioned amateur gardener, who devoted much of his leisure and means to the cultivation of rare plants, and this side of his nature finds here its sole expression in the journals.

The records of these two journeys, separated by six years in time, are found together in a small purple cloth notebook, 4 inches by 6½, with a paper label marked 1879 (in ink) and 1885 (in pencil) in Parkman's hand. A loose page refers to his visit to Beaufort.

1879 & 1885

[The front end papers list the following names:[1] "Alphonsine La Rue, Marie Louise, Marie Luce, Paul, Luc, Joseph" and also this series of numbers: "200, 100, 200, 100, 100."—Ed.]

Quebec, 9 Aug., 1879. Journal de Franquet, 1752.[2] Church of Caughnawaga. No seats. Men *"sont assis, ou si mieux l'on aime dire, accroupis sur leur cul."* Women separated by a balustrade from men. (Copy p. 52-53, 72.)

At *Two Mountains,* was a post commanded by Benoist, and a fort belonging to Sulpitians, adjoining (containing ?) the church. A square, bastioned—with loopholed wall 12 ft. high—refuge for families. Iroq[uois], Algonkins, Nipissings, Iroq. live in log houses. About the *"jour des trépassés,"* they go hunting with wives & children —generally come back at Christmas. After Ash Wednesday they go again for furs. They raise beans etc.

Many F[rench] traders in the village.

At a dance, a widow was allowed to dance with an E[nglish] scalp on a pole to comfort her for the loss of her husband, who had been killed.

A very curious acct. of Two Mts. (pp. 64-75).

"Balises" of *"sapin"* [spruce] planted on ice of river to guide travellers.

Officers at Montreal engage greatly in trade.

Quarrels among officers at Ft. Frédéric [Crown Point], because Lusignan, the commander, traded with E. and would let nobody else trade—even in ginsing. Hence great dissatisfaction. Abuses like this ruin the service. Trade of officers should be prohibited.

Varin withdrew right to trade from Lusignan and gave it to the *"garde-magasin,"* who was thought to share profits with him— Lusignan extremely wroth.

Mentions Carillon [Ticonderoga].

The portage of St. Sacrement [Lake George] is the chief road by wh[ich] our Inds. carry on contreband trade with E.

Proposes a *"fort de pieux"* [stockade] at Carillon & another at R[ivière]-au-Chicot, with an Ind. settlement *"à titre de mission."*

Fort Frédéric is in a ruinous state.

Description of Ft. Fréd. (copy p. 112, 113).

12 houses near St. John [St. Jean]. There was a habitant named La Bonté some distance below I(s)le-aux-Noix.

Chambly impregnable without cannon. Land cleared all around it.

Description of Chambly (copy 127-129.).

The curé of St. Ours (133).

Sorel (copy 134, 135).

St. Francis (139-141). Becancourt, only 19 *"cabanes."* All Inds. had gone to trade in N. England or to gather ginsing. Cabins closed.

Lorette. (Copy 150-160.)

At St. Louis, Inds., set on, says F[ranquet], by Jesuits, opposed the establishment of a garrison. The village has now an imperfect palisade & is surrounded by trees & bushes. The fort is of *"pieux"* on 2 sides.

At 2 Mts. the Algonquins & Nipissings have 113 warriors, and the Iroq. 105: a total of 1,060 souls. There is a stone fort, enclosing church & presbetery, and an *"enceinte de pieux"* for the whole village except the part occupied by this fort.

Bigot (Copy 218.).

Country manners (221).

Two Mts. (220-224).

St. Francis—51 cabins of logs, *"carrés longs,"* covered with bark and planks.

Jean Langelier,[3] Bureau du Registraire
Hon. Luc Letellier de St. Just,[4] P.Q., Canada

---

11 Aug., Quebec. The high ground on which the prison stands is evidently that on wh. Wolfe took his stand before the battle.[5]

From this to the Buttes à Neveu is 600 paces.

Send to Abbé Bois:[6] *Book of Roses, Jesuits, La Salle.*
To Evanturel:[7] *La Salle*, etc.
["] Faucher de St. Maurice:[8] *La Salle.*
["] Jean Langelier: *La Salle.*
["] La Rue: entire set, except *old Regime.*

"Attack of July 31, [17]59," contemporary engraving from drawing made on the spot by Capt. Hervey Smith [Smyth] (shown me by Faucher de St. Maurice). This one of a set of contemporary engravings, including views of Quebec, Miramichi, Gaspé, etc.—large & well executed.[9]

Alfred Garneau[10] has collected many odds & ends in Canadian history. Says that in *Memoirs of Academy of Inscriptions*[11] is a curious incident, recorded by Bougainville, of the attack on Carillon, 1758.

Mr. & Mrs. William M. McPherson:[12] Steamer[a] *Dunara Castle*, Martin Orme & Co., leaves Glasgow every Thursday for outside Hebrides. *Deck cabin.*

John Henderson, (Tiree) Scotland; Woodlands, Maidenhead.

Dec. 29, 1757. In a letter of this date, Wolfe suggests to Pitt the capture of Quebec, as the true way to end the war. He became the victim of his own project. Grant's *Mem. of Wolfe.*[13]

---

morue[14]	Basque: *macaillaioua* Esp.: *baccaliau* Gascon: *mouru*[b]

---

23 Aug., Forts Lawrence [&] Beauséjour [Nova Scotia]. About 2 miles apart. Lawrence[15]—of which the traces are slight—stood on a rising ground, with marsh, of great extent on each side. On the side towards Beauséjour, wh. is plainly visible near the end of the long high ridge—beyond the marsh, runs the Missiguash [Misseguash], filled with water to the brim at high tides, but at low tides a great winding ditch of reddish mud. Tide rises at least 20 feet. Marshes covered

---

[a] Remainder of this entry is in another hand.—Ed.
[b] "The above from a semi-Basque Gascon, on the steamer from Sydney."—F.P.

with coarse grass. Low wooded hills in extreme distance—fir & spruce, as everywhere.

The view from Beauséjour[16] is of vast extent. On one side, Ft. Lawrence in full view, 2 miles off across the marsh. On the other, the great Tant(r)amar marsh, traversed by the Aulac, in character like the Missiguash. Westward, another vast tract of marsh, with Cumberland basin beyond, visible to a great distance—muddy shores, bare at low tide. *Aboiteaux*[c] everywhere (the word is still in use). Bricks are made of this red mud.

Ramparts of Beauséjour well preserved. Magazine—capacious casements, extremely well built of stone & brick. One curtain is of stone. In front of it, towards Cumberland Basin,[17] an immense stone structure, apparently a bomb-proof, in tolerable preservation. On this side the ground slopes towards the basin. Five bastions, with deep ditches and embrasures towards east or land side, where the ground is level. Foundations of 2 ranges of barracks. The fort is visible from a great distance, being much higher than Ft. Lawrence.

When at Pictou, visited Micmac village. Lazy beggars. Those on Cape Breton work well at farming and coopering. Near Truro, they make butter firkins. Though tolerably industrious here as at Cape Breton, they are said not to increase.

Mr. Gillies, Sydney

On Wed., 20 Aug., visited Louisbourg; 21 Aug., Sydney to Hawksbury; 22, Hawkesbury to Pictou, & thence to Truro and Amherst; 23, Visited Beauséjour & site of Ft. Lawrence. Thence to St. John.

The 42[d] [Highlanders] at Ticonderoga: "on the top of their breastwork, they had plenty of wall pieces. . . . They took care to cut down monstrous large oak trees which covered all the ground from the foot of their breastwork about the distance of a cannon shot every way in their front. . . . Even those who were mortally wounded

[c] A special dike, allowing the water to enter at the flood, and retaining it at the ebb.—Ed.

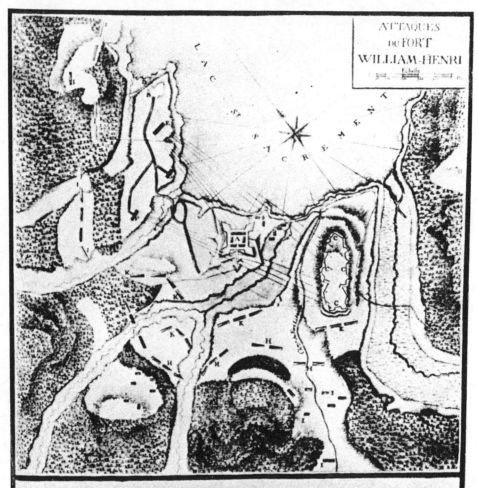

Attaques du Fort William-Henri, 1757
Line engraving after Engineer Lieutenant Therbu
(Coverdale Collection No. 1797)

cried to their companions not to mind or lose a thought upon them, but to follow their officers and to mind the honor of their country. Nay, their ardor was such that it was difficult to bring them off. When shall we have so fine a regt. again?" Letter from Lieut. Wᵐ. Grant, in Maclauchlan's *Highlands*, II, 340 (1875).

Plan of Ty[conderoga] in *The Scot's Mag.*, Aug. 1758.

Capt. John Campbell with a few men forced their way over the breastwork & were bayonnetted. (Maclauchlan, II, 339)

St. John, 24 Aug. Ulysse de Fabremont, Belgian, says that he saw a Mr. Wiggin(?) at Halifax who said he had doc[ument]s wh. he wanted to give me. F.B. Webster, Counsellor at Law, 121 Bank St., Cleveland, O., can probably give his address, as it was to him that he spoke about the docs.

St. John, 24 Aug. Tides not less than 30 feet. At slack water—that is, when the rising tide overcomes the downward current—vessels of considerable size go up over the falls. At this time, there are a few minutes of still water, after which the course of the current is reversed, and the tide rushes up with great force over what was before the fall. In spring freshets, however, the river keeps the mastery and the downward current maintains itself. Large ships are built above the falls.[18]

1885

South Carolina and Florida Notes

9 Mar. [*1885*], *Beaufort, S. C.* Wide entrance, low shores on each side, long strips of white sand with bushes and pine trees behind. Harbor forks not far from entrance, Beaufort River on right, Broad River on

left. Port Royal a little above fork. Archer's Creek, close to Port
Royal connects the two rivers, thus;

Sandy soil: live oak, cypress in flower, holly, myrtles, cherry,
eleagnus, Spanish moss abundant. Peaches & wild cherry in flower.
Also narcissus.

Harbor well given on a county map of Beaufort County
pub[lished] in 1873 at Charleston.

A great marsh, covered with tall grass, and bordered by distant
woods. At the spot marked *x* is a small coquina fort,[20] said to be
older than St. Augustine. It is near the bank of the river.

10 Mar., 1885, Fernandina, Fla. [21] Harbor bordered by broad meadows
of rank grass or rushes, intersected by creeks & inlets.

R.R. from Fernandina to Jacksonville. "Saw" palmetto in abundance—dwarf—said never much to exceed 6 feet, while the cabbage
palm is a considerable tree. Sandy soil covered with pine, chiefly
long-leaved. Little or no underbrush. Ground beneath covered with
low, coarse grass. Occasional vast meadows, of rank grass or rushes,
looking dark and dingy at this season, traversed by creeks and
rivers; woods, chiefly pine, in the distance, sometimes dim and faint,
sometimes nearer, like islands or promontories studded with the tall
pines, sometimes massed together, sometimes apart, their irregular
tops shaped something like the Italian pines. Cherries, oranges,
roses in bloom at Jacksonville.

Jacksonville, 11 Mar. Red-bud maples in early seed. Yellow jasamine,
rubia, wild cherry in flower. Magnolia—dark-green lustrous leaves—

bloom in June or a little earlier. Andromedas in bud. A delicious warm balmy morning. Mocking birds in many porches.

Fort George, 11 Mar., Evening. Came down this P.M. from Jacksonville —about 25 miles by course of steamer, 18 direct.

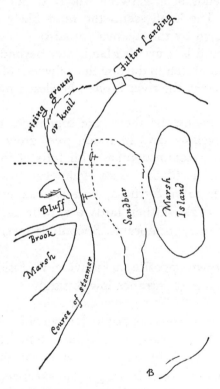

12 Mar. Returned to Jacksonville. River[22] nearly a mile wide at entrance, widening as you enter. Brimful of lazy, breathless water, quivering under the setting sun. Marshes of bulrushes or rank grass, almost level with the river, forming islands, or stretching to the lines of forest, faint in the haze, that bound the view to right & left. These are traversed by creeks or broad belts of torpid water.

Pelican Bank[23] is destroyed by the Eads system of jetties. It was in the entrance.

About 5 miles from the entrance, a long ridge of fine yellowish sand, covered thickly with pines & deciduous trees, rises on the farther side of a sedgy marsh, and abuts on the river, forming St. John's Bluff. The tide here is very strong and the bluff is constantly cut away, as are the sandy shores into which it slopes away above. About ¼ of a mile above is a sandy knoll, half cut away, and behind it a meadow extends back between woody slopes (Q. The vale of Laudonnière?).[24] The knoll seems the most likely site of the fort. (See the plan drawn by the steamer captain).

Opposite the bluff is a marsh island, and beyond this, across the river, vast marshes stretch to the dim line of woods of the north shore. For some miles above, the river is often bordered by marshes, inter sected by creeks.

Towards Jacksonville the shores are sometimes ten feet or even more high. Fine yellow sand in which trees grow well. The main feature is tall, bare-stemmed pines with tufts of foliage at the top often mixed with deciduous trees. Palmetto (dwarf), occasional magnolia, cabbage palm, & yucca, with live oak, etc.

Saw a golden eagle. Other birds are pelicans, white & grey, herons, egrets, cranes, cormorants. Spoonbills rare. Flamingoes are only seen above.

River a dark brown opposite Jacksonville. Profusion of animal and vegetable life. Shores at entrance low & sandy.[25]

Friday, [*March*] *13th.* Woods opposite Jacksonville. Tall, lank, bare-stemmed pines. Wire grass, etc., below. Sun easily penetrates. Palmetto thickets. Pools of stagnant water. Marshes of bulrushes. Masses of deciduous trees & magnolia—creepers, Spanish moss, sometimes choking the trees like tattered cobwebs, slowly killing them. Liquid amber, maples, live oak, etc.

Up the river to Palatka, 75 miles. 3, 4, or 6 miles wide—low, wooded shores, pine mixed with young foliage of deciduous trees. Thunder, heavy rain. Waves pitted with the great drops. Water coffee-color. Calm at sunset. Water suffused with red. Heat lightning. Forest fires in distance.

The Entrance of Louisbourg Harbour, 1779
Aquatint by J. F. W. Des Barres, from the Atlantic Neptune
(Coverdale Collection No. 52)

Soft, pea-green, young foliage of deciduous cypress.

Sat., [March] 14ᵗʰ. From Palatka to mouth of Ocklawaha. Forests on nearly same level as water. Chiefly deciduous. Many trees killed or nearly so by Spanish moss. A few intervals of sandy banks several feet high. The pine here reappears.

Entered Ocklawaha. A decided current. Water not so dark as main river. Swamps on either hand with pools of dead water. No pine. A tangled mixture of tropical & northern vegetation. Ash, maple, cabbage palm, cypress, sweet gum, "bay." Mistletoe (or something like it, clinging to ash & other trees) and two curious parasites, one like a tuft of bristly hair, the other like a pine-apple growing out of the trunks of trees. Palms taller & more numerous as we went southward. Evening. Grating of pine knots burning on pilot house. Effect very striking. Occasional yells of birds disturbed in the forest.

Not only the cypress but also the ash, & perhaps other trees growing in the water of the swamp, have their stems enlarged into a cone shape at the base. It is melancholy to see the effect of the Spanish moss. The tall trees, especially cypress, for mile upon mile, are covered with it, a few opening leaves alone visible above the dismal drapery. At rare intervals, sandy banks interrupt the swamp— always with a settlement. The yellow water lily and many other water weeds fill the coves & line long reaches of shore, and masses of floating vegetation collect among half sunk rotten logs.

Sun. [March] 15ᵗʰ, Daybreak. The steamer—a little tug—makes her way through a solitude, varied by an occasional small alligator, large turtles, the large brown bird whose cries were heard so often in the night, a white heron, a blue heron, etc. Numerous leaping fish. The stream scarce wide enough at times for the tug to pass, brushing against the boughs. Strong current. Entered the stream from Silver Spring—20 or 30 yards wide, very deep, water of a pellucid, greenish blue, tinting the white sand & limestone of the bottom, where the waterweeds did not hide it. Black bass, cat-fish, garfish large & small, and many large turtles, plainly seen 20 feet below. Reached the spring at about 11½. Extensive marshes for some miles below.

From Silver Spring to Ocala. The usual sand, covered with pine &

wiregrass. Then some shell limestone, and an undulating country, dry & uninteresting. Deciduous oaks.

Saw this A.M. many palms of from 40 to 60 or perhaps even 70 feet.

Mon., 16ᵗʰ Mar. Ocala to Palatka. Rolling or flat country. Sand, whitish or yellow. Pine, long bare stems, wire grass, with palmetto beneath. Occasional shell limestone. Hummock land at intervals with magnolias, bay, *cornus florida*, gum, maples, and sometimes numerous palms, rarely over 30 feet. Some *mag. glauca.* One or two cypress swamps. Orange lake, water & marsh interspersed. Many small lakes & ponds, sometimes covered with weeds. A heron & other game. Deciduous oaks. Marshy places choked with matted vegetation.

Tues., [March] 17ᵗʰ, Daybreak, St. John's below Sanford. Narrow stream, between marshes, and woody islands. Tall, reedy grass, 8 or 10 feet high along banks. Willows. Extensive grassy meadows, backed with woods and interspersed with tufts or bushes, trees, & rank vegetation. Morning mists. Fish leaping. White cranes abundant; blue & white herons also. Large hawks. A bushy point alive with singing birds, like blackbirds. Maple, ash, gum, cypress, laurel, etc. Banks low & swampy almost everywhere. Palms numerous, sometimes large tracts of them—hundreds together. Water covered in in coves and along banks with bright green glistening leaves of yellow water lily.

Back to Palatka. Stream very tortuous. Strange floating water plant, drifting with the current. Alligator 8 or 10 feet long, lying in the mud. Continuous swamp, with intervals of sandy banks, in every instance occupied by settlers. Lake George—wide, low banks. Ducks of several kinds. Stream wider below. Swamp, with a few intervals of dry banks. Strange climbing plants, one with a fruit like a gourd, hanging through winter. Mistletoe. Palms numerous in some places below L. George.

18 Mar., Palatka to Jacksonville by rail. Pine, with hummock land. The decidous or hummock growth alway[s] in wet places, usually with water visible. The water indeed seems even in the pine lands to be near the surface.

From Jacksonville to St. Augustine. Pine, bare lank stems in innumerable multitude. Beneath, tufted wiregrass, palmetto in extensive tracts, pools of water. Frequent wet hummock land, often forming an impervious jungle of dense matted bushes & trees, creepers etc. Occasional cabbage palms. Extensive meadows of rank grass near St. Augustine.[26]

Thursday, Mar. 19. Anastatia [Anastasia] Island.[27] Bordered by extensive marshes, deep mud, and rank grasses on the side opposite St. Augustine. The island is of sand over coquina, covered in most parts with a jungle of low bushes, bay, myrtle, etc., with tracts of large yucca and palmetto, occasional prickly pear; sometimes mere wire grass, in ragged patches. On eastern side a wide beach formed of fragments of shell from the disintegrated coquina. Waves breaking in the sand shallows across the channel, which follows the shore.

Menagerie. Rattlesnake—*alive, 7 feet long.* Water mocassin, 4 to 5 feet. Hooping or sandhill crane. Black vulture. Darter or snake bird (*Plotus*). American barn owl. Opossum. Red tailed hawk. Gray fox. Lynx. Gopher. Gopher-snake. Ground rattlesnake.

Anastasia Island extends about 13 miles to inlet wh. is narrow.

Dr. DeWitt Webb, St. Augustine.

---

21 Mar. From St. Augustine to Jacksonville. Near St. A., marshes of bulrushes. Then higher levels covered with palmetto, then pine woods with palmetto, wire grass, & stunted bushes beneath. Gopher holes. Frequent hummock tracts of great extent, always low & wet— deciduous trees, palms, bushes, tangled vines, fallen logs, black mud, water-weeds. Almost impervious.

1889 - 1892 Notebook

Introduction

THIS last notebook summarizes aptly enough the closing years of Parkman's life. The opening pages (here printed as an appendix) are devoted to a careful account of his battle against insomnia: the date, the amount of sleeping draught taken, and the number of hours of sleep thus gained, from December 1889 to November 1892. The historical notes consist largely of references and queries for *A Half-Century of Conflict*, the last link in the chain of his history, and one which he feared might not be completed before death came or his strength gave out. Then there are lists of people who were to receive his new book or the revised editions of earlier works; the roll reads like a *Who's Who in America* in the 1890's, with an international supplement. As he neared the end of his lifelong task, his work was at last receiving the popular recognition it deserved. And, to the end, he kept on revising the books which had already appeared and sifting the sources for new material, for at sixty-nine Parkman's passion for history was as consuming as in his youth. The next-to-last summer of his life was devoted to preparing the new chapters on Acadia which he added to the revised edition of *The Old Regime*, published a few months before his death. It is appropriate that the very last note that he made in his journals concerned the correction of a slip in one of his early books.

Parkman's last years were a race against time. After 1884 his powers of work were sharply reduced by the insomnia from which he could get little relief, despite the aid of such eminent physicians as Dr. S. Weir Mitchell of Philadelphia. In a letter written to Abbé Casgrain in the spring of 1889, Parkman revealed his plight: "Two or three hours of sleep in the 24—which have been until lately my average allowance for long periods together—are not enough to wind up the human machine. . . . Though I have slept better in the last year, it is still an open question whether I shall manage to supply the missing link between that objectionable work [*Montcalm and Wolfe*] and its predecessor, *Count Frontenac*." He had written the more important *Montcalm and Wolfe*, the last in chronological order of the series and its crowning piece, before tackling the period from 1700 to 1750, in the fear that he might not be able to complete his life-work; but he struggled doggedly on as best he could, harboring his slender resources of energy, and in March 1892 he finished the book and with it the great historical epic he had planned in his youth. The great history of *France and England in North America* had been written, in the face of all the misfortunes and setbacks which had beset his path. It had taken nearly half a century, but Parkman permitted himself only a brief comment in his last preface:

The manuscript material collected for the preparation of the series now comprises about seventy volumes, most of them folios. . . . The collection was begun forty-five years ago, and its formation has been exceedingly slow, having been retarded by difficulties which seemed insurmountable, and for years were so in fact. Hence the completion of the series has required twice the time that would have sufficed under less unfavorable conditions.

Few others had traveled the same path far enough and grown sufficiently weary in the same service to appreciate what Parkman felt at the completion of the task and what a great triumph its achievement was. But one of the few, his cousin Henry Adams, wrote to assure him that "You have had the singular good fortune to complete successfully a great work which puts you at the head of our living historians; and I leave the dead ones out of account only because we cold-blooded Yanks detest the appearance of exaggeration so much more than we love what the French call *mesure*." Such a letter, among the flood of congratulations which poured in upon Parkman, surely offered some reward for his long struggle.

This last record is written in pencil and ink on the pages of a black leather-covered notebook, $4\frac{1}{4}$ by $7\frac{1}{8}$ inches.

1889 - 1892

Send some book to: Hon. John George Bourinot,[1] etc., etc., etc., Ottawa; also T. Roosevelt[2].

Change statement about Vetch[3] being relieved from fine in consequence of his scheme against *Canada*.

Benoni Stebbins[4]—his character *as a boy* (Miss C. A. Baker).[5]

"No trained soldier in Mass."? Vetch might be called one.[6]

The growth in Jamaica Pond is *oscillaria roseata*, a *European* species (Faxon).

Smith's, *Hist. N.Y.*,[7] 194

Juchereau,[8] 458, 473, 491

"The Four Kings of Canada,"[9] *Mag. Am. Hist.*, Mar. 1878

Articles [on] Vetch and Nicholson[10] in Appleton's *Cyc[lopedia of American Biography]*.

Consult *Mém. des Commissaires*,[11] II, *338*, 340, 642 (Capture of Annapolis).

Also Poore MSS.,[12] III, 25, 29 (*ibid*).

"Journal of the Voyage of the Sloop Mary, 1701," (O'Callaghan, 1866).

"Journals of Mad. Knight and Rev. Mr. Buckingham" (H. C. 6374,12)

N. H. [New Hampshire] *Provincial Papers*, II, 504-513 (Attack on P[ort] Royal, 1707)

Brymner, *Report 1887*, for Acadian matters about 1705.[13]

Acadians (after conquest), Poore Mss., III, 19, 20, 37, 40.

1708. "The *coup* struck by the Canadians *où Mars, plus féroce qu'en*

595

Europe, a donné carrière à sa rage ([at] Haverhill) makes me fear reprisals." *De Goutin au Min[istre], 29 Dec., 1708.*[14]

Send book to:

Theodore Roosevelt[ans.]	S. Weir Mitchell
Mrs. French	Col. Dodge[ans.]
Pres. Eliot	Barrett Wendell[ans.]
Mrs. H. Parkman	Capt. J. G. Bourke[ans.]
B. A. Gould[ans.]	Geo. Sheldon[ans.]
Justin Winsor[ans.]	Miss C. Alice Baker
C. S. Sargent[ans.]	James Grant Wilson[ans.]
G. E. Ellis[ans.]	Prof. A. L. Perry, Williams-
St. Botolph Club	town[ans.]
Chauncy Hall[ans.]	E. Rameau de St. Père
Hon. Geo. Bournot,[ans.] Ottawa	B. D.[ans.]
Mr. Brice	Mrs. Fiske[ans.]
Casgrain[ans.]	Dr. Oliver[ans.]
Henry Adams[ans.]	D. D. Slade[ans.]
Jas. F. Hunnewell	

E. Rameau[15] is preparing a new and enlarged edition of his book on Acadians & Canadians.

Modify statement about character of Nicholson.[16]

Read the following in [*Le*] *Canada-Français* I, 1re livraison, docs.:[17] 28 Nov. 1730, "*Estat de l'Acadie*"; 1735-1739, "*Lettres de Maillard.*"

On Dudley's meeting with Inds. at Casco in 1703, compare Rale's acct. (see Francis, *Life of Rale*,[18] 231).

Tanguay,[19] 1871, contains a list of English persons taken in the 17th century and baptized in Canada.

Examine: "Remarks out of the Fryar Sebastian Rale's Letters from Narridgwock, Feb. 7, 1720" in the *Common Place Book* of Rev. Henry Flynt[20] (Mass. Hist. Soc.).

Examine: Letter of Rev. Joseph Baxter to Rale (April, 1719).[21]
(Given to Mass. Hist. Soc. by Mr. Daniel Adams of Medfield)
"Journal of Baxter," in N. E. *Hist. & Gen. Reg.*, 1867, p. 45.
Flynt's *Common Place Book*, in Mass. Hist. Soc.
"Strong box" of Rale, Mass. Hist. Soc.?[22]
Rale's *Abenaki Dictionary*[23] (H.C.)

Frye, see if his name is in *Quinquennial Cat*[*alogue*], *H*[*arvard*] *C*[*ollege*].
Bouton, *Lovewell's Great Fight*.
Fox, *History of Dunstable*.
Corr[*espondence*] *Officielle*, 3me Série, Vol. VIII, *Vaudreuil et Begon au Min*[*istre*], *14 oct., 1723*, pp. 51-59 (see Calendar, 125).

Louisbourg:
Mass. Hist. [Soc.] *Coll*[*ections*], 2 ser., III, 192.
Hist. Mag., 2 ser., VIII, 23, 25, 97.
Mass. Hist. *Coll.*, 4 ser., V, 398 (Niles)[24]
Coll. Essex Institute VI, 182 (Craft's "Journal"[25])
    "   "   "   III, 186.
Mass. Hist. *Coll.*, 1 ser., VI, 108-112, 117.
Hist. Mag., IX, V, 63; 2 ser., V, 396.
W^m. Vaughan[26] in Harvard *Quinquennial*.
Raynal, VII, 106.
Gents. Mag., 1758, 102-XV, 649; XVIII, 105.
Pepperell's journal, *Journal or Minutes of an Expedition made against Louisbourg*,[27] (Am. Ant. Soc., Worcester).
N. E. *Hist. Gen. Reg.*, XXIV, 367; XXV, 249.
New France, I, II (F. P[arkman] [Papers], Mass. Hist. Soc.).

1890, July.
Examine Douglass's *Summary*.[28]
    "   Viscount Bing[Byng]'s account of the capture of Louisbourg in "Exodus of the Western Nations."
Examine *Alloa* [Père Alloüez, S. J.?] often cited by Brown.

Robert Bancroft, descended from Col. Hale, told E.S.P.[a] of the

_____
[a] Parkman's sister Eliza, who served as his amanuensis.—Ed.

diary of a soldier named Benjamin Cleves, in N. E. Historic-Genealogy Society—said to be good. Also of a curious letter to Col. Hale from a friend in Boston, written after the siege, and expressing anxiety as to the consequences of the excessive consumption of punch. Bancroft[29] has a copy of it. (Bancroft promises me a copy, Sept. 1.) (I have it.)

Stephen Williams[30]—look him up in Appleton's *Cyc.*

Jesuits, 257, correct "*evening* mass."

Appendix

Accounts

E. W. S. P.[b] ½		10.25
" "		6.48
E. W. S. P. ½		22.16
E. W. S. [P.] ½		37.25

3 July	recd. per F. C. Welch, B. & L. R.R.	175 ⎱ returned to	
	B. & A. " "	80 ⎰ Welch for deposit	
10 "	Welch, bal. of acct.	1,532.16	del. by post.
		625	Mass. Bk.

3 July	Paid S. S. Pierce	23.00
9 July	M. W. Quinlan	111.58
	Craffey, shoing	20.50
	Fenno, fodder	12.96
	Clough & Stuckley	13.60
	Balkam & Co.	9.25
	Dr. Williams	5.00
	Dr. Richardson	5.00
	Grant, saddler	4.15
31 July	Rowe, wood & hay	44.33
4 Aug	M. D. Ayers, carpenter	30.25
	S. S. Pierce	28
5 Aug	H. W. Beckwith	5
8 "	Bickford's Exp.	4.85
" "	Burnham & Co.	74.50
1 Sept.	Henry Lee	20
4 Sept.	S. S. Pierce	22
"	Saltonstall Portrait	10
	Journ. of Archaeology	5

[b] Parkman's sister Eliza, who ran his household and often acted as his secretary. —Ed.

1891

Receipts:

sent to Welch for deposit ⎱ June, Thompson-Houston   43.75
                          ⎰ 10 July, F. C. Welch,   1,622.78

11 July

1 Sept. Boston & Maine, R. I. (sent to F. C. W. for deposit, 2 Sept.) 30

E. S. P.

Pratt, butcher,	28.72$\frac{1}{2}$	14.36
Fodder	16.69$\frac{1}{2}$	8.34
Horse shoer	10$\frac{1}{2}$	5.00
Quinlan, sundries	82.50	12.
Burnham, coal	17.25$\frac{1}{2}$	8.62
Beckwith, carriage	5$\frac{1}{2}$	2.50
Rowe, wood	$7.$\frac{1}{2}$	3.50
Fallon, fish	$\frac{1}{2}$	3.44

1891

27 June, check to D. Foy, clothes   45.

 9 July D.D. Lee, veterinarian   2.

10 Dec. Pulford & Son, 65 St. James st., S.W.
                £ 15.17.

Look after:

Hansas Bonds (Jeffries)

10 New Sh[are]s B. & A. R.R.

Thompson-Houston shares (30 June, 1892 notice rcd. of readiness to
exchange for N. Y. Electric shares—sent to Welch for execution this day).
(Receipts are in Lee's vaults—of wh. I have key, 7 July.)

Books on La Tour [Latour][31] to go to Portsmouth:

Hutchinson 1.	Rameau, *Colonie Féodale*, I
Mém. des Commissaires	Moreau, *Acadie*, I
4 Mass. Hist. Coll. IV	Winthrop, *N. England*
” ” ” VII	2 Mass. Hist. Coll VI (Hubbard)

Notes made on:

Mar. [18] '92 *Corr. Officielle*, Copy	Sir Wm Alexander (Prince Soc.)
1857 Vol. I	Hazard, *State Papers*, I, II.
Poore MSS. (Quebec	Bradford, *Hist. Plymouth*
ed.) I, II	Williamson
Hutchinson Papers	Palfrey
Memorial Hist. Boston.	*N. Y. Col. Docs.* IV, IX

29 Sept., 1892.

Guarantee fund of *Good Government*[32] published by Civil Service Reform League yearly for 3 years from 1 July 1892— $15.

Oregon Trail

(ans.)	X B.Derby—Lit. & Brown 16 Oct.	(ans.)	XC. H. Cordner
”	Mrs. H. Parkman	(ans.)	J. T. Coolidge—L. & B. 16 Oct.
	Col. Dodge	(ans.)	G. P. Coffin
(ans.)	Casgrain—L. & B. 16 Oct.	(ans.)	Bijorby
given (ans.)	X Mrs Fiske	(ans.)	M. A. B.—L. & B. 25 Oct.
	X Mrs. C. S. Sargent	(ans.)	Mrs. J. Q. Adams 25 Oct.
” (ack.)	” Q[uincy] A. S[haw]		
(ans.)	John Bartlett—L. & B. 16 Oct.	(ans.)	Mrs. John Lowell, 30 Dec. 1893
” (ack.)	” Julius H. Ward	(ack.)	Mrs. Mary B. Hall, 25 Dec. 1893
” (ack.)	” E. S. P.		

Medicine and Sleep

	1889				30	7
12 Dec. Sulph.	30	6 hrs	30 Ap.		30	7
————		6	4 May		30	5½
	1890		13 ”		30	6½
8 Jan.	30	7	16 ”		30	6½
17 ”	30	6	20 ”		30	6½
1 Feb.	30	8	28 ”		30	5
15 ”	28	5½	4 June		30	7
18 ”	30	6	7 ”		30	6½
25 ”	30	6½	14 ”		30	5½
4 Mar.	30	8	21 ”		30	6½
14 ”	45	6	24 ”		30	6
21 ”	30	6½	26 ”		30	7
25 ”	30	6	1 July		30	5
29 ”	30	6	7 ”		30	6
4 Ap.	30	7	9 July		30	7
7 ”	15	6½	16 ”		30	5
9 ”	20	10 4	22 ”		30	6
14 ”	30	6	24 ”		30	6
16 ”	30	6	31 ”		30	7
			17 Aug.			

Date	Drug		
27 Aug.		30	6
1 Sept.		"	6
6 "		"	7
12 "		"	5
17 "		"	7
19 "		"	8
26 "		"	6½
2 Oct.		"	5
7 "		"	3½
13 "		37	5
29 "		37	6½
1 Nov.	New Drug		6½
5 Nov.	Sulph.	37	6
7 "	Ch^ld.		6
14 "	Sul.	37	6
18 "	Ch^ld.		5
26 "	Sul.	37	6
29 "	Nit. Soda		5
1 Dec.	Ch^ld		5½
3 "	Sul.	30	6½
8 "	Ch^ld		4
12 "	Sul.	37	7½
22 "	Sul.	37	6½
29 "	Sul.	30	5

1891

Date	Drug		
10 Jan.	Sul.	37	6
18 Jan.	Sul.	37	6
27 Jan.	"	37	6
6 Feb.	Sul.	37	7
15 "	"	37	7
6 Mar.	"	37	7
17 "	"	37	7
22 "	"	37	5
2 April	"	37	6
8 "	"	37	5½
17 "	"	37	7
27 "	"	37	7
4 May	"	37	7
10 "	"	37	5

Date	Drug		
17 May	Sul.	37	7½
25 "	"	37	8
30	"(3D)"	37	5¼
2 June	"	37	6
4 "	"	37	6½
12 "	"	37	5½
18 "	"	36	5
21 June	"	37	6
25 "	"	37	6½
3 July	"	37	4
9 "	"	37	6
19 "	"	37	7½
25 "	"	37	6
31 July	"	37	7 hrs.
6 Aug.	"	37	7 "
13 "	"	37	7 "
17 Aug.	"	37	6½
21 "	"	30	6½
28 "	"	30	6½
3 Sept.	"	37	6½
7 "	"	37	8 hrs.
11 "	"	30	6 "
15 "	"	30	6½
19 "	"	30	5
21 "	"	37	5½
25 "	"	37	6
29 "	"	37	6
7 Oct.	"	37	5½
11 "	"	37	5
15 "	"	37	6½
20 "	"	37	6½
23 "	"	30	5½
27 "	"	30	6
31 "	"	30	6
4 Nov.	"	30	6
8 "	"	30	7
17 "	"	30	5½
21 "	"	30	5
25 "	"	30	5
30 "	"	37 grs.	6

8 Dec.	Sul.	37	4½		14 May	Sul.	30	6
14 "	"	30	5½		21 "	"	30	6
20 "	"	30	5		27 "	"	30	6½
27 "	"	30	6¼		5 June	"	30	6
					14 "	"	30	6
	1892				21 "	"	30	3½
					24 "	"	37	5
5 Jan.	"	30	5		1 July	"	37	6½
9 "	"	30	5		9 "	"	30	5
13 "	"	37	7		20 "	"	30	7
23 "	"	37	5		26 "	"	30	6
1 Feb.	"	37	6		10 Aug.	"	30	6
7 "	"	37	6½		5 Sept.	"	30	6½
11 "	"	37	7		12 "	"	30	7
18 "	"	37	7		19 "	"	30	6½
27 "	"	30	7		25 "	"	30	4
5 Mar.	"	30	6		5 Oct.	"	30	6
10 "	"	30	6½		9 "	"	30	6
15 "	"	30	7		16 "	"	30	7
22 "	"	30	6½		22 "	"	30	6
30 "	"	30	3½		22 "	"	30	5
6 April	"	30	6		2 Nov.	"	37	7
12 "	"	30	5½		9 "	"	30	5
19 "	"	30	5½		16 "	"	36	4
24 "	"	30	3½·					
30 "	"	30	5½					

NOTES

VII. THE OREGON TRAIL
VOLUME I

[1] During his three days in New York, Parkman saw Ramsay Crooks, head of the northern department of the American Fur Company, who gave him letters of recommendation to the principals of the western department: George H. Moore, author of *The Indian Wars of the United States* (*Philadelphia, 1843*) and one Allen. (*1846 Account Book.*)

[2] Henry Whitney Bellows (1814-82), a graduate of Harvard College and the Divinity School, became pastor in 1839 of the first Unitarian church in New York City. Parkman probably had an introduction from his father, one of the leading Boston Unitarians. Bellows was a famous preacher and lyceum lecturer, and an editor of *The Christian Inquirer* and *The Christian Examiner*. During the Civil War he founded and directed the U. S. Sanitary Commission, the forerunner of the Red Cross.

[3] Mr. Kay, like most bookish Easterners of the period, was interested in the social theories of Charles Fourier and in the attempt to put them into practice at Brook Farm. Parkman had no use for the Transcendentalists, whom he called the "she-philosophers of West Roxbury."

[4] Henry Rowe Schoolcraft (1793-1864), explorer and ethnologist, first visited the Indian country on a geological trip through Missouri and Arkansas in 1817-18. He served as geologist on Governor Lewis Cass's expedition to the Lake Superior copper country in the summer of 1820, and described it in his *Narrative Journal of Travels Through the North-Western Regions of the United States* (1821). Two years later he was appointed Indian agent for the tribes of Lake Superior. He married the grand-daughter of an Ojibwa chief, and negotiated many treaties with the Indians. From 1836 to 1841 he was Superintendent of Indian Affairs for Michigan, and devoted much of his time to studying and writing about the Indians. His best known works are *Algic Researches* (1839), *Oneota* (1844-45), *Notes on the Iroquois* (1846), and his tremendous compilation, *Indian Tribes of the United States* (1851-57). In the *North American Review* for July, 1866 (CIII, 1-18) Parkman critized this last work savagely, for Schoolcraft was guilty of many inaccuracies and some deliberate fudging.

[5] In Philadelphia, Parkman consulted on historical matters William B. Reed, a lawyer; Dr. Alfred Elwyn; John Jordan, Jr.; C. A. Poulson, Jr.; and Francis J. Fisher, Jr.—many of whom are mentioned in his acknowledgments in the preface to *Pontiac*.

[6] In Harrisburg, Parkman saw Samuel Brenizer, to whom he returned some borrowed papers; and Neville B. Craig, editor of *Olden Time*, who told him that S. P. Hildreth had the St. Clair papers. (*1846 Account Book.*)

[7] [Carlisle] "Armstrong family. The Col. had two sons—[one] of the [*sic*] youngest, Genl. A., has a son living near Baltimore—others, one of them called Koskiusko, in N. Y. Dr. A. of Carlisle thinks the family papers in their hands." (*1846 Account Book.*)

"Baird of Reading (formerly of Carlisle) has collected materials for a history of Cumberland Cnty." (*1846 Account Book.*)

[8] Colonel Henry Bouquet (1719-66), a Swiss professional soldier, came to America with his compatriot Frederick Haldimand of the Royal Americans in 1754, after joining the British service. Bouquet took a leading part in the French and Indian War. In 1758 he marched with General Forbes against Fort Duquesne and commanded there, after it had been renamed Fort Pitt, until 1762. In the following year he returned and broke up the Indian siege, in the "dangerous enterprise" of which Parkman speaks (cf. *Pontiac*, II, 61-78). In the winter of 1763-64 Bouquet organized and led an expedition against the Ohio Indians, which resulted in the signing of a treaty of peace. Parkman wrote an introduction for William Smith's *Historical Account of Bouquet's Expedition* (Cincinnati, 1868), and revised the translation of Dumas' biographical account of Bouquet which prefaces it.

[9] "Colonel" James Smith led the Pennsylvania rangers in 1763 and 1765. In the latter year he waylaid a government pack train at Bloody Run (see *Pontiac*, II, 292-96). His narrative may be found in Samuel G. Drake's *Tragedies of the Wilderness*.

[10] General Edward Braddock cut a road from Fort Cumberland to Fort Pitt in the course of the expedition of 1755 against what was then Fort Duquesne, which ended in his defeat and death at the Monongahela. Bouquet's road from Fort Loudon to Fort Pitt was to the north of Braddock's road, along the course Parkman followed.

[11] The battle of Bushy Run in 1763 is described in *Pontiac*, II, 67-8.

[12] Jared Sparks (1789-1866), the first professor of history in an American university, began teaching at Harvard in 1839, after an earlier career as a Unitarian clergyman. He edited the *North American Review* (1824-30); published a *Life and Writings of Washington* (1834-37) and the *Works and Life of Franklin* (1836-40); and studied the history of the American Revolu-

tion in European sources (1840-41). He also edited the *Library of American Biography*, to which he made many contributions. He was Parkman's historical mentor, and later his guide and critic. He was president of Harvard from 1849 to 1853.

[13] Two Mr. Biddles of Pittsburg are mentioned in Parkman's notes: Richard, to whom he was referred by William B. Reed of Philadelphia, and John W.

[14] Fort Pitt was built by General Stanwix in 1759 on the ruins of Fort Duquesne, after the capture of the latter by Bouquet in 1758. It was named after the elder William Pitt.

[15] A fortification was first built at the junction of the Alleghany and Monongahela rivers, on the present site of Pittsburgh, by Virginians under Captain Trent in 1754. After the Great Meadows fight, the place was newly fortified and named Fort Duquesne by the French. In 1755, under Contrecoeur, it served as a base for the Indians with whom Beaujeu defeated Braddock. It was captured by Bouquet in 1758 and renamed Fort Pitt.

[16] *"La Belle Rivière"* was the old French name for the Ohio.

[17] Francis Fauvel-Gouraud published his *Phreno-Mnemotechny or the Art of Memory* (New York, 1845) after lecturing on his system, which he claimed was "founded on a purely philosophical basis and operates through the intellectual and not the mechanical action of the mind."

[18] Fort Massiac, or Massac, on the Ohio River in southern Illinois, was built by the French as Fort Ascension in 1757, and renamed after the Marquis de Massiac in the following year. It was abandoned in 1759, but another fort was built on the same site in 1794 by the Americans, on the orders of Anthony Wayne.

[19] The Planters' House in St. Louis, opened in 1841, was the best-known hostelry of the metropolis of the old West.

[20] Henry Clay (1777-1852), the "Great Pacificator," author of the Missouri Compromise, had been the Whig candidate for the presidency in 1844. Parkman admired him as the white hope of the Whigs, whom the New England Federalists supported against the Jacksonian Democrats.

[21] Quincy Adams Shaw, Parkman's cousin and companion on the Oregon Trail trip, was a lover of sport and travel, but not of history; and hence only joined the expedition at St. Louis, where they outfitted. He later acted as Parkman's amanuensis for the composition of *The Oregon Trail*, and helped to shape it into a record of holiday adventure rather than a history.

[22] Madame Julia Jarrot of Cahokia, a native of Ste. Geneviève and the

daughter of the wealthy Vital Ste. Gem of Kaskaskia, was the widow of
Nicolas Jarrot, one of the principal inhabitants of the place in 1809. The
Jarrot mansion was a center of hospitality, and according to local legend
Lafayette was entertained there in 1825.

[23] Passed Midshipman Selim E. Woodworth, U.S.N., was the son of
Samuel Woodworth, editor of the New York *Mirror* and author of "The
Old Oaken Bucket." From Oregon young Woodworth made his way to
California, where he was put in charge of the relief expeditions which
sought to rescue the Donner Party early in 1847. He himself never
ventured farther into the mountains than Summit Valley, and his conduct has been severely criticized. He was characterized by the milder-
mouthed Californians as a martinet, a drunkard, and an egotist. During
the Civil War he returned to the Navy and rose to the rank of Commodore.

[24] Pascal Louis Cerré, whose sister Marie Thérèse married Auguste
Chouteau, the older half-brother of Pierre. A son, Michel Sylvestre Cerré,
a veteran of the Upper Missouri fur trade, entered the mountain trade
while supplying Captain Bonneville, and later was with the American
Fur Company and Pierre Chouteau, Jr. & Company. The Cerrés ranked
close to the Chouteaus among the first families of the St. Louis fur trade.

[25] Pontiac (1720-69), head of the Ottowa, Ojibwa, and Pottowatomie
confederation, was perhaps the greatest leader the North American
Indians ever produced. In 1746 he helped the French at Detroit to repel
an attack by the northern tribes, and in 1755 he led the Ottawas at
Braddock's defeat. After the fall of New France in 1760, he organized a
great Indian uprising against the new masters of the continent. In 1763
he destroyed many of the British forts on the Great Lakes and massacred
their garrisons. No less than eight of the twelve frontier posts were
captured by Pontiac, and only in 1766 did Sir William Johnson succeed
in subduing the Indians and making a treaty of peace. Pontiac was
assassinated by a Kaskaskia Indian three years later. Parkman's first
historical work, *The Conspiracy of Pontiac* (1851), was devoted to this period
of American history; and it is interesting to see from this and earlier notes,
and the later use of Pontiac's name for Parkman's horse, that the young
historian's mind was already full of his subject.

[26] "*April 17.* Tradition here [St. Louis] says that Pontiac was killed in a
drunken fray near Cahokia." (1846 Account Book.)

"Baptiste Vallée of St. Geneviève must have seen Pontiac." (1846
Account Book.)

[27] Thomas Fitzpatrick (1798-1854), "Broken Hand" or "White

Head," was perhaps the greatest of the mountain men, and played a notable part in the opening of the West. He was with W. H. Ashley's fur brigade on the second voyage up the Missouri in 1823, and in March 1824 was among the first white men to use South Pass. He was once Jed Smith's partner and Kit Carson's tutor in the ways of the wilderness. In 1834 he headed the Rocky Mountain Fur Company, with Jim Bridger and Milton Sublette as partners, and later joined the American Fur Company, which became Pratte, Chouteau & Company. He twice guided the misnamed "Pathfinder" Frémont along the routes long known to the mountain men, and led the first emigrant trains to set out for the West Coast by the Oregon Trail. He guided Father De Smet, S.J. and his fellow missionaries all the way into the Flathead country. In 1845 he showed Colonel Kearny and his dragoons the road to South Pass, and led Lieutenant Abert safely through the hostile country from Bent's Fort along the Purgatoire and the Canadian to Fort Gibson. In this summer of 1846 he was to guide the Army of the West to Santa Fe, and the California expedition as far as Socorro, returning to St. Louis with dispatches for Washington in November. With an unmatched experience as a trapper, explorer, Indian fighter, and trader, he was named as the first Indian agent for the Plains tribes, a post which he held until his death. Parkman could have had no better informant. Cf. L. R. Hafen & W. J. Ghent, *Broken Hand* (Denver, 1931).

[28] Lieutenant James William Abert, Topographical Engineers, U. S. A., mapped much of the West. He was the son of Colonel J. J. Abert, the Chief of Engineers, who sent Frémont on his expedition of 1842. Young Abert accompanied Frémont in 1845, and on his orders made a survey of the Purgatoire. His first report, dated 1845, deals with the Bent's Fort–St. Louis route; his second, in Major W. H. Emory's *Notes on the Topographical Survey*, App. 6 & 7, covers the Fort Leavenworth–Bent's Fort route and New Mexico.

[29] Fitzpatrick's picture of the Western tribes is strikingly modern on the whole, though faulty in some respects. Of the tribes which Fitzpatrick left out of his two main divisions, the Pawnees and Arikaras belong to the Caddoan linguistic group, the Mandans to the Siouan, the Cheyennes to the Algonkin, and the Kiowas to the Kiowan. The first great group of which Fitzpatrick speaks was the Siouan, which was second in numbers only to the Algonkin among the Indians north of Mexico. To this group belong all the tribes which Fitzpatrick includes, save the Sauks and Foxes, which are Algonkin. Other Western tribes also included in this Siouan group are the Crows and Assiniboins. Fitzpatrick lumps the

Iroquoian group, including the Mohawks and Tuscaroras, with the Algonkin, which includes the Shawnees, Delawares, Chippewas, and most of
the Indians of the Northeast and the Great Lakes, as well as the Blackfeet,
Arapahos, and Cheyennes of the West. Properly speaking, the Iroquoian
group includes only the Hurons, the Tobacco Nation, Neutrals, Iroquois,
Conestogas, the Tuscarora Confederation, and the Cherokees.

Owing to the peculiar geographical position of the Crows, their Siouan
dialect was known by such linguistically different tribes as the Nez
Percés, Blackfeet, and Gros Ventres, as well as by the Siouan Dakotas
and Mandans. It was often used by traders as an intertribal language,
instead of sign talk.

The Comanches, Utes, Bannocks, and Shoshonies all belong to the
Shoshonean group, as Fitzpatrick has it. But the Nez Percés and Chinooks
belong to the Penutian family, while the Flatheads and Spokans were
Salishan tribes, usually considered to be Algonkin. The Salish, who were
known as Flatheads from the tribal designation in sign language (which
referred to their ancient practice of deforming the heads of their children),
and as Diggers for their digging up of wild roots for food, differed very
widely from the Plains Indians.

[30] Jefferson Barracks, an army cantonment near St. Louis, was an
important military center during the Mexican and Civil wars.

[31] "*Vide Poche*" ("Empty Pocket") was the nickname of Carondelet,
the poor French suburb of St. Louis.

[32] The Crows, a Siouan tribe closely related to the Hidatsa or Gros
Ventres of the Missouri, were divided into two main bands, the River
Crows of the Yellowstone and the Mountain Crows of the Rockies. The
latter, with whom Fitzpatrick and Parkman were concerned, were much
more important than the Dakotas to the mountain fur trade, because of
their strategic position. They produced better buffalo robes than any other
tribe, and their language was used as a common medium of communication in the trade which centered about their territory in the valley of the
Big Horn. After the Crows separated from the Hidatsa in the eighteenth
century, their chief enemies were the Dakotas, Sioux, Blackfeet, Pawnees,
and Arapahos. They were nomadic hunters, living on the buffalo and
planting only a little tobacco for use in their religious ritual. Prince
Maximilian of Wied considered them the proudest of the Indians, and
pointed out that they more often plundered than killed the whites. The
Crows were expert horse thieves and robbers, but professed friendship
with the whites, many of whom resided among them at various times.
Two mulattoes, Edward Rose and James P. Beckwith, even became Crow

chiefs. The Crows were noted for their magnificent social discipline, which enabled them to spare themselves the ravages of liquor, use of which they long prohibited, while other tribes were weakened by it. They were, however, sexually dissolute.

[33] Dixon and R. Ewing followed much the same route as Parkman through the West, while R. G. Jacob went all the way to the Pacific Coast. All three went as far as Fort Laramie with W. H. Russell's or Lillburn W. Boggs' emigrant party, which Parkman saw assembling at Independence and later met at Richard's Post near Laramie. Here Jacob joined Edwin Bryant's horseback party to California, which was the first group of the 1846 emigration to reach the coast. Jacob then joined the California Battalion with Bryant, and went campaigning under Frémont. Dixon and Ewing went southward from Fort Laramie to Bent's Fort, and returned to Westport along the Santa Fe Trail. Parkman expected to keep them company, but they left without him while he was with the Sioux in the mountains.

[34] Pierre Chouteau (1758-1849), whose older half-brother Auguste accompanied Pierre Laclède to the site of St. Louis in November 1763, and in the following spring founded there the first center of a fur-trading enterprise which later covered the whole West. Chouteau and his son Pierre, Jr. (1789-1865), who acted as his father's clerk before he was sixteen and went into business for himself in 1813, lent their names to places as far north as Dakota and as far south as New Mexico; Kansas City was first known as Chouteau's Landing. Pratte, Chouteau & Company, of which the younger Chouteau was a leading partner, bought the Western Department and Upper Missouri Outfit of the American Fur Company in 1834, when John Jacob Astor sold out and a syndicate headed by Ramsay Crooks bought the Northern Department. Both outfits retained the old name in their field operations. By 1846 the St. Louis firm had become Pierre Chouteau, Jr. & Company, and it then operated Fort Laramie. Parkman found "the magic of a dream and the enchantment of an Arabian tale" in old Chouteau's memories of St. Louis' growth from outpost to metropolis, and gives an eloquent account of them in *Pontiac*, II, 274n. It would seem that he confused Pierre Chouteau, who only came to St. Louis in 1764, with Auguste, the co-founder.

[35] This sentence is taken almost word for word from the 1846 Account Book.

[36] Liguest P. Chouteau, a son of the elder Pierre, is quoted as an authority on Pontiac's death in *Pontiac*, II, 325. Pontiac led the Ottawas

at Braddock's defeat and was given a French officer's uniform by Montcalm shortly before the battle of the Plains of Abraham (*Pontiac*, I, 192*n*). Liguest was Pierre Laclède's last name, usually dropped.

[37] "Mr. Liguest P. Chouteau tells me, as coming from his father, that Pontiac had a high command over the Inds. in Montcalm army—that the English hired an Indian to kill him at Cahokia—that the Spanish requested his body, and buried it at St. Louis." (1846 Account Book.)

[38] The Kansa(s) or Kaw Indians were a tribe of Siouan stock who lived in the valley of the Kansas. Their mud-hut village stood a few miles above the river's mouth. The Kaws lived at peace with both whites and their Indian neighbors, growing corn and hunting. As they became more dependent upon the government, they grew lazy and demoralized, like those Parkman saw begging on the steamer.

[39] Henry Chatillon (1816-?), Parkman's hunter and guide on the Oregon Trail trip, was one of the St. Louis French who played so great a role in opening up the West. He had earned his living as a hunter on the plains and in the mountains since he was fifteen, and was considered one of the best hunters in the West. He was engaged for Parkman by P. Chouteau, Jr. & Company, whose trading posts he had long supplied with buffalo meat, as he later did the Missouri steamboats. The steamboat captains employed hunters to precede them up the river, leaving their kill on the river banks to be picked up by the boat's yawl and thus providing a welcome variation to the staple diet of pork and beans. H. M. Chittenden, the historian of the fur trade and of early navigation on the Missouri, mentions Chatillon as hunter for Captain Joseph La Barge, and calls him "a fine man, an excellent hunter, and sensible and gentlemanly in his relations" (*Early Steamboat Navigation on the Missouri* [New York, 1903], 126). Chatillon's real home was the plains and the mountains —he had just returned from four years there when Parkman engaged him at St. Louis, and he was perfectly willing to leave on another expedition after only three days in St. Louis—and like many another mountain man, he had taken an Indian wife. This woman, Bear Robe, who died during his expedition with Parkman, was the daughter of old Bull Bear, the great chief of the Oglalas—probably the chief here referred to by Parkman—and the relationship doubtless did much to explain the immunity with which the small party passed through the Indian country. It was certainly responsible for Parkman having the opportunity to live with an Indian village as it pursued its normal life. Chatillon was known as "Yellow Whiteman" by the Sioux, and as late as 1931 he was remembered by the descendants of Bull Bear's band (cf. G. E. Hyde, *Red Cloud's*

Folk [Norman, Oklahoma, 1937], 59). Parkman judged that Chatillon had:

A natural refinement and delicacy of mind, such as is rare even in women. His manly face was a mirror of uprightness, simplicity, and kindness of heart; he had, moreover, a keen perception of character, and a tact that would preserve him from flagrant error in any society. Henry had not the restless energy of an Anglo-American. He was content to take things as he found them; and his chief fault arose from an excess of easy generosity, not conducive to thriving in the world. Yet it was commonly remarked of him, that whatever he might choose to do with what belonged to himself, the property of others was always safe in his hands. His bravery was as much celebrated in the mountains as his skill in hunting; but it is characteristic of him that in a country where the rifle is the chief arbiter between man and man, he was very seldom involved in quarrels. Once or twice, indeed, his quiet good-nature had been mistaken and presumed upon, but the consequences of the error were such that no one was ever known to repeat it. No better proof of the intrepidity of his temper could be asked, than the common report that he had killed more than thirty grizzly bears. He was a proof of what unaided nature will sometimes do. I have never, in the city or in the wilderness, met a better man than my true-hearted friend, Henry Chatillon. (*Oregon Trail*, 17-18)

Parkman gave Chatillon his rifle at the end of the trip; and though the latter could neither read nor write—in one of the notebooks Parkman wrote out his own name and Chatillon's, evidently for the latter's benefit—he kept up a correspondence with Parkman through the aid of others until 1867. The two men then met again in St. Louis, where Chatillon had retired to spend his last years.

⁴⁰ Independence, six miles from the Missouri, founded in 1827, was the second starting point of the Santa Fe and California-Oregon trails, after Franklin was washed away by the Missouri in 1828. It was the main outfitting center of the westward movement from about 1832 to 1840. It gradually lost ground before the rise of Westport, founded six years later and ten miles farther west, which was near the good landing at Kansas and beyond the Blue River (of the Missouri), which was hard for wagons to ford.

⁴¹ Albert Speyer, a Prussian Jew who was a Santa Fe trader of many years standing, carried two wagonloads of arms and ammunition consigned to Mexico on this trip. He was accompanied by Dr. Adolphe Wislizenus, a German geologist, naturalist, and political refugee, who had already followed the Oregon Trail as far as Fort Hall in 1839 and written a book about it, and was now planning to investigate the flora and

fossils of the Southwest. After Speyer's train had set off, Colonel Kearny learned that these munitions were destined for General Manuel Armijo, the governor of New Mexico, with whose brother Speyer was probably in partnership. Kearny sent two troops of dragoons under Captain Benjamin Moore to intercept the shipment, but Speyer had too great a start and reached Santa Fe safely. On his way thence to Chihuahua the arms were seized by the Mexicans, against whom Speyer later made claim for payment, though he was escorted on this journey by General Armijo, who was fleeing from Santa Fe. George Frederick Ruxton met them on the trail. Speyer later quit the Santa Fe trade and set up business in New York, where he killed himself after going bankrupt.

[42] Westport, now part of Kansas City, stood approximately at the present intersection of the Santa Fe road and Grand Avenue. The landing on the Missouri near Westport was first known as Chouteau's and later as Kansas. Westport was predestined to be a center of the westward movement, for if freight for Santa Fe were landed farther up the Missouri, the Kansas River had to be crossed; if farther downstream, a longer wagon haul was demanded. Westport had the good grass, water, and wood essential for wagon trains, and its outfitting establishments soon rivaled those of St. Louis and Independence.

[43] Colonel Chick, who kept a store as well as a tavern at Kansas Landing, probably also speculated in land and outfits. He befriended all the westward-moving world, and his hospitality is frequently mentioned by travelers.

[44] The Sauks, like the Kickapoos and Pottowatomies, were of Algonkin stock and had been forced out of their home in northern Illinois and Wisconsin when the whites moved in. The Sauks and their close kinsmen the Foxes waged the Black Hawk War. These Eastern tribes were established on reservations in present-day Kansas and Oklahoma which were created by the government after 1830.

[45] The center of the Shawnee Methodist Mission was the large brick building which still stands two miles west of the Missouri line in the midst of Kansas City. The Shawnees and the Delawares were Algonkins from the eastern seaboard. The Wyandots (Hurons) had been driven out of their original home in Ontario near Georgian Bay by the Six Nations and the Sioux about 1650, and in 1842 they migrated to Kansas from Ohio and Michigan. In 1856 Parkman saw the other surviving section of the Huron nation at Lorette, near Quebec, where they had taken refuge with their Jesuit missionaries after the fall of Huronia in the seventeenth century. The Delawares, once the most important tribe of Algonkin stock

and hence given the title of "grandfather" by other Indians, were "made women" after their conquest by the Iroquois about 1720, and forbidden to make war or to hold land. They slowly migrated westward and south-westward, and became the only forest tribe that really mastered the Plains culture. In small bands they roved everywhere in the West, and were magnificent scouts, trailers, hunters, and trappers. They were the Ishmaels of the Plains Indians, since every man's hand had been against them and theirs was against every Indian's. They accompanied the fur-trapping brigades of the mountain men as trusted and valued master craftsmen of life on the plains and in the mountains. They were with Jim Bridger, Kit Carson, and Frémont, and later served as scouts for the U. S. Army. The Plains Indians had a healthy respect for the Delawares' prowess as warriors. Their Kansas reservation was established in 1835.

[46] This party, with which Parkman and Shaw joined forces, consisted of Captain Bill Chandler, a retired Irish officer of the British Army who had served in Canada and Jamaica; his brother Jack, an amiable non-entity; and Romaine, an English traveler who had "once been upon the Western prairies." The Britishers parted company with Parkman at the forks of the Platte, on June 10. Cf. *Knickerbocker Magazine* (June 1847) XXIX, No. 6, 506. Shaw later met the Captain in New York.

[47] The Noland House was run by Smallwood Noland, "Uncle Wood," who prided himself on the fact that his was the largest hotel in Missouri outside St. Louis. It was also the westernmost American hotel of the period, and the most famous of all frontier taverns.

[48] In *The Oregon Trail* (p. 9) Parkman identifies this party as being from Illinois. Many of the emigrants were men of substance and reputation, despite Parkman's low opinion of them, such as Jessy Quinn Thornton, James Frazier Reed, and the Donners, all well-to-do Illinois folk then in Independence awaiting the formation of a wagon train for Oregon. Cf. B. DeVoto, *Year of Decision* (Boston, 1943).

[49] McGee's establishment is not mentioned in other traveler's accounts of Westport.

[50] General Lewis Cass (1782-1866), after serving under Hull and Harrison in the War of 1812, became governor of the territory of Michigan in 1813, and during his eighteen years in that office collected documents on Pontiac's siege of Detroit, which he later put at Parkman's disposal. In 1839, while Minister to France, he commissioned Pierre Margry to collect papers in the Paris archives dealing with the old Northwest. A close friend and frequent companion of Schoolcraft, he was much interested in the Indians, about whom he wrote many articles for the *North*

American Review and his *Inquiries Concerning the Indians Living Within the United States* (n. p., 1823). He was an unsuccessful candidate for the Democratic nomination for the presidency in 1844, and in 1846 a leader in the Senate of the "54°40' or Fight" school of thought. He ran for president in 1848.

[51] Probably Albert G. Boone, a nephew of the great Daniel, who conducted an outfitting and trading business at Westport under the firm name of Boone and Hamilton. Daniel Boone, Jr. first explored this region, and three of his sons traveled westward with Boggs' or Russell's party, which Parkman frequently encountered. Boggs' wife, Panthea Grant Boone, was a granddaughter of the original Daniel.

[52] Vogel was probably one of the St. Louis Germans who worked their way westward as small traders, having emigrated from Germany after the disturbances of the 1830's. The Giessner Emigrant Society was established in Hesse in 1834 to aid those bound for America, and the first parties came to St. Louis in 1834 under the leadership of Frederick Muench and Paul Follenius.

[53] The first of five ferries, on the Kansas River between its mouth and Topeka. Fording was not practical at this point when the river was swollen in the spring, though calked wagons could be floated across without serious difficulty.

[54] This fort on the Missouri above Kansas City was then the westernmost outpost of the United States. It was built in 1827 by General Henry Leavenworth (1783-1834), who had led the punitive expedition against the Arikaras of the Upper Missouri four years before and who died while negotiating a peace with the Indians on the Southwest frontier. Fort Leavenworth was long the headquarters of the First Dragoons, a crack regiment and the only body of troops accustomed to Western conditions. In 1846 the fort became the base of the Army of the West for the Mexican Campaign.

[55] Colonel Stephen Watts Kearny (1794-1848), uncle of General Phil Kearny of Civil War fame, was the commanding officer on the Western frontier, with headquarters at Fort Leavenworth. In the preceding year he had led a party of the First Dragoons west to Laramie in a show of force designed to quiet the increasingly unruly Sioux—and perhaps to pave the way for American intervention in Oregon. Later in the summer of 1846, as general, he led the Army of the West against Santa Fe, and in the following year to California. Lieutenant Jefferson Davis, later president of the Confederate States, was adjutant of the First Dragoons.

[56] The Kickapoos were of Algonkin stock. They were first encountered

by the French in Wisconsin, and later moved to the Ohio Valley, where they fought for the British during the Revolution and the War of 1812. They had only recently been moved by the U. S. Government to this Kansas reservation.

[57] The Pottowatomies belonged to the central or Great Lakes division of the Algonkin linguistic group, like the Sauks, Foxes, and Kickapoos. Parkman had seen Ojibwa bark lodges at Sault Ste. Marie in 1845.

[58] A young Englishman with this uncommon name accompanied Father De Smet, S.J., into the buffalo country with Bidwell's Oregon party of 1841. References to him may be found in both De Smet's *Life, Letters and Travels* (New York, 1905), 276, 280, 295, 1,348-9; and in "De Smet's Letters & Sketch," *Early Western Travels*, XXVII (Cleveland, 1906), 198, 235-6. Father De Smet described Romaine as "jealous of the honor of his nation," and "of a good English family, and like most of his countrymen, fond of travel." He may have been one of the numerous British agents who were pursuing secret missions in the West at this period, before the Oregon question was settled, or simply one of the many well-heeled sportsmen who were drawn to the region by the magnificent hunting. Parkman gives a fuller account of him in the *Knickerbocker Magazine* (June 1847), 508.

[59] Captain Chandler, as a retired British officer who had served in Canada, may have had other purposes than sport in mind. He and his brothers reached the Oregon settlements, and visited the Sandwich (Hawaiian) Islands before returning home by way of Panama, New Orleans, and New York. Cf. *Knickerbocker Magazine* (November 1847).

[60] The "new fort up the Missouri," which two companies of the First Dragoons under Captain Philip St. George Cooke built just below Table Creek in the early summer of 1846, was Fort Kearney, which was soon abandoned. The name was then given to the fort on the Platte, not far from the junction of the Independence and St. Joseph trails with the Nebraska City road, which had been called Fort Child at its establishment in 1848. Through some error of the War Department or the Post Office, this placename has long been misspelled "Kearney," though it was intended to perpetuate the memory of Stephen Watts Kearny.

[61] The dragoon trail from Clough Creek to which Parkman refers was that followed by Kearny's First Dragoons in their sweep through the West in 1845.

[62] The St. Joseph's Trail commenced at Ellwood on the west bank of the Missouri, opposite St. Joseph, Missouri, and proceeded westward by Mosquito Creek, the Kickapoo Agency, Wolf Creek, and the Nemaha to

Marysville on the east bank of the Big Blue, where one route from Independence joined it. The junction with the Independence Crossing route was six miles to the west. St. Joseph, two days by steamer up the Missouri from Independence, was considered to be seventy miles farther west. The settlement was named in the French-Canadian fashion after Joseph Robidoux, who did much to promote its growth.

[63] There were no organized parties of Mormons ahead of Parkman on the trail—Parkman never encountered any until he reached the Pueblo—but the camp at Independence had been full of rumors of the proposed westward movement of the Latter-day Saints from their temporary resting place at Nauvoo. The emigrants from Illinois and Missouri, notably Lillburn W. Boggs (who as governor of Missouri had ordered his militia to exterminate the Mormons and had been filled with buckshot in his own home by a Destroying Angel) had reason to fear the Saints, who were supposed to be on the march in thousands, with "ten brass field pieces" and every man "armed with a rifle, a bowie knife, and a brace of large revolving pistols" (DeVoto, *Year of Decision*, 149). Boggs' or Russell's party had requested a military escort as protection against the Mormons, but Colonel Kearny had refused to supply it. Parkman evidently shared the emigrants' alarm, for he observed: "No one could predict what would be the result when large armed bodies of these fanatics should encounter the most impetuous and reckless of their old enemies on the prairie" (*Oregon Trail*, 47). He himself was later mistaken for one of the "fanatics" when he met emigrant trains on the trail, to his vast annoyance.

[64] Sorel, one cf the Britishers' two hunters, was doubtless a French Canadian. The name is that of one of the oldest settlements on the St. Lawrence, at the mouth of the Richelieu.

[65] The Little Nemaha is about halfway between St. Joseph and Marysville. It was a steep-banked but not difficult crossing.

[66] Romaine, who had inspired the Chandlers to make the trip, proved to be "the most uncomfortable man" the Captain ever met, for he was "determined to have everything his own way." (*Knickerbocker Magazine*, June 1847, 505.) Jack Chandler, the brother of Captain Bill, was a nonentity among the members of the party. His easy-going good-nature, however, made him more popular with Parkman and Shaw than either the apprehensive Captain or the overbearing Romaine.

[67] The fur companies bought cheap and sold dear, in order to keep the trappers and hunters dependent upon them, after the classic company-store pattern. The account book (cf. Appendix, p. 491) shows that Park-

man paid $3 for a shirt at Laramie. This reduction and the comparatively low price for whiskey quoted by Chatillon show the effect of competition from the traders Richard and Bissonnette upon what had been a monopoly of the American Fur Company. The independent traders sold flour for 40% less, and bacon for 30% less, than the prevailing prices at Fort Laramie. Osborne Russell estimated the usual mark-up in the mountains as 2,000% on St. Louis prices (*Journal of a Trapper* [Boise, 1921], 63).

[68] This was the early practice in the fur trade, but the Indians now brought most of their furs to the trading posts, as under the Hudson's Bay Company system. Parkman met some of the old "winterers" at Laramie, for every big company post still sent out a few traders to travel with the various bands and to induce them to come to the post with their furs.

[69] The Little Vermillion was sometimes known as the Black Vermillion.

[70] Chatillon seems to be alluding to the Owns-Alone feast, for women who had reached the age of forty or more and had been strictly true to the marriage relation. Cf. Clark Wissler, "Oglala Societies," *Anthropological Papers of the American Museum of Natural History*, XI, 1 (New York, 1916), 76-7. Chatillon, doubtless because of his Sioux wife, as Parkman suggests, makes a little too much of Sioux chastity. Their women were more promiscuous within the tribe, for instance, than the Cheyenne or Arapaho women. The right of a brother-in-law to take liberties was undisputed and universally practiced, and this right was often assumed by nonrelatives. The Sioux girl here mentioned probably did not like the young man in question, and felt insulted rather than degraded.

[71] Boisverd or Boisvert, the Britishers' second hunter, was also a French Canadian.

[72] Wright, a St. Louis man, was the Britishers' muleteer. Missouri mule skinners were already noted for the adequacy of their vocabulary.

[73] The main Oregon Trail left the Santa Fe Trail near Gardner, Kansas, crossed the Waukarusa and the Kansas near Topeka, and struck overland to the Little Vermillion and the Vermillion. One route then followed the east bank of the Big Blue to the junction with the St. Joseph's road near Marysville, Kansas, while another crossed the Big Blue at Independence Crossing just short of it. It then followed the east bank of the Little Blue and reached the Platte near Grand Island (Hastings, Nebraska), after crossing the Pawnee Trail. It then continued along the south bank to the forks of the Platte, from which various routes crossed to the North Platte, whose south bank it followed well beyond Fort Laramie.

[74] Romaine might well be expected to know something about rafting across streams after his journey with Father De Smet in 1841, which he does not seem to have discussed with Parkman. The *Knickerbocker* version gives a fuller account of his annoying omniscience (June, 1847).

[75] Delorier, or Deslauriers, Parkman and Shaw's muleteer from Kansas Landing, was considered a true French Canadian—St. Jean Baptiste is the patron saint of French Canadians—by Parkman. He was loyal and indefatigable, cheerful and polite to his *bourgeois*, or boss, even when the going was rough, but somewhat stupid.

[76] Here Parkman probably garbled some of the wealth of information about the Indians which he was receiving. No such ceremony is known to have existed among the Plains tribes. A "white" buffalo—that is, an albino or unusually blond one—was about the most valuable object in the world to the Plains Indians, who regarded it as having great magical power. Its owner would only give it away under the compulsion of some dream or other magical instruction, or to obtain some even more greatly desirable object, or to propitiate the spirits after a disaster. Such an act called for a feast, and the guests would be duly impressed by the gift of the cherished possession. The *quid pro quo* inevitably expected by an Indian in return for a gift has given us the expression "Indian giving."

[77] Anything could be a "medicine," but usually personal medicines were parts of or objects associated with animals, birds, or insects. An Indian's personal medicine was usually revealed to him during the initiatory fast later mentioned by Parkman (p. 444). In the course of the trance produced by the various ordeals, a dream or vision occurred in which somebody or something analyzed the individual's character and forecast his future. The personal medicine was usually associated with the apparition, which if human was usually considered to be an animal or a bird which had temporarily taken on the form of a man, but the medicine might be merely some inanimate object involved in the vision—a tree, plant, or stone. Anything connected with these things was a medicine object. In his medicine bundle the Indian carried part of the bird or beast or thing in question, and perhaps some of the objects associated with his vision. This bundle was his most sacred possession, to be opened only by himself and usually only when alone, with the proper incantations and ritual.

Woodpeckers and rattlesnakes were no more powerful medicine with the Sioux and Kaws than with other Indians. All living objects were venerated for their medicine power, but special veneration was paid to the personal medicine.

[78] This passage indicates Parkman's anthropological naivete, in that he was still unfamiliar with personal medicines and the most nearly universal of primitive tabus, that affecting mothers-in-law. Not calling someone by his true name is a common practice among all primitives. Prince Maximilian of Wied displayed a much more profound understanding of Indian customs more than ten years earlier.

Parkman later witnessed Sioux mourning, for Chatillon's wife Bear Robe at his Chugwater camp, and for the warriors killed by the Snakes while in the Laramie Mountains. See pp. 448, 450, 459.

[79] Keatley, or Kearsley, the captain of the emigrant train that Parkman met near the Big Blue (the "Mormons" of earlier entries), resigned his charge because of the insubordination of his party. Such changes of leadership were typical of the emigrants, who carried the principle of the town meeting into the wilderness, and were restless under discipline. Kearsley joined Parkman's party with four ox-drawn wagons, an unwelcome addition since the emigrants moved at a much slower pace than the sportsmen.

[80] Bull Bear (Mahto-Tatonka in *The Oregon Trail*) was the head chief of the Oglala Sioux after 1835, and Henry Chatillon's father-in-law. His portrait was painted by Alfred Jacob Miller for Captain William Drummond Stewart in 1837. He was a good friend of the whites, but quarreled with the Pawnees over buffalo-hunting near the forks of the Platte in 1834, when his band were lured southward from the old Oglala Post on the south fork of the Cheyenne to trade at Fort William. From about 1840 Bull Bear's bands hunted west of the Laramie River, while Smoke's, the other division of the Oglalas, took over the Platte Forks range. The two divisions of the tribe met to trade horses, and in November 1841 Bull Bear was killed at Smoke's camp on the Chugwater in a drunken brawl. The tribe then split into two factions for forty years. After Bull Bear's death his band became "a body without a head," as old Red Water put it; for the chief's son of the same name, despite his courage, ambition, and activity, lacked his father's qualities of leadership. Among the Sioux the chiefs had little authority except in wartime, and the young warriors frequently disobeyed them.

[81] Henry Fraeb—the name frequently appears as Frapp—was a mountain man and small trader. He was a partner of Fitzpatrick in the Rocky Mountain Fur Company from 1830 to 1834, and later a partner of Peter A. Sarpy, with whom he built an American Fur Company fort on St. Vrain's Fork of the South Platte. While leading a group of free trappers in the Green River country, Frapp was killed in 1841 at Battle Creek, a

tributary of the Little Smoke near Dixon, Wyoming, by a mixed band of Sioux and Cheyennes in the first of a series of outbreaks which were increasing just as Parkman traveled through the West, because of the growing impatience of the Indians with the invasion of their hunting lands by the whites. This situation did much to hasten the decline of the roving trapper and hunter.

[82] Cf. Osborne Russell's dreams of "cool springs, rich feasts, and cool shade" (*Journal*, 39) while traveling on the prairie. Parkman was entering upon the subhumid region of the Plains, which appalled many an eastern forest-dweller. The increasing altitude produced mountain sickness in many travelers, with the usual symptoms of headaches, nervousness, and depression, or vomiting; while the alkali water gave almost every traveler dysentery.

[83] Similar self-mutilation, more common among the Cheyennes and the Mandans than the Tetons, is still practiced by the Canadian Sioux, as part of the sun dance. The idea of penance entered into such practices, but they were primarily coming-of-age ordeals, intended to demonstrate fitness and to induce a mystical consciousness. They were part of the highly symbolic sun-gaze dance, which most of the Plains Indians celebrated in some form as their great religious ceremony during the summer solstice. Cf. R. Walker, "Oglala Sun Dance," *Anthropological Papers of the American Museum of Natural History*, XVI (New York, 1921), 116-19. The participants were chosen by the priests, who were controlled by the war chief. Such selection was an honor. The ceremony lasted eight days, three or four of fasting and one to four of dancing to a ritual of chanted songs, and included both secret and public rites. The warrior societies paraded when the sun dance lodge was dedicated, and the chiefs then signaled out the bravest for public commendation. This lodge contained an altar on which a buffalo skull and pipe were placed; but the center pole, which represented the sun, was the focus of the dance, towards which the painted participants danced, blowing eagle-wing whistles to the accompaniment of chants and drums. At the conclusion of the ceremonies the dancers broke their fast and were purified in the sweat lodge. The sun dance lodge was usually abandoned to the elements as sacred after the ceremony.

[84] A grave marked "Mary Ellis—Died May 7, 1845. Aged two months." is mentioned in *The Oregon Trail*, 65. J. Q. Thornton notes several such graves of children who died on the trail during the long trek westward, in his *Oregon and California in 1848* (New York, 1849).

[85] The Indians' favorite method of hunting buffalo was to surround a herd with mounted men and break it up, so that the fat cows, which were

normally protected in the center of the herd by bulls on the flanks, could be killed easily. For excellent descriptions of "running" buffalo on horseback and "approaching" on foot, see *Oregon Trail*, 401-4. Henry Chatillon was considered the master of the latter technique; Kit Carson of the former. Later in the journal Parkman describes a surround in the Laramie Basin (p. 460).

[86] *Pommes blanches*, commonly called "prairie turnips" or "prairie potatoes," were breadroot (*Psoralea esculenta*), a near relative of skunkweed.

[87] Turner, a member of Robinson's Oregon train of some forty wagons, was known to Parkman from a meeting at Westport. Unarmed travel on the plains in the Pawnee country was distinctly dangerous (Cf. *Oregon Trail*, 73). This part of the trail was crossed by the north-south artery of Pawnee movement, the "Pawnee Trail" from the Platte villages to the Big Bend of the Arkansas which is shown on Frémont's map.

[88] "54° 40′ or fight" was the slogan of the warhawks who were ready to fight England for Oregon. Few New Englanders were of that persuasion.

[89] Pierre D. Papin, the *bourgeois* or boss of Fort Laramie, was a famous fur trader. His grave is six miles due south of the Mitchell Pass Museum, near Scott's Bluff, Nebraska. Of the eleven boats of the convoy which he took down the Platte, nine contained property of the American Fur Company—still so-called in the Indian country, though now really Pierre Chouteau, Jr. & Company—while the two others were laden with the furs of free trappers and hunters. Only eight boats arrived at St. Louis on July 7, after a two month's voyage which had taken a toll of one quarter of the shipment, according to the *Missouri Republican* of that date, which reported that the cargo was assigned to Chouteau & Company. The abandonment of beaver hats in favor of silk ones about 1840 and the virtual extinction of the beaver in the mountains had shifted the staple of the fur trade from beaver plews to buffalo robes and deerskins. By 1846 Fort Laramie's main trade was in robes, since the post was the center of the best buffalo country for five hundred miles. Each boatload probably consisted of 1,100 buffalo robes, since ten hides made a pack. This was a big load for any boat which could move on the Platte, whose navigation was always dangerous, and overloading may have been responsible for the heavy loss in transit.

[90] For Parkman's tour of Sicily in 1844, see the European Journal, p. 128.

[91] The Honorable Charles Augustus Murray's account of the Pawnees in his *Travels in North America* (London, 1839) was highly regarded by such Indian authorities of the day as George Catlin, who had also visited this tribe.

[92] For Parkman's experience in the Roman convent, see European Journal, p. 190.

[93] The Side or South Fork is now known as the South Platte. Parkman traversed it at the Lower California Crossing, near Brulé, Nebraska—the hardest ford of the trip.

[94] Ash Hollow is a canyon extending southward from the North Platte into the badlands between the two branches of the river. It was close to the scene of General William S. Harney's massacre of the Brulés in 1855, which won him the nickname of "Squaw Killer."

[95] Lawrence Fork is a southern tributary of the North Platte, near Bridgeport, Nebraska.

[96] Frédéric was one of Papin's assistants at Fort Laramie. Parkman had met him with the boats on the lower Platte (cf. Oregon Trail, 86-7).

[97] Chimney Rock, on the Platte opposite Bayard, Nebraska, was the first great landmark of the Oregon Trail encountered by the westbound traveler. It was a column of weather-worn marl and limestone. In 1842 Charles Preuss, who accompaned Frémont's expedition of that year, estimated that it towered some two hundred feet above the river.

[98] This refers to the fur company's practice of treating trappers or wintering traders when they returned to the fixed posts in the spring with their winter's catch. These Yellowstone blowouts were similar to the annual summer rendezvous held in the mountains for some sixteen years after 1825, when W. H. Ashley introduced the system of bringing a supply train out from the frontier to a prearranged meeting-place in the Rockies, where company trappers, free trappers, and Indians were all on hand to cash in on their winter's work. The first received their wages and a new outfit, while the free traders and the Indians bartered their furs for whatever equipment and supplies they needed. A blowout started while the trading was still going on, for an essential part of the train's equipment was the flat alcohol kegs, which were soon broached. There was much guzzling of food and drink and a great deal of gambling, usually at the trapper's expense and to the trader's profit. There were horse races, wrestling matches, shooting contests, and some real fights. In one way or another most of the trapper's year's earnings found its way back to the company before the train set out for the frontier with the furs.

[99] This party of five men returning to the East from the Oregon settlements was probably that of Joel Palmer, whose Journal of Travels over the Rocky Mountains is a classic description of the emigration of 1845.

[100] It is not clear which of the famous Robidoux brothers was guiding this party. Joseph, the founder of St. Joseph, Missouri, is the most likely

one, as Antoine joined the Army of the West as interpreter at Fort Leavenworth on June 4, and accompanied it to Santa Fe and California.

101 In 1846 the area known as Oregon included the present states of Oregon, Washington, and Idaho, with those parts of Montana and Wyoming that lie west of the Continental Divide. The goal of most of the emigrants in 1846 was the Willamette Valley. There, at Oregon City, the capital of the provisional government, modeled on that of Iowa, had been established in 1843, with a governor, a judicial system, and five counties. Oregon remained virtually an independent republic until it was given territorial status in 1848.

102 Scott's Bluff, twenty miles west of Chimney Rock, was another landmark of the trail. It was named after a sick trapper who was brought down the Platte by bull boat one spring. The boat was wrecked and he was abandoned by his companions, who were unable to carry him. He struggled on sixty miles by himself to the spring rendezvous of the winterers at Scott's Bluff, but found them already gone. His bones were later discovered beside the spring at the Bluff.

103 This probably refers to a warrior's voluntary announcement that he was tired of living or in love with death, which gave him complete freedom to do anything he liked with anyone's women or property until the next fight, when he had to "count a coup"—kill an enemy or perform a deed of great valor at the risk of his life—and was not allowed to flee. There was various rituals and private medicines practiced before a battle which were intended to make warriors invulnerable. Indians usually considered that they were so when they started to fight.

104 The Apaches were of Athapascan stock, like the Kiowas and the Sarsi, and they ranged over southeastern Arizona and southwestern New Mexico. They were bitter enemies of the whites and systematically raided the flocks and herds of the New Mexicans, whom they contemptuously called their sheepherders, for more than a century.

105 James Kirker was an Irish-American who was hired by the Mexican governor of Chihuahua to destroy the Apaches. With a band of mountain men and Delawares, he gathered scalps, receiving a bounty of $50 per brave and $25 per woman or child. He appears by name in Mayne Reid's Scalp Hunters, and was probably the model for its hero.

106 Old Smoke, chief of the other main division of the Oglalas besides Bull Bear's band, was a good friend of Henry Chatillon and proved a valuable informant to Parkman.

107 Horse Creek, not far west of Scott's Bluff, flows into the North Platte from the southwest, near the Wyoming-Nebraska boundary. About 1815

the Kiowas held a fair there, trading the horses and Spanish goods which they brought up from the south to the northern tribes.

[108] Identified in *Oregon Trail*, 113, as the Hog. Later referred to as Lalamie. In the journal Parkman used the Indian names or their English or French equivalents at random; in the book he generally used English versions.

[109] Parkman evidently confused Fort Bernard, half-built in the summer of 1845 or in the following winter by the brothers John and Peter Richard, with the new Fort Laramie, built in 1841 about a mile up the Laramie from the old fort and named Fort John after John B. Sarpy, an officer of the American Fur Company. The Richard brothers traded under the license of Pratte, Cabanné & Company, and their fort was named after Bernard Pratte. Bissonnette represented the company there in 1845, and probably was trading under their license in 1846, since Parkman refers to his partnership with Richard. John Richard, probably the one Parkman encountered, was an explosive French Canadian in bad odor with his rivals. Such posts as this sought to break the monopoly of the American Fur Company by supplying the Indians with illicit liquor and by selling trade goods more cheaply than the company posts did.

[110] This was Fort Platte, a quarter of a mile up Laramie Creek from the old Fort Laramie (the name commemorates Joseph Laramée, a trapper drowned there in 1821). It was built in 1840 or 1841 by Lancaster P. Lupton, a lieutenant of dragoons who went west with Colonel Dodge in 1835 and resigned from the army in the following year to enter the fur trade. The fort was sold to Sabille, Adams & Company in 1842. This small firm had some sort of working arrangement with Pratte, Cabanné & Company, and both the Richards and Bissonnette worked for it. In the following year Pratte, Cabanné & Company took over direct control of Fort Platte, which offered lively opposition to Fort Laramie. The Indian agents, bribed by the American Fur Company, made the trade too hot for the opposition, however, and in 1845 Pratte, Cabanné & Company abandoned Fort Platte and established Fort Bernard, six or eight miles to the east.

[111] This was the second Fort Laramie, three-quarters of a mile up Laramie Creek from Fort Platte and a mile above the site where the original fort was built by Sublette & Campbell, who named it Fort William after Sublette. In the following year the Rocky Mountain Fur Company, which was supplied with outfits by Sublette & Campbell, ceased to exist; and three former partners of it, Milton Sublette, Jim Bridger, and Thomas Fitzpatrick, formed a new company which bought

Fort William. This firm, which operated as a trapping and trading company, first contracted with Lucien Fontenelle to sell its furs and buy its supplies, and then with Pratte, Chouteau & Company, who bought it out in 1836 and acquired the fort. In 1846 the successor of this company, Pierre Chouteau, Jr. & Company, operated Fort Laramie, while the former partner Pratte ran the opposition establishment at Fort Bernard. In 1841 Fort Laramie was rebuilt on the new site upstream where Parkman found it. It was at first called Fort John on the Laramie, after John B. Sarpy, but usage gradually condensed its name to Fort Laramie, as in the case of Fort William on the Laramie.

Charles Preuss, who visited the new fort with Frémont in 1842, thus describes it:

... a quadrangular structure, built of clay, after the fashion of the Mexicans, who are generally employed in building them. The walls are about fifteen feet high, surrounded with a wooden palisade, and form a portion of a range of houses, which entirely surround a yard of about one hundred and thirty feet square. Every apartment has its door and window—all, of course, opening on the inside. There are two large entrances, opposite each other, and midway the wall, one of which is a large and public entrance; the other smaller and more private—a sort of postern gate. Over the great entrance is a square tower with loopholes, and, like the rest of the work, built of earth. At two of the angles, and diagonally opposite each other, are large square bastions, so arranged as to sweep the four faces of the walls.

When the whites first established themselves at Fort Laramie, no one Indian tribe claimed the surrounding territory, though many hunted there, so the importance of the site for trade purposes was obvious. It was the crossroads of the old Indian route through South Pass which became the Oregon Trail, and of the north-south trade route along the Front Range of the Rockies which is as old as Indian legend in the West. It was the center of a country rich in beaver and buffalo. All these favorable conditions were responsible for the bitter competition among the fur companies for the control of the Laramie trade.

[112] James Bordeaux, acting bourgeois of Fort Laramie in Papin's absence when Parkman visited it, is mentioned by many Western travelers. He was the "author" of a description of the Gratton Massacre which may be found in the 1854 Report of the Commissioner for Indian Affairs.

[113] "Colonel" Pierre Louis Vasquez (1798-?), the St. Louis-born son of Don Benito Vasquez, a Spanish grandee and militia captain of Louisiana, was one of the leading mountain men. He was a partner of Jim Bridger, and married an American wife.

Simoneau was a noted French-Canadian mountain man, who was considered Henry Chatillon's chief rival for the title of best hunter in the West.

Monthalon, the clerk of the fort, was notable in the illiterate West for his ability to read and write and keep books.

[114] These Iroquois had been brought West as trappers by the North-West Company, but they failed to adapt themselves to a country so radically different from any they had known. They introduced the idea of Christianity among the Western Indians, and the desire of the Flatheads and the Nez Percés to have the Bible and "blackrobes" probably stems from them. It is a curious coincidence that Parkman should be greeted at Fort Laramie with news of the Iroquois, after he had traveled two-thirds of the way across the continent in order to be able to recreate their history in the East.

VOLUME II

[115] The high prices charged for provisions and supplies at Fort Laramie by the American Fur Company were notorious. The company paid good prices for buffalo robes and such few furs as were still taken, but got most of its money back by exorbitant charges for supplies, of which it had a virtual monopoly. Few mountain men could get their provisions from the nearest settlements, eight hundred miles to the east, and the company had ways of dealing with the feeble opposition offered by such rivals as Pratte, Cabanné & Company. Parkman had good reason to be bitter at the prices, for he had to make extensive purchases at Fort Laramie, amounting to $105.50. Chatillon, wise in mountain ways, bought some supplies from the opposition at Fort Bernard, who charged ten cents less a pound for flour and three and a half cents less a pound for bacon. Cf. Appendix, p. 494.

[116] Many mountain men took squaws, both for domestic comfort and occupational security. They fed them and supplied them with work curing robes and skins, in exchange for the wilderness version of the comforts of home. Sometimes they had more than one "wife," since a solitary white man's safety among the Indians was partly dependent upon the number of his savage relatives who might be expected to avenge his death. When a trapper made a trading visit to a normally hostile or semihostile tribe, he was usually given a squaw for the duration of his visit by the chief, who wanted to trade and to protect the trapper. In such cases the squaw was

a business asset, but also a liability because her relatives had to be shown with presents that he loved her. From the squaw's point of view, trappers were extremely desirable husbands, gentler than any Indian and furnishing their wives with store clothes and ornaments, knives and utensils, and other articles that they would never otherwise have seen.

[117] Parkman gives an account of the role of the "soldiers," the misnamed Indian police, on p. 445. (See also *Oregon Trail*, 263, 301, 303.) The Indian term *akiata*, usually translated "soldier," means "those who see there is general order in camp, when traveling, and who oversee the buffalo hunt." Among the Sioux the "soldiers" were chosen from the most reputed warriors by the chiefs. Before their contact with the British, the Sioux had no chiefs and were controlled by the "soldiers." Cf. C. Wissler, "Oglala Societies," *Anthropological Papers of the American Museum of Natural History*, XI, 1 (New York, 1912), 7-74.

[118] Finch, a trapper, had been held up by the Pawnees earlier in June.

[119] Jack Hill was a trapper allied by marriage to Smoke's band.

[120] Old Lalamie or Lomalomie, the Hog, is described at length in *Oregon Trail*, 113-14. He offered to become Parkman's uncle by swapping a niece for his horse, but this alliance was declined.

[121] Paul Dorion was the grandson of the half-breed voyageur Pierre Dorion, who had briefly assisted Sacajawea on Lewis and Clark's expedition, and with his Iowa squaw Marie Aioe had accompanied Wilson Hunt's Astorians. Parkman had read about the elder Dorions in Washington Irving's books. He named the mare, for whom he traded his horse Pontiac, Pauline, so evidently he ranked Paul Dorion with his other Indian heroes: Pontiac, the great chief of the Ottawas, and Hendrick, the Mohawk leader who was killed at Bloody Pond.

[122] Raymond, a willing but timorous and thick-skulled *engagé*, was hired by Parkman when he left Fort Laramie for the Chugwater camp at the end of June. He was the only member of the party to accompany Parkman during his stay with the Sioux in the mountains, and he stayed with him until Bent's Fort, where he was paid off with $38 at the end of August, having received a $3 shirt as advance wages when engaged at Laramie. Raymond died in 1848 on Frémont's criminally foolish attempt to cross the Rockies in the winter. Cf. Appendix, pp. 494-95, and *Oregon Trail*, xvi.

[123] Parkman first met Reynal at Fort Bernard. The trader joined forces with him when he left Fort Laramie to meet the Whirlwind (Tunica)'s village. Reynal's squaw Margot and her two nephews, the Horse (His Horses), and the Hail Storm were also members of the party; and it was their village of the Oglalas that Parkman joined in Laramie Basin, after

the proposed war party broke up. Chatillon's relatives did not cross the mountains to hunt buffalo, and since he stayed behind with Shaw at Fort Laramie, Reynal replaced him as Parkman's interpreter.

[124] This was the *travois* or *traineau* used by most of the Plains tribes. The lodge poles were bound together with rawhide to form an A-shaped frame, to which a basket for carrying baggage was tied. The heavier ends of the poles were fastened on either side of a rude packsaddle, while the other ends dragged on the ground.

[125] The Laramie Mountains were called the Black Hills on Frémont's map, which Parkman had with him, and in common speech at this time, because of the thick growth of cedar which covered them as it does the Black Hills of Dakota, where the name has survived. Cedar made excellent lodge poles, which was one reason why this region was a favorite resort of the Indians.

[126] Wild sage and absinthe are the same plant. There are numerous species of sage, and their relationship was not always recognized.

[127] Practically all of the secret societies were "mystic associations," and tricks with fire were performed by the medicine men among their other jugglery. The subject has received little study from ethnologists, but it is clear that the Plains Indians, like all Indians and most primitives, made a cult of prestidigitation.

[128] This might be merely a reference to the desperate deeds of valor performed by any Indian while on the warpath under the compulsion of some omen or dream. But more probably it refers to the cult of dedication to death described in note 103. Some members of the cult did everything by contraries and were known by that name. A contrary would say: "I do not want the best part of that deer," and the owner of the deer was obliged to give him the choicest part. Followers of the cult were much in demand as good warriors and war party leaders. If they failed, they were subject to intolerable derision; but if they succeeded, they gained great honor and were privileged characters.

[129] Cf. note 83, p. 621.

[130] Parkman here confuses the sun dance, the purification rituals required by some medicines before going to war, and the initiatory ordeals of puberty. Fasting was part of most Sioux religious ceremonies, for it helped to bring on the desired visions.

[131] The war bonnet was a dress uniform and a lodge garment, and not war medicine as Parkman here suggests.

[132] La Bonté's camp was at the mouth of Big Timber or La Bonté's Creek, on the Platte about sixty miles above Fort Laramie. It marked the

beginning of the worst stretch of the Oregon Trail east of the Continental Divide. La Bonté was a historical person who became the fictional hero of George Frederick Ruxton's *Life in the Far West* (London, 1848).

133 The scalp of the Whirlwind's son hung in Papin's room at Fort Laramie, which Parkman and Shaw occupied in the *bourgeois'* absence. It had been taken, along with those of nine other Oglala warriors, during the previous summer by the Shoshonies (Snakes), who had left it at the fort in an attempt to propitiate the Whirlwind, with whom they had asked Vasquez to intercede. Revenge for the Snake victory of the previous year was the motive of the great muster of the Sioux, which to Parkman's disappointment failed to come off.

134 Mentioned earlier as the Man Afraid of his Horses. Called the Horse in *Oregon Trail*. He later became a head chief of the Oglala. Cf. G. E. Hyde, *Red Cloud's Folk*.

135 Tunica is earlier referred to as the Whirlwind; in *The Oregon Trail* he is also called by the latter name.

136 This was the emigrant train which Parkman had seen assembling at Independence in May. It was first headed by Colonel W. H. "Owl" Russell, veteran of the Black Hawk War, former secretary of Henry Clay, and an orator with a low flashpoint. Much given to drink, he had earned his nickname by bellowing in reply to the whooing of owls one exalted night: "Colonel William H. Russell of Kentucky, sir, a bosom friend of Henry Clay." The company, which included the annalists Jessy Quinn Thornton and Edwin Bryant as well as the famous Donner Party, had rejected Russell's leadership in favor of that of Lillburn W. Boggs, former governor of Missouri, mortal enemy of the Mormons, and the husband of Daniel Boone's granddaughter. It was the most notable emigrant party to travel the Oregon Trail this year, and contained a far higher proportion of educated and cultivated people than most trains.

137 The Miniconques, or Minneconjous, were a band of Sioux who belonged to the same Teton division of the nation as the Oglalas. The Sioux had long ranged from the Missouri westward, but under pressure from Eastern tribes pushed out by the whites, they had for some years been moving southwestward again, thus impinging upon the Cheyennes to the south and the Crows to the northwest.

138 William P. May, a trader, was killed by the northern Arapahos this same year. He was the May who was robbed of his furs on the Yellowstone by Kelsey in 1843.

139 The Minneconjous, who arrived after Parkman left Fort Bernard, did break up and return home, having lost their warlike purpose in floods

of liquor supplied by the emigrants, according to Parkman, and perhaps by Richard, who had a bad name for selling drink to the Indians. Paul Dorion and the Canadian free trappers were displeased, since liquor made normally friendly Indians untrustworthy.

[140] This party included Jim Clyman, returning from California after crossing the Salt Desert and Wasatch Mountains with Lansford Hastings, whose new cutoff trail to California was to lead the Donner Party to its doom. The veteran Clyman urged the emigrants at Richard's post to take the old Fort Hall route, but in vain. Clyman was an epitome of the new West, as DeVoto has pointed out in *Year of Decision*. He was born in Virginia in 1792 on a farm belonging to George Washington. By way of Pennsylvania, Ohio, and the Sangamon he worked his way westward, reaching St. Louis in the spring of 1823. He joined the second expedition of W. H. Ashley in that year and spent the next four years in the Rockies, helping to blaze the South Pass route. He then returned to Illinois, keeping a store and serving as a private in the same company as Abraham Lincoln during the Black Hawk War. Then he took up a timber claim in Wisconsin, where he spent six years. In 1844 he went to Oregon with Ford's company, and 1845 to Sutter's Fort in California. Such a man had much to tell Parkman, but the latter was too much concerned with his letters to Boston to waste time on uncouth non-Indians.

[141] Tucker was one of the mountain men who had greeted Henry Chatillon on his arrival at Fort Laramie on June 15.

[142] Identified as Rouleau in *Oregon Trail*, 161. The two traders killed by the Arapahos were Boot and May, the latter of whom Parkman had met at Fort Laramie.

[143] There is a full account of Bear Robe's death and funeral in *Oregon Trail*, 165-68.

[144] Bissonnette was trading in the summer of 1846 on the license of Pratte, Cabanné & Company, and probably was in partnership with the Richard brothers of Fort Bernard. He was a friend of Paul Dorion and Nat Sabille, and may have been a son of Antoine Bissonnette, the *engagé* of Manuel Lisa on his expedition to the Upper Missouri, who was killed as a deserter by Lisa's aide Drouillard at the mouth of the Osage in 1807.

[145] The party included Morin, Séraphin, Rouleau, and Gingras. Cf. *Oregon Trail*, 169.

[146] This quarrel between Bordeaux and the trapper Perrault is described in *Oregon Trail*, 156-57.

[147] Wife-stealing was sometimes ritualistic—at least one secret society among the Crows made it a prerogative—sometimes a kind of joke, and

sometimes a quite legitimate way of getting a wife, under the proper circumstances. Sometimes it was purely a business transaction, when a man wanted a particular woman. It was not, as Parkman thought, "a way of becoming great," though refusing to make payment for a stolen wife indicated a certain toughness; the injured husband would demand or take compensation unless afraid of the offender.

[148] Le Borgne ("One Eye") in *Oregon Trail*, where he is called "the Nestor of the tribe" (179).

[149] Mad Wolfe was a nephew of Le Borgne. Parkman judged that he "seemed, but for his face, the Pythian Apollo himself." (*Oregon Trail*, 190).

[150] Shaw had a homeopathic medical kit and applied simple remedies to the Indians, as a means of winning their goodwill. This incident takes place in Smoke's lodge in the book.

[151] Liberties might be taken with a young girl by a brother-in-law. Cf. note 70.

[152] The Strong Hearts, like the Arrow Breakers whose activities Parkman later records, were one of the secret societies, partly religious and partly military in character, which extended through the tribes. Each had a tutelary deity or totem, to whom respect was paid in the ritual, described in *Oregon Trail*, 198, 302, 358. Among the Plains Indians these societies were largely military.

[153] Bitter Cottonwood Creek, near Wendover, Wyoming, was named after the narrow-leaved cottonwoods of bitter taste which line its banks. This was the third camp site for the emigrants after Fort Laramie, though the faster outfits usually pushed on to Horseshoe Creek, where there was better grass.

[154] Parkman had visited Dixville Notch in the White Mountains in 1841 and 1842. Cf. pp. 24, 33-34, 82, 83.

[155] Mt. Auburn, a pleasant stretch of countryside along the Charles River on the outskirts of Cambridge, Massachusetts, has long been the Valhalla of the Bostonian as an exclusive cemetery.

[156] It was not likely that they would meet Snakes here, although it was possible; but in any case the Snakes were well disposed toward the whites at this time. It was only barely possible that they might encounter Gros Ventres, while Arapahos were much more likely to be found in this region. Raymond was clearly reluctant to wander further into the mountains with only one companion, and seems to have tried to frighten Parkman into returning to Fort Laramie.

[157] This was one of the periodic breakups which had given the Oglalas their name of Scattered or Divided People. Le Borgne and all Bull Bear's

relations had remained behind with the Whirlwind, who had lost his zeal for warring on the Snakes. Cf. *Oregon Trail*, 235.

[158] Practically all the tribes had many thunderbird myths. The Thunderbird was usually considered a great spirit, whose conflict with another deity—usually a monster—produced thunder and lightning. The swastika was a thunderbird symbol.

[159] Heap of Hail is called Hail Storm in the book. His great crony was the Rabbit.

[160] Red Water, the elder statesman of the reduced band, is also called Mene-Seela in *Oregon Trail*, 271, where Parkman gives a fuller account of him.

[161] These were the "Mormon crickets," the black crickets who were the victims of Brigham Young's miracle of the sea gulls at Great Salt Lake.

[162] Red Water's story is given in finished form in *Oregon Trail*, 271-72.

[163] The Plains Indians made pemmican by drying strips of buffalo meat in the sun, pulverizing it, mixing it with tallow and some such flavoring matter as crushed wild cherries, and packing it in intestines or rawhide bags with more tallow. It was the best of all concentrated foods, the mainstay of the early explorers and the fur traders when fresh or ordinary meat failed.

[164] This was the White Shield, whose brother had been killed the previous year by the Snakes and who became Parkman's friend. Cf. pp. 461-65 and *Oregon Trail*, 287-91.

[165] Reynal's wife was following Indian etiquette when she gave the feast for her helpers. Ceremonies were prescribed for the occasion, and one of the women was there because she had the ritualistic right to cut and shape the skins.

[166] The ordinary trapper's rifle—the best was made by the Hawken brothers of St. Louis and sold for $40—was only accurate at ranges of two hundred yards or less. It was shorter and heavier than the long Kentucky rifle. It was not a much better weapon than the Indian's bow, which could kill at seventy-five to hundred and fifty yards, though the rifle was more accurate within this range and could be discharged much more rapidly. The maximum range of the Hawken was five or six hundred yards, and it fired a 32-to-the-pound bullet. Parkman had a superior rifle, which Chatillon liked to use and which he received as a gift at the end of the trip.

[167] Rouville was a trapper who had once been an acrobatic rider in the circus. This may have given him a bond with Parkman, who had taken lessons from a circus rider while a Harvard student. Parkman's party now

consisted of Shaw, Chatillon, and Deslauriers, whom he had rejoined at Fort Laramie, and Raymond.

168 Nathaniel Sabille was one of the famous brothers whose name was well known though continually misspelled in the West. Frémont's map assigns it in the form "Sibille" to one of the southern tributaries of Laramie Creek, which has retained this version, though the modern town on the North Fork of this stream is called "Sibylee." "Sybil" is another common variant.

169 Antoine Le Rouge was a half-breed. Cf. *Oregon Trail*, 356-57.

170 Probably Andrew Sublette, since Milton had died in 1835 and William in 1845, and Solomon was presumably guiding emigrants this year. Parkman credits this hold-up to Smoke's young men (cf. *Oregon Trail*, 347).

171 This was Wales B. Bonney, returning alone from Oregon to get his family. Near Fort Bridger he was met by Lansford Hastings, who got him to carry an open letter to the emigrants about the Hastings Cutoff on the California Trail. Parkman later referred to Bonney as a "bare-faced rascal," which he was.

172 During his sweep to South Pass in 1845, Colonel Kearny had announced his intention of returning the following summer, but the outbreak of the Mexican War in the spring of 1846 called him to the command of the Army of the West, while it took the First Dragoons to Santa Fe, Taos, and San Diego.

173 The movement of the Army of the West along the Santa Fe Trail, and Zachary Taylor's victories of Palo Alto (May 8) and Resaca de la Palma (May 9), which resulted in the American occupation of Matamoras. The news had taken three months to reach Parkman. Cf. *Oregon Trail*, 354-55.

174 Another reference to the sun dance, of which Parkman had evidently gained no clear understanding.

175 Another reference to the Owns-Alone ceremony. Cf. note 70.

176 This cluster of abandoned forts was a memorial to the vanished trade in beaver plews (from the French *plus*, for top-grade skins), which had once centered in the South Park region. It was also evidence of the keen competition in the trade. After coming West with Colonel Dodge's dragoons in 1835, Lieutenant Lancaster P. Lupton resigned his commission—supposedly after cursing Andrew Jackson—and entered the fur trade on the South Platte in the following year. In 1837 the American Fur Company, disturbed at this invasion of its Fort Laramie territory, subsidized Peter Sarpy and Henry Fraeb in the building of a competing

post, Fort Jackson, six miles from Fort Lupton. In 1839 it also subsidized the building of the third post by Andrew Sublette and Louis Vasquez, which was named after the latter. The Bent brothers, who also drew furs from this region, established Fort George in this region in 1841, under Marcellin St. Vrain. The forts had been abandoned when Parkman saw them because the trade had shifted to buffalo robes, while beaver had become scarce. Fort Lupton was on the right bank of the South Platte, ten miles above the mouth of St. Vrain's Fork, opposite which on the right bank stood Fort George or St. Vrain.

177 Parkman thus camped near the site of Denver, Colorado. He was following southward the established trail linking Fort Laramie, the Pueblo, Bent's Fort, and Taos.

178 Richard, the *bourgeois* of Fort Bernard, was taking some buffalo robes to Taos, and guided William Crosby and John Brown's party of Mississippi Mormons from the Platte to the trapper's winter stockade at the Pueblo. Here they were later joined by the sick detachment of the Mormon Battalion and another group of unfit sent back from Santa Fe by Captain Philip St. George Cooke after he took over command of the battalion. Crosby and Brown's party left Fort Bernard soon after their meeting with Jim Clyman at Ash Hollow on July 2, when they learned that there were no other Mormons ahead of them on the trail. The party consisted of nineteen wagons, twenty-four men, women, and children, and five Negro slaves. They had left Mississippi in April, under instructions to meet the main Mormon body—which did not move until the following year—along the Oregon Trail.

179 Possibly the camp of Dr. Edwin James, who accompanied Major Long's expedition to the Rockies in 1820. On July 12 he camped on the Fontaine qui Bouille, twenty-five miles from Pikes Peak, which he and two other men then climbed, returning to their camp on July 15.

180 The Lower Pueblo (Pueblo, Colorado), was chiefly a trapper's winter quarters, although it was also a natural stopping place on the north-south trade route which linked Mexico and the Platte. There had been some sort of post at this place since 1806, when Zeb Pike built a breastwork there. During 1846 it accidentally became a Mormon outpost. The fort Parkman visited was probably that built in 1842 by Jim Beckwith.

181 Any Indian was apt to make a brother of a white whom he liked, by exchanging knives or other gifts (any Indian expected a gift in return for the one he gave). The Sioux made brothers among the whites as well as the Crows, but the latter did it more frequently and meant more by it. The Crows really liked the whites and saw that it was to their

advantage to get along well with them. Their refusal to wage war on the whites made them unpopular among other Indians, but it helped them to keep more of their original country than any other Plains tribe. Their reservation in their original homeland—Absaroka, in the Big Horn and Little Big Horn country—is on extremely good agricultural and grazing land, among the best set aside for reservations.

182 Bent's Old Fort, or Fort William, five hundred and thirty miles from Independence by the mountain route of the Santa Fe Trail, stood on the north bank of the Arkansas near the mouth of the Purgatoire or "Picket-wire." It was a crossroads of the West like Fort Laramie and, until the Oregon and California emigration really got under way, far more important and better known. A little to the southwest the trail forked, one branch leading to Taos. To the west a trail led up the Fontaine qui Bouille to South Park. Northward was the route to the Platte.

Bent's was one of the largest of the trading posts and the first permanent settlement in Colorado. It boasted warehouses, a smithy, a wagon shop, storerooms, dormitories, and such unlikely luxuries as a billiard table and an icehouse. A staff of 150 men was permanently employed at the fort. It was a magnet for mountain men, Santa Fe traders, and the Cheyennes, Arapahos, Utes, Kiowas, and Comanches. Parkman bought $49 worth of supplies and paid off Raymond while at Bent's.

183 Holt, the trader in charge of the fort in the absence of the Bents, invited Parkman and Shaw to dinner, which was served on a table covered with a white cloth—their first civilized meal since dining with Colonel Kearny at Fort Leavenworth in May.

184 Seventy-five invalid officers and soldiers had been left behind at Bent's by the Army of the West, whose raw militia suffered heavy losses from dysentery on the march to Santa Fe.

185 Evidently a rumor about James Magoffin's mission to conquer Santa Fe by fifth-column tactics was abroad, although this may have been simply the judgment of experts on Governor Armijo's fortitude. The courage of the Mexicans was not highly regarded by Americans in the Southwest. The garrison of Santa Fe was known to be small and worthless, and there was a question whether militia could be raised to reinforce it. Part of Kearny's command and many natives of Santa Fe thought that the Mexicans would not fight.

186 Hodgman, christened "*Tête Rouge*" by Chatillon because of his red hair, was a slightly unbalanced young Missourian who found marching to the Halls of Montezuma too much for his constitution. He was one of the casualties left at Bent's by Kearny.

[187] Munroe, an Iowan, had found the West less promising than reputed, and was heading homeward. Parkman characterized him as "open, warm-hearted, and intelligent" (*Oregon Trail*, 379).

[188] Ben, called Jim Gurney in the book and Jim hereafter in the journal, was a Boston sailor who had reached California by sea, and probably was a deserter from his ship, preferring to beat his way home overland rather than around Cape Horn. Parkman liked him best of the four new members of the party.

[189] The homesick emigrant, who was really lovesick according to Jim Gurney, was a Missourian named Ellis.

Bridger's Fort was in the valley of Black's Fork of the Green River. It was established in the summer of 1843 to cater to the emigrants, to whom it offered a blacksmith's shop for wagon repairs, horses, and supplies.

[190] Probably Marcellin St. Vrain, since Parkman later met Céran on the Santa Fe Trail. Céran, who had useful connections from his marriage into the New Mexican gentry, helped Colonel Sterling Price to put down the Taos Rising in January 1847, as a captain of volunteers.

[191] Originally there were four Bent brothers in the trade. One was dead by August 1846, and two more were killed within a year. Charles Bent, American governor of New Mexico, was murdered on January 19, 1847 in his own home at Taos by a Pueblo mob. William Bent and a number of his trappers had been engaged as scouts by Kearny when he set out for Santa Fe on August 1.

[192] William Magoffin, a younger brother of James and Samuel, who were magnates of the Santa Fe carrying trade. William later studied medicine, served in the Confederate Army, and eventually settled in Minnesota.

[193] Ewing was the Kentuckian whom Parkman had met at St. Louis and again at Fort Bernard, and with whom he had planned to travel from Laramie to Bent's and Westport. But Ewing had become impatient while Parkman was in the mountains with the Indians and had gone ahead, probably with Richard's Mormon party. Between the Caches and Pawnee Fork, on the homeward stretch of the Santa Fe Trail, he killed a Pawnee who tried to steal his horses, and by thus arousing the Indians once more caused Parkman to run risks.

[194] Parkman's "poison" was dysentery, very prevalent on the Plains and a cause of much illness in the Army of the West. It was often caused by the alkali water and the change to an exclusive diet of fresh meat. This is the first specific reference to Parkman's illness in the journal. In the book he depicts himself as struggling against collapse from it soon after his arrival at Fort Laramie.

195 Here Parkman encountered the main part (later known as the Great Southern Herd) of the Plains buffalo herd, which was gradually being divided into two parts by the emigrant traffic. Before this he had only encountered small bands.

VOLUME III

196 Colonel Sterling Price's Second Missouri Volunteers were mounted infantry, hastily recruited for the Mexican War from Monroe, Platte City, and St. Louis counties. Price was made commandant of New Mexico when Doniphan moved on Chihuahua with the First Missouri late in 1846. He suppressed the Santa Fe Conspiracy of December 1846 and the Taos Rising of the following January, which his "undisciplined ragamuffins" had done much to cause. The Second Missouri was considerably inferior to the First, which under the inspired leadership of Doniphan performed military miracles, although its discipline never appealed to West Pointers.

197 The Ridge Road was a short cut on the Santa Fe Trial across a long bend in the Arkansas River, to the west of Pawnee Fork and the Big Bend.

198 The Mormon Battalion, on its march from Fort Leavenworth to Santa Fe, was under the command of Lieutenant Andrew Jackson Smith of the First Dragoons. Smith was replaced on October 2 by Captain Philip St. George Cooke, who marched the battalion from Santa Fe to California. The detachment had been born in May 1846, when President Polk welcomed Elder Little's suggestion that a Mormon battalion be enlisted for the defense of California. This amounted, from the Mormon point of view, to the free transportation westward of five hundred men and a sum in pay and allowances which would enable the main body to move. Brigham Young recruited over five hundred men, who were accompanied by a good many wives, relatives, and children. Since many of the young Mormons were unwilling to serve a government they had cursed for years, the ranks were filled with unfit elders; and when Cooke took over from Smith, he weeded out nearly a third of the command and sent them to the Pueblo, where some women and children had already been sent by Smith. Beset by mumps, dysentery, and the irreconcilability of the ways of Saints with West Pointers, they nevertheless made better time from Fort Leavenworth to Santa Fe than Price's command. They constituted without doubt one of the oddest units which ever saw service in the United States Army. During their entire service they saw no action,

except when they were attacked on the Arizona desert by a large herd of wild cattle, who gored some of the brethren, and when at Los Angeles they were ordered to massacre the bloodthirsty dogs of the town. Cf. DeVoto, *Year of Decision*.

[199] The Santa Fe Trail, a well-established trade route of eight hundred miles from Independence to Santa Fe by way of either Bent's Fort (the Mountain Route) or the Cimarron Crossing (the Desert Route), saw its busiest season in the summer of 1846. In addition to the regular traders' trains of enormous wagons, twice the size of the prairie schooners of the Oregon emigrants, Kearny's army, his wagon trains and those of his supports, Price's Second Missouri, the Mormon Battalion, commissary trains, scouts, couriers, ambulances, and detachments of discharged and invalided soldiers passed over it. The Army chose the less vulnerable Mountain Route and used Bent's Fort as a base. From this point onward, Parkman encountered wagon train after wagon train, and grew weary of answering the same inevitable questions. He might have paid the price of civility more cheerfully if he had realized that the volume of traffic over the trail probably saved his small party from mishap at the hands of the Indians, who were far more dangerous on the Santa Fe route than on the Oregon Trail. The southern part was within reach of the Apaches, while the eastern was the land of the thieving Pawnees, who still took scalps as readily as horses at this period. The middle section was a no man's land raided by the southern Arapahos, the southern Cheyennes, and most notably the Kiowas and Comanches, the most dangerous Indians of the West at this period, who fortunately for Parkman were more concerned with the vulnerable Texans and Mexicans this year. In the following summer the Comanches killed forty-seven men and burned three hundred wagons on the trail, including Army supply trains. As Parkman saw, traffic along the trail followed established routines, except for such parties of greenhorns as the Second Missouri. Beyond Council Grove the trains traveled in formation of two or four parallel lines. A corral was formed at night. The route, which had even been surveyed, was mostly through country bountifully supplied with buffalo, and offering abundant grass in normal years, and water in reasonable plenty, except on the Cimarron Crossing Route. Forty-five or fifty days was the usual running time from Independence to Santa Fe.

[200] This train was making very poor time. It was half a day out from Council Grove, and thus had covered only a sixth of the total distance. At the same rate of progress, it would take almost twice as long as usual to make the trip to Santa Fe.

201 Bent & St. Vrain freighted their own goods from Independence to their trading post of Bent's Fort, whose trade extended far to the north, west, southwest, and southeast. They had smaller posts in the Indian country, and agents living with the tribes. The original partnership was formed in 1831 by Charles Bent and Céran de Hault de Lassus de St. Vrain (1802-70), the son of a French naval officer who had settled at Ste. Geneviève near St. Louis. Céran St. Vrain early entered the fur trade, working for Bernard and Sylvestre Pratte. Like most Santa Fe traders, he became a Mexican citizen, and he married an aristocratic New Mexican girl. With Cornelio Vigil, he owned some four million acres in the Purgatoire and other valleys. Charles Bent had likewise married a Mexican wife, while his brother William, the resident manager of Bent's Fort, was the husband of the Cheyenne Owl Woman. Thus through marriage the firm had excellent connections with Santa Fe, Taos, and one of the main tribes on the trail which was its lifeline. Their wagon train was late this year, because Kearny had held up the traders until his army reached Santa Fe.

202 George Catlin (1796-1872), author of *Manners, Customs, and Institutions of the North American Indians* (1841) and *The North American Indian Portfolio* (1844), was a painter and ethnologist, who abandoned his early career as a lawyer in 1832 to study the Indians, who he realized were beginning to die out. His paintings were widely exhibited in the United States before he took them to Europe in 1840, where Parkman had seen them in London in 1844. They are now in the National Museum at Washington, D. C.

Joe Chadwick was Catlin's companion on some of his Western travels. He was killed in Texas in 1838, one of four hundred prisoners shot on Santa Anna's orders. Bernard DeVoto points out that this same train included Lewis Garrard, whose *Wah-To-Yah*, a forgotten classic, is a better book about the West in 1846 than Parkman's famous work.

203 Perhaps Major John Dougherty, long Indian agent for the Pawnees, who supplied Catlin with his views on the Indian question (Cf. *Manners*, II, 26). These are summed up in a sentence in one of his reports to the Secretary of War, which Catlin quotes approvingly: "It is my decided opinion, that, so long as the Fur Traders and trappers are permitted to reside among the Indians, all the efforts of the Government to better their condition will be fruitless; or, in a great measure, checked by the strong influence of these men over the tribes."

204 The Wyandots had been granted lands in Ohio and Michigan under a treaty of 1817, only to have much of this land sold to white settlers two

years later, regardless of the agreement. This payment in 1846 was a reparation. The Wyandots moved to Kansas in 1845 and later established themselves in Oklahoma.

205 John B. Clapp signed Parkman's and Shaw's "passport" to the trading posts on behalf of Pierre Chouteau, Jr. & Company.

206 Robert Campbell (1804-79) had been Thomas Fitzpatrick's partner in the only firm which gave serious opposition to the American Fur Company. Like his partner, he was an Irishman who drifted to St. Louis. He was with Ashley on the second Missouri expedition in 1825, and became one of his principal lieutenants. He later was associated with Fitzpatrick, Jed Smith, Jim Bridger, and the Sublettes. He saved William Sublette's life in the fight against the Blackfeet at Pierre's Hole in 1832, which was chronicled by Washington Irving. In 1835 he returned to St. Louis, and until 1842 devoted himself to the affairs of the firm which he formed with Fitzpatrick in that year. He then went into real estate and banking, and became active in politics. He did much to train and equip the Mounted Volunteers in 1846. He was an Indian commissioner in 1851 and 1869.

207 Brantz L. Mayer wrote on Mexican history and archaeology and was the founder of the Maryland Historical Society.

208 John Ledyard (1751-89) of Connecticut was the famous explorer who left Dartmouth to become a sailor. He was with Captain Cook on the latter's last voyage in the Pacific, and formed the dream of opening up the trade of the Pacific Northwest. Jefferson knew him, and shared his interest in the Northwest. Ledyard's most ambitious effort in a colorful career was his attempt to walk across Russia and Siberia, which was frustrated by Catherine the Great's police. His story was familiar to Parkman from Jared Spark's *Life* in the Library of American Biography.

209 John Romeyn Brodhead collected papers bearing on the colonial history of New York from the French archives. These papers were of vital importance to Parkman's work.

210 Parkman contributed five sketches of frontier life to the *Knickerbocker Magazine* in 1845. The editor, Gaylord Clark, was rewarded for his encouragement of the young writer by the opportunity to serialize *The Oregon Trail*, which first appeared in the *Knickerbocker* from 1847 to 1849.

211 Ramsay Crooks knew better than anyone else the whole empire of the American Fur Company, of which he was the administrative head for many years.

212 These notes refer to sources for *The Conspiracy of Pontiac*, and reveal

the wide range of Parkman's research for the work which did not appear until 1851.

213 Dr. Edwin James was Major Long's annalist and one of the first men to climb Pikes Peak. Cf. note 179.

214 This note suggests that Parkman had been offered the use of W. L. Stone, Sr.'s collection of materials for a life of Sir William Johnson. The work was eventually undertaken by Stone's son.

VIII. 1856 & 1866 NOTEBOOK

1 Parkman was seeking a title for the great history to which he had decided to devote his life. These tentative titles are not far removed from his final choice, "France and England in North America," but evidently his concept of the history as a struggle between two colonial systems for domination in the New World had not yet clearly emerged.

2 This work of Faillon saw the light as Part II of the first volume of his *Histoire de la Colonie française en Canada* (Montreal, 1865-66). Abbé Etienne-Michel Faillon (1799-1870), a Sulpician, first came to Canada in 1849 as official visitor of his order. He went back to Paris in the following year, but returned to Montreal in 1854 and again 1858, when he spent three years in historical work. His history, which he did not live to complete, stops short at 1600, although he had prepared the materials up to 1710. "His other Canadian works to which Parkman refers include biographies of Madame d'Youville (1852), Soeur Bourgeoys (1853), and Madamoiselle Jeanne Mance (1854). Parkman opened a correspondence with him early in 1856, and on March 13 Faillon, then in Paris, wrote that he put himself at Parkman's disposal and offered to persuade the Bishop of Boston to open the ecclesiastical libraries to the young Protestant historian.

3 The publication of Schmitt's *Catalogue de l'Histoire du France* was begun in 1855 by the Bibliothèque Impériale in 1855. Parkman probably got this information from Faillon.

4 While a political exile in Paris from 1840 to 1845, L. J. Papineau did research on the old regime of New France at the Archives de l'Etat. He had many important documents copied, and brought them back to Canada when he returned. The greater part were destroyed with the Parliamentary Library in the fire of 1849, when an English mob sacked the government buildings in Montreal.

This entry was crossed out, probably indicating that Parkman had examined the collection.

[5] General Lewis Cass, while Governor of the Michigan Territory (1813-31) collected materials on the early history of the region. In 1839 Cass, while Minister to France, employed Pierre Margry to compile relevant documents from the French archives. Cass had placed his Detroit MSS. in Parkman's hands for the writing of *Pontiac*, while Parkman had visited Detroit in the summer of 1845 for firsthand information. This entry was crossed out, probably indicating that Parkman had examined the collection.

[6] Charles Etienne Arthur Gayarré (1805-95) collected historical material from public and private archives while spending eight years in France under doctor's orders. This was used as the foundation of his *Histoire de la Louisiane* (1846-7) and of his later and more complete *History of Louisiana* (New Orleans, 1851-66).

[7] Benjamin F. French collected documents for his *Historical Memoirs of Louisiana* (New York, 1853).

[8] Pierre-Joseph-Marie Chaumonot, S.J. (1611-93), *La vie du R. P. Pierre Joseph Marie Chaumonot, De la Compagnie de Jésus, Missionaire dans la Nouvelle France, Ecrite par lui-même par ordre de son Supérieur, l'an 1688 (Nouvelle York, Isle de Manate, A la presse Crémoisy de Jean-Marie Shea, MDCCCLVIII). Bib. Can.* 101.

Nicolas Perrot (1644?-1717?), *Mémoire sur les moeurs, coustumes et religion des sauvages de l'Amérique Septentrionale par Nicolas Perrot publiée pour la première fois par le R. P. J. Tailhan de la Compagnie de Jésus* (Leipzig & Paris, 1864). *Bib. Can.* 130. Evidently Shea did not print Perrot, if Parkman was correct in supposing that he intended to do so.

Claude Dablon, S.J. (1619?-97), *Relation de ce qui s'est passé de plus remarquables aux missions des pères de la Compagnie de Jésus en la Nouvelle France les années 1672 et 1673. Par le R. P. Claude Dablon, Recteur du Collège de Québec & Supérieur des Missions de la Compagnie de Jésus en la Nouvelle France (A la Nouvelle York, De la Presse Crémoisy de Jean-Marie Shea, MDCCCLVI. Bib. Can.* 70. Also his *Relation de ce qui s'est passé de plus remarquables aux missions des pères de la Compagnie de Jésus en la Nouvelle France les années 1673 à 1679. Par le R. P. Claude Dablon, Recteur du Collège de Québec & Supérieur des Missions de la Compagnie de Jésus en la Nouvelle France (A la Nouvelle York, De la Presse Crémoisy de Jean-Marie Shea, MDCCCLX).*

· Mère St. Augustin [Marie de Tranchepain], *Relation du voyage des premières Ursulines à la Nouvelle Orléans et de leur établissement en cette ville. Par la Rev. Mère St. Augustin de Tranchepain, Supérieure. Avec les lettres circulaires de quel-*

ques-unes de ses Soeurs, et de la dite Mère. (*Nouvelle York, Isle de Manate, De la Presse Crémoisy de Jean-Marie Shea, MDCCCLIX*). This last volume carries a note that it was printed after *"la Chronique du monastère."* Marie Hachard's *Relation du voyage des religieuses Ursulines de Rouen à la Nouvelle Orléans en 1727* was reprinted at Rouen in a small edition in 1865.

[9] George Bancroft wrote to Parkman on August 9, 1856: "As to what papers there are at Rome, there can be no difficulty. Were my old friend B. U. Campbell alive, he would undertake it for us. I think Mrs. George Ripley, wife of George Ripley of the *Tribune*, will easily interest Archbishop Hughes in your behalf. . . . I don't believe much remains in Rome, But the search is worth making." (Massachusetts Historical Society Parkman Papers, cxxvii, 89).

[10] The Biddle Papers in Bancroft's possession were thus described in his letter of July 31, 1856 to Parkman: "I have also three MS. volumes relating to the French settlements on the St. John, in Florida, given to me by Mr. Biddle, the historian of Cabot." In his letter of August 9, 1856 to Parkman, Bancroft speaks of the pleasure he takes in lending him "the family papers obtained by Mr. Biddle." (Massachusetts Historical Society Parkman Papers, cxxvii, 88.)

[11] F. X. Garneau's picture of the colonization of New France, in his classic *Histoire du Canada*, has not been greatly changed by subsequent investigation, though the topic is one which has received a great deal of attention among French-Canadian historical workers.

[12] Parkman seems to have heard in Quebec of the plan to publish Perrot, perhaps from Père Félix Martin, S.J., who was the most historically-minded of the small group of Jesuits who resumed the work of the order in Canada in 1842.

[13] Montcalm was buried in an unmarked grave in the chapel of the Ursuline Convent at Quebec. Lord Aylmer, in visiting the convent in 1830, was surprised to find that no memorial marked the last resting place of the great general. At his own expense he caused the present marble plaque to be installed during the following year, at the spot traditionally supposed to be the grave. In 1833 only one 82-year old nun, Soeur St. Ignace, still remained who remembered Montcalm's funeral and the place where he was buried. Under her guidance, the grave was found and opened. Only some fragments of the bier and some bones were discovered and these fell into dust except for the skull, which was perfectly preserved and since has been carefully guarded, almost as a sacred relic, by the convent. (Martin, *Montcalm*, 267 n.)

[14] Dablon, in Chapter IV of his *Relation* of 1670-71, describes Père

Chaumonot's Huron colony at Lorette and the image to which Parkman refers:

Their village is situated near a Chapel which they built in union with the settlers of the place, and in which honor is paid to a picture in relief of the Blessed Virgin, made from the wood of an oak in whose heart there was found, sixty years ago, one of like size,—in the village of Foye in the province of Liége, one league from the Town of Dinant. It is a precious pledge of the affection of the Queen of Heaven toward this Tribe and all the settlers of the district. That Mother of mercy has already made herself known there by so many favors, which pass for miracles in the opinion of all their recipients, that all Canada has recourse to her. (Thwaites, *Jesuit Relations*, LIV, 287).

In Père Félix Martin's edition of Chaumonot's *Autobiographie* (Paris, 1885), there are two mentions of this image: "l'image de la sainte Vierge, faite sur celle de la vraie Lorette, d'où on nous l'a envoyée" (p. 198) and "le P. Poncet, ayant repassé en France, a eu soin de m'envoyer non seulement une Vierge faite sur celle de Lorette (ainsi que je l'ai déjà dit), mais aussi une coiffe ou bonnet de taffetas blanc qui a été sur la tète de l'image, laquelle est dans la Sainte Maison d'Italie" (203).

[15] C.-P. Drolet (1795-1873), whose mother was English-speaking, was deputy clerk of the Court of Appeals and registrar of the Vice-Admiralty Court in Quebec. He was admitted to the bar in 1827 and sat in the Legislative Assembly as member for Saguenay from February 1836 until the dissolution of 1838. He was one of the most active *Patriotes* in the Quebec district during the Papineau Rebellion, and helped the Americans Dodge and Theller to escape from the Citadel on the night of October 15, 1838.

[16] Charles Panet, Jr. (1838-86) was admitted to the bar in 1859 and became clerk of the House of Commons in 1875. He was a brother-in-law of F. R. Angers. At the time of Parkman's visit to Quebec he lived at 67 St. Louis St., not far from Parkman's customary stopping place, Russell's Hotel (now the St. Louis) on the same street.

[17] Narcisse Fages had his notary's office at 6 St. George (now St. John's) St.

[18] Thomas Sterry Hunt (1826-92) was a native of Norwich, Connecticut. He was a student of Benjamin Silliman at Yale, and soon after his graduation became chemist and mineralogist for the Geological Survey of Canada under Sir William Logan. He was the first professor of chemistry at Laval University in Quebec, and a fellow of the Royal Society of London, the Geological Society of France, the Imperial Geological Institute of Vienna, and the Imperial Leopold Academy of Germany.

He became a naturalized British subject, but died in New York City, after spending most of his life in Canada.

¹⁹ Mgr. Charles-Félix Cazeau (1807-81) was a native of Quebec. He was ordained in 1830 and immediately was attached to the archbishop's staff as a secretary. He became vicar-general in 1850 and a domestic prelate in 1875. He was an honorary canon of the chapter of Quebec. Mgr. Cazeau and Mgr. Hamel, rector of Laval, were brought into Parkman's circle of friends by Abbé Casgrain and Dr. LaRue.

²⁰ Henry Black (1799-1873) was judge of the Vice-Admiralty Court of Quebec for more than fifty years. He was admitted to the bar in 1820, and nominated for the bench by the Imperial Government shortly afterwards. He was a member of the Special Council under Poulett Thomson, from April 1840 to February 1841, and was one of Quebec's two members in the Assembly under the Union.

²¹ Georges-Barthélemi Faribault (1789-1866) was the founder and "perpetual" archival secretary of the Quebec Literary and Historical Society, in whose work of publishing historical documents he took a leading part. Faribault knew much of Quebec history at first hand: as a boy he was a pupil of John Fraser, a Scots veteran of Wolfe's army, and he studied law with J. A. Panet, first Speaker of Quebec's Assembly. Faribault became associated with the assembly as a clerk and translator in 1822, and was its assistant clerk 1840-55. He was an impassioned collector of books and documents relating to the history of Canada. His first collection of 1,600 volumes was lost in the Montreal Parliamentary fire of 1849. Faribault was sent to Europe by the assembly in 1851 to acquire a new library. He assembled 2,000 volumes, of which 700 were lost in the Quebec Parliamentary fire of 1854. Discouraged and broken in health by this double tragedy to his lifework, he resigned his official post. Nevertheless, before his death he had amassed another notable collection, for he left 400 MSS., 1,000 volumes, and an album of maps, plans, portraits, and views relating to Canada to Laval University.

²² Félix Martin, S.J. (1804-86), was born in Brittany, ordained in Switzerland, and came to Canada in 1842, when the Jesuits returned to their best-known mission field. After serving at Sandwich as superior for Ontario (1844-47), he became superior of the Montreal house in 1847, a post he held for ten years. He was the founder and first rector of the Collège Ste. Marie on Bleury Street. In 1857 he was sent abroad by the government to search the French and Roman archives for materials bearing on the early history of Canada. On his return he was named rector of the Jesuit residence in Quebec, and there he remained until he

was finally recalled to France in 1862. Père Martin was an earnest historical worker and the author of *Le Marquis Montcalm au Canada* and of biographies of the Jesuit martyrs Jogues, Brébeuf, Chaumonot, etc.

[23] Jacques Viger (1787-1858) was a journalist, militia officer, antiquarian, and the first mayor of Montreal. A son of a member of the Legislative Assembly, he first took to political journalism as an editor of *Le Canadian* of Quebec (1808-9). In the War of 1812 he served as a captain of the *Voltigeurs*; and after long service as inspector of streets and bridges in Montreal, he became mayor in 1833. For fifty years Viger copied notes, MSS., letters, maps, plans, and everything which might possibly serve history into a collection of notebooks, which he refered to as *Ma Saberdache*. This collection of forty-four notebooks, five opuscules, and an album of views is now in the Archives de la Séminaire de Québec. Many of Viger's materials were published by Michel Bibaud in his *Bibliothèque Canadienne*, to which Viger was an anonymous contributor.

[24] Louis-Joseph Papineau (1786-1871), the first great political genius of the French Canadians, was a lawyer, long Speaker of the Legislative Assembly, and the leader of the *Patriote* uprising of 1837, which is commonly known by his name. He was first elected to the Assembly in 1808, served as a captain in the militia in 1812, and became Speaker in 1815, a post that he held almost continuously until the Assembly was dissolved on the outbreak of the rebellion twenty-three years later. Papineau went to London with John Neilson in 1822-23 to combat the project of joining Upper and Lower Canada in one Union. As the spearhead and spokesman of the French-Canadian resistance to the autocratic rule of the English governors and their placemen, Papineau at first favored constitional resistance and an anti-British embargo rather than revolutionary means. But in his speeches he was frequently carried away into more violent utterances than he intended; and upon the outbreak of the troubles in the autumn of 1837, Lord Gosford ordered his arrest and put a price upon his head. Papineau fled from Montreal to St. Denis and then to St. Hyacinthe, finally taking refuge in the United States about November 25 when he was indicted for treason. He then spent two years at Albany, Philadelphia, and Saratoga Springs; but after all hope of resistance in Canada had collapsed, he went to Paris, where he became intimate with Béranger, Louis Blanc, and Lamennais. He did research work in the Archives d'Etat and had copies made of many documents concerning the French regime in Canada. Thanks to Lafontaine's efforts, Papineau was permitted to return to Canada in 1845, and to retire to his seigneury

of Petite Nation at Montebello, where Parkman visited him in 1856. Here he had one of the best historical libraries then existing in Canada.

[25] John Tanner (1780-1847), *A Narrative of the Captivity and Adventures of John Tanner (U. S. Interpreter at the Saut de Ste. Marie) during thirty years residence among the Indians in the interior of North America* (New York, 1830). *Bib. Can.* 1612.

[26] Philip Alegambe, S.J., *Bibliotheca scriptorum societas Jesu, post excusum anno MDCVIII catalogum P. Ribadeneirae, nunc novo apparatu librorum ad annum reparatae salutis MDCXLII editorum concinnata et illustrium virorum elogiis adornata, a P. Alegambe* (Antwerp, 1643). See also his *Mortes illustrae, et gesta eorum de Societate Iesu* (Rome, 1657). Cf. Thwaites, *Jesuit Relations,* LXXXI.

[27] Samuel de Champlain (1570-1635), the navigator, geographer, founder of Port Royal (Annapolis Royal) and of Quebec, the "Father of New France."

[28] Viger's *Album* was a collection of pictures and prints which formed part of its owner's collection of Canadiana. The *Album* is now in the Bibliothèque Municipale of Montreal, while the rest of the collection is in the Archives de la Séminaire de Québec.

[29] Père Pierre-François-Xavier de Charlevoix, S.J. (1682-1761), the first historian of New France. Born in France, he was sent out in 1720 to investigate the true boundaries of Acadia and the possibilities of explorations in the West. Leaving Quebec in early March 1721, he traveled by way of Montreal, the upper St. Lawrence, and the Great Lakes to Michilimackinac; thence by Fort St. Joseph, the Kanakakee, and the Illinois to the Mississippi at Cahokia; and thence to New Orleans, which he reached on January 5, 1722. Returning to Paris by way of Santo Domingo early in the following year, he published his *Journal d'un Voyage fait par ordre de la Cour dans l'Amérique Septentrionale par le Père de Charlevoix, S.J.*, together with his *Histoire et Description générale de la Nouvelle-France*, at Paris in 1744.

[30] Père Joseph-François Lafiteau, S.J. (1681-1746), the missionary, teacher, and writer. He came to Quebec in 1711 and spent five years studying the Iroquois at the mission of Saut-St.-Louis near Montreal. He was the discoverer of ginseng in Canada. He returned to France in 1717, where he remained as procurer of the Canadian missions in Paris and as a historical writer.

[31] Abbé François Picquet (1708-81) was a Sulpician missionary, the founder of La Présentation. He came to Canada in 1734 and began the study of Indian dialects while ministering to the Indians at Montreal. In

1739 he was attached to the mission at the Lake of Two Mountains (Oka), and devoted himself to developing the colony, which included Algonquins, Nipissings, Hurons, Ottawas, and even Iroquois. In 1744 he replaced the primitive fort by a small modern one constructed on European lines, using his own money and royal funds. His Indians were active in war from 1743-48. In 1749, under La Galissonière and Bigot, Picquet decided to build a fort at the mission of La Présentation (Ogdensburg, New York), with the aim of drawing the Iroquois away from the English. In 1753 he took three Iroquois to France and introduced them to Louis XV, who gave him books and a silver statue of the Virgin for the church at Oka. Early in the following year Picquet returned to his post, strongly favored by Vaudreuil and by Montcalm, who called him the "Patriarch of the Five Nations." After Picquet had accompanied his warriors to Oswego and Fort George in 1757 and to Ticonderoga in the following year, the English put a price on his head. Nothing daunted, Picquet built and launched two 10-gun corvettes on the lakes in the spring of 1759; and in May and June accompanied La Corne's force in the attack on Oswego. After its failure, Picquet moved his mission to Ile Picquet (Big Isle), and until the summer of 1760 tried to check the desertion of the Indians to the English. On September 8 of that year he left Montreal with twenty-five French and two groups of Indians for New Orleans, by way of the Ottawa Valley, lakes Huron and Michigan, and the Wisconsin and Mississippi rivers. He reached New Orleans in July of the following year and remained there until the peace of April 1763 sealed the fate of New France. He then returned to France.

[32] Père Emmanuel Crespel (1703?-75), a Recollet, was at Quebec from 1724 to 1726; accompanied an expedition against the Foxes west of Lake Michigan in 1728; visited Niagara, Fort Frontenac, and Fort Frédéric (Crown Point); and was shipwrecked on Anticosti Island while returning to France in 1736. He published a journal of his experiences, *Voyages du R. P. Emanuel Crespel dans le Canada, et son naufrage en revenant en France. Mis au jour par le S^r. Louis Crespel son Frère (A Francfort sur le Meyn, MDCCXLII. Bib. Can.* 183. This was republished at Amsterdam in 1757, and an English translation appeared in London in 1797. The French version was republished at Quebec in 1884 by Abbé L.-E. Bois.

[33] Luc de La Corne, Sieur de Chaptes et de St. Luc (1711-84), early adopted the military life. He served against the Sauks and Foxes of Wisconsin in 1734, at Fort Clinton in 1741, at Crown Point and Saratoga in 1746-47, at La Présentation in 1752, and at Ticonderoga in 1758. He organized the ambush of Abercromby's wagon train at Fort Lydius and

the less successful attempt to intercept Haldimand's march on Niagara in 1759. He was a brilliant leader of mixed parties of French and Indians, and was a favorite of the tribes, whose languages he spoke. He was wounded at Ste. Foye in 1761 and in the following year was one of the seven survivors of the wreck of the *Augusta*, which was returning to France with most of the officials of the colony. From 1775 until his death he sat in the Legislative Council, and he served in command of the savages at Wood Creek under Burgoyne in 1777. His third wife was Marguerite Boucher de Boucherville, whose daughter Marie-Marguerite Lennox married Jacques Viger in 1808, after the death of her first husband.

[34] The Caughnawaga fort was begun in 1747 and completed in 1754. There is a plan of it in the Public Archives at Ottawa. For a description, see E. J. Devine, *History of Caughnawaga* (Montreal, 1922), 243-44.

[35] The Mission of Two Mountains near Montreal was settled by some nine hundred Iroquois about 1720, after the abandonment of Saut-au-Recollet. They were later joined by Nipissings and Algonquins from Ile-aux-Tourtes.

[36] The Hôpital-Général, or Monastery of the Religieuses Hospitalières de la Miséricorde de Jésus, was founded at Quebec in 1692 by Bishop Saint-Vallier as a home for the old and infirm, under the direction of a sister of the Congrégation de Notre Dame. In 1693 he put four nuns from the Hôtel-Dieu in charge of the new establishment, and in 1710 added two wings to the original quarters in the old Recollet Convent of Notre-Dame-des-Anges. During his thirteen years of exile in France he raised funds for the hospitalization of thirty persons. Provision was made for the care of the insane there until the Beauport asylum was opened in 1846; and the nuns also conducted a boarding school for girls until 1868. Part of the buildings were reserved for those who chose to spend the remainder of their lives there, as Bishop Saint-Vallier did.

[37] Bishop Jean-Baptiste de Saint-Vallier (1653-1727) was one of the most remarkable prelates of New France. After serving as a court chaplain under Louis XIV and as a military chaplain in Flanders in 1678, he refused the bishoprics of Tours and Marseilles. He first visited Canada in 1685 as bishop-elect and grand-vicar. He was consecrated at St. Sulpice in Paris in 1688 and reached Quebec that autumn. After conflicts with Frontenac, the governor, he was captured by the English while on his way to France in 1704, and spent five years in England and four in France before he could return to his diocese. He spent 600,000 livres, a third of the sum being his own, on the works of the Church in Quebec. He was buried in the chapel of the Hôpital-Général.

[38] The Soeurs de la Congrégation were founded at Montreal in 1658 by Venerable Marguerite Bourgeoys (1620-1700). The congregation is devoted to the education and instruction of youth.

[39] The Soeurs de la Charité de l'Hôpital-Général de Montréal (Soeurs Grises), or Grey Nuns, were founded at Montreal in 1737 by Madame d'Youville (Venerable Marie-Marguerite Dufrust, dame d'Youville) (1701-71). Madame d'Youville, born at Varennes and educated by the Ursulines of Quebec, was the daughter of an officer killed in service. She married a spendthrift, who left her penniless and with two children to support. Founding a successful small business, she gave much of her time to devotions and to charity. In 1737 she formed, with three other Montreal women, a community devoted to the service of the poor, and in 1747 took on the Hôpital-Général when the Frères Charon gave it up because of financial difficulties. The court had ordered the combination of the Hôpitals-Généraux of Montreal and Quebec, but Madame d'Youville managed to have this order rescinded through petition to the Bishop and to the Intendant Bigot. Before her death in 1771 she paid off all except 7,000 livres of the total debt of 48,000 which she had inherited from the Fréres Charon; and had established two new wards for poor patients, an asylum for the insane or perverted, and a home for foundling children. All this was accomplished despite the effort of founding and developing her new community, the wartime trials of 1759-60, and the destruction of the hospital by fire in 1765.

[40] The Soeurs Servantes du Coeur Immaculé de Marie founded the Asile du Bon-Pasteur de Québec in 1850 as a refuge for repentant young girls and for the education and instruction of children.

[41] The Hôtel-Dieu of Quebec was founded in 1639 at Sillery by Mères St. Ignace, St. Bernard, and St. Bonaventure (the oldest of whom was then 29), of the Congrégation des Hospitalières de la Miséricorde de Jésus. The institution was moved to Quebec in 1646.

[42] The Quebec house of the Religieuses Ursulines was founded in 1639 by Madame de la Peltrie, with Venerable Mère Marie de l'Incarnation as the first superior. The Ursulines are famous for their education of girls.

[43] At present this division of the land at Charlesbourg can best be observed from the church steeple or from a plane.

[44] *Lettres de la Vénérable Mère Marie de l'Incarnation, Première Supérieure des Ursulines de la Nouvelle-France, divisées en deux parties* (Paris, 1681). This edition by Dom Claude Martin, which was exceedingly scarce, has been superseded by Dom Jamet's, in Vol. III-IV (1935-1937) of his *Escrits Spirituels et Temporels de Marie de l'Incarnation.*

On November 1(?), 1857 Parkman referred to his difficulties in finding this volume in a letter to George Bancroft (M.H.S., Bancroft Papers, 1857, June to December):

Dear Sir,

I observe, cited by you, the name of a book which I have chased in vain in the United States, Canada, and France—the *Lettres de Marie de l'Incarnation*. It is rare, and though I know of one or two copies, they are fast locked up in convent libraries. I should be very much your debtor, if you can aid me in gaining an opportunity to consult either this or another kindred book—Juchereau's *Histoire de l'Hôtel-Dieu de Québec*. The latter is comparatively numerous: but, being chiefly in unaccomodating hands, I fear I must go to Canada to consult it.

I remain, Dear Sir,

Respectfully yours,

Francis Parkman.

The Know-Nothing disturbances and the rise of that party to complete power in Massachusetts had not left Boston Catholics in a mood to be helpful to Protestant students.

[45] Abbé Edouard-Gabriel Plante (1813-69) became chaplain of the Hôpital-Général de Québec in 1851, after serving for eleven years as vicar of the Basilica. He was passionately devoted to Canadian history and amassed a remarkable library, which included the original editions of Champlain, Sagard, Lescarbot, a collection of the *Jesuit Relations*, Denys, Boucher, Lafiteau, and Leclerq. He left his books to Laval University.

[46] R. P. P.-F.-X. de Charlevoix (1682-1761), *Vie de la Mère Marie de l'Incarnation* (Paris, Chez Claude Briasson, 1724). According to Dom Jamet, the modern editor of Marie de l'Incarnation, this is merely an "easy and intelligent popularization" of Dom Claude Martin's biography.

[47] Louis Bertrand Latour (1700-80), *Histoire de l'Hôtel-Dieu de Québec* (Montaubon, Chez Jerome Legier, 1751).

[48] Jeanne-Françoise Juchereau [Mère de St. Ignace] (1650-1723), *Les Annales de l'Hôtel-Dieu de Québec, 1636-1716, Composées par les Reverends Mères Jeanne-Françoise Juchereau de St. Ignace et Marie Andrée Duplessis de Ste. Hélène, Anciennes Religieuses.* This was the basis, after much cutting and alteration, of Latour's *Historie.* It has recently been edited from the original text by Dom Jamet (Quebec, 1939).

[49] Père Paul Ragueneau, S.J. (1608-80), *La Vie de la Mère Catherine de Saint-Augustin, Religieuse Hospitalière de la Miséricorde de Québec en la Nouvelle-France (A Paris, Chez Florentin Lambert, M.DC.LXXI)*. A facsimile was printed at Quebec in 1923.

[50] Margry's list of documents on Louisiana cannot be traced.

[51] *Les Voyages Aventureux du Capitaine Jan Alfonce Santongeois,* an abridgement of his *Cosmographie,* was published at Poictiers in 1559 and translated in Hakluyt's *Voyages,* (Glasgow, 1904) VIII, 275. It also appears in French in M. Musset's *Récueil de Voyages et documents pour servir à l'histoire de la Géographie.* Alphonse, who served as pilot to Roberval in 1542-43 gives some account of the Saguenay, which he took for an inland sea and a possible northwest passage.

[52] M. Adolphe de Puibusque (?-1863) was a French writer who married an English Canadian, and spent three years in Canada.

[53] This passage is crossed out.

[54] Pierre Margry (1818-94) was drawn into his lifework in 1839 by his employment by General Lewis Cass, then U. S. Minister to France, to collect documents in the French archives relating to the history of the Old Northwest. When John Romeyn Brodhead came to Paris to gather documents bearing on the early history of New York, Margry was recommended to him by Cass. At some uncertain date Margry became attached to the Archives de la Marine et des Colonies, of which he eventually became the conservator. Exhausting his own archives, he sought further materials on the colonial history of France wherever they were to be found, in public or private hands. After his death his immense collection of transcripts went to the Bibliothèque Nationale. There is an account of it in the library's *Inventaire Sommaire* for 1898-99. The existence of this treasure house of materials became known to historians by the publication of *Relations et mémoires inédites pour servir à l'histoire de la France dans les pays d'outremer* (Paris, 1867), and Margry was besieged by requests to use it, which he refused. Parkman had many dealings with Margry in the late 1860's and early 1870's, and obtained the appropriation by the American Congress of $10,000 to underwrite the publication in six volumes of Margry's *Découvertes et établissements des Français dans l'ouest et dans le sud de l'Amérique Septentrionale, 1614-1754* (Paris, 1876-86).

[55] Penicaut, *Relation ou annales véritables de ce qui s'est passé dans le pays de la Louisiane . . . 1669, continué jusqu'en 1722* (in Margry's *Découvertes,* V, 375-586).

[56] Pierre-Joseph-Oliver Chauveau (1820-90), lawyer, statesman, and man of letters, studied law in Quebec under Parkman's friend Judge George O'Kill Stuart. He was Superintendent of Public Instruction from 1855-67, and was the first Prime Minister of Quebec under Confederation. His most famous book is *Charles Guérin* (1853), one of the first French-Canadian novels. He was also the author of a study of Garneau (1883).

[57] This collection is no longer preserved at the Parliamentary Library

in Quebec. It may have been among the papers taken to Ottawa when the government moved to the new capital in 1867.

⁵⁸ *La Bibliothèque Canadienne, ou Miscellanées Historiques, Scientifiques, et Littéraires* (Vol. I, 1822; Vol. II, 1825-26), edited by Michel Bibaud.

⁵⁹ *La Revue Canadienne*, the longest-lived French-Canadian magazine, was first published in January 1864 by E. Senécal.

⁶⁰ David Dale Owen (1807-60), the geologist son of Robert Owen and Ann Dale of New Lanark, made a survey of the Dubuque and Mineral Point districts of Wisconsin and Iowa for the Federal Land Commissioner. His report was published in *House Document No. 239 (26 Cong. I Sess.)*, April 2, 1840. He made a more complete survey of Wisconsin, Iowa, and Minnesota which may be found in his *Report of Geological Survey of Wisconsin, Iowa, and Minnesota . . . 1852.*

⁶¹ Munsell's Historical Series, No. VIII: John Dawson Gilmary Shea (1824-92), *Early Voyages Up and Down the Mississippi by Cavelier, St. Cosme, Le Sueur, Gravier, and Guigues* (Albany, 1851). *Bib. Can.* 167.

⁶² Abbé Henri-Raymond Casgrain (1831-1904), completing his studies at the Quebec Seminary, traveled in France and Italy before serving as a vicar at Beauport and at the Basilica of Quebec. In 1861 he became chaplain to the Convent of the Bon Pasteur, where he made his home until his death. In that same year he published his *Légendes Canadiennes*, and in 1864 his *Histoire de la Mère Marie de l'Incarnation*, as well as several of the biographical sketches which were later collected in *Biographies canadiennes* (1879), which includes a life of Parkman. He was the leading spirit of the literary revival of the 1860's, which was largely the work of Quebec writers. He was to become Parkman's closest friend in Quebec, and his rival in the same historical field.

⁶³ Jacques Duperron Baby of Windsor, Ontario, a prominent trader who supplied the garrison of Detroit with provisions during the siege of 1763. He was a friend of Pontiac, the great Indian leader. Parkman visited his grandson at Windsor in 1845.

⁶⁴ *Le Foyer Canadien*, the organ of Abbé Casgrain's literary group, began publication in January 1863 and ceased to appear in December 1866.

⁶⁵ Chevalier James Johnstone (1720-1800), *A Dialogue in Hades, a parallel of military errors, of which the French and English armies were guilty during the campaign of 1759 in Canada* (Quebec, 1866). In Quebec Literary & Historical Society *Documents*, II Series.

⁶⁶ Philippe Joseph Aubert de Gaspé (1786-1871), *Mémoires*. *Bib. Can.* 4464.

⁶⁷ Eugene Vétromile (1819-81), *The Abenakis and Their History, Or*

Historical Notes on the Aborigines of Acadia (New York, 1866). *Bib. Can.* 4546.

[68] Abbé Joseph-Pierre-Anselme Maurault (1819-71), *Histoire des Abenakis depuis 1605 jusqu'à nos jours* ([Sorel?] 1866). *Bib. Can.* 4520.

IX. FIRST PARIS NOTEBOOK

[1] Pierre Margry had lived on the same street, formerly known as Rue de la Harpe, in 1845, at the outset of the studies which brought him into contact with Parkman. (Note by Margry in his presentation copy of the *Jesuits*, dated "25 Jan. 1869" by Parkman.)

[2] This portrait of Anne de La Grange-Trianon, Comtesse de Frontenac (1632?-1707?), painted as Minerva, is reproduced as the frontispiece of *Frontenac and New France* (Part V of *France and England in North America*). An account of the portrait and of the Countess herself is given in the opening pages of that work.

[3] Parkman evidently changed his opinion of this bust of Montcalm, for it does not figure among the illustrations to *Montcalm and Wolfe*.

[4] Henri Joutel (1640?-1735), *Journal historique du dernier voyage que feu M. de La Salle fit dans le Golfe de Mexique* (Paris, 1713). Joutel, who accompanied La Salle as intendant on his expedition of 1684-87, repudiated this altered and abridged version of his journal, which Margry printed in full in *Découvertes*, III, 91-534. An English translation of the first printed text was published at London in 1714, and reprinted at Albany in 1906 in a new edition by Henry Reed Stiles. The Caxton Club of Chicago also issued an English version, c. 1895. (*Bib. Can.* 96, 230).

[5] This baptismal certificate furnished the basis of a footnote on the first page of *La Salle*.

[6] These letters of La Salle and Beaujeu, who was in charge of the ships, are printed in *Découvertes*, II, 519-52.

[7] The passage in the *Histoire de M*[r]. *de La Salle* upon which Margry based his accusation against Nicolas Perrot (1644-1717), the interpreter, is cited in *La Salle*, 116 n.

[8] Parkman did not accept Margry's view of Beaujeu. Cf. *La Salle*, 389-90 n.

[9] The copies sent to New York were those selected by John Romeyn Brodhead in 1841-45, in his capacity of historical agent for the State.

They were printed in E. B. O'Callaghan, *Documents Relating to the Colonial History of New York* (Albany, 1853-83), IX-X ("Paris Documents"). In 1845 the Canadian government authorized Louis Joseph Papineau, then in Paris, to obtain copies of documents in the French archives relating to the history of Canada. Of the ten MS. volumes he gathered from the Archives des Colonies, six were destroyed in the Montreal Parliament fire of 1849, while four volumes, calendared in the *Catalogue de la Bibliothèque du Parlement* (Quebec, 1858), 1448, were preserved in the library of the Quebec Literary and Historical Society. In 1851 Georges-Barthélemi Faribault gathered what were known as the second and third series of Paris documents, to replace those lost in the fire of 1849. These are calendared in the 1858 *Catalogue*, 1499-1611.

The letters of Antoine Laumet de la Mothe Cadillac (1658-1730), who commanded at Michilimackinac, Detroit, and in Louisiana, were used by Parkman in *The Old Regime* (Part IV of *France and England in North America*). In the preface he mentions his reliance upon the Archives de la Marine et Colonies and upon Margry's aid. These papers were later printed in Margry, *Découvertes*, V, 75-346. It evidently did not take Parkman long to discover that Margry was holding back the La Salle papers, which were not made available until the publication of the first three volumes of the *Découvertes* in 1879.

[10] While American Minister to Paris from 1836 to 1842, General Lewis Cass collected materials on the history of the old Northwest—the Great Lakes region. Papineau made a selection from the Paris archives in 1845.

[11] L. Dussieux, *Le Canada sous la Domination Française* (Paris, 1862), 283-376.

[12] Sir Thomas Phillips, as Margry told Parkman on February 25.

[13] As later entries in this notebook indicate, Parkman established relations with the Marquis de Montcalm and was given permission "to copy all the letters written by his ancestor, General Montcalm, when in America, to members of his family in France." (*Montcalm and Wolfe*, Preface, viii).

[14] Frontenac's dispatch to Colbert of November 2, 1672 is cited in *Frontenac*, 25.

[15] R. Thomassy, "De la Salle et ses Relations inédites," in *Géologie pratique de la Louisiane* (Paris, 1860).

[16] Cited *La Salle*, 374.

[17] This map, rudely sketched by Parkman in his notebook, is Harrisse No. 228. Harrisse, in his *Notes sur la Nouvelle France* (Paris, 1872), 205, like Parkman (*La Salle*, 383 n.), assigns it to the engineer Minet, Beaujeu's

chartmaker, and considers it a copy of No. 226. Harrisse found it among the working drawings of the great cartographer Guillaume Delisle (1675-1726); and hazards the guess that "Minet" became "Minuty" either through the copyist's misreading, or through an attempt to latinize the engineer's name.

[18] Probably a preliminary sketch for Harrisse No. 241: "Carte de l'Amérique Septentrionale, dressée par Raudin, l'ingénieur et l'obligé du Cte. de Frontenac," 1689. Harrisse was only able to find an outline tracing of this lost map (reproduced in J. Winsor, *Narrative and Critical History of America*, IV, 235). The tracing is now in the Barlow Collection. J. Winsor, *The Kohl Collection* (Washington, 1904), 110.

[19] Parkman may have seen the lost map of Raudin, which, like the sketch, shows the Mississippi as the Buade. Harrisse dates this map 1689.

[20] Harrisse No. 263: "Carte de la Rivière de Mississippi sur les mémoires de M. le Sueur qui en a pris avec la boussole tous les tours et détours depuis la mer jusqu'à la Rivière St. Pierre et a pris la hauteur du pôle en plusieurs endroits. Par Guillaume De L'Isle Géographe, de l'Académie Royale des Sciences, 1702." This map was based on information supplied by Pierre Charles Le Sueur (1657-1702?), long a fur trader among the Sioux of the upper Mississippi, who ascended the river from Louisiana in 1700 in search of a copper mine in the same region, after his fur trading activities had been banned by Louis XIV's edict of 1698.

[21] In 1730 Pierre Gaultier de Varennes, sieur de la Vérendrye, came down to Quebec from his post of command at the trading posts on Lake Nipigon. While urging his plans of discovery in the West, he showed the governor, the Marquis de Beauharnois, a map drawn by the Indian Aughagah or Ochagach. This map was evidently sent to France, for a tracing of it was reproduced in Philippe Buache's "Carte Physique des terrains les plus élevés de la partie occidentale du Canada, 1754." The original "Carte tracée par les Cris" is reproduced in L. J. Burpee, *Journals and Letters of La Vérendrye and His Sons* (Toronto, 1937), 192; while Buache's map, with its inset "Carte tracée par le Sauvage Ockagach," is found in the same work, p. 53. A further "Carte contenant les nouvelles découvertes de l'Ouest, 1737," which went to France with De Beauharnois' letter of October 14, 1737, is reproduced opposite p. 116. There are four variants of this map, two of them copies by La Galissonnière, head of the department of nautical charts at Paris. Christopher Dufrost, sieur de La Jemeraye —La Vérendrye's nephew, who died in 1735 while trying to establish a new post west of the Lake of the Woods—is supposed to have drawn the "Carte d'une partie du lac Supérieur, avec la découverte de la rivière

depuis le grand portage A jusqu'à la barrière B," (*ibid*, 488), but it contains information which must have been obtained after his death.

²² This map, to which Parkman refers in *La Salle* (469 n.), seems to be distinct from Harrisse No. 260: "Carte du Mississipy à la Coste de la Floride avec ses environs, 1700." The latter shows La Salle's fort and a route marked "Chemin Par où les Espagnols ont Esté à la Baye St. Louis." Since Parkman refers to the map he saw as a manuscript in Margry's collection, it may have been a tracing from that listed by Harrisse, with an altered legend.

²³ Harrisse No. 360: "Carte de la Rivière Longue et de quelques autres qui se déchargent dans le grand fleuve de Mississippi, 1689." This map, which is found in the first volume of Lahontan's *Nouveaux Voyages* and reproduced in *Narrative and Critical History*, IV, 261, shows an east-west route marked down the "Rivière des Ilinois" from the village of the "Oumamis de Chegakoi." On the "Carte générale de Canada" in the second volume, the river is still given as the "Ilinois," but the "Portage Ilinois" of the first map becomes "Portage de Chegakou V[ers] des Ilinois" and the "Chegakou Oumanis" village is shown. Parkman's "Chacagou" might well be a misreading or a phonetic equivalent, but where he got "Rivière à la Roche" from Lahontan remains a mystery.

²⁴ This "Tabula Novae Franciae Anno 1660" (Harrisse No. 329; Kohl No. 210) appeared in *Historia canadensis, seu Novae Franciae Libri Decem, ad annum usque Christi M.DC.LVI. Auctore P. Francisco Creuxio, e Societate Iesu* (Paris, 1664). Père du Creux's work was based upon the *Jesuit Relations*, which he followed in too detailed a fashion for Charlevoix's taste. The map was reproduced in Père Bressani's *Relation abrégée* (*Bib. Can.* 45), translated and edited by Père Félix Martin, S.J., at Montreal in 1852. It is also given in facsimile in J. G. Shea, *Mississippi Valley* (New York, 1853), 50, and partially in *Narrative and Critical History*, IV, 148 & 389. It almost corresponds in extent to Champlain's great map of 1632 (Harrisse No. 322).

²⁵ Harrisse No. 348; Kohl No. 178: "Le Canada faict par le Sr. Champlain où sont la Nouvelle France, la Nouvelle Angleterre, etc., avec les nations voisines et autres terres nouvellement découvertes suivant les mémoires du P. du Val Géographe du Roy," 1677. Duval's map was based on Champlain's of 1632. An earlier version appeared in 1664 (Harrisse No. 331), while Winsor (*Narrative and Critical History*, IV, 388 n.) mentions one of 1660 in the Kohl Collection.

²⁶ Harrisse No. 359; Kohl No. 213: "Partie occidentale du Canada ou de la Nouvelle France où sont les nations des Illinois, de Trace, les

Iroquois, et plusieurs autres Peuples; avec la Louisiane Nouvellement découverte etc.," 1688. This map was republished in the following year on a reduced scale, annexed to the "Partie orientale, 1689" (Harrisse No. 361), as "L'Amérique Septentrionale, ou la Partie Septentrionale des Indes Occidentales" (Harrisse No. 362). The western portion is sketched in *Narrative and Critical History*, IV, 232. Coronelli was the Venetian cartographer; and his work was "corrected and augmented" by the Sieur Tillemon.

[27] Kohl No. 240: "Partie de l'Amérique Septentrionale qui comprend le cours de l'Ohio, etc.," 1755, by Robert de Vaugondy. De Vaugondy (1688-1766), the cartographical heir of the Sansons, was royal geographer in 1760.

[28] Atlas F & G: "Carte du Canada et de La Louisiane qui forment La Nouvelle France et des Colonies Angloises où sont représentés les Pays contestés Dressée sur les observations et sur plusieurs Cartes particulières et même Angloises Par J. B. Nolin Géographe . . . 1756."

[29] Kohl No. 240: "Canada et Louisiane par le Sieur le Rouge, ingénieur géographe du Roi," 1755.

[30] N. Bellin's "Carte de la partie orientale de la Nouvelle France ou du Canada, 1744" appeared in the first volume of Père Charlevoix's *Histoire et description de la Nouvelle France* (Paris, 1744).

[31] Harrisse No. 354; Kohl No. 127: "Partie de la Nouvelle France . . . par . . . Hubert Jaillot, 1685." This map, based almost entirely on Canadian sources according to Kohl, shows the French and English posts on Hudson's Bay. Jaillot was royal geographer in 1736.

[32] Harrisse No. 238; Kohl No. 233: "Parties les Plus Occidentales du Canada. *Pierre Raffeix Jesuite*," 1688. The map is sketched and the marginal inscriptions are given in *Narrative and Critical History*, IV, 233. Raffeix's suggested route runs from Lake Ontario, not Lake Erie, up the Cheneseco, with a portage to the headwaters of the Alleghany, and thus by the Ohio to the Mississippi.

[33] "Canada, Louisiane et terres Angloises. Par le sr. d'Anville. 1755." This is a three-sheet map (pl. 28-28a-28b) from Jean Baptiste Bourguignon d'Anville's *Atlas général* (Paris, 1743-80). Cf. P. L. Phillips, *Geographical Atlases* (Washington, 1909), 573.

[34] "Amérique Septentrionale. Par le sr. d'Anville, 1746." A one-sheet map (No. 10-11) in D'Anville's 1727-80 *Atlas général* and two sheets (pl. 27) in the 1743-80 edition (Phillips, 571).

[35] "Carte de l'Amérique Septentrionale Depuis le 28 degré de latitude jusqu'au 72. Par N. Bellin Ingénieur de la Marine et du Depost des

Plans . . .," 1755. In Library of Congress; photo-lithograph copy in Public Archives, Ottawa, Tray 54.

36 "Nouvelle Carte particulière de l'Amérique où sont exactement marquées la Nouvelle Bretagne, le Canada ou Nouvelle France, la Nouvelle Ecosse, la Nouvelle Angleterre, la Nouvelle York, la Pensilvanie, Mary Land, La Caroline Septentrionale, l'Ile de Terre Neuve, le Grand Banc, etc.," from Henry Popple, *Atlas* (Amsterdam, 1733).

37 Parkman's account of Montcalm in *Montcalm and Wolfe*, I, 351-60, is based chiefly on an unpublished autobiography, *Mémoires pour servir à l'Histoire de ma Vie*, "preserved by his descendents." Parkman uses the current Marquis' characterization of his ancestor's mother—"a woman of remarkable force of character and who held great influence over her son" (*Montcalm and Wolfe*, I, 359)—without adopting the suggestion that Madame de St. Véran induced him to take the American command offered by D'Argenson. The family name was De Montcalm-Gozon de St. Véran; the Marquis' wife was known as Madame de Montcalm, his mother as Madame de St. Véran. The portrait is reproduced as frontispiece to *Montcalm and Wolfe*, I.

38 Sir Thomas Phillips (1792-1872) was one of the great book and manuscript collectors of his day, and maintained a private press at his residence, Middle Hill, at Broadway. He later removed to Thirlestane House, Cheltenham, where Parkman saw him.

39 The original draft of this letter, pasted in Margry's presentation copy of *The Jesuits*, came to light in Rutland, Vermont, in the spring of 1942. Through the courtesy of the present owner of the volume, Richard B. McCormack of Chicago, the text of this important letter is here given in full:

–Cette lettre a été adressée par moi à Ste. Beuve qui m'avait prié de lui donner les moyens de répondre à Parkman sur un sujet qu'il ne connaissait pas–

Monsieur

Vous trouverez avec ce billet le Volume de M. Parkman sur lequel vous m'avez fait l'honneur de me demander un mot. Ce volume, intitulé, comme vous le savez, *Les Jésuites dans l'Amérique du Nord*, fait partie d'une série de livres de cet auteur sur l'action de la France dans ce continent, action dont il me semble avoir été amené à reconnaitre l'importance par son [livre] de La Conspiration de Pontiac–La révolte des Hurons et des autres nations voisines des Lacs contre les Anglais, qui eut lieu sous les ordres de ce chef après la [?] perte du Canada, ayant dû montrer à M. Parkman l'attachement de ces nations pour les Français. Il a voulu sans doute étudier les circonstances dans lesquelles s'étaient formées nos relations avec les tribus indiennes, et comment notre puissance s'était établie dans le continent qu'elles parcouraient plus qu'elles ne le possédaient, suivant l'expression du Général Cass.

Le premier volume que M. Parkman a donné en conséquence sur ce sujet contient la tentative d'établissement des Français à la Caroline du Nord sous Charles IX et la vie de Samuel de Champlain fondateur de la puissance française sur le Saint Laurent.

Le second volume est celui que vous m'avez confié.

Et il précède, à qu'il paraît, un troisième ouvrage qui aura pour sujet la Découverte de l'Ouest.

Il est difficile de juger une de ces parties sans les autres. Néanmoins pour vous être agréable, je vous dirai ce que j'ai aperçu du second volume.

Dans cette partie l'auteur Américain a cru pouvoir détacher comme présentant un tableau capable de frapper l'attention le rôle des Jésuites dans l'Amérique du Nord pendant 20 ans de 1634 à 1654.

Il lui a paru que durant ce temps ils ont prétendu former en Canada un Empire analogue à celui qu'ils avaient fondé au Paraguay. Et il attribue aux victoires des Iroquois, ennemis des Hurons et des nations Algonquines dont les Jésuites étaient les missionaires, d'avoir eu pour résultat la chute du projet de La Compagnie.

Suivant moi, l'auteur a raison quand il expose ce dessein des Jésuites. Ils l'avouent eux-mêmes, mais il se trompe quand il ne voit qu'une cause aussi indirecte à la fin de la domination des Jésuites là où il y en a plusieurs bien plus nettement apparentes pour ceux qui ont suivi les faits de plus près que M. Parkman.

La première de ces causes a été la Cession d'Indépendance des colons qui ne pouvaient se faire à un tel régime de compression que celui qu'avaient établi les Jésuites. Et lorsque le nombre des colons augmente, les R.R.P.P. eurent la main forcée, parce que les habitants s'aidèrent contre eux d'autres forces contraires aux vues de la Société de Jésus.

La création du gouvernement Royal, en se substituant à celui des compagnies commerciales absorbé par les Jésuites, favorisa naturellement les habitants pour établir sa propre indépendance, et à cet effet il opposa également les Sulpiciens et les Récollets aux Jésuites.

Ce qui prouve à la fois la justice de la vue de M. Parkman sur le but des Jésuites, et son erreur sur ce qu'il croit avoir amené le fin de leur domination, c'était le rôle de cette Société dans l'ouest même, et dans la vallée du Mississippi après l'établissement du Gouvernement Royal sur les bords du Saint Laurent—Les français étant restés peu nombreux dans l'ouest et au sud. Les Jésuites prétendirent bien y demeurer les maîtres. Et ils firent une guerre acharnée, rarement ouverte, presque toujours souterraine, à ceux qui vinrent dans ces régions en rivaux, soit pour établir l'autorité Royale, soit pour élever des missions, soit pour trafiquer en dehors d'eux, tandis que la Société continuait de lutter sur les bords du Saint Laurent pour garder du pouvoir tout ce qu'elle pourrait. Pendant 30 ans je la vois dans toutes les cabales, dans tous les remuements des partis qui divisent le pays, et peu s'y faut que ses menées n'aient pas pour conséquence la ruine entière de la colonie.

Le livre de M. Parkman est donc un livre insuffisant et faux dans ses déductions par l'insuffisance de ses lumières—Néanmoins il a ceci de bon qu'il laisse apercevoir une partie de la vérité, ce qui rendra aux autres plus facile de la faire entendre toute entière—D'un autre côté il concourt à faire reconnaître sous certains aspects la grandeur de notre colonisation et par là, Monsieur, il mérite que vous lui encouragiez à continuer son oeuvre, quoiqu'à mon sens également il ne fasse que résumer avec un peu plus de lest d'esprit les travaux historiques publiés tant en France qu'en Canada par des ecclésiastiques—Seulement il est nécessaire que vous sachiez au moins pour vous que tout est loin d'être dit sur ces matières.

Je pense, Monsieur, que ces quelques mots vous suffiront pour répondre à M. Parkman. Et pour justifier auprès de vous le plaisir que me conféra toujours l'occasion de vous témoigner les sentiments avec lesquels

> J'ai l'honneur d'être
> Votre très humble et très obéissant
> serviteur

J'espère, parce que je le souhaite,
que votre santé est meilleure que   Pierre Margry,
le jour où j'ai eu l'honneur de vous   11 Rue du Mont Thabor
voir après un contretemps.

After receiving this letter, Ste. Beuve wrote a brief and guarded note to Parkman, congratulating him upon his work but not criticizing it. Cf. Massachusetts Historical Society, Parkman Papers, 128, 60.

40 Cf. *La Salle*, 317 n., for Parkman's account of the small fieldpiece found at Ottawa, Illinois, and for a comparison of it with the Paris specimens.

41 In the spring of 1759 Bougainville brought the news, which he had heard before sailing from France, that one of Montcalm's daughters had died (*Montcalm and Wolfe*, II, 179).

42 J. E. Roy, in his *Rapport sur les Archives de France relatives à l'histoire du Canada* (Ottawa, 1911), 324, says that the Archives de Guerre go back continuously to the reign of Louis XIV, with a few scattered dossiers, documents, and registers of earlier date.

43 No mention of this map is found in the standard works on French cartography.

44 This might be any of a dozen or more plans of Louisbourg. N. Bellin did a "Port de Louisbourg dans l'Isle Royale, 1764" which is mentioned in J. S. McLennan, *Louisbourg* (London, 1918), 433, as being in the Bibliothèque Nationale (FF. 4693 pl. 23). The manuscript Parkman saw may have the basis of this engraved map.

45 In *Montcalm and Wolfe* (I, 76) Parkman refers to his use of the Detroit

map made c. 1750 by the French engineer Gaspard Chaussegros de Léry (1682-1756). N. Bellin's "La Rivière du Detroit" and its inset "Plan du Fort du Detroit," in *Le Petit Atlas Maritime* (Paris, 1764), are based upon two manuscript sketches of De Léry, made in 1749 and 1752.

[46] Probably maps by Robert de Vaugondy from his *Atlas Universel* (Paris, 1757).

[47] The papers upon which Margry based his views were published in his *Découvertes*, II, 357-471, and were used by Parkman in the eleventh edition of *The Discovery of the Great West*, which was reentitled *La Salle and the Discovery of the Great West*.

[48] Harrisse No. 225: "Carte de la Louisiane, May 1685," by Minet. Harrisse says that Minet cut partially away the original outline of the river's mouth, and pasted the second version beneath it. He also thinks that the map was made after Minet's return to France, and that it was based upon Franquelin's manuscript map of 1684. Cf. Thomassy, 208; J. G. Shea, *Peñalosa* (New York, 1882), 21; G. Gravier, *La Salle* (Paris, 1870), 283; Delisle, *Journal des Savans*, xix, 211. The map is sketched in *Narrative and Critical History*, IV, 237.

[49] Cf. *La Salle*, 114.

[50] Cf. T. Chapais, *Montcalm* (Quebec, 1911), 226.

[51] *Lettres de monsieur le marquis de Montcalm . . . 1757, 1758, 1759* (London, 1777). *Bib. Can.* 289. These are the Roubaud letters, given to George III about 1764 by the renegade Jesuit, circulated in manuscript in 1775, and then printed. Roubaud claimed the author was an Englishman known to Chatham (cf. *Canadian Archives Report*, 1885, xiii-xxi, cxxxviii-cxliii). Parkman and Justin Winsor uncovered Roubaud's forgery in Massachusetts Historical Society *Proceedings*, XI(1869), 112-28; *ibid*, II Series, 3 (1887), 202-5.

X. MT. DESERT NOTEBOOK

[1] Mt. Desert Island, off the Maine coast near the mouth of the Penobscot, was discovered and named by Champlain in 1604. It was first settled by the Jesuits in 1609, but their colony was destroyed four years later by Samuel Argall. In 1688 the island was granted to the Sieur de la Mothe Cadillac, but no general settlement was established until 1762, when Massachusetts granted half the island to Governor Francis Bernard.

Despite its growing popularity as a summer resort, in 1870 the island was still reached only by stage from Bangor or by steamer twice a week from Portland.

² Grand Manan Island, off the New Brunswick coast near the entrances of Passamaquoddy Bay and the Bay of Fundy, was discovered by Champlain in 1604 and is mentioned by Lescarbot (1609) and Biard (1611).

³ Pemaquid was an early settlement on the Maine coast, near the modern town of Boothbay Harbor, which fell victim to the French and Indians. See *Frontenac*, 235-37, 397-401.

⁴ Mt. Katahdin, the unattained goal of Parkman's youthful excursion along the Canadian boundary in the summer of 1842, evidently still held some lure for him. It can hardly be said to be "very accessible" even today. The region about Katahdin was first explored in 1837 by Dr. Charles T. Jackson, the state geologist, whom Parkman met in the White Mountains in 1841; and Thoreau visited it in September 1846. At the entrance of Somes Sound on Mt. Desert Island was the site of the settlement of St. Sauveur, founded by the Jesuits Biard and Massé in 1609 and destroyed by Samuel Argall in 1613.

⁵ Parkman first visited Center Harbor on Lake Winnepesaukee in New Hampshire in 1838 with his father. He describes the place in the 1841 Journal.

XI. ACADIAN NOTEBOOK

[Parkman probably used "A New Map of Nova Scotia Compiled from the Latest Surveys expressly for the *Historical and Statistical Account of Nova Scotia*, 1829," which serves as frontispiece to T. C. Haliburton's book of that title (Halifax, 1829). This map gives the old French and Indian names in italics, along with the current English names.]

¹ Digby or Annapolis Gut is the narrow entrance to the Annapolis Basin, the Port Royal of the French first settlers.

² A fort was built on this site about 1643 by Charles de Menou de Charnisay, Sieur d'Aulnay (Parkman prefers the spelling "d'Aunay"). The place was always fortified until Port Royal was surrendered to the English under Colonel Nicholson in 1710. The Annapolis River was variously known under the French regime as Rivière du Port Royal and Rivière du Dauphin (Lescarbot). Allen's River was called Rivière de

l'Equille, "because that was the first fish caught there" (Lescarbot, II, 234). *Equille* is a local Norman word for sand eel.

[3] Perhaps Judge Chipman of Halifax, Haliburton's informant.

[4] These French remains on the Lequille may have been the ruins of the mill which appears on Lescarbot's "Figure du Port Royal en La Nouvelle France, 1609."

[5] There is still a small Micmac settlement on the Bear River reservation, partly in Digby and partly in Annapolis County. The river's name is a corruption of Hébert, the name given to it by Champlain after the apothecary Louis Hébert, later the first habitant of Quebec.

[6] The French Acadian settlement at Clare, the region between the Sissiboo River and St. Mary's Bay, dates from 1768, when, on the recommendation of Lieutenant Governor Michael Francklyn, grants there were given to returning Acadians who took the English oath of allegiance. Joseph Dugas was the first settler, but he was soon joined by many compatriots, including numbers returning from exile in Massachusetts. More lands were granted in 1771, 1772, and 1775; and today the bulk of the French population of Nova Scotia is concentrated in this region.

[7] Minas Basin was named by Champlain after the mines he sought in the region.

[8] Lyon's Cove does not appear on most maps. Cape Blomidon stands at the entrance of the Minas Basin and is the landfall for vessels approaching from the Bay of Fundy.

[9] In 1621, Sir William Alexander obtained from James I a grant of the whole peninsula (in which the name of Nova Scotia was first used instead of Acadia) as a fief of the Scottish Crown. James' grant was based on the claim that the territory belonged to England by right of Cabot's discovery. This claim had also served as the legal excuse for Samuel Argall's descent upon Port Royal in 1613, when he and his Virginian freebooters laid waste the Sieur de Monts' settlement of Port Royal. This settlement, like that of Sir William Alexander which replaced it, was at Lower Granville, opposite, not on, Goat Island. The Scots arrived in 1628, and made their headquarters on the site of the old French fort which Argall had destroyed. The little colony, never very successful, surrendered to De Razilly in August 1632 under the terms of the treaty of St. Germain-en-Laye, and thus closed the short-lived attempt to make a New Scotland.

[10] Perreau is undoubtedly a phonetic equivalent for Perrot, in which form the name is given on Haliburton's map. François-Marie Perrot was governor of Acadia, 1684-86, and remained as a trader after his dismissal from office.

[11] The Gaspereau was named after the small herring which frequent this tidal stream.

[12] The Triassic red sandstone formation of the Minas Basin culminates in the basaltic promontory of Cape Blomidon.

[13] The Jemseg River flows into the St. John about thirty-five miles upstream above the city of St. John. In 1659 Colonel Thomas Temple, acting under a grant given him by Oliver Cromwell and as governor of Acadia, established a fort at the mouth of the Jemseg as a trading post with the Indians. When Acadia was restored to France in 1667 by the Treaty of Breda, Fort Jemseg was taken over by the French. In the summer of 1674 it was captured by a Dutch force under Captain Jurriaen Aernouts. The fort was rebuilt by Villebon in 1690, after having returned to French hands, but was abandoned in favor of the fort at Nashwaak in 1692.

[14] Fort Nashwaak or St. Joseph, built by Villebon in 1692, at the Junction of the Nashwaak River with the St. John, was the headquarters for many French and Indian raids on the New England settlements. After Villebon's attack in 1696 on the English stronghold of Fort William Henry at Pemaquid, a retaliatory expedition under Colonel John Ha(w)thorne who supplanted Captain Ben Church in command after the latter's attack on Chignecto, was sent from New England to attack Fort Nashwaak, but retired without having done more than ineffectually bombard the French stronghold. In 1698 Villebon abandoned Nashwaak in favor of the fort at the mouth of the St. John.

[15] Parkman here confuses the sites of Latour's and D'Aulnay's forts, a common error until the matter was settled by Dr. W. F. Ganong's exhaustive research, to the early results of which a footnote in *The Old Regime* (39) refers. The place called "Old Fort," at Carleton on the west side of the harbor, overlooking Navy Island, was the site of D'Aulnay's fort and later of a succession of French and English establishments. Latour's fort was on the east side of the harbor at Portland Point. Its site is now marked by a brass tablet at the head of Portland Street. D'Aulnay destroyed Latour's fort in 1645 and built a new one on the opposite side of the harbor. After D'Aulnay's death by drowning in 1650, Latour returned to St. John as governor of Acadia, and lived there until his death in 1666. Since he made his headquarters at the fort built by his rival, it became known by his name; and thus arose the confusion into which Parkman, like many others, fell. (For Ganong's evidence, see *Transactions of the Royal Society of Canada*, IX, 1891, Pt. II, 61, and V, 1899, 276; and *New Brunswick Magazine*, I, 20, 165. Hannay's case against the Old

Fort site is in *New Brunswick Magazine*, I, 89. See also Ganong's note in Denys, *Acadia*, 114-15.)

[16] This French fort at the mouth of the Nerepis River was variously known as Fort Boishébert, Beauhébert, or Nerepis. It was built in 1749, upon the site of an ancient Indian fort and village, by Charles des Champs de Boishébert et Raffetot, who had served under his uncle M. de Ramezay at the unsuccessful siege of Annapolis Royal in 1746 and at the defeat of the British under Colonel Noble at Grand Pré in January 1747. Boishébert's original orders in 1749 were to rebuild and garrison the fort at the mouth of the St. John; but meeting opposition from the Nova Scotian government, which claimed the territory as British, he moved upriver to Nerepis. Here he built the small fort which goes by his name and contented himself with keeping watch on the English and preventing their settlement in the region by encouraging raids by the Indians, whom he secretly supplied with arms and supplies. As delivery of these by sea was difficult, De la Jonquière, the governor of Canada, tried to improve the land route from Quebec to Lake Témiscouata. In 1754, under a more aggressive French policy, Boishébert was ordered to rebuild Villebon's old fort at St. John, and the fort at Nerepis was abandoned.

[17] Pierre-Louis Morin was a Quebec surveyor and cartographer, who made maps for Parkman.

[18] Thomas Sterry Hunt (1826-1892), geologist and pioneer organic chemist, early became absorbed in the natural sciences, and was a private student and assistant of Professor Benjamin Silliman, Jr. at Yale. In 1846 he was appointed to the Geological Survey of Vermont, and in the following year became chemist to the Geological Survey of Canada under Sir William Logan, which post he held until 1872. He was professor of chemistry at Laval University in Quebec when Parkman met him.

[19] Digby is a township in the county of Annapolis, which includes the township of Clare where the bulk of the French population of the province is concentrated, though descendents of the Acadians are also found in Cape Breton and Halifax County. It is probable that Parkman meant to write "The French in Annapolis Cty."

[20] Horace Gray (1828-1902), Massachusetts jurist and United States Supreme Court justice, was, like Parkman, a lover of sport and country life. Since he was a member of the Harvard class of 1845, he had probably known Parkman since the latter's law school days. Gray was, with C. C. Langdell, an early advocate of the case system.

XII. SECOND PARIS NOTEBOOK

[1] These working drawings of the cartographer Guillaume Delisle (1675-1726) are mentioned by Harrisse in his account of the French archives (*Notes*, xxvii). Photostats in Public Archives, Ottawa.

[2] No record of this study has been found. Sebastien Crémoisy (1585/6-1669) was the printer of the *Jesuit Relations*, which appeared in annual volumes from 1632 to 1673. The books which bear his imprint are often called by his name.

[3] Le Rocher was the site of Fort St. Louis of the Illinois, and was later known as Starved Rock (cf. *La Salle*, 314). In Margry, *Découvertes*, III, 607-22, there are documents relating to the fate of La Salle's other colony, Fort St. Louis of Texas, which was often confused with Le Rocher. Parkman may have made, in this instance, the very error which he later warned his readers against, since no papers of the sort he describes seem to exist.

[4] Harrisse (*Notes*, xxiii-xxiv) mentions twenty-three portfolios, No. 122-43, devoted to North America, which contained materials relating to La Salle, Joliet, Bourgmont, Le Gardeur, and the La Vérendryes. Parkman's reference is correct.

[5] Probably Harrisse No. 208: "Carte de 80 x 50 c., représente le 'Messipi' du 49 au 42 d. où la revière 'Misconsing' vient aboutir. Le Lac Supérieur est nommé: Almepigou," 1679. Cf. *La Salle*, 481-482, where Parkman maintains that this map was "made by or for Du Lhut."

[6] Harrisse No. 209: "Carte de 68 x 43 cent. représentant tous les grands lacs. Le cartouche est vide, et on remarque à l'Ouest un grand nombre d'animaux tels que chameaux et rennes. La rivière des Illinois ne porte que la légende suivante: 'Rivière descendante dans le fleuve Mississippi,'" 1679. Harrisse considers this map to be the work of Franquelin.

[7] Jean Baptiste Louis Franquelin (1652-1718), who came to Canada in 1672, was the first "*hydrographe du roi*" in Canada. He made his first map in 1678; was named "*hydrographe royal*" in 1687; and left Quebec in 1695, probably to work for Vauban. He was succeeded by Louis Joliet. A great number of his maps and sketches are preserved in the Dépôt des Cartes de la Marine. For a list of his published maps, see C. de La Roncière, *Catalogue général des Manuscrits des bibliothèques publiques de France, Bibliothèques de la Marine* (Paris, 1907).

[8] Harrisse No. 258: "Carte en quatre sections de 90 x 53 cent. chacune,

dressée par M. de Fonville, Enseigne d'une compagnie de volontaires de la marine et dédiée au comte de Maurepas. Elle est datée de Québec 1699." De la Roncière (227) notes that this map includes views of Quebec from the east and northwest.

⁹ Harrisse No. 240: "Carte de l'Amérique Septentrionale entre les 25 et 65 degrés de latitude et depuis environ 240. jusqu'aux 340 de longit. . . . Par Jean Baptiste Louis Franquelin," 1689. Harrisse notes that this map includes a very fine view of Quebec from the east.

¹⁰ Harrisse No. 214: "Carte gnlle. de la France Septentrionale contenant la découverte du pays des Ilinois Faite par le Sieur Jolliet," 1681. Parkman notes: "This map, which is inscribed with a dedication by the Intendant Duchesneau to the minister Colbert, was made some time after the voyage of Joliet and Marquette. It is an elaborate piece of work, but very inaccurate. . . . This map, which is an early effort of the engineer Franquelin, does more credit to his skill as a designer than to his geographical knowledge, which appears in some respects behind his time." (*La Salle*, 480-81).

¹¹ Harrisse No. 219: "Carte de l'Amérique Septentrionale et partie de la Méridionale Depuis l'embouchure de la Rivière St. Laurent jusqu'à l'Isle de Cayenne, avec les nouvelles découvertes de la Rivière Mississippi, ou Colbert," 1682. Parkman dates this map 1682 or 1683, and believes that Du Luth supplied data for it (*La Salle*, 455).

¹² In the "*grandes archives*," Harrisse found many boxes of "instructions, reports, travel notes, and memorials, for the most part unpublished." (*Notes*, xxiii-xxiv). Carton 5, No. 18, contained material relating to Le Gardeur and La Vérendrye.

¹³ Carton 5, No. 15, contained manuscript material dealing with Joliet's voyage to Labrador in 1694 (*Notes*, xxiv).

¹⁴ Harrisse Nos. 253 & 254: "Plan de la ville et du Château de Québec en la présente année 1695." and "Plan de Québec en 1699. Fait ce 30 Mars par Levasseur de Neré, Ingénieur."

¹⁵ Harrisse No. 240: "Carte de l'Amérique Septentrionale . . . par Jean Baptiste Louis Franquelin," 1689.

¹⁶ Harrisse No. 259: "Partie de l'Amérique Septentrionale . . . par Jean Baptiste Louis Franquelin, Géographe du Roy, 1699."

¹⁷ Harrisse No. 219: "Carte de l'Amérique Septentrionale et partie de la Méridionale," 1682.

¹⁸ Harrisse No. 421: "*Trés-humble remontrance et mémoires des choses nécessaires pour l'entretien et exécution de l'entreprise faicte en la Nouvelle France, présentées au Roy, et du temps qu'elle a été découverte*," 1621.

[19] Harrisse No. 443: "Dépêche du Cardinal de Richelieu à M. de Châteauneuf, Ambassadeur à Londres, lui recommandant la poursuite de la restitution du Canada," 1629.

[20] Harrisse No. 501: "Lettre du P. Nickel, Général des Jésuites, au P. Cellot, Provincial de la Compagnie en France. Rome 16 Octobre 1656."

[21] Cf. Harrisse, *Notes*, 151.

[22] Margry had the "Relation de Joutel" well "mislaid," since it was not "found" until the publication of *Découvertes* was under way. It was printed for the first time in full in *Découvertes*, III, 91-534.

[23] There is a Brienne Collection of 362 volumes in the Bibliothèque Nationale, Nos. 6972-7328, which may be what Parkman meant, since there is no collection of this name in the British Museum.

[24] The Jesuits had no special collections of documents in their Paris house. In 1864 Père J. Tailhan had published Nicolas Perrot's *Mémoire sur les Moeurs, Coustumes, et Religion des Sauvages de l'Amérique septentrionale*, one of Charlevoix's manuscript sources.

[25] Probably "A *correct plan* of the environs of Quebec, and of the battle fought on the 13th sept., 1759 together with a particular detail of the French lines and batteries and also of the encampments, batteries and attacks of the British army [etc.]. Engraved by Thomas Jefferys. 16 x 35. [London], T. Jefferys." A. Doughty & G. W. Parmelee, *Siege of Quebec* (Quebec, 1901), VI, 292, No. 39.

[26] "Carte Des Environs de Québec En La Nouvelle France Mesurée très exactement en 1688 Par le Sr. De Villeneuve Ingr." Cf. Harrisse No. 230. This map gives a table of the names and surnames of the inhabitants of Quebec by parishes.

[27] Harrisse No. 230: "Carte Des Enuirons De Québec En La Nouvelle France Mesuré Sur Le Lieu Très-Exactement En 1685, Et 1686. Par Le Sr. Devilleneuve Ingénieur Du Roy."

[28] Cf. Harrisse No. 195: "Véritable plan Québec Comme il est l'an 1664 et la fortification que l'on y puisse faire."

[29] Harrisse No. 251: "Carte de la Coste de la Nouvelle Angleterre depuis le Cap Anne jusqu'à la Pointe Nevresing, où est compris le Chemin par Terre et par Mer de Boston à Manathes. Par J. B. L. Franquelin. Hydrographe du Roy, 1693." Harrisse notes that this map contains a "Plan de Manathes ou Nouvelle Yorc. Vérifié par le Sr. de la Motte."

[30] Harrisse No. 259: "Partie de l'Amérique Septentrionale où est compris la Nouvelle France . . . Par Jean Baptiste Louis Franquelin, Géographe

du Roy 1699." Harrisse believes this to be a copy made by F. de la Croix, for Franquelin was succeeded as royal hydrographer by Joliet in 1695.

[31] Harrisse No. 240: "Carte de l'Amérique Septentrionale . . . Franquelin," 1689.

[32] Harrisse No. 258: "Carte en quatre sections de 90 x 53 cent. chacune, dressée par M. de Fonville . . . 1689."

[33] Cf. *Frontenac*, 12-13.

[34] Abbé Faillon's papers were later transferred to the Montreal Sulpicians, and number much more than the "4 Ms. vols." shown Parkman.

[35] The Archives of the Dépôt des Cartes de la Marine, No. 359, contained two plans of Quebec in 1694 and 1695 (Harrisse Nos. 252 & 253). No. 369 probably held later plans of the city and of the fortifications.

[36] D'Avezac had recently published an essay on the Cabots in J. G. Kohl's *History of the Discovery of Maine* (Portland, 1869).

[37] Probably Nicolas de la Salle's *Récit* of 1685, published by Margry in *Découvertes*, I, 547-70, and in an English translation by the Caxton Club of Chicago in 1898 (*Bib. Can. 88*). Nicolas de la Salle was also the author of the letter dated Toulon, 3 Sept. 1698, which gives an account of Louisiana. He was "the son of a naval officer at Toulon, and was not related to the Caveliers." (*La Salle*, 463 n.)

[38] These notes indicate that Parkman had discovered that the missing La Salle papers were concentrated in Margry's hands.

[39] See note 37.

[40] Samuel L. M. Barlow was a noted collector of Americana.

[41] The Fonds Clerembault was one of the manuscript collections, named after the individuals who formed them under Louis XIV and Louis XV, which contained some of the most valuable Canadian material in the Bibliothèque Nationale. Cf. Harrisse, *Notes*, xxix.

XIII. 1878 NOTEBOOK

[1] These lines, on the ridge which crosses the plateau half a mile from the fort, were first formed by the abatis built by Montcalm's army in a single day against Abercromby's attack in 1758 (cf. *Montcalm and Wolfe*, II, 104-6). They are clearly shown on Lieutenant E. Meyer's "Sketch of the Country Round Tyconderoga" (*Montcalm and Wolfe*, II, 99) and in Skinner's "A Perspective View of Lake George" (Samuel, *Seven Years'*

War in Canada, 44), but are best seen in Engineer Lieutenant Thérbu's "Plan du Fort Carillon."

² The Indian path over Mt. Defiance to Lake Champlain was probably used by Sir William Johnson and the Indians, who were stationed on the mountain during Abercromby's attack on Ticonderoga. The path to Trout Brook is shown on Meyer's "Sketch" (*Montcalm and Wolfe*, II, 99).

³ Lord George Augustus Howe (1724-58) was killed on July 8 near the junction of Trout Brook with the outlet of Lake George, not far from the portage to the sawmill and the lower falls. Cf. *Johnson Papers*, II, 872.

⁴ The best map of the head of Lake George is "A Plan of Fort William Henry and the English Camps and Retrenchments with the French different Camps and Attack there upon" (*Johnson Papers*, II, 728). This is from the famous "Set of Plans and forts in America, reduced from actual surveys" (London, 1763). Unfortunately the plan is poorly reproduced and most of the legend is unreadable. A more useful map of the battlefield is Engineer Lieutenant Thérbu's "Attaques du Fort William-Henri". Samuel Blodget's "A Perspective View of the Battle Near Lake George" has been frequently reproduced, *e.g.*, Bancroft, *History of the United States*, IV, 210. On this map, see Massachusetts Historical Society *Collections*, II Series, IV, 153.

⁵ Fort George was laid out by Amherst and Montresor in June 1759, on the hill at the head of Lake George which had formed part of Johnson's camp in 1755, of Munro's in 1757, and of Abercromby's in 1758. It was finished about a month later, but the capture of Ticonderoga and Crown Point rendered it useless.

⁶ According to Blodget's "Perspective View" the old road did run into Johnson's camp.

⁷ Artillery Cove and Lévis' camp are shown on Thérbu's "*Attaques*."

⁸ Brown's was a crossroads tavern near the toll gate on the plank road to Lake George.

⁹ The site of Fort William Henry was first fortified by Sir William Johnson on the advice of Captain Eyre in 1755. Robert Rogers used the camp as his base in 1755-56. The fort was surveyed by Montresor in March 1757 and captured by Montcalm in the following July.

¹⁰ The Whitehall–Fort Anne–Fort William Henry area is best shown in the map supposedly used by Montcalm, "Carte, depuis le fort St-Frédéric jusqu'à Orange ou Albanie, du Lac de St-Sacrement & de la situation des Forts construits dans cette partie de l'Amérique Septentrionale, 1757," which is reproduced in *Knox's Historical Journal*, III, 28.

¹¹ The stream that enters the head of South Bay is Mt. Hope Brook.

[12] Fort Anne (Fort de la Reine), a military post on Wood Creek on the portage from the head of South Bay to Fort Edward, was built by Colonel Nicholson in 1709. It was later captured and destroyed by the French, but rebuilt.

[13] Wood Creek, called Rivière-au-Chicot on Montcalm's plan, is now a canal between Whitehall and the Hudson. Half-Way Brook is a tributary which joins the main stream at Fort Anne.

[14] These are the Drowned Lands, near the northern end of which are the Two Rocks (Deux Rochers).

[15] Pierre de Sales de Laterrière (1747-1815), *Mémoires de Pierre de Sales Laterrière et de ses traverses* (Edition intime. Quebec, 1873). *Bib. Can.* 832. This book was published in 1871 in an edition of one hundred copies by Alfred Garneau, the historian's son, who doubtless brought it to Parkman's attention. It is a valuable source for the social history of the post-conquest period, and a most entertaining book.

[16] In Abbé Casgrain's *Histoire de l'Hôtel-Dieu de Québec* (Quebec, 1878), he lists Mere Juchereau de St. Ignace's work of the same name (Montauban, 1751) in his bibliography and remarks: "*Cette histoire a été écrite d'après les renseignements de la mère de St-Ignace et rédigée par la mère Duplessis de Ste-Hélène.*" The original manuscript, in the writing of Mère de Ste-Hélène and signed by Mère de St. Ignace, is in the Hôtel-Dieu of Quebec.

[17] Possibly a descendent of John Neilson (1776-1848), editor of the Quebec *Gazette*, friend of Louis-Joseph Papineau, delegate to London of the Quebec Asembly, and Speaker of the Legislative Council in 1844.

[18] The Archives de la Séminaire de Québec contain a rich store of historical material on the French and English periods. Parkman's friend Abbé Casgrain knew them well, and used their resources both to help and to refute his friend's work.

[19] James Macpherson Le Moine (1825-1912), *Maple Leaves: Canadian History—Literature—Sport. New Series* (Quebec, 1873).

[20] The Buttes à Neveu is the highest point on the Plains of Abraham.

[21] Wolfe's Ravine is where the British troops climbed the Heights of Abraham on the night of September 12, 1759.

[22] Major Robert Stobo (1727-?), a Scots officer of the Virginia Regiment, held hostage by the French in the Fort Necessity affair of 1754, was condemned to death for breaking his parole by corresponding with the British forces. He was reprieved; twice escaped to Louisbourg in 1756 and 1759; and came back to Quebec as a spy. He was not involved in the Battle of the Plains, for he left Wolfe to join Amherst on September 7.

De Vitré's son, Lieutenant John Denis De Vitré, memorialized William

Pitt for losses suffered as a result of his father's action (cf. Viger, *Siège de Québec en 1759* [Quebec, 1836] 38-41), so it seems clear that his share in Wolfe's victory was established.

[23] Abbé Louis-Edouard Bois (1813-89) developed an interest in historical pursuits while vicar at St. Jean-Port Joli, where he saw much of the historically minded Aubert de Gaspé family. He worked as an antiquarian and compiler while curé of St. François de Beauce and of Maskinongé. He had a major part in the production of the Laverdière edition of the *Jesuit Relations* (Quebec, 1858) and of the *Collection des anciens documents*. He was a member of the Literary and Historical Society of Quebec and was awarded the degree of *docteur-ès-lettres* by Laval. His admirable library is now in the Séminaire de Nicolet.

[24] *Siège de Québec en 1759. Copié d'après un manuscrit apporté de Londres par l'honorable D. B. Viger, lors de son retour en Canada en Septembre 1834—Mai 1835. Copié d'un manuscrit déposé à la bibliothèque de Hartwell en Angleterre* (Quebec, 1836). *Bib. Can.* 299. Viger made a copy of this MS. in the library of Dr. John Lee at Hartwell House, who got it from Captain Alex Schomberg, an English naval officer present at the siege, who edited the MS. The journal, written at four ten-day intervals by one of the beseiged, covers the period from May 1 to September 10, 1759, just before the Battle of the Plains.

[25] Frédéric-Georges Baby (1832-1906), lawyer, cabinet minister, judge. He was Sir John MacDonald's Minister of Internal Revenue in 1878, and later became a Supreme Court justice. He was a founder of the Société Historique de Montréal and president of the Numismatic and Antiquarian Society of Montreal. His papers now belong to the University of Montreal and are being calendared.

[26] Théophile-Pierre Bédard (1837-1900), lawyer, journalist, and historian, began with *Journal de Québec*, but turned to the civil service and became archivist and registrar. In 1869 he published his *Historie de cinquante ans* (1791-1841), which shares more of the vices than the virtues of Robert Christie's history, to which it was a rejoinder. He published a "Table analytique des Jugements et Deliberations du Conseil Superieur, 1717-31" in the *Rapports du Secrétaire et Registraire de Québec pour 1892 et 1893*.

[27] James Macpherson Le Moine (1825-1912), born in Quebec of a French-Canadian father and a Scots mother, wrote with equal facility in English and French. He was a lawyer, but did not long practice, since he became inspector of internal revenue for Quebec in 1869 and held this office until his death. His five series of *Maple Leaves*, *L'Album du Touriste* (Quebec, 1872), *Quebec Past & Present* (Quebec, 1876), *Chronicles*

of the St. Lawrence (1888), and *The Explorations of Jonathan Oldbuck* (1889) are perhaps the best known of the almost innumerable books, pamphlets, and discourses he produced. In addition to his historical interests, he was an ornithologist, and he wrote widely for Canadian and American magazines. His home, Spencer Grange, in Sillery was a center of hospitality for the artistic and the literary. He was president of the Royal Society of Canada and several times president of the Literary and Historical Society of Quebec. He was knighted by Queen Victoria in 1897.

28 Lieutenant Colonel R. S. Beatson, *Notes on the Plains of Abraham* (Gibraltar, 1858). According to Doughty (*Siege of Quebec*, VI, 155): "The book is exceedingly rare and the only copies we have knowledge of are in the possession of the Gibraltar Garrison Library and Sir J. M. Le Moine."

29 Montcalm died in the home of M. André Arnoux, St. Louis Street (probably on the site of No. 59) at 5 A.M. September 14, 1759, the day following the battle, and was buried in the Ursulines' Chapel at nine that night (cf. Chapais, *Montcalm*, 666-75). Chapais supports De Folignée's story of the shell-hole grave (cf. Doughty, *Siege*, IV, 207).

30 George Robert Gleig (1796-1888), *Lives of Eminent British Military Commanders* (London, 1831-32).

31 This "Plan of the Town & Basin of Quebec" is No. 14 in Doughty's list of plans and engravings, *Siege*, VI, 285 & n.

32 The relevant portion of Parkman's letter to Le Moine, dated Montreal November 17, 1878, is as follows:

> Your Historical Society has done a great deal for Canadian history, but there is, I think, no particular in which it has done better service than in collecting and printing memoirs and journals concerning the great crisis of 1759. I trust it will continue this good work. A great deal may thus be saved that would otherwise perish and be forgotten. There must be a great number of letters, papers and maps in private hands, subject to fire and all sorts of accidents, which might be saved at moderate expense and the preservation of which is essential to a full knowledge of that important period.

This letter is printed in Literary and Historical Society of Quebec *Transactions*, New Series, XIII (1877-79), 159.

33 Joseph Marmette (1844-95), historian, novelist, and archivist, presented Parkman with copies of most of his books. His chief works were *François de Bienville* (Quebec, 1870), *Le Chévalier de Mornac* (Montreal, 1873), and *Bigot* (Quebec, 1874), as well as other popular romantic novels about the French Regime. In 1880 Chapleau made him joint commissioner with Hector Fabre at Paris, where he studied in the French archives.

Upon his return to Canada in 1884, he became assistant director of the Ottawa archives, for whom he later visited Paris in search of documents.

34 Mgr. Thomas Hamel (1830-1913) was associated with Laval University all of his life, except for four years of graduate study in Paris. He became superior of the Seminary and rector of the University in 1871 and held the post until 1880, and again from 1883 to 1886. He was librarian from 1886 to 1908. A scientist, he was president of the Royal Society of Canada.

35 Dr. Hubert La Rue (1833-81), one of Parkman's closest friends in Quebec, was a physician, professor, and man of letters. He did graduate work at Louvain and Paris after completing his classical course at Laval, and then returned to occupy a new chair which he held until his death. He wrote a vast number of pamphlets and magazine articles, gave innumerable lectures, and was a founder of the *Soirées Canadiennes* of 1860. His wife was a daughter of Judge Panet and Lucie Casgrain.

36 Louis Dupont du Chambon de Vergor (1710-?), an Acadian who was an accomplice of the Intendant Bigot and plundered both people and government, was in ill repute for his surrender of Fort Beauséjour in 1755 to Monckton after Pichon's betrayal. Bougainville gave him command of the post at Anse au Foulon (Wolfe's Cove), and he is suspected of having been bought by the English.

XIV. 1879 & 1885 NOTEBOOK

1 This is a list of the children of Dr. Hubert La Rue, Parkman's friend and frequent host in Quebec. Alphonsine died the following year; and only four of the ten La Rue children survived their father, who died at the age of forty-eight in 1889.

2 It is not clear on what text these notes are based, for the *Journal de Franquet* was first published in the *Annuaire du Institut Canadien de Québec* (1885), 29-240. A note in the foreword reads: "Une copie en fut transcrite et mise dans nos archives nationales en 1854." Parkman evidently made his notes from a text in Quebec. In 1889 a general edition was published: Louis Franquet (1697-1768), *Voyages et Mémoires sur le Canada par Franquet* (Quebec, 1889). *Bib. Can.* 229. Parkman's page references do not agree with either of these editions.

3 Jean C. Langelier (1845-1910) was a journalist and publicist who

became deputy registrar of Quebec in 1887. As a young man he wrote for *La Minerve* and *Le Courier de St. Hyacinthe*; and then produced a long series of pamphlets on agriculture, colonization, railroads, and public works. His most scholarly work was a *Liste des terres concedées par la couronne, 1763-1870*.

4 Luc Letellier de St. Just (1820-81) was lieutenant governor of Quebec from 1876-79. In the latter year a dispute over his powers with the premier, Charles de Boucherville, was settled against him by the governor general in council, and it was established that the lieutenant governor, like the king whom he represents, reigns but does not govern. Letellier, who had fought for Maximilian in Mexico and traveled widely, was a friend of Sir James Macpherson Le Moine; and Parkman saw much of him during his visits to Quebec.

5 Wolfe's line of battle was drawn up somewhat nearer the city than the site of the prison. His deathplace is about as far in the opposite direction.

6 Parkman had met Abbé Louis-Edouard Bois, for forty-one years the historically minded *curé* of Maskinongé, in the previous year. Bois was a friend of Le Moine, who gives a biographical sketch with bibliography in *Monographies et esquisses*, 467-68.

7 Joseph-Eudore Evanturel (1852-1919) was one of Parkman's copyists in Quebec. He published his *Premières Poésies* in 1878. He later became a civil servant in Quebec, and died a pillar of the Boston St. Jean-Baptiste Society.

8 Narcisse-Henri-Edouard Faucher de St. Maurice (1847-97) was one of the most colorful figures of Quebec at this period. A son of the seigneur of Beaumont, he had fought for Maximilian in Mexico in 1864 and was twice wounded. He was clerk of the Legislative Council of Quebec from Confederation until 1881, and a member of the Assembly. As a yachtsman he sailed the lower St. Lawrence and described his voyages in several books, as he also did his travels in Europe and North Africa. He was later editor of the *Journal de Québec* and of *Le Canadien*. As a historically minded sportsman, he was a welcome addition to Parkman's circle of Quebec friends.

9 "A view of the Fall of Montmorenci and the attack made by General Wolfe on the French Intrenchments near Beauport, with the Grenadiers of the Army, July 31st, 1759." Engraved by William Elliott (Coverdale Collection, No. 21). One of Smyth's St. Lawrence set, "Six Elegant Views of the Most Remarkable Places in the River and Gulph of St. Lawrence, from the Originals drawn on the spot by Captain Hervey Smyth, Aid de Camp to the late General Wolfe, 1760." The others, some of which

Parkman mentions, are: "A View of the City of Quebec," "A View of Cape Rouge," "A View of Gaspe Bay," "A View of Miramichi," and "A View of the Pierced Island" (Coverdale Collection, Nos. 19-25).

10 Alfred Garneau (1836-1904), the son of François-Xavier Garneau, the first great French-Canadian historian, was a poet and an antiquarian who served the provincial government as a translator and as librarian of the Parliamentary Library.

11 The Academy of Inscriptions was a section of the French Academy.

12 William M. McPherson was Quebec agent for the Dominion Line Steamships, with offices at 92 St. Peter Street.

13 This letter of December 29, 1757 from Wolfe to Pitt is not given in Doughty's *Siege of Quebec*. Grant's *Memoir of Wolfe* is not listed in *Bib. Can.*

14 The French-Canadian word for codfish, *morue*, is supposedly derived from the Gascon *mouru*. Spaniards, Basques, and Gascons were active in the St. Lawrence fisheries before the period of French settlement, as a few place names along the lower St. Lawrence indicate. Lescarbot gives the Basque word for cod as *bacaillos* (II, 24).

15 Fort Lawrence, named after Major (later Governor) Charles Lawrence, who built it in the autumn of 1750, stood on or near the site of the village of Beaubassin (burned in that same year) on a ridge parallel with the higher ridge of Beauséjour, about a mile and a quarter across the marshes of the Missequash River. It was square, consisting of four bastions connected by curtains, with a ditch and picket palisade. After Monckton captured Beauséjour in 1755, the latter replaced Lawrence as the British stronghold. Fort Lawrence was dismantled and evacuated in 1756, but part of the ditch on the south side can still be seen.

16 Fort Beauséjour (called Cumberland, after its conquest by Monckton in 1755) was named after an early settler of the place. It was begun in 1751 as a counterweight to Fort Lawrence and was still unfinished at the time it was besieged by Monckton, thanks to Abbé Le Loutre's insistence that all available men work on the *aboiteaux* or dikes on the marsh west of Beauséjour. The fort was a "pentagon of earthworks about 280 feet in width," consisting of five bastions and connecting curtains. It was surrounded by a deep ditch and a fifteen-foot picket palisade. Casements were built along the walls for protection from cannon fire, but during Monckton's siege these were found not to be bombproof. De Vergor, the commandant, and Le Loutre, who played a role reminiscent of the modern Russian Army political commissars, surrendered the fort on June 16, 1755 after a siege of twelve days. The fort was greatly strengthened by the English, as indicated by Lieutenant Colonel Moore's report in

1784. The "immense stone structure" which Parkman noticed was the magazine, built of stone and brick outside the main entrance, this being the best preserved portion of the fortifications in an 1870 watercolor sketch. See J. C. Webster, *Forts of Chegnecto* (Shediac, 1930), 78. Its base still remains. Barracks stood within both the pentagon and the extension of the glacis in a spur toward the south, which was added by the English. The walls still stand, but the buildings have disappeared, the glacis has been leveled, and the casements have fallen in.

[17] Cumberland Basin is now called Chegnecto Bay.

[18] The reversing falls of St. John, New Brunswick, are one of the great sights of the Maritime Provinces.

1885

[19] For Parkman's use of these notes on Beaufort, South Carolina (the Port Royal of Jean Ribaut in 1562), see *Pioneers*, 39-41.

[20] Not Ribaut's "Charlesfort." Cf. *Pioneers*, 41 n.

[21] For Ribaut's arrival at Fernandina, Florida, see *Pioneers*, 38-39.

[22] The St. John's River was Ribaut and Laudonnière's "River of May." Cf. *Pioneers*, 51-52.

[23] Pelican Bank was the sand bar which Ribaut (*Pioneers*, 36) and Laudonnière (*ibid*, 50) crossed in their boats, since it blocked the entrance of ships to the harbor which has since become the port of Jacksonville.

[24] For the Vale of Laudonnière see *Pioneers*, 55 & n.

[25] Cf. *Pioneers*, 59-60 for the use Parkman made of these notes.

[26] Parkman used these notes in his description of Menendez' march on Fort Caroline in 1565 (*Pioneers*, 121).

[27] Anastasia Island was the scene of Menendez' massacre of the shipwrecked French in 1565 (*Pioneers*, 133-47).

XV. 1889-1892 NOTEBOOK

[1] Sir John George Bourinot (1837-1902), a Nova Scotian educated at Toronto, became Clerk of the House of Commons in 1880 and for many years was honorary secretary of the Royal Society of Canada. He was a historian and an authority on constitutional government. His chief works are *Canada under British Rule*, a *Manual of the Constitutional History of Canada*, and *Parliamentary Procedure and Government in Canada*.

[2] Theodore Roosevelt (1858-1919) dedicated *The Winning of the West*,

which he had written in an interlude of his political career, to Parkman, saying that "your works stand alone and that they must be the models for all historical treatments of the founding of new communities and the growth of the frontier here in the wilderness." He found it difficult to thank Parkman for the gift of *A Half-Century of Conflict:* "It must have been rather hard for any one to whom Gibbon, for instance, sent his work to find perfectly fit words to use in acknowledging the gift."

³ Captain Samuel Vetch (1668-1732), a Scot who came to New York in 1699, was accused of illicit trade while acting as Governor Dudley's emissary to Vaudreuil in the matter of the Deerfield captives in 1705. He was the author of the plan for the reduction of Canada during the War of the Spanish Succession, and with Colonel Nicholson was joint leader of the expedition of 1709. The statement to which Parkman refers appears in *A Half-Century of Conflict*, I, 103-4.

⁴ Benoni Stebbins, a sergeant in the county militia, was killed in the Deerfield massacre of 1704. See *Half-Century*, I, 63-6.

⁵ Miss C. Alice Baker of Cambridge, Massachusetts, a descendent of one of the Deerfield captives, did considerable research on the massacre.

⁶ For Vetch's military qualifications, see *Half-Century*, I, 122.

⁷ William Smith (1728-93), *The History of the Late Province of New-York, from its first discovery* (London, 1756 and New York, 1829). *Bib. Can.* 266.

⁸ Jeanne-Françoise Juchereau, Mère de St. Ignace (1650-1723). *Histoire de l'Hôtel-Dieu de Québec.* Ed. by Dom Latom. (Montaubon, 1751.)

⁹ John R. Bartlett, "The Four Kings of Canada," *Magazine of American History*, March 1878. This is an account of the five Mohawk chiefs whom Peter Schuyler took to London in 1710. One died on the voyage; the others were presented to Queen Anne, one as emperor of the Mohawks and the others as kings. See *Half-Century*, I, 142.

¹⁰ Samuel Vetch and Colonel Francis Nicholson were the joint leaders and instigators of the campaign against Canada in 1709. Nicholson commanded the force moving north by the Champlain route while Vetch was to accompany the British fleet which was to sail to Quebec from Boston. After the collapse of this campaign, Nicholson was named to command the expedition against Port Royal in the following year, with Vetch as his adjutant general. This effort was successful. See *Half-Century*, I, 120-55.

¹¹ *Mémoires des Commissionaires du roi et ceux de Sa Majesté britannique Sur les possessions & les droits respectifs des deux Couronnes en Amérique.* 4 vols. (Paris, 1755-7). *Bib. Can.* 235.

¹² Benjamin Perley Poore had collected and copied documents in Paris

bearing on the colonial history of the Commonwealth. These copies, kept at the Statehouse in Boston, are commonly called the Paris Documents.

13 Dr. Douglas Brymner (1823-1902) was the Dominion Archivist from 1872 until his death. His annual reports were eagerly awaited by Parkman, who provided the Public Archives at Ottawa with copies of his own collection of Paris documents.

14 The letters of De Goutin, a magistrate who acted as intendant at Port Royal and reported to Paris, are valuable sources on Acadian history from 1700 to 1710. The originals are in the Archives de la Marine et des Colonies at Paris, with some copies in the *Correspondance Officielle* at Ottawa. See *Half-Century*, I, 119 n.

15 E. Rameau de St. Père (1820-99) was the author of *La France aux Colonies* (Paris, 1859), of which a new edition appeared as *Une Colonie Féodale* in 1889. Parkman reviewed the earlier book in the *Nation* for December 27, 1877 (XXV, 400) and April 4, 1878 (XXVI, 230). Parkman and Rameau held violently opposing views on the Acadian question.

16 The character of Colonel Francis Nicholson is sketched in *Half-Century*, I, 148.

17 *Le Canada-Français*, a magazine published by Laval University at Quebec, printed in three separate volumes, *Collection de Documents inédits* (Quebec 1888-90), Abbé Casgrain's Acadian material, before it was collected in *Un Pèlerinage au Pays d'Evangéline*.

18 Dr. Convers Francis' "Life of Rale" may be found in Jared Sparks's *Library of American Biography*, New Series, VII.

19 Abbé Cyprien Tanguay (1819-1902), *Dictionnaire Généalogique des Familles Canadiennes* (Quebec, 1871).

20 The original of the Reverend Henry Flynt's *Common Place Book* is in the library of the Massachusetts Historical Society. It is quoted in *Half-Century*, I, 222, 230-1. Père Sebastien Rale, Rasles, or Rasle, S.J. (1657-1724) was assigned to the Abenaki Mission in 1691, after spending two years in the Illinois country, and devoted the rest of his life to keeping the Abenaki loyal to the French. He took an active part in their war efforts and was killed in a New England raid on one of their villages.

21 The letter of the Rev. Joseph Baxter to Rale (April 1719), belonging to the Massachusetts Historical Society, is summarized in *Half-Century*, I, 229-30. Baxter was Rale's rival as spiritual guide and political director of the Abenakis, and carried on a polemical correspondence in Latin with him on the relative merits of their faiths, their Latin, and their tempers.

22 Rale's papers were seized by Colonel Westbrook's expedition against

Norridgewock in 1721, which had the capture of the missionary as its main object. Rale escaped, but his strongbox was captured; and the papers it contained supplied clear evidence that he was acting as an agent of the Canadian authorities in exciting his flock against the English. Some of these papers, including a letter from Vaudreuil to Rale (Quebec, Sept. 25, 1721), are preserved in the Archives of Massachusetts. See *Half-Century*, I, 238 & n.

23 Rale was a good linguist, like many of the other Jesuit missionaries. His *Abenaki Dictionary* is preserved in the Harvard College Library. It was published in 1833.

24 Niles based his *Indian and French Wars* largely on Penhallow's *History of Wars of New England with the Eastern Indians*, but frequently blundered in his copying. See *Half-Century*, I, 46 n.

25 Benjamin Crafts (?-1746) was a private in Colonel Hale's Essex Regiment. His journal is quoted in *Half-Century*, II, 148.

26 William Vaughan (1703-?) of Damariscotta, son of the lieutenant governor of New Hampshire, was second in command of Pepperrell's expedition against Louisbourg in 1745. He is the supposed author of the attack, and played a leading role in the siege. See *Half-Century*, II, 64-5, 98-118.

27 Sir William Pepperrell (1696-1759), born in Maine and a member of the General Court of Massachusetts from 1727 until his death, commanded the expedition against Louisbourg and captured the fortress in 1745. He was subsequently made a baronet, and lieutenant general in 1759. His papers are in the Massachusetts Historical Society. A journal appended to Shirley's letter to Newcastle (Oct. 28, 1745) bears the names of Pepperrell, Waldo, Moore, Lothrop, and Gridley, who attest its accuracy. This may be the journal referred to by Parkman. See *Half-Century*, II, 144 n.

28 William Douglass (1691?-1752), *A summary, Historical and Political, of the First Planting, Progressive Improvements, and Present State of the British Settlements in North America* (London, 1760). *Bib. Can.* 225. Originally issued serially in Boston, 1747-52.

29 Robert Hale Bancroft was a descendent of Colonel Robert Hale of the Essex regiment in the Louisbourg expedition of 1745. See *Half-Century*, II, 107 n. The letter from John Payne of Boston to Colonel Hale is given in II, 88-9 n.

30 The Rev. Stephen Williams (1693-?) of Longmeadow, Massachusetts, son of the Rev. John Williams of Deerfield, was captured as a boy of eleven at the time of the massacre. He was the author of an *Account of the*

Captivity of Stephen Williams and of manuscript diary of the winter after the capture of Louisbourg, where he served as chaplain. Parkman owned the later diary, and refers feelingly to its "detestable" handwriting. See *Half-Century*, II, 150 n.

[31] These "Latour books" were the materials upon which Parkman based the new section, "The Feudal Chiefs of Acadia," which he added to the 1893 edition of *The Old Regime*.

[32] *"Good Government* was the organ of the Civil Service Reform League. Parkman's support was probably recruited by his friend E. L. Godkin of the *Nation* or by Theodore Roosevelt, who had been named a Civil Service Commissioner in 1889 by President Cleveland. It was a period of revolt on the part of the established elements of the community against boss and machine rule in politics. The object of the League was close to Parkman's heart. See his "The Failure of Universal Suffrage," *North American Review*, July-August 1878 (CXXVII, 1-20).

Index

685

Joint Occupancy, 401, 402
Joliet, Louis, 559, 668
Joly, 528
Jonas, 256
Jones, Josiah (Capt.), 359, 362
Jones, Col., 268
Jones, Mr. and Mrs., 306
Jones, Mrs. Stephen, 261, 359
Jones, Stephen, 261, 269
Jordan, John Jr., 294, 369, 490, 605
Josselyn, John, 97, 351–52
Journal de Franquet, 676
Journal de Québec, 567, 674, 677
Journal des Savans, 663
Journal du dernier voyage de M. de la Salle, 377
Journal d'un Voyage . . . par . . . Charlevoix, 648
Journal historique du dernier voyage . . . La Salle, 655
Journal of Archaeology, 599
Journal of a Trapper, 618
"Journal of Baxter," 597
"Journal of Mad. Knight . . . ," 595
Journal of the Expulsion of the Acadians, 379
Journal of the Late Siege, 324, 379
"Journal of the Voyage of the Sloop Mary," 595
Journal of Travels in 1817, 380
Journal of Travels Over the Rocky Mountains, 623
Journal or Minutes of . . . Louisbourg, 597
Journals and Letters of La Vérendrye and His Sons, 657
Joutel, Henri, 324, 377, 528, 529, 534, 561, 655
Juchereau, Mère Jeanne-Françoise, 520, 572, 595, 652, 680
Juniata Crossing, 407
Jupiter, temple of, 155

Kalispeks, 413
Kalm, Peter, 369
Kansas, 392, 413, 415, 417, 611; *see also* Caws
Kansas City, 392, 613
Kansas R., 418, 421, 611, 613
Kaskaskia, Ill., 607
Katahdin, Mt., *see* Mt. Katahdin
Kay, 405, 604
Kearney, Fort, *see* Fort Kearney
Kearney, Stephen Watts (Col.), 402, 422, 469, 473, 608, 613, 615, 616, 617, 634, 636, 637, 639, 640

Kearny, Phil (Gen.), 615
Kearsley, 428, 429, 432, 620
Keathley, *see* Kearlsey
Keatley, *see* Kearsley
Keene, N.H., 332, 367
Keith, William (Sir), 325, 379
Kelsey, 630
Kenfield, 69
Kennebec, 366
Kerney, 90
Kickapoo Agency, 616
Kickapoos, 392, 422, 613, 615–16
Killington, Mt., 342
Kinderhook, N.Y., 44
King, Thomas Starr, 94, 350
King George's War, xiii
King Philip's War, 260, 359
King's Arms, 119
Kingsford, William, 547
King William's War, xiii, 328
Kinsés, 413
Kiowas, 396, 397, 412, 608, 625, 636, 639
Kirker, James, 624
Knapp, 94, 349
Knickerbocker Magazine, 349, 387, 400, 486, 614, 616, 617, 641
Knight, 440
Knight, Artemus (Capt.), 83, 343-44
Knox, John, 229, 327, 381
Kohl, J. G., 671
Kohl Collection, 657
Konkapot, John (Capt.), 263, 360–61
Kosciusko, 359
Kutenais, 413

La Barge, Joseph (Capt.), 611
La Bonté, 580, 630
La Bonté's Camp, 445, 451, 453–54, 629-30
La Bonté's Creek, 629
La Cara, 242, 244
Lachine, Ont., 352
Laclède, Pierre, 610
La Corne, Luc de, 519, 649–50
Lacroix, François, 306-8
Lafayette, Marquis de, 607
Lafiteau, Père Joseph-François-Henri, 324, 377, 519, 648, 652
Lafontaine, 647
La Forest, 560
La Galissonière, 649, 657
Lahontan, 531, 658

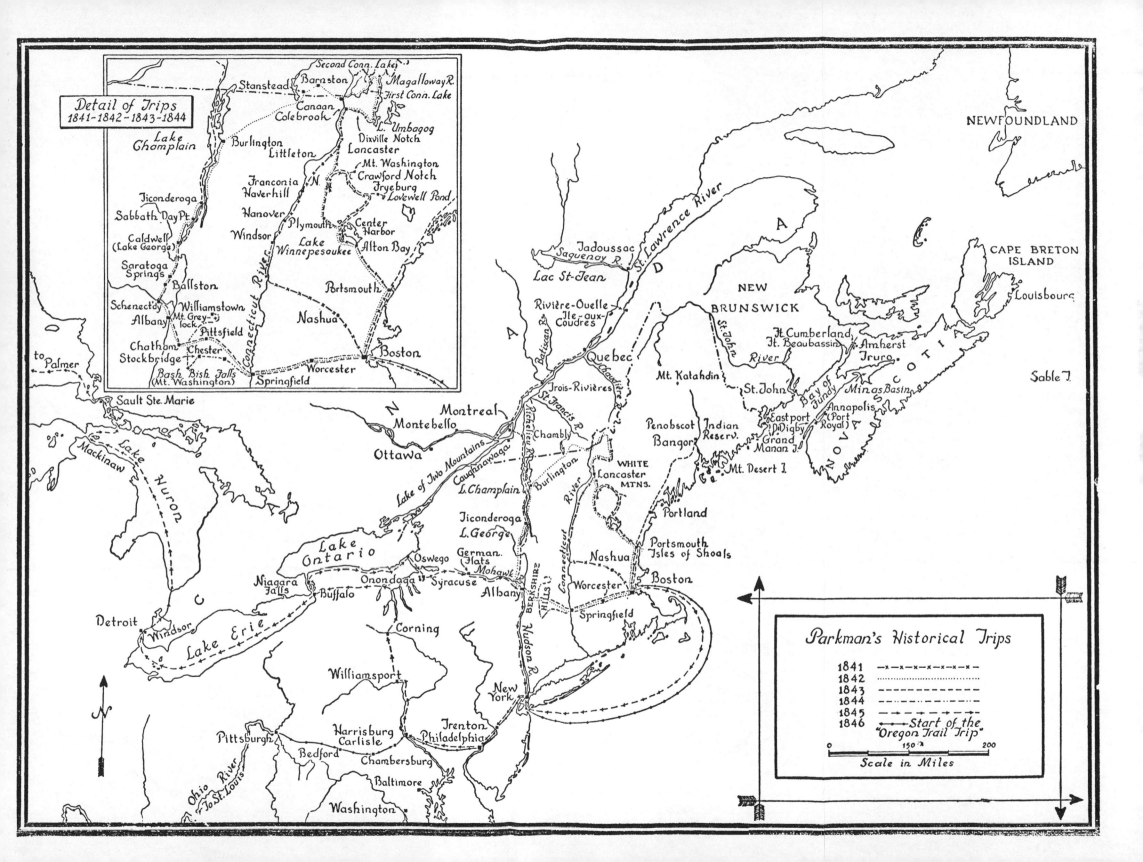

Detail of Trips
1841-1842-1843-1844

Lake Champlain

Second Conn. Lake
Stanstead
Barnston
Magalloway R.
First Conn. Lake
Canaan
Colebrook
L. Umbagog
Burlington
Littleton
Dixville Notch
Lancaster
Franconia
Haverhill
N.
Mt. Washington
Crawford Notch
Fryeburg
Lovewell Pond
Hanover
Plymouth
Center Harbor
Windsor
Lake Winnepesoukee
Alton Bay
Ticonderoga
Sabbath Day Pt.
Caldwell (Lake George)
Saratoga Springs
Ballston
Portsmouth
Schenectdy
Williamstown
Albany
Mt. Greylock
Pittsfield
Nashua
Chatham
Stockbridge
Chester
to Palmer
Bash Bish Falls (Mt. Washington)
Springfield
Worcester
Boston
Connecticut River

NEWFOUNDLAND

CAPE BRETON ISLAND

Louisbourg

Sable I.

NEW BRUNSWICK

NOVA SCOTIA

Jadoussac
Saguenay R.
Lac St-Jean
St. Lawrence River
A
D
A

Rivière-Ouelle
Ile-aux-Coudres
Batiscan R.
Quebec
Chaudière
St. John River
Ft. Cumberland
Ft. Beaubassin
Amherst
Truro
Minas Basin
St. John
Bay of Fundy
Eastport
Digby
Grand Manan I.
Annapolis (Port Royal)

Mt. Katahdin

Trois-Rivières
St. Francis R.
Richelieu R.
Montreal
Montebello
Chambly
Penobscot
Bangor
Indian Reserv.
Mt. Desert I.
Portland
Ottawa
Lake of Two Mountains
Caughnawaga
L. Champlain
Burlington
WHITE MTNS.
Lancaster
Portsmouth
Isles of Shoals

Sault Ste. Marie

Lake Huron
Mackinaw

Lake Ontario
Oswego
Onondaga
Syracuse
German Flats
Mohawk
Albany
BERKSHIRE HILLS
Connecticut River
Nashua
Worcester
Springfield
Boston

Niagara Falls
Buffalo

Detroit
Windsor
Lake Erie
C

Corning

Williamsport

New York

Hudson R.

Pittsburgh
Bedford
Chambersburg
Baltimore
Washington
Harrisburg
Carlisle
Trenton
Philadelphia

Ohio River
To St. Louis

Parkman's Historical Trips

1841 —x—x—x—x—x—
1842 ·············
1843 — — — — —
1844 —··—··—··—
1845 →→→→→→
1846 •—•—•→ Start of the "Oregon Trail Trip"

0   150   200
Scale in Miles